# Implementing SSL/TLS Using Cryptography and PKI

# Implementing SSL/TLS Using Cryptography and PKI

### Joshua Davies

Wiley Publishing, Inc.

**Implementing SSL/TLS Using Cryptography and PKI**

Published by
**Wiley Publishing, Inc.**
10475 Crosspoint Boulevard
Indianapolis, IN 46256
www.wiley.com

Copyright © 2011 by Wiley Publishing, Inc., Indianapolis, Indiana

Published simultaneously in Canada

ISBN: 978-0-470-92041-1
ISBN: 978-1-118-03875-8 (ebk)
ISBN: 978-1-118-03876-5 (ebk)
ISBN: 978-1-118-03877-2 (ebk)

Manufactured in the United States of America

10 9 8 7 6 5 4 3 2 1

For general information on our other products and services please contact our Customer Care Department within the United States at (877) 762-2974, outside the United States at (317) 572-3993 or fax (317) 572-4002.

Wiley also publishes its books in a variety of electronic formats. Some content that appears in print may not be available in electronic books.

**Library of Congress Control Number:** 2010942196

*For my wife, Lupita, who may not always understand but always accepts, supports, and encourages.*

# About the Author

**Joshua Davies** has been hacking on computers since his father brought home the family's first computer, a TI-99/4A, in 1982. He holds a Bachelor's degree in computer science from Valdosta State University and a Masters degree in computer science from the University of Texas at Arlington. He has been programming professionally since 1990 and as a result has never had to do any real work. He is currently responsible for security architecture at `Travelocity` `.com` and previously worked internationally as a consultant for One, Inc. whose client list included AT&T, Nieman Marcus, Intermedia, and the Mexican telecommunications giant Pegaso. He prefers to work in C or assembler, but often codes in Java since it pays the bills. He currently resides in Dallas, Texas with his wife and two children.

# About the Technical Editor

**David Chapa** is a Senior Analyst with the Enterprise Strategy Group covering the Data Protection segment with a focus on Disaster Recovery, Backup/Recovery as a Service, and Availability Solutions. David has invested over 25 years in the computer industry, focusing specifically on data protection, data disaster recovery, and business resumption practices. He has held several senior level technical positions with companies such as Cheyenne Software, OpenVision, ADIC, Quantum, and NetApp. Prior to joining ESG, as Director of Data Protection Strategy and Global Alliances for NetApp, David continued to evangelize "Recovery and Backup," his mantra for over a decade now, and the benefits of integrating software solutions with disk-based backup. In his role with ESG, David will bring all of this expertise, knowledge, and passion to raise a greater holistic awareness around data protection. David is an energetic and dynamic speaker who brings a great deal of experiential knowledge, humor, and keen insight to his audience. He has been a featured speaker at VERITAS Vision, CA World, SNW, Chicago Software Association, and CAMP/IT Conferences, and has served as panelist on various discussions related to disaster recovery, compliance, and the use of disk, tape, and cloud for recovery and backup strategies.

David has written several articles and blogs over the years. In addition, he is the co-author of *Implementing Backup and Recovery*, the Technical Editor of *Cloud Security*, *Security 2020*, and *Web Commerce Security Design and Development* with Wiley and Sons, and is recognized worldwide as an authority on the subject of backup and recovery. David is also a member of SNIA's Data Protection and Capacity Optimization (DPCO) Committee, whose mission is to foster the growth and success of the storage market in the areas of data protection and capacity optimization technologies.

# Credits

**Executive Editor**
Carol Long

**Project Editor**
Maureen Spears

**Technical Editor**
David A. Chapa

**Production Editor**
Kathleen Wisor

**Copy Editor**
Charlotte Kughen

**Editorial Director**
Robyn B. Siesky

**Editorial Manager**
Mary Beth Wakefield

**Freelancer Editorial Manager**
Rosemarie Graham

**Marketing Manager**
Ashley Zurcher

**Production Manager**
Tim Tate

**Vice President and Executive Group Publisher**
Richard Swadley

**Vice President and Executive Publisher**
Barry Pruett

**Associate Publisher**
Jim Minatel

**Project Coordinator, Cover**
Katie Crocker

**Proofreader**
Nancy Bell

**Indexer**
Robert Swanson

**Cover Designer**
Ryan Sneed

# Acknowledgments

My name is the name on the cover of this book, but I can't possibly take all of the credit for the finished product. I can't thank the staff at John Wiley and Sons enough for their hard work and dedication in bringing this book to print — Charlotte Kughen for tirelessly correcting my overly casual use of the English language, David Chapa for his encouragement and gentle feedback, Maureen Spears for her infinite patience with me every time I asked to make last-minute changes long after the time for last-minute changes had passed (I'm sure some day you'll look back on this and laugh) and finally to Carol Long for understanding what I was trying to accomplish and expending so much effort to get the green light for this project in the first place.

Thanks to the OpenSSL development team for their excellent software, which I made such heavy use of while developing and testing the code in this book, and to Thomas Hruska of Shining Light Productions for his feedback as well. Many thanks to the IETF TLS working group who volunteer their time to generate free, openly accessibly specifications for no compensation beyond the satisfaction that they are making the world a better, safer place. I've enjoyed debating and discussing the finer points of TLS with all of you while I was lurking on the mailing list over the past three years. This book is in no small part the culmination of the understanding I've achieved from listening to all of you.

I must, of course, acknowledge the support and encouragement I received from my university professors long after graduation — especially to Dr. Roger Lamprey, Dr. Gergely Zaruba, and Dr. Farhad Kamangar. I have no idea what they're paying you, but I'm sure it's far less than you deserve.

A special thank you goes to Troy Magennis of Travelocity, who encouraged me to take the leap from thinking about writing a book to finally sitting down and making it happen. Your example and inspiration were invaluable.

Thank you to my parents and my brother and sisters who are five of the most different, unique, and interesting people on the planet. It's amazing that we're all related, but somehow we pull it off. Finally, thank you to my family for their support as I wrote this book. This took far longer and much more effort than I ever anticipated. For putting up with my long absences and lost evenings and weekends as I wrote, re-wrote, and re-re-wrote: Lupita, Dylan, and Isabelle — you are my purpose on this earth and my reason for being — I hope I can always make you proud.

And, of course, thanks to Tornado the cat for keeping my lap warm night after night as I wrote after everybody else had gone to bed.

# Contents at a Glance

# Contents

# Introduction

This book examines the *Secure Sockets Layer* (SSL) and *Transport Layer Security* (TLS) protocols in detail, taking a bottom-up approach. SSL/TLS is a standardized, widely implemented, peer-reviewed protocol for applying cryptographic primitives to arbitrary networked communications. It provides privacy, integrity, and some measure of authenticity to otherwise inherently untrustworthy network connections. Rather than just present the details of the protocol itself, this book develops, incrementally, a relatively complete SSL/TLS library. First, all of the relevant cryptographic protocols are examined and developed, and then the library itself is built piece by piece.

All of the code developed in this book is C (not C++) code. It's been tested on both Windows and Linux systems and should run as advertised on either. Although this is a code-heavy book, non-C programmers — or even non-programmers in general — will still be able to get quite a bit from it. All of the protocols and examples are presented in general form as well as in source code form so that if you're interested in a higher-level overview, you can skip the code examples and the book should still make sense.

I chose C instead of C++ (or Java or Python or Perl, and so on) as a good "least-common-denominator" language. If you can program in any other procedural language, you can program in C; and if you can understand an implementation in C, you can understand an implementation in any other language. This book takes full advantage of the C programming language, though. I use pointer syntax in particular throughout the book. If you plan on following along with the code samples, make sure you're comfortable with C and pointers. I do my best to avoid the sort of excessive macro-ization and gratuitous typedef-ing that make professional C code easy to maintain but hard to read.

You might be wondering, though, why I present the source code of yet another (partially incomplete) implementation when there are so many good, tried-and-tested open-source implementations of SSL available. Effectively, production-grade libraries have (at least) five primary concerns regarding their source code:

1. It must work.

2. It must be secure.

3. It should be as fast as reasonably possible.

4. It must be modular/extensible.

5. It must be easy to read/understand.

When a higher-numbered concern conflicts with a lower-numbered concern, the lower-numbered concern wins. This must be the case for code that's actually used by real people to perform real tasks. The upshot is that the code is not always pretty, nor is it particularly readable, when security/speed/modularity take precedence. The priorities for the code in this book are

1. It must work.

2. It should be as readable as possible.

Note that security, speed, and modularity aren't concerns. In fact, the code presented in this book (somewhat ironically) is *not* particularly secure. For example, when the algorithms call for random bytes, the code in this book just returns sequentially numbered bytes, which is the exact opposite of the random bytes that the algorithm calls for. This is done to simplify the code as well as to make sure that what you see if you try it out yourself matches what you see in the book.

There isn't any bounds-checking on buffers or verification that the input matches what's expected, which are things that a proper library ought to be doing. I've omitted these things to keep this book's (already long) page count under control, as well as to avoid obscuring the purpose of the example code with hundreds of lines of error checking. At various times throughout the book, you'll see code comments such as `// TODO make this random` or `// TODO check the length before using`. I've placed these comments in the code to draw your attention to the functionality that was intentionally omitted.

Of course, if you're coding in a hostile environment — that is, if you're working with any production quality code — you should prefer a well-established library such as OpenSSL, GnuTLS, or NSS over home-grown code any day. This book, however, should help you understand the internals of these libraries so that, when it comes time to use one, you know exactly what's going on at all stages.

## Supplemental Web Sites

Every aspect of the Internet itself — including SSL/TLS — is described by a series of documents written and maintained by the *Internet Engineering Task Force* (IETF). These documents are referred to (somewhat confusingly) as *Requests for Comments* or, more commonly, just *RFCs*. Each such RFC describes, authoritatively, some aspect of some protocol related to the Internet. And at the time of this writing, there are over 5000 such documents. Although I doubt that anybody, anywhere, has actually read all of them, you'll need to be familiar with quite a few in order to do any serious Internet programming. As such, I'll refer to these RFCs by number throughout the book. Rather than provide a link to each inline, I'll just refer to them as, e.g., RFC 2246. If you want to see RFC 2246 (the authoritative document that describes TLS 1.0 itself), you can visit the IETF's website at `www.ietf.org`. Each RFC is stored in a document under `http://www .ietf.org/rfc/rfcnnnn.txt`, where *nnnn* is the RFC number itself.

In addition, SSL/TLS borrows heavily from a couple of related standards bodies — the *International Telecommuncation Union* (ITU) "X series" of documents and RSA laboratories' *Public Key Cryptography Standards* (PKCS). The ITU standards can be found at `http://www.itu.int/rec/T-REC-X/en` and the PKCS standards can be found at `http://www.rsa.com/rsalabs/node.asp?id=2124`. I'll refer to RFC's, X-series documents, and PKCS standards throughout the book. You may want to bookmark these locations in a browser for quick reference, if you'd like to compare the text to the official standards documents. All of the standards documents referenced in this book are freely available and downloadable, so I don't make any great effort to repeat them. Instead, I try to explain the background information that the standards documents always seem to take for granted. I'm assuming that, if you're interested in the low-level details, you can always refer to the standards document itself.

## Roadmap and Companion Source Code

I've been around and reading technical documentation since before there was an Internet, or even CD-ROM drives. Back in my day, readers of code-heavy books such as this one couldn't just download the samples from a companion website or an included CD-ROM. If you wanted to see the code samples in action, you had to type them in by hand. Although typing code can be tedious at times, I've found that it's also the best way to completely absorb the material. So, Luddite that I am, I tend to eschew code downloads when I read technical material.

This book has been designed so that somebody who wants to follow along can do so. However, I also recognize that not every reader is a dinosaur like myself — er, I mean not everyone is quite so meticulous. Changes to code presented previously are listed in boldface, so it's easy to see what's been modified and what's been left unchanged.

The companion website at `http://www.wiley.com/go/implementingssl` has two download files — one for GCC for those following along on a Linux platform and one for Visual Studio for those following along on Windows. Each download is split into two sections: one that includes the finished code for each chapter and another for somebody who might want to follow along. I urge you to download at least the code for following along because it includes Makefiles and headers that aren't specifically reproduced in this book. This book's code is heavily self-referential — especially in the second half — so you want to be sure to build correctly. The downloadable Makefiles ensure that you can.

Because this book is about SSL, I try my best not to get too hung up on unrelated implementation details. However, the code presented here does work and is somewhat nontrivial, so some "implementation asides" are unavoidable.

## Outline of the Book

Chapter 1, "Understanding Internet Security," examines the basics of Internet communication and what is and is not vulnerable to attackers. To motivate the remainder of the book, a basic working HTTP example is developed here. Later chapters incrementally add security features to this beginning HTTP example.

Chapter 2, "Protecting Against Eavesdroppers with Symmetric Cryptography," examines the aspect of communications security that most people think of first, which is scrambling data in flight so that it can't be intercepted or read by unauthorized parties. There are many internationally recognized standard algorithms in this space, which SSL/TLS rely heavily on. Chapter 2 examines three of these standards in detail: DES, AES and RC4. The code developed here will be reused in Chapter 6 when the actual TLS library is built.

Chapter 3, "Secure Key Exchange over an Insecure Medium with Public Key Cryptography," looks at the problem of exchanging keys when the underlying communications channel can't be trusted. The thorny problem of how to take an unencrypted link and turn it into an encrypted one is examined here. There are also several standards in this area — RSA, Diffie-Hellman, and Elliptic-Curve Cryptography are examined in detail in this chapter.

Chapter 4, "Authenticating Communications Using Digital Signatures," examines a less prominent, but equally as important, aspect of secure communications. While cryptography protects data from eavesdroppers, authentication protects data against forgers. The standards MD-5, SHA-1, SHA-256, HMAC, DSA, and ECDSA are all examined in detail in this chapter. Each of these plays a key role in TLS as discussed further in Chapter 6.

Chapter 5, "Creating a Network of Trust Using X.509 Certificates," discusses the final piece of the PKI puzzle that the previous two chapters began, digital certificates. Digital certificates and the Public-Key Infrastructure that support them are required to guard against active attacks. TLS depends greatly on certificates, so this chapter develops an ASN.1 parser and an X.509 certificate reader, which is used in the next chapter to authenticate web sites securely.

Chapter 6, "A Usable, Secure Communications Protocol: Client-Side TLS," ties together all of the concepts from the previous four chapters into a working TLS implementation. This chapter looks at TLS from the perspective of the client and ends with a working HTTPS implementation.

Chapter 7, "Adding Server-Side TLS 1.0 Support," takes the foundation of TLS from Chapter 6 and expands it to the web server example from Chapter 1, developing an SSL-enabled mini–web server. Since the server needs to store private keys, which are, by their nature, especially sensitive, Chapter 7 also examines the topic of using password to securely encrypt data at rest.

Chapter 8, "Advanced SSL Topics," covers the rest of TLS 1.0 — there are several optional elements that a compliant implementation ought to support, but which are not as widespread as the most common case covered in Chapters 6 and 7. Client authentication, server name identification, export grade cryptography, session resumption, and session renegotiation are all explored in depth here.

Chapter 9, "Adding TLS 1.2 Support to Your TLS Library," implements the latest version of the TLS protocol, 1.2, on top of the TLS 1.0 implementation that Chapters 6–8 developed. Here you see elliptic curve cryptography put to use. Additionally, AEAD-mode ciphers are examined, since TLS 1.2 is the first version of TLS to permit this mode.

Chapter 10, "Other Applications of SSL," takes a look at the non-HTTP uses that SSL/TLS has been put to. The STARTTLS extension and DTLS are examined here. Also, S/MIME and DNSSEC — not strictly TLS, but related — are covered in this chapter. Finally, Chapter 10 ends by looking at how HTTPS supports HTTP proxies, which is, overall, an interesting compromise.

## How to Read This Book

This book was written to be read cover to cover. Additionally, if you have some background in C programming, you will want to read through, and probably compile and run, the code samples. If you're not a programmer, or not particularly comfortable with the C programming language, you can skip over the code samples and just read the text descriptions of the relevant protocols — the book was written to make sense when read this way. The benefit of the code samples is that it's impossible to omit any detail — accidentally or intentionally — when writing code, so if you can understand the code, it will cement your understanding of the text preceding it. I've made every effort to ensure that the text and diagrams describe the protocols exactly. If, however, in spite of my best efforts, my descriptions are for any reason unclear, you can always step through the code to see exactly what's going on.

Although this is a book about SSL/TLS, the first half of the book just sets the stage for SSL/TLS by presenting all of the protocols and standards they rely on. If you're just looking for a description of TLS, and have a reasonable understanding of cryptography and PKI in general, you should be able to safely skip ahead to Chapter 6 and start there with the overview of TLS itself. However, at some point, you should jump back and read Chapters 2–5, since there are a lot of implementation details that can bite you in surprising ways when using cryptographic libraries. My primary motivation in writing this book was to present, in detail, the interplay between the SSL and TLS protocols and the cryptographic routines that they rely on.

# Understanding Internet Security

How secure is the data that you transmit on the Internet? How vulnerable is your personal data to hackers? Even computer-literate, experienced programmers find it's hard to answer these questions with certainty. You probably know that standard encryption algorithms are used to protect data — you've likely heard of public-key algorithms such as RSA and DSA — and you may know that the U.S. government's Data Encryption Standard has been replaced by an Advanced Encryption Standard. Everybody knows about the lock icon in their browsers that indicates that the session is protected by HTTPS. You've most likely heard of PGP for e-mail security (even if you gave up on it after failing to convince your friends to use it).

In all likelihood, though, you've also heard of *man in the middle attacks, timing attacks, side-channel attacks,* and various other attacks that aim to compromise privacy and security. Anybody with a web browser has been presented with the ominous warning message that "This site's security cannot be trusted — either the certificate has expired, or it was issued by a certificate authority you have chosen not to trust." Every week, you can read about some new zero-day exploit uncovered by security researchers that requires a round of frantic patching. As a professional programmer, you may feel you ought to know exactly what that means — yet trying to decipher these messages and determine whether you should really be worried or not takes you down the rabbit hole of IETF, PKCS, FIPS, NIST, ITU, and ASN. You may have tried to go straight to the source and read RFC 2246, which describes TLS, but you may have discovered, to your chagrin, that RFC 2246 presumes a background in symmetric cryptography, public-key cryptography, digital signature algorithms, and X.509 certificates. It's unclear where to even begin. Although there are a handful of books that describe SSL and "Internet Security," none are targeted at the technically inclined reader who wants, or needs, to know the details.

A mantra among security professionals is that the average programmer doesn't understand security and should not be trusted with it until he verses himself in it. This is good, but ultimately unhelpful, advice. Where does one begin? What the security professionals are really trying to tell you is that, as a practitioner rather than a casual user, it's not enough to treat security as a black box or a binary property; you need to know what the security is doing and how it's doing it so that you know what you are and aren't protected against. This book was written for you — the professional programmer who understands the basics of security but wants to uncover the details without reading thousands of pages of dry technical specifications (only some of which are relevant).

This book begins by examining sockets and socket programming in brief. Afterward, it moves on to a detailed examination of cryptographic concepts and finally applies them to SSL/TLS, the current standard for Internet security. You examine what SSL/TLS does, what it doesn't do, and how it does it. After completing this book, you'll know exactly how and where SSL fits into an overall security strategy and you'll know what steps yet need to be taken, if any, to achieve additional security.

## What Are Secure Sockets?

The Internet is a *packet-switching* network. This means that, for two hosts to communicate, they must *packetize* their data and submit it to a router with the destination address prepended to each packet. The router then analyzes the destination address and routes the packet either to the target host, or to a router that it believes is closer to the target host. The *Internet Protocol* (IP), outlined in RFC 971, describes the standard for how this packetization is performed and how addresses are attached to packets in headers.

A packet can and probably will pass through many routers between the sender and the receiver. If the contents of the data in that packet are sensitive — a password, a credit card, a tax identification number — the sender would probably like to ensure that only the receiver can read the packet, rather than the packet being readable by any router along the way. Even if the sender trusts the routers and their operators, routers can be compromised by malicious individuals, called *attackers* in security terminology, and tricked into forwarding traffic that's meant for one destination to another, as shown in `http://www.securesphere` `.net/download/papers/dnsspoof.htm`. If you'd like to get an idea just how many different hosts a packet passes through between you and a server, you can use the *traceroute* facility that comes with every Internet-capable computer to print a list of the hops between you and any server on the Internet.

An example of a traceroute output is shown below:

```
[jdavies@localhost]:~$ traceroute www.travelocity.com
traceroute to www.travelocity.com (151.193.224.81), 30 hops max, 40 byte packets
 1 192.168.0.1 (192.168.0.1) 0.174 ms 0.159 ms 0.123 ms
 2 * * *
 3 172.216.125.53 (172.216.125.53) 8.052 ms 7.978 ms 9.699 ms
 4 10.208.164.65 (10.208.164.65) 10.731 ms 9.895 ms 9.489 ms
 5 gig8-2.dllatxarl-t-rtr1.tx.rr.com (70.125.217.92) 12.593 ms 10.952 ms
13.003 ms
 6 gig0-1-0.dllatxl3-rtr1.texas.rr.com (72.179.205.72) 69.604 ms 37.540 ms
14.015 ms
 7 ae-4-0.cr0.dfw10.tbone.rr.com (66.109.6.88) 13.434 ms 13.696 ms 15.259 ms
 8 ae-1-0.pr0.dfw10.tbone.rr.com (66.109.6.179) 15.498 ms 15.948 ms 15.555 ms
 9 xe-7-0-0.edge4.Dallas3.Level3.net (4.59.32.17) 18.653 ms 22.451 ms 16.034
ms
10 ae-11-60.car1.Dallas1.Level3.net (4.69.145.3) 19.759 ms
ae-21-70.car1.Dallas1.Level3.net (4.69.145.67) 17.455 ms
ae-41-90.car1.Dallas1.Level3.net (4.69.145.195) 16.469 ms
11 EDS.car1.Dallas1.Level3.net (4.59.113.86) 28.853 ms 25.672 ms 26.337 ms
12 151.193.129.61 (151.193.129.61) 24.763 ms 26.032 ms 25.481 ms
13 151.193.129.99 (151.193.129.99) 28.727 ms 25.441 ms 26.507 ms
14 151.193.129.173 (151.193.129.173) 26.642 ms 23.995 ms 28.462 ms
15 * * *
```

Here, I've submitted a traceroute to `www.travelocity.com`. Each router along the way is supposed to respond with a special packet called an ICMP timeout packet, as described in RFC 793, with its own address. The routers that cannot or will not do so are represented with * * * in the preceding code. Typically the routers don't respond because they're behind a firewall that's configured not to forward ICMP diagnostic packets. As you can see, there are quite a few hops between my home router and Travelocity's main web server.

In network programming parlance, the tenuous connection between a sender and a receiver is referred to as a *socket*. When one host — the *client* — is ready to establish a connection with another — the *server* — it sends a *synchronize* (SYN) packet to the server. If the server is willing to accept the connection, it responds with a SYN and acknowledge packet. Finally, the client acknowledges the acknowledgment and both sides have agreed on a connection. This three-packet exchange is referred to as the *TCP handshake* and is illustrated in Figure 1-1. The connection is associated with a pair of numbers: the *source port* and the *destination port*, which are attached to each subsequent packet in the communication. Because the server is sitting around, always listening for connections, it must advertise its destination port ahead of time. How this is done is protocol-specific; some protocols are lucky enough to have "magic numbers" associated with them that are well-known (in other words, you, the programmer are supposed to know them). This is the *Transport Control Protocol* (TCP); RFC

793 describes exactly how this works and how both sides agree on a source and destination port and how they sequence these and subsequent packets.

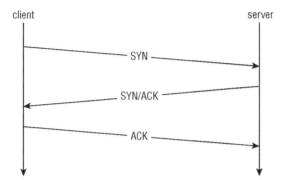

**Figure 1-1:** TCP three-way handshake

TCP and IP are usually implemented together and called *TCP/IP*. A *socket* refers to an established TCP connection; both sides, client and server, have a socket after the *three-way handshake* described above has been completed. If either side transmits data over this socket, TCP guarantees, to the best of its ability, that the other side sees this data in the order it was sent. As is required by IP, however, any intermediate router along the way also sees this data.

*SSL* stands for *Secure Sockets Layer* and was originally developed by Netscape as a way to allow the then-new browser technology to be used for e-commerce. The original specification proposal can be found in `http://www.mozilla.org/projects/security/pki/nss/ssl/draft02.html`. Although it has since been standardized and renamed *Transport Layer Security* (*TLS*), the name SSL is much more recognizable and in some ways describes better what it does and what it's for. After a socket has been established between the client and the server, SSL defines a second handshake that can be performed to establish a secure channel over the inherently insecure TCP layer.

# "Insecure" Communications: Understanding the HTTP Protocol

*HTTP*, or *Hypertext Transport Protocol*, which is officially described in RFC 2616, is the standard protocol for web communication. Web clients, typically referred to as *browsers*, establish sockets with web servers. HTTP has a well-known destination port of 80. After the socket has been established, the web browser begins following the rules set forth by the HTTP protocol to request documents. HTTP started out as a fairly simple protocol in which the client issued a GET command and a description of what it would like to get, to which the server responded with either what the client requested in document form or an error indicating why it could not or did not give the client that document. Either way, the socket would be closed after this. If the client wanted another document, it would create another socket and request another document. Over the years, HTTP has been refined quite a bit and optimized for bandwidth, speed, and security features.

HTTP was also the primary motivator for SSL. Originally, SSL didn't stand on its own; it was designed as an add-on to HTTP, called HTTPS. Although SSL was subsequently decoupled from HTTP, some of its features were optimized for HTTP, leaving it to be a bit of a square peg in a round hole in some other contexts. Because HTTP and SSL go so well together, in this book I motivate SSL by developing an HTTP client and adding security features to it incrementally, finally arriving at a working HTTP/SSL implementation.

## Implementing an HTTP Client

Web browsers are complex because they need to parse and render HTML — and, in most cases, render images, run Javascript, Flash, Java Applets and leave room for new, as-yet-uninvented add-ons. However, a web client that only retrieves a document from a server, such as the wget utility that comes standard with most Unix distributions, is actually pretty simple. Most of the complexity is in the socket handling itself — establishing the socket and sending and receiving data over it.

Start with all of the includes that go along with socket communication — as you can see, there are quite a few, shown in Listing 1-1.

**Listing 1-1:** "http.c" header includes

```
/**
 * This test utility does simple (non-encrypted) HTTP.
 */

#include <stdio.h>
#include <stdlib.h>
#include <errno.h>
#include <string.h>
#include <sys/types.h>
#ifdef WIN32
#include <winsock2.h>
#include <windows.h>
#else
#include <netdb.h>
#include <sys/socket.h>
#include <netinet/in.h>
#include <unistd.h>
#endif
```

The main routine is invoked with a URL of the form `http://www.server`
`.com/path/to/document.html`. You need to separate the host and the path using
a utility routine `parse_url`, shown in Listing 1-2.

**Listing 1-2:** "http.c" parse_url

```
/**
 * Accept a well-formed URL (e.g. http://www.company.com/index.html) and return
 * pointers to the host part and the path part. Note that this function
 * modifies the uri itself as well. It returns 0 on success, -1 if the URL is
 * found to be malformed in any way.
 */
int parse_url( char *uri, char **host, char **path )
{
  char *pos;

  pos = strstr( uri, "//" );

  if ( !pos )
  {
    return -1;
  }

  *host = pos + 2;

  pos = strchr( *host, '/' );

  if ( !pos )
  {
    *path = NULL;
  }
  else
  {
    *pos = '\0';
    *path = pos + 1;
  }

  return 0;
}
```

You scan through the URL, looking for the delimiters `//` and `/` and replace
them with null-terminators so that the caller can treat them as C strings. Notice
that the calling function passes in two pointers to pointers; these should be
null when the function starts and will be modified to point into the `uri` string,
which came from `argv`.

The main routine that coordinates all of this is shown in Listing 1-3.

**Listing 1-3:** "http.c" main

```
#define HTTP_PORT    80

/**
 * Simple command-line HTTP client.
```

```
 */
int main( int argc, char *argv[ ] )
{
  int client_connection;
  char *host, *path;
  struct hostent *host_name;
  struct sockaddr_in host_address;
#ifdef WIN32
  WSADATA wsaData;
#endif

  if ( argc < 2 )
  {
    fprintf( stderr, "Usage: %s: <URL>\n", argv[ 0 ] );
    return 1;
  }

  if ( parse_url( argv[ 1 ], &host, &path ) == -1 )
  {
    fprintf( stderr, "Error - malformed URL '%s'.\n", argv[ 1 ] );
    return 1;
  }

  printf( "Connecting to host '%s'\n", host );
```

After the URL has been parsed and the host is known, you must establish a socket to it. In order to do this, convert it from a human-readable host name, such as www.server.com, to a dotted-decimal IP address, such as 100.218.64.2. You call the standard gethostbyname library function to do this, and connect to the server. This is shown in Listing 1-4.

**Listing 1-4:** "http.c" main (continued)

```
  // Step 1: open a socket connection on http port with the destination host.
#ifdef WIN32
  if ( WSAStartup( MAKEWORD( 2, 2 ), &wsaData ) != NO_ERROR )
  {
    fprintf( stderr, "Error, unable to initialize winsock.\n" );
    return 2;
  }
#endif

  client_connection = socket( PF_INET, SOCK_STREAM, 0 );

  if ( !client_connection )
  {
    perror( "Unable to create local socket" );
    return 2;
  }

  host_name = gethostbyname( host );

  if ( !host_name )
```

*(Continued)*

```
{
  perror( "Error in name resolution" );
  return 3;
}

host_address.sin_family = AF_INET;
host_address.sin_port = htons( HTTP_PORT );
memcpy( &host_address.sin_addr, host_name->h_addr_list[ 0 ],
        sizeof( struct in_addr ) );

if ( connect( client_connection, ( struct sockaddr * ) &host_address,
      sizeof( host_address ) ) == -1 )
{
  perror( "Unable to connect to host" );
  return 4;
}

printf( "Retrieving document: '%s'\n", path );
```

Assuming nothing went wrong — the socket structure could be created, the hostname could be resolved to an IP address, the IP address was reachable, and the server accepted your connection on the well-known port 80 — you now have a usable (cleartext) socket with which to exchange data with the web server. Issue a GET command, display the result, and close the socket, as shown in Listing 1-5.

**Listing 1-5:** "http.c" main (continued)

```
http_get( client_connection, path, host );

display_result( client_connection );

printf( "Shutting down.\n" );

#ifdef WIN32
  if ( closesocket( client_connection ) == -1 )
#else
  if ( close( client_connection ) == -1 )
#endif
  {
    perror( "Error closing client connection" );
    return 5;
  }

#ifdef WIN32
  WSACleanup();
#endif

  return 0;
}
```

An HTTP GET command is a simple, plaintext command. It starts with the three ASCII-encoded letters GET, all in uppercase (HTTP is case sensitive), a space, the path to the document to be retrieved, another space, and the token

HTTP/1.0 or HTTP/1.1 depending on which version of the HTTP protocol the client understands.

**NOTE** At the time of this writing, there are only two versions of HTTP; the differences are immaterial to this book.

The GET command itself is followed by a carriage-return/line-feed pair (0x0A 0x0D) and a colon-separated, CRLF-delimited list of *headers* that describe how the client wants the response to be returned. Only one header is required — the Host header, which is required to support *virtual hosting*, the situation where several hosts share one IP address or vice-versa. The Connection header is not required, but in general you should send it to indicate to the client whether you want it to Keep-Alive the connection — if you plan on requesting more documents on this same socket — or Close it. If you omit the Connection: Close header line, the server keeps the socket open until the client closes it. If you're just sending a single request and getting back a single response, it's easier to let the server just close the connection when it's done sending. The header list is terminated by an empty CRLF pair.

A minimal HTTP GET command looks like this:

```
GET /index.html HTTP/1.1
Host: www.server.com
Connection: close
```

The code to format and submit a GET command over an established socket is shown in Listing 1-6. Note that the input is the socket itself — the connection argument — the path of the document being requested, and the host (to build the host header).

**Listing 1-6:** "http.c" http_get

```
#define MAX_GET_COMMAND 255
/**
 * Format and send an HTTP get command. The return value will be 0
 * on success, -1 on failure, with errno set appropriately. The caller
 * must then retrieve the response.
 */
int http_get( int connection, const char *path, const char *host )
{
  static char get_command[ MAX_GET_COMMAND ];

  sprintf( get_command, "GET /%s HTTP/1.1\r\n", path );
  if ( send( connection, get_command, strlen( get_command ), 0 ) == -1 )
  {
    return -1;
  }

  sprintf( get_command, "Host: %s\r\n", host );
  if ( send( connection, get_command, strlen( get_command ), 0 ) == -1 )
  {
```

*(Continued)*

```
    return -1;
  }

  sprintf( get_command, "Connection: close\r\n\r\n" );
  if ( send( connection, get_command, strlen( get_command ), 0 ) == -1 )
  {
    return -1;
  }

  return 0;
}
```

Finally, output the response from the server. To keep things simple, just dump the contents of the response on stdout. An HTTP response has a standard format, just like an HTTP request. The response is the token `HTTP/1.0` or `HTTP/1.1` depending on which version the server understands (which does not necessarily have to match the client's version), followed by a space, followed by a numeric code indicating the status of the request — errored, rejected, processed, and so on — followed by a space, followed by a textual, human-readable, description of the meaning of the status code.

Some of the more common status codes are shown in Table 1-1.

**Table 1-1:** Common status codes

| STATUS | MEANING |
|--------|---------|
| 200 | Everything was OK, requested document follows. |
| 302 | Requested document exists, but has been moved – new location follows. |
| 403 | Forbidden: Requested document exists, but you are not authorized to view it. |
| 404 | Requested document not found. |
| 500 | Internal Server Error. |

There are quite a few more status codes, as described in RFC 2616. The response status line is followed, again, by a CRLF, and a series of colon-separated, CRLF-delimited headers, a standalone CRLF/blank line end-of-headers marker, and the document itself. Here's an example HTTP response:

```
HTTP/1.1 200 OK
Date: Tue, 13 Oct 2009 19:34:51 GMT
Server: Apache
Last-Modified: Fri, 27 Oct 2006 01:53:57 GMT
ETag: "1876a-ff-316f5740"
Accept-Ranges: bytes
```

```
Content-Length: 255
Vary: Accept-Encoding
Connection: close
Content-Type: text/html; charset=ISO-8859-1

<html>
<head>
<TITLE>Welcome to the server</TITLE>
</head>
<BODY BGCOLOR=ffffff>
This is the server's homepage
</BODY>
</html>
```

Here's an example of a 404 "not found" error:

```
HTTP/1.1 404 Not Found
Date: Tue, 13 Oct 2009 19:40:53 GMT
Server: Apache
Last-Modified: Fri, 27 Oct 2006 01:53:58 GMT
ETag: "1875d-c5-317e9980"
Accept-Ranges: bytes
Content-Length: 197
Vary: Accept-Encoding
Connection: close
Content-Type: text/html; charset=ISO-8859-1

<!DOCTYPE HTML PUBLIC "-//IETF//DTD HTML 2.0//EN">
<html><head>
<title>404 Not Found</title>
</head><body>
<h1>Not Found</h1>
<p>The requested URL was not found on this server.</p>
</body></html>
```

Even though the document requested was not found, a document was returned, which can be displayed in a browser to remind the user that something has gone wrong.

For testing purposes, you don't care about the response itself, as long as you get one. Therefore, don't make any efforts to parse these responses — just dump their contents, verbatim, on stdout as shown in Listing 1-7.

**Listing 1-7:** "http.c" display_result

```
#define BUFFER_SIZE 255

/**
 * Receive all data available on a connection and dump it to stdout
 */
void display_result( int connection )
{
  int received = 0;
```

*(Continued)*

```
static char recv_buf[ BUFFER_SIZE + 1 ];

while ( ( received = recv( connection, recv_buf, BUFFER_SIZE, 0 ) ) > 0 )
{
  recv_buf[ received ] = '\0';
  printf( "%s", recv_buf );
}
printf( "\n" );
}
```

This is all that's required to implement a bare-bones web client. Note, however, that because the socket created was a cleartext socket, everything that's transmitted between the client and the server is observable, in plaintext, to every host in between. In general, if you want to protect the transmission from eavesdroppers, you establish an SSL context — that is, *secure the line* — prior to sending the GET command.

## Adding Support for HTTP Proxies

One important topic related to HTTP is the HTTP proxy. Proxies are a bit tricky for SSL. Notice in Listing 1-4 that a socket had to be created from the client to the server before a document could be requested. This means that the client had to be able to construct a SYN packet, hand that off to a router, which hands it off to another router, and so on until it's received by the server. The server then constructs its own SYN/ACK packet, hands it off, and so on until it's received by the client. However, in corporate intranet environments, packets from outside the corporate domain are not allowed in and vice versa. In effect, there is no route from the client to the server with which it wants to connect.

In this scenario, it's typical to set up a *proxy server* that can connect to the outside world, and have the client funnel its requests through the proxy. This changes the dynamics a bit; the client establishes a socket connection with the proxy server first, and issues a GET request to it as shown in Figure 1-2. After the proxy receives the GET request, the proxy examines the request to determine the host name, resolves the IP address, connects to that IP address on behalf of the client, re-issues the GET request, and forwards the response back to the client. This subtly changes the dynamics of HTTP. What's important to notice is that the client establishes a socket with the proxy server, and the GET request now includes the full URL.

Because you may well be reading this behind such a firewalled environment, and because proxies present some unique challenges for SSL, go ahead and add proxy support to the minimal HTTP client developed in the preceding section.

First of all, you need to modify the main routine to accept an optional proxy specification parameter. A proxy specification includes, of course, the hostname of the proxy server itself, but it also typically allows a username and password to be passed in, as most HTTP proxies are, or at least can be, authenticating. The standard format for a proxy specification is

```
http://[username:password@]hostname[:port]/
```

where `hostname` is the only part that's required. Modify your main routine as shown in Listing 1-8 to accept an optional proxy parameter, preceded by `-p`.

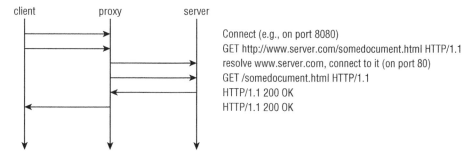

**Figure 1-2:** HTTP Proxies

**Listing 1-8:** "http.c" main (with proxy support)

```c
int main( int argc, char *argv[ ] )

{
  int client_connection;
  char *proxy_host, *proxy_user, *proxy_password;
  int proxy_port;
  char *host, *path;
  struct hostent *host_name;
  struct sockaddr_in host_address;
  int ind;
#ifdef WIN32
  WSADATA wsaData;
#endif

  if ( argc < 2 )
  {
    fprintf( stderr,
      "Usage: %s: [-p http://[username:password@]proxy-host:proxy-port]\
<URL>\n",
      argv[ 0 ] );
    return 1;
  }
  proxy_host = proxy_user = proxy_password = host = path = NULL;
  ind = 1;
  if ( !strcmp( "-p", argv[ ind ] ) )
  {
    if ( !parse_proxy_param( argv[ ++ind ], &proxy_host, &proxy_port,
```

*(Continued)*

```
                                    &proxy_user, &proxy_password ) )
  {
    fprintf( stderr, "Error - malformed proxy parameter '%s'.\n",
      argv[ 2 ] );
    return 2;
  }
  ind++;
}
if ( parse_url( argv[ ind ], &host, &path ) == -1 )
```

If the first argument is -p, take the second argument to be a proxy specification in the canonical form and parse it. Either way, the last argument is still a URL.

If parse_proxy_param succeeds, proxy_host is a non-null pointer to the host-name of the proxy server. You need to make a few changes to your connection logic to support this correctly, as shown in Listing 1-9. First you need to establish a socket connection to the proxy host rather than the actual target HTTP host.

**Listing 1-9:** "http.c" main (with proxy support) (continued)

```
if ( proxy_host )
{
  printf( "Connecting to host '%s'\n", proxy_host );
  host_name = gethostbyname( proxy_host );
}
else
{
  printf( "Connecting to host '%s'\n", host );
  host_name = gethostbyname( host );
}
host_address.sin_family = AF_INET;
host_address.sin_port = htons( proxy_host ? proxy_port : HTTP_PORT );
memcpy( &host_address.sin_addr, host_name->h_addr_list[ 0 ],
        sizeof( struct in_addr ) );
...
http_get( client_connection, path, host, proxy_host,
          proxy_user, proxy_password );
```

Finally, pass the proxy host, user, and password to http_get. The new parse_proxy_param function works similarly to the parse_url function in Listing 1-2: pass in a pointer to the argv string, insert nulls at strategic places, and set char * pointers to the appropriate places within the argv string to represent the individual pieces, as shown in Listing 1-10.

**Listing 1-10:** "http.c" parse_proxy_param

```
int parse_proxy_param( char *proxy_spec,
        char **proxy_host,
        int *proxy_port,
        char **proxy_user,
        char **proxy_password )
{
```

```
char *login_sep, *colon_sep, *trailer_sep;
// Technically, the user should start the proxy spec with
// "http://". But, be forgiving if he didn't.
if ( !strncmp( "http://", proxy_spec, 7 ) )
{
 proxy_spec += 7;
}
```

In Listing 1-11, check to see if an authentication string has been supplied. If the @ symbol appears in the proxy_spec, it must be preceded by a "username:password" pair. If it is, parse those out; if it isn't, there's no error because the username and password are not strictly required.

**Listing 1-11:** "http.c" parse_proxy_param (continued)

```
login_sep = strchr( proxy_spec, '@' );

if ( login_sep )
{
  colon_sep = strchr( proxy_spec, ':' );
  if ( !colon_sep || ( colon_sep > login_sep ) )
  {
    // Error - if username supplied, password must be supplied.
    fprintf( stderr, "Expected password in '%s'\n", proxy_spec );
    return 0;
  }
  *colon_sep = '\0';
  *proxy_user = proxy_spec;
  *login_sep = '\0';
  *proxy_password = colon_sep + 1;
  proxy_spec = login_sep + 1;
}
```

Notice that, if a username and password are supplied, you modify the proxy_spec parameter to point to the character after the @. This way, proxy_spec now points to the proxy host whether an authentication string was supplied or not.

Listing 1-12 shows the rest of the proxy parameter parsing — the user can supply a port number if the proxy is listening on a non-standard port.

**Listing 1-12:** "http.c" parse_proxy_param (continued)

```
// If the user added a "/" on the end (as they sometimes do),
// just ignore it.
trailer_sep = strchr( proxy_spec, '/' );
if ( trailer_sep )
{
  *trailer_sep = '\0';
}

colon_sep = strchr( proxy_spec, ':' );
if ( colon_sep )
```

*(Continued)*

```
  {
    // non-standard proxy port
    *colon_sep = '\0';
    *proxy_host = proxy_spec;
    *proxy_port = atoi( colon_sep + 1 );
    if ( *proxy_port == 0 )
    {
      // 0 is not a valid port; this is an error, whether
      // it was mistyped or specified as 0.
      return 0;
    }
  }
  else
  {
    *proxy_port = HTTP_PORT;
    *proxy_host = proxy_spec;
  }
  return 1;
}
```

The port number is also optional. If there's a : character before the end of the proxy specification, it denotes a port; otherwise, assume the standard HTTP port 80.

At this point, you have all the pieces you need for HTTP proxy support except for the changes to the actual `http_get` routine. Remember that, in ordinary, "proxy-less" HTTP, you start by establishing a connection to the target HTTP host and then send in a `GET /path HTTP/1.0` request line. However, when connecting to a proxy, you need to send a whole hostname because the socket itself has just been established between the client and the proxy. The request line becomes `GET http://host/path HTTP/1.0`. Change `http_get` as shown in Listing 1-13 to recognize this case and send a proxy-friendly `GET` command if a proxy host parameter was supplied.

**Listing 1-13:** http_get (modified for proxy support)

```
int http_get( int connection,
       const char *path,
       const char *host,
       const char *proxy_host,
       const char *proxy_user,
       const char *proxy_password )
{
  static char get_command[ MAX_GET_COMMAND ];
  if ( proxy_host )
  {
    sprintf( get_command, "GET http://%s/%s HTTP/1.1\r\n", host, path );
  }
  else
  {
```

```
    sprintf( get_command, "GET /%s HTTP/1.1\r\n", path );

}
```

If the proxy is non-authenticating, this is all you need to do. If the proxy is an authenticating proxy, as most are, you need to supply an additional HTTP header line including the proxy authorization string.

```
Proxy-Authorization: [METHOD] [connection string]
```

**[METHOD]**, according to RFC 2617, is one of BASIC or DIGEST. It's also common to see the non-standard NTLM in Microsoft environments. BASIC is, clearly, the simplest of the three, and the only one you'll support — hopefully, if you're behind a proxy, your proxy does, too. The format of *connection string* varies depending on the METHOD. For BASIC, it's base64_encode('username:password').

## Reliable Transmission of Binary Data with Base64 Encoding

You may be somewhat familiar with *Base 64* encoding, or at least be familiar with the term. In early modem-based communication systems, such as e-mail relay or UUCP systems, an unexpected byte value outside of the printable ASCII range 32–126 could cause all sorts of problems. Early modems interpreted byte code 6 as an acknowledgment, for example, wherever it occurred in the stream. This created problems when trying to transmit binary data such as compressed images or executable files. Various (incompatible) encoding methods were developed to map binary data into the range of printable ASCII characters; one of the most popular was Base64.

Base64 divides the input into 6-bit chunks — hence the name *Base64* because $2^6$=64 — and maps each 6-bit input into one of the printable ASCII characters. The first 52 combinations map to the upper- and lowercase alphabetic characters A–Z and a–z; the next 10 map to the numerals 0–9. That leaves two combinations left over to map. There's been some historical contention on exactly what these characters should be, but compatible implementations map them, arbitrarily, to the characters + and /. An example of a Base64 encoding is shown in Figure 1-3.

Because the input stream is, obviously, a multiple of 8 bits, dividing it into 6-bit chunks creates a minor problem. Because 24 is the least-common-multiple of 6 and 8, the input must be padded to a multiple of 24 bits (three bytes). Although Base64 could just mandate that the encoding routine add padding bytes to ensure alignment, that would complicate the decoding process. Instead the encoder adds two = characters if the last chunk is one byte long, one = character if the last chunk is two bytes long, and no = characters if the input is an even multiple of three bytes. This 6:8 ratio also means that the output is one third bigger than the input.

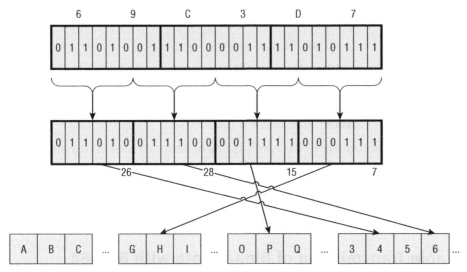

**Figure 1-3:** Base64 Encoding

As you see in Listing 1-14, Base64 encoding is pretty simple to implement after you understand it; most of the complexity deals with non-aligned input:

**Listing 1-14:** "base64.c" base64_encode

```
static char *base64 =
 "ABCDEFGHIJKLMNOPQRSTUVWXYZabcdefghijklmnopqrstuvwxyz0123456789+/";
void base64_encode( const unsigned char *input, int len, unsigned char *output )
{
  do
  {
    *output++ = base64[ ( input[ 0 ] & 0xFC ) >> 2 ];

    if ( len == 1 )
    {
      *output++ = base64[ ( ( input[ 0 ] & 0x03 ) << 4 ) ];
      *output++ = '=';
      *output++ = '=';
      break;
    }

    *output++ = base64[
        ( ( input[ 0 ] & 0x03 ) << 4 ) | ( ( input[ 1 ] & 0xF0 ) >> 4 ) ];

    if ( len == 2 )
    {
      *output++ = base64[ ( ( input[ 1 ] & 0x0F ) << 2 ) ];
      *output++ = '=';
      break;
    }

    *output++ = base64[
```

```
         ( ( input[ 1 ] & 0x0F ) << 2 ) | ( ( input[ 2 ] & 0xC0 ) >> 6 ) ];
    *output++ = base64[ ( input[ 2 ] & 0x3F ) ];
    input += 3;
  }
  while ( len -= 3 );

  *output = '\0';
}
```

Here, the output array is already assumed to have been allocated as 4/3 * len. The input masks select 6 bits of the input at a time and process the input in 3-byte chunks.

Base64 decoding is just as easy. Almost. Each input byte corresponds back to six possible output bits. This mapping is the exact inverse of the encoding mapping. However, when decoding, you have to be aware of the possibility that you can receive invalid data. Remember that the input is given in 8-bit bytes, but not every possible 8-bit combination is a legitimate Base64 character — this is, in fact, the point of Base64. You must also reject non-aligned input here; if the input is not a multiple of four, it didn't come from a conformant Base64 encoding routine. For these reasons, there's a bit more error-checking that you need to build into a Base64 decoding routine; when encoding, you can safely accept anything, but when decoding, you must ensure that the input actually came from a real Base64 encoder. Such a Base64 decoder is shown in Listing 1-15.

**Listing 1-15:** "base64.c" base64_decode

```
static int unbase64[] =
{
  -1, -1, -1, -1, -1, -1, -1, -1, -1, -1, -1, -1, -1, -1, -1, -1, -1,
  -1, -1, -1, -1, -1, -1, -1, -1, -1, -1, -1, -1, -1, -1, -1,
  -1, -1, -1, -1, -1, -1, -1, -1, -1, -1, 62, -1, -1, -1, 63, 52,
  53, 54, 55, 56, 57, 58, 59, 60, 61, -1, -1, -1, 0, -1, -1, -1,
  0, 1, 2, 3, 4, 5, 6, 7, 8, 9, 10, 11, 12, 13, 14, 15,
  16, 17, 18, 19, 20, 21, 22, 23, 24, 25, -1, -1, -1, -1, -1, -1,
  26, 27, 28, 29, 30, 31, 32, 33, 34, 35, 36, 37, 38, 39, 40, 41,
  42, 43, 44, 45, 46, 47, 48, 49, 50, 51, -1, -1, -1, -1, -1, -1
};

int base64_decode( const unsigned char *input, int len, unsigned char *output )
{
  int out_len = 0, i;

  assert( !( len & 0x03 ) ); // Is an even multiple of 4

  do
  {
    for ( i = 0; i <= 3; i++ )
    {
      // Check for illegal base64 characters
      if ( input[ i ] > 128 || unbase64[ input[ i ] ] == -1 )
```

*(Continued)*

```
    {
      fprintf( stderr, "invalid character for base64 encoding: %c\n",
          input[ i ] );
      return -1;
    }
  }
  *output++ = unbase64[ input[ 0 ] ] << 2 |
       ( unbase64[ input[ 1 ] ] & 0x30 ) >> 4;
  out_len++;
  if ( input[ 2 ] != '=' )
  {
    *output++ = ( unbase64[ input[ 1 ] ] & 0x0F ) << 4 |
         ( unbase64[ input[ 2 ] ] & 0x3C ) >> 2;
    out_len++;
  }

  if ( input[ 3 ] != '=' )
  {
    *output++ = ( unbase64[ input[ 2 ] ] & 0x03 ) << 6 |
         unbase64[ input[ 3 ] ];
    out_len++;
  }

  input += 4;
 }
 while ( len -= 4 );

 return out_len;
}
```

Notice that `unbase64` was declared as a static array. Technically you could have computed this from `base64`, but because this never changes, it makes sense to compute this once and hardcode it into the source. The –1 entries are non-base64 characters. If you encounter one in the decoding input, halt.

What does all of this Base64 stuff have to do with proxy authorization? Well, `BASIC` authorization has the client pass a username and a password to the proxy to identify itself. In a minor nod to security, HTTP requires that this username and password be Base64 encoded before being transmitted. This provides some safeguard (but not much) against accidental password leakage. Of course, even a lazy attacker with access to a packet sniffer could easily Base64 decode the proxy authorization line. In fact, the open-source Wireshark packet sniffer decodes it for you! Still, it's required by the specification, so you have to support it.

To support proxy authorization, add the following to `http_get` as shown in Listing 1-16.

**Listing 1-16:** "http.c" http_get (with proxy support) (continued)

```
  sprintf( get_command, "Host: %s\r\n", host );
  if ( send( connection, get_command, strlen( get_command ), 0 ) == -1 )
  {
```

```
      return -1;
  }

  if ( proxy_user )
  {
    int credentials_len = strlen( proxy_user ) + strlen( proxy_password ) + 1;
    char *proxy_credentials = malloc( credentials_len );
    char *auth_string = malloc( ( ( credentials_len * 4 ) / 3 ) + 1 );
    sprintf( proxy_credentials, "%s:%s", proxy_user, proxy_password );
    base64_encode( proxy_credentials, credentials_len, auth_string );
    sprintf( get_command, "Proxy-Authorization: BASIC %s\r\n", auth_string );
    if ( send( connection, get_command, strlen( get_command ), 0 ) == -1 )
    {
      free( proxy_credentials );
      free( auth_string );
      return -1;
    }
    free( proxy_credentials );
    free( auth_string );
  }
  sprintf( get_command, "Connection: close\r\n\r\n" );
```

Now, if you invoke your http `main` routine with just a URL, it tries to connect directly to the target host; if you invoke it with parameters:

`./http -p http://user:password@proxy-host:80/ http://some.server.com/path`

You connect through an authenticating proxy and request the same page.

## Implementing an HTTP Server

Because you probably also want to examine server-side SSL, develop a server-side HTTP application — what is usually referred to as a *web server* — and add SSL support to it, as well. The operation of a web server is pretty straightforward. It starts by establishing a socket on which to listen for new requests. By default, it listens on port 80, the standard HTTP port. When a new request is received, it reads an HTTP request, as described earlier, from the client, forms an HTTP response that either satisfies the request or describes an error condition, and either closes the connection (in the case of HTTP 1.0) or looks for another request (in the case of HTTP 1.1+).

The main routine in Listing 1-17 illustrates the outer shell of an HTTP server — or any other internet protocol server, for that matter.

**Listing 1-17:** "webserver.c" main routine

```
#define HTTP_PORT 80

int main( int argc, char *argv[ ] )
{
```

*(Continued)*

```
    int listen_sock;
    int connect_sock;
    int on = 1;
    struct sockaddr_in local_addr;
    struct sockaddr_in client_addr;
    int client_addr_len = sizeof( client_addr );
#ifdef WIN32
    WSADATA wsaData;

    if ( WSAStartup( MAKEWORD( 2, 2 ), &wsaData ) != NO_ERROR )
    {
      perror( "Unable to initialize winsock" );
      exit( 0 );
    }
#endif

    if ( ( listen_sock = socket( PF_INET, SOCK_STREAM, 0 ) ) == -1 )
    {
      perror( "Unable to create listening socket" );
      exit( 0 );
    }

    if ( setsockopt( listen_sock,
            SOL_SOCKET,
            SO_REUSEADDR,
            &on, sizeof( on ) ) == -1 )
    {
      perror( "Setting socket option" );
      exit( 0 );
    }

    local_addr.sin_family = AF_INET;
    local_addr.sin_port = htons( HTTP_PORT );
    local_addr.sin_addr.s_addr = htonl( INADDR_LOOPBACK );
    //local_addr.sin_addr.s_addr = htonl( INADDR_ANY );

    if ( bind( listen_sock,
          ( struct sockaddr * ) &local_addr,
          sizeof( local_addr ) ) == -1 )
    {
      perror( "Unable to bind to local address" );
      exit( 0 );
    }

    if ( listen( listen_sock, 5 ) == -1 )
    {
      perror( "Unable to set socket backlog" );
      exit( 0 );
    }

    while ( ( connect_sock = accept( listen_sock,
```

```
                    ( struct sockaddr * ) &client_addr,
                    &client_addr_len ) ) != -1 )
  {
    // TODO: ideally, this would spawn a new thread.
    process_http_request( connect_sock );
  }

  if ( connect_sock == -1 )
  {
    perror( "Unable to accept socket" );
  }

  return 0;
}
```

This code is standard sockets fare. It issues the four required system calls that are required for a process to act as a TCP protocol server: `socket`, `bind`, `listen`, and `accept`. The `accept` call will *block* — that is, not return — until a client somewhere on the Internet calls `connect` with its IP and port number. The inside of this `while` loop handles the request. Note that there's nothing HTTP specific about this loop yet; this could just as easily be an e-mail server, an ftp server, an IRC server, and so on. If anything goes wrong, these calls return –1, `perror` prints out a description of what happened, and the process terminates.

There are two points to note about this routine:

- The call to `setsockopt( listen_socket, SOL_SOCKET, SO_REUSEADDR, &on, sizeof( on ) )`. This enables the same process to be restarted if it terminates abnormally. Ordinarily, when a server process terminates abnormally, the socket is left open for a period of time referred to as the `TIME_WAIT` period. The socket is in `TIME_WAIT` state if you run `netstat`. This enables any pending client `FIN` packets to be received and processed correctly. Until this `TIME_WAIT` period has ended, no process can listen on the same port. `SO_REUSEADDR` enables a process to take up ownership of a socket that is in the `TIME_WAIT` state, so that on abnormal termination, the process can be immediately restarted. This is probably what you always want, but you have to ask for it explicitly.

- Notice the arguments to `bind`. The `bind` system call tells the OS which port you want to listen on and is, of course, required. However, `bind` accepts a port as well as an interface name/IP address. By supplying an IP address here, you can specify that you're only interested in connections coming into a certain interface. You can take advantage of that and bind this socket with the loopback address (127.0.0.1) to ensure that only connections from this machine are accepted (see Listing 1-18).

**Listing 1-18:** "webserver.c" remote connection exclusion code

```
local_addr.sin_family = AF_INET;
local_addr.sin_port = htons( HTTP_PORT );
local_addr.sin_addr.s_addr = htonl( INADDR_LOOPBACK );
//local_addr.sin_addr.s_addr = htonl( INADDR_ANY );

if ( bind( listen_sock, ( struct sockaddr * ) &local_addr,
           sizeof( local_addr ) ) == -1 )
```

If you uncomment the line below (INADDR_ANY), or just omit the setting of local_addr.sin_addr.s_addr entirely, you accept connections from any available interface, including the one connected to the public Internet. In this case, as a minor security precaution, disable this and only listen on the loopback interface. If you have local firewall software running, this is unnecessary, but just in case you don't, you should be aware of the security implications.

Now for the HTTP-specific parts of this server. Call process_http_request for each received connection. Technically, you ought to spawn a new thread here so that the main thread can cycle back around and accept new connections; however, for the current purpose, this bare-bones single-threaded server is good enough.

Processing an HTTP request involves first reading the request line that should be of the format

```
GET <path> HTTP/1.x
```

Of course, HTTP supports additional commands such as POST, HEAD, PUT, DELETE, and OPTIONS, but you won't bother with any of those — GET is good enough. If a client asks for any other functionality, return an error code 501: Not Implemented. Otherwise, ignore the path requested and return a canned HTML response as shown in Listing 1-19.

**Listing 1-19:** "webserver.c" process_http_request

```
static void process_http_request( int connection )
{
  char *request_line;
  request_line = read_line( connection );
  if ( strncmp( request_line, "GET", 3 ) )
  {
   // Only supports "GET" requests
    build_error_response( connection, 501 );
  }
  else
  {
   // Skip over all header lines, don't care
    while ( strcmp( read_line( connection ), "" ) );

    build_success_response( connection );
  }

#ifdef WIN32
```

```
    if ( closesocket( connection ) == -1 )
#else
    if ( close( connection ) == -1 )
#endif
    {
      perror( "Unable to close connection" );
    }
}
```

Because HTTP is line-oriented — that is, clients are expected to pass in multiple CRLF-delimited lines that describe a request — you need a way to read a line from the connection. `fgets` is a standard way to read a line of text from a file descriptor, including a socket, but it requires that you specify a maximum line-length up front. Instead, develop a simple (and simplistic) routine that autoincrements an internal buffer until it's read the entire line and returns it as shown in Listing 1-20.

**Listing 1-20:** "webserver.c" read_line

```
#define DEFAULT_LINE_LEN 255

char *read_line( int connection )
{
  static int line_len = DEFAULT_LINE_LEN;
  static char *line = NULL;
  int size;
  char c;    // must be c, not int
  int pos = 0;

  if ( !line )
  {
    line = malloc( line_len );
  }

  while ( ( size = recv( connection, &c, 1, 0 ) ) > 0 )
  {
    if ( ( c == '\n' ) && ( line[ pos - 1 ] == '\r' ) )
    {
      line[ pos - 1 ] = '\0';
      break;
    }
    line[ pos++ ] = c;

    if ( pos > line_len )
    {
      line_len *= 2;
      line = realloc( line, line_len );
    }
  }

  return line;
}
```

There are three problems with this function:

- It keeps reallocating its internal buffer essentially forever. A rogue client could take advantage of this, send a malformed request with no CRLF's and crash the server.

- It reads one byte at a time from the socket. Each call to `recv` actually invokes a system call, which slows things down quite a bit. For optimal efficiency, you should read a buffer of text, extract a line from it, and store the remainder for the next invocation.

- Its use of static variables makes it non-thread-safe.

You can ignore these shortcomings, though. This implementation is good enough for your requirements, which is to have a server to which you can add SSL support.

To wrap up the web server, implement the functions `build_success_response` and `build_error_response` shown in Listing 1-21.

**Listing 1-21:** "webserver.c" build responses

```
static void build_success_response( int connection )
{
  char buf[ 255 ];
  sprintf( buf, "HTTP/1.1 200 Success\r\nConnection: Close\r\n\
Content-Type:text/html\r\n\
\r\n<html><head><title>Test Page</title></head><body>Nothing here</body></html>\
\r\n" );

  // Technically, this should account for short writes.
  if ( send( connection, buf, strlen( buf ), 0 ) < strlen( buf ) )
  {
    perror( "Trying to respond" );
  }
}

static void build_error_response( int connection, int error_code )
{
  char buf[ 255 ];
  sprintf( buf, "HTTP/1.1 %d Error Occurred\r\n\r\n", error_code );

  // Technically, this should account for short writes.
  if ( send( connection, buf, strlen( buf ), 0 ) < strlen( buf ) )
  {
    perror( "Trying to respond" );
  }
}
```

Again, these don't add up to a fantastic customer experience, but work well enough to demonstrate server-side SSL.

You can run this and either connect to it with the sample HTTP client developed in the section "Implementing an HTTP client" or connect with any standard web browser. This implements RFC-standard HTTP, albeit a microscopically small subset of it.

## Roadmap for the Rest of This Book

SSL was originally specified by Netscape, when it became clear that e-commerce required secure communication capability. The first release of SSL was SSLv2 (v1 was never released). After its release, SSLv2 was found to have significant flaws, which will be examined in greater detail in Chapter 6. Netscape later released and then turned over SSLv3 to the IETF, which promptly renamed it TLS 1.0 and published the first official specification in RFC 2246. In 2006, TLS 1.1 was specified in RFC 4346 and in 2008, TLS 1.2 was released and is specified in RFC 5246.

The rest of this book is dedicated to describing every aspect of what SSL does and how it does it. In short, SSL encrypts the traffic that the higher-level protocol generates so that it can't be intercepted by an eavesdropper. It also authenticates the connection so that, in theory, both sides can be assured that they are indeed communicating with who they think they're communicating with.

SSL support is now standard in every web browser and web server, open- or closed-source. Although SSL was originally invented for secure HTTP, it's been retrofitted, to varying degrees of success, to work with other protocols. In theory, SSL is completely specified at the network layer, and any protocol can just layer invisibly on top of it. However, things aren't always so nice and neat, and there are some drawbacks to using SSL with protocols other than HTTP. Indeed, there are drawbacks even to using it with HTTP. I guess you can say that nothing is perfect. You come back to the details of HTTPS, and how it differs from HTTP, in Chapter 6 after you've examined the underlying SSL protocol.

Additionally, there are several open-source implementations of the SSL protocol itself. By far the most popular is Eric A. Young's *openssl*. The ubiquitous Apache server, for example, relies on the openssl library to provide SSL support. A more recent implementation is GnuTLS. Whereas openssl 0.9.8e (the most recent version as of this writing) implements SSLv2, SSLv3 and TLS 1.0, GnuTLS implements TLS 1.0, 1.1 and 1.2. Therefore it's called TLS rather than SSL because it doesn't technically implement SSL at all. Also, Sun's Java environment has SSL support built in. Because Sun's JDK has been open-sourced, you can also see the details of how Sun built in SSL. This is interesting, as OpenSSL and GnuTLS are written in C but most of Sun's SSL implementation is written in Java. Throughout the book, you examine how these three different implementations work. Of course, because this book walks through yet another C-based implementation, you are able to compare and contrast these popular implementations with the approach given here.

# Protecting Against Eavesdroppers with Symmetric Cryptography

Encryption refers to the practice of scrambling a message such that it can only be read (*descrambled*) by the intended recipient. To make this possible, you must scramble the message in a reversible way, but in such a way that only somebody with a special piece of knowledge can descramble it correctly. This special piece of knowledge is referred to as the *key,* evoking an image of unlocking a locked drawer with its one and only *key* to remove the contents. Anybody who has the key can descramble — *decrypt,* in crypto-speak — the scrambled message. In theory, at least, no one without the key can decrypt the message.

When computers are used for cryptography, messages and keys are actually numbers. The message is converted to (or at least treated as) a number, which is numerically combined with the key (also a number) in a specified way according to a cryptographic algorithm. As such, an attacker without the key can try all keys, starting at "1" and incrementing over and over again, until the correct key is found. To determine when he's hit the right combination, the attacker has to know something about the message that was encrypted in the first place, obviously. However, this is usually the case. Consider the case of an HTTP exchange. The first four characters of the first request are likely to be "G E T ." The hypothetical attacker can just do a decryption using a proposed key, check the first four letters, and if they don't match, move on to the next.

This sort of attack is called a *brute force* attack. To be useful and resistant to brute-force attacks, keys should be fairly large numbers, and algorithms should accept a huge range of potential keys so that an attacker has to try for a very, very long time before hitting on the right combination. There's no defense against a brute-force attack; the best you can hope for is to ensure that an attacker spends so much time performing one that the data loses its value before a brute force attack might be successful.

The application of encryption to SSL is obvious — encrypting data is effectively the point. When transmitting one's credit card number over the public Internet, it's reassuring to know that only the intended recipient can read it. When you transmit using an SSL-enabled algorithm, such as HTTPS, all traffic is encrypted prior to transmission, and must subsequently be decrypted before processing.

There are two very broad categories of cryptographic algorithms — symmetric and public. The difference between the two is in key management:

- Symmetric algorithms are the simpler of the two, at least conceptually (although the implementations are the other way around), and are examined in this chapter.

- Public algorithms, properly *public key algorithms,* are the topic of the next chapter.

With symmetric cryptography algorithms, the same key is used both for encryption and decryption. In some cases, the algorithm is different, with decryption "undoing" what encryption did. In other cases, the algorithm is designed so that the same set of operations, applied twice successively, cycle back to produce the same result; encryption and decryption are actually the same algorithms. In all cases, though, both the sender and the receiver must both agree what the key is before they can perform any encrypted communication. This key management turns out to be the most difficult part of encryption operations and is where public-key cryptography enters in Chapter 3. For now, just assume that this has been worked out and look at what to do with a key after you have one.

> **NOTE** This chapter is the most technically dense chapter in this book; this is the nature of symmetric cryptography. If you're not entirely familiar with terminology such as *left shift* and *big endian*, you might want to take a quick look at Appendix A for a refresher.

## Understanding Block Cipher Cryptography Algorithms

Julius Caesar is credited with perhaps the oldest known symmetric cipher algorithm. The so-called *Caesar cipher* — a variant of which you can probably find as a diversion in your local newspaper — assigns each letter, at random, to a number. This mapping of letters to numbers is the key in this simple algorithm. Modern cipher algorithms must be much more sophisticated than Caesar's in order to withstand automated attacks by computers. Although the basic premise remains — substituting one letter or symbol for another, and keeping track of that substitution for later — further elements of confusion and diffusion were added over the centuries to create modern cryptography algorithms. One such hardening technique is to operate on several characters at a time, rather than just one. By far the most common category of symmetric encryption algorithm is the *block cipher algorithm*, which operates on a fixed range of bytes rather than on a single character at a time.

In this section you examine three of the most popular block cipher algorithms — the ones that you'll most likely encounter in modern cryptographic implementations. These algorithms will likely remain relevant for several decades — changes in cryptographic standards come very slowly, and only after much analysis by cryptographers and cryptanalysts.

## Implementing the Data Encryption Standard (DES) Algorithm

The *Data Encryption Standard* (DES) algorithm, implemented and specified by IBM at the behest of the NSA in 1974, was the first publicly available computer-ready encryption algorithm. Although for reasons you see later, DES is not considered particularly secure any more, it's still in widespread use (!) and serves as a good starting point for the study of symmetric cryptography algorithms in general. Most of the concepts that made DES work when it was first introduced appear in other cryptographic algorithms. DES is specified at the following web site: http://csrc.nist.gov/publications/fips/fips46-3/fips46-3.pdf.

DES breaks its input up into eight-byte blocks and scrambles them using an eight-byte key. This scrambling process involves a series of fixed *permutations* — swapping bit 34 with bit 28, bit 28 with bit 17, and so on — rotations, and XORs. The core of DES, though, and where it gets its security, is from what the standard calls *S boxes* where six bits of input become four bits of output in a fixed, but non-reversible (except with the key) way.

Like any modern symmetric cryptographic algorithm, DES relies heavily on the XOR operation. The logic table for XOR is shown in Table 2-1:

**Table 2-1:** XOR Operation

| INPUT | | OUTPUT |
| --- | --- | --- |
| A | B | A XOR B |
| 0 | 0 | 0 |

*(Continued)*

**Table 2-1** *(continued)*

| INPUT | | OUTPUT |
|---|---|---|
| 0 | 1 | 1 |
| 1 | 0 | 1 |
| 1 | 1 | 0 |

If any of the input bits are 1, the output is 1, unless *both* of the inputs bits are one. This is equivalent to addition modulo 2 and is referred to that way in the official specification. One interesting and important property of XOR for cryptography is that it's reversible. Consider:

$$
\begin{array}{r}
0011 \\
\oplus\ 0101 \\
\hline
0110
\end{array}
$$

However:

$$
\begin{array}{r}
0110 \\
\oplus\ 0101 \\
\hline
0011
\end{array}
$$

This is the same operation as the previous one, but reversed; the output is the input, but it's XORed against the same set of data. As you can see, you've recovered the original input this way. You may want to take a moment to look at the logic of the XOR operation and convince yourself that this is always the case.

To make your implementation match the specification and most public descriptions of the algorithm, you operate on byte arrays rather than taking advantage (where you can) of the wide integer types of the target hardware. DES is described using *big endian* conventions — that is, the most significant bit is bit 1 — whereas the Intel x86 conventions are *little endian* — bit 1 is the least-significant bit. To take full advantage of the hardware, you'd have to reverse quite a few parts of the specification, which you won't do here.

Instead, you operate on byte (unsigned char) arrays. Because you work at the bit level — that is, bit 39 of a 64-bit block, for example — you need a few support macros for finding and manipulating bits within such an array. The bit manipulation support macros are outlined in Listing 2-1.

**Listing 2-1:** "des.c" bit macros

```
// This does not return a 1 for a 1 bit; it just returns non-zero
#define GET_BIT( array, bit ) \
    ( array[ ( int ) ( bit / 8 ) ] & ( 0x80 >> ( bit % 8 ) ) )
#define SET_BIT( array, bit ) \
```

```
      ( array[ ( int ) ( bit / 8 ) ] |= ( 0x80 >> ( bit % 8 ) ) )
#define CLEAR_BIT( array, bit ) \
      ( array[ ( int ) ( bit / 8 ) ] &= ~( 0x80 >> ( bit % 8 ) ) )
```

Although this is a bit dense, you should see that GET_BIT returns 0 if an array contains a 0 at a specific bit position and non-zero if an array contains a 1. The divide operator selects the byte in the array, and the shift and mod operator selects the bit within that byte. SET_BIT and CLEAR_BIT work similarly, but actually update the position. Notice that the only difference between these three macros is the operator between the array reference and the mask: & for get, |= for set, and &= ~ for clear.

Because this example XORs entire arrays of bytes, you need a support routine for that as shown in Listing 2-2.

**Listing 2-2:** "des.c" xor array

```
static void xor( unsigned char *target, const unsigned char *src, int len )
{
  while ( len-- )
  {
    *target++ ^= *src++;
  }
}
```

This overwrites the target array with the XOR of it and the src array.

Finally, you need a permute routine. The permute routine is responsible for putting, for instance, the 57th bit of the input into the 14th bit of the output, depending on the entries in a permute_table array. As you'll see in the code listings that follow, this function is the workhorse of the DES algorithm; it is called dozens of times, with different permute_tables each time.

**Listing 2-3:** "des.c" permutation

```
/**
 * Implement the initial and final permutation functions. permute_table
 * and target must have exactly len and len * 8 number of entries,
 * respectively, but src can be shorter (expansion function depends on this).
 * NOTE: this assumes that the permutation tables are defined as one-based
 * rather than 0-based arrays, since they're given that way in the
 * specification.
 */
static void permute( unsigned char target[],
          const unsigned char src[],
          const int permute_table[],
          int len )
{
  int i;
  for ( i = 0; i < len * 8; i++ )
```

*(Continued)*

```
    {
      if ( GET_BIT( src, ( permute_table[ i ] - 1 ) ) )
      {
        SET_BIT( target, i );
      }
      else
      {
        CLEAR_BIT( target, i );
      }
    }
}
```

Now, on to the steps involved in encrypting a block of data using DES.

## DES Initial Permutation

DES specifies that the input should undergo an initial permutation. The purpose of this permutation is unclear, as it serves no cryptographic purpose (the output would be just as secure without this). It may have been added for optimization for certain hardware types. Nevertheless, if you don't include it, your output will be wrong, and you won't be able to interoperate with other implementations. The specification describes this permutation in terms of the input bits and the output bits, but it works out to copying the second bit of the last byte into the first bit of the first byte of the output, followed by the second bit of the next-to-last byte into the second bit of the first byte of the output, and so on, so that the first byte of output consists of the second bits of all of the input bytes, "backward." (Remember that the input is exactly eight-bytes long, so given an 8-bit byte, taking the second bit of each input byte yields one byte of output.) The second byte of the output is the fourth bit of each of the input bytes, again backward. The third is built from the sixth bits, the fourth from the eighth bits, and the fifth comes from the first bits, and so on. So, given an 8-byte input as shown in Figure 2-1:

**Figure 2-1:** Unpermuted 8-byte input

The first byte of output comes from the second bits of each input byte, backward as shown in Figure 2-2.

The second byte of output comes from the fourth bits of each input byte, backward as shown in Figure 2-3.

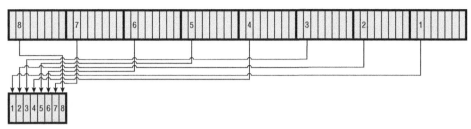

**Figure 2-2:** First byte of output

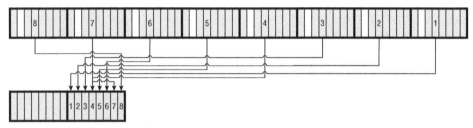

**Figure 2-3:** Second byte of output

and so on for bytes 3 and 4; the fifth byte of output comes from the first bit of input as shown in Figure 2-4:

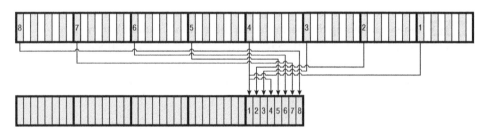

**Figure 2-4:** Five permuted bytes

and so on until all of the input bits were exhausted.

You can code this all in a very terse loop without using a lookup table on that basis, something like what's shown in Listing 2-4.

**Listing 2-4:** Terse initial permutation

```
for ( i = 1; i != 8; i = ( i + 2 ) % 9 )
{
  for ( j = 7; j >= 0; j-- )
```

*(Continued)*

```
  {
    output[ ( i % 2 ) ? ( ( i - 1 ) >> 1 ) : ( ( 4 + ( i >> 1 ) ) ) ] |=
                ( ( ( input[ j ] & ( 0x80 >> i ) ) >> ( 7 - i ) ) << j );
  }
}
```

However, the specification is given in terms of permutations, so you do the same, using the permute routine. The `permute_table` for the initial permutation is shown in Listing 2-5.

**Listing 2-5:** "des.c" initial permutation table

```
static const int ip_table[] = {
    58, 50, 42, 34, 26, 18, 10, 2,
    60, 52, 44, 36, 28, 20, 12, 4,
    62, 54, 46, 38, 30, 22, 14, 6,
    64, 56, 48, 40, 32, 24, 16, 8,
    57, 49, 41, 33, 25, 17, 9,  1,
    59, 51, 43, 35, 27, 19, 11, 3,
    61, 53, 45, 37, 29, 21, 13, 5,
    63, 55, 47, 39, 31, 23, 15, 7 };
```

This specifies that the 58th bit of the input is the first bit of the output; the 50th bit of the input is the second bit of the output; and so on. You may want to convince yourself that this is the same as described above.

> **NOTE** When examining the permutation table above, remember the structure of the GET_BIT and SET_BIT macros. The first bit, bit 58, works out to be byte #58/8 = 7, bit #58%8 = 2. Remember that DES considers bytes to be ordered according to *big endian* conventions, which means that bit 2 is the next-to-the-most significant bit.

After the input has been so permuted, it is combined with the key in a series of 16 rounds, each of which consists of the following:

1. Expand bits 32–64 of the input to 48 bits (described in the expansion function in Listing 2-10).

2. XOR the expanded right half of the input with the key.

3. Use the output of this XOR to look up eight entries in the *s-box* table and overwrite the input with these contents.

4. Permute this output according to a specific p-table.

5. XOR this output with the left half of the input (bits 1–32) and swap sides so that the XORed left half becomes the right half, and the (as of yet untouched) right-half becomes the left half. On the next round, the same series of operations are applied again, but this time on what used to be the right half.

This five step procedure is referred to as the *Feistel function* after its originator. Graphically, the rounds look like Figure 2-5.

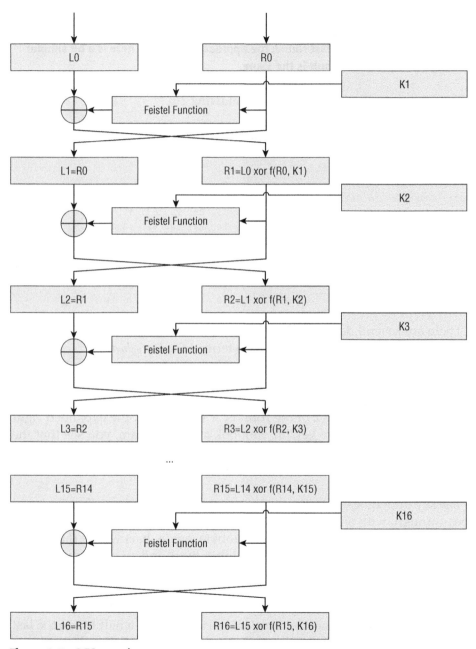

**Figure 2-5:** DES overview

Finally, the halves are *swapped* one last time, and the output is subject to the inverse of the initial permutation — this just undoes what the initial permutation did.

> **NOTE** The specification suggests that you should implement this last step by just not swapping in the last round; the approach presented here is a bit simpler to implement and the result is the same.

The final permutation table is show in Listing 2-6.

**Listing 2-6:** "des.c" final permutation table

```
/**
 * This just inverts ip_table.
 */
static const int fp_table[] = { 40,  8, 48, 16, 56, 24, 64, 32,
                                39,  7, 47, 15, 55, 23, 63, 31,
                                38,  6, 46, 14, 54, 22, 62, 30,
                                37,  5, 45, 13, 53, 21, 61, 29,
                                36,  4, 44, 12, 52, 20, 60, 28,
                                35,  3, 43, 11, 51, 19, 59, 27,
                                34,  2, 42, 10, 50, 18, 58, 26,
                                33,  1, 41,  9, 49, 17, 57, 25 };
```

There are several details missing from the description of the rounds. The most important of these details is what's termed the *key schedule*.

## DES Key Schedule

In the description of step 2 of the rounds, it states "XOR the expanded right half of the input with the key." If you look at the diagram, you see that the input to this XOR is shown as K1, K2, K3, … K15, K16. As it turns out, there are 16 different 48-bit keys, which are generated deterministically from the initial 64-bit key input.

The key undergoes an initial permutation similar to the one that the input goes through, with slight differences — this time, the first byte of the output is equal to the first bits of each input byte (again, backward); the second byte is equal to the second bit of each input byte; and so on. However, the key itself is specified as two 28-bit halves — the second half works backward through the input bytes so that the first byte of the second half is the seventh bit of each input byte; the second byte is the sixth bit; and so on. Also, because the key halves are 28 bits each, there are only three and a half bytes; the last half byte follows the pattern but stops after four bits. Finally, although the key input is 8 bytes (64 bits), the output of two 28-bit halves is only 56 bits.

Eight of the key bits (the least-significant-bit of each input byte) are discarded and not used by DES.

Again, the DES specification presents this as a bit-for-bit permutation, so you will, too. This permutation table is shown in Listing 2-7.

**Listing 2-7:** "des.c" key permutation table 1

```
static const int pc1_table[] = { 57, 49, 41, 33, 25, 17,  9, 1,
                                 58, 50, 42, 34, 26, 18, 10, 2,
                                 59, 51, 43, 35, 27, 19, 11, 3,
                                 60, 52, 44, 36,
                                 63, 55, 47, 39, 31, 23, 15, 7,
                                 62, 54, 46, 38, 30, 22, 14, 6,
                                 61, 53, 45, 37, 29, 21, 13, 5,
                                 28, 20, 12,  4 };
```

If you look carefully at this table, you see that bits 8, 16, 24, 32, 40, 48, 56, and 64 — the LSBs of each input byte — never appear. Early DES implementations used more fault-prone hardware than you are probably used to — the LSBs of the keys were used as *parity bits* to ensure that the key was transmitted correctly. Strictly speaking, you should ensure that the LSB of each byte is the sum (modulo 2) of the other seven bits. Most implementers don't bother, as you can probably trust your hardware to hang on to the key you loaded into it correctly.

At each round, each of the two 28-bit halves of this 56-bit key are rotated left once or twice — once in rounds 1, 2, 9, and 16, twice otherwise. These rotated halves are then permuted (surprise) according to the second permutation table in Listing 2-8.

**Listing 2-8:** "des.c" key permutation table 2

```
static const int pc2_table[] = { 14, 17, 11, 24,  1,  5,
                                  3, 28, 15,  6, 21, 10,
                                 23, 19, 12,  4, 26,  8,
                                 16,  7, 27, 20, 13,  2,
                                 41, 52, 31, 37, 47, 55,
                                 30, 40, 51, 45, 33, 48,
                                 44, 49, 39, 56, 34, 53,
                                 46, 42, 50, 36, 29, 32 };
```

This produces a 48-bit subkey from the 56-bit (rotated) key. Due to the rotation, this means that each round has a unique key K1, K2, K3, ..., K15, K16. These subkeys are referred to as the *key schedule*.

Notice that the key schedule is independent of the encryption operations and can be precomputed and stored before encryption or decryption even begins. Most DES implementations do this as a performance optimization, although this one doesn't bother.

The independent rotations of the two key-halves are shown in Listing 2-9:

**Listing 2-9:** "des.c" rotate left

```
/**
 * Perform the left rotation operation on the key. This is made fairly
 * complex by the fact that the key is split into two 28-bit halves, each
 * of which has to be rotated independently (so the second rotation operation
 * starts in the middle of byte 3).
 */
static void rol( unsigned char *target )
{
  int carry_left, carry_right;

  carry_left = ( target[ 0 ] & 0x80 ) >> 3;

  target[ 0 ] = ( target[ 0 ] << 1 ) | ( ( target[ 1 ] & 0x80 ) >> 7 );
  target[ 1 ] = ( target[ 1 ] << 1 ) | ( ( target[ 2 ] & 0x80 ) >> 7 );
  target[ 2 ] = ( target[ 2 ] << 1 ) | ( ( target[ 3 ] & 0x80 ) >> 7 );

  // special handling for byte 3
  carry_right = ( target[ 3 ] & 0x08 ) >> 3;
  target[ 3 ] = ( ( ( target[ 3 ] << 1 ) |
( ( target[ 4 ] & 0x80 ) >> 7 ) ) & ~0x10 ) | carry_left;

  target[ 4 ] = ( target[ 4 ] << 1 ) | ( ( target[ 5 ] & 0x80 ) >> 7 );
  target[ 5 ] = ( target[ 5 ] << 1 ) | ( ( target[ 6 ] & 0x80 ) >> 7 );
  target[ 6 ] = ( target[ 6 ] << 1 ) | carry_right;
}
```

Here you see that each byte of the key, which is in a 7-byte array, is left-shifted by one place, and the MSB of the next byte is used as the LSB. The only complicating factor here is that the key is in a 7-byte array, but the dividing point between the two halves is in the middle of the third byte.

## DES Expansion Function

Notice in the previous section that the subkeys are 48-bits long, but the input halves that are to be XORed are 32 bits long. Now, you can't properly XOR a 32-bit input with a 48-bit key, so the input is expanded — some bits are duplicated — before being XORed. The output of the expansion function is illustrated in Figure 2-6.

The output is split into eight six-bit blocks (which works out to six eight-bit bytes), with the first and last bits of each block overlapping the preceding and following blocks. Note that the first and last block wrap around and use the last bit of the input as the first bit of output and the first bit of input as the last bit of output. Again, rather than specifying this in code, you use a permutation table as shown in Listing 2-10:

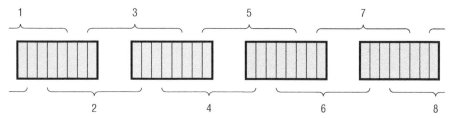

**Figure 2-6:** DES expansion function

**Listing 2-10:** "des.c" expansion table

```
static const int expansion_table[] = {
      32,  1,   2,   3,   4,   5,
       4,  5,   6,   7,   8,   9,
       8,  9,  10,  11,  12,  13,
      12, 13,  14,  15,  16,  17,
      16, 17,  18,  19,  20,  21,
      20, 21,  22,  23,  24,  25,
      24, 25,  26,  27,  28,  29,
      28, 29,  30,  31,  32,   1 };
```

After this has been XORed with the correct subkey for this round, it is fed into the s-box lookup. The s-boxes are what makes DES secure. It's important that the output not be a linear function of the input; if it was, a simple statistical analysis would reveal the key. An attacker knows, for example, that the letter "E" is the most common letter in the English language — if he knew that the plaintext was ASCII-encoded English, he could look for the most frequently occurring byte of output, assume that was an "E", and work backward from there (actually, in ASCII-encoded English text, the space character 32 is more common than the "E"). If he was wrong, he could find the second-most occurring character, and try again. This sort of cryptanalysis has been perfected to the point where it can be performed by a computer in seconds. Therefore, the s-boxes are *not* permutations, rotations or XORs but are lookups into a set of completely random tables.

Each six-bits of the input — the expanded right-half XORed with the sub-key — correspond to four bits of table output. In other words, each six bits of input is used as an index into a table of four-bit outputs. In this way, the expanded, XORed right half is reduced from 48-bits to 32. The s-boxes are described in a particularly confusing way by the DES specification. Instead, I present them here as simple lookup tables in Listing 2-11. Note that each six-bit block has its own unique s-box.

**Listing 2-11:** "des.c" s-boxes

```
static const int sbox[8][64] = {
 { 14, 0, 4, 15, 13, 7, 1, 4, 2, 14, 15, 2, 11, 13, 8, 1,
    3, 10, 10, 6, 6, 12, 12, 11, 5, 9, 9, 5, 0, 3, 7, 8,
    4, 15, 1, 12, 14, 8, 8, 2, 13, 4, 6, 9, 2, 1, 11, 7,
   15, 5, 12, 11, 9, 3, 7, 14, 3, 10, 10, 0, 5, 6, 0, 13 },
 { 15, 3, 1, 13, 8, 4, 14, 7, 6, 15, 11, 2, 3, 8, 4, 14,
    9, 12, 7, 0, 2, 1, 13, 10, 12, 6, 0, 9, 5, 11, 10, 5,
    0, 13, 14, 8, 7, 10, 11, 1, 10, 3, 4, 15, 13, 4, 1, 2,
    5, 11, 8, 6, 12, 7, 6, 12, 9, 0, 3, 5, 2, 14, 15, 9 },
 { 10, 13, 0, 7, 9, 0, 14, 9, 6, 3, 3, 4, 15, 6, 5, 10,
    1, 2, 13, 8, 12, 5, 7, 14, 11, 12, 4, 11, 2, 15, 8, 1,
   13, 1, 6, 10, 4, 13, 9, 0, 8, 6, 15, 9, 3, 8, 0, 7,
   11, 4, 1, 15, 2, 14, 12, 3, 5, 11, 10, 5, 14, 2, 7, 12 },
 { 7, 13, 13, 8, 14, 11, 3, 5, 0, 6, 6, 15, 9, 0, 10, 3,
    1, 4, 2, 7, 8, 2, 5, 12, 11, 1, 12, 10, 4, 14, 15, 9,
   10, 3, 6, 15, 9, 0, 0, 6, 12, 10, 11, 1, 7, 13, 13, 8,
   15, 9, 1, 4, 3, 5, 14, 11, 5, 12, 2, 7, 8, 2, 4, 14 },
 { 2, 14, 12, 11, 4, 2, 1, 12, 7, 4, 10, 7, 11, 13, 6, 1,
    8, 5, 5, 0, 3, 15, 15, 10, 13, 3, 0, 9, 14, 8, 9, 6,
    4, 11, 2, 8, 1, 12, 11, 7, 10, 1, 13, 14, 7, 2, 8, 13,
   15, 6, 9, 15, 12, 0, 5, 9, 6, 10, 3, 4, 0, 5, 14, 3 },
 { 12, 10, 1, 15, 10, 4, 15, 2, 9, 7, 2, 12, 6, 9, 8, 5,
    0, 6, 13, 1, 3, 13, 4, 14, 14, 0, 7, 11, 5, 3, 11, 8,
    9, 4, 14, 3, 15, 2, 5, 12, 2, 9, 8, 5, 12, 15, 3, 10,
    7, 11, 0, 14, 4, 1, 10, 7, 1, 6, 13, 0, 11, 8, 6, 13 },
 { 4, 13, 11, 0, 2, 11, 14, 7, 15, 4, 0, 9, 8, 1, 13, 10,
    3, 14, 12, 3, 9, 5, 7, 12, 5, 2, 10, 15, 6, 8, 1, 6,
    1, 6, 4, 11, 11, 13, 13, 8, 12, 1, 3, 4, 7, 10, 14, 7,
   10, 9, 15, 5, 6, 0, 8, 15, 0, 14, 5, 2, 9, 3, 2, 12 },
 { 13, 1, 2, 15, 8, 13, 4, 8, 6, 10, 15, 3, 11, 7, 1, 4,
   10, 12, 9, 5, 3, 6, 14, 11, 5, 0, 0, 14, 12, 9, 7, 2,
    7, 2, 11, 1, 4, 14, 1, 7, 9, 4, 12, 10, 14, 8, 2, 13,
    0, 15, 6, 12, 10, 9, 13, 0, 15, 3, 3, 5, 5, 6, 8, 11 }
};
```

Also note that I have taken the liberty to reorder these, as they're given out-of-order in the specification.

After substitution, the input block undergoes a final permutation, shown in Listing 2-12.

**Listing 2-12:** "des.c" final input block permutation

```
static const int p_table[] = { 16,  7, 20, 21,
                               29, 12, 28, 17,
                                1, 15, 23, 26,
                                5, 18, 31, 10,
```

```
                 2,   8, 24, 14,
                32, 27,  3,  9,
                19, 13, 30,  6,
                22, 11,  4, 25 };
```

All of this is performed on the right-half of the input, which is then XORed with the left half, becoming the new right-half, and the old right-half, before any transformation, becomes the new left half.

Finally, the code to implement this is shown in Listing 2-13. This code accepts a single eight-byte block of input and an eight-byte key and returns an encrypted eight-byte output block. The input block is not modified. This is the DES algorithm itself.

**Listing 2-13:** "des.c" des_block_operate

```c
#define DES_BLOCK_SIZE 8 // 64 bits, defined in the standard
#define DES_KEY_SIZE 8 // 56 bits used, but must supply 64 (8 are ignored)
#define EXPANSION_BLOCK_SIZE 6
#define PC1_KEY_SIZE 7
#define SUBKEY_SIZE 6

static void des_block_operate( const unsigned char plaintext[ DES_BLOCK_SIZE ],
               unsigned char ciphertext[ DES_BLOCK_SIZE ],
               const unsigned char key[ DES_KEY_SIZE ] )
{
  // Holding areas; result flows from plaintext, down through these,
  // finally into ciphertext. This could be made more memory efficient
  // by reusing these.
  unsigned char ip_block[ DES_BLOCK_SIZE ];
  unsigned char expansion_block[ EXPANSION_BLOCK_SIZE ];
  unsigned char substitution_block[ DES_BLOCK_SIZE / 2 ];
  unsigned char pbox_target[ DES_BLOCK_SIZE / 2 ];
  unsigned char recomb_box[ DES_BLOCK_SIZE / 2 ];

  unsigned char pc1key[ PC1_KEY_SIZE ];
  unsigned char subkey[ SUBKEY_SIZE ];
  int round;
  // Initial permutation
  permute( ip_block, plaintext, ip_table, DES_BLOCK_SIZE );

  // Key schedule computation
  permute( pc1key, key, pc1_table, PC1_KEY_SIZE );
  for ( round = 0; round < 16; round++ )
  {
    // "Feistel function" on the first half of the block in 'ip_block'

    // "Expansion". This permutation only looks at the first
    // four bytes (32 bits of ip_block); 16 of these are repeated
    // in "expansion_table".
    permute( expansion_block, ip_block + 4, expansion_table, 6 );
```

*(Continued)*

```
// "Key mixing"
// rotate both halves of the initial key
rol( pc1key );
if ( !( round <= 1 || round == 8 || round == 15 ) )
{
  // Rotate twice except in rounds 1, 2, 9 & 16
  rol( pc1key );
}

permute( subkey, pc1key, pc2_table, SUBKEY_SIZE );

xor( expansion_block, subkey, 6 );

// Substitution; "copy" from updated expansion block to ciphertext block
memset( ( void * ) substitution_block, 0, DES_BLOCK_SIZE / 2 );
substitution_block[ 0 ] =
  sbox[ 0 ][ ( expansion_block[ 0 ] & 0xFC ) >> 2 ] << 4;
substitution_block[ 0 ] |=
  sbox[ 1 ][ ( expansion_block[ 0 ] & 0x03 ) << 4 |
  ( expansion_block[ 1 ] & 0xF0 ) >> 4 ];
substitution_block[ 1 ] =
  sbox[ 2 ][ ( expansion_block[ 1 ] & 0x0F ) << 2 |
  ( expansion_block[ 2 ] & 0xC0 ) >> 6 ] << 4;
substitution_block[ 1 ] |=
  sbox[ 3 ][ ( expansion_block[ 2 ] & 0x3F ) ];
substitution_block[ 2 ] =
  sbox[ 4 ][ ( expansion_block[ 3 ] & 0xFC ) >> 2 ] << 4;
substitution_block[ 2 ] |=
  sbox[ 5 ][ ( expansion_block[ 3 ] & 0x03 ) << 4 |
  ( expansion_block[ 4 ] & 0xF0 ) >> 4 ];
substitution_block[ 3 ] =
  sbox[ 6 ][ ( expansion_block[ 4 ] & 0x0F ) << 2 |
  ( expansion_block[ 5 ] & 0xC0 ) >> 6 ] << 4;
substitution_block[ 3 ] |=
  sbox[ 7 ][ ( expansion_block[ 5 ] & 0x3F ) ];

// Permutation
permute( pbox_target, substitution_block, p_table, DES_BLOCK_SIZE / 2 );

// Recombination. XOR the pbox with left half and then switch sides.
memcpy( ( void * ) recomb_box, ( void * ) ip_block, DES_BLOCK_SIZE / 2 );
memcpy( ( void * ) ip_block, ( void * ) ( ip_block + 4 ),
  DES_BLOCK_SIZE / 2 );
xor( recomb_box, pbox_target, DES_BLOCK_SIZE / 2 );
memcpy( ( void * ) ( ip_block + 4 ), ( void * ) recomb_box,
  DES_BLOCK_SIZE / 2 );
}

// Swap one last time
```

```
memcpy( ( void * ) recomb_box, ( void * ) ip_block, DES_BLOCK_SIZE / 2 );
memcpy( ( void * ) ip_block, ( void * ) ( ip_block + 4 ), DES_BLOCK_SIZE / 2 );
memcpy( ( void * ) ( ip_block + 4 ), ( void * ) recomb_box,
    DES_BLOCK_SIZE / 2 );

// Final permutation (undo initial permutation)
permute( ciphertext, ip_block, fp_table, DES_BLOCK_SIZE );
}
```

This code is a bit long, but if you followed the descriptions of the permutations and the Feistel function, you should be able to make sense of it.

## DES Decryption

One of the nice things about the way DES was specified is that decryption is the exact same as encryption, except that the key schedule is inverted. Instead of the original key being rotated left at each round, it's rotated right. Otherwise, the routines are identical. You can easily add decryption support to des_block_operate, as illustrated in Listing 2-14.

**Listing 2-14:** "des.c" des_block_operate with decryption support

```
typedef enum { OP_ENCRYPT, OP_DECRYPT } op_type;
static void des_block_operate( const unsigned char plaintext[ DES_BLOCK_SIZE ],
                unsigned char ciphertext[ DES_BLOCK_SIZE ],
                const unsigned char key[ DES_KEY_SIZE ],
                op_type operation )
{
...
  for ( round = 0; round < 16; round++ )
  {
    permute( expansion_block, ip_block + 4, expansion_table, 6 );

    // "Key mixing"
    // rotate both halves of the initial key
    if ( operation == OP_ENCRYPT )
    {
      rol( pc1key );
      if ( !( round <= 1 || round == 8 || round == 15 ) )
      {
        // Rotate twice except in rounds 1, 2, 9 & 16
        rol( pc1key );
      }
    }

    permute( subkey, pc1key, pc2_table, SUBKEY_SIZE );

    if ( operation == OP_DECRYPT )
    {
```

(Continued)

```
      ror( pc1key );
      if ( !( round >= 14 || round == 7 || round == 0 ) )
      {
        // Rotate twice except in rounds 1, 2, 9 & 16
        ror( pc1key );
      }
    }
    xor( expansion_block, subkey, 6 );
...
}
```

That's it. The substitution boxes and all the permutations are identical; the only difference is the rotation of the key. The `ror` function, in Listing 2-15, is the inverse of the `rol` function.

**Listing 2-15:** "des.c" rotate right

```
static void ror(unsigned char *target )
{
  int carry_left, carry_right;

  carry_right = ( target[ 6 ] & 0x01 ) << 3;

  target[ 6 ] = ( target[ 6 ] >> 1 ) | ( ( target[ 5 ] & 0x01 ) << 7 );
  target[ 5 ] = ( target[ 5 ] >> 1 ) | ( ( target[ 4 ] & 0x01 ) << 7 );
  target[ 4 ] = ( target[ 4 ] >> 1 ) | ( ( target[ 3 ] & 0x01 ) << 7 );

  carry_left = ( target[ 3 ] & 0x10 ) << 3;
  target[ 3 ] = ( ( ( target[ 3 ] >> 1 ) |
      ( ( target[ 2 ] & 0x01 ) << 7 ) ) & ~0x08 ) | carry_right;

  target[ 2 ] = ( target[ 2 ] >> 1 ) | ( ( target[ 1 ] & 0x01 ) << 7 );
  target[ 1 ] = ( target[ 1 ] >> 1 ) | ( ( target[ 0 ] & 0x01 ) << 7 );
  target[ 0 ] = ( target[ 0 ] >> 1 ) | carry_left;
}
```

# Padding and Chaining in Block Cipher Algorithms

As shown earlier, DES operates on eight-byte input blocks. If the input is longer than eight bytes, the `des_block_operate` function must be called repeatedly. If the input isn't aligned on an eight-byte boundary, it has to be padded. Of course, the padding must follow a specific scheme so that the decryption routine knows what to discard after decryption. If you adopt a convention of padding with 0 bytes, the decryptor needs to have some way of determining whether the input actually ended with 0 bytes or whether these were padding bytes. National Institute for Standards and Technology (NIST) publication 800-38A (http://csrc .nist.gov/publications/nistpubs/800-38a/sp800-38a.pdf) recommends that a "1" bit be added to the input followed by enough zero-bits to make up eight bytes. Because you're working with byte arrays that must end on an 8-bit (one-byte) boundary, this means that, if the input block is less than eight bytes, you add the byte 0x80 (128), followed by zero bytes to pad. The decryption routine just starts at the end of the decrypted output, removing zero bytes until 0x80 is encountered, removes that, and returns the result to the caller.

Under this padding scheme, an input of, for example, "abcdef" (six characters) needs to have two bytes added to it. Therefore, "abcdef" would become

61 62 63 64 65 66 80 00

a  b  c  d  e  f

This would be encrypted under DES (using, say, a key of the ASCII string *password*) to the hex string: 25 ac 8f c5 c4 2f 89 5d. The decryption routine would then decrypt it to a, b, c, d, e, f, 0x80, 0x00, search backward from the end for the first occurrence of 0x80, and remove everything after it. If the input string happened to actually end with hex byte 0x80, the decryptor would see 0x80 0x80 0x0 ... and still correctly remove only the padding.

There's one wrinkle here; if the input *did* end on an eight-byte boundary that happened to contain 0 bytes following a 0x80, the decryption routine would remove legitimate input. Therefore, if the input ends on an eight-byte boundary, you have to add a whole block of padding (0x80 0x0 0x0 0x0 0x0 0x0 0x0 0x0) so that the decryptor doesn't accidentally remove something it wasn't supposed to.

You can now implement a `des_encrypt` routine, as shown in Listing 2-16, that uses `des_block_operate` after padding its input to encrypt an arbitrarily sized block of text.

**Listing 2-16:** "des.c" des_operate with padding support

```
static void des_operate( const unsigned char *input,
            int input_len,
            unsigned char *output,
            const unsigned char *key,
            op_type operation )
{
  unsigned char input_block[ DES_BLOCK_SIZE ];

  assert( !( input_len % DES_BLOCK_SIZE ) );

  while ( input_len )
  {
    memcpy( ( void * ) input_block, ( void * ) input, DES_BLOCK_SIZE );
    des_block_operate( input_block, output, key, operation );

    input += DES_BLOCK_SIZE;
    output += DES_BLOCK_SIZE;
    input_len -= DES_BLOCK_SIZE;
  }
}
```

des_operate iterates over the input, calling des_block_operate on each eight-byte block. The caller of des_operate is responsible for padding to ensure that the input is eight-byte aligned, as shown in Listing 2-17.

**Listing 2-17:** "des.c" des_encrypt with NIST 800-3A padding

```
void des_encrypt( const unsigned char *plaintext,
        const int plaintext_len,
        unsigned char *ciphertext,
        const unsigned char *key )
{
  unsigned char *padded_plaintext;
  int padding_len;

  // First, pad the input to a multiple of DES_BLOCK_SIZE

  padding_len = DES_BLOCK_SIZE - ( plaintext_len % DES_BLOCK_SIZE );
  padded_plaintext = malloc( plaintext_len + padding_len );

  // This implements NIST 800-3A padding
  memset( padded_plaintext, 0x0, plaintext_len + padding_len );
  padded_plaintext[ plaintext_len ] = 0x80;

  memcpy( padded_plaintext, plaintext, plaintext_len );

  des_operate( padded_plaintext, plaintext_len + padding_len, ciphertext,
            key, OP_ENCRYPT );
  free( padded_plaintext );
}
```

The des_encrypt variant shown in Listing 2-17 first figures out how much padding is needed — it will be between one and eight bytes. Remember, if the input is already eight-byte aligned, you must add a *dummy* block of eight bytes on the end so that the decryption routine doesn't remove valid data. des_encrypt then allocates enough memory to hold the padded input, copies the original input into this space, sets the first byte of padding to 0x80 and the rest to 0x0 as described earlier.

Another approach to padding, called PKCS #5 padding, is to append the number of padding bytes as the padding byte. This way, the decryptor can just look at the last byte of the output and then strip off that number of bytes from the result (with 8 being a legitimate number of bytes to strip off). Using the "abcdef" example again, the padded input now becomes

61 62 63 64 65 66 02 02

a  b  c  d  e  f

Because two bytes of padding are added, the number 2 is added twice. If the input was "abcde," the padded result is instead.

61 62 63 64 65 03 03 03

a   b   c   d   e

`des_encrypt` can be changed simply to implement this padding scheme as shown in Listing 2-18.

**Listing 2-18:** "des.c" des_encrypt with PKCS #5 padding

```
// First, pad the input to a multiple of DES_BLOCK_SIZE

padding_len = DES_BLOCK_SIZE - ( plaintext_len % DES_BLOCK_SIZE );
padded_plaintext = malloc( plaintext_len + padding_len );
// This implements PKCS #5 padding.
memset( padded_plaintext, padding_len, plaintext_len + padding_len );

memcpy( padded_plaintext, plaintext, plaintext_len );

des_operate( padded_plaintext, plaintext_len + padding_len, ciphertext,
            key, OP_ENCRYPT );
```

So, of these two options, which does SSL take? Actually, neither. SSL takes a somewhat simpler approach to padding — the number of padding bytes is output explicitly. If five bytes of padding are required, the very last byte of the decrypted output is 5. If no padding was necessary, an extra 0 byte is appended on the end.

### Implementing Cipher Block Chaining

A subtler issue with this implementation of DES is that two identical blocks of text, encrypted with the same key, produce the same output. This can be useful information for an attacker who can look for repeated blocks of ciphertext to determine the characteristics of the input. Even worse, it lends itself to *replay attacks*. If the attacker knows, for example, that an encrypted block represents a password, or a credit card number, he doesn't need to decrypt it to use it. He can just present the same ciphertext to the authenticating server, which then dutifully decrypts it and accepts it as though it were encrypted using the original key — which, of course, it was.

The simplest way to deal with this is called *cipher block chaining* (CBC). After encrypting a block of data, XOR it with the results of the previous block. The first block, of course, doesn't have a previous block, so there's nothing to XOR it with. Instead, the encryption routine should create a random eight-byte *initialization vector* (sometimes also referred to as *salt*) and XOR the first block with that. This initialization vector doesn't necessarily have to be strongly protected or strongly randomly generated. It just has to be different every time so that encrypting a certain string with a certain password produces different output every time.

Incidentally, you may come across the term *ECB* or *Electronic Code Book* chaining, which actually refers to encryption with no chaining (that is, the encryption routine developed in the previous section) and mostly serves to distinguish non-CBC from CBC. There are other chaining methods as well, such as *OFB* (*output feedback*), which I discuss later.

You can add support for initialization vectors into `des_operate` easily as shown in Listing 2-19.

**Listing 2-19:** "des.c" des_operate with CBC support and padding removed from des_encrypt

```
static void des_operate( const unsigned char *input,
            int input_len,
            unsigned char *output,
            const unsigned char *iv,
            const unsigned char *key,
            op_type operation )
{
  unsigned char input_block[ DES_BLOCK_SIZE ];

  assert( !( input_len % DES_BLOCK_SIZE ) );

  while ( input_len )
  {
    memcpy( ( void * ) input_block, ( void * ) input, DES_BLOCK_SIZE );
    xor( input_block, iv, DES_BLOCK_SIZE ); // implement CBC
    des_block_operate( input_block, output, key, operation );
    memcpy( ( void * ) iv, ( void * ) output, DES_BLOCK_SIZE ); // CBC

    input += DES_BLOCK_SIZE;
    output += DES_BLOCK_SIZE;
    input_len -= DES_BLOCK_SIZE;
  }
}


...
void des_encrypt( const unsigned char *plaintext,
        const int plaintext_len,
        unsigned char *ciphertext,
        const unsigned char *iv,
        const unsigned char *key )
{
  des_operate( plaintext, plaintext_len, ciphertext,
          iv, key, OP_ENCRYPT );
}
```

As you can see, this isn't particularly complex. You just pass in a DES_BLOCK_SIZE byte array, XOR it with the first block — before encrypting it — and then keep track of the output on each iteration so that it can be XORed, before encryption, with each subsequent block.

Notice also that, with each operation, you overwrite the contents of the `iv` array. This means that the caller can invoke `des_operate` again, pointing to the same `iv` memory location, and encrypt streamed data.

At decryption time, then, you first decrypt a block, and then XOR that with the *encrypted* previous block.

But what about the first block? The initialization vector must be remembered and transmitted (or agreed upon) before decryption can continue. To support CBC in decryption, you have to change the order of things just a bit as shown in Listing 2-20.

**Listing 2-20:** "des.c" des_operate with CBC for encrypt or decrypt

```
while ( input_len )
{
  memcpy( ( void * ) input_block, ( void * ) input, DES_BLOCK_SIZE );
  if ( operation == OP_ENCRYPT )
  {
    xor( input_block, iv, DES_BLOCK_SIZE ); // implement CBC
    des_block_operate( input_block, output, key, operation );
    memcpy( ( void * ) iv, ( void * ) output, DES_BLOCK_SIZE ); // CBC
  }

  if ( operation == OP_DECRYPT )
  {
    des_block_operate( input_block, output, key, operation );
    xor( output, iv, DES_BLOCK_SIZE );
    memcpy( ( void * ) iv, ( void * ) input, DES_BLOCK_SIZE ); // CBC
  }

  input += DES_BLOCK_SIZE;
  output += DES_BLOCK_SIZE;
  input_len -= DES_BLOCK_SIZE;
}
```

And finally, the decrypt routine that passes in the initialization vector and removes the padding that was inserted, using the PKCS #5 padding scheme, is shown in Listing 2-21.

**Listing 2-21:** "des.c" des_decrypt

```
void des_decrypt( const unsigned char *ciphertext,
        const int ciphertext_len,
        unsigned char *plaintext,
        const unsigned char *iv,
        const unsigned char *key )
{
  des_operate( ciphertext, ciphertext_len, plaintext, iv, key, OP_DECRYPT );
  // Remove any padding on the end of the input
  //plaintext[ ciphertext_len - plaintext[ ciphertext_len - 1 ] ] = 0x0;
}
```

The commented-out line at the end of listing 2-21 illustrates how you might remove padding. As you can see, removing the padding is simple; just read the contents of the last byte of the decrypted output, which contains the number of padding bytes that were appended. Then replace the byte at that position, from the end with a null terminator, effectively discarding the padding. You don't want this in a general-purpose decryption routine, though, because it doesn't deal properly with binary input and because, in SSL, the caller is responsible for ensuring that the input is block-aligned.

To see this in action, you can add a `main` routine to your des.c file so that you can do DES encryption and decryption operations from the command line. To enable compilation of this as a test app as well as an included object in another app — which you do when you add this to your SSL library — wrap up the main routine in an `#ifdef` as shown in Listing 2-22.

**Listing 2-22:** "des.c" command-line test routine

```
#ifdef TEST_DES
int main( int argc, char *argv[ ] )
{
  unsigned char *key;
  unsigned char *iv;
  unsigned char *input;
  unsigned char *output;
  int out_len, input_len;

  if ( argc < 4 )
  {
    fprintf( stderr, "Usage: %s <key> <iv> <input>\n", argv[ 0 ] );
    exit( 0 );
  }

  key = argv[ 1 ];
  iv = argv[ 2 ];
  input = argv[ 3 ];

  out_len = input_len = strlen( input );
  output = ( unsigned char * ) malloc( out_len + 1 );
  des_encrypt( input, input_len, output, iv, key );

  while ( out_len-- )
  {
    printf( "%.02x", *output++ );
  }
  printf( "\n" );

  return 0;
}
#endif
```

Notice that the input must be an even multiple of eight. If you give it bad data, the program just crashes unpredictably. The output is displayed in hexadecimal because it's almost definitely not going to be printable ASCII. Alternatively, you could have Base64-encoded this, but using hex output leaves it looking the same as the network traces presented later. You have to provide a -DTEST_DES flag to the compiler when building this:

```
gcc -DTEST_DES -g -o des des.c
```

After this has been compiled, you can invoke it via

```
[jdavies@localhost ssl]$ ./des password initialz abcdefgh
71828547387b18e5
```

Just make sure that the input is block-aligned. The key and the initialization vector must be eight bytes, and the input must be a multiple of eight bytes.

What about decryption? You likely want to see this decrypted, but the output isn't in printable-ASCII form and you have no way to pass this in as a command-line parameter. Expand the input to allow the caller to pass in hex-coded values instead of just printable-ASCII values. You can implement this just like C does; if the user starts an argument with "0x," the remainder is assumed to be a hex-coded byte array. Because this hex-parsing routine is useful again later, put it into its own utility file, shown in Listing 2-23.

**Listing 2-23:** "hex.c" hex_decode

```
/**
 * Check to see if the input starts with "0x"; if it does, return the decoded
 * bytes of the following data (presumed to be hex coded). If not, just return
 * the contents. This routine allocates memory, so has to be free'd.
 */
int hex_decode( const unsigned char *input, unsigned char **decoded )
{
  int i;
  int len;

  if ( strncmp( "0x", input, 2 ) )
  {
    len = strlen( input ) + 1;
    *decoded = malloc( len );
    strcpy( *decoded, input );
    len--;
  }
  else
  {
    len = ( strlen( input ) >> 1 ) - 1;
    *decoded = malloc( len );
    for ( i = 2; i < strlen( input ); i += 2 )
    {
      (*decoded)[ ( ( i / 2 ) - 1 ) ] =
        ( ( ( input[ i ] <= '9' ) ? input[ i ] - '0' :
( ( tolower( input[ i ] ) ) - 'a' + 10 ) ) << 4 ) |
        ( ( input[ i + 1 ] <= '9' ) ? input[ i + 1 ] - '0' :
```

*(Continued)*

```
( ( tolower( input[ i + 1 ] ) ) - 'a' + 10 ) );
    }
  }

  return len;
}
```

Whether the input starts with "0x" or not, the `decoded` pointer is initialized and filled with either the unchanged input or the byte value of the hex-decoded input — minus, of course, the "0x" leader. While you're at it, go ahead and move the simple `hex_display` routine that was at the end of des.c's `main` routine into a reusable utility function as shown in Listing 2-24.

**Listing 2-24:** "hex.c" show_hex

```
void show_hex( const unsigned char *array, int length )
{
  while ( length-- )
  {
    printf( "%.02x", *array++ );
  }
  printf( "\n" );
}
```

Now, des.c's `main` function becomes what's shown in Listing 2-25.

**Listing 2-25:** "des.c" main routine with decryption support

```
int main( int argc, char *argv[ ] )
{
  unsigned char *key;
  unsigned char *iv;
  unsigned char *input;
  int key_len;
  int input_len;
  int out_len;
  int iv_len;
  unsigned char *output;

  if ( argc < 4 )
  {
    fprintf( stderr, "Usage: %s [-e|-d] <key> <iv> <input>\n", argv[ 0 ] );
    exit( 0 );
  }

  key_len = hex_decode( argv[ 2 ], &key );
  iv_len = hex_decode( argv[ 3 ], &iv );
  input_len = hex_decode( argv[ 4 ], &input );

  out_len = input_len;
```

```
output = ( unsigned char * ) malloc( out_len + 1 );

if ( !( strcmp( argv[ 1 ], "-e" ) ) )
{
  des_encrypt( input, input_len, output, iv, key );
  show_hex( output, out_len );
}
else if ( !( strcmp( argv[ 1 ], "-d" ) ) )
{
  des_decrypt( input, input_len, output, iv, key );
  show_hex( output, out_len );
}
else
{
  fprintf( stderr, "Usage: %s [-e|-d] <key> <iv> <input>\n", argv[ 0 ] );
}

free( input );
free( iv );
free( key );
free( output );

return 0;
}
```

Now you can decrypt the example:

```
[jdavies@localhost ssl]$ ./des -d password initialz \
    0x71828547387b18e5
6162636465666768
```

Notice that the output here is hex-coded; 6162636465666768 is the ASCII representation of abcdefgh. The key and initialization vector were also changed to allow hex-coded inputs. In general, real DES keys and initialization vectors are not printable-ASCII characters, but they draw from a larger pool of potential input bytes.

## Using the Triple-DES Encryption Algorithm to Increase Key Length

DES is secure. After forty years of cryptanalysis, no feasible attack has been demonstrated; if anybody has cracked it, they've kept it a secret. Unfortunately, the 56-bit key length is built into the algorithm. Increasing the key length requires redesigning the algorithm completely because the s-boxes and the permutations are specific to a 64-bit input. 56 bits is not very many, these days. $2^{56}$ possible keys means that the most naïve brute-force attack would need to try, on the average, $2^{55}$ ($2^{56}$ / 2), or 36,028,797,018,963,968 (about 36,000 trillion operations) before it hit the right combination. This is not infeasible; my modern laptop can repeat the non-optimized decrypt routine shown roughly 7,500 times per second. This means it would take me about 5 trillion seconds, or about 150,000 years for me to search the entire keyspace. This is a long time, but the brute-forcing process is infinitely parallelizable. If I had two computers to dedicate to the task, I could have the first search keys from $0$–$2^{55}$ and the second search keys from $2^{55}$–$2^{56}$. They would crack the key in about 79,000 years. If, with significant optimizations, I could increase the decryption time to 75,000 operations per second (which is feasible), I'd only need about 7,500 years with two computers. With about 7,500 computers, I'd only need a little less than two years to search through half the keyspace.

In fact, optimized, parallelized hardware has been shown to be capable of cracking a DES key by brute force in just a few days. The hardware is not cheap, but if the value of the data is greater than the cost of the specialized hardware, alternative encryption should be considered.

The proposed solution to increase the keyspace beyond what can feasibly be brute-forced is called *triple DES* or *3DES*. 3DES has a 168-bit (56 * 3) key. It's called triple-DES because it splits the key into three 56-bit keys and repeats the DES rounds described earlier three times, once with each key. The clearest and most secure way to generate the three keys that 3DES requires is to just generate 168 bits, split them cleanly into three 56-bit chunks, and use each independently. The 3DES specification actually allows the same 56-bit key to be used three times, or to use a 112-bit key, split it into two, and reuse one of the two keys for one of the three rounds. Presumably this is allowed for backward-compatibility reasons (for example, if you have an existing DES key that you would like to or need to reuse as is), but you can just assume the simplest case where you have 168 bits to play with — this is what SSL expects when it uses 3DES as well.

One important wrinkle in the 3DES implementation is that you don't encrypt three times with the three keys. Instead you encrypt with one key, *decrypt* that with a different key — remember that decrypting with a mismatched key produces garbage, but reversible garbage, which is exactly what you want when doing cryptographic work — and finally encrypt that with yet a third key. Decryption, of course, is the opposite — decrypt with the third key, encrypt that with the second, and finally decrypt that with the first. Notice that you reverse the order of the keys when decrypting; this is important! The Encrypt/Decrypt/Encrypt procedure makes cryptanalysis more difficult. Note that the "use the same key three times" option mentioned earlier is essentially useless. You encrypt with a key, decrypt with the same key, and re-encrypt again with the same key to produce the exact same results as encrypting one time.

Padding and cipher-block-chaining do not change at all. 3DES works with eight-byte blocks, and you need to take care with initialization vectors to ensure that the same eight-byte block encrypted twice with the same key appears different in the output.

Adding support for 3DES to `des_operate` is straightforward. You add a new `triplicate` flag that tells the function that the key is three times longer than before and call `des_block_operate` three times instead of once, as shown in Listing 2-26.

**Listing 2-26:** "des.c" des_block_operate with 3DES support

```
static void des_operate( const unsigned char *input,
             int input_len,
             unsigned char *output,
             const unsigned char *iv,
             const unsigned char *key,
             op_type operation,
             int triplicate )
{
  unsigned char input_block[ DES_BLOCK_SIZE ];

  assert( !( input_len % DES_BLOCK_SIZE ) );

  while ( input_len )
  {
    memcpy( ( void * ) input_block, ( void * ) input, DES_BLOCK_SIZE );
    if ( operation == OP_ENCRYPT )
    {
      xor( input_block, iv, DES_BLOCK_SIZE ); // implement CBC
      des_block_operate( input_block, output, key, operation );
      if ( triplicate )
      {
        memcpy( input_block, output, DES_BLOCK_SIZE );
        des_block_operate( input_block, output, key + DES_KEY_SIZE,
                OP_DECRYPT );
        memcpy( input_block, output, DES_BLOCK_SIZE );
        des_block_operate( input_block, output, key + ( DES_KEY_SIZE * 2 ),
                operation );
      }
      memcpy( ( void * ) iv, ( void * ) output, DES_BLOCK_SIZE ); // CBC
    }

    if ( operation == OP_DECRYPT )
    {
      if ( triplicate )
      {
        des_block_operate( input_block, output, key + ( DES_KEY_SIZE * 2 ),
                operation );
        memcpy( input_block, output, DES_BLOCK_SIZE );
        des_block_operate( input_block, output, key + DES_KEY_SIZE,
                OP_ENCRYPT );
        memcpy( input_block, output, DES_BLOCK_SIZE );
        des_block_operate( input_block, output, key, operation );
      }
```

*(Continued)*

```
      else
      {
        des_block_operate( input_block, output, key, operation );
      }
      xor( output, iv, DES_BLOCK_SIZE );
      memcpy( ( void * ) iv, ( void * ) input, DES_BLOCK_SIZE ); // CBC
    }

    input += DES_BLOCK_SIZE;
    output += DES_BLOCK_SIZE;
    input_len -= DES_BLOCK_SIZE;
  }
}
```

If you were paying close attention in the previous section, you may have noticed that des_block_operate accepts a key as an array of a fixed size, whereas des_operate accepts a pointer of indeterminate size. Now you can see why it was designed this way.

Two new functions, des3_encrypt and des3_decrypt, are clones of des_encrypt and des_decrypt, other than the passing of a new flag into des_operate, shown in Listing 2-27.

**Listing 2-27:** "des.c" des3_encrypt

```
void des_encrypt( const unsigned char *plaintext,
  ...
{
  des_operate( plaintext, plaintext_len, ciphertext,
        iv, key, OP_ENCRYPT, 0 );
}

void des3_encrypt( const unsigned char *plaintext,...
{
  des_operate( padded_plaintext, plaintext_len + padding_len, ciphertext,
        iv, key, OP_ENCRYPT, 1 );
}
void des_decrypt( const unsigned char *ciphertext,
  ...
{
  des_operate( ciphertext, ciphertext_len, plaintext, iv, key, OP_DECRYPT, 0 );
}
void des3_decrypt( const unsigned char *ciphertext,
  ...
{
  des_operate( ciphertext, ciphertext_len, plaintext, iv, key, OP_DECRYPT, 1 );
}
```

You may be wondering why you created two new functions that are essentially clones of the others instead of just adding a triplicate flag to `des_encrypt` and `des_decrypt` as you did to `des_operate`. The benefit of this approach is that `des_encrypt` and `des3_encrypt` have identical function signatures. Later on, when you actually start developing the SSL framework, you take advantage of this and use function pointers to refer to your bulk encryption routines. You see this at work in the next section on AES, which is the last block cipher bulk encryption routine you examine. Notice also that I've removed the padding; for SSL purposes, you want to leave the padding up to the caller.

You can easily extend the test main routine in des.c to perform 3DES as shown in Listing 2-28; just check the length of the input key. If the input key is eight bytes, perform "single DES"; if it's 24 bytes, perform 3DES. Note that the block size, and therefore the initialization vector, is still eight bytes for 3DES; it's just the key that's longer.

**Listing 2-28:** "des.c" main routine with 3DES support

```
...
  if ( !( strcmp( argv[ 1 ], "-e" ) ) )
  {
    if ( key_len == 24 )
    {
      des3_encrypt( input, input_len, output, iv, key );
    }
    else
    {
      des_encrypt( input, input_len, output, iv, key );
    }

    show_hex( output, out_len );
  }
  else if ( !( strcmp( argv[ 1 ], "-d" ) ) )
  {
    if ( key_len == 24 )
    {
      des3_decrypt( input, input_len, output, iv, key );
    }
    else
    {
      des_decrypt( input, input_len, output, iv, key );
    }
```

For example,

```
[jdavies@localhost ssl]$ ./des -e twentyfourcharacterinput initialz abcdefgh
c0c48bc47e87ce17
[jdavies@localhost ssl]$ ./des -d twentyfourcharacterinput initialz \
    0xc0c48bc47e87ce17
6162636465666768
```

## Faster Encryption with the Advanced Encryption Standard (AES) Algorithm

3DES works and is secure — that is, brute-force attacks against it are computationally infeasible, and it has withstood decades of cryptanalysis. However, it's clearly slower than it needs to be. To triple the key length, you also have to triple the operation time. If DES itself were redesigned from the ground up to accommodate a longer key, processing time could be drastically reduced.

In 2001, the NIST announced that the *Rijndael* algorithm (`http://csrc.nist.gov/publications/fips/fips197/fips-197.pdf`) would become the official replacement for DES and renamed it the *Advanced Encryption Standard*. NIST evaluated several competing block-cipher algorithms, looking not just at security but also at ease of implementation, relative efficiency, and existing market penetration.

If you understand the overall workings of DES, AES is easy to follow as well. Like DES, it does a non-linear s-box translation of its input, followed by several permutation- and shift-like operations over a series of rounds, applying a key-schedule to its input at each stage. Just like DES, AES relies heavily on the XOR operation — particularly the reversibility of it. However, it operates on much longer keys; AES is defined for 128-, 192-, and 256-bit keys. Note that, assuming that a brute-force attack is the most efficient means of attacking a cipher, 128-bit keys are *less* secure than 3DES, and 192-bit keys are about the same (although 3DES does throw away 24 bits of key security due to the parity check built into DES). 256-bit keys are much more secure. Remember that every extra bit doubles the time that an attacker would have to spend brute-forcing a key.

### AES Key Schedule Computation

AES operates on 16-byte blocks, regardless of key length. The number of rounds varies depending on key length. If the key is 128 bits (16 bytes) long, the number of rounds is 10; if the key size is 192 bits (24 bytes) long, the number of rounds is 12; and if the key size is 256 bits (32 bytes), the number of rounds is 14. In general, rounds = (key-size in 4-byte words) + 6. Each round needs 16 bytes of keying material to work with, so the key schedule works out to 160 bytes (10 rounds * 16 bytes per round) for a 128-bit key; 192 bytes (12 * 16) for a 192-bit key; and 224 bytes (14 * 16) for a 256-bit key. (Actually there's one extra key permutation at the very end, so AES requires 176, 208, and 240 bytes of keying material). Besides the number of rounds, the key permutation is the only difference between the three algorithms.

So, given a 16-byte input, the AES key schedule computation needs to produce 176 bytes of output. The first 16 bytes are the input itself; the remaining 160 bytes are computed four at a time. Each four bytes are a permutation of the previous four bytes. Therefore, key schedule bytes 17–20 are a permutation of key bytes

13–16; 21–24 are a permutation of key bytes 17–20; and so on. Three-fourths of the time, this permutation is a simple XOR operation on the previous "key length" four bytes — bytes 21–24 are the XOR of bytes 17–20 and bytes 5–8. Bytes 25–28 are the XOR of bytes 21–24 and bytes 9–12. Graphically, in the case of a 128-bit key, this can be depicted as shown in Figure 2-7.

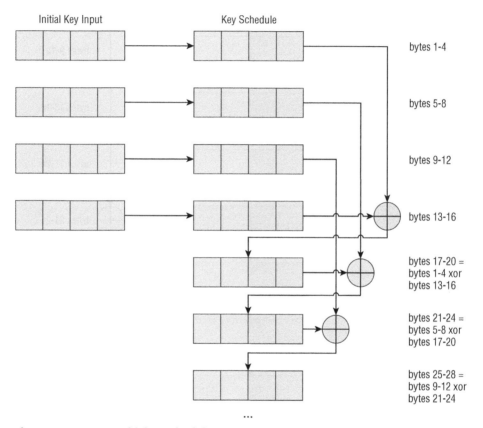

**Figure 2-7:** AES 128-bit key schedule computation

For a 192-bit key, the schedule computation is shown in Figure 2-8. It's just like the 128-bit key, but copies all 24 input bytes before it starts combining them.

And the 256-bit key is the same, but copies all 32 input bytes.

This is repeated 44, 52 or 60 times (rounds * 4 + 1) to produce as much keying material as needed — 16 bytes per round, plus one extra chunk of 16 bytes.

This isn't the whole story, though — every four iterations, there's a complex transformation function applied to the previous four bytes before it is XORed with the previous key-length four bytes. This function consists of first rotating the four-byte word, then applying it to a substitution table (AES's s-box), and XORing it with a *round constant*.

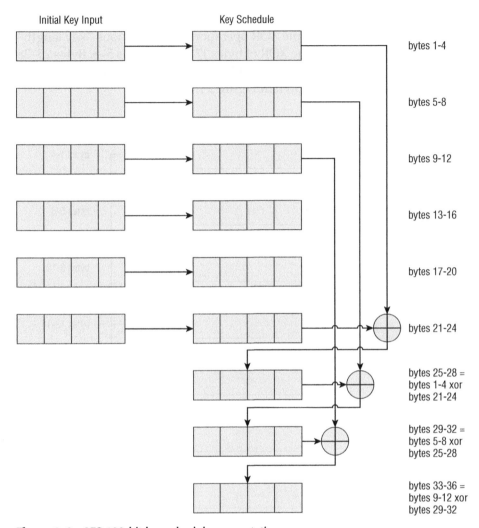

**Figure 2-8:** AES 192-bit key schedule computation

Rotation is straightforward and easy to understand. The first byte is overwritten with the second, the second with the third, the third with the fourth, and the fourth with the first, as shown in Figure 2-9 and Listing 2-29.

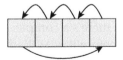

**Figure 2-9:** AES rotation

**Listing 2-29:** "aes.c" rot_word

```
static void rot_word( unsigned char *w )
{
  unsigned char tmp;

  tmp = w[ 0 ];
  w[ 0 ] = w[ 1 ];
  w[ 1 ] = w[ 2 ];
  w[ 2 ] = w[ 3 ];
  w[ 3 ] = tmp;
}
```

The substitution involves looking up each byte in a translation table and then replacing it with the value found there. The translation table is $16 \times 16$ bytes; the row is the high-order nibble of the source byte and the column is the low-order nibble. So, for example, the input byte 0x1A corresponds to row 1, column 10 of the lookup table, and input byte 0xC5 corresponds to row 12, column 5.

Actually, the lookup table values can be computed dynamically. According to the specification, this computation is "the affine transformation (over $GF(2^8)$) of $b_i + b_{(i+4)\%8} + b_{(i+5)\%8} + b_{(i+6)\%8} + b_{(i+7)\%8} + c_i$ after taking the multiplicative inverse in the finite field $GF(2^8)$". If that means anything to you, have at it.

This isn't something you'd want to do dynamically anyway, though, because the values never change. Instead, hardcode the table as shown in Listing 2-30, just as you did for DES:

**Listing 2-30:** "aes.c" sbox

```
static unsigned char sbox[ 16 ][ 16 ] = {
{ 0x63, 0x7c, 0x77, 0x7b, 0xf2, 0x6b, 0x6f, 0xc5,
  0x30, 0x01, 0x67, 0x2b, 0xfe, 0xd7, 0xab, 0x76 },
{ 0xca, 0x82, 0xc9, 0x7d, 0xfa, 0x59, 0x47, 0xf0,
  0xad, 0xd4, 0xa2, 0xaf, 0x9c, 0xa4, 0x72, 0xc0 },
{ 0xb7, 0xfd, 0x93, 0x26, 0x36, 0x3f, 0xf7, 0xcc,
  0x34, 0xa5, 0xe5, 0xf1, 0x71, 0xd8, 0x31, 0x15 },
{ 0x04, 0xc7, 0x23, 0xc3, 0x18, 0x96, 0x05, 0x9a,
  0x07, 0x12, 0x80, 0xe2, 0xeb, 0x27, 0xb2, 0x75 },
{ 0x09, 0x83, 0x2c, 0x1a, 0x1b, 0x6e, 0x5a, 0xa0,
  0x52, 0x3b, 0xd6, 0xb3, 0x29, 0xe3, 0x2f, 0x84 },
{ 0x53, 0xd1, 0x00, 0xed, 0x20, 0xfc, 0xb1, 0x5b,
  0x6a, 0xcb, 0xbe, 0x39, 0x4a, 0x4c, 0x58, 0xcf },
{ 0xd0, 0xef, 0xaa, 0xfb, 0x43, 0x4d, 0x33, 0x85,
  0x45, 0xf9, 0x02, 0x7f, 0x50, 0x3c, 0x9f, 0xa8 },
{ 0x51, 0xa3, 0x40, 0x8f, 0x92, 0x9d, 0x38, 0xf5,
  0xbc, 0xb6, 0xda, 0x21, 0x10, 0xff, 0xf3, 0xd2 },
{ 0xcd, 0x0c, 0x13, 0xec, 0x5f, 0x97, 0x44, 0x17,
```

*(Continued)*

```
        0xc4, 0xa7, 0x7e, 0x3d, 0x64, 0x5d, 0x19, 0x73 },
    { 0x60, 0x81, 0x4f, 0xdc, 0x22, 0x2a, 0x90, 0x88,
        0x46, 0xee, 0xb8, 0x14, 0xde, 0x5e, 0x0b, 0xdb },
    { 0xe0, 0x32, 0x3a, 0x0a, 0x49, 0x06, 0x24, 0x5c,
        0xc2, 0xd3, 0xac, 0x62, 0x91, 0x95, 0xe4, 0x79 },
    { 0xe7, 0xc8, 0x37, 0x6d, 0x8d, 0xd5, 0x4e, 0xa9,
        0x6c, 0x56, 0xf4, 0xea, 0x65, 0x7a, 0xae, 0x08 },
    { 0xba, 0x78, 0x25, 0x2e, 0x1c, 0xa6, 0xb4, 0xc6,
        0xe8, 0xdd, 0x74, 0x1f, 0x4b, 0xbd, 0x8b, 0x8a },
    { 0x70, 0x3e, 0xb5, 0x66, 0x48, 0x03, 0xf6, 0x0e,
        0x61, 0x35, 0x57, 0xb9, 0x86, 0xc1, 0x1d, 0x9e },
    { 0xe1, 0xf8, 0x98, 0x11, 0x69, 0xd9, 0x8e, 0x94,
        0x9b, 0x1e, 0x87, 0xe9, 0xce, 0x55, 0x28, 0xdf },
    { 0x8c, 0xa1, 0x89, 0x0d, 0xbf, 0xe6, 0x42, 0x68,
        0x41, 0x99, 0x2d, 0x0f, 0xb0, 0x54, 0xbb, 0x16 },
};
```

Performing the substitution is a matter of indexing this table with the high-order four bits of each byte of input as the row and the low-order four bits as the column, which is illustrated in Listing 2-31.

**Listing 2-31:** "aes.c" sub_word

```
static void sub_word( unsigned char *w )
{
    int i = 0;

    for ( i = 0; i < 4; i++ )
    {
        w[ i ] = sbox[ ( w[ i ] & 0xF0 ) >> 4 ][ w[ i ] & 0x0F ];
    }
}
```

Finally, the rotated, substituted value is XORed with the round constant. The low-order three bytes of the round constant are always 0, and the high-order byte starts at 0x01 and shifts left every four iterations, so that it becomes 0x02 in the eighth iteration, 0x04 in the twelfth, and so on. Therefore, the first round constant, applied at iteration #4 if the key length is 128 bits, iteration #6 if the key length is 192 bits, and iteration #8 if the key length is 256 bits, is 0x01000000. The second round constant, applied at iteration #8, #12, or #16 depending on key length, is 0x02000000. The third at iteration #12, #18, or #24 is 0x04000000, and so on.

If you've been following closely, though, you may notice that for a 128-bit key, the round constant is left-shifted 10 times because a 128-bit key requires 44 iterations with a left-shift occurring every four iterations. However, if you left-shift a single byte eight times, you end up with zeros from that point on. Instead, AES mandates that, when the left-shift overflows, you XOR the result — which in this case is zero — with 0x1B. Why 0x1B? Well, take a look at the first 51 iterations of this simple operation – left shift and XOR with 0x1B on overflow:

01, 02, 04, 08, 10, 20, 40, 80, 1b, 36, 6c, d8, ab, 4d, 9a, 2f, 5e, bc, 63, c6, 97, 35, 6a, d4, b3, 7d, fa, ef, c5, 91, 39, 72, e4, d3, bd, 61, c2, 9f, 25, 4a, 94, 33, 66, cc, 83, 1d, 3a, 74, e8, cb, 8d

After the 51st iteration, it wraps back around to 0x01 and starts repeating.

This strange-looking formulation enables you to produce unique values simply and quickly for quite a while, although the key schedule computation only requires 10 iterations (this comes up again in the *column mixing* in the actual encryption/decryption process). Of course, you could have just added one each time and produced 255 unique values, but the bit distribution wouldn't have been as diverse. Remember that you're XORing each time; you want widely differing bit values when you do this.

So, for a 128-bit key, the actual key schedule process looks more like what's shown in Figure 2-10.

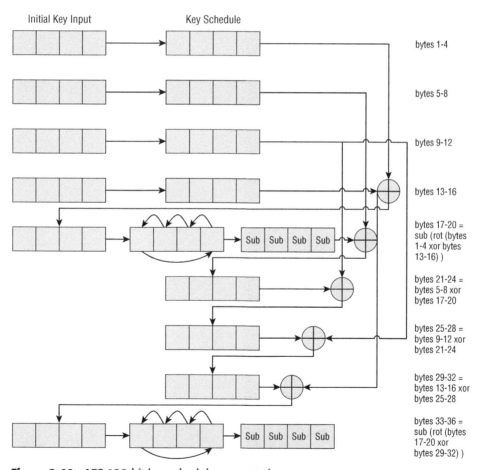

**Figure 2-10:** AES 128-bit key schedule computation

The 192-bit key schedule is the same, except that the rotation, substitution and round-constant XOR is applied every sixth iteration instead of every fourth. For a 256-bit key, rotation, substitution, and XORing happens every eighth iteration. Because every eight iterations doesn't work out to that many, a 256-bit key schedule adds one small additional wrinkle — every fourth iteration, substitution takes place, but rotation and XOR — only take place every eighth iteration.

The net result of all of this is that the key schedule is a non-linear, but repeatable, permutation of the input key. The code to compute an AES key schedule is shown in Listing 2-32.

**Listing 2-32:** "aes.c" compute_key_schedule

```
static void compute_key_schedule( const unsigned char *key,
                int key_length,
                unsigned char w[ ][ 4 ] )
{
  int i;
  int key_words = key_length >> 2;
  unsigned char rcon = 0x01;

  // First, copy the key directly into the key schedule
  memcpy( w, key, key_length );
  for ( i = key_words; i < 4 * ( key_words + 7 ); i++ )
  {
    memcpy( w[ i ], w[ i - 1 ], 4 );
    if ( !( i % key_words ) )
    {
      rot_word( w[ i ] );
      sub_word( w[ i ] );
      if ( !( i % 36 ) )
      {
        rcon = 0x1b;
      }
      w[ i ][ 0 ] ^= rcon;
      rcon <<= 1;
    }
    else if ( ( key_words > 6 ) && ( ( i % key_words ) == 4 ) )
    {
     sub_word( w[ i ] );
    }
    w[ i ][ 0 ] ^= w[ i - key_words ][ 0 ];
    w[ i ][ 1 ] ^= w[ i - key_words ][ 1 ];
    w[ i ][ 2 ] ^= w[ i - key_words ][ 2 ];
    w[ i ][ 3 ] ^= w[ i - key_words ][ 3 ];
  }
}
```

Here, key_length is given in bytes, and w is the key schedule array to fill out. First copy key_length bytes directly into w, and then perform

( ( `key_length` / 4 ) + 6 ) * 4 iterations of the key schedule computation described above — if the iteration number is an even multiple of the key size, a rotation, substitution and XOR by the round constant of the previous four-byte word is performed. In any case, the result is XORed with the value of the previous key_length word.

The following code:

```
else if ( ( key_words > 6 ) && ( ( i % key_words ) == 4 ) )
{
  sub_word( w[ i ] );
}
```

covers the exceptional case of a 256-bit key. Remember, for a 256-bit key, you have to perform a substitution every four iterations.

### AES Encryption

With the key schedule computation defined, you can look at the actual encryption process. AES operates on 16-byte blocks of input, regardless of key size; the input is treated as a 4 × 4 two-dimensional array of bytes. The input is mapped *vertically* into this array as shown in Figure 2-11.

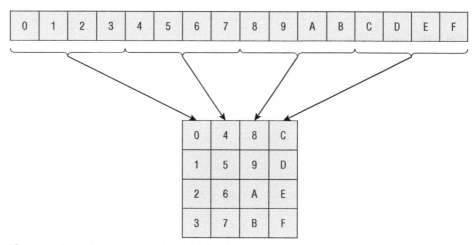

**Figure 2-11:** AES state mapping initialization

This 4 × 4 array of input is referred to as the *state*. It should come as no surprise that the encryption process, then, consists of permuting, substituting, and combining the keying material with this state to produce the output.

The first thing to do is to XOR the state with the first 16 bytes of keying material, which comes directly from the key itself (see Figure 2-12). This is illustrated in Listing 2-33.

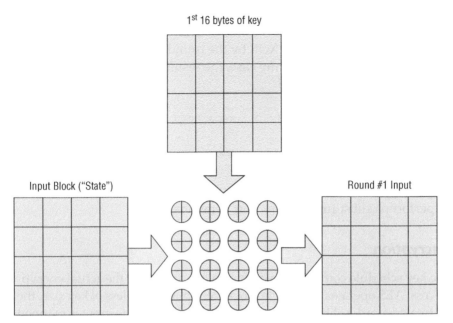

**Figure 2-12:** AES key combination

**Listing 2-33:** "aes.c" add_round_key

```
static void add_round_key( unsigned char state[ ][ 4 ],
                           unsigned char w[ ][ 4 ] )
{
  int c, r;

  for ( c = 0; c < 4; c++ )
  {
    for ( r = 0; r < 4; r++ )
    {
      state[ r ][ c ] = state[ r ][ c ] ^ w[ c ][ r ];
    }
  }
}
```

Note that this is done before the rounds begin.

Each round consists of four steps: a substitution step, a *row-shifting* step, a *column-mixing* step, and finally a key combination step.

Substitution is performed on each byte individually and comes from the same table that the key schedule substitution came from, as in Listing 2-34.

**Listing 2-34:** "aes.c" sub_bytes

```c
static void sub_bytes( unsigned char state[ ][ 4 ] )
{
  int r, c;

  for ( r = 0; r < 4; r++ )
  {
    for ( c = 0; c < 4; c++ )
    {
      state[ r ][ c ] = sbox[ ( state[ r ][ c ] & 0xF0 ) >> 4 ]
                            [ state[ r ][ c ] & 0x0F ];
    }
  }
}
```

Row shifting is a rotation applied to each row. The first row is rotated zero places, the second one place, the third two, and the fourth three. Graphically, this can be viewed as shown in Figure 2-13.

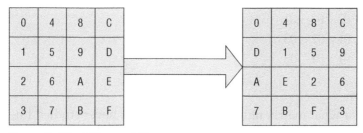

**Figure 2-13:** AES row shift

In code, this is shown in Listing 2-35.

**Listing 2-35:** "aes.c" shift_rows

```c
static void shift_rows( unsigned char state[ ][ 4 ] )
{
  int tmp;

  tmp = state[ 1 ][ 0 ];
  state[ 1 ][ 0 ] = state[ 1 ][ 1 ];
  state[ 1 ][ 1 ] = state[ 1 ][ 2 ];
  state[ 1 ][ 2 ] = state[ 1 ][ 3 ];
  state[ 1 ][ 3 ] = tmp;

  tmp = state[ 2 ][ 0 ];
  state[ 2 ][ 0 ] = state[ 2 ][ 2 ];
```

*(Continued)*

```
    state[ 2 ][ 2 ] = tmp;
    tmp = state[ 2 ][ 1 ];
    state[ 2 ][ 1 ] = state[ 2 ][ 3 ];
    state[ 2 ][ 3 ] = tmp;

    tmp = state[ 3 ][ 3 ];
    state[ 3 ][ 3 ] = state[ 3 ][ 2 ];
    state[ 3 ][ 2 ] = state[ 3 ][ 1 ];
    state[ 3 ][ 1 ] = state[ 3 ][ 0 ];
    state[ 3 ][ 0 ] = tmp;
}
```

Note that for simplicity and clarity, the position shifts are just hardcoded at each row. The relative positions never change, so there's no particular reason to compute them on each iteration.

*Column mixing* is where AES gets a bit confusing and where it differs considerably from DES. The column mix step is actually defined as a matrix multiplication of each column in the source array with the matrix:

$$\begin{bmatrix} 02 & 03 & 01 & 01 \\ 01 & 02 & 03 & 01 \\ 01 & 01 & 02 & 03 \\ 03 & 01 & 01 & 02 \end{bmatrix}$$

### Multiplying Matrices

If you don't remember what matrix multiplication is, or you never studied linear algebra, this works out to multiplying each element of each column with each element of each row and then adding the results to come up with the target column. (Don't worry, I show you some code in just a second). If you *do* remember linear algebra, don't get too excited because AES redefines the terms *multiply* and *add* to mean something completely different than what you probably consider *multiply* and *add*.

An ordinary, *traditional* 4×4 matrix multiplication can be implemented as in Listing 2-36.

**Listing 2-36:** Example matrix multiplication

```
static void matrix_multiply( unsigned char m1[4][4],
             unsigned char m2[4][4],
             unsigned char target[4][4])
{
  int r, c;
  for ( r = 0; r < 4; r++ )
  {
    for ( c = 0; c < 4; c++ )
    {
      target[ r ][ c ] =
```

```
        m1[ r ][ 0 ] * m2[ 0 ][ c ] +
        m1[ r ][ 1 ] * m2[ 1 ][ c ] +
        m1[ r ][ 2 ] * m2[ 2 ][ c ] +
        m1[ r ][ 3 ] * m2[ 3 ][ c ];
    }
  }
}
```

As you can see, each element of the target matrix becomes the sum of the rows of the first matrix multiplied by the columns of the second. As long as the first matrix has as many rows as the second has columns, two matrices can be multiplied this way. This code can be made even more general to deal with arbitrarily sized matrices, but C's multidimensional array syntax makes that tricky, and you won't need it for AES.

If you multiply something, there ought to be a way to *unmultiply* (that is, divide) it. And certainly if you're using this in an encryption operation you need a well-defined way to undo it. Matrix division is not as clear-cut as matrix multiplication, however. To undo a matrix multiplication, you must find a matrix's *inverse*. This is another matrix which, when multiplied, as defined above, will yield the *identity matrix*:

$$\begin{bmatrix} 01 & 00 & 00 & 00 \\ 00 & 01 & 00 & 00 \\ 00 & 00 & 01 & 00 \\ 00 & 00 & 00 & 01 \end{bmatrix}$$

If you look back at the way matrix multiplication was defined, you can see why it's called the identity matrix. If you multiply this with any other (four-row) matrix, you get back the same matrix. This is analogous to the case of multiplying a number by 1 — when you multiply any number by the number 1 you get back the same number.

The problem with the standard matrix operations, as they pertain to encryption, is that the inversion of the matrix above is:

$$\begin{bmatrix} 02 & 03 & 01 & 01 \\ 01 & 02 & 03 & 01 \\ 01 & 01 & 02 & 03 \\ 03 & 01 & 01 & 02 \end{bmatrix} = \begin{bmatrix} -0.1143 & 0.0857 & -0.3143 & 0.4857 \\ 0.4857 & -0.1143 & 0.0857 & -0.3143 \\ -0.3143 & 0.4857 & -0.1143 & 0.0857 \\ 0.0857 & -0.3143 & 0.4857 & -0.1143 \end{bmatrix}$$

As you can imagine, multiplying by this inverted matrix to decrypt would be terribly slow, and the inclusion of floating point operations would introduce round-off errors as well. To speed things up, and still allow for invertible matrices,

AES redefines the add and multiply operations for its matrix multiplication. This means also that you don't have to worry about the thorny topic of matrix inversion, which is fortunate because it's as complex as it looks (if not more so).

*Adding* in AES is actually redefined as *XORing*, which is nothing at all like adding. *Multiplying* is repeated adding, just as in ordinary arithmetic, but it's done modulo 0x1B (remember this value from the key schedule?). The specification refers to this as a *dot product* — another linear algebra term, but again redefined. If your head is spinning from this mathematicalese, perhaps some code will help.

To multiply two bytes — that is, to compute their dot product in AES — you XOR together the xtime values of the multiplicand with the multiplier. What are xtime values? They're the "left-shift and XOR with 0x1B on overflow" operation that described the round constant in the key schedule computation. In code, this works out to Listing 2-37.

**Listing 2-37:** "aes.c" dot product

```
unsigned char xtime( unsigned char x )
{
  return ( x << 1 ) ^ ( ( x & 0x80 ) ? 0x1b : 0x00 );
}

unsigned char dot( unsigned char x, unsigned char y )
{
  unsigned char mask;
  unsigned char product = 0;

  for ( mask = 0x01; mask; mask <<= 1 )
  {
    if ( y & mask )
    {
      product ^= x;
    }
    x = xtime( x );
  }

  return product;
}
```

This probably doesn't look much like multiplication to you — and, honestly, it isn't — but this is algorithmically how you'd go about performing binary multiplication if you didn't have a machine code implementation of it to do the heavy lifting for you. In fact, this concept reappears in the next chapter when the topic of arbitrary-precision binary math is examined.

Fortunately, from an implementation perspective, you can just accept that this is "what you do" with the bytes in a column-mixing operation.

### Mixing Columns in AES

Armed with this strange multiplication operation, you can implement the matrix multiplication that performs the column-mixing step in Listing 2-38.

**Listing 2-38:** "aes.c" mix_columns

```
static void mix_columns( unsigned char s[ ][ 4 ] )
{
  int c;
  unsigned char t[ 4 ];

  for ( c = 0; c < 4; c++ )
  {
    t[ 0 ] = dot( 2, s[ 0 ][ c ] ) ^ dot( 3, s[ 1 ][ c ] ) ^
             s[ 2 ][ c ] ^ s[ 3 ][ c ];
    t[ 1 ] = s[ 0 ][ c ] ^ dot( 2, s[ 1 ][ c ] ) ^
             dot( 3, s[ 2 ][ c ] ) ^ s[ 3 ][ c ];
    t[ 2 ] = s[ 0 ][ c ] ^ s[ 1 ][ c ] ^ dot( 2, s[ 2 ][ c ] ) ^
             dot( 3, s[ 3 ] [ c ] );
    t[ 3 ] = dot( 3, s[ 0 ][ c ] ) ^ s[ 1 ][ c ] ^ s[ 2 ][ c ] ^
             dot( 2, s[ 3 ][ c ] );
    s[ 0 ][ c ] = t[ 0 ];
    s[ 1 ][ c ] = t[ 1 ];
    s[ 2 ][ c ] = t[ 2 ];
    s[ 3 ][ c ] = t[ 3 ];
  }
}
```

Remembering that adding is XORing and mutiplying is dot-ing, this is a straightforward matrix multiplication. Compare this to Listing 2-35.

And that's it. Each round consists of substituting, shifting, column mixing, and finally adding the round key. Encrypting a block of AES, then, can be done as shown in Listing 2-39.

**Listing 2-39:** "aes.c" aes_block_encrypt

```
static void aes_block_encrypt( const unsigned char *input_block,
               unsigned char *output_block,
               const unsigned char *key,
               int key_size )
{
  int r, c;
  int round;
  int nr;
  unsigned char state[ 4 ][ 4 ];
  unsigned char w[ 60 ][ 4 ];

  for ( r = 0; r < 4; r++ )
  {
```

*(Continued)*

```
  for ( c = 0; c < 4; c++ )
  {
    state[ r ][ c ] = input_block[ r + ( 4 * c ) ];
  }
}
// rounds = key size in 4-byte words + 6
nr = ( key_size >> 2 ) + 6;

compute_key_schedule( key, key_size, w );

add_round_key( state, &w[ 0 ] );

for ( round = 0; round < nr; round++ )
{
  sub_bytes( state );
  shift_rows( state );
  if ( round < ( nr - 1 ) )
  {
    mix_columns( state );
  }
  add_round_key( state, &w[ ( round + 1 ) * 4 ] );
}

for ( r = 0; r < 4; r++ )
{
  for ( c = 0; c < 4; c++ )
  {
    output_block[ r + ( 4 * c ) ] = state[ r ][ c ];
  }
}
}
```

Notice this same routine handles 128-, 192-, or 256-bit key sizes; the only difference between the three is the number of rounds, and the amount of key material that therefore needs to be computed. Rather than computing the size of w — the key schedule array — dynamically, it just statically allocates enough space for a 256-bit key schedule (60 * 4). It then copies the input into the state matrix, applies the first round key, and starts iterating. Also, it skips column mixing on the very last iteration. Finally, it copies from state array back into the output, and the block is encrypted.

## AES Decryption

Unlike DES, AES's decryption operation isn't the same as encryption. You have to go back and undo everything that you did during the encryption step. This starts, of course, with re-applying the round keys in reverse order, unmixing the columns, unshifting the rows, and unsubstituting the bytes.

Do everything in exactly the inverse order that you did it when encrypting. This means that the loops occur in different orders. Look at the expanded set of operations for an encryption:

1. AddRound Key

2. SubBytes

3. ShiftRows

4. MixColumns

5. AddRoundKey

6. SubBytes

7. ShiftRows

8. MixColumns

9. AddRoundKey

...

42. SubBytes

43. ShiftRows

44. AddRoundKey

This means that the decrypt loop won't be the same as the encrypt loop. It starts with an `AddRoundKey` and is then followed by `invShiftRows`, `invSubBytes`, `addRoundKey`, and `invMixColumns`:

1. AddRound Key
2. SubBytes
3. ShiftRows
4. MixColumns
5. AddRoundKey
6. SubBytes
7. ShiftRows
8. MixColumns
9. AddRoundKey
...
42. SubBytes
43. ShiftRows
44. AddRoundKey

And then, a final `invShiftRows`, `invSubBytes` and `addRoundKey`. Notice that `shiftRows`, `subBytes` and `mixColumns` all need specific inversion routines whereas `addRoundKey` is its own inverse, because it's just applying the XOR operation. This is shown in Listing 2-40.

**Listing 2-40:** "aes.c" inversion routines

```
static void inv_shift_rows( unsigned char state[ ][ 4 ] )
{
  int tmp;

  tmp = state[ 1 ][ 2 ];
  state[ 1 ][ 2 ] = state[ 1 ][ 1 ];
  state[ 1 ][ 1 ] = state[ 1 ][ 0 ];
  state[ 1 ][ 0 ] = state[ 1 ][ 3 ];
  state[ 1 ][ 3 ] = tmp;

  tmp = state[ 2 ][ 0 ];
  state[ 2 ][ 0 ] = state[ 2 ][ 2 ];
  state[ 2 ][ 2 ] = tmp;
  tmp = state[ 2 ][ 1 ];
  state[ 2 ][ 1 ] = state[ 2 ][ 3 ];
  state[ 2 ][ 3 ] = tmp;

  tmp = state[ 3 ][ 0 ];
  state[ 3 ][ 0 ] = state[ 3 ][ 1 ];
  state[ 3 ][ 1 ] = state[ 3 ][ 2 ];
  state[ 3 ][ 2 ] = state[ 3 ][ 3 ];
  state[ 3 ][ 3 ] = tmp;
}

static unsigned char inv_sbox[ 16 ][ 16 ] = {
{ 0x52, 0x09, 0x6a, 0xd5, 0x30, 0x36, 0xa5, 0x38,
  0xbf, 0x40, 0xa3, 0x9e, 0x81, 0xf3, 0xd7, 0xfb },
{ 0x7c, 0xe3, 0x39, 0x82, 0x9b, 0x2f, 0xff, 0x87,
  0x34, 0x8e, 0x43, 0x44, 0xc4, 0xde, 0xe9, 0xcb },
{ 0x54, 0x7b, 0x94, 0x32, 0xa6, 0xc2, 0x23, 0x3d,
  0xee, 0x4c, 0x95, 0x0b, 0x42, 0xfa, 0xc3, 0x4e },
{ 0x08, 0x2e, 0xa1, 0x66, 0x28, 0xd9, 0x24, 0xb2,
  0x76, 0x5b, 0xa2, 0x49, 0x6d, 0x8b, 0xd1, 0x25 },
{ 0x72, 0xf8, 0xf6, 0x64, 0x86, 0x68, 0x98, 0x16,
  0xd4, 0xa4, 0x5c, 0xcc, 0x5d, 0x65, 0xb6, 0x92 },
{ 0x6c, 0x70, 0x48, 0x50, 0xfd, 0xed, 0xb9, 0xda,
  0x5e, 0x15, 0x46, 0x57, 0xa7, 0x8d, 0x9d, 0x84 },
{ 0x90, 0xd8, 0xab, 0x00, 0x8c, 0xbc, 0xd3, 0x0a,
  0xf7, 0xe4, 0x58, 0x05, 0xb8, 0xb3, 0x45, 0x06 },
{ 0xd0, 0x2c, 0x1e, 0x8f, 0xca, 0x3f, 0x0f, 0x02,
  0xc1, 0xaf, 0xbd, 0x03, 0x01, 0x13, 0x8a, 0x6b },
{ 0x3a, 0x91, 0x11, 0x41, 0x4f, 0x67, 0xdc, 0xea,
  0x97, 0xf2, 0xcf, 0xce, 0xf0, 0xb4, 0xe6, 0x73 },
{ 0x96, 0xac, 0x74, 0x22, 0xe7, 0xad, 0x35, 0x85,
  0xe2, 0xf9, 0x37, 0xe8, 0x1c, 0x75, 0xdf, 0x6e },
{ 0x47, 0xf1, 0x1a, 0x71, 0x1d, 0x29, 0xc5, 0x89,
  0x6f, 0xb7, 0x62, 0x0e, 0xaa, 0x18, 0xbe, 0x1b },
{ 0xfc, 0x56, 0x3e, 0x4b, 0xc6, 0xd2, 0x79, 0x20,
  0x9a, 0xdb, 0xc0, 0xfe, 0x78, 0xcd, 0x5a, 0xf4 },
{ 0x1f, 0xdd, 0xa8, 0x33, 0x88, 0x07, 0xc7, 0x31,
  0xb1, 0x12, 0x10, 0x59, 0x27, 0x80, 0xec, 0x5f },
```

```
{ 0x60, 0x51, 0x7f, 0xa9, 0x19, 0xb5, 0x4a, 0x0d,
  0x2d, 0xe5, 0x7a, 0x9f, 0x93, 0xc9, 0x9c, 0xef },
{ 0xa0, 0xe0, 0x3b, 0x4d, 0xae, 0x2a, 0xf5, 0xb0,
  0xc8, 0xeb, 0xbb, 0x3c, 0x83, 0x53, 0x99, 0x61 },
{ 0x17, 0x2b, 0x04, 0x7e, 0xba, 0x77, 0xd6, 0x26,
  0xe1, 0x69, 0x14, 0x63, 0x55, 0x21, 0x0c, 0x7d },
};

static void inv_sub_bytes( unsigned char state[ ][ 4 ] )
{
  int r, c;

  for ( r = 0; r < 4; r++ )
  {
    for ( c = 0; c < 4; c++ )
    {
      state[ r ][ c ] = inv_sbox[ ( state[ r ][ c ] & 0xF0 ) >> 4 ]
                                [ state[ r ][ c ] & 0x0F ];
    }
  }
}
```

`inv_shift_rows` and `inv_sub_bytes` are fairly straightforward; notice that the s-boxes that AES uses are not invertible like DES's were. You need two sets of s-boxes to encrypt and decrypt. There's no computation involved in the inverted s-box. If you turn back to the "forward" s-box, you see that, for example, `substitution(0x75) = sbox[7][5] = 0x9d`. Conversely, `inv_substitution(0x9d) = inv_sbox[9][d] = 0x75`.

Inverting column mixing involves performing a matrix multiplication of each column by the inversion of the matrix that the encryption operation multiplied it by. Of course, this isn't just any matrix multiplication, and it's not just any matrix inversion. It's the matrix multiplication and inversion "considered as polynomials over $GF(2^8)$ and multiplied modulo $x^4 + 1$ with a fixed polynomial $a^{-1}(x)$, given by $a^{-1}(x) = \{0b\}x^3 + \{0d\}x^2 + \{09\}x + \{0e\}$". This dense phrase means performing another "matrix multiplication" against the matrix:

$$\begin{bmatrix} 0e & 0b & 0d & 09 \\ 09 & 0e & 0b & 0d \\ 0d & 09 & 0e & 0b \\ 0b & 0d & 09 & 0e \end{bmatrix}$$

which is the inversion, after redefining addition and multiplication as described earlier, of the forward matrix. In code, this is shown in Listing 2-41.

**Listing 2-41:** "aes.c" inv_mix_columns

```
static void inv_mix_columns( unsigned char s[ ][ 4 ] )
{
  int c;
```

*(Continued)*

```
unsigned char t[ 4 ];

for ( c = 0; c < 4; c++ )
{
  t[ 0 ] = dot( 0x0e, s[ 0 ][ c ] ) ^ dot( 0x0b, s[ 1 ][ c ] ) ^
           dot( 0x0d, s[ 2 ][ c ] ) ^ dot( 0x09, s[ 3 ][ c ] );
  t[ 1 ] = dot( 0x09, s[ 0 ][ c ] ) ^ dot( 0x0e, s[ 1 ][ c ] ) ^
           dot( 0x0b, s[ 2 ][ c ] ) ^ dot( 0x0d, s[ 3 ][ c ] );
  t[ 2 ] = dot( 0x0d, s[ 0 ][ c ] ) ^ dot( 0x09, s[ 1 ][ c ] ) ^
           dot( 0x0e, s[ 2 ][ c ] ) ^ dot( 0x0b, s[ 3 ][ c ] );
  t[ 3 ] = dot( 0x0b, s[ 0 ][ c ] ) ^ dot( 0x0d, s[ 1 ][ c ] ) ^
           dot( 0x09, s[ 2 ][ c ] ) ^ dot( 0x0e, s[ 3 ][ c ] );
  s[ 0 ][ c ] = t[ 0 ];
  s[ 1 ][ c ] = t[ 1 ];
  s[ 2 ][ c ] = t[ 2 ];
  s[ 3 ][ c ] = t[ 3 ];
}
}
```

And the AES block decryption operation is shown in Listing 2-42.

**Listing 2-42:** "aes.c" aes_block_decrypt

```
static void aes_block_decrypt( const unsigned char *input_block,
               unsigned char *output_block,
               const unsigned char *key,
               int key_size )
{
  int r, c;
  int round;
  int nr;
  unsigned char state[ 4 ][ 4 ];
  unsigned char w[ 60 ][ 4 ];

  for ( r = 0; r < 4; r++ )
  {
    for ( c = 0; c < 4; c++ )
    {
      state[ r ][ c ] = input_block[ r + ( 4 * c ) ];
    }
  }
  // rounds = key size in 4-byte words + 6
  nr = ( key_size >> 2 ) + 6;

  compute_key_schedule( key, key_size, w );

  add_round_key( state, &w[ nr * 4 ] );

  for ( round = nr; round > 0; round-- )
  {
    inv_shift_rows( state );
    inv_sub_bytes( state );
```

```
      add_round_key( state, &w[ ( round - 1 ) * 4 ] );
      if ( round > 1 )
      {
        inv_mix_columns( state );
      }
    }

    for ( r = 0; r < 4; r++ )
    {
      for ( c = 0; c < 4; c++ )
      {
        output_block[ r + ( 4 * c ) ] = state[ r ][ c ];
      }
    }
  }
```

With the block operations defined, encryption and decryption are simple enough, as shown in Listing 2-43.

**Listing 2-43:** "aes.c" aes_encrypt and aes_decrypt

```
#define AES_BLOCK_SIZE 16

static void aes_encrypt( const unsigned char *input,
            int input_len,
            unsigned char *output,
            const unsigned char *iv,
            const unsigned char *key,
            int key_length )
{
  unsigned char input_block[ AES_BLOCK_SIZE ];

  while ( input_len >= AES_BLOCK_SIZE )
  {
    memcpy( input_block, input, AES_BLOCK_SIZE );
    xor( input_block, iv, AES_BLOCK_SIZE ); // implement CBC
    aes_block_encrypt( input_block, output, key, key_length );
    memcpy( ( void * ) iv, ( void * ) output, AES_BLOCK_SIZE ); // CBC
    input += AES_BLOCK_SIZE;
    output += AES_BLOCK_SIZE;
    input_len -= AES_BLOCK_SIZE;
  }
}

static void aes_decrypt( const unsigned char *input,
            int input_len,
            unsigned char *output,
            const unsigned char *iv,
            const unsigned char *key,
            int key_length )
{
  while ( input_len >= AES_BLOCK_SIZE )
```

*(Continued)*

```
  {
    aes_block_decrypt( input, output, key, key_length );
    xor( output, iv, AES_BLOCK_SIZE );
    memcpy( ( void * ) iv, ( void * ) input, AES_BLOCK_SIZE ); // CBC
    input += AES_BLOCK_SIZE;
    output += AES_BLOCK_SIZE;
    input_len -= AES_BLOCK_SIZE;
  }
}
```

Notice the similarities between `aes_encrypt`/`aes_decrypt` and `des_oper-ate`. CBC and block iteration are implemented the same in both cases. In fact, CBC and block iteration are the same for all block ciphers. If you were going to be implementing many more block ciphers, it would be worth the investment to generalize these operations so you could just pass in a function pointer to a generic `block_operate` function. Don't bother here, though, because you're finished with block ciphers.

Finally — you do want the AES encryption/decryption routines to be interchangeable with the DES and 3DES encryption/decryption routines. For that to be possible, the method signatures must be the same. Therefore, go ahead and implement a couple of top-level functions as shown in Listing 2-44.

**Listing 2-44:** "aes.c" AES encryption and decryption routines

```
void aes_128_encrypt( const unsigned char *plaintext,
          const int plaintext_len,
          unsigned char ciphertext[],
          const unsigned char *iv,
          const unsigned char *key )
{
  aes_encrypt( plaintext, plaintext_len, ciphertext, iv, key, 16 );
}

void aes_128_decrypt( const unsigned char *ciphertext,
          const int ciphertext_len,
          unsigned char plaintext[],
          const unsigned char *iv,
          const unsigned char *key )
{
  aes_decrypt( ciphertext, ciphertext_len, plaintext, iv, key, 16 );
}

void aes_256_encrypt( const unsigned char *plaintext,
          const int plaintext_len,
          unsigned char ciphertext[],
          const unsigned char *iv,
          const unsigned char *key )
{
  aes_encrypt( plaintext, plaintext_len, ciphertext, iv, key, 32 );
}
```

```
void aes_256_decrypt( const unsigned char *ciphertext,
          const int ciphertext_len,
          unsigned char plaintext[],
          const unsigned char *iv,
          const unsigned char *key )
{
  aes_decrypt( ciphertext, ciphertext_len, plaintext, iv, key, 32 );
}
```

Here the function name dictates the key length. This isn't a good approach for general scalability, but because AES is only defined for a few specific key lengths, you're safe in this case. Notice that there's no `aes_192_encrypt/_decrypt` pair here. AES 192 actually isn't used in SSL, so I don't cover it here.

AES is widely supported. In fact, recent Intel chips include assembly-level AES instructions!

Of course, you want to be able to test this out, so create a main routine in aes.c, blocked off by an #ifdef so that this file can be included in other applications, as shown in Listing 2-45:

**Listing 2-45:** "aes.c" main routine for testing

```
#ifdef TEST_AES
int main( int argc, char *argv[ ] )
{
  unsigned char *key;
  unsigned char *input;
  unsigned char *iv;
  int key_len;
  int input_len;
  int iv_len;

  if ( argc < 5 )
  {
    fprintf( stderr, "Usage: %s [-e|-d] <key> <iv> <input>\n", argv[ 0 ] );
    exit( 0 );
  }

  key_len = hex_decode( argv[ 2 ], &key );
  iv_len = hex_decode( argv[ 3 ], &iv );
  input_len = hex_decode( argv[ 4 ], &input );

  if ( !strcmp( argv[ 1 ], "-e" ) )
  {
    unsigned char *ciphertext = ( unsigned char * ) malloc( input_len );

    if ( key_len == 16 )
    {
      aes_128_encrypt( input, input_len, ciphertext, iv, key );
    }
```

*(Continued)*

```
      else if ( key_len == 32 )
      {
        aes_256_encrypt( input, input_len, ciphertext, iv, key );
      }
      else
      {
        fprintf( stderr, "Unsupported key length: %d\n", key_len );
        exit( 0 );
      }

      show_hex( ciphertext, input_len );

      free( ciphertext );
    }
    else if ( !strcmp( argv[ 1 ], "-d" ) )
    {
      unsigned char *plaintext = ( unsigned char * ) malloc( input_len );

      if ( key_len == 16 )
      {
        aes_128_decrypt( input, input_len, plaintext, iv, key );
      }
      else if ( key_len == 32 )
      {
        aes_256_decrypt( input, input_len, plaintext, iv, key );
      }
      else
      {
        fprintf( stderr, "Unsupported key length %d\n", key_len );
        exit( 0 );
      }

      show_hex( plaintext, input_len );
      free( plaintext );
    }
    else
    {
      fprintf( stderr, "Usage: %s [-e|-d] <key> <iv> <input>\n", argv[ 0 ] );
    }

    free( iv );
    free( key );
    free( input );
  }
#endif
```

This checks the length of the key and invokes aes_128_decrypt or aes_256_
decrypt. Its operation is identical to the operation of the DES tester routine
described earlier.

## Other Block Cipher Algorithms

There are actually dozens, if not hundreds, of other block cipher algorithms. Two additional algorithms specifically named in the TLS standard are IDEA and RC2, although support for them has been deprecated with TLS 1.2. They weren't widely implemented because both were patented. What's worse is that RC2 uses a 40-bit (!) key. AES isn't mentioned in the specification because Rijndael hadn't yet been named as the NIST's new encryption standard when RFC 2246 was drafted. RFC 3268, issued in 2002, defined the addition of AES to SSL/TLS.

Other block ciphers known or believed to be secure are blowfish, twofish, FEAL, LOKI, and Camelia. See Bruce Schneier's book *Applied Cryptography* (Wiley, 1996) for a thorough (although now somewhat dated) discussion of many block ciphers. By far the most common ciphers used in SSL, though, are 3DES and AES. There's one more encryption routine I'd like to discuss because it's treated a bit differently than the others, as it is a *stream cipher*.

# Understanding Stream Cipher Algorithms

*Stream cipher algorithms* are technically the same as block cipher algorithms; they just operate on a block size of one byte. Conceptually, the only difference is that there's no need for padding or for CBC. Design-wise, however, stream ciphers tend to be quite a bit different. Whereas block ciphers are concerned with shuffling bits around within the block, stream ciphers concentrate on generating a secure stream of bytes whose length is the same as the plaintext and then simply XORing those bytes with the plaintext to produce the ciphertext. Stream ciphers derive all of their cryptographic security from the keystream generation function.

With block ciphers, you take a key, generate a key schedule and then mix that key schedule with the permuted, shifted, rotated, sliced, diced, and chopped-up block one after another. Optionally, you apply CBC to each block to ensure that identical blocks look different in the output stream.

Stream ciphers work somewhat similarly, but they generate a key schedule that is as long as the *entire* block of data to be encrypted. After the key schedule is generated, the input block is simply XORed with the input. To decrypt, the key schedule is similarly generated and XORed with the encrypted ciphertext to recover the original plaintext. Therefore, all of the security is in the key schedule generation.

Stream ciphers are also interesting from a design perspective because they're treated somewhat differently than block ciphers; making the SSL layer treat block and stream ciphers interchangeably is a bit tricky. Only one stream cipher has been widely implemented in SSL; this is the RC4 algorithm, examined in the next section.

## Understanding and Implementing the RC4 Algorithm

RC4 was invented by Ron Rivest (whose name comes up again in Chapter 3), who also invented RC2 (and RC5 and RC6). RC4 is actually not an open standard like AES and DES are. In fact, in spite of the fact that it's specifically named as one of the five encryption algorithms available for use with SSL, the details of how RC4 works have never been officially published. However, they've been widely distributed, and an IETF draft specification of the algorithm — referred to as an *RC4-compatible* algorithm for trademark purposes — has been submitted for review although it's not yet officially published.

After the complexity of DES and AES, you may be pleasantly surprised at the simplicity of RC4. First, a 256-byte *key schedule* is computed from the key, which can be essentially any length. After that, each byte of the plaintext is XORed with one byte of the key schedule after permuting the key schedule. This goes on until the plaintext is completely encrypted. Decrypting is the *exact* same process. Because there's no concept of CBC, there's no need for an initialization vector either. An example of the RC4 operation is shown in Listing 2-46.

**Listing 2-46:** "rc4.c" rc4_operate

```
static void rc4_operate( const unsigned char *plaintext,
             int plaintext_len,
             unsigned char *ciphertext,
             const unsigned char *key,
             int key_len )
{
  int i, j;
  unsigned char S[ 256 ];
  unsigned char tmp;

  // KSA (key scheduling algorithm)
  for ( i = 0; i < 256; i++ )
  {
    S[ i ] = i;
  }
```

S is the key schedule. The first step in computing the key schedule is to initialize each element with its index as shown in Figure 2-14:

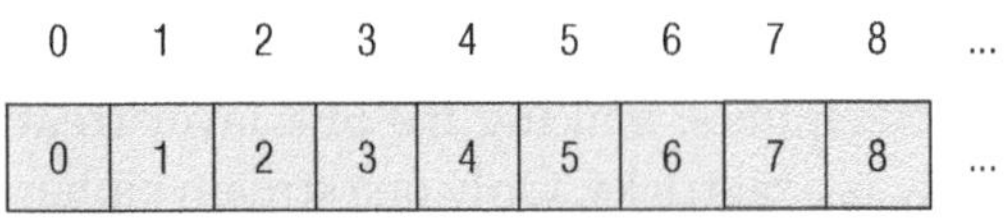

**Figure 2-14:** Initial RC4 key schedule

Next, the key is combined with the key schedule:

```
j = 0;
for ( i = 0; i < 256; i++ )
{
  j = ( j + S[ i ] + key[ i % key_len ] ) % 256;
  tmp = S[ i ];
  S[ i ] = S[ j ];
  S[ j ] = tmp;
}
```

Given a key of "password" (0x70617373776f7264), for example, the first few computations are illustrated in Figure 2-15.

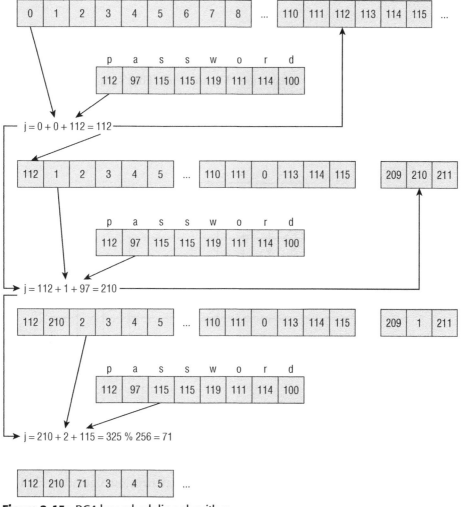

**Figure 2-15:** RC4 key scheduling algorithm

After 256 such iterations, the s array is completely permuted, with each ordinal from 0 to 255 appearing once and only once.

With the key schedule computed, encryption — or decryption, remembering that they're identical — can begin:

```
i = 0;
j = 0;
while ( plaintext_len-- )
{
  i = ( i + 1 ) % 256;
  j = ( j + S[ i ] ) % 256;
  tmp = S[ i ];
  S[ i ] = S[ j ];
  S[ j ] = tmp;
  *(ciphertext++) = S[ ( S[ i ] + S[ j ] ) % 256 ] ^ *(plaintext++);
}
}
```

First, the key schedule is permuted, again. The permutation is a bit simpler and doesn't involve the key itself. Then the input is XORed with a byte of the key schedule to produce the output (see Figure 2-16). That's all there is to it.

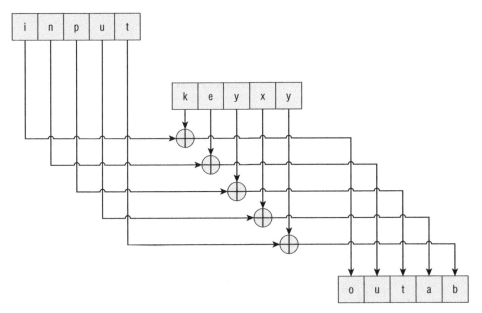

**Figure 2-16:** RC4 encryption and decryption

RC4 is simple — too simple, in fact. It's been shown to be fairly straightforward to crack, yet, like DES, it continues to be a popular encryption algorithm choice. In fact, *WEP*, the *Wired Equivalent Privacy* encryption routine built into — and often the only option for — most wireless devices mandates its use! You should add support for it because it's the only stream cipher defined for use in SSL, and because its implementation is so simple; however, you should almost definitely prefer 3DES or AES-256 for encryption of any valuable data.

As you can see, there are effectively no restrictions on the key length; the key can be as long as 256 bytes (it could be longer, but the remaining bytes wouldn't factor into the key scheduling algorithm). There are two standard, common key lengths though — 40 bits and 128 bits. 40 bits is just 5 bytes (!) and is trivially crackable. 128 bits is a decent-sized key for most crypto purposes.

Put together a simple main routine to test this, as shown in Listing 2-47.

**Listing 2-47:** "rc4.c" main routine for testing

```
#ifdef TEST_RC4
int main( int argc, char *argv[ ] )
{
  unsigned char *key;
  unsigned char *input;
  unsigned char *output;
  int key_len;
  int input_len;

  if ( argc < 4 )
  {
    fprintf( stderr, "Usage: %s [-e|-d] <key> <input>\n", argv[ 0 ] );
    exit( 0 );
  }

  key_len = hex_decode( argv[ 2 ], &key );
  input_len = hex_decode( argv[ 3 ], &input );

  output = malloc( input_len );
  rc4_operate( input, input_len, output, key, key_len );
  printf( "Results: " );
  show_hex( output, input_len );

  free( key );
  free( input );

  return 0;
}
#endif
```

Again, you can use the `hex_decode` convenience function to allow you to pass in arbitrary byte arrays and not just printable-ASCII input.

```
[jdavies@localhost ssl]$ ./rc4 -e abcdef abcdefghijklmnop
Results: daf70b86e76454eb975e3bfe2cce339c
```

This works, but there's a problem with this routine, if you plan to use it in a larger program. Every call starts over at the beginning of the key space. You want to treat each call as if it was the next part of a very long string, which means you need to keep track of the state of the algorithm. You can't just make i, j, and s static variables. In addition to not being thread-safe, you need to keep multiple RC4 contexts around. Instead, define a structure to store the rc4 state in, as shown in Listing 2-48.

**Listing 2-48:** "rc4.h" rc4_state structure

```
#define RC4_STATE_ARRAY_LEN  256

typedef struct
{
  int i;
  int j;
  unsigned char S[ RC4_STATE_ARRAY_LEN ];
}
rc4_state;
```

Now, instead of initializing this on each invocation, let the caller pass in a pointer to this structure. It is updated as rc4_operate completes, and the caller can pass it back in to the next invocation to pick up where it left off, so that the output looks like one, long, continuous stream of encrypted data.

The only remaining issue is when to do the initial key scheduling algorithm; the one illustrated in Figure 2-15. This should be done one time, but never again afterward. You can sort of "cheat," here, as shown in Listing 2-49. The rc4_operate algorithm checks the state parameter; if the s array starts with two zeros — an impossible state — assume that the caller is passing in an uninitialized rc4_state structure. Otherwise, it is accepted as provided.

**Listing 2-49:** "rc4.c" rc4_operate with persistent state

```
static void rc4_operate( const unsigned char *plaintext,
            int plaintext_len,
            unsigned char *ciphertext,
            const unsigned char *key,
            int key_len,
            rc4_state *state )
{
  int i, j;
  unsigned char *S;
  unsigned char tmp;

  i = state->i;
  j = state->j;
  S = state->S;

  // KSA (key scheduling algorithm)
```

```
if ( S[ 0 ] == 0 && S[ 1 ] == 0 )
{
  // First invocation; initialize the state array
  for ( i = 0; i < 256; i++ )
  {
    S[ i ] = i;
  }
...
  i = 0;
  j = 0;
}
...
  *(ciphertext++) = S[ ( S[ i ] + S[ j ] ) % 256 ] ^ *(plaintext++);
}

state->i = i;
state->j = j;
}
```

Now, it's up to the caller to initialize a new `rc4_state` structure, fill it with 0's (or zero out at least the first two elements), and pass it into each `rc4_operate` call. Technically, you probably ought to define an `rc4_initialize` function that does this to make it more explicit — while you're at it, you could and should define similar functions for DES and AES that compute the key schedule and store it somewhere so it doesn't need to be recomputed on each iteration. I leave this as an exercise for you.

One last tweak: Because there are "standard" rc4 key sizes, create a couple of wrapper functions that identify the key lengths explicitly, as shown in Listing 2-50.

**Listing 2-50:** "rc4.c" key-length wrapper functions

```
void rc4_40_encrypt( const unsigned char *plaintext,
        const int plaintext_len,
        unsigned char ciphertext[],
        void *state,
        const unsigned char *key )
{
  rc4_operate( plaintext, plaintext_len, ciphertext, key, 5,
    ( rc4_state * ) state );
}

void rc4_40_decrypt( const unsigned char *ciphertext,
        const int ciphertext_len,
        unsigned char plaintext[],
        void *state,
        const unsigned char *key )
{
  rc4_operate( ciphertext, ciphertext_len, plaintext, key, 5,
    ( rc4_state * ) state );
```

*(Continued)*

```
}

void rc4_128_encrypt( const unsigned char *plaintext,
          const int plaintext_len,
          unsigned char ciphertext[],
          void *state,
          const unsigned char *key )
{
  rc4_operate( plaintext, plaintext_len, ciphertext, key, 16,
    ( rc4_state * ) state );
}

void rc4_128_decrypt( const unsigned char *ciphertext,
          const int ciphertext_len,
          unsigned char plaintext[],
          void *state,
          const unsigned char *key )
{
  rc4_operate( ciphertext, ciphertext_len, plaintext, key, 16,
    ( rc4_state * ) state );
}
```

If you compare these functions to des_encrypt, des3_encrypt and aes_encrypt, notice that they're almost identical except that the fourth parameter, the state, is a void pointer rather than an unsigned char pointer to an initialization vector. In fact, go ahead and change all eight encrypt/decrypt functions to accept void pointers and cast them to the proper type. This commonality enables you to switch from one encryption function to another by just changing a function pointer. You will take advantage of this flexibility in Chapter 6, when TLS itself is examined — all of the functions developed in this chapter will be reused there.

## Converting a Block Cipher to a Stream Cipher: The OFB and COUNTER Block-Chaining Modes

Actually, a block cipher can be converted into a stream cipher. If you look at the way CBC works, notice that the initialization vector is XORed with the input and then the result is encrypted. What if you reverse that? What if you encrypt the CBC, and then XOR that with the input? As it turns out, you end up with a cipher just as secure as one that had its initialization vector applied first and then encrypted. This method of chaining is called OFB or *output-feedback* mode. The principal benefit of OFB is that the input doesn't have to be block-aligned. As long as the initialization vector itself is of the correct block length — which it is for every block except the very last — the final block can just truncate its output. The decryptor recognizes this short block and updates its output accordingly.

OFB isn't used in SSL. CTR mode didn't make it into TLS until version 1.2, so this topic is revisited in Chapter 9 when AEAD encryption in TLS 1.2 is discussed.

# CHAPTER 3

# Secure Key Exchange over an Insecure Medium with Public Key Cryptography

Chapter 2 examined symmetric or *private/shared key* algorithms. The fundamental challenge in applying private key algorithms is keeping the private key private — or, to put it another way, exchanging keys without letting an interested eavesdropper see them. This may seem like an insoluble problem; you can't establish keys over an insecure channel, and you can't establish a secure channel without keys. Perhaps surprisingly, there is a solution: *public-key cryptography*. With public-key algorithms, there are actually two keys, which are mathematically related such that an encrypt operation performed with one can only be decrypted using the other one. Furthermore, to be usable in a cryptography setting, it must be impossible, or at least mathematically infeasible, to compute one from the other after the fact. By far the most common public-key algorithm is the *RSA* algorithm, named after its inventors Ron *Rivest*, Adi *Shamir*, and Leonard *Adleman*. You may recall Rivest from Chapter 2 as the inventor of RC4.

You may notice a difference in the technical approach between this chapter and the last. Whereas symmetric/shared key algorithms are based on shifting and XORing bits, asymmetric/public key algorithms are based entirely on properties of natural numbers. Whereas symmetric encryption algorithms aim to be as complex as their designers can get away with while still operating reasonably quickly, public-key cryptography algorithms are constrained by their own mathematics. In general, public-key cryptography aims to take advantage of problems that computers are inherently bad at and as a result don't translate nearly as easily to the domain of programming as symmetric cryptography does.

In fact, the bulk of this chapter simply examines how to perform arithmetic on arbitrarily large numbers. Once that's out of the way, the actual process of public key cryptography is surprisingly simple.

# Understanding the Theory Behind the RSA Algorithm

The theory behind RSA public-key cryptosystems is actually very simple. The core is modulus arithmetic; that is, operations modulo a number. For example, you're most likely familiar with C's mod operator %; ($x$ % 2) returns 0 if $x$ is even and 1 if $x$ is odd. RSA public-key cryptography relies on this property of a finite number set. If you keep incrementing, eventually you end up back where you started, just like the odometer of a car. Specifically, RSA relies on three numbers $e$, $d$, and $n$ such that $(m^e)^d$ % n=m — here $m$ is the message to be encrypted and converted to a number.

Not all numbers work this way; in fact, finding three numbers $e$, $d$, and $n$ that satisfy this property is complex, and forms the core of the RSA specification. After you've found them, though, using them to encrypt is fairly straightforward. The number $d$ is called the *private key*, and you should never share it with anybody. $e$ and $n$ together make up the *public key*, and you can make them available to anybody who cares to send you an encoded message. When the sender is ready to send you something that should remain private, he first converts the message into a number $m$ and then computes $m^e$ % n and sends you the result $c$. When you receive it, you then compute $c^d$ % n and, by the property stated above, you get back the original message $m$.

Pay special attention to the nomenclature here. Most people, when first introduced to the RSA algorithm, find it confusing and "backward" that encryption is done with the *public* key and decryption with the *private* key. However, if you think about it, it makes sense: The public key is the one that's shared with anybody, anywhere, and thus you can use it to encrypt messages. You don't care how many people can see your public key because it can only be used to encrypt messages that you alone can read. It's the decryption that must be done privately, thus the term *private key*.

The security of the system relies on the fact that even if an attacker has access to $e$ and $n$ — which he does because they're public — it's computationally infeasible for him to compute $d$. For this to be true, $d$ and $n$ have to be enormous — at least 512 bit numbers (which is on the order of $10^{154}$) — but most public key cryptosystems use even larger numbers. 1,024- or even 2,048-bit numbers are common.

As you can imagine, computing anything to the power of a 2,048-bit number is bound to be more than a bit computationally expensive. Most common computers these days are 32-bit architectures, meaning that they can only perform native computations on numbers with 32 or fewer bits. Even a 64-bit architecture isn't going to be able to deal with this natively. And even if you could find a 2,048-bit architecture, the interim results are on the order of millions of bits! To make this possible on any hardware, modern or futuristic, you need an arbitrary precision math module, and you need to rely on several tricks to both speed up things and minimize memory footprint.

# Performing Arbitrary Precision Binary Math to Implement Public-Key Cryptography

Developing an arbitrary precision binary math module — one that can efficiently represent and process numbers on the order of 2,048 bits — is not difficult, although it's somewhat tedious at times. It's important that the numeric representation be constrained only by available memory and, in theory, virtual memory — that is, disk space (to oversimplify a bit). The number must be able to grow without bounds and represent, exactly, any size number. In theory, this is straightforward; any integer can be represented by an array of C chars, which are eight bits each. The *least-significant-bit* (LSB) of the next-to-last char represents $2^8$, with the *most-significant-bit* (MSB) of the last being $2^7$. As the integer being represented overflows its available space, more space is automatically allocated for it.

**NOTE** For a more detailed understanding of LSB and MSB, see Appendix A.

As such, define a new type, called huge, shown in Listing 3-1.

**Listing 3-1:** "huge.h" huge structure

```
typedef struct
{
  unsigned int size;
  unsigned char *rep;
}
huge;
```

Each huge is simply an arbitrarily-sized array of chars. As it's manipulated — added to, subtracted from, multiplied or divided by — its size will be dynamically adjusted to fit its contents so that the size member always indicates the current length of rep.

## Implementing Large-Number Addition

Addition and subtraction are perhaps more complex than you might expect. After all, adding and subtracting numbers is fundamentally what computers do; you'd expect that it would be trivial to extend this out to larger numbers. However, when dealing with arbitrarily-sized numbers, you must deal with inputs of differing sizes and the possibility of overflow. A large-number add routine is shown in Listing 3-2.

**Listing 3-2:** "huge.c" add routine

```c
/**
 * Add two huges - overwrite h1 with the result.
 */
void add( huge *h1, huge *h2 )
{
  unsigned int i, j;
  unsigned int sum;
  unsigned int carry = 0;

  // Adding h2 to h1. If h2 is > h1 to begin with, resize h1.
  if ( h2->size > h1->size )
  {
    unsigned char *tmp = h1->rep;
    h1->rep = ( unsigned char * ) calloc( h2->size,
      sizeof( unsigned char ) );
    memcpy( h1->rep + ( h2->size - h1->size ), tmp, h1->size );
    h1->size = h2->size;
    free( tmp );
  }

  i = h1->size;
  j = h2->size;

  do
  {
    i--;
    if ( j )
    {
      j--;
      sum = h1->rep[ i ] + h2->rep[ j ] + carry;
    }
    else
    {
      sum = h1->rep[ i ] + carry;
    }

    carry = sum > 0xFF;
    h1->rep[ i ] = sum;
  }
  while ( i );

  if ( carry )
  {
```

```
      // Still overflowed; allocate more space
      expand( h1 );
   }
}
```

This routine adds the value of h2 to h1, storing the result in h1. It does so in three stages. First, allocate enough space in h1 to hold the result (assuming that the result will be about as big as h2). Second, the addition operation itself is actually carried out. Finally, overflow is accounted for.

**Listing 3-3:** "huge.c" add routine (size computation)

```
if ( h2->size > h1->size )
{
   unsigned char *tmp = h1->rep;
   h1->rep = ( unsigned char * ) calloc( h2->size,
      sizeof( unsigned char ) );
   memcpy( h1->rep + ( h2->size - h1->size ), tmp, h1->size );
   h1->size = h2->size;
   free( tmp );
}
```

If h1 is already as long as or longer than h2, in listing 3-3, nothing needs to be done. Otherwise, allocate enough space for the result in h1, and carefully copy the contents of h1 into the right position. Remember that the chars are read right-to-left, so if you allocate two new chars to hold the result, those chars need to be allocated at the *beginning* of the array, so the old contents need to be copied. Note the use of calloc here to ensure that the memory is cleared.

If h1 is three chars and h2 is five, you see something like Figure 3-1.

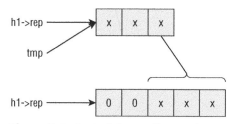

**Figure 3-1:** Large Integer alignment

Note that if h2 is smaller than h1, h1 is not changed at all, which means that h1 and h2 do not necessarily line up, that is, you can add a three-char number to a five-char number — so you have to be careful to account for this when implementing. This is the next step in the addition operation, shown in Listing 3-4.

**Listing 3-4:** "huge.c" add routine (addition loop)

```
i = h1->size;
j = h2->size;

do
{
  i--;
  if ( j )
  {
    j--;
    sum = h1->rep[ i ] + h2->rep[ j ] + carry;
  }
  else
  {
    sum = h1->rep[ i ] + carry;
  }

  carry = sum > 0xFF;
  h1->rep[ i ] = sum;
}
while ( i );
```

Most significantly, start at the end of each array, which, again, could be two different sizes, although h2 is guaranteed to be equal to or smaller in length than h1. Each char can be added independently, working right-to-left, keeping track of overflow at each step, and propagating it backward to the subsequent char, as shown in figure 3-2.

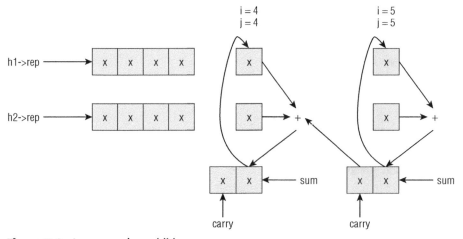

**Figure 3-2:** Large number addition

Note that the overflow cannot be more than one bit. To convince yourself that this is true, consider adding two four-bit numbers. The largest such (unsigned) number is 15 (binary 1111). If you add 15 and 15, you get:

$$1111(15)$$
$$+\ \underline{1111(15)}$$
$$11110(30)$$

As you can see, the result fits into five bits. Also notice that although if you add four bits to four bits and they overflow, they wrap. The wrapped result is the lower four bits of the correct response. Therefore, you can just add the two ints, keep track of whether they overflowed, and carry this overflow (of one bit) into the next addition.

Notice that sum — the temporary workspace for each addition operation — is itself an int. You check for overflow by comparing it to MAXCHAR (0xFF). Although the Intel instruction set does keep track of whether or not an operation — such as an add — overflowed and updates an overflow bit (also called a carry bit), the C language has never standardized access to such a bit, in spite of the fact that every microprocessor or microcontroller defines one. Because you don't have access to the overflow bit, you have to check for it on each add operation.

The only other point to notice is that you must continue until you've looped through all of the bytes of h1. You can't stop after you hit the last (actually, the first because you're working backward) byte of h2 because there may be a carry bit that needs to be propagated backward. In one extreme case, which actually does occur in cryptographic applications, h1 may be 0x01FFFFFEFF and h2 may be 0x0100. In this case, each byte of h1 overflows all the way to the very first. Thus, the while loop continues until i is 0, even if there's nothing left to do with h2 (for example, j = 0).

Finally, there's a possibility that you can get to the end of the add operation and still have a carry bit left over. If this is the case, you need to expand h1 by exactly one char and set its lower-order bit to 1 as shown in Listing 3-5.

**Listing 3-5:** "huge.c" add (overflow expansion)

```
// Still overflowed; allocate more space
if ( carry )
{
  expand( h1 );
}
```

Here you call the function expand, shown in listing 3-6, which is defined for precisely this purpose.

**Listing 3-6:** "huge.c" expand

```
/**
 * Extend the space for h by 1 char and set the LSB of that int
 * to 1.
 */
void expand( huge *h )
```

*(Continued)*

```
{
  unsigned char *tmp = h->rep;
  h->size++;
  h->rep = ( unsigned char * )
    calloc( h->size, sizeof( unsigned char ) );
  memcpy( h->rep + 1, tmp,
    ( h->size - 1 ) * sizeof( unsigned char ) );
  h->rep[ 0 ] = 0x01;
  free( tmp );
}
```

The code in Listing 3-6 should look familiar. It is a special case of the expansion of h1 that was done when h2 was larger than h1. In this case, the expansion is just a bit simpler because you know you're expanding by exactly one char.

## Implementing Large-Number Subtraction

Another thing to note about this add routine — and the huge datatype in general — is that you use unsigned chars for your internal representation. That means that there's no concept of negative numbers or two's-complement arithmetic. As such, you need a specific subtract routine, shown in Listing 3-7.

**Listing 3-7:** "huge.c" subtract

```
static void subtract( huge *h1, huge *h2 )
{
  int i = h1->size;
  int j = h2->size;
  int difference; // signed int - important!
  unsigned int borrow = 0;

  do
  {
    i--;

    if ( j )
    {
      j--;
      difference = h1->rep[ i ] - h2->rep[ j ] - borrow;
    }
    else
    {
      difference = h1->rep[ i ] - borrow;
    }
    borrow = ( difference < 0 ) ;
    h1->rep[ i ] = difference;
  }
  while ( i );
```

```
if ( borrow && i )
{
  if ( !( h1->rep[ i - 1 ] ) ) // Don't borrow i
  {
    printf( "Error, subtraction result is negative\n" );
    exit( 0 );
  }
  h1->rep[ i - 1 ]--;
}


  contract( h1 );
}
```

The subtract routine looks a lot like the add routine, but in reverse. Note that there's no allocation of space at the beginning. Because you're subtracting, the result always uses up less space than what you started with. Also, there's no provision in this library yet for negative numbers, so behavior in this case is undefined if h2 is greater than h1.

Otherwise, subtracting is pretty much like adding: You work backward, keeping track of the borrow from the previous char at each step. Again, although the subtraction operation wraps if h2->rep[ j ] > h1->rep[ i ], the wrap ends up in the right position. To see this, consider the subtraction 30 − 15 (binary 11110 − 1111). To keep things simple, imagine that a char is four bits. The integer 30 then takes up two four-bit chars and is represented as:

(0001 1110) : (1 14 )

whereas 15 takes up one char and is represented as 1111 (15). When subtracting, start by subtracting 15 from 14 and end up "wrapping" back to 15 as illustrated in Table 3-1.

**Table 3-1:** Subtraction Wrapping Behavior

| DECIMAL | BINARY | |
|---------|--------|---|
| 0 | 0000 | ← b. wrap back around to the bottom |
| 1 | 0001 | |
| 2 | 0010 | |
| 3 | 0011 | |
| 4 | 0100 | |
| 5 | 0101 | |
| 6 | 0110 | |
| 7 | 0111 | |
| 8 | 1000 | |

*(Continued)*

**Table 3-1** *(continued)*

| DECIMAL | BINARY | |
|---------|--------|---|
| 9 | 1001 | |
| 10 | 1010 | |
| 11 | 1011 | |
| 12 | 1100 | |
| 13 | 1101 | |
| 14 | 1110 | ← a. start here, go backward 15 steps |
| 15 | 1111 | ← c. end here |

Because 15 is greater than 14, you set the borrow bit and subtract one extra from the preceding char, ending up with the representation (0 15) (0000 1111), which is the correct answer.

To be a bit more memory efficient, you should also contract the response before returning. That is, look for extraneous chars ints on the left side and remove them, as shown in Listing 3-8.

**Listing 3-8:** "huge.c" contract

```
/**
 * Go through h and see how many of the left-most bytes are unused.
 * Remove them and resize h appropriately.
 */
void contract( huge *h )
{
  int i = 0;

  while ( !( h->rep[ i ] ) && ( i < h->size ) ) { i++; }

  if ( i && i < h->size )
  {
    unsigned char *tmp = &h->rep[ i ];
    h->rep = ( unsigned char * ) calloc( h->size - i,
      sizeof( unsigned char ) );
    memcpy( h->rep, tmp, h->size - i );
    h->size -= i;
  }
}
```

This happens in two steps. First, find the leftmost non-zero char, whose position is contained in i. Second, resize the array representation of h. This works, obviously, just like expansion but in reverse.

As shown earlier, addition and subtraction are somewhat straightforward; you can take advantage of the underlying machine architecture to a large extent;

most of your work involves memory management and keeping track of carries and borrows.

## Implementing Large-Number Multiplication

Multiplication and division aren't quite so easy, unfortunately. If you tried to multiply "backward" one char at a time as you did with addition, you'd never even come close to getting the right result. Of course, multiplication is just successive adding — multiplying five by three involves adding five to itself three times — $5 + 5 + 5 = 3 * 5 = 15$. This suggests an easy implementation of a multiplication algorithm. Remember, though, that you're going to be dealing with astronomical numbers. Adding five to itself three times is not a terribly big deal — it wouldn't even be a big deal if you did it in the reverse and added three to itself five times. But adding a 512-bit number to itself $2^{512}$ times would take ages, even on the fastest desktop computer. As a result, you have to look for a way to speed this up.

When you were in elementary school, you were probably taught how to do multi-digit multiplication like this:

$$
\begin{array}{r}
123 \\
\times \quad 456 \\
\hline
738 \\
6150 \\
+ \ 49200 \\
\hline
56088
\end{array}
$$

You may have never given much thought to what you were doing, or why this works, but notice that you've shortened what might otherwise have been 123 addition operations down to 3. A more algebraic way to represent this same multiplication is

$$(400 + 50 + 6) * 123$$

$$(4 * 10^2 + 5 * 10^1 + 6 * 10^0) * 123$$

$(4 * 10^2) * 123 + (5 * 10^1) * 123 + (6 * 10^0) * 123$
(distributivity of multiplication)

$$4 * 123 * 10^2 + 5 * 123 * 10^1 + 6 * 123 * 10^0$$

$$492 * 10^2 + 615 * 10^1 + 123 * 10^0$$

Because multiplying by $10^n$ just involves concatenating $n$ zeros onto the result, this is simply

$$49200 + 6150 + 738 = 56088$$

What you actually did at each step was to first multiply 123 by one of the digits of 456, and then shift it left — that is, concatenate a zero. Can you do the same thing with binary multiplication? Yes, you can. In fact, it's significantly easier because the interim multiplications — the multiplication by the digits of 456 — are unnecessary. You either multiply by 1 or 0 at each step, so the answer is either the first number or just 0. Consider the multiplication of 12 (binary 1100) by 9 (1001):

$$
\begin{array}{r}
1100 \\
\times\ 1001 \\
\hline
1100 \\
00000 \\
000000 \\
+\ 1100000 \\
\hline
1101100
\end{array}
$$

Here, the 12 is left-shifted 0 times and 3 times, because the bits at positions 0 and 3 of the multiplicand 1001 are set. The two resulting values — 1100 and 1100000 — are added together to produce $2^6 + 2^5 + 2^3 + 2^2 = 108$, the expected answer.

Now you've reduced what might have been an $O(2^n)$ operation to a simple $O(n)$ operation, where $n$ is the number of bits of the smaller of the two operators. In practice, it really doesn't matter if you try to optimize and use the smaller number to perform the multiplication, so this implementation just takes the numbers as given.

In code, this algorithm is implemented as shown in Listing 3-9 and illustrated in Figure 3-3.

**Listing 3-9:** "huge.c" multiply

```
/**
 * Multiply h1 by h2, overwriting the value of h1.
 */
void multiply( huge *h1, huge *h2 )
{
  unsigned char mask;
  unsigned int i;
  huge temp;

  set_huge( &temp, 0 );
  copy_huge( &temp, h1 );

  set_huge( h1, 0 );

  i = h2->size;
  do
  {
```

```
      i--;
      for ( mask = 0x01; mask; mask <<= 1 )
      {
        if ( mask & h2->rep[ i ] )
        {
          add( h1, &temp );
        }
        left_shift( &temp );
      }
    }
  while ( i );
}
```

First, notice that you need a couple of utility routines: copy_huge, free_huge, and set_huge. The implementations of the first two are straightforward in Listing 3-10.

**Listing 3-10:** "huge.c" copy_huge and free_huge

```
void copy_huge( huge *tgt, huge *src )
{
  if ( tgt->rep )
  {
    free( tgt->rep );
  }

  tgt->size = src->size;
  tgt->rep = ( unsigned char * )
    calloc( src->size, sizeof( unsigned char ) );
  memcpy( tgt->rep, src->rep,
      ( src->size * sizeof( unsigned char ) ) );
}

void free_huge( huge *h )
{
  if ( h->rep )
  {
    free( h->rep );
  }
}
```

To be more generally useful, set_huge is perhaps a bit more complex than you would expect. After all, what you're doing here is copying an int into a byte array. However, you need to be as space-efficient as possible, so you need to look at the int in question and figure out the minimum number of bytes that it can fit into. Note that this space-efficiency isn't merely a performance concern;

the algorithms illustrated here don't work at all if the `huge` presented includes extraneous leading zeros. And, of course, you have to deal with little-endian/big-endian conversion. You can accomplish this as shown in Listing 3-11.

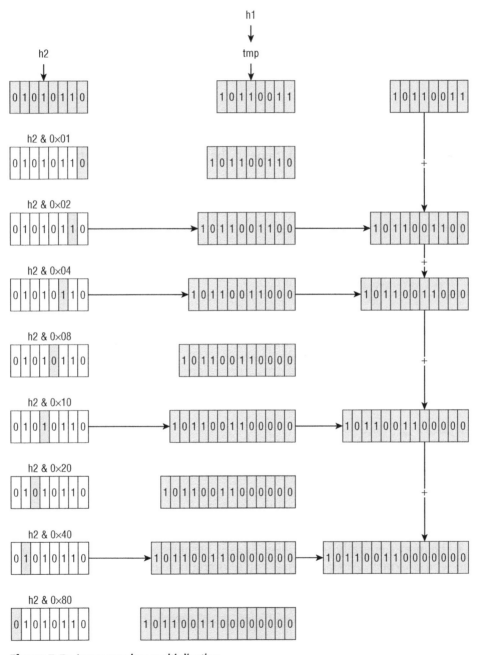

**Figure 3-3:** Large number multiplication

**Listing 3-11:** "huge.c" set_huge

```
void set_huge( huge *h, unsigned int val )
{

  unsigned int mask, i, shift;

  h->size = 4;

  // Figure out the minimum amount of space this "val" will take
  // up in chars (leave at least one byte, though, if "val" is 0).
  for ( mask = 0xFF000000; mask > 0x000000FF; mask >>=8 )
  {
    if ( val & mask )
    {
      break;
    }
    h->size--;
  }

  h->rep = ( unsigned char * ) malloc( h->size );

  // Now work backward through the int, masking off each 8-bit
  // byte (up to the first 0 byte) and copy it into the "huge"
  // array in big-endian format.
  mask = 0x000000FF;
  shift = 0;
  for ( i = h->size; i; i-- )
  {
    h->rep[ i - 1 ] = ( val & mask ) >> shift;
    mask <<= 8;
    shift += 8;
  }
}
```

Notice that at the top of the multiply routine you see

```
set_huge( &temp, 0 );
```

but then you overwrite it immediately with a call to copy_huge. This is necessary because the huge temp is allocated on the stack and is initialized with garbage values. Because copy_huge immediately tries to free any pointer allocated, you need to ensure that it's initialized to NULL. set_huge accomplishes this.

Start multiplying by setting aside a temporary space for the left-shifted first operand, copy that into the temporary space, and reset h1 to 0. Then, loop through each char of h2 (backward, again), and check each bit of each char. If the bit is a 1, add the contents of temp to h1. If the bit is a zero, do nothing. In either case, left-shift temp by one position. Left-shifting a huge is, of course, a separate operation that works on one char at a time, right-to-left.

**Listing 3-12:** "huge.c" left_shift

```
void left_shift( huge *h1 )
{
  int i;
  int old_carry, carry = 0;

  i = h1->size;
  do
  {
    i--;
    old_carry = carry;
    carry = ( h1->rep[ i ] & 0x80 ) == 0x80;
    h1->rep[ i ] = ( h1->rep[ i ] << 1 ) | old_carry;
    // Again, if C exposed the overflow bit...
  }
  while ( i );

  if ( carry )
  {
    expand( h1 );
  }
}
```

Because each `char` can overflow into the next-leftmost `char`, it's necessary to manually keep track of the carry bit and expand the result if it overflows, just as you did for addition.

This double-and-add approach to multiplication is important when dealing with binary arithmetic. In fact, you've seen it once before, in Chapter 2, when you implemented AES multiplication in terms of the `dot` and `xtime` operations. It comes up later when I redefine multiplication yet again in the context of elliptic curves. However, this is not the most efficient means of performing binary multiplication. Karatsuba's algorithm, originally published by Anatolii Karatsuba in the "Proceedings of the USSR Academy of Sciences" in 1962, is actually much faster, albeit much more complicated to implement — I won't cover it here, but you can consult a book on advanced algorithms if you're curious. However, this routine runs well enough on modern hardware, so just leave it as is.

## Implementing Large-Number Division

Finally, what about division? Division is, of course, the inverse of multiplication, so it makes sense that you ought to be able to reverse the multiplication process and perform a division. Consider the multiplication of 13 by 5, in binary:

$$
\begin{array}{r}
1101 \\
\times \quad 101 \\
\hline
\end{array}
$$

$$
\begin{array}{rl}
1101 & (1) \\
00000 & (0) \\
+ \quad 110100 & (1) \\
\hline
1000001 &
\end{array}
$$

To reverse this, you have as input 100001 and 1101, and you want to recover 101. You can do this by subtracting and right-shifting:

$$
\begin{array}{rl}
1000001 & (65) \\
- \quad 110100 & \\
\hline
001101 & (13\ \text{left shifted twice} = 13 * 2^2 = 13 * 4 = 52) \\
- \quad 011010 & (52\ \text{right-shifted once — do nothing}) \\
\hline
001101 & \\
- \quad 001101 & (52\ \text{right-shifted twice — back to the original value of 13}) \\
\hline
000000 &
\end{array}
$$

If you just keep track of which iterations involved a subtraction — that is, which right-shifts yielded a value less than the current value of the dividend — you get "subtract" "nothing" "subtract" or, in binary, 101, which is exactly the value you were looking for.

Of course, there's one immediate problem with implementing this: How do you know to left-shift 13 twice before subtracting it? You could look at the bit-length of the dividend — 65 in the example — and compare it to the bit-length of the divisor (13), which tells you that you need to left-shift by two positions. However, finding the bit-length of a value is somewhat non-trivial. An easier (and faster) approach is just to keep left-shifting the divisor until it's greater than the dividend.

Finally, you're doing integer division here — there's no compensation for *uneven* division. So what happens if you divide 14 by, say, 5?

$$
\begin{array}{rl}
1100 & \\
- \quad 1010 & (5\ \text{left-shifted once}) \\
\hline
0100 & \\
- \quad 101 & (\text{do nothing},\ 5 > 4) \\
\hline
0100 &
\end{array}
$$

Now you get a quotient of 10 (2) and the dividend, at the end of the operation, is 4, which happens to be the remainder of the division of 14 by 5. Remember the discussion of the importance of modular arithmetic to the RSA cryptosystem? As it turns out, you almost never call divide for the quotient. Instead, you are interested in the remainder (or *modulus*). The complete division routine is implemented in Listing 3-13.

**Listing 3-13:** "huge.c" divide

```
/**
 * dividend = numerator, divisor = denominator
 *
 * Note that this process destroys divisor (and, of course,
 * overwrites quotient). The dividend is the remainder of the
 * division (if that's important to the caller). The divisor will
 * be modified by this routine, but it will end up back where it
 * "started".
 */
void divide( huge *dividend, huge *divisor, huge *quotient )
{
  int bit_size, bit_position;

  // "bit_position" keeps track of which bit, of the quotient,
  // is being set or cleared on the current operation.
  bit_size = bit_position = 0;

  // First, left-shift divisor until it's >= than the dividend
  while ( compare( divisor, dividend ) < 0 )
  {
    left_shift( divisor );
    bit_size++;
  }

  // overestimates a bit in some cases
  quotient->size = ( bit_size / 8 ) + 1;
  quotient->rep = ( unsigned char * )
    calloc(quotient->size, sizeof( unsigned char ) );
  memset( quotient->rep, 0, quotient->size );

  bit_position = 8 - ( bit_size % 8 ) - 1;

  do
  {
    if ( compare( divisor, dividend ) <= 0 )
    {
      subtract( dividend, divisor );  // dividend -= divisor
      quotient->rep[ ( int ) ( bit_position / 8 ) ] |=
        ( 0x80 >> ( bit_position % 8 ) );
    }

    if ( bit_size )
    {
```

```
        right_shift( divisor );
    }
    bit_position++;
  }
  while ( bit_size-- );
}
```

Start by left shifting the divisor until it's greater than or equal to the dividend. Most of the time, this means you "overshoot" a bit, but that's not a problem because you compare again when you start the actual division.

```
  while ( compare( divisor, dividend ) < 0 )
  {
    left_shift( divisor );
    bit_size++;
  }
```

## Comparing Large Numbers

Notice the call to the compare function. Remember the subtract function a while ago — in theory, you could just call subtract here, and check to see if the result is negative. Two problems with that approach are that a) subtract overwrites its first operator, and b) you don't have any provision for negative numbers. Of course, you could work around both of these, but a new compare function, shown in Listing 3-14, serves better.

**Listing 3-14:** "huge.c" compare

```
/**
 * Compare h1 to h2. Return:
 * 0 if h1 == h2
 * a positive number if h1 > h2
 * a negative number if h1 < h2
 */
int compare( huge *h1, huge *h2 )
{
  int i, j;

  if ( h1->size > h2->size )
  {
    return 1;
  }

  if ( h1->size < h2->size )
  {
    return -1;
  }

  // Otherwise, sizes are equal, have to actually compare.
```

*(Continued)*

```
    // only have to compare "hi-int", since the lower ints
    // can't change the comparison.
    i = j = 0;

    // Otherwise, keep searching through the representational integers
    // until one is bigger than another - once we've found one, it's
    // safe to stop, since the "lower order bytes" can't affect the
    // comparison
    while ( i < h1->size && j < h2->size )
    {
      if ( h1->rep[ i ] < h2->rep[ j ] )
      {
        return -1;
      }
      else if ( h1->rep[ i ] > h2->rep[ j ] )
      {
        return 1;
      }
      i++;
      j++;
    }

    // If we got all the way to the end without a comparison, the
    // two are equal
    return 0;
}
```

If the sizes of the `huge`s to be compared are different, you don't have to do any real comparison. A five-`char` huge always has a larger value than a three-`char` huge, assuming you've been diligent in compressing representations to remove leading 0's:

```
    if ( h1->size > h2->size )
    {
      return 1;
    }

    if ( h1->size < h2->size )
    {
      return -1;
    }
```

Otherwise, you need to do a char-by-char comparison. You can safely stop at the first non-equal char, though. If the first char of `h1` is larger than the first char of `h2`, the lower-order integers can't change the comparison.

```
    while ( i < h1->size && j < h2->size )
    {
      if ( h1->rep[ i ] < h2->rep[ j ] )
      {
        return -1;
      }
    }
```

```
    else if ( h1->rep[ i ] > h2->rep[ j ] )
    {
        return 1;
    }
    i++;
    j++;
}
```

Of course, if you go through both `h1` and `h2`, and they're both the same size, and each char is equal, then they both represent equal numbers.

Referring to the original `divide` function, the second step is to allocate space for the quotient by keeping track of how many times the dividend was left shifted. The quotient can't be any bigger than this, which overallocates just a bit, but not so much that you need to worry about it.

```
quotient->size = ( bit_size / 8 ) + 1;
quotient->rep = ( unsigned char * )
    calloc( quotient->size, sizeof( unsigned char ) );
memset( quotient->rep, 0, quotient->size );
```

Finally, start the "compare and subtract" loop. If the current dividend, after being left-shifted, is less than the current divisor, then the quotient should have that bit position set, and the current dividend should be subtracted from the divisor. In all cases, the dividend should be right-shifted by one position for the next loop iteration. Although the comparison, subtraction and right-shift operators are easy to understand — they just call the compare and subtract functions coded earlier — the setting of the "current" bit of the quotient is somewhat complex:

```
quotient->rep[ ( int ) ( bit_position / 8 ) ] |=
    ( 0x80 >> ( bit_position % 8 ) );
```

Remember that `bit_position` is absolute. If `quotient` is a 128-bit number, `bit_position` ranges from 0 to 127. So, in order to set the correct bit, you need to determine which `char` this refers to in the array of chars inside `quotient` and then determine which bit inside that char you need to set (that is, `or`). This may look familiar; this is essentially the SET_BIT macro developed in Chapter 2.

Finally, right-shift the divisor at each step except the last:

```
if ( bit_size )
{
    right_shift( divisor );
}
```

Technically, you could get away with always right-shifting and not skipping this on the last step, but by doing this, you guarantee that divisor is reset to the value that was passed in to the function originally. This is useful behavior because you are calling "divide" over and over again with the same argument, which keeps you from having to make a temporary copy of the divisor.

`right_shift`, the reverse of `left_shift`, is shown in Listing 3-15.

**Listing 3-15:** "huge.c" right_shift

```
static void right_shift( huge *h1 )
{
  int i;
  unsigned int old_carry, carry = 0;

  i = 0;
  do
  {
    old_carry = carry;
    carry = ( h1->rep[ i ] & 0x01 ) << 7;
    h1->rep[ i ] = ( h1->rep[ i ] >> 1 ) | old_carry;
  }
  while ( ++i < h1->size );

  contract( h1 );
}
```

## Optimizing for Modulo Arithmetic

One optimization you might as well make is to allow the caller to indicate that the quotient is unimportant. For public-key cryptography operations you never actually care what the quotient is; you're interested in the remainder, which the `dividend` operator is turned into after a call to `divide`. Extend `divide` just a bit to enable the caller to pass in a NULL pointer for `quotient` that indicates the quotient itself should not be computed, as shown in Listing 3-16.

**Listing 3-16:** "huge.c" divide

```
void divide( huge *dividend, huge *divisor, huge *quotient )
{
  int i, bit_size, bit_position;

  bit_size = bit_position = 0;

  while ( compare( divisor, dividend ) < 0 )
  {
    left_shift( divisor );
    bit_size++;
  }

  if ( quotient )
  {
    quotient->size = ( bit_size / 8 ) + 1;
    quotient->rep = ( unsigned char * )
      calloc( quotient->size, sizeof( unsigned char ) );
    memset( quotient->rep, 0, quotient->size );
  }
```

```
bit_position = 8 - ( bit_size % 8 ) - 1;

do
{
  if ( compare( divisor, dividend ) <= 0 )
  {
    subtract( dividend, divisor );
    if ( quotient )
    {
      quotient->rep[ ( int ) ( bit_position / 8 ) ] |=
        ( 0x80 >> ( bit_position % 8 ) );
    }
  }

  if ( bit_size )
  {
    right_shift( divisor );
  }
  bit_position++;
}
while ( bit_size-- );
}
```

One note about the choice to use chars–that is, bytes — instead of ints for the huge arrays: You could reduce the number of add and subtract operations by a factor of four if you represent huges as integer arrays rather than char arrays. This is actually how OpenSSL, GMP, and Java implement their own arbitrary-precision math libraries. However, this introduces all sorts of problems later on when you try to convert from big endian to little endian. You also need to keep close track of the exact non-padded size of the huge. A three-byte numeral uses up one int; however, you'd need to remember that the leading byte of that int is just padding. RSA implementations in particular are very finicky about result length; if they expect a 128-byte response and you give them 129 bytes, they error out without even telling you what you did wrong.

## Using Modulus Operations to Efficiently Compute Discrete Logarithms in a Finite Field

The *modulus* operation — that is, the remainder left over after a division operation — is important to modern public-key cryptography and is likely going to remain important for the foreseeable future. In general, and especially with respect to the algorithms currently used in SSL/TLS, public-key operations require that all mathematical operations — addition, subtraction, multiplication, division — be performed in such a finite field. In simple terms, this just means that each operation is followed by a modulus operation to truncate it into a finite space.

Given the importance of modulus arithmetic to public-key cryptography, it's been the subject of quite a bit of research. Every computational cycle that can be squeezed out of a modulus operation is going to go a long way in speeding up public-key cryptography operations. There are a couple of widely implemented ways to speed up cryptography operations: the Barrett reduction and the Montgomery reduction. They work somewhat similarly; they trade a relatively time-consuming up-front computation for faster modulus operations. If you're going to be computing a lot of moduli against a single value — which public-key cryptography does — you can save a significant amount of computing time by calculating and storing the common result.

I don't cover these reductions in detail here. The divide operation shown earlier computes moduli fast enough for demonstration purposes, although you can actually observe a noticeable pause whenever a private-key operation occurs. If you're interested, the Barrett reduction is described in detail in the journal "Advances in Cryptology '86" (`http://www.springerlink.com/content/c4f3rqbt5dxxyad4/`), and the Montgomery reduction in "Math Computation vol. 44" (`http://www.jstor.org/pss/2007970`).

## Encryption and Decryption with RSA

You now have enough supporting infrastructure to implement RSA encryption and decryption. How the exponents $d$ and $e$ or the corresponding modulus $n$ are computed has not yet been discussed, but after you've correctly determined them, you just need to pass them into the encrypt or decrypt routine. How you specify the message $m$ is important; for now, just take the internal binary representation of the entire message to be encrypted as $m$. After you have done this, you can implement encryption as shown in Listing 3-17.

**Listing 3-17:** "rsa.c" rsa_compute

```
/**
 * Compute c = m^e mod n.
 */
void rsa_compute( huge *m, huge *e, huge *n, huge *c )
{
  huge counter;
  huge one;

  copy_huge( c, m );
  set_huge( &counter, 1 );
  set_huge( &one, 1 );
  while ( compare( &counter, e ) < 0 )
  {
    multiply( c, m );
    add( &counter, &one );
  }
```

```
    divide( c, n, NULL );

    free_huge( &counter );
    free_huge( &one );
    // Remainder (result) is now in c
}
```

Remember that encryption and decryption are the exact same routines, just with the exponents switched; you can use this same routine to encrypt by passing in $e$ and decrypt by passing in $d$. Just keep multiplying $m$ by itself (notice that $m$ was copied into $c$ once at the beginning) and incrementing a counter by 1 each time until you've done it $e$ times. Finally, divide the whole mess by $n$ and the result is in $c$. Here's how you might call this:

```
    huge e, d, n, m, c;

    set_huge( &e, 79 );
    set_huge( &d, 1019 );
    set_huge( &n, 3337 );

    set_huge( &m, 688 );
    rsa_compute( &m, &e, &n, &c );
    printf( "Encrypted to: %d\n", c.rep[ 0 ] );

    set_huge( &m, 0 );
    rsa_compute( &c, &d, &n, &m );
    printf( "Decrypted to: %d\n", m.rep[ 0 ] );
```

## Encrypting with RSA

Because this example uses small numbers, you can verify the accuracy by just printing out the single int representing $c$ and $m$:

```
Encrypted to: 1570
Decrypted to: 688
```

The encrypted representation of the number 688 is 1,570. You can decrypt and verify that you get back what you put in.

However, this public exponent 79 is a small number for RSA, and the modulus 3,337 is microscopic — if you used numbers this small, an attacker could decipher your message using pencil and paper. Even with these small numbers, $688^{79}$ takes up 1,356 bytes. And this is for a small $e$. For reasons you see later, a more common $e$ value is 65,537.

> **NOTE** Note that everybody can, and generally does, use the same $e$ value as long as the $n$ — and by extension, the $d$ — are different.

A 32-bit integer raised to the power of 65,537 takes up an unrealistic amount of memory. I tried this on my computer and, after 20 minutes, I had computed

68849422, which took up 58,236 bytes to represent. At this point, my computer finally gave up and stopped allocating memory to my process.

First, you need to get the number of multiplications under control. If you remember when I first discussed huge number multiplication, the naïve implementation that would have involved adding a number $m$ to itself $n$ times to compute $m \times n$ was rejected. Instead, you developed a technique of doubling and adding. Can you do something similar with exponentiation? In fact, you can. Instead of doubling and adding, *square and multiply*. By doing so, you reduce 65,537 operations down to $\log_2 65,537 = 17$ operations.

Fundamentally, this works the same as double and add; cycle through the bits in the exponent, starting with the least-significant bit. If the bit position is 1, perform a multiplication. At each stage, square the running exponent, and that's what you multiply by at the 1 bits. Incidentally, if you look at the binary representation of 65,537 = 10000000000000001, you can see why it's so appealing for public-key operations; it's big enough to be useful, but with just two 1 bits, it's also quick to operate on. You square $m$ 17 times, but only multiply the first and 17th results.

> **NOTE** Why 65,537? Actually, it's the smallest prime number (which $e$ must be) that can feasibly be used as a secure RSA public-key exponent. There are only four other prime numbers smaller than 65,537 that can be represented in just two 1 bits: 3, 5, 17, and 257, all of which are far too small for the RSA algorithm. 65,537 is also the largest such number that can be represented in 32 bits. You could, if you were so inclined, take advantage of this and speed up computations by using native arithmetic operations.

If it's not clear that this should work for exponentiation as well as for multiplication, consider $x^{10}$. This, expanded, is

$$xxxxxxxxxx$$
$$(xxxxx)(xxxxx)$$
$$(xxxxx)^2$$
$$[(xx)(xx)x]^2$$
$$[(xx)^2x]^2$$
$$[((x^2)^2)x]^2$$

Notice how you can successively split the $x$'s in half, reducing them to squaring operations each time. It should be clear that you can do this with any number; you may have a spare $x$ left over, if the exponent is an odd number, but that's OK.

If you look at the binary representation of the decimal number 10 (1010 in binary) and you work backward through its binary digits, squaring at each step, you get:

$$x \qquad 0$$
$$x^2 \qquad 1 \quad \leftarrow \text{multiply}$$
$$(x^2)^2 \qquad 0$$
$$((x^2)^2)^2 \quad 1 \quad \leftarrow \text{multiply}$$

multiplying the two "hits" together, you get $x^2((x^2)^2)^2$ or $[((x^2)^2)x]^2$ which is what you got when you deconstructed decimal 10 in the first place.

Listing 3-18 shows how you can implement this in code. Compare this to the implementation of multiply in Listing 3-9.

**Listing 3-18:** "huge.c" exponentiate

```
/**
 * Raise h1 to the power of exp. Return the result in h1.
 */
void exponentiate( huge *h1, huge *exp )
{
  int i = exp->size, mask;
  huge tmp1, tmp2;

  set_huge( &tmp1, 0 );
  set_huge( &tmp2, 0 );

  copy_huge( &tmp1, h1 );
  set_huge( h1, 1 );

  do
  {
    i--;
    for ( mask = 0x01; mask; mask <<= 1 )
    {
      if ( exp->rep[ i ] & mask )
      {
        multiply( h1, &tmp1 );
      }

      // Square tmp1
      copy_huge( &tmp2, &tmp1 );
      multiply( &tmp1, &tmp2 );
    }
  }
  while ( i );

  free_huge( &tmp1 );
  free_huge( &tmp2 );
}
```

This works; you've drastically reduced the number of multiplications needed to compute an exponentiation. However, you still haven't addressed the primary problem of memory consumption. Remember that you allocated 56 *kilobytes* of memory to compute an interim result — just throw it away when you compute the modulus at the end of the operation. Is this really necessary? As it turns out, it's not. Because the modulus operator is distributive — that is, $(abc)$ % $n = [a$ % $n * b$ % $n * c$ % $n]$ % $n$, you can actually compute the modulus at each step. Although this results in more computations, the memory savings are drastic. Remember that multiplications take as many addition operations as there are bits in the representation as well, so reducing the size of the numbers being multiplied actually speeds things up considerably.

Listing 3-19, then, is the final RSA computation $(m^e)$ % $n$, with appropriate speed-ups.

**Listing 3-19:** "huge.c" mod_pow

```
/**
 * Compute c = m^e mod n.
 *
 * Note that this same routine is used for encryption and
 * decryption; the only difference is in the exponent passed in.
 * This is the "exponentiate" algorithm, with the addition of a
 * modulo computation at each stage.
 */
void mod_pow( huge *h1, huge *exp, huge *n, huge *h2 )
{
  unsigned int i = exp->size;
  unsigned char mask;
  huge tmp1, tmp2;

  set_huge( &tmp1, 0 );
  set_huge( &tmp2, 0 );

  copy_huge( &tmp1, h1 );
  set_huge( h2, 1 );

  do
  {
    i--;
    for ( mask = 0x01; mask; mask <<= 1 )
    {
      if ( exp->rep[ i ] & mask )
      {
        multiply( h2, &tmp1 );
        divide( h2, n, NULL );
      }
      // square tmp1
      copy_huge( &tmp2, &tmp1 );
```

```
      multiply( &tmp1, &tmp2 );
      divide( &tmp1, n, NULL );
    }
  }
  while ( i );

  free_huge( &tmp1 );
  free_huge( &tmp2 );

  // Result is now in "h2"
}
```

Besides the introduction of a call to `divide`, for its side effect of computing a modulus, and the substitution of m and c for h1, Listing 3-19 is identical to the `exponentiate` routine in Listing 3-18. This works, and performs reasonably quickly, using a reasonable amount of memory, even for huge values of *m*, *e*, and *n*. Given a message *m* and a public key *e* and *n*, you encrypt like this:

```
huge c;
mod_pow( &m, &e, &n, &c );
```

## Decrypting with RSA

Decryption is identical, except that you swap *e* with *d* and of course you switch *c* and *m*:

```
huge m;
mod_pow( &c, &d, &n, &e );
```

There is one subtle, but fatal, security flaw with this implementation of decrypt, however. Notice that you multiply and divide $\log_2 d$ times as you iterate through the bits in *d* looking for 1 bits. This is not a problem. However, you do an additional multiply and divide at each 1 bit in the private exponent *d*. These multiply and divide operations are reasonably efficient, but not fast. In fact, they take long enough that an attacker can measure the time spent decrypting and use this to determine how many 1 bits were in the private exponent, which is called a *timing attack*. This information drastically reduces the number of potential private keys that an attacker has to try before finding yours. Remember, part of the security of the RSA public key cryptosystem is the infeasibility of a brute-force attack. The most straightforward way to correct this is to go ahead and perform the multiply and divide even at the 0 bits of the exponent, but just throw away the results. This way, the attacker sees a uniform duration for every private key operation. Of course, you should only do this for the private-key operations. You don't care if an attacker can guess your public key (it's public, after all).

It may occur to you that, if the modulus operation is distributive throughout exponentiation, it must also be distributive throughout multiplication and even addition. It is perfectly reasonable to define "modulus-aware" addition and multiplication routines and call those from exponentiation routine. This would actually negate the need for the division at each step of the exponentiation. There are actually many additional speed-ups possible; real implementations, of course, enable all of these. However, this code is performant enough.

## Encrypting a Plaintext Message

So, now that you have a working RSA encrypt and decrypt algorithm, you're still missing two important pieces of the puzzle. The first is how keys are generated and distributed. The topic of key distribution actually takes up all of Chapter 5. The second topic is how to convert a plaintext message into a number $m$ to be passed into `rsa_compute`. Each `rsa_compute` operation returns a result mod $n$. This means that you can't encrypt blocks larger than $n$ without losing information, so you need to chop the input up into blocks of length $n$ or less. On the flip side, if you want to encrypt a very small amount of data, or the non-aligned end of a long block of data, you need to pad it to complicate brute-force attacks.

Just like the previous chapter's symmetric algorithms, RSA works on blocks of data. Each block includes a header and some padding (of at least 11 bytes), so the resulting input blocks are `modulus_length` -11 bytes minimum. The header is pretty simple: It's a 0 byte, followed by a *padding identifier* of 0, 1, or 2. I examine the meaning of the different padding bytes later. For RSA encryption, always use padding identifier 2, which indicates that the following bytes, up to the first 0 byte, are padding and should be discarded. Everything following the first 0 byte, up to the length of the modulus $n$ in bytes, is data.

> **NOTE** Unlike the symmetric algorithms of the previous chapter, RSA pads at the beginning of its block.

To implement this in code, follow these steps:

1. Define an `rsa_key` type that holds the modulus and exponent of a key, as shown in Listing 3-20. Notice that it doesn't matter whether it's a public or a private key. Each includes a modulus and an exponent; the only difference is which exponent.

**Listing 3-20:** "rsa.h" rsa_key structure

```
typedef struct
{
  huge *modulus;
  huge *exponent;
}
rsa_key;
```

2. Define an `rsa_encrypt` routine that takes in the data to be encrypted along with the public key. Notice also that the `output` is a pointer to a pointer.

Due to the way padding works, it's difficult for the caller to figure out how much space the decrypted data takes up (a one-byte payload could encrypt to a 256-byte value!). As a result, listing 3-21 allocates space in the target output array.

**Listing 3-21:** "rsa.c" rsa_encrypt

```
/**
 * The input should be broken up into n-bit blocks, where n is the
 * length in bits of the modulus. The output will always be n bits
 * or less. Per RFC 2313, there must be at least 8 bytes of padding
 * to prevent an attacker from trying all possible padding bytes.
 *
 * output will be allocated by this routine, must be freed by the
 * caller.
 *
 * returns the length of the data encrypted in output
 */
int rsa_encrypt( unsigned char *input,
                 unsigned int len,
                 unsigned char **output,
                 rsa_key *public_key )
{
  int i;
  huge c, m;
  int modulus_length = public_key->modulus->size;
  int block_size;
  unsigned char *padded_block = ( unsigned char * )
    malloc( modulus_length );
  int encrypted_size = 0;

  *output = NULL;

  while ( len )
  {
    encrypted_size += modulus_length;
    block_size = ( len < modulus_length - 11 ) ?
      len : ( modulus_length - 11 );
    memset( padded_block, 0, modulus_length );
    memcpy( padded_block + ( modulus_length - block_size ),
      input, block_size );
    // set block type
    padded_block[ 1 ] = 0x02;

    for ( i = 2; i < ( modulus_length - block_size - 1 ); i++ )
    {
      // TODO make these random
      padded_block[ i ] = i;
    }
```

*(Continued)*

```
        load_huge( &m, padded_block, modulus_length );
        mod_pow( &m, public_key->exponent, public_key->modulus, &c );

        *output = ( unsigned char * ) realloc( *output, encrypted_size );

        unload_huge( &c, *output + ( encrypted_size - modulus_length ),
          modulus_length );

        len -= block_size;
        input += block_size;
        free_huge( &m );
        free_huge( &c );
    }

    free( padded_block );

    return encrypted_size;
}
```

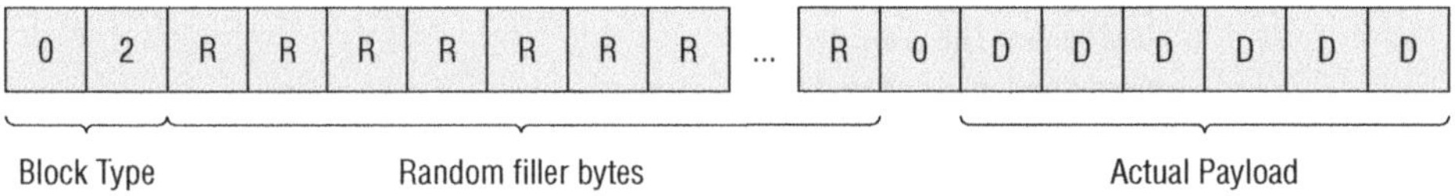

| 0 | 2 | R | R | R | R | R | R | R | ... | R | 0 | D | D | D | D | D | D |
|---|---|---|---|---|---|---|---|---|-----|---|---|---|---|---|---|---|---|

Block Type          Random filler bytes                          Actual Payload

**Figure 3-4:** RSA Padding

3. Figure out how long the block size is. It should be the same as the length of the modulus, which is usually 512, 1024, or 2048 bits. There's no fundamental reason why you couldn't use any other modulus lengths if you wanted, but these are the usual lengths. The encrypted result is the same length as the modulus:

   ```
   int modulus_length = public_key->modulus->size;
   ```

4. Allocate that much space and then fill up this block with the padding, as described earlier, and encrypt it using `rsa_compute`.

   ```
   unsigned char *padded_block = ( unsigned char * )
     malloc( modulus_length );
   ```

5. Operate on the input data until there is no more. Figure out if you're dealing with a whole block (`modulus-length – 11` bytes) or less than that, copy the input to the end of the block (remember that in RSA, the padding goes at the beginning), and set the padding type to 2.

   ```
   while ( len )
   {
     encrypted_size += modulus_length;
     block_size = ( len < modulus_length - 11 ) ?
       len : ( modulus_length - 11 );
   ```

```
memset( padded_block, 0, modulus_length );
memcpy( padded_block + ( modulus_length - block_size ),
  input, block_size );
// set block type
padded_block[ 1 ] = 0x02;
```

6. Technically speaking, you ought to follow this with random bytes of padding, up to the beginning of the data. Throw security out the window here, and just pad with sequential bytes:

```
for ( i = 2; i < ( modulus_length - block_size - 1 ); i++ )
{
  // TODO make these random
  padded_block[ i ] = i;
}
```

7. RSA-encrypt the padded block:

```
load_huge( &m, padded_block, modulus_length );
rsa_compute( &m, public_key->exponent, public_key->modulus, &c );
```

Notice the new function load_huge. This function essentially just memcpy's a block into a huge, as shown in Listing 3-22:

**Listing 3-22:** "huge.c" load_huge

```
/**
 * Given a byte array, load it into a "huge", aligning integers
 * appropriately
 */
void load_huge( huge *h, const unsigned char *bytes, int length )
{
  while ( !( *bytes ) )
  {
    bytes++;
    length--;
  }

  h->size = length;
  h->rep = ( unsigned char * ) malloc( length );
  memcpy( h->rep, bytes, length );
}
```

**NOTE** One interesting point to note here is that you start by skipping over the zero bytes. This is an important compatibility point. Most SSL implementations (including OpenSSL, GnuTLS, NSS and JSSE) zero-pad positive numbers so that they aren't interpreted as negative numbers by a two's-complement-aware large number implementation. This one isn't, and zero-padding actually confuses the comparison routine, so just skip them.

8. Returning to the `rsa_encrypt` function; now you've encrypted the input block, and the result is in huge c. Convert this huge c into a byte array:

```
*output = ( unsigned char * ) realloc( *output, encrypted_size );

unload_huge( &c, *output + ( encrypted_size - modulus_length ),
    modulus_length );
```

9. Allocate space for the output at the end of the `output` array — if this is the first iteration, the end is the beginning — and `unload_huge`, shown in Listing 3-23, into it.

**Listing 3-23:** "huge.c" unload_huge

```
void unload_huge( const huge *h, unsigned char *bytes, int length )
{
  memcpy( bytes + ( length - h->size ), h->rep, length );
}
```

10. Adjust `len` and `input` and free the previously allocated `huge`s for the next iteration.

```
len -= block_size;
input += block_size;
free_huge( &m );
free_huge( &c );
}
```

If the input is less than *modulus_length* - *11* bytes (which, for SSL/TLS, is actually always the case), there will only be one iteration.

## Decrypting an RSA-Encrypted Message

Decryption is, of course, the opposite.

You operate on blocks of `modulus_length` at a time, decrypt the block — again using `rsa_compute`, but this time with the private key — and remove the padding, as shown in Listing 3-24.

**Listing 3-24:** "rsa.c" rsa_decrypt

```
/**
 * Convert the input into key-length blocks and decrypt, unpadding
 * each time.
 * Return -1 if the input is not an even multiple of the key modulus
 * length or if the padding type is not "2", otherwise return the
 * length of the decrypted data.
 */
int rsa_decrypt( unsigned char *input,
                 unsigned int len,
                 unsigned char **output,
                 rsa_key *private_key )
```

```
{
  int i, out_len = 0;
  huge c, m;
  int modulus_length = private_key->modulus->size;
  unsigned char *padded_block = ( unsigned char * ) malloc(
    modulus_length );

  *output = NULL;

  while ( len )
  {
    if ( len < modulus_length )
    {
      fprintf( stderr, "Error - input must be an even multiple \
        of key modulus %d (got %d)\n",
        private_key->modulus->size, len );
      free( padded_block );
      return -1;
    }

    load_huge( &c, input, modulus_length );
    mod_pow( &c, private_key->exponent,
      private_key->modulus, &m );

    unload_huge( &m, padded_block, modulus_length );

    if ( padded_block[ 1 ] > 0x02 )
    {
      fprintf( stderr, "Decryption error or unrecognized block \
        type %d.\n", padded_block[ 1 ] );
      free_huge( &c );
      free_huge( &m );
      free( padded_block );
      return -1;
    }

    // Find next 0 byte after the padding type byte; this signifies
    // start-of-data
    i = 2;
    while ( padded_block[ i++ ] );

    out_len += modulus_length - i;
    *output = realloc( *output, out_len );
    memcpy( *output + ( out_len - ( modulus_length - i ) ),
      padded_block + i, modulus_length - i );

    len -= modulus_length;
    input += modulus_length;
```

*(Continued)*

```
      free_huge( &c );
      free_huge( &m );
  }

  free( padded_block );

  return out_len;
}
```

This should be easy to follow, after the description of `rsa_encrypt` in Listing 3-21 — the primary differences are that the input is always a multiple of `modulus_length`; exit with an error if this is not the case. The block-length computation is simpler. Check for padding type 2; most likely, if the decrypted padding type is not 2, this represents a decryption error (for example, you decrypted using the wrong private key). Remove the padding and copy the resultant output, one block at a time, into the output array.

> **NOTE**   The previously described padding algorithm is called PKCS1.5 padding. There are other, even more secure padding algorithms such as OAEP. For now, though, PKCS1.5 padding is just fine; the attacks that OAEP guards against are all theoretical attacks, although interesting. Additionally, TLS v1.0 mandates this padding, so there's not much point in implementing another format unless it is used outside of SSL.
>
> Note also that, technically speaking, you should also permit CBC chaining, as well as other chaining algorithms such as OFB. However, SSL never uses RSA for more than a single block, so this won't be examined here. If you're interested, the discussion on CBC in the previous chapter should make it simple to add this feature.

## Testing RSA Encryption and Decryption

Finally, develop a `main` routine, shown in Listing 3-25, that you can use to test this out. How to compute $e$, $d$, and $n$ has still not been covered, so hardcode some default values that are used if nothing is passed in.

**Listing 3-25:** "rsa.c" test main routine

```
#ifdef TEST_RSA
const unsigned char TestModulus[] = {
0xC4, 0xF8, 0xE9, 0xE1, 0x5D, 0xCA, 0xDF, 0x2B,
0x96, 0xC7, 0x63, 0xD9, 0x81, 0x00, 0x6A, 0x64,
0x4F, 0xFB, 0x44, 0x15, 0x03, 0x0A, 0x16, 0xED,
0x12, 0x83, 0x88, 0x33, 0x40, 0xF2, 0xAA, 0x0E,
0x2B, 0xE2, 0xBE, 0x8F, 0xA6, 0x01, 0x50, 0xB9,
0x04, 0x69, 0x65, 0x83, 0x7C, 0x3E, 0x7D, 0x15,
```

```
0x1B, 0x7D, 0xE2, 0x37, 0xEB, 0xB9, 0x57, 0xC2,
0x06, 0x63, 0x89, 0x82, 0x50, 0x70, 0x3B, 0x3F
};

const unsigned char TestPrivateKey[] = {
0x8a, 0x7e, 0x79, 0xf3, 0xfb, 0xfe, 0xa8, 0xeb,
0xfd, 0x18, 0x35, 0x1c, 0xb9, 0x97, 0x91, 0x36,
0xf7, 0x05, 0xb4, 0xd9, 0x11, 0x4a, 0x06, 0xd4,
0xaa, 0x2f, 0xd1, 0x94, 0x38, 0x16, 0x67, 0x7a,
0x53, 0x74, 0x66, 0x18, 0x46, 0xa3, 0x0c, 0x45,
0xb3, 0x0a, 0x02, 0x4b, 0x4d, 0x22, 0xb1, 0x5a,
0xb3, 0x23, 0x62, 0x2b, 0x2d, 0xe4, 0x7b, 0xa2,
0x91, 0x15, 0xf0, 0x6e, 0xe4, 0x2c, 0x41
};

const unsigned char TestPublicKey[] = { 0x01, 0x00, 0x01 };

int main( int argc, char *argv[ ] )
{
  int exponent_len;
  int modulus_len;
  int data_len;
  unsigned char *exponent;
  unsigned char *modulus;
  unsigned char *data;
  rsa_key public_key;
  rsa_key private_key;

  if ( argc < 3 )
  {
    fprintf( stderr, "Usage: rsa [-e|-d] [<modulus> <exponent>] <data>\n" );
    exit( 0 );
  }

  if ( argc == 5 )
  {
    modulus_len = hex_decode( argv[ 2 ], &modulus );
    exponent_len = hex_decode( argv[ 3 ], &exponent );
    data_len = hex_decode( argv[ 4 ], &data );
  }
  else
  {
    data_len = hex_decode( argv[ 2 ], &data );
    modulus_len = sizeof( TestModulus );
    modulus = TestModulus;
    if ( !strcmp( "-e", argv[ 1 ] ) )
    {
      exponent_len = sizeof( TestPublicKey );
      exponent = TestPublicKey;
    }
```

*(Continued)*

```
    else
    {
      exponent_len = sizeof( TestPrivateKey );
      exponent = TestPrivateKey;
    }
  }

  public_key.modulus = ( huge * ) malloc( sizeof( huge ) );
  public_key.exponent = ( huge * ) malloc( sizeof( huge ) );
  private_key.modulus = ( huge * ) malloc( sizeof( huge ) );
  private_key.exponent = ( huge * ) malloc( sizeof( huge ) );

  if ( !strcmp( argv[ 1 ], "-e" ) )
  {
    unsigned char *encrypted;
    int encrypted_len;

    load_huge( public_key.modulus, modulus, modulus_len );
    load_huge( public_key.exponent, exponent, exponent_len );

    encrypted_len = rsa_encrypt( data, data_len, &encrypted, &public_key );
    show_hex( encrypted, encrypted_len );
    free( encrypted );
  }
  else if ( !strcmp( argv[ 1 ], "-d" ) )
  {
    int decrypted_len;
    unsigned char *decrypted;

    load_huge( private_key.modulus, modulus, modulus_len );
    load_huge( private_key.exponent, exponent, exponent_len );

    decrypted_len = rsa_decrypt( data, data_len, &decrypted, &private_key );

    show_hex( decrypted, decrypted_len );

    free( decrypted );
  }
  else
  {
    fprintf( stderr, "unrecognized option flag '%s'\n", argv[ 1 ] );
  }

  free( data );
  if ( argc == 5 )
  {
    free( modulus );
    free( exponent );
  }
}
#endif
```

If called with only an input, this application defaults to the hardcoded keypair. If you run this, you see

```
jdavies@localhost$ rsa -e abc
40f73315d3f74703904e51e1c72686801de06a55417110e56280f1f8471a3802406d2110011e1f38
7f7b4c43258b0a1eedc558a3aac5aa2d20cf5e0d65d80db3
```

The output is hex encoded as before. Notice that although you only encrypted three bytes of input, you got back 64 bytes of output. The modulus is 512 bits, so the output must also be 512 bits.

You can see this decoded:

```
jdavies@localhost$ rsa -d \ 0x40f73315d3f74703904e51e1c7\
2686801de06a55417110e56280f1f8471a3802406d2110011e1f387f\
7b4c43258b0a1eedc558a3aac5aa2d20cf5e0d65d80db3
616263
```

The decryption routine decrypts, removes the padding, and returns the original input "616263" (the hex values of the ASCII characters $a$, $b$, and $c$). Note that if you try to decrypt with the public key, you get gibberish; once encrypted, the message can *only* be decrypted using the private key.

---

**PROCEDURE FOR GENERATING RSA KEYPAIRS**

Although code to generate RSA keypairs isn't examined here, it's not prohibitively difficult to do so. The procedure is as follows:

1. Select two random prime numbers $p$ and $q$.

2. Compute the modulus $n = pq$.

3. Compute the totient function (p-1)(q-1)

4. Select a random public exponent e < φ(n) (as previously mentioned, 65,537 is a popular choice).

5. Perform a modular inversion (to be introduced shortly) to compute the private exponent $d$: $de \% n = 1$.

---

You also likely noticed that your computer slowed to a crawl while decrypting; encrypting isn't too bad, because of the choice of public exponent (65,537). Decrypting is slow — not unusably slow, but also not something you want to try to do more than a few times a minute. It should come as no surprise to you that reams of research have been done into methods of speeding up the RSA decryption operation. None of them are examined here; they mostly involve keeping track of the interim steps in the original computation of the private key and taking advantage of some useful mathematical properties thereof.

So, because public-key cryptography can be used to exchange secrets, why did Chapter 2 spend so much time (besides the fact that it's interesting) looking at private-key cryptography? Well, public-key cryptography is painfully slow. There are actually ways to speed it up — the implementation presented here is slower than it could be, even with all the speed-ups employed — but it's still not realistic to apply RSA encryption to a data stream in real time. You would severely limit the network utilization if you did so. As a result, SSL actually calls on you to select a symmetric-key algorithm, generate a key, encrypt that key using an RSA public key, and, after that key has been sent and acknowledged, to begin using the symmetric algorithm for subsequent communications. The details of how precisely to do this is examined in painstaking detail in Chapter 6.

## Achieving Perfect Forward Secrecy with Diffie-Hellman Key Exchange

The security in RSA rests in the difficulty of computing first the private exponent $d$ from the public key $e$ and the modulus $n$ as well as the difficulty in solving the equation m$^x$%n=c for m. This is referred to as the *discrete logarithm* problem. These problems are both strongly believed (but technically not proven) to be impossible to solve other than by enumerating all possible combinations. Note that although RSA can be used as a complete cryptography solution, its slow runtime limits its practical uses to simple encryption of keys to be used for symmetric cryptography. Another algorithm that relies similarly on the difficulty of factoring large prime numbers and the discrete logarithm problem is *Diffie-Hellman* key exchange, named after its inventors, Whitfield Diffie and Martin Hellman and originally described by Diffie and Hellman in the "Journal IEEE Transactions on Information Theory 22" in 1976. One significant difference between RSA and Diffie-Hellman is that although RSA can be used to encrypt arbitrary bits of data, Diffie-Hellman can only be used to perform a key exchange because neither side can predict what value both sides will ultimately agree upon, even though it's guaranteed that they'll both arrive at the same value. This ability to encrypt arbitrary data using RSA, although desirable in some contexts, is something of a double-edged sword. One potential drawback of the RSA algorithm is that, if the private key is ever compromised, any communication that was secured using that private key is now exposed. There's no such vulnerability in the Diffie-Hellman key exchange algorithm. This property — communications remaining secure even if the private key is uncovered — is referred to as *perfect forward secrecy*.

Diffie-Hellman key agreement relies on the fact that

$$g^{ab}\%p = g^{ba}\%p = (g^a\%p)^b\%p = (g^b\%p)^a\%p$$

$g$ and $p$ are agreed on by both sides, either offline or as part of the key exchange. They don't need to be kept secret and SSL/TLS transmits them in the clear. The server chooses a value $a$ at random and the client chooses a value $b$ at random. Then the server computes

$$Ys = (g^a\%p)$$

And the client computes

$$Yc = (g^b\%p)$$

The server transmits $Ys$ to the client and the client transmits $Yc$ to the server. At this point, they each have enough to compute the final value $z = g^{ab}\%p$:

| Client | Server |
|:---:|:---:|
| $(g^a\%p)^b\%p$ | $(g^b\%p)^a\%p$ |
| $(Ys)^b\%p$ | $(Yc)^a\%p$ |
| Z | Z |

And $z$ is the key that both sides use as the symmetric key. The server knows the value $a$ (because it chose it), and the client knows the value $b$ (because, again, it chose it). Neither knows the other's value, but they don't need to. Nor can an eavesdropper glean the value of $z$ without either $a$ or $b$, neither of which has been shared. You can think of each side as computing one-half of an exponentiation and sharing that half with the other side, which then completes the exponentiation. Because the exponentiation operation is done mod $p$, it can't be feasibly inverted by an attacker, unless the attacker has solved the discrete logarithm problem.

Using the mod_pow function developed earlier for RSA, this is simple to implement in code as shown in Listing 3-26.

**Listing 3-26:** "dh.c" Diffie-Hellman key agreement

```
static void dh_agree( huge *p, huge *g, huge *e, huge *Y )
{
  mod_pow( g, &e, p, Y );
}

static void dh_finalize( huge *p, huge *Y, huge *e, huge *Z )
{
  mod_pow( Y, &e, p, &Z );
}
```

In fact, there's not much point in defining new functions to implement this because all they do is call mod_pow. Given $p$, $g$, and $a$, the server does something like

```
huge Ys, Yc, Z;
dh_agree( p, g, a, &Ys );
send_to_client( &Ys );
receive_from_client( &Yc );
dh_finalize( p, Yc, a, Z );
// ... use "Z" as shared key
```

At the same time, the client does:

```
huge Ys, Yc, Z;
dh_agree( p, g, b, &Yc );
```

```
send_to_server( &Yc );
receive_from_server( &Ys );
dh_finalize( p, &Ys, b, &Z );
// ... use "Z" as shared key
```

Notice also that the client doesn't need to wait for $Ys$ before computing $Yc$, assuming $p$ and $g$ are known to both sides. In SSL, the server picks $p$ and $g$, and transmits them along with $Ys$, but Diffie-Hellman doesn't actually require that key exchange be done this way.

One particularly interesting difference between RSA and DH is that RSA is very, very picky about what values you can use for $e$, $d$, and $n$. As you saw earlier, not every triple of numbers works (in fact, relative to the size of all natural numbers, very few do). However, DH key exchange works with essentially any random combination of $p$, $g$, $a$, and $b$. What guidance is there for picking out "good" values? Of course, you want to use large numbers, especially for $p$; other than using a large number — 512-bit, 1024-bit, and so on — you at least want to ensure that the bits are securely randomly distributed.

It also turns out that some choices of $p$ leave the secret $z$ vulnerable to eavesdroppers who can employ the *Pohlig-Hellman* attack. The attack itself, originally published by Stephen Pollig and Martin Hellman in the journal "IEEE Transactions on Information Theory" in 1978, is mathematically technical, but it relies on a $p - 1$ that has no large prime factors. The math behind the attack itself is outside of the scope of this book, but guarding against it is straightforward, as long as you're aware of the risk. Ensure that the choice $p - 1$ is not only itself large, but that it includes at least one large prime factor. RFC 2631 recommends that $p = jq + 1$ where $q$ is a large prime number and $j$ is greater than or equal to 2. Neither $q$ nor $j$ needs to be kept secret; in fact, it's recommended that they be shared so that the receiver can verify that $p$ is a good choice.

In most implementations, $g$ is actually a very small number — 2 is a popular choice. As long as $p$, $a$, and $b$ are very large, you can get away with such a small $g$ and still be cryptographically secure.

# Getting More Security per Key Bit: Elliptic Curve Cryptography

Although the concept and theory of elliptic curves and their application in cryptography have been around for quite a while (Miller and Koblitz described the first ECC cryptosystem in 1985), elliptic curves only managed to find their way into TLS in the past few years. TLS 1.2 introduced support for *Elliptic-Curve Cryptography* (ECC) in 2008. Although it hasn't, at the time of this writing, found its way into any commercial TLS implementations, it's expected that ECC will become an important element of public-key cryptography in the future. I explore the basics of ECC here — enough for you to add support for it in the chapter 9, which covers TLS 1.2 — but overall, I barely scratch the surface of the field.

ECC — elliptic-curves in general, in fact — are complex entities. An elliptic-curve is defined by the equation $y^2 = x^3 + ax + b$. $a$ and $b$ are typically fixed and, for public-key cryptography purposes, small numbers. The mathematics behind ECC is extraordinarily complex compared to anything you've seen so far. I won't get any deeper into it than is absolutely necessary.

Figure 3-5 shows the graph of $y^2 = x^3 + ax + b$, the elliptic curve defined by $a = -1$, $b = 0$. Notice the discontinuity between 0 and 1; $\sqrt{x^3 - ax}$ has no solutions between 0 and 1 because $x^3 - x < 0$.

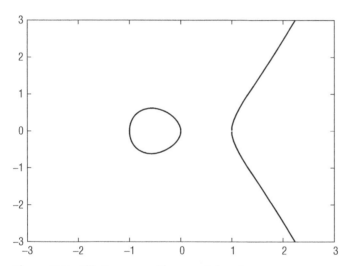

**Figure 3-5:** Elliptic curve with $a = -1$, $b = 0$

Cryptographic operations are defined in terms of multiplicative operations on this curve. It's not readily apparent how one would go about "multiplying" anything on a curve, though. Multiplication is defined in terms of addition, and "addition," in ECC, is the process of drawing a line through two points and finding it's intersection at a third point on the curve as illustrated in Figure 3-6.

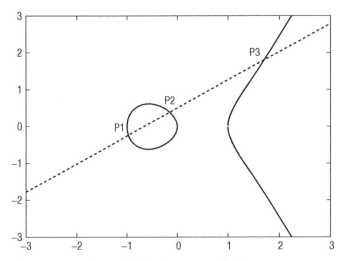

**Figure 3-6:** Point multiplication on an elliptic curve

So, given two points $p_1 = (x_1, y_1)$, $p_2 = (x_2, y_2)$, "addition" of points $p_3 = p_1 + p_2$ is defined as:

$$x_3 = \lambda^2 - x_1 - x_2$$
$$y_3 = \lambda(x_1 - x_3) - y_1$$

where

$$\lambda = \frac{y_2 - y_1}{x_2 - x_1}$$

(that is, the slope of the line through $p_1$ and $p_2$). You may be able to spot a problem with this definition, though: How do you add a point to itself? A point all by itself has no slope — $\lambda = \frac{0}{0}$ in this case. So you need a special rule for "doubling" a point. Given $p_1 = (x_1, y_1)$, $2p_1$ is defined as:

$$x_3 = \lambda^2 - 2x_1$$
$$y_3 = \lambda (x_1 - x_3) - y_1$$

where

$$\lambda = \frac{3x_1^2 + a}{2y_1}$$

Remember that $a$ was one of the constants in the definition of the curve.

So, armed with a point addition and a point-doubling routine, you can define multiplication of a point by a scalar in terms of double and add. Recall that, for integer operations, double-and-add was a "nice" speed-up. In terms of elliptic curves, though, it's a necessity because you can't add a point to itself a given number of times. Notice also that multiplication of points is meaningless; you can add two points together, but you can only meaningfully multiply a point by a scalar value.

Whew! I warned you elliptic curves were complex. However, that's not all. As a programmer, you can likely still spot a problem with this definition: the division operation in the definition of λ. Whenever you divide integers, you get fractions, and fractions create all sorts of problems for cryptographic systems, which need absolute precision. The solution to this problem, which is probably not a surprise to you at this point, is to define everything modulo a prime number.

But — how do you divide modulo a number?

## How Elliptic Curve Cryptography Relies on Modular Inversions

Recall that addition modulo a number $n$ is pretty straightforward: Perform the addition normally and then compute the remainder after dividing by $n$. Multiplication and exponentiation are the same; just perform the operation as you normally would and compute the remainder. The distributivity of the modulus operator enables you to implement this as multiple operations each followed by modulo, but the end result is the same.

What about division modulo $n$? Can you divide $x$ by $y$ and then compute the remainder when divided by $n$? Consider an example. $5 \times 6 = 30$ and $30 \% 13 = 4$ (because $2 * 13 = 26$ and $30 - 26 = 4$). Division mod $n$ ought to return 6 if you apply it to 5. In other words, you need an operation that, given 4, 5, and 13, returns 6. Clearly, normal division doesn't work at all: $(5 \times 6) \% 13 = 4$, but $(4 / 5) \% 13 = 0.8$, not 6. In fact, division modulo $n$ isn't particularly well defined.

You can't really call it division, but you do need an operation referred to as the *modular inverse* to complete elliptic-curve operations. This is an operation on $x$ such that

$$x^{-1}x\%n = 1$$

So, going back to the example of $(5 \times 6) \% 13 = 4$, you want to discover an operation to compute a number which, when multiplied by 4 and then computed $\% 13$ returns 6, inverting the multiplication.

## Using the Euclidean Algorithm to compute Greatest Common Denominators

Such an operation exists, but it's not easily expressible; it's not nearly as simple as modulus addition or multiplication. Typically, $x^{-1}$ is computed via the extended Euclidean algorithm. The *normal* (that is, non-extended) Euclidean algorithm is an efficient way to discover the greatest common denominator (GCD) of two numbers; the largest number that divides both evenly. The idea of the algorithm is to recursively subtract the smaller of the two numbers from the larger until one is 0. The other one is the GCD. In code, this can be implemented recursively as in Listing 3-27.

**Listing 3-27:** gcd (small numbers)

```
int gcd( int x, int y )
{
  if ( x == 0 ) { return y; }
  if ( y == 0 ) { return x; }

  if ( x > y )
  {
    return gcd( x - y, y );
  }
  else
  {
    return gcd( y - x, x );
  }
}
```

So, for example, given $x = 105$, $y = 252$:

| ITERATION | X | Y |
| --- | --- | --- |
| 0 | 105 | 252 |
| 1 | 147 | 105 |
| 2 | 42 | 105 |
| 3 | 63 | 42 |
| 4 | 21 | 42 |
| 5 | 21 | 21 |
| 6 | 0 | 21 |

This tells you that 21 is the largest number that evenly divides both 105 and 252 — 105/21 – 5, and 252/21 = 12. The actual values of the division operations aren't particularly important in this context. What's important is that 21 is the largest number that divides both without leaving a fractional part.

It may not be intuitively clear, but it can be proven that this will always complete. If nothing else, any two numbers always share a GCD of 1. In fact, running the GCD algorithm and verifying that the result is 1 is a way of checking that two numbers are *coprime* or *relatively prime*, in other words they share no common factors.

## Computing Modular Inversions with the Extended Euclidean Algorithm

Although certainly interesting, it's not yet clear how you can use the Euclidean algorithm to compute the modular inverse of a number as defined earlier. The extended Euclidean algorithm actually runs this same process in reverse, starting from 0 up to the GCD. It also computes, in the process, two numbers $y_1$ and $y_2$ such that $ay_1 + zy_2 = gcd(a,z)$; if $z$ is a prime number, $y_1$ is also the solution to a $^{-1}$ a%z = 1, which is exactly what you're looking for.

The extended Euclidean algorithm for computing modular inverses is described algorithmically in FIPS-186-3, Appendix C.1. Listing 3-28 presents it in C code form.

**Listing 3-28:** "ecc_int.c" extended Euclidean algorithm (small numbers)

```
int ext_euclid( int z, int a )
{
  int i, j, y2, y1, y, quotient, remainder;

  i = a;
  j = z;
  y2 = 0;
  y1 = 1;

  while ( j > 0 )
  {
    quotient = i / j;
    remainder = i % j;
    y = y2  - ( y1 * quotient );
    i = j;
    j = remainder;
    y2 = y1;
    y1 = y;
  }
  return ( y2 % a );
}
```

Returning again to the example above of 5 and 6 % 13, remember that $(5 \times 6) \% 13 = 4$. `ext_euclid` tells you what number $x$ satisfied the relationship $(4x) \% 13 = 6$, thus inverting the multiplication by 5. In this case, $z = 5$ and $a = 13$.

| QUOTIENT | REMAINDER | Y | $Y^2$ | $Y^1$ |
|---|---|---|---|---|
| 2 | 3 | −2 | 0 | 1 |
| 1 | 2 | 3 | 1 | −2 |
| 1 | 1 | −5 | −2 | 3 |
| 2 | 0 | 13 | 3 | −5 |

Halt because remainder = 0.

The solution, `ext_euclid(5,13)` = y1 % a = -5 % 13 = -5. You can check this result by verifying that $(4 \times -5) \% 13 = -20 \% 13 = 6$ because $13 \times -2 = -26$ and $-20 - (-26) = 6$.

Of course, it should come as no surprise that, to compute secure elliptic curve parameters, you are dealing with numbers far too large to fit within a single 32-bit integer, or even a 64-bit integer. Secure ECC involves inverting 1,024- or 2,048-bit numbers, which means you need to make use of the huge library again.

You may see a problem here, though. When you inverted the multiplication of 5 modulo 13, you got a negative result, and the interim computation likewise involved negative numbers, which the huge library was not equipped to handle. Unfortunately, there's just no way around it. You need negative number support in order to compute modular inverses that are needed to support ECC.

## Adding Negative Number Support to the Huge Number Library

You may be familiar with two's complement binary arithmetic. In two's complement binary arithmetic, the lower half of the bit space represents positive numbers and the upper half represents negative numbers. This enables you to take advantage of the natural wrapping behavior of digital registers to efficiently perform signed operations. Given, say, a 4-bit register (to keep things small), you'd have the following:

| | |
|---|---|
| 0000 | 0 |
| 0001 | 1 |
| 0010 | 2 |
| 0011 | 3 |
| 0100 | 4 |
| 0101 | 5 |
| 0110 | 6 |
| 0111 | 7 |

| | |
|---|---|
| 1000 | −8 |
| 1001 | −7 |
| 1010 | −6 |
| 1011 | −5 |
| 1100 | −4 |
| 1101 | −3 |
| 1110 | −2 |
| 1111 | −1 |

If you subtract 3 (0011) from 1 (0001), the counters naturally wrap and end up back on 1110, which is chosen to represent −2. Multiplication preserves sign as well − 2 × −3 = 0010 × 1101:

$$
\begin{array}{r}
1101 \\
\times\ 0010 \\
\hline
0000 \quad (0) \\
11010 \quad (1) \\
000000 \quad (0) \\
+\ 0000000 \quad (0) \\
\hline
0011010
\end{array}
$$

Truncate the leading three digits and you get the correct result: 1010, or −6.

This truncation creates a problem when you're trying to implement arbitrary precision binary math, though. Consider 7 × 7, which overflows this four-bit implementation:

$$
\begin{array}{r}
0111 \\
\times\ 0111 \\
\hline
0111 \quad (1) \\
01110 \quad (1) \\
011100 \quad (1) \\
+\ 0000000 \quad (0) \\
\hline
11001
\end{array}
$$

You've computed the correct answer — 49 — but according to the rule stated earlier, you should throw away the first bit and end up with an incorrect answer of −7. You could, of course, check the magnitude of each operand, check to see if it would have overflowed, and adjust accordingly, but this is an awful lot of trouble to go to. It also negates the benefit of two's complement arithmetic. In general, two's complement arithmetic only works correctly when bit length is fixed. Instead, just keep track of signs explicitly and convert the "huge" data type to a sign/magnitude representation.

---

**COMPUTING WITH A FIXED-PRECISION NUMERIC REPRESENTATION**

As an aside, it would be possible to create, say, a fixed-precision 2,048-bit numeric representation and perform all calculations using this representation; if you do, then you can, in fact, make use of two's complement arithmetic to handle negative numbers. You can get away with this in the context of public-key cryptography because all operations are performed modulo a fixed 512-, 1024-, or 2048-bit key. Of course, in the future, you might need to expand this out to 4,096 bits and beyond. The downside of this approach is that every number, including single-byte numbers, take up 256 bytes of memory, so you trade memory for speed. I'm not aware of any arbitrary-precision math library that works this way, however; OpenSSL, GnuTLS (via GMP, via gcrypt), NSS and Java all take the "sign/magnitude" approach that's examined here.

---

When negative numbers enter the mix, additions and subtractions essentially become variants of the same operation; keep an explicit "add" and "subtract" routine for clarity, but additions become subtractions when the signs of the operators differ and vice versa.

Treat adding and subtracting as occurring in two separate stages — first, computing the magnitude of the result, and then computing the sign. The magnitude of the result depends, of course, on the operation requested and the operator's values as well as the signs of each; the sign depends on the operation and the sign of each value, as well as whether the addend (or subtrahend) is greater than the summand (or minuend). Table 3-2 summarizes, hopefully, the preceding paragraph.

**Table 3-2:** Negative Number Operations

| OPERATION REQUESTED | X SIGN | Y SIGN | ABS(X) > ABS(Y)? | MAGNITUDE | SIGN |
|---|---|---|---|---|---|
| add | + | + | N | x + y | + |
| add | + | − | N | x − y | + |
| add | − | + | N | x − y | − |
| add | − | − | N | x + y | − |
| add | + | + | Y | y + x | + |
| add | + | − | Y | y − x | − |

| OPERATION REQUESTED | X SIGN | Y SIGN | ABS(X) > ABS(Y)? | MAGNITUDE | SIGN |
|---|---|---|---|---|---|
| add | − | + | Y | $y - x$ | + |
| add | − | − | Y | $y + x$ | − |
| subtract | + | + | N | $x - y$ | + |
| subtract | + | − | N | $x + y$ | + |
| subtract | − | + | N | $x + y$ | − |
| subtract | − | − | N | $x - y$ | − |
| subtract | + | + | Y | $y - x$ | − |
| subtract | + | − | Y | $y + x$ | + |
| subtract | − | + | Y | $y + x$ | − |
| subtract | − | − | Y | $y - x$ | + |

To summarize, when adding or subtracting, if $x$ is greater than $y$, invert the operation if the signs of the operators are different. Perform the operation as requested if the signs are the same. If $x$ is less than $y$, swap the operators first. Of course, $x + y$ is the same as $y + x$. This gives the magnitude. The sign of the operation can be determined, essentially independently, as the following: If $x$ is greater than $y$, the result has the same sign as $x$, whether adding or subtracting. Otherwise, if adding, and the operators have the same sign, the result has the same sign as $x$; if they differ, the result has the same sign as $y$. When subtracting, and $x$ is less than $y$, the sum has the opposite sign as $x$ if $x$ and $y$ have the same sign, and the opposite sign as $y$ if $x$ and $y$ have different signs. You may find it worthwhile to work through a few examples to convince yourself that we've covered every case, except for the exceptional case where $x = y$, which is dealt with specially because 0 is neither positive nor negative.

Follow these steps to support arbitrary-sized negative number addition and subtraction.

1. Add an element to the huge struct from Listing 3-1 to keep track of its sign, as shown in Listing 3-29. Let 0 represent positive and 1 represent negative:

**Listing 3-29:**  "huge.h" huge structure with negative number support

```
typedef struct
{
  int sign;
  unsigned int size;
  unsigned char *rep;
}
huge;
```

2. There are three initializer functions that create huges: set_huge, copy_huge, and load_huge. Each needs to be updated to initialize the sign bit, as shown in Listing 3-30.

**Listing 3-30:** "huge.c" initializer routines with negative number support included

```
void set_huge( huge *h, unsigned int val )
{
  unsigned int mask, i, shift;
  // Negative number support
  h->sign = 0;   // sign of 0 means positive
  ...

void copy_huge( huge *tgt, huge *src )
{
  if ( tgt->rep )
  {
    // TODO make this a little more efficient by reusing "rep"
    // if it's big enough
    free( tgt->rep );
  }

  tgt->sign = src->sign;
  ...

void load_huge( huge *h, const unsigned char *bytes, int length )
{
  while ( !( *bytes ) )
  {
    bytes++;
    length--;
  }

  h->sign = 0;
  ...
```

Notice that there's no way to initialize a huge as a negative number; you don't need one and, in fact, negative numbers get in the way if, for example, you treat a high 1 bit as a negative number indicator in load_huge. If a computation results in a negative number, the routines keep track of it internally.

3. Because the current add and subtract routines do a good job of computing magnitudes of arbitrarily sized numbers — provided, of course, that h1 is greater than h2 in the case of subtraction — those routines can be used unchanged to compute magnitudes, and you can do sign computation and swapping in a separate routine. As such, rename add and subtract and make them static as shown in Listing 3-31.

**Listing 3-31:** "huge.c" add_magnitude and subtract_magnitude

```
/**
 * Add two huges - overwrite h1 with the result.
 */
static void add_magnitude( huge *h1, huge *h2 )
{
  unsigned int i, j;
  unsigned int sum;
  unsigned int carry = 0;
  ...

/**
 * Subtract h2 from h1, overwriting the value of h1.
 */
static void subtract_magnitude( huge *h1, huge *h2 )
{
  int i = h1->size;
  int j = h2->size;
  int difference; // signed int - important!
  unsigned int borrow = 0;
  ...
  if ( borrow && i )
  {
    if ( h1->rep[ i - 1 ] ) // Don't borrow i
    {
      // negative reults are now OK
      h1->rep[ i - 1 ]--;
    }
  }
}
```

Nothing else changes in these routines.

4. Now, create two new routines named `add` and `subtract` that invoke `add_magnitude` and `subtract_magnitude`, after performing the rules described by Table 3-2 as shown in Listing 3-32. These new routines have the same method signatures as the old `add` and `subtract`. In fact, they end up taking their places, which means you need to relink anything linked using the old object file. This won't be a problem because your Make rules are set up correctly.

**Listing 3-32:** "huge.c" add with negative number support

```
void add( huge *h1, huge *h2 )
{
  int result_sign;

  // First compute sign of result, then compute magnitude
  if ( compare( h1, h2 ) > 0 )
```

*(Continued)*

```
  {
    result_sign = h1->sign;

    if ( h1->sign == h2->sign )
    {
      add_magnitude( h1, h2 );
    }
    else
    {
      subtract_magnitude( h1, h2 );
    }
  }
  else
  {
    huge tmp;

    // put h1 into tmp and h2 into h1 to swap the operands
    set_huge( &tmp, 0 ); // initialize
    copy_huge( &tmp, h1 );
    copy_huge( h1, h2 );

    if ( h1->sign == tmp.sign )
    {
      result_sign = h1->sign;
      add_magnitude( h1, &tmp );
    }
    else
    {
      result_sign = h2->sign;
      subtract_magnitude( h1, &tmp );
    }

    free_huge( &tmp );
  }

  // Use the stored sign to set the result
  h1->sign = result_sign;
}
```

5.  This routine embodies the signing rules described by the first half of Table 3-2. If h1 is greater than h2 (see Figure 3-7), add or subtract, depending on whether the signs of the two operands are the same or different, and preserve the sign of h1. h2 never changes regardless. If h1 is less than h2, swap them; you want to preserve h2 as before, so copy h1 into a temporary object and h2 into h1.

    The net effect here is that you add or subtract h1 from h2, overwriting h1, just as if the operation had been called with the operators reversed, but not touching h2, which is what you want.

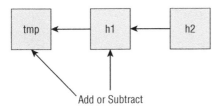

Add or Subtract

**Figure 3-7:** Arithmetic routines with negative numbers

6. Subtracting is similar, in Listing 3-33.

**Listing 3-33:** "huge.c" subtract with negative number support

```
void subtract( huge *h1, huge *h2 )
{
  int result_sign;

  // First compute sign of result, then compute magnitude
  if ( compare( h1, h2 ) > 0 )
  {
    result_sign = h1->sign;

    if ( h1->sign == h2->sign )
    {
      subtract_magnitude( h1, h2 );
    }
    else
    {
      add_magnitude( h1, h2 );
    }
  }
  else
  {
    huge tmp;

    // put h1 into tmp and h2 into h1 to swap the operands
    set_huge( &tmp, 0 ); // initialize
    copy_huge( &tmp, h1 );
    copy_huge( h1, h2 );

    if ( h1->sign == tmp.sign )
    {
      result_sign = !( h1->sign );
      subtract_magnitude( h1, &tmp );
    }
    else
    {
      result_sign = !( h2->sign );
      add_magnitude( h1, &tmp );
```

*(Continued)*

```
    }

    free_huge( &tmp );
  }

  // Use the stored sign to set the result
  h1->sign = result_sign;
}
```

In fact, you can probably see how you could collapse these two functions into one single function if you were so inclined.

7. Multiplication and division are even easier. The magnitudes of the results are the same as they were in the unsigned case, and the sign of the result is positive if the signs are equal and negative if the signs are unequal. This is illustrated in Listing 3-34.

**Listing 3-34:** "huge.c" multiply with negative number support

```
void multiply( huge *h1, huge *h2 )
{
  unsigned char mask;
  unsigned int i;
  int result_sign;
  huge temp;

  set_huge( &temp, 0 );
  copy_huge( &temp, h1 );

  result_sign = !( h1->sign == h2->sign );
...
  }
  while ( i );

  h1->sign = result_sign;
}
```

8. To support signed numbers at division time, you don't even need to remember a temporary sign because quotients are always initialized dynamically as shown in Listing 3-35.

**Listing 3-35:** "huge.c" divide with negative number support

```
void divide( huge *dividend, huge *divisor, huge *quotient )
{
  int i, bit_size, bit_position;
  ...
  if ( quotient )
  {
    quotient->sign = !( dividend->sign == dividend->sign );
```

```
    quotient->size = ( bit_size / 8 ) + 1;
    quotient->rep = ( unsigned char * ) malloc( quotient->size );
    memset( quotient->rep, 0, quotient->size );
}
...
```

9. Because you're keeping track of your own negative numbers, you don't want subtract doing it for you:

```
if ( compare( divisor, dividend ) <= 0 )
{
    subtract_magnitude( dividend, divisor );   // dividend -= divisor
```

10. Finally, you need to account for negative modulus operations. As it turns out, although negative number modulus operations come up in computations, they're not that well defined. Consider, for example, 17 % 7. This is equal to 3 because $7 \times 2 = 14$ and $17 - 14 = 3$. Now, you might be tempted to say that $-17 \% 7 = -3$ because $-17 / 7 = \text{round}( -2.42 ) = -2, 7 \times -2 = -14$, and $-17 - (-14) = -3$.

Although that's a perfectly valid definition of the modulus operation, it's not the one that's been standardized on (at least not for cryptographic computations — it *is* the standard that the C programming language follows!). Instead, $-17 \% 7 = 4$. Why? $7 \times -3 = -21$, and $-17 - (-21) = 4$.

## Supporting Negative Remainders

If you view this on a number line, this starts to make (some) sense, as shown in Figure 3-8.

**Figure 3-8:** Positive remainder operations

To figure the remainder, find the first multiple, on the number line, to the *left* of your target and then figure the distance between the two points. This means, first of all, that modulus operations always return positive values and second that

$$(-x \% y) != -(x \% y)$$

(as convenient as that would have been when coding it). This also means that you can't rely on the dividend being updated to be the modulus when one of the parameters is negative. However, there's a simple solution: subtract divisor one more time before exiting, if dividend is negative. Consider the earlier example above of ⁻17 % 7. The division operation proceeds as follows:

1. Left-shift (double) 7 until the result is greater than 17 (28)

2. Right- shift divisor once (14)

3. Subtract 14 from 17 (dividend = 3)

4. Right-shift divisor again (7)

The division is complete because the divisor has shifted back to its initial position. Now the dividend contains −3 — seven positions away from the desired result of 4. Subtracting -divisor yields the correct answer, 4.

Unfortunately, in some contexts, specifically the extended Euclidean algorithm developed here, the modulus of a negative and a positive must be negative. As a result, you have to keep track of when and where you need the positive modulus versus the negative modulus.

With signed-number support, you can now implement the extended Euclidean algorithm for computing modular inverses for arbitrarily sized integers, as shown in Listing 3-36.

**Listing 3-36:** "huge.c" inv routine

```
void inv( huge *z, huge *a )
{
  huge i, j, y2, y1, y, quotient, remainder, a_temp;

  set_huge( &i, 1 );  // initialize for copy
  set_huge( &j, 1 );  // initialize for copy
  set_huge( &remainder, 1 );  // initialize for copy
  set_huge( &y, 1 );

  set_huge( &a_temp, 1 );

  set_huge( &y2, 0 );
  set_huge( &y1, 1 );

  copy_huge( &i, a );
  copy_huge( &j, z );
  if ( z->sign )
  {
    divide( &j, a, NULL );
    // force positive remainder always
    j.sign = 0;
    subtract( &j, a );
  }

  while ( !( ( j.size == 1 ) && ( !j.rep[ 0 ] ) ) )
  {
    copy_huge( &remainder, &i );
```

```
    copy_huge( &i, &j );
    divide( &remainder, &j, &quotient );

    multiply( &quotient, &y1 ); // quotient = y1 * quotient
    copy_huge( &y, &y2 );
    subtract( &y, &quotient );   // y = y2 - ( y1 * quotient )

    copy_huge( &j, &remainder );
    copy_huge( &y2, &y1 );
    copy_huge( &y1, &y );
  }

  copy_huge( z, &y2 );
  copy_huge( &a_temp, a );
  divide( z, &a_temp, NULL );   // inv_z = y2 % a

  if ( z->sign )
  {
    z->sign = 0;
    subtract( z, &a_temp );
    if ( z->sign )
    {
      z->sign = 0;
    }
  }
}
```

Fundamentally, this works the same as the native int algorithm presented in Listing 3-28; I've added the equivalent operations as comments so that you can compare the two. The only difference is that I moved the assignment of i to j up to the top because the subsequent divide overwrites j. This doesn't affect functionality because i isn't used again in the body of the loop. The only reason for coding it this way is to cut down on the number of temporary huges that need to be allocated and freed.

Finally, notice the last section where inv_z is computed:

```
divide( inv_z, &a_temp, NULL );   // inv_z = y2 % a

if ( inv_z->sign )
{
  inv_z->sign = 0;
  subtract( inv_z, &a_temp );
}
```

The default divide operation returns the negative modulus. You need the positive one (if it's negative), which you can recover by swapping the signs and subtracting a one more time. The divide call inside the loop, however, must preserve negative moduli or the routine doesn't work correctly.

## Making ECC Work with Whole Integers: Elliptic-Curve Cryptography over F$_p$

Now that modular inversions have been defined, you can return to the subject of ECC. ECC over a *prime finite field* (denoted F$_p$) is just like "regular" ECC, but everything is performed modulo a prime number $p$. The point-addition and point-doubling algorithms become:

$$x_3 = (\lambda - x_1 - x_2)\%p$$
$$y_3 = (\lambda(x_1 - x_3) - y_1)\%p$$
$$\lambda = (y_2 - y_1) * (x_2 - x_1)^{-1}\%p$$

and

$$x_3 = (\lambda^2 - 2x_1)\%p$$
$$y_3 = \lambda(x_1 - x_3) - y_1)\%p$$
$$\lambda = (3x_1^2 + a) * (2y_1)^{-1}\%p$$

Point multiplication (by a scalar) is still defined in terms of "double-and-add."

There's just one more definitional issue must be addressed here. Recall that the general form of double-and-add is the following:

```
sum = 0
double = multiplicand
while ( bits in multilpier )
{
  if ( bit set in multiplier )
  {
    sum += double;
  }
  double *= 2;
}
```

You have `sum += double` and `double *= 2` defined for ECC points, but what about `sum = 0`? You need a "point" which is zero. You can't just use the point (0, 0). Unless $b = 0$ it's not *on* the curve, and if b = 0, (0, 0) is just another point.

ECC sort of sidesteps this by defining a non-existent *point at infinity*, which you just have to keep track of. A point is either the point at infinity (for example, 0), or it's something else, in which case it has a legitimate $x$ and $y$ coordinate.

## Reimplementing Diffie-Hellman to Use ECC Primitives

So what does all of this *elliptic-curve* stuff have to do with public-key cryptography? Recall that RSA and *classic* Diffie-Hellman get their security and feasibility from the fact that exponentiation modulo a number is solvable. There's an O($n$) algorithm to raise a number to an $n$-bit power modulo a given prime, but there's no known feasible inverse operation. There's no (known) algorithm to compute a discrete logarithm in polynomial time. Well, for elliptic curves, there's an $O(n)$ algorithm to multiply a point by a scalar $n$, but no feasible inverse operation. You can't "divide" a point by a scalar and find the original point. This property of being able to perform an operation in one direction in a reasonable amount of time, but not invert it, makes it usable as a public-key cryptosystem.

Diffie-Hellman can be redefined in terms of elliptic-curve operations. The private key is a scalar, and the public key is that scalar, multiplied by another shared point G. The two entities, A and B, which want to perform a secure key exchange, each have a private scalar and a public point, plus another shared point and, of course, the $a$, $b$, and $p$ that define an elliptic-curve and its prime field. If A multiplies his private key by B's public-key and B multiplies his private key by A's public key, they both arrive at the same point Z because they started at the same shared point G. Z can't be computed by anybody else without access to one of the private keys, so Z can be used as a shared secret. Typically the x-coordinate of Z is used and the y-coordinate is discarded.

At this point, your head may be spinning. An example might help clarify things. To keep things semi-readable, just stick to integer arithmetic for now and use small (less than 32-bit) values as an example.

1. Start off with a few definitions as shown in Listing 3-37.

**Listing 3-37:** "ecc_int.h" structure definitions

```
typedef struct
{
  int x;
  int y;
}
point;

typedef struct
{
  int private_key;
  point public_key;
}
key_pair;

/**
 * Describe y^2 = (x^3 + ax + b) % p
 */
typedef struct
{
  int p;
  int a;
  int b;
  point G;   // base point
}
domain_parameters;
```

> **NOTE** If you look at other texts on elliptic curves, notice that they also define n the *order* of the curve and *h* the *cofactor* of the curve. *h* is used to speed things up in advanced ECC implementations and isn't discussed here. n is discussed in Chapter 4.

2. You also need a modular inversion routine. You examined one for the huge implementation earlier, but because you're just doing integer arithmetic here, you can use the simple ext_euclid routine from Listing 3-25. This is wrapped up in Listing 3-38.

**Listing 3-38:** "ecc_int.c" invert routine

```
/**
 * Extended Euclidean algorithm to perform a modular inversion
 * of x by y (e.g. (x/y) % p).
 */
static int invert( int x, int y, int p )
{
  int inverse = ext_euclid( y, p );
  return x * inverse;
}
```

3. Now, define an add_points operation (modulo a prime p), shown in Listing 3-39.

**Listing 3-39:** "ecc_int.c" add_points routine

```
static void add_points( point *p1, point *p2, int p )
{
  point p3;
  int lambda = invert( p2->y - p1->y, p2->x - p1->x, p );

  p3.x = ( ( lambda * lambda ) - p1->x - p2->x ) % p;
  p3.y = ( ( lambda * ( p1->x - p3.x ) ) - p1->y ) % p;

  p1->x = p3.x;
  p1->y = p3.y;
}
```

Compare this to the equations defining point addition, in the previous section. Notice that the result is returned in p1, just as with the huge routines.

4. You also need a double_point routine, shown in Listing 3-40.

**Listing 3-40:** "ecc_int.c" double_point routine

```
static void double_point( point *p1, int p, int a )
{
  point p3;
  int lambda = invert( 3 * ( p1->x * p1->x ) + a, 2 * p1->y, p );
```

```
    p3.x = ( ( lambda * lambda ) - ( 2 * p1->x ) ) % p;
    p3.y = ( ( lambda * ( p1->x - p3.x ) ) - p1->y ) % p;

    p1->x = p3.x;
    p1->y = p3.y;
}
```

5. Finally, you can implement multiplication in terms of double and add, shown in Listing 3-41.

**Listing 3-41:** "ecc_int.c" multiply_point routine

```
static void multiply_point( point *p1, int k, int a, int p )
{
  point dp;
  int mask;
  int paf = 1;

  dp.x = p1->x;
  dp.y = p1->y;

  for ( mask = 0x00000001; mask; mask <<= 1 )
  {
    if ( mask & k )
    {
      if ( paf )
      {
        paf = 0;
        p1->x = dp.x;
        p1->y = dp.y;
      }
      else
      {
        add_points( p1, &dp, p );
      }
    }
    double_point( &dp, p, a );
  }
}
```

**NOTE** Notice the `paf` flag that indicates that `p1` is the point at infinity (that is, the ECC equivalent of "zero"). It's not particularly pretty, but it works. Otherwise, this should look fairly familiar. The same routine has effectively been implemented twice now — once for large integer multiplication and once for large integer exponentiation.

6. To implement Diffie-Hellman, you need a set of domain parameters T and a private key each for A and B. You can't just make up random domain parameters; in this case, just hardcode them:

```
domain_parameters T;
key_pair A;
key_pair B;
point Z1, Z2;

T.p = 23;
T.a = 1;
T.b = 1;
T.G.x = 5;
T.G.y = 19;
```

7. Obviously, you want most of these numbers to be much larger — although the value 1 for *a* and *b* is fairly typical in real ECC. A and B each have private keys — random numbers which are again hardcoded here:

```
A.private_key = 4;
B.private_key = 2;
```

The public keys are not random. They're = `private_key * G`:

```
A.public_key.x = T.G.x;
A.public_key.y = T.G.y;
multiply_point( &A.public_key, A.private_key, T.a, T.p );
B.public_key.x = T.G.x;
B.public_key.y = T.G.y;
multiply_point( &B.public_key, B.private_key, T.a, T.p );
```

This is important for key agreement. At this point, A's public key is the point (13, 16) and B's public key is the point (17, 3). Of course, they would compute these individually, after having agreed on the domain parameters.

8. Finally, there's the matter of key agreement. A sends B his public key (13, 16) and B sends A his public key (17, 3), and each computes the final point z:

```
Z1.x = A.public_key.x;
Z1.y = A.public_key.y;
multiply_point( &Z1, B.private_key, T.a, T.p );

Z2.x = B.public_key.x;
Z2.y = B.public_key.y;
multiply_point( &Z2, A.private_key, T.a, T.p );
```

A and B have both computed ZZ = (5, −4). In this case, by convention, ZZ.x = 5 is the shared secret — although of course, they could have used ZZ.y = −4, as long as both sides agreed on this convention beforehand.

## Why Elliptic-Curve Cryptography?

As you can see, ECC is quite a bit more complex than "modulus" cryptography such as RSA or classic Diffie-Hellman. So, why bother with it? Speed. ECC can provide the same security with an 80-bit private key as RSA can provide with a

512-bit private key because every single bit (provably) contributes to the security of the cryptosystem. Remember that the public-key operations are $O(n)$, where $n$ is the number of bits in the private key. ECC is fast enough, and has a small enough operating footprint, that it can be used in smartcard implementations.

Although ECC is popular in the banking industry, it's only just now beginning to find its way into TLS. OpenSSL 1.0, although it includes elliptic-curve operations, doesn't support TLS 1.2, and therefore doesn't support online ECC. GnuTLS does support TLS 1.2 and ECC, but is disabled by default. I'm not aware of any commercial (or open source) website or browser that supports TLS 1.2 at the time of this writing. Still, you can expect to see ECC gain in popularity in the coming years simply because of its speed advantages over RSA and DH.

I revisit ECC again in Chapter 4 when I examine ECDSA, and it will be added to the TLS library in Chapter 9 which covers TLS 1.2.

# Authenticating Communications Using Digital Signatures

In Chapter 3, you examined public key cryptography in detail. Public key cryptography involves generating two mathematically related *keys*, one of which can be used to encrypt a value and the other of which can be used to decrypt a value previously encrypted with the other. One important point to note is that it technically doesn't matter which key you use to perform the encryption, as long as the other one is available to perform the decryption. The RSA algorithm defines a *public key* that is used to encrypt, and a *private key* that is used to decrypt. However, the algorithm works if you reverse the keys — if you encrypt something with the private key, it can be decrypted with — and *only* with — the public key.

At first glance, this doesn't sound very useful. The public key, after all, is public. It's freely shared with anybody and everybody. Therefore, if a value is encrypted with the private key, it can be decrypted by anybody and everybody as well. However, the nature of public/private keypairs is such that it's also impossible — or, to be technically precise, mathematically infeasible — for anybody except the holder of the private key to generate something that *can* be decrypted using the public key. After all, the encryptor must find a number $c$ such that $c^e \% n = m$ for some arbitrary $m$. By definition, $c = m^d$ satisfies this condition and it is believed to be computationally infeasible to find another such number $c$.

As a result, the private key can also be used to prove identity. The holder of the private key generates a message $m$, and sends it to the receiver (unencrypted). Then the holder of the private key encrypts $m$ using the private key $(d,n)$ and sends the resulting *c* to the receiver. The receiver uses the public key (*e,n*) to "decrypt" *c*. If the decrypted value is exactly equal to *m*, the message is verified. The receiver is confident that it was truly sent by somebody with access to the private key. Note that, in this scenario, anybody can read *m* — it is sent in cleartext. In this case, you're just proving identity. Of course, this sort of *digital signature* can be easily combined with encryption. The sender could encrypt the request, sign the encrypted value, and send that on for the receiver to verify. An eavesdropper could, of course, decrypt the signature, but all he would get is the encrypted string, which he can't decrypt without the key.

There's another benefit to this approach as well. If anything changed in transit — due to a transmission error or a malicious hacker — the decrypted value won't match the signature. This guarantees not only that the holder of the private key sent it, but that what was received is *exactly* what was sent.

There's one problem with this approach to digital signatures, though. You've essentially doubled, at least, the length of each message. And, as you recall from the previous chapter, public key cryptography is too slow for large blocks of information. In general, you use public key operations to encode a symmetric key for subsequent cryptography operations. Obviously, you can't do this for digital signatures; you're trying to prove that somebody with access to the private key generated the message. What you need is a shortened representation of the message that can be computed by both sides. Then the sender can encrypt that using the private key, and the receiver can compute the same shortened representation, decrypt it using the public key and verify that they're identical.

## Using Message Digests to Create Secure Document Surrogates

Such a shortened representation of a message is referred to as a *message digest*. The simplest form of a message digest is a *checksum*. Given a byte array of arbitrary length, add up the integer value of each byte (allowing the sum to overflow), and return the total, for example, Listing 4-1.

**Listing 4-1:** checksum

```
int checksum( char *msg )
{
  int sum = 0;
  int i;

  for ( i = 0; i < strlen( msg ); i++ )
  {
    sum += msg[ i ];
  }
```

```
      return sum;
}
```

Here, the message "abc" sums to 294 because, in ASCII, $a = 97$, $b = 98$ and $c = 99$; "abd" sums to 295. Because you just ignore overflow, you can compute a digest of any arbitrarily sized message.

The problem with this approach is that it can be easily reversed. Consider the following scenario: I want to send a message that says, "Please transfer $100 to account 123," to my bank. My bank wants to ensure that this message came from me, so I digitally sign it. First I compute the checksum of this message: 2,970. I then use my private key to compute the signature. Using the mini-key pair $e = 79$, $d = 1019$, $n = 3337$ from Chapter 3, this encodes (without any padding) to $2970^{1019} \% 3337 = 2552$. The bank receives the message, computes the same checksum, decodes 2552 using the public key and computes $2552^{79} \% 3337 = 2970$. Because the computed checksum matches the encrypted checksum, the message can be accepted as authentic because nobody else can solve $x^{79} \% 3337 = 2970$.

However, there's a problem with this simple checksum digest routine. Although an attacker who might want to submit, "Please transfer $1,000,000 to account 3789," which sums to 3171, is not able to solve $x^{79} \% 3337 = 3171$, he can instead look for ways to change the message itself so that it sums to 2970. Remember that the signature itself is public, transmitted over a clear channel. If the attacker can do this, he can reuse my original signature of 2552. As it turns out, it's not hard to work backward from 2970 to engineer a *collision* by changing the message to "Transfer $1,000,000 to account 3789 now!" (Notice that I dropped the "please" from the beginning and inserted "now!") A bank employee might consider this rude, but the signature matches. You may have to play tricks with null terminators and backspace characters to get the messages to collide this way, but for $1,000,000, an attacker would consider it well worth the effort. Note that this would have been a vulnerability even if you had encoded the whole message rather than the output of the digest algorithm.

Therefore, for cryptographic security, you need a more secure message digest algorithm. Although it may seem that cryptography would be the hardest category of secure algorithms to get right, message digests actually are. The history of secure message digest algorithms is littered with proposals that were later found to be insecure — that is, not properly collision resistant.

## Implementing the MD5 Digest Algorithm

One of the earliest secure message digest algorithms in the literature is MD2 (MD1 appears never to have been released). It was followed by MD4 (rather than MD3), which was finally followed by MD5 and is the last of the MD series of message digest algorithms. All were created by Dr. Ron Rivest, who was also one-third of the RSA team.

## Understanding MD5

The goal of MD5, specified in RFC 1321, or any secure hashing algorithm, is to reduce an arbitrarily sized input into an $n$-bit *hash* in such a way that it is very unlikely that two messages, regardless of length or content, produce identical hashes — that is, collide — and that it is impossible to specifically reverse engineer such a collision. For MD5, $n = 128$ bits. This means that there are $2^{128}$ possible MD5 hashes. Although the input space is vastly larger than this, $2^{128}$ makes it highly unlikely that two messages will share the same MD5 hash. More importantly, it should be impossible, assuming that MD5 hashes are evenly, randomly distributed, for an attacker to compute a useful message that collides with another by way of brute force.

MD5 operates on 512-bit (64-byte) blocks of input. Each block is reduced to a 128-bit (16-byte) hash. Obviously, with such a 4:1 ratio of input blocks to output blocks, there will be at least a one in four chance of a collision. The challenge that MD5's designer faced is making it difficult or impossible to work backward to find one.

If the message to be hashed is greater than 512 bits, each 512-bit block is hashed independently and the hashes are added together, being allowed to overflow, and the result is the final sum. This obviously creates more potential for collisions.

Unlike cryptographic algorithms, though, message digests do not have to be reversible — in fact, this irreversibility is the whole point. Therefore, algorithm designers do not have to be nearly as cautious with the number and type of operations they apply to the input. The more operations, in fact, the better; this is because operations make it more difficult for an attacker to work backward from a hash to a message. MD5 applies 64 transformations to each input block. It first splits the input into 16 32-bit chunks, and the current hash into four 32-bit chunks referred to tersely as A, B, C, and D in the specification. Most of the operations are done on A, B, C, and D, which are subsequently added to the input. The 64 operations themselves consist of 16 repetitions of the four *bit flipping* functions F, G, H, and I as shown in Listing 4-2.

**Listing 4-2:** "md5.c" bit manipulation routines

```
unsigned int F( unsigned int x, unsigned int y, unsigned int z )
{
    return ( x & y ) | ( ~x & z );
}


unsigned int G( unsigned int x, unsigned int y, unsigned int z )
{
    return ( x & z ) | ( y & ~z );
}
```

```
unsigned int H( unsigned int x, unsigned int y, unsigned int z )
{
  return ( x ^ y ^ z );
}

unsigned int I( unsigned int x, unsigned int y, unsigned int z )
{
  return y ^ ( x | ~z );
}
```

The purpose of these functions is simply to shuffle bits in an unpredictable way; don't look for any deep meaning here.

Notice that this is implemented using unsigned integers. As it turns out, MD5, unlike any of the other cryptographic algorithms in this book, operates on little-endian numbers, which makes implementation a tad easier on an Intel-based machine — although MD5 has an odd concept of "little endian" in places.

The function F is invoked 16 times — once for each input block — and then G is invoked 16 times, and then H, and then I. So, what are the inputs to F, G, H, and I? They're actually permutations of A, B, C, and D — remember that the hash was referred to as A, B, C, and D. The results of F, G, H, and I are added to A, B, C, and D along with each of the input blocks, as well as a set of constants, shifted, and added again. In all cases, adds are performed modulo 32 — that is, they're allowed to silently overflow in a 32-bit register. After all 64 operations, the final values of A, B, C, and D are concatenated together to become the hash of a 512-bit input block.

More specifically, each of the 64 transformations on A, B, C, and D involve applying one of the four functions F, G, H, or I to some permutation of A, B, C, or D, adding it to the other, adding the value of input block (i % 4), adding the value of 4294967296 * abs(sin(i)), rotating by a per-round amount, and adding the whole mess to yet one more of the A, B, C, or D hash blocks.

### A Secure Hashing Example

If this is all making your head spin, it's supposed to. Secure hashing algorithms are necessarily complex. In general, they derive their security from their complexity:

1. Define a ROUND macro that will be expanded 64 times, as shown in Listing 4-3.

**Listing 4-3:** "md5.c" ROUND macro

```
#define BASE_T 4294967296.0

#define ROUND( F, a, b, c, d, k, s, i ) \
  a = ( a + F( b, c, d ) + x[ k ] + \
```

*(Continued)*

```
        ( unsigned int ) ( BASE_T * fabs( sin( ( double ) i ) ) ) ); \
  a = ( a << s ) | ( a >> ( 32 - s ) ); \
  a += b;
```

This macro takes as input the function to be performed, a, b, c and d; a value k which is an offset into the input; a value s which is an amount to rotate; and a value i which is the operation number. Notice that i is used to compute the value of 4294967296 * abs(sin(i)) on each invocation. Technically speaking, these values ought to be precomputed because they'll never change.

2. Using this macro, the MD5 block operation function is straightforward, if a bit tedious, to code, as in Listing 4-4:

**Listing 4-4:** "md5.c" md5_block_operate function

```c
// Size of MD5 hash in ints (128 bits)
#define MD5_RESULT_SIZE 4

void md5_block_operate( const unsigned char *input,
                unsigned int hash[ MD5_RESULT_SIZE ] )
{
  unsigned int a, b, c, d;
  int j;
  unsigned int x[ 16 ];

  a = hash[ 0 ];
  b = hash[ 1 ];
  c = hash[ 2 ];
  d = hash[ 3 ];

  for ( j = 0; j < 16; j++ )
  {
     x[ j ] = input[ ( j * 4 ) + 3 ] << 24 |
                    input[ ( j * 4 ) + 2 ] << 16 |
                    input[ ( j * 4 ) + 1 ] << 8 |
                    input[ ( j * 4 ) ];
  }

  // Round 1
  ROUND( F, a, b, c, d, 0, 7, 1 );
  ROUND( F, d, a, b, c, 1, 12, 2 );
  ROUND( F, c, d, a, b, 2, 17, 3 );
  ROUND( F, b, c, d, a, 3, 22, 4 );
  ROUND( F, a, b, c, d, 4, 7, 5 );
  ROUND( F, d, a, b, c, 5, 12, 6 );
  ROUND( F, c, d, a, b, 6, 17, 7 );
  ROUND( F, b, c, d, a, 7, 22, 8 );
  ROUND( F, a, b, c, d, 8, 7, 9 );
  ROUND( F, d, a, b, c, 9, 12, 10 );
```

```
ROUND( F, c, d, a, b, 10, 17, 11 );
ROUND( F, b, c, d, a, 11, 22, 12 );
ROUND( F, a, b, c, d, 12, 7, 13 );
ROUND( F, d, a, b, c, 13, 12, 14 );
ROUND( F, c, d, a, b, 14, 17, 15 );
ROUND( F, b, c, d, a, 15, 22, 16 );

// Round 2
ROUND( G, a, b, c, d, 1, 5, 17 );
ROUND( G, d, a, b, c, 6, 9, 18 );
ROUND( G, c, d, a, b, 11, 14, 19 );
ROUND( G, b, c, d, a, 0, 20, 20 );
ROUND( G, a, b, c, d, 5, 5, 21 );
ROUND( G, d, a, b, c, 10, 9, 22 );
ROUND( G, c, d, a, b, 15, 14, 23 );
ROUND( G, b, c, d, a, 4, 20, 24 );
ROUND( G, a, b, c, d, 9, 5, 25 );
ROUND( G, d, a, b, c, 14, 9, 26 );
ROUND( G, c, d, a, b, 3, 14, 27 );
ROUND( G, b, c, d, a, 8, 20, 28 );
ROUND( G, a, b, c, d, 13, 5, 29 );
ROUND( G, d, a, b, c, 2, 9, 30 );
ROUND( G, c, d, a, b, 7, 14, 31 );
ROUND( G, b, c, d, a, 12, 20, 32 );

// Round 3
ROUND( H, a, b, c, d, 5, 4, 33 );
ROUND( H, d, a, b, c, 8, 11, 34 );
ROUND( H, c, d, a, b, 11, 16, 35 );
ROUND( H, b, c, d, a, 14, 23, 36 );
ROUND( H, a, b, c, d, 1, 4, 37 );
ROUND( H, d, a, b, c, 4, 11, 38 );
ROUND( H, c, d, a, b, 7, 16, 39 );
ROUND( H, b, c, d, a, 10, 23, 40 );
ROUND( H, a, b, c, d, 13, 4, 41 );
ROUND( H, d, a, b, c, 0, 11, 42 );
ROUND( H, c, d, a, b, 3, 16, 43 );
ROUND( H, b, c, d, a, 6, 23, 44 );
ROUND( H, a, b, c, d, 9, 4, 45 );
ROUND( H, d, a, b, c, 12, 11, 46 );
ROUND( H, c, d, a, b, 15, 16, 47 );
ROUND( H, b, c, d, a, 2, 23, 48 );

// Round 4
ROUND( I, a, b, c, d, 0, 6, 49 );
ROUND( I, d, a, b, c, 7, 10, 50 );
ROUND( I, c, d, a, b, 14, 15, 51 );
ROUND( I, b, c, d, a, 5, 21, 52 );
ROUND( I, a, b, c, d, 12, 6, 53 );
ROUND( I, d, a, b, c, 3, 10, 54 );
```

*(Continued)*

```
ROUND( I, c, d, a, b, 10, 15, 55 );
ROUND( I, b, c, d, a, 1, 21, 56 );
ROUND( I, a, b, c, d, 8, 6, 57 );
ROUND( I, d, a, b, c, 15, 10, 58 );
ROUND( I, c, d, a, b, 6, 15, 59 );
ROUND( I, b, c, d, a, 13, 21, 60 );
ROUND( I, a, b, c, d, 4, 6, 61 );
ROUND( I, d, a, b, c, 11, 10, 62 );
ROUND( I, c, d, a, b, 2, 15, 63 );
ROUND( I, b, c, d, a, 9, 21, 64 );

hash[ 0 ] += a;
hash[ 1 ] += b;
hash[ 2 ] += c;
hash[ 3 ] += d;
}
```

3. Create a work area to hold the a, b, c, and d values from the current hash. You see in just a minute how this is initialized — this is important. Then, split the input, which is required to be exactly 512 bits, into 16 integers. Notice that you convert to integers using little-endian conventions, rather than the big-endian conventions you've been following thus far:

```
for ( j = 0; j < 16; j++ )
{
    x[ j ] = input[ ( j * 4 ) + 3 ] << 24 |
             input[ ( j * 4 ) + 2 ] << 16 |
             input[ ( j * 4 ) + 1 ] << 8 |
             input[ ( j * 4 ) ];

}
```

Technically speaking, because you know you're compiling to a 32-bit little-endian architecture, you could actually memcpy into x — or even forgo it completely if you are willing to be fast and loose with your typecasting. The rest of the function consists of 64 expansions of the ROUND macro. You can probably see how, if you just index hash directly, rather than using the work area variables a, b, c, and d, you can change this from a macro expansion to a loop. In fact, if you want to get a bit tricky, you could follow the pattern in the k's and s's and code the whole thing in a terse loop. You can replace md5_block_operate with the shorter, but more divergent — in terms of the specification — function shown in Listing 4-5.

**Listing 4-5:** Alternate md5_block_operate implementation

```
static int s[ 4 ][ 4 ] = {
  { 7, 12, 17, 22 },
  { 5, 9, 14, 20 },
  { 4, 11, 16, 23 },
  { 6, 10, 15, 21 }
};
```

```
void md5_block_operate( const unsigned char *input,
                unsigned int hash[ MD5_RESULT_SIZE ] )
{
  int a, b, c, d, x_i, s_i;
  int i, j;
  unsigned int x[ 16 ];
  unsigned int tmp_hash[ MD5_RESULT_SIZE ];

  memcpy( tmp_hash, hash, MD5_RESULT_SIZE * sizeof( unsigned int ) );

  for ( j = 0; j < 16; j++ )
  {
    x[ j ] = input[ ( j * 4 ) + 3 ] << 24 |
        input[ ( j * 4 ) + 2 ] << 16 |
        input[ ( j * 4 ) + 1 ] << 8 |
        input[ ( j * 4 ) ];
  }

  for ( i = 0; i < 64; i++ )
  {
    a = 3 - ( ( i + 3 ) % 4 );
    b = 3 - ( ( i + 2 ) % 4 );
    c = 3 - ( ( i + 1 ) % 4 );
    d = 3 - ( i % 4 );

    if ( i < 16 )
    {
      tmp_hash[ a ] += F( tmp_hash[ b ], tmp_hash[ c ], tmp_hash[ d ] );
      x_i = i;
    }
    else if ( i < 32 )
    {
      tmp_hash[ a ] += G( tmp_hash[ b ], tmp_hash[ c ], tmp_hash[ d ] );
      x_i = ( 1 + ( ( i - 16 ) * 5 ) ) % 16;
    }
    else if ( i < 48 )
    {
      tmp_hash[ a ] += H( tmp_hash[ b ], tmp_hash[ c ], tmp_hash[ d ] );
      x_i = ( 5 + ( ( i - 32 ) * 3 ) ) % 16;
    }
    else
    {
      tmp_hash[ a ] += I( tmp_hash[ b ], tmp_hash[ c ], tmp_hash[ d ] );
      x_i = ( ( i - 48 ) * 7 ) % 16;
    }
    s_i = s[ i / 16 ][ i % 4 ];
    tmp_hash[ a ] += x[ x_i ] + ( unsigned int )
    ( BASE_T * fabs( sin( ( double ) i + 1 ) ) );
    tmp_hash[ a ] = ( tmp_hash[ a ] << s_i ) | ( tmp_hash[ a ] >> ( 32 - s_i ) );
```

*(Continued)*

```
      tmp_hash[ a ] += tmp_hash[ b ];
  }

  hash[ 0 ] += tmp_hash[ 0 ];
  hash[ 1 ] += tmp_hash[ 1 ];
  hash[ 2 ] += tmp_hash[ 2 ];
  hash[ 3 ] += tmp_hash[ 3 ];
}
```

The longer implementation in Listing 4-5 follows the specification more closely; the shorter implementation is a bit difficult to read, but it yields the same results.

**NOTE** Actually, the specification includes C code! The implementation there is a bit different than this one, though. The reason is covered later.

This produces a 128-bit hash on a 512-bit block. If the input is greater than 512 bits, just call the function again, this time passing the output of the previous call as the initializer. If this is the first call, initialize the hash code to the cryptographically meaningless initializer in Listing 4-6.

**Listing 4-6:** "md5.c" md5 initial hash

```
unsigned int md5_initial_hash[ ] = {
  0x67452301,
  0xefcdab89,
  0x98badcfe,
  0x10325476
};
```

Notice that this initializer doesn't have any quasi-mystical cryptographic security properties; it's just the byte sequence 0123456789abcdef (in little-endian form), followed by the same thing backward. It doesn't much matter what you initialize the hash to — although 0's would be a bad choice — as long as every implementation agrees on the starting value.

### Securely Hashing Multiple Blocks of Data

If you need to encrypt less than 512 bits, or a bit string that's not an even multiple of 512 bits, you pad the last block. However, you can't just pad with 0's or just with 1's. Remember, 512 0's is a legitimate input to MD5. So is one 0. You need some way to ensure that 512 0's hashes to a different value than one 0. Therefore, MD5 requires that the last eight bytes of the input be set to the length, in bits (remember that you may want to hash a value that's not an even multiple of eight bits) of the input preceding it. This means that MD5 is essentially undefined for lengths greater than $2^{64}$ bits, and that if the input happens to be between 448 (512 – 64) and 512 bits, you need to add an extra 512-bit block of padding just to store the length. A sole "1" bit follows the last bit of input, followed by enough 0's to pad up to 448 bits, followed by the length of the message itself in bits.

> **NOTE** According to the specification, if the length is greater than $2^{64}$ bits, you can throw away the high-order bits of the length. This won't come up with any of the values that are hashed in this book.

Now, the MD5 specification has a strange formulation for the length. Rather than just being a little-endian 64-bit integer, it's instead stored as "low-order 32 bits" and "high-order 32 bits."

The code to process an arbitrarily sized input into an MD5 hash, including padding and iteration over multiple blocks, is shown in Listing 4-7.

**Listing 4-7:** "md5.c" md5 hash algorithm

```
#define MD5_BLOCK_SIZE 64
#define MD5_INPUT_BLOCK_SIZE 56
#define MD5_RESULT_SIZE 4

int md5_hash( const unsigned char *input,
      int len,
      unsigned int hash[ MD5_RESULT_SIZE ] )
{
  unsigned char padded_block[ MD5_BLOCK_SIZE ];
  int length_in_bits = len * 8;

  // XXX should verify that len < 2^64, but since len is only 32 bits, this won't
  // be a problem.

  hash[ 0 ] = md5_initial_hash[ 0 ];
  hash[ 1 ] = md5_initial_hash[ 1 ];
  hash[ 2 ] = md5_initial_hash[ 2 ];
  hash[ 3 ] = md5_initial_hash[ 3 ];

  while ( len >= MD5_INPUT_BLOCK_SIZE )
  {
    // Special handling for blocks between 56 and 64 bytes
    // (not enough room for the 8 bytes of length, but also
    // not enough to fill up a block)
    if ( len < MD5_BLOCK_SIZE )
    {
      memset( padded_block, 0, sizeof( padded_block ) );
      memcpy( padded_block, input, len );
      padded_block[ len ] = 0x80;
      md5_block_operate( padded_block, hash );

      input += len;
      len = -1;
```

*(Continued)*

```
    }
    else
    {
       md5_block_operate( input, hash );

       input += MD5_BLOCK_SIZE;
       len -= MD5_BLOCK_SIZE;
    }
  }

  // There's always at least one padded block at the end, which includes
  // the length of the message
  memset( padded_block, 0, sizeof( padded_block ) );
  if ( len >= 0 )
  {
    memcpy( padded_block, input, len );
    padded_block[ len ] = 0x80;
  }

  // Only append the length for the very last block
  // Technically, this allows for 64 bits of length, but since we can only
  // process 32 bits worth, we leave the upper four bytes empty
  // This is sort of a bizarre concept of "little endian"...
  padded_block[ MD5_BLOCK_SIZE - 5 ] = ( length_in_bits & 0xFF000000 ) >> 24;
  padded_block[ MD5_BLOCK_SIZE - 6 ] = ( length_in_bits & 0x00FF0000 ) >> 16;
  padded_block[ MD5_BLOCK_SIZE - 7 ] = ( length_in_bits & 0x0000FF00 ) >> 8;
  padded_block[ MD5_BLOCK_SIZE - 8 ] = ( length_in_bits & 0x000000FF );

  md5_block_operate( padded_block, hash );

  return 0;
}
```

**NOTE** Notice that this code requires that the entire input to be hashed be available when this function is called. As it turns out, you can't assume that this is always be the case. I address this shortcoming later.

Now, follow these steps:

1.  Initialize the hash response to the standard starting value defined earlier.

2.  Iterate through 512-bit blocks, calling md5_block_operate until you come to the last, or next-to-last block depending on whether the last block aligns on less than 448 bits or not.

3.  If the last block is between 448 and 512 bits (56 and 64 bytes), pad by adding a "1" bit, which is always hex 0x80 because this implementation never accepts non-byte-aligned input, and fill the rest of the buffer with 0's.

4.  The length is appended to the next block. Set len = −1 as a reminder for the next section not to append another "1" bit.

```
// Special handling for blocks between 56 and 64 bytes
// (not enough room for the 8 bytes of length, but also
// not enough to fill up a block)
if ( len < MD5_BLOCK_SIZE )
{
  memset( padded_block, 0, sizeof( padded_block ) );
  memcpy( padded_block, input, len );
  padded_block[ len ] = 0x80;
  md5_block_operate( padded_block, hash );

  input += len;
  len = -1;
}
```

5. Append the length, the padding bits and a trailing "1" bit — if it hasn't already been added — and operate on the final block. There will be $448 - l$. These are $l$ bits of padding, where $l$ is the length of the input in bits. Note that this always happens, even if the input is 1 bit long.

```
// There's always at least one padded block at the end, which includes
// the length of the message
memset( padded_block, 0, sizeof( padded_block ) );
if ( len >= 0 )
{
  memcpy( padded_block, input, len );
  padded_block[ len ] = 0x80;
}

// Only append the length for the very last block
// Technically, this allows for 64 bits of length, but since we can only
// process 32 bits worth, we leave the upper four bytes empty
// This is sort of a odd concept of "little endian"...
padded_block[MD5_BLOCK_SIZE - 5] = (length_in_bits & 0xFF000000)>>24;
padded_block[MD5_BLOCK_SIZE - 6] = (length_in_bits & 0x00FF0000)>>16;
padded_block[MD5_BLOCK_SIZE - 7] = (length_in_bits & 0x0000FF00)>>8;
padded_block[MD5_BLOCK_SIZE - 8] = (length_in_bits & 0x000000FF);

md5_block_operate( padded_block, hash );
```

6. Because input greater than $2^{32}$ isn't allowed in this implementation, leave the last four bytes empty (0) in all cases.

And you now have a 128-bit output that is essentially unique to the input.

## MD5 Vulnerabilities

If you gathered 366 people in a room, there's a 100 percent chance that two of them will share the same birthday. There are only 365 birthdays to go around, so with 366 people at least two must have the same birthday (367 if you want to count Feb. 29 and Mar. 1 as two distinct birthdays). This is clear. Here's a question for you, though: How many people would you have to gather in a room to have a 50 percent chance that two of them share the same birthday? You might hazard a guess that it would take about 183 — half the people, half the chance.

As it turns out, the answer is stunningly lower. If 23 people are gathered together in a room, there's a 50 percent chance that two of them share the same birthday. To resolve this seeming paradox, consider this: If there are $n$ people in a room, there are $365^n$ possible birthdays. The first person can have any of 365 birthdays; the second can have any of 365 birthdays; and so on. However, there are only 365*364 ways that two people can have unique birthdays. The first person has "used up" one of the available birthdays. Three people can only have 365*364*363 unique birthday combinations. In general, $n$ people can have $\frac{365!}{(365-n)!}$ *unique* combinations of birthdays. So, there are $365^n - \frac{365!}{(365-n)!}$ ways that at least two people share a birthday — that is, that the birthday combinations are not unique. The math is complex, but clear: With $n$ possibilities, you need $n + 1$ instances to guarantee a repeat, but you need $\approx 1.1772\sqrt{n}$ to have a 50% chance of a repeat. This surprising result is often referred to as the *birthday paradox*.

This doesn't bode well for MD5. MD5 produces 128 bits for each input. $2^{128}$ is a mind-bogglingly large number. In decimal, it works out to approximately 340 million trillion trillion. However, $1.1772\sqrt{2^{128}} \approx 2.2 \times 10^{19}$. That's still a lot, but quite a few less than $2^{128}$. Remember that the purpose of using MD5 rather than a simple checksum digest was that it ought to be impossible for an attacker to engineer a collision. If I deliberately go looking for a collision with a published hash, I have to compute for a long time. However, if I go looking for two documents that share a hash, I need to look for a much shorter time, albeit still for a long time. And, as you saw with DES, this brute-force *birthday attack* is infinitely parallelizable; the more computers I can add to the attack, the faster I can get an answer.

This vulnerability to a birthday attack is a problem that all digest algorithms have; the only solution is to make the output longer and longer until a birthday attack is infeasible in terms of computing power. As you saw with symmetric cryptography, this is a never-ending arms race as computers get faster and faster and protocol designers struggle to keep up. However, MD5 is even worse off than this. Researchers have found cracks in the protocol's fundamental design.

In 2005, security researchers Xiaoyan Wang and Hongbo Yu presented their paper "How to break MD5 and other hash functions" (`http://merlot.usc.edu/csac-s06/papers/Wang05a.pdf`), which detailed an exploit capable of producing targeted MD5 collisions in 15 minutes to an hour using commodity hardware. This is not a theoretical exploit; Magnus Daum and Stefaun Lucks illustrate an actual real-world MD-5 collision in their paper `http://th.informatik.uni-mannheim.de/people/lucks/HashCollisions/`.

In spite of this, MD5 is fairly popular; TLS mandates its use! Fortunately for the TLS-using public, it does so in a reasonably secure way — or, at least, a not terribly insecure way — so that the TLS protocol itself is not weakened by the inclusion of MD5.

# Increasing Collision Resistance with the SHA-1 Digest Algorithm

*Secure Hash Algorithm* (*SHA-1*) is similar to MD5. The only principal difference is in the block operation itself. The other two superficial differences are that SHA-1 produces a 160-bit (20-byte) hash rather than a 128-bit (16-byte) hash, and SHA-1 deals with big-endian rather than little-endian numbers. Like MD5, SHA-1 operates on 512-bit blocks, and the final output is the sum (modulo 32) of the results of all of the blocks. The operation itself is slightly simpler; you start by breaking the 512-bit input into 16 4-byte values x. You then compute 80 four-byte w values from the original input where the following is rotated left once:
`W[0<t<16]` = `x[t]`, and `W[17<7<80]` = `W[ t - 3 ] xor W[ t - 8 ] xor W[ t - 14 ] xor W[ t - 16 ]`

This w array serves the same purpose as the `4294967296 * abs(sin(i))` computation in MD5, but is a bit easier to compute and is also based on the input.

After that, the hash is split up into five four-byte values a, b, c, d, and e, which are operated on in a series of 80 rounds, similar to the operation in MD5 — although in this case, somewhat easier to implement in a loop. At each stage, a rotation, an addition of another hash integer, an addition of an indexed constant, an addition of the w array, and an addition of a function whose operation depends on the round number is applied to the active hash value, and then the hash values are cycled so that a new one becomes the active one.

## Understanding SHA-1 Block Computation

If you understood the MD5 computation in Listing 4-4, you should have no trouble making sense of the SHA-1 block computation in Listing 4-8.

**Listing 4-8:** "sha.c" bit manipulation, initialization and block operation

```
static const int k[] = {
  0x5a827999, // 0 <= t <= 19
  0x6ed9eba1, // 20 <= t <= 39
  0x8f1bbcdc, // 40 <= t <= 59
  0xca62c1d6 // 60 <= t <= 79
};


// ch is functions 0 - 19
unsigned int ch( unsigned int x, unsigned int y, unsigned int z )
```

*(Continued)*

```
{
  return ( x & y ) ^ ( ~x & z );
}

// parity is functions 20 - 39 & 60 - 79
unsigned int parity( unsigned int x, unsigned int y, unsigned int z )
{
  return x ^ y ^ z;
}

// maj is functions 40 - 59
unsigned int maj( unsigned int x, unsigned int y, unsigned int z )
{
  return ( x & y ) ^ ( x & z ) ^ ( y & z );
}

#define SHA1_RESULT_SIZE 5

void sha1_block_operate( const unsigned char *block,
unsigned int hash[ SHA1_RESULT_SIZE ] )
{
  unsigned int W[ 80 ];
  unsigned int t = 0;
  unsigned int a, b, c, d, e, T;

  // First 16 blocks of W are the original 16 blocks of the input
  for ( t = 0; t < 80; t++ )
  {
    if ( t < 16 )
    {
      W[ t ] = ( block[ ( t * 4 ) ] << 24 ) |
               ( block[ ( t * 4 ) + 1 ] << 16 ) |
               ( block[ ( t * 4 ) + 2 ] << 8 ) |
               ( block[ ( t * 4 ) + 3 ] );
    }
    else
    {
      W[ t ] = W[ t - 3 ] ^
               W[ t - 8 ] ^
               W[ t - 14 ] ^
               W[ t - 16 ];
      // Rotate left operation, simulated in C
      W[ t ] = ( W[ t ] << 1 ) | ( ( W[ t ] & 0x80000000 ) >> 31 );
    }
  }

  a = hash[ 0 ];
  b = hash[ 1 ];
  c = hash[ 2 ];
  d = hash[ 3 ];
  e = hash[ 4 ];
```

```
for ( t = 0; t < 80; t++ )
{
  T = ( ( a << 5 ) | ( a >> 27 ) ) + e + k[ ( t / 20 ) ] + W[ t ];

  if ( t <= 19 )
  {
    T += ch( b, c, d );
  }
  else if ( t <= 39 )
  {
    T += parity( b, c, d );
  }
  else if ( t <= 59 )
  {
    T += maj( b, c, d );
  }
  else
  {
    T += parity( b, c, d );
  }

  e = d;
  d = c;
  c = ( ( b << 30 ) | ( b >> 2 ) );
  b = a;
  a = T;
}

hash[ 0 ] += a;
hash[ 1 ] += b;
hash[ 2 ] += c;
hash[ 3 ] += d;
hash[ 4 ] += e;
}
```

Regarding Listing 4-8:

1. The constants k are defined — one for each set of 20 rounds.

2. The functions ch, maj, and parity are defined: ch for rounds 0–19, maj for rounds 40–59, and parity for the remaining rounds. Like MD5's F, G, H, and I, these four functions just shuffle the bits of their input randomly.

3. The block operation function computes the w array. Notice that you're using unsigned ints here, rather than four-byte blocks, so you have to be careful to account for endian-ness as usual. The benefit is that you only have to keep track of this transformation once, at the beginning of the computation, and from that point you can use native operations on a 32-bit architecture.

4. After w has been computed, the individual five hash integers are copied into a, b, c, d, and e for computation; at each round, a new T value is computed according to

```
T = ( ( a << 5 ) | ( a >> 27 ) ) + e + k[ ( t / 20 ) ] + W[ t ] +
ch/parity/maj(b,c,d);
```

5. a, b, c, d, and e are then rotated through each other, just as in MD5, and, for good measure, c is rotated left 30 positions as well. Although the mechanics are slightly different, this is very similar to what was done with MD5.

You don't really have to try to make sense of the mechanics of this. It's supposed to be impossible to do so. As long as the details are correct, you can safely think of the block operation function as a true black-box function.

### Understanding the SHA-1 Input Processing Function

The input processing function of SHA-1 is almost identical to that of MD5. The length is appended, in bits, at the very end of the last block, each block is 512 bits, the hash must be initialized to a standard value before input begins, and the hash computations of each block are added to one another, modulo 32, to produce the final result. The function in Listing 4-9, which computes SHA-1 hashes of a given input block, differs from md5_hash in only a few places, which are highlighted in bold .

**Listing 4-9:** "sha.c" SHA-1 hash algorithm

```
#define SHA1_INPUT_BLOCK_SIZE 56
#define SHA1_BLOCK_SIZE 64

unsigned int sha1_initial_hash[ ] = {
  0x67452301,
  0xefcdab89,
  0x98badcfe,
  0x10325476,
  0xc3d2e1f0
};

int sha1_hash( unsigned char *input, int len,
        unsigned int hash[ SHA1_RESULT_SIZE ] )
{
  unsigned char padded_block[ SHA1_BLOCK_SIZE ];
  int length_in_bits = len * 8;


  hash[ 0 ] = sha1_initial_hash[ 0 ];
  hash[ 1 ] = sha1_initial_hash[ 1 ];
```

```
hash[ 2 ] = sha1_initial_hash[ 2 ];
hash[ 3 ] = sha1_initial_hash[ 3 ];
hash[ 4 ] = sha1_initial_hash[ 4 ];

while ( len >= SHA1_INPUT_BLOCK_SIZE )
{
  if ( len < SHA1_BLOCK_SIZE )
  {
    memset( padded_block, 0, sizeof( padded_block ) );
    memcpy( padded_block, input, len );
    padded_block[ len ] = 0x80;
    sha1_block_operate( padded_block, hash );

    input += len;
    len = -1;
  }
  else
  {
    sha1_block_operate( input, hash );

    input += SHA1_BLOCK_SIZE;
    len -= SHA1_BLOCK_SIZE;
  }
}

memset( padded_block, 0, sizeof( padded_block ) );
if ( len >= 0 )
{
  memcpy( padded_block, input, len );
  padded_block[ len ] = 0x80;
}

padded_block[ SHA1_BLOCK_SIZE - 4 ] = ( length_in_bits & 0xFF000000 ) >> 24;
padded_block[ SHA1_BLOCK_SIZE - 3 ] = ( length_in_bits & 0x00FF0000 ) >> 16;
padded_block[ SHA1_BLOCK_SIZE - 2 ] = ( length_in_bits & 0x0000FF00 ) >> 8;
padded_block[ SHA1_BLOCK_SIZE - 1 ] = ( length_in_bits & 0x000000FF );

sha1_block_operate( padded_block, hash );

return 0;
}
```

In fact, sha1_hash and md5_hash are so similar it's almost painful *not* to just go ahead and consolidate them into a common function. Go ahead and do so.

Because md5_block_operate and sha1_block_operate have identical method signatures (what a coincidence!), you can just pass the block_operate function in as a function pointer as in Listing 4-10.

**Listing 4-10:** "digest.h" digest_hash function prototype

```
int digest_hash( unsigned char *input,
        int len,
        unsigned int *hash,
        void (*block_operate)(const unsigned char *input, unsigned int hash[] ));
```

Because `SHA1_BLOCK_SIZE` and `MD5_BLOCK_SIZE` are actually identical, there's not much benefit in using two different constants. You could pass the block size in as a parameter to increase flexibility, but there are already quite a few parameters, and you don't need this flexibility — at least not yet. The initialization is different because SHA has one extra four-byte integer, but you can just initialize outside of the function to take care of that.

### *Understanding SHA-1 Finalization*

The only remaining difference is the finalization. Remember that MD5 had sort of an odd formulation to append the length to the end of the block in little-endian format. SHA doesn't; it sticks with the standard big endian. You could probably code your way around this, but a better approach is to just refactor this into another function in Listing 4-11 and Listing 4-12.

**Listing 4-11:** "md5.c" md5_finalize

```
void md5_finalize( unsigned char *padded_block, int length_in_bits )
{
  padded_block[ MD5_BLOCK_SIZE - 5 ] = ( length_in_bits & 0xFF000000 ) >> 24;
  padded_block[ MD5_BLOCK_SIZE - 6 ] = ( length_in_bits & 0x00FF0000 ) >> 16;
  padded_block[ MD5_BLOCK_SIZE - 7 ] = ( length_in_bits & 0x0000FF00 ) >> 8;
  padded_block[ MD5_BLOCK_SIZE - 8 ] = ( length_in_bits & 0x000000FF );
}
```

**Listing 4-12:** "sha.c" sha1_finalize

```
void sha1_finalize( unsigned char *padded_block, int length_in_bits )
{
  padded_block[ SHA1_BLOCK_SIZE - 4 ] = ( length_in_bits & 0xFF000000 ) >> 24;
  padded_block[ SHA1_BLOCK_SIZE - 3 ] = ( length_in_bits & 0x00FF0000 ) >> 16;
  padded_block[ SHA1_BLOCK_SIZE - 2 ] = ( length_in_bits & 0x0000FF00 ) >> 8;
  padded_block[ SHA1_BLOCK_SIZE - 1 ] = ( length_in_bits & 0x000000FF );
}
```

So the final "digest" function looks like Listing 4-13, with two function parameters.

**Listing 4-13:** "digest.c" digest_hash

```
#define DIGEST_BLOCK_SIZE 64
#define INPUT_BLOCK_SIZE 56
```

```c
/**
 * Generic digest hash computation. The hash should be set to its initial
 * value *before* calling this function.
 */
int digest_hash( unsigned char *input,
                        int len,
                                        unsigned int *hash,
                        void (*block_operate)(const unsigned char *input,
                                        unsigned int hash[] ),
                        void (*block_finalize)(unsigned char *block, int length ) )
{
  unsigned char padded_block[ DIGEST_BLOCK_SIZE ];
  int length_in_bits = len * 8;

  while ( len >= INPUT_BLOCK_SIZE )
  {
    // Special handling for blocks between 56 and 64 bytes
    // (not enough room for the 8 bytes of length, but also
    // not enough to fill up a block)
    if ( len < DIGEST_BLOCK_SIZE )
    {
     memset( padded_block, 0, sizeof( padded_block ) );
     memcpy( padded_block, input, len );
     padded_block[ len ] = 0x80;
     block_operate( padded_block, hash );

     input += len;
     len = -1;
    }
    else
    {
     block_operate( input, hash );

     input += DIGEST_BLOCK_SIZE;
     len -= DIGEST_BLOCK_SIZE;
    }
  }

  memset( padded_block, 0, sizeof( padded_block ) );
  if ( len >= 0 )
  {
    memcpy( padded_block, input, len );
    padded_block[ len ] = 0x80;
  }

  block_finalize( padded_block, length_in_bits );

  block_operate( padded_block, hash );

  return 0;
}
```

This single function is now responsible for computing both MD5 and SHA-1 hashes. To compute an MD5 hash, call

```
unsigned int hash[ 4 ];
memcpy( hash, md5_initial_hash, 4 * sizeof( unsigned int ) );
digest_hash( argv[ 2 ], strlen( argv[ 2 ] ), hash, 4, md5_block_operate,
 md5_finalize );
```

and to compute an SHA-1 hash, call

```
unsigned int hash[ 5 ];
memcpy( hash, sha1_initial_hash, 5 * sizeof( unsigned int ) );
digest_hash( argv[ 2 ], strlen( argv[ 2 ] ), hash, 5, sha1_block_operate,
 sha1_finalize );
```

If you were paying close attention, you may have also noticed that the first four integers of the sha1_initial_hash array are the same as the first four integers of the md5_initial_hash array. Technically you could even use one initial_hash array and share it between the two operations.

There's one final problem you run into when trying to use digest as in Listing 4-13. The output of md5 is given in big-endian format, whereas the output of SHA-1 is given in little-endian format. In and of itself, this isn't really a problem, but you want to be able to treat digest as a black box and not care which algorithm it encloses. As a result, you need to decide which format you want to follow. Arbitrarily, pick the MD5 format, and reverse the SHA-1 computations at each stage. The changes to sha.c are detailed in Listing 4-14.

**Listing 4-14:** "sha.c" SHA-1 in little-endian format

```
unsigned int sha1_initial_hash[ ] = {
  0x01234567,
  0x89abcdef,
  0xfedcba98,
  0x76543210,
  0xf0e1d2c3
};

...

void sha1_block_operate( const unsigned char *block, unsigned int hash[ 5 ] )
{
...
    W[ t ] = ( W[ t ] << 1 ) | ( ( W[ t ] & 0x80000000 ) >> 31 );
  }
}

  hash[ 0 ] = ntohl( hash[ 0 ] );
  hash[ 1 ] = ntohl( hash[ 1 ] );
  hash[ 2 ] = ntohl( hash[ 2 ] );
  hash[ 3 ] = ntohl( hash[ 3 ] );
  hash[ 4 ] = ntohl( hash[ 4 ] );
```

```
  a = hash[ 0 ];
  b = hash[ 1 ];
  c = hash[ 2 ];
  d = hash[ 3 ];
...
  hash[ 3 ] += d;
  hash[ 4 ] += e;

  hash[ 0 ] = htonl( hash[ 0 ] );
  hash[ 1 ] = htonl( hash[ 1 ] );
  hash[ 2 ] = htonl( hash[ 2 ] );
  hash[ 3 ] = htonl( hash[ 3 ] );
  hash[ 4 ] = htonl( hash[ 4 ] );
}
```

Notice that all this does is reverse the hash values prior to each `sha1_block_operate` call so that you can use the native arithmetic operators to work on the block. It then re-reverses them on the way out. Of course, you also have to reverse `sha1_initial_hash`.

Now you can call `digest` and treat the `hash` results uniformly, whether the hash algorithm is MD5 or SHA-1. Go ahead and build a test `main` routine and see some results as shown in Listing 4-15.

**Listing 4-15:** "digest.c" main routine

```
#ifdef TEST_DIGEST
int main( int argc, char *argv[ ] )
{
  unsigned int *hash;
  int hash_len;
  int i;
  unsigned char *decoded_input;
  int decoded_len;

  if ( argc < 3 )
  {
    fprintf( stderr, "Usage: %s [-md5|-sha] [0x]<input>\n", argv[ 0 ] );
    exit( 0 );
  }

  decoded_len = hex_decode( argv[ 2 ], &decoded_input );

  if ( !( strcmp( argv[ 1 ], "-md5" ) ) )
  {
    hash = malloc( sizeof( int ) * MD5_RESULT_SIZE );
    memcpy( hash, md5_initial_hash, sizeof( int ) * MD5_RESULT_SIZE );
    hash_len = MD5_RESULT_SIZE;
    digest_hash( decoded_input, decoded_len, hash,
      md5_block_operate, md5_finalize );
  }
```

*(Continued)*

```
    else if ( !( strcmp( argv[ 1 ], "-sha1" ) ) )
    {
      hash = malloc( sizeof( int ) * SHA1_RESULT_SIZE );
      memcpy( hash, sha1_initial_hash, sizeof( int ) * SHA1_RESULT_SIZE );
      hash_len = SHA1_RESULT_SIZE;
      digest_hash( decoded_input, decoded_len, hash,
        sha1_block_operate, sha1_finalize );
    }
    else
    {
      fprintf( stderr, "unsupported digest algorithm '%s'\n", argv[ 1 ] );
      exit( 0 );
    }


    {
      unsigned char *display_hash = ( unsigned char * ) hash;

      for ( i = 0; i < ( hash_len * 4 ); i++ )
      {
        printf( "%.02x", display_hash[ i ] );
      }
      printf( "\n" );
    }

    free( hash );
    free( decoded_input );

    return 0;
}
#endif
```

Compile and run this to see it in action:

```
jdavies@localhost$ digest -md5 abc
900150983cd24fb0d6963f7d28e17f72

jdavies@localhost$ digest -sha1 abc
a9993e364706816aba3e25717850c26c9cd0d89d
```

Notice that the SHA-1 output is a bit longer than the MD5 output; MD5 gives you 128 bits, and SHA-1 gives you 160.

## Even More Collision Resistance with the SHA-256 Digest Algorithm

Even SHA, with its 160 bits of output, is no longer considered sufficient to effectively guard against hash collisions. There have been three new standardized SHA extensions named *SHA-256*, *SHA-384* and *SHA-512*. In general, the SHA-*n* algorithm produces *n* bits of output. You don't examine them all here, but go ahead and add support for SHA-256 because it's rapidly becoming the minimum required standard where secure hashing is concerned (you'll also need it later in this chapter, to support elliptic-curve cryptography). At the time of this writing, the NIST is evaluating proposals for a new SHA standard, which will almost certainly have an even longer output.

Everything about SHA-256 is identical to SHA-1 except for the block process-ing itself and the output length. The block size, padding, and so on are all the same. You can reuse the `digest_hash` function from Listing 4-13 verbatim, if you just change the `block_operate` function pointer.

SHA-256's block operation is similar; `ch` and `maj` reappear, but the parity func-tion disappears and four new functions, which are identified in the specification as $\Sigma^1$, $\Sigma^0$, $\sigma^1$ and $\sigma^0$ are introduced:

$$\Sigma^0 (x) = \text{rotr}( x, 2 ) \wedge \text{rotr}( x, 13 ) \wedge \text{rotr}( x, 22 )$$

$$\Sigma^1 (x) = \text{rotr}( x, 6 ) \wedge \text{rotr}( x, 11 ) \wedge \text{rotr}( x, 25 )$$

$$\sigma^0 (x) = \text{rotr}( x, 7 ) \wedge \text{rotr}( x, 18 ) \wedge \text{shr}( x \wedge 3 )$$

$$\sigma^1 (x) = \text{rotr}( x, 17 ) \wedge \text{rotr}( x, 19 )\wedge \text{shr}( x, 10 )$$

This choice of nomenclature doesn't translate very well into code, so call $\Sigma$ sigma_rot (because the last operation is a rotr — "rotate right") and $\sigma$ sigma_shr (because the last operation is a shr — "shift right"). In code, this looks like Listing 4-16.

**Listing 4-16:** "sha.c" SHA-256 sigma functions

```
unsigned int rotr( unsigned int x, unsigned int n )
{
  return ( x >> n ) | ( ( x ) << ( 32 - n ) );
}

unsigned int shr( unsigned int x, unsigned int n )
{
  return x >> n;
}

unsigned int sigma_rot( unsigned int x, int i )
{
  return rotr( x, i ? 6 : 2 ) ^ rotr( x, i ? 11 : 13 ) ^ rotr( x, i ? 25 : 22 );
}

unsigned int sigma_shr( unsigned int x, int i )
{
  return rotr( x, i ? 17 : 7 ) ^ rotr( x, i ? 19 : 18 ) ^ shr( x, i ? 10 : 3 );
}
```

The block operation itself should look familiar; instead of just a, b, c, d and e, you have a-h because there are eight 32-bit integers in the output now. There's a 64-int (instead of an 80-int) w that is precomputed, and a static k block. There's also a 64-iteration round that's applied to a-h where they shift positions each round and whichever input is at the head is subject to a complex computation. The code should be more or less self-explanatory; even if you can't see why this works, you should be more than convinced that the output is a random permutation of the input, which is what you want from a hash function. This is shown in Listing 4-17.

**Listing 4-17:** "sha.c" SHA-256 block operate

```
void sha256_block_operate( const unsigned char *block,
                           unsigned int hash[ 8 ] )
{
  unsigned int W[ 64 ];
  unsigned int a, b, c, d, e, f, g, h;
  unsigned int T1, T2;
  int t, i;

  /**
   * The first 32 bits of the fractional parts of the cube roots
   * of the first sixty-four prime numbers.
   */
  static const unsigned int k[] =
  {
    0x428a2f98, 0x71374491, 0xb5c0fbcf, 0xe9b5dba5, 0x3956c25b, 0x59f111f1,
    0x923f82a4, 0xab1c5ed5, 0xd807aa98, 0x12835b01, 0x243185be, 0x550c7dc3,
    0x72be5d74, 0x80deb1fe, 0x9bdc06a7, 0xc19bf174, 0xe49b69c1, 0xefbe4786,
    0x0fc19dc6, 0x240ca1cc, 0x2de92c6f, 0x4a7484aa, 0x5cb0a9dc, 0x76f988da,
    0x983e5152, 0xa831c66d, 0xb00327c8, 0xbf597fc7, 0xc6e00bf3, 0xd5a79147,
    0x06ca6351, 0x14292967, 0x27b70a85, 0x2e1b2138, 0x4d2c6dfc, 0x53380d13,
    0x650a7354, 0x766a0abb, 0x81c2c92e, 0x92722c85, 0xa2bfe8a1, 0xa81a664b,
    0xc24b8b70, 0xc76c51a3, 0xd192e819, 0xd6990624, 0xf40e3585, 0x106aa070,
    0x19a4c116, 0x1e376c08, 0x2748774c, 0x34b0bcb5, 0x391c0cb3, 0x4ed8aa4a,
    0x5b9cca4f, 0x682e6ff3, 0x748f82ee, 0x78a5636f, 0x84c87814, 0x8cc70208,
    0x90befffa, 0xa4506ceb, 0xbef9a3f7, 0xc67178f2
  };

  // deal with little-endian-ness
  for ( i = 0; i < 8; i++ )
  {
    hash[ i ] = ntohl( hash[ i ] );
  }

  for ( t = 0; t < 64; t++ )
  {
    if ( t <= 15 )
    {
      W[ t ] = ( block[ ( t * 4 ) ] << 24 ) |
               ( block[ ( t * 4 ) + 1 ] << 16 ) |
```

```
                       ( block[ ( t * 4 ) + 2 ] << 8 ) |
                       ( block[ ( t * 4 ) + 3 ] );
      }
      else
      {
        W[ t ] = sigma_shr( W[ t - 2 ], 1 ) +
                 W[ t - 7 ] +
                 sigma_shr( W[ t - 15 ], 0 ) +
                 W[ t - 16 ];
      }
    }

    a = hash[ 0 ];
    b = hash[ 1 ];
    c = hash[ 2 ];
    d = hash[ 3 ];
    e = hash[ 4 ];
    f = hash[ 5 ];
    g = hash[ 6 ];
    h = hash[ 7 ];

    for ( t = 0; t < 64; t++ )
    {
      T1 = h + sigma_rot( e, 1 ) + ch( e, f, g ) + k[ t ] + W[ t ];
      T2 = sigma_rot( a, 0 ) + maj( a, b, c );
      h = g;
      g = f;
      f = e;
      e = d + T1;
      d = c;
      c = b;
      b = a;
      a = T1 + T2;
    }

    hash[ 0 ] = a + hash[ 0 ];
    hash[ 1 ] = b + hash[ 1 ];
    hash[ 2 ] = c + hash[ 2 ];
    hash[ 3 ] = d + hash[ 3 ];
    hash[ 4 ] = e + hash[ 4 ];
    hash[ 5 ] = f + hash[ 5 ];
    hash[ 6 ] = g + hash[ 6 ];
    hash[ 7 ] = h + hash[ 7 ];

    // deal with little-endian-ness
    for ( i = 0; i < 8; i++ )
    {
      hash[ i ] = htonl( hash[ i ] );
    }
}
```

Notice that there are quite a few more k values for SHA-256 than for SHA-1, and that σ shows up only in the computation of w and Σ in the main loop. You also have to have an `initial hash` in Listing 4-18.

**Listing 4-18:** "sha.c" SHA-256 initial hash

```
static const unsigned int sha256_initial_hash[] =
{
  0x67e6096a,
  0x85ae67bb,
  0x72f36e3c,
  0x3af54fa5,
  0x7f520e51,
  0x8c68059b,
  0xabd9831f,
  0x19cde05b
};
```

These are presented here backward (that is, in little-endian format) with respect to the specification. If you want to invoke this, you need to call the same `digest_hash` function developed earlier:

```
unsigned int hash[ 8 ];
memcpy( hash, sha256_initial_hash, 8 * sizeof( unsigned int ) );
digest_hash( argv[ 2 ], strlen( argv[ 2 ] ), hash, 8, sha256_block_operate,
  sha1_finalize );
```

Notice that the finalize pointer points to `sha1_finalize` — finalization is exactly the same for SHA-256 as it is for SHA-1, so there's no reason to define a new function here.

## Preventing Replay Attacks with the HMAC Keyed-Hash Algorithm

Related to message digests (and particularly relevant to SSL) are HMACs, speci-fied in RFC 2104. To understand the motivation for HMAC, consider the secure hash functions (MD5 and SHA) examined in the previous three sections. Secure hashes are reliable, one-way functions. You give them the input, they give you the output, and nobody — not even you — can work backward from the output to uncover the input. Right?

Well, not exactly — or at least, not always. Imagine that a company maintains a database of purchase orders, and to verify that the customer is in posses-sion of the credit card number used to place an order, a secure hash of the credit card number is stored for each order. The customer is happy, because her credit card number is not being stored in a database for some hacker to steal; and the company is happy, because it can ask a customer for her credit card number and then retrieve all orders that were made using that card for customer service purposes. The company just asks the customer for the credit card number again, hashes it, and searches the database on the hash column.

Unfortunately, there's a problem with this approach. Although there are a lot of potential hash values — even for a small hash function such as MD5 — there aren't that many credit card numbers. About 10,000 trillion. In fact, not every 16-digit number is a valid credit card number, and the LUHN consistency check that verifies the validity of a credit card number is a public algorithm. In cryptography terms, this isn't actually a very big number. A motivated attacker might try to compute the MD5 hash — or whatever hash was used — of all 10,000 trillion possible credit card numbers and store the results, keyed back to the original credit card number. This might take months to complete on a powerful cluster of computers, but after it's computed this database could be used against *any* database that stores an MD5 hash of credit card numbers. Fortunately, this direct attack is infeasible for a different reason. This would require 320,000 trillion bytes of memory — about 320 petabytes. The cost of this storage array far outweighs the value of even the largest database of credit card numbers.

So far, so good. An attacker would have to spend months mounting a targeted attack against the database or would have to have an astronomical amount of storage at his disposal. Unfortunately, Martin Hellman, in his paper "A Cryptanalytic Time — Memory Trade-Off", came up with a way to trade storage space for speed. His concept has been refined into what are now called *rainbow tables*. The idea is to start with an input, hash it, and then arbitrarily map that hash back to the input space. This arbitrary mapping doesn't undo the hash — that's impossible — it just has to be repeatable. You then take the resulting input, hash it, map it back, and so on. Do this $n$ times, but only store the first and the last values. This way, although you have to go through every possible input value, you can drastically reduce the amount of storage you need.

When you have a hash code you want to map back to its original input, look for it in your table. If you don't find it, apply your back-mapping function, hash that, and look in the table again. Eventually, you find a match, and when you do, you have uncovered the original input. This approach has been successfully used to crack passwords whose hashes were stored rather than their actual contents; rainbow tables of common password values are available for download online; you don't even have to compute them yourself.

The easiest way to guard against this is to include a secret in the hash; without the secret, the attacker doesn't know what to hash in the first place. This is, in fact, the idea behind the HMAC. Here, both sides share a secret, which is combined with the hash in a secure way. Only a legitimate holder of the secret can figure out $H(m,s)$ where $H$ is the secure hash function, $m$ is the message, and $s$ is the secret.

A weak, naïve, shared-secret MAC operation might be:

$$h(m) \oplus s$$

where *h* refers to a secure digest. The problem with this approach is its vulnerability to *known plaintext attacks*. The attack works like this: The attacker convinces somebody with the MAC secret to hash and XOR the text "abc" or some other value that is known to the attacker. This has the MD5 hash 900150983cd24fb0 d6963f7d28e17f72. Remember that the attacker can compute this as well — an MD5 hash never changes. The holder of the secret then XORs this value with the secret and makes the result available.

Unfortunately, the attacker can then XOR the hash with the result and recover the secret. Remember that a $\oplus$ b $\oplus$ b = a, but a $\oplus$ b $\oplus$ a = b as well. So *hash $\oplus$ secret $\oplus$ hash = secret*. Since *mac = (hash $\oplus$ secret)*, *mac $\oplus$ hash = secret*, and the secret has been revealed.

### Implementing a Secure HMAC Algorithm

A more secure algorithm is specified in RFC 2104 and is the standard for combining shared secrets with secure hash algorithms. Overall, it's not radically different in concept than XORing the shared secret with the result of a secure hash; it just adds a couple of extra functions.

An HMAC-hash prepends one block of data to the data to be hashed. The prepended block consists of 64 bytes of 0x36, XORed with the shared secret. This means that the shared secret can't be longer than 64 bytes. If it is, it should be securely hashed itself, and the results of that hash used as the shared secret. This result (the prepended block, plus the input data itself) is then hashed, using a secure hash algorithm. Finally, this hash is appended to a new block of data that consists of one block of the byte 0x5C, XORed again with the shared secret (or its computed hash as described previously), and hashed again to produce the final hash value. Figure 4-1 illustrates this process.

This double-hash technique stops the attacker in the known-plaintext attack described earlier from computing the hash code and XORing it against the secret to recover it. All of this complexity is carefully designed to create a repeatable process. Remember, if "abc" hashes to "xyz" for me, it must hash that way for you no matter when you run it or what type of machine you're on — but in such a way that can't be reversed or forged. It seems complicated (and it is), but after it's implemented, it can be treated as a black box.

Using the `digest` algorithm above, you can put together an HMAC implementation that can work with any hash algorithm in Listing 4-19.

**Listing 4-19:** "hmac.c" HMAC function

```
/**
 * Note: key_length, text_length, hash_block_length are in bytes.
 * hash_code_length is in ints.
 */
void hmac( const unsigned char *key,
```

```
        int key_length,
        const unsigned char *text,
        int text_length,
        void (*hash_block_operate)(const unsigned char *input, unsigned int hash[] ),
        void (*hash_block_finalize)(const unsigned char *block, int length ),
        int hash_block_length,
        int hash_code_length,
        unsigned int *hash_out )
{
  unsigned char *ipad, *opad, *padded_block;
  unsigned int *hash1;
  int i;

  // TODO if key_length > hash_block_length, should hash it using "hash_
  // function" first and then use that as the key.
  assert( key_length < hash_block_length );

  hash1 = ( unsigned int * ) malloc( hash_code_length * sizeof( unsigned int )
);
  ipad = ( unsigned char * ) malloc( hash_block_length );
  padded_block = ( unsigned char * ) malloc( text_length + hash_block_length );

  memset( ipad, 0x36, hash_block_length );

  memset( padded_block, '\0', hash_block_length );
  memcpy( padded_block, key, key_length );
  for ( i = 0; i < hash_block_length; i++ )
  {
    padded_block[ i ] ^= ipad[ i ];
  }

  memcpy( padded_block + hash_block_length, text, text_length );
  memcpy( hash1, hash_out, hash_code_length * sizeof( unsigned int ) );
  digest_hash( padded_block, hash_block_length + text_length, hash1,
   hash_code_length, hash_block_operate, hash_block_finalize );

  opad = ( unsigned char * ) malloc( hash_block_length );

  memset( opad, 0x5C, hash_block_length );

  free( padded_block );
  padded_block = ( unsigned char * ) malloc(
   ( hash_code_length * sizeof( int ) ) + hash_block_length );
  memset( padded_block, '\0', hash_block_length );
  memcpy( padded_block, key, key_length );

  for ( i = 0; i < hash_block_length; i++ )
  {
    padded_block[ i ] ^= opad[ i ];
```

*(Continued)*

```
    }

    memcpy( padded_block + hash_block_length, hash1,
        hash_code_length * sizeof( int ) );
    digest_hash( padded_block,
        hash_block_length + ( hash_code_length * sizeof( int ) ), hash_out,
        hash_code_length, hash_block_operate, hash_block_finalize );

    free( hash1 );
    free( ipad );
    free( opad );
    free( padded_block );
}
```

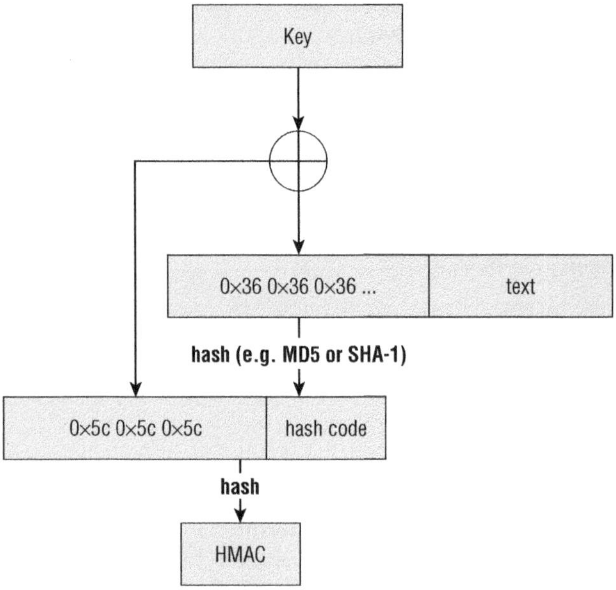

**Figure 4-1:** HMAC Function

The method signature is a behemoth, repeated in Listing 4-20.

**Listing 4-20:** "hmac.h" HMAC function prototype

```
void hmac( const unsigned char *key,
    int key_length,
    const unsigned char *text,
    int text_length,
    int (*hash_block_operate)(const unsigned char *input, unsigned int hash[] ),
    int (*hash_block_finalize)(unsigned char *block, int length ),
    int hash_block_length,
    int hash_code_length,
    unsigned int *hash_out )
```

Here, `key` and `key_length` describe the shared secret; `text` and `text_length` describe the data to be HMAC-ed; `hash_block_operate` and `hash_block_finalize` describe the hash operation; `hash_block_length` describes the length of a block in bytes (which is always 64 for MD5 and SHA-1); `hash_code_length` is the length of the resultant hash in `int`s (4 for MD5, 5 for SHA-1); and `hash_out` is a pointer to the hash code to be generated.

Because you don't need to deal with shared secrets that are greater than 64 bytes for SSL, just ignore them:

```
// TODO if key_length > hash_block_length, should hash it using "hash_
// function" first and then use that as the key.
assert( key_length < hash_block_length );
```

**NOTE** Note that `hash_out` must be initialized properly, according to the secure hashing algorithm. Alternatively, you could have added an initialization parameter, but you're already up to nine parameters here.

Remember that HMAC requires that you compute an initial hash based on the text to be hashed, prepended with a block of 0x36s XORed with the shared secret, called the key here. This section of the HMAC function builds this block of data:

```
hash1 = ( unsigned int * ) malloc( hash_code_length * sizeof( unsigned int ) );

ipad = ( unsigned char * ) malloc( hash_block_length );
padded_block = ( unsigned char * ) malloc( text_length + hash_block_length );

memset( ipad, 0x36, hash_block_length );

memset( padded_block, '\0', hash_block_length );
memcpy( padded_block, key, key_length );
for ( i = 0; i < hash_block_length; i++ )
{
  padded_block[ i ] ^= ipad[ i ];
}
```

You allocate a new block of memory as long as the text to be hashed plus one extra block, fill it with 0x36s, and XOR that with the key. Finally, compute the hash of this new data block:

```
memcpy( padded_block + hash_block_length, text, text_length );
memcpy( hash1, hash_out, hash_code_length * sizeof( unsigned int ) );
digest_hash( padded_block, hash_block_length + text_length, hash1,
  hash_code_length, hash_block_operate, hash_block_finalize );
```

Notice that you're hashing into an internal block called `hash1`, and remember that HMAC requires you to hash *that* hash. There's a minor implementation problem here, though. The caller of `digest_hash` must preinitialize the hash code to its proper initialization value. You could ask the caller of this function to pass the correct initialization value in as a parameter, but you can "cheat" instead to save an input parameter. Because you know that the caller of `hmac` had to initialize `hash_out`, copy that value into `hash1` to properly initialize it.

### Completing the HMAC Operation

Now you have the first hash code computed in `hash1`, according to the secure hashing algorithm that was passed in. To complete the HMAC operation, you need to prepend that with another block of 0x5Cs, XORed with the shared secret, and hash it:

```
opad = ( unsigned char * ) malloc( hash_block_length );

memset( opad, 0x5C, hash_block_length );

free( padded_block );
padded_block = ( unsigned char * ) malloc( hash_code_length +
  ( hash_block_length * sizeof( int ) ) );
memset( padded_block, '\0', hash_block_length );
memcpy( padded_block, key, key_length );

for ( i = 0; i < hash_block_length; i++ )
{
  padded_block[ i ] ^= opad[ i ];
}
```

Notice that this frees and reallocates `padded_block`. You may wonder why you'd want to reallocate here because you already allocated this temporary space to compute the first hash value. However, consider the case where `text_length` is less than `hash_code_length`, which sometimes it is. In this case, you'd have too little space for the prepended hash code. You could make this a bit more efficient by allocating `max( hash_code_length, text_length )` at the top of the function, but this implementation is good enough.

Finally, compute the hash into `hash_out`, which is the return value of the function

```
memcpy( padded_block + hash_block_length, hash1,
  hash_code_length * sizeof( int ) );
digest_hash( padded_block,
  hash_block_length + ( hash_code_length * sizeof( int ) ), hash_out,
  hash_code_length, hash_block_operate, hash_block_finalize );
```

## Creating Updateable Hash Functions

Notice that, in order to compute an HMAC, you had to build an internal buffer consisting of a padded, XORed key followed by the text to be hashed. However, the hash functions presented here don't ever need to go back in the data stream.

After block #N has been hashed, subsequent operations won't change the hash of block #N. They are just added to it, modulo 32. Therefore, you can save memory and time by allowing the hash operation to save its state and pick back up where it left off later — that is, feed it a block of data, let it update the hash code, and then feed it another, and so on.

Of course, the padding requirements of MD5 and SHA make this a little trickier than it sounds at first. You need to keep track of the running bit-length of the input so that it can be appended later on. This is, incidentally, how a 32-bit architecture can hash an input of more than $2^{32}$ bits. Plus, for additional flexibility, you'd want to allow the caller to pass in less than a single block at a time and accumulate the blocks yourself.

You could store this running state in a static global, but this would cause thread-safety problems (if you ever wanted to use this routine in a threaded context, anyway). Instead, you'd do better to pass a context object into the hashing function, with a routine named something like `hash_update` that would also take the data to be added to the running hash, and another routine named `hash_finalize` that would add the final padding blocks and return the result. This is, in fact, the only non-superficial difference between the MD5 code included in RFC 1321 and the MD5 implementation presented here. You need to be able to compute running hashes for SSL, so implement this extension for MD5 and SHA. Change your `digest` function to allow running updates and improve the HMAC implementation a bit.

### Defining a Digest Structure

Because you can no longer call `digest` in one shot, but must instead keep track of a long-running operation, define a `context` structure that stores the state of an ongoing digest computation as shown in Listing 4-21.

**Listing 4-21:** "digest.h" digest context structure declaration

```
typedef struct
{
  unsigned int *hash;
  int hash_len;
  unsigned int input_len;

  void (*block_operate)(const unsigned char *input, unsigned int hash[] );
  void (*block_finalize)(const unsigned char *block, int length );

  // Temporary storage
  unsigned char block[ DIGEST_BLOCK_SIZE ];
  int block_len;
}
digest_ctx;
```

hash and hash_len are fairly straightforward; this is the hash code as it has been computed with the data that's been given so far. input_len is the number of bytes that have been passed in; remember input_len needs to be tracked in order to append the length in bits to the virtual buffer before computing the final hash code. Go ahead and stick the block_operate and block_finalize function pointers in here so that you don't have to further pollute your function call signatures. Finally, there's a block of temporary storage; if a call to update is made with less than a full block (or with a non-aligned bit left over), store it here, along with its length, and pass it on to block_operate when there's enough data to make a full block. This is shown in Listing 4-22.

**Listing 4-22:** "digest.c" update digest function

```
void update_digest( digest_ctx *context, const unsigned char *input, int input_
len )
{
  context->input_len += input_len;

  // Process any left over from the last call to "update_digest"
  if ( context->block_len > 0 )
  {
    // How much we need to make a full block
    int borrow_amt = DIGEST_BLOCK_SIZE - context->block_len;

    if ( input_len < borrow_amt )
    {
      memcpy( context->block + context->block_len, input, input_len );
      context->block_len += input_len;
      input_len = 0;
    }
    else
    {
      memcpy( context->block + context->block_len, input, borrow_amt );
      context->block_operate( context->block, context->hash );
      context->block_len = 0;
      input += borrow_amt;
      input_len -= borrow_amt;
    }
  }

  while ( input_len >= DIGEST_BLOCK_SIZE )
  {
    context->block_operate( input, context->hash );

    input += DIGEST_BLOCK_SIZE;
    input_len -= DIGEST_BLOCK_SIZE;
  }

  // Have some non-aligned data left over; save it for next call, or
  // "finalize" call.
```

```
if ( input_len > 0 )
{
  memcpy( context->block, input, input_len );
  context->block_len = input_len;
}
}
```

This is probably the most complex function presented so far, so it's worth going through carefully:

1. Update the input length. You have to append this to the very last block, whenever that may come.

   ```
   context->input_len += input_len;


   // Process any left over from the last call to "update_digest"
   if ( context->block_len > 0 )

   {

   ...

   }
   ```

2. Check to see if you have any data left over from a previous call. If you don't, go ahead and process the data, one block at a time, until you run out of blocks:

   ```
   while ( input_len >= DIGEST_BLOCK_SIZE )
   {
     context->block_operate( input, context->hash );

     input += DIGEST_BLOCK_SIZE;
     input_len -= DIGEST_BLOCK_SIZE;
   }
   ```

   This ought to look familiar; it's the main loop of the original `digest` function from Listing 4-13.

3. Process one entire block, update the hash, increment the input pointer and decrement the length counter. At the end, `input_len` is either 0 or some integer less than the block size, so just store the remaining data in the context pointer until the next time `update_digest` is called:

   ```
   if ( input_len > 0 )
   {
     memcpy( context->block, input, input_len );
     context->block_len = input_len;
   }
   ```

   At this point, you know that `input_len` is less than one block size, so there's no danger of overrunning the temporary buffer `context->block`.

4. Next time `update_digest` is called, check to see if there's any data left over from the previous call. If so, concatenate data from the input buffer onto

the end of it, process the resulting block, and process whatever remaining blocks are left.

```
if ( context->block_len > 0 )
{
  // How much we need to make a full block
  int borrow_amt = DIGEST_BLOCK_SIZE - context->block_len;

  if ( input_len < borrow_amt )
  {
```

5. `borrow_amt` is the number of bytes needed to make a full block. If you *still* don't have enough, just add it to the end of the temporary block and allow the function to exit.

```
    memcpy( context->block + context->block_len, input, input_len );
    context->block_len += input_len;
    input_len = 0;
}
```

Otherwise, go ahead and copy `borrow_amt` bytes into the temporary block, process that block, and continue:

```
else
{
  memcpy( context->block + context->block_len, input, borrow_amt );
  context->block_operate( context->block, context->hash );
  context->block_len = 0;
  input += borrow_amt;
  input_len -= borrow_amt;
}
```

### Appending the Length to the Last Block

So, the caller calls `update_digest` repeatedly, as data becomes available, allowing it to compute a running hash code. However, to complete an MD5 or SHA-1 hash, you still have to append the length, in bits, to the end of the last block. The function `finalize_digest` handles what used to be the complex logic in `digest_hash` to figure out if the remaining data consists of one or two blocks — that is, if there's enough space for the end terminator and the length on the end of the remaining block as shown in Listing 4-23.

**Listing 4-23:** "digest.c" finalize digest

```
/**
 * Process whatever's left over in the context buffer, append
 * the length in bits, and update the hash one last time.
 */
void finalize_digest( digest_ctx *context )
{
  memset( context->block + context->block_len, 0, DIGEST_BLOCK_SIZE -
```

```
   context->block_len );
context->block[ context->block_len ] = 0x80;
// special handling if the last block is < 64 but > 56
if ( context->block_len >= INPUT_BLOCK_SIZE )
{
  context->block_operate( context->block, context->hash );
  context->block_len = 0;
memset( context->block + context->block_len, 0, DIGEST_BLOCK_SIZE -
  context->block_len );
}
// Only append the length for the very last block
// Technically, this allows for 64 bits of length, but since we can only
// process 32 bits worth, we leave the upper four bytes empty
context->block_finalize( context->block, context->input_len * 8 );

  context->block_operate( context->block, context->hash );
}
```

This logic was described when it was originally presented in the context of MD5.

Listing 4-24 shows how you initialize the MD5 digest context.

**Listing 4-24:** "md5.c" MD5 digest initialization

```
void new_md5_digest( digest_ctx *context )
{
  context->hash_len = 4;
  context->input_len = 0;
  context->block_len = 0;
  context->hash = ( unsigned int * )
   malloc( context->hash_len * sizeof( unsigned int ) );
memcpy( context->hash, md5_initial_hash,
   context->hash_len * sizeof( unsigned int ) );
memset( context->block, '\0', DIGEST_BLOCK_SIZE );
  context->block_operate = md5_block_operate;
  context->block_finalize = md5_finalize;
}
```

Listing 4-25 shows how you initialize the SHA-1 context.

**Listing 4-25:** "sha.c" SHA-1 digest initialization

```
void new_sha1_digest( digest_ctx *context )
{
  context->hash_len = 5;
  context->input_len = 0;
  context->block_len = 0;
  context->hash = ( unsigned int * )
  malloc( context->hash_len * sizeof( unsigned int ) );
memcpy( context->hash, sha1_initial_hash,
  context->hash_len * sizeof( unsigned int ) );
```

*(Continued)*

```
  memset( context->block, '\0', DIGEST_BLOCK_SIZE );
  context->block_operate = sha1_block_operate;
  context->block_finalize = sha1_finalize;
}
```

And finally, Listing 4-26 shows how you initialize the SHA-256 context.

**Listing 4-26:** "sha.c" SHA-256 digest initialization

```
void new_sha256_digest( digest_ctx *context )
{
  context->hash_len = 8;
  context->input_len = 0;
  context->block_len = 0;
  context->hash = ( unsigned int * ) malloc( context->hash_len *
    sizeof( unsigned int ) );
  memcpy( context->hash, sha256_initial_hash, context->hash_len *
    sizeof( unsigned int ) );
  memset( context->block, '\0', DIGEST_BLOCK_SIZE );
  context->block_operate = sha256_block_operate;
  context->block_finalize = sha1_finalize;
}
```

Of course if you want to support more hash contexts, just add more of them here.

After the contexts have been initialized, they're just passed to `update_digest` as new data becomes available, and passed to `finalize_digest` after all the data to be hashed has been accumulated.

### Computing the MD5 Hash of an Entire File

An example might help to clarify how these updateable digest functions work. Consider a real-world example — computing the MD5 hash of an entire file:

```
// hash a file; buffer input
digest_ctx context;
const char *filename = "somefile.tmp";
char buf[ 400 ]; // purposely non-aligned to exercise updating logic
int bytes_read;
int f = open( filename, O_RDONLY );

if ( !f )
{
  fprintf( stderr, "Unable to open '%s' for reading: ", filename );
  perror( "" );
  exit( 0 );
}

new_md5_digest( &context );
```

```
while ( ( bytes_read = read( f, buf, 400 ) ) > 0 )
{
  update_digest( &context, buf, bytes_read );
}

finalize_digest( &context );

if ( bytes_read == -1 )
{
  fprintf( stderr, "Error reading file '%s': ", filename );
  perror( "" );
}

close( f );

{
  unsigned char *hash = ( unsigned char * ) context.hash;

  for ( i = 0; i < ( context.hash_len * 4 ); i++ )
  {
    printf( "%.02x", hash[ i ] );
  }
  printf( "\n" );
}

free( context.hash );
```

Pay special attention to how this works:

1. A new MD5 digest structure is initialized by calling `new_md5_digest` from Listing 4-24.

2. The file is opened and read, 400 bytes at a time.

3. These 400-byte blocks are passed into `update_digest` from Listing 4-22, which is responsible for computing the hash "so far," on top of the hash that's already been computed.

4. Before completing, `finalize_digest` from Listing 4-23 is called to append the total length of the file as required by the digest structure and the final hash is computed.

5. At this point, the `context` parameter can no longer be reused; if you wanted to compute another hash, you'd have to initialize another context.

The benefit of this approach is that rather than reading the whole file into memory and calling `md5_hash` from Listing 4-7 (which would produce the exact same result), the whole file doesn't need to be stored in memory all at once.

The hash is converted to a char array at the end so that it prints out in canonical order — remember that MD5 is little-endian; however, it's customary to display a hash value in big-endian order anyway.

> **NOTE** This update_digest/finalize_digest/digest_ctx all but invents C++.
> (Don't worry, I promise it won't happen again.) In fact, if C and C++ weren't so
> difficult to interoperate, I'd just turn `digest` into a new superclass with three
> subclasses, md5digest, sha1digest, and sha256digest.

This new updateable hash operation simplifies HMAC a bit because you
don't need to do so much copying to get the buffers set up correctly as shown
in Listing 4-27.

**Listing 4-27:** "hmac.c" modified HMAC function to use updateable digest functions

```c
void hmac( unsigned char *key,
     int key_length,
     unsigned char *text,
     int text_length,
     digest_ctx *digest )
{
  unsigned char ipad[ DIGEST_BLOCK_SIZE ];
  unsigned char opad[ DIGEST_BLOCK_SIZE ];
  digest_ctx hash1;
  int i;

  // TODO if key_length > hash_block_length, should hash it using
  // "hash_function" first and then use that as the key.
  assert( key_length < DIGEST_BLOCK_SIZE );

  // "cheating"; copy the supplied digest context in here, since we don't
  // know which digest algorithm is being used
  memcpy( &hash1, digest, sizeof( digest_ctx ) );
  hash1.hash = ( unsigned int * ) malloc(
  hash1.hash_len * sizeof( unsigned int ) );
  memcpy( hash1.hash, digest->hash, hash1.hash_len * sizeof( unsigned int ) );

  memset( ipad, 0x36, DIGEST_BLOCK_SIZE );

  for ( i = 0; i < key_length; i++ )
  {
    ipad[ i ] ^= key[ i ];
  }

  update_digest( &hash1, ipad, DIGEST_BLOCK_SIZE );
  update_digest( &hash1, text, text_length );
  finalize_digest( &hash1 );

  memset( opad, 0x5C, DIGEST_BLOCK_SIZE );

  for ( i = 0; i < key_length; i++ )
```

```
  {
    opad[ i ] ^= key[ i ];
  }

  update_digest( digest, opad, DIGEST_BLOCK_SIZE );
  update_digest( digest, ( unsigned char * ) hash1.hash,
  hash1.hash_len * sizeof( int ) );
  finalize_digest( digest );

  free( hash1.hash );
}
```

Although `update_digest` and `finalize_digest` themselves are practically impenetrable if you don't already know what they're doing, HMAC is actually much easier to read now that you've shunted memory management off to `update_digest`. Now you simply XOR the key with a block of 0x36s, update the digest, update it again with the text, finalize, XOR the key with another block of 0x5Cs, update another digest, update it again with the result of the first digest, and finalize that. The only real "magic" in the function is at the beginning.

```
  memcpy( &hash1, digest, sizeof( digest_ctx ) );
  hash1.hash = ( unsigned int * ) malloc(
    hash1.hash_len * sizeof( unsigned int ) );
  memcpy( hash1.hash, digest->hash, hash1.hash_len * sizeof( unsigned int ) );
```

Remember that the `hmac` function can be called with an MD5, SHA-1, or SHA-256 context. However, the function has no way of knowing which it was called with. There are multitudes of ways to work around that: You could pass in a flag or add an initializer function to the `digest_ctx` structure, but the simplest way is to just `memcpy` the whole initialized structure at the start of the function. You know it was initialized prior to invocation; the only thing to be careful of is that `hash` was dynamically allocated, so you need to reallocate and recopy it. If you were doing this in C++, this would be the sort of thing you'd use a copy constructor for. OK, really, I promise to stop talking C++ now.

You can develop a `main` routine in Listing 4-28 to test this out.

**Listing 4-28:** "hmac.c" main routine

```
#ifdef TEST_HMAC
int main( int argc, char *argv[ ] )
{
  int i;
  digest_ctx digest;
  int key_len;
  unsigned char *key;
  int text_len;
  unsigned char *text;
```

*(Continued)*

```
  if ( argc < 4 )
  {
    fprintf( stderr, "usage: %s [-sha1|md5] [0x]<key> [0x]<text>\n", argv[ 0 ] );
    exit( 0 );
  }

  if ( !( strcmp( argv[ 1 ], "-sha1" ) ) )
  {
    new_sha1_digest( &digest );
  }
  else if ( !( strcmp( argv[ 1 ], "-md5" ) ) )
  {
    new_md5_digest( &digest );
  }
  else
  {
    fprintf( stderr, "usage: %s [-sha1|md5] <key> <text>\n", argv[ 0 ] );
    exit( 1 );
  }

  key_len = hex_decode( argv[ 2 ], &key );
  text_len = hex_decode( argv[ 3 ], &text );

  hmac( key, key_len, text, text_len, &digest );

  for ( i = 0; i < digest.hash_len * sizeof( int ); i++ )
  {
    printf( "%.02x", ( ( unsigned char *) digest.hash )[ i ] );
  }
  printf( "\n" );

  free( digest.hash );
  free( key );
  free( text );

  return 0;
}
#endif
```

To compute an HMAC, call it like this:

```
jdavies@localhost$ hmac -md5 Jefe "what do ya want for nothing?"
750c783e6ab0b503eaa86e310a5db738
```

### Where Does All of This Fit into SSL?

You may still be wondering what all this has to do with SSL. After all, you have secure key exchange and symmetric cryptography. Where does the HMAC function fit in?

SSL requires that every record first be HMAC'ed before being encrypted. This may seem like overkill — after all, HMAC guarantees the integrity of a record. But because you're using symmetric cryptography, the odds are infinitesimally small that an attacker could modify a record in such a way that it decrypts meaningfully, at least without access to the session key. Consider a secure application that transmits the message, "Withdraw troops from Bunker Hill and move them to Normandy beach." If you run this through the AES algorithm with the key "passwordsecurity" and the initialization vector "initializationvc," you get:

0xc99a87a32c57b80de43c26f762556a76bfb3040f7fc38e112d3ffddf4a5cb703
989da2a11d253b6ec32e5c45411715006ffa68b20dbc38ba6fa03fce44fd581b

So far, so good. An attacker can't modify the message and move the troops — say, to Fort Knox — without the key. If he tries to change even one bit of the message, it decrypts to gibberish and is presumably rejected.

He can, however, cut half of it off. The attacker could modify the encrypted message to be

0xc99a87a32c57b80de43c26f762556a76bfb3040f7fc38e112d3ffddf4a5cb703

This message is received and decrypted correctly to "Withdraw troops from Bunker Hill." The recipient has no way to detect the modification. For this reason, some hash function must be used to verify the integrity of the message after it's been decrypted. SSL mandates that every record be protected this way with an HMAC function. You examine this in more detail when the details of the SSL protocol are discussed.

Also, SSL uses the HMAC function quite a bit as a pseudo-random number generator. Because the output is not predictably related to the input, the HMAC function is actually used to generate the keying material from a shared secret. In fact, the HMAC function is used to generate the final HMAC secret!

## Understanding Digital Signature Algorithm (DSA) Signatures

Now it's time to return to the primary topic of this chapter — digital signatures. Recall from the beginning of this chapter that, in order to properly support digital signatures, you must first compute a secure hash of the document/message that you want to sign, and then perform a public-key operation on that secure hash using a private key. By now, you should have a very good understanding of secure hash algorithms, but not the actual mechanics of what to do with those secure hashes because this hasn't yet been covered.

RSA support for digital signatures is straightforward — compute a secure hash over the bytes to be signed and "encrypt" it using a private key. The recipient then verifies the same signature by computing the secure hash of the same set of bytes, "decrypting" using the associated public key, and comparing the two. The only difference between an RSA digital signature and an RSA encryption (other than the fact that encryption is done with a public key and signing is done with a private key) is that the padding type from Listing 3-21 is 0x01, instead of 0x02, and the padding bytes are all 1s instead of random bytes.

However, RSA isn't the only game in town, at least not when it comes to digital signatures. A competing standard is the U.S. government's *Digital Signature Algorithm*, specified in FIPS 186-3.

### Implementing Sender-Side DSA Signature Generation

If you were pleasantly surprised by the simplicity and elegance of the RSA algorithm, where encryption, decryption, signatures, and verification were all essentially the same operation with different parameters, DSA is going to be a bit of a shock to your system. The signature and verification operations are both completely different, and both are fairly complex. They also take quite a few extra parameters.

A DSA signature accepts five input parameters, including the message to be signed, and returns two output parameters. The input parameters are named $g$, $p$, $q$, and $x$ (and, of course, the message itself). $g$, $p$, and $q$ are part of the public key, and $x$ is the private key. Like RSA, the signature is performed on a secure hash of the message to be signed. However, the hash algorithm is somewhat part of the signature, so you can't necessarily just pick a random signature algorithm and try to apply it. DSA is certified for SHA-1 and SHA-256; if you try to use it with some other hash algorithm, "behavior is undefined."

So, to generate the two-element DSA signature, whose elements are named $r$ and $s$ by the standard (apparently nobody ever told the FIPS people the general rule on using meaningful variable names), you perform the following computations:

$$k = (c \% (q - 1)) + 1$$
$$r = (g^k \% p) \% q$$
$$z = \text{hash}(\text{ message }), \text{truncated to sizeof}(q)$$
$$s = ((k^{-1} \% q) * (z + xr)) \% q$$

where $(k^{-1} \% q)$ means the inverse mod $q$, as defined in Chapter 3, of $k$.

What about this $c$? $c$ is just a random number — securely generated, of course — whose length in bits is the same as $q$. After performing these operations, you've generated $r$ and $s$, which make up the signature.

To slightly minimize the method signatures, define a new structure named dsa_params in Listing 4-29 to hold the general parameters $g$, $p$, and $q$.

**Listing 4-29:** "dsa.h" dsa_params structure

```
typedef struct
{
  huge g;
  huge p;
  huge q;
}
dsa_params;
```

Define the structure in Listing 4-30 to hold the actual signature.

**Listing 4-30:** "dsa.h" dsa_signature structure

```
typedef struct
{
  huge r;
  huge s;
}
dsa_signature;
```

So now, in code, the signature algorithm can be implemented as shown in Listing 4-31.

**Listing 4-31:** "dsa.c" DSA signature generation algorithm

```
void dsa_sign( dsa_params *params,
       huge *private_key,
       unsigned int *hash,
       int hash_len,
       dsa_signature *signature )
{
  huge k;
  huge z;
  huge q;

  set_huge( &q, 1 );

  generate_message_secret( params, &k );
  // r = ( g ^ k % p ) % q
  mod_pow( &params->g, &k, &params->p, &signature->r );
  copy_huge( &q, &params->q );
  divide( &signature->r, &q, NULL );

  // z = hash(message), only approved with SHA
  load_huge( &z, ( unsigned char * ) hash,
    ( (hash_len * 4 ) < params->q.size ) ?
    (hash_len * 4 ) : params->q.size );
```

*(Continued)*

```
  // s = ( inv(k) * ( z + xr ) ) % q
  inv( &k, &params->q );
  set_huge( &signature->s, 0 );
  copy_huge( &signature->s, private_key );
  multiply( &signature->s, &signature->r );
  add( &signature->s, &z );
  multiply( &signature->s, &k );
  copy_huge( &q, &params->q );
  divide( &signature->s, &q, NULL );

  free_huge( &z );
}
```

Notice that this keeps essentially the same variable names that the specification suggests, although it does call $x$ private_key to make it a bit clearer what it does. You should be able to follow the last parts of the code. I've added comments to indicate what each section is doing with respect to the overall algorithm. Note that this calls the inv routine defined in Listing 3-36 to compute $(k^{-1}\,\%\,q)$ as part of the computation of $s$. Also, the caller passes in the hash, not the message itself; this makes the routine a bit more flexible, although DSA is only officially approved for use with SHA. The signature function doesn't know or care what the original message was.

The computation of k is delegated to its own routine in Listing 4-32.

**Listing 4-32:** "dsa.c" message secret generation

```
static void generate_message_secret( dsa_params *params, huge *k )
{
  int i;
  huge q;
  huge one;

  set_huge( &q, 0 ); // initialize this so that copy works
  set_huge( &one, 1 );

  copy_huge( &q, &params->q );
  subtract( &q, &one );

  // XXX the extra + 8 aren't really necessary since we're not generating
  // a random "c"
  k->sign = 0;
  k->size = params->q.size + 8;
  k->rep = malloc( k->size );
  // TODO this should be filled with random bytes
  for ( i = 0; i < k->size; i++ )
  {
    k->rep[ i ] = i + 1;
  }
```

```
  // k will become k % ( q - 1 );
  divide( k, &q, NULL );
  add( k, &one );
}
```

The whole `dsa_params` structure is passed here, although technically only q is required.

So, given a message, a set of DSA parameters, and a private key, you can compute a DSA signature for the message. Remember that a DSA signature consists of two separate elements. Because r and s are both computed mod q, they are of the same length as q, but they have to be separated somehow in the output. This is in contrast to an RSA signature which is just a single, very long, number. You'll see in Chapter 5 that this comes up as a bit of an issue in SSL/TLS.

### Implementing Receiver-Side DSA Signature Verification

Now you may be saying, "OK, that DSA signature algorithm was a little complex, but it wasn't *that* bad." Get ready to see the signature verification algorithm.

Remember that the purpose of this whole thing is for the holder of the private key to be able to transmit, in some authenticated way, the public key and the signature to anybody else and allow that person to verify that only the holder of the private key could have produced that signature over the given message. With RSA, verification was a trivial extension of signature generation. You "encrypt" a hash using the private key, and the recipient "decrypts" using the public key and compares the hashes. If the two match, the signature is verified.

Because DSA isn't encrypting or decrypting anything, DSA signature verification is a bit more complex. The recipient has the DSA parameters $g$, $p$, and $q$, the public key $y$ and the signature elements $r$ and $s$ — along with, of course, the message itself. From this, it needs to check to see if $r$ and $s$ were generated from $g$, $p$, $q$, $x$, and the message. The DSA way to accomplish this is to perform the following operations:

$$w = s^{-1} \% q$$

$$z = hash(\ message\ ),\ truncated\ to\ sizeof(\ q\ )$$

$$u1 = (\ zw\ ) \% q$$

$$u2 = (\ rw\ ) \% q$$

$$v = (\ (\ g^{u1}\ y^{u2}\ ) \% p\ ) \% q$$

If everything went correctly, $v$ is equal to $r$. Otherwise, something went wrong or the signature is faked.

The signature part, then, is in $r$; $s$ is just transmitted to allow the recipient to invert enough of the original computation to recover $r$. The security is mostly in the secrecy of the parameter $k$ — which, you'll recall, was generated randomly in the signature stage. Since $s$ depends on $k$ and the private key $x$ — and $x$ and $y$ are of course mathematically related — $v$ depends on $s$ and $y$. The whole complicated mess described in this section just repeats the computation

$$r = ( g^k \% p ) \% q$$

without having access to $k$.

In code, this can be implemented as in Listing 4-33.

**Listing 4-33:** "dsa.c" DSA signature verification algorithm

```
int dsa_verify( dsa_params *params,
                              huge *public_key,
                              unsigned int *hash,
                              int hash_len,
                              dsa_signature *signature )
{
  int match;
  huge w, z, u1, u2, q, p;

  set_huge( &q, 1 );
  set_huge( &p, 1 );
  set_huge( &w, 0 );

  // w = inv(s) % q
  copy_huge( &w, &signature->s );
  inv( &w, &params->q );

  // z = hash(message), truncated to sizeof(q)
  load_huge( &z, ( unsigned char * ) hash,
    ( (hash_len * 4 ) < params->q.size ) ?
    (hash_len * 4 ) : params->q.size );

  // u1 = (zw) % q
  multiply( &z, &w );
  copy_huge( &q, &params->q );
  divide( &z, &params->q, NULL );   // u1 = z

  // u2 = (rw) % q
  multiply( &w, &signature->r );
  copy_huge( &q, &params->q );
  divide( &w, &q, NULL ); // u2 = w

  // v = ( ( ( g^u1) % p * (y^u2) %p ) % p ) % q
  mod_pow( &params->g, &z, &params->p, &u1 );
  mod_pow( public_key, &w, &params->p, &u2 );
  multiply( &u1, &u2 );
  copy_huge( &p, &params->p );
  divide( &u1, &p, NULL );
```

```
copy_huge( &q, &params->q );
divide( &u1, &q, NULL ); // u1 is "v" now

// Check to see if v & s match
match = !compare( &u1, &signature->r );

free_huge( &w );
free_huge( &z );
free_huge( &u1 );
free_huge( &u2 );

return match;
}
```

As with the signing algorithm, I've added comments so that you can match what the code is doing with the algorithm. Notice that this doesn't use u1 and u2 exactly as they're shown in the algorithm, instead putting u1 and u2 into z and w because you don't need them again, and then using u1 and u2 to hold the mod_pow values later on.

Also notice how:

$$v = ( ( g^{u1} \, y^{u2} ) \, \% \, p ) \, \% \, q$$

is put together. You don't want to compute $g^{u1}$, then compute $y^{u2}$ and then multiply them by each other to finally figure out "mod p" of the whole mess. You want to be able to use your mod_pow algorithm to keep the memory constraints manageable. So instead, factor the $v$ computation out into

$$v = ( ( ( g^{u1} \, \% \, p ) * ( y^{u2} \, \% \, p ) ) \, \% \, p ) \, \% \, q$$

by the distributivity of the modulus operator. Now you can use mod_pow to compute $(g^{u1}) \, \% \, p$ and $( y^{u2} \, \% \, p)$, multiply these together, which results in at most $2p$ bits, and then apply the modulus operation twice.

You can put together a main routine to test this but, like RSA's $e$, $d$, and $n$, the DSA parameters $g$, $p$, $q$, $x$, and $y$ must be specifically related and you haven't yet seen how. So just hardcode a sample set in the routine in Listing 4-34 to show how it can be called.

**Listing 4-34:** "dsa.c" test main routine

```
#ifdef TEST_DSA
int main( int argc, char *argv[] )
{
  unsigned char priv[] = {
0x53, 0x61, 0xae, 0x4f, 0x6f, 0x25, 0x98, 0xde, 0xc4, 0xbf, 0x0b, 0xbe, 0x09,
  0x5f, 0xdf,  0x90, 0x2f, 0x4c, 0x8e, 0x09 };
  unsigned char pub[] = {
0x1b, 0x91, 0x4c, 0xa9, 0x73, 0xdc, 0x06, 0x0d, 0x21, 0xc6, 0xff, 0xab, 0xf6,
```

*(Continued)*

```
  0xad, 0xf4, 0x11, 0x97, 0xaf, 0x23, 0x48, 0x50, 0xa8, 0xf3, 0xdb, 0x2e, 0xe6,
  0x27, 0x8c, 0x40, 0x4c,  0xb3, 0xc8, 0xfe, 0x79, 0x7e, 0x89, 0x48, 0x90, 0x27,
  0x92, 0x6f, 0x5b, 0xc5, 0xe6, 0x8f,  0x91, 0x4c, 0xe9, 0x4f, 0xed, 0x0d, 0x3c,
  0x17, 0x09, 0xeb, 0x97, 0xac, 0x29, 0x77, 0xd5,  0x19, 0xe7, 0x4d, 0x17 };
  unsigned char P[] = {
0x00, 0x9c, 0x4c, 0xaa, 0x76, 0x31, 0x2e, 0x71, 0x4d, 0x31, 0xd6, 0xe4, 0xd7,
  0xe9, 0xa7,  0x29, 0x7b, 0x7f, 0x05, 0xee, 0xfd, 0xca, 0x35, 0x14, 0x1e, 0x9f,
  0xe5, 0xc0, 0x2a, 0xe0,  0x12, 0xd9, 0xc4, 0xc0, 0xde, 0xcc, 0x66, 0x96, 0x2f,
  0xf1, 0x8f, 0x1a, 0xe1, 0xe8, 0xbf,  0xc2, 0x29, 0x0d, 0x27, 0x07, 0x48, 0xb9,
  0x71, 0x04, 0xec, 0xc7, 0xf4, 0x16, 0x2e, 0x50,  0x8d, 0x67, 0x14, 0x84, 0x7b
};
  unsigned char Q[] = {
0x00, 0xac, 0x6f, 0xc1, 0x37, 0xef, 0x16, 0x74, 0x52, 0x6a, 0xeb, 0xc5, 0xf8,
  0xf2, 0x1f,  0x53, 0xf4, 0x0f, 0xe0, 0x51, 0x5f };
  unsigned char G[] = {
0x7d, 0xcd, 0x66, 0x81, 0x61, 0x52, 0x21, 0x10, 0xf7, 0xa0, 0x83, 0x4c, 0x5f,
  0xc8, 0x84,  0xca, 0xe8, 0x8a, 0x9b, 0x9f, 0x19, 0x14, 0x8c, 0x7d, 0xd0, 0xee,
  0x33, 0xce, 0xb4, 0x57,  0x2d, 0x5e, 0x78, 0x3f, 0x06, 0xd7, 0xb3, 0xd6, 0x40,
  0x70, 0x2e, 0xb6, 0x12, 0x3f, 0x4a,  0x61, 0x38, 0xae, 0x72, 0x12, 0xfb, 0x77,
  0xde, 0x53, 0xb3, 0xa1, 0x99, 0xd8, 0xa8, 0x19,  0x96, 0xf7, 0x7f, 0x99 };
  dsa_params params;
  dsa_signature signature;
  huge x, y;
  unsigned char *msg = "abc123";
  digest_ctx ctx;

  // TODO load these from a DSA private key file instead
  load_huge( &params.g, G, sizeof( G ) );
  load_huge( &params.p, P, sizeof( P ) );
  load_huge( &params.q, Q, sizeof( Q ) );
  load_huge( &x, priv, sizeof( priv ) );
  load_huge( &y, pub, sizeof( pub ) );

  new_sha1_digest( &ctx );
  update_digest( &ctx, msg, strlen( msg ) );
  finalize_digest( &ctx );

  dsa_sign( &params, &x, ctx.hash, ctx.hash_len, &signature );

  printf( "DSA signature of abc123 is:" );
  printf( "r:" );
  show_hex( signature.r.rep, signature.r.size );
  printf( "s:" );
  show_hex( signature.s.rep, signature.s.size );

  if ( dsa_verify( &params, &y, ctx.hash, ctx.hash_len, &signature ) )
  {
    printf( "Verified\n" );
  }
  else
```

```
{
    printf( "Verificiation failed\n" );
}

free_huge( &x );
free_huge( &y );

    return 0;
}
#endif
```

The output of this function isn't too interesting.

```
jdavies@localhost$ ./dsa
DSA signature of abc123 is:
r: 14297f2522458d809b6c5752d3975a00bb0d89e0
s: 2f6e24ed330faf27700470cc6074552e58cbea3a
Verifying:
Verified
```

But it illustrates how DSA signatures are generated. You can see a noticeable pause when this example runs; public-key cryptography strikes again.

> **NOTE** DSA keys consist of the parameters $p$, $q$, and $g$, a private key $x$, and a public key $y$. $q$ must be a (random) prime number; $p - 1$ must be a multiple of $q$; and $g$ is a small number (usually 2). $x$, the private key, is random, and $y = g^x$ % $p$. In general, rather than compute their own $p$, $q$, and $g$, most implementations use standardized DSA parameters. As long as $x$ is random, the security of the algorithm isn't weakened by the sharing of parameters.

### How to Make DSA Efficient

As you can imagine, it takes a bit longer to compute or verify a DSA signature than it does to compute or verify an RSA signature. The parameters $p$ and $y$ need to be at least 512 bits to be secure (2,048 bits is common). $q$ and $x$ can be a bit shorter; typically these are 160 bits, to match the output from an SHA-1 hash, and can still be secure as long as $p$ and $y$ are long. Still, this requires a lot of computation and a lot of memory compared to RSA.

However, if you look at the signature algorithm, you notice that the only part that depends on the message is $s$ — $r$ can actually be precomputed before the message is known, as long as $q$ is known because the secret parameter $k$ depends on it. Because $p$, $g$, and $q$ are part of the public key, a very speed-conscious implementation could create a table of $r$ and $k$ values and speed up the signature process quite a bit.

Also, notice that RSA verification involves a modular exponentiation of an enormous parameter $d$, which is 1,024 bits for reasonable security. This takes a long time to process. In contrast, DSA signature verification only requires modular exponentiation of *u1* and *u2*, which are both the same length as *q*, which is 160 bits. On the other hand, you have to compute a modular inverse for every signature verification.

Finally, notice that although `mod_pow` is aware of, and optimized for, the fact that it's operating in a Galois field (that is, the final result is computed modulo a target *p*), the DSA implementation here does several multiplication and addition operations only to throw away all but the "mod p" bits of the results. If you reworked your add and multiply operations to be aware of their field, you could cut down quite a bit on the amount of memory you'd need to set aside to compute interim results. You could even speed up `mod_pow` this way. This optimization won't be explored here; see Michael Brown's paper "Software Implementations of the NIST Elliptic Curves over Prime Fields" (www.eng.auburn.edu/users/hamilton/security/pubs/Software_Implementation_of_the_NIST_Elliptic.pdf) for a good discussion on optimal arithmetic operations in a Galois field. The paper itself is about elliptic-curve cryptography, but a lot of it is applicable to large-number modular arithmetic in general.

DSA is not particularly common, or popular, in spite of being a U.S. government standard (in fact, I wasn't able to find any U.S. government web sites using SSL with DSA, including the NIST web site, which published the DSA standard in the first place!). Still, it's worth examining both because support for it is a mandatory part of TLS as well as because supporting it demonstrates how flexible you need to be on signature algorithms.

## Getting More Security per Bit: Elliptic Curve DSA

DSA has been defined using ECC primitives, just like DH was. For the most part, ECDSA works like DSA, but it uses elliptic-curve keypairs instead of public/private keypairs. Instead of *r* being ( $g^k$ % p ) % q, *r* is just *G* — the *generator point* that is part of an elliptic-curve's definition — multiplied by *k*. *s* is computed identically; remember that in an elliptic-curve keypair, the private key is just an integer. Signature verification is also almost identical up until the computation of *v* (which is compared to *r* and, if they're identical, indicates that the signature is verified). Even this computation is similar; you just replace the `mod_pow` operations with ECC point-multiplication operations.

However, for ECDSA, you can't "cheat" and just use integer operations like in the ECDH implementation of the last chapter; remember that there's a hash computation that's used in the signature generation process. The smallest hash examined so far is MD5, which outputs 128 bits — quite a few more than you can fit into a 32-bit `int`. In fact, ECDSA is only defined for an SHA-256 hash, unlike "regular" DSA, which used a plain-old 160-bit

SHA-1 hash. Because you're going to be dealing with a 256-bit integer, at least, go ahead and rewrite the elliptic-curve math functions from Chapter 3 to work with `huge` integers.

### *Rewriting the Elliptic-Curve Math Functions to Support Large Numbers*

The implementations are, obviously, not drastically different than with 32-bit integers; a few things are shuffled around to reduce the number of temporary `huge` objects, though, so you might want to compare this code carefully to the ECC code in Chapter 3.

If you recall, ECC involves two operations: point addition — which works on two distinct points in a Cartesian plane, whose X-values must be different — and point multiplication — which works on one point and a scalar value. To implement, follow these steps:

1. Redefine the `point`, `elliptic_curve`, and `ecc_key` structures in Listing 4-35 to work with `huge`s instead of points.

**Listing 4-35:** "ecc.h" elliptic curve structure declarations

```
typedef struct
{
  huge x;
  huge y;
}
point;

typedef struct
{
  huge p;
  huge a;
  huge b;
  point G;
  huge n; // n is prime and is the "order" of G
  huge h; // h = #E(F_p)/n (# is the number of points on the curve)
}
elliptic_curve;

typedef struct
{
  huge d;  // random integer < n; this is the private key
  point Q; // Q = d * G; this is the public key
}
ecc_key;
```

2. You need an `add_points` operation in Listing 4-36.

**Listing 4-36:** "ecc.c" point addition implementation

```
void add_points( point *p1, point *p2, huge *p )
{
  point p3;
  huge denominator;
  huge numerator;
  huge invdenom;
  huge lambda;

  set_huge( &denominator, 0 );
  copy_huge( &denominator, &p2->x );      // denominator = x2
  subtract( &denominator, &p1->x );       // denominator = x2 - x1
  set_huge( &numerator, 0 );
  copy_huge( &numerator, &p2->y );        // numerator = y2
  subtract( &numerator, &p1->y );         // numerator = y2 - y1
  set_huge( &invdenom, 0 );
  copy_huge( &invdenom, &denominator );
  inv( &invdenom, p );
  set_huge( &lambda, 0 );
  copy_huge( &lambda, &numerator );
  multiply( &lambda, &invdenom );         // lambda = numerator / denominator
  set_huge( &p3.x, 0 );
  copy_huge( &p3.x, &lambda );      // x3 = lambda
  multiply( &p3.x, &lambda );       // x3 = lambda * lambda
  subtract( &p3.x, &p1->x );        // x3 = ( lambda * lambda ) - x1
  subtract( &p3.x, &p2->x );        // x3 = ( lambda * lambda ) - x1 - x2

  divide( &p3.x, p, NULL );         // x3 = ( ( lamdba * lambda ) - x1 - x2 ) % p

  // positive remainder always
  if ( p3.x.sign )
  {
    p3.x.sign = 0;
    subtract( &p3.x, p );
    p3.x.sign = 0;
  }

  set_huge( &p3.y, 0 );
  copy_huge( &p3.y, &p1->x );       // y3 = x1
  subtract( &p3.y, &p3.x );         // y3 = x1 - x3
  multiply( &p3.y, &lambda );       // y3 = ( x1 - x3 ) * lambda
  subtract( &p3.y, &p1->y );        // y3 = ( ( x1 - x3 ) * lambda ) - y

  divide( &p3.y, p, NULL );
  // positive remainder always
  if ( p3.y.sign )
  {
    p3.y.sign = 0;
    subtract( &p3.y, p );
    p3.y.sign = 0;
  }
```

```
// p1->x = p3.x
// p1->y = p3.y
copy_huge( &p1->x, &p3.x );
copy_huge( &p1->y, &p3.y );

free_huge( &p3.x );
free_huge( &p3.y );
free_huge( &denominator );
free_huge( &numerator );
free_huge( &invdenom );
free_huge( &lambda );
}
```

I've left comments indicating the int operations that the huge operation blocks correspond to so you can cross-reference this implementation back to the easier-to-understand integer-based operation in Listing 3-39.

3. Recall that multiplication is defined in terms of "double-and-add" — in this case, not as a performance optimization, but because adding a point to itself is actually not defined, so you need a double_point operation in Listing 4-37.

**Listing 4-37:** "ecc.c" point-doubling algorithm

```
static void double_point( point *p1, huge *a, huge *p )
{
  huge lambda;
  huge l1;
  huge x1;
  huge y1;

  set_huge( &lambda, 0 );
  set_huge( &x1, 0 );
  set_huge( &y1, 0 );
  set_huge( &lambda, 2 );     // lambda = 2;
  multiply( &lambda, &p1->y ); // lambda = 2 * y1
  inv( &lambda, p );          // lambda = ( 2 * y1 ) ^ -1 (% p)

  set_huge( &l1, 3 );         // l1 = 3
  multiply( &l1, &p1->x );     // l1 = 3 * x
  multiply( &l1, &p1->x );     // l1 = 3 * x ^ 2
  add( &l1, a );              // l1 = ( 3 * x ^ 2 ) + a
  multiply( &lambda, &l1 );    // lambda = [ ( 3 * x ^ 2 ) + a ] / [ 2 * y1 ] ) % p
  copy_huge( &y1, &p1->y );
  // Note - make two copies of x2; this one is for y1 below
  copy_huge( &p1->y, &p1->x );
  set_huge( &x1, 2 );
  multiply( &x1, &p1->x );     // x1 = 2 * x1

  copy_huge( &p1->x, &lambda ); // x1 = lambda
```

*(Continued)*

```
multiply( &p1->x, &lambda );  // x1 = ( lambda ^ 2 );
subtract( &p1->x, &x1 );    // x1 = ( lambda ^ 2 ) - ( 2 * x1 )
divide( &p1->x, p, NULL );   // [ x1 = ( lambda ^ 2 ) - ( 2 * x1 ) ] % p

if ( p1->x.sign )
{
  subtract( &p1->x, p );
  p1->x.sign = 0;
  subtract( &p1->x, p );
}
subtract( &p1->y, &p1->x );  // y3 = x3 - x1
multiply( &p1->y, &lambda ); // y3 = lambda * ( x3 - x1 );
subtract( &p1->y, &y1 );    // y3 = ( lambda * ( x3 - x1 ) ) - y1
divide( &p1->y, p, NULL );   // y3 = [ ( lambda * ( x3 - x1 ) ) - y1 ] % p
if ( p1->y.sign )
{
  p1->y.sign = 0;
  subtract( &p1->y, p );
  p1->y.sign = 0;
}

free_huge( &lambda );
free_huge( &x1 );
free_huge( &y1 );
free_huge( &l1 );
}
```

4. Finally, you can implement `multiply_point` in Listing 4-38, the really important function, in terms of `double_point` and `add_points`.

**Listing 4-38:** "ecc.c" point-multiplication algorithm

```
void multiply_point( point *p1, huge *k, huge *a, huge *p )
{
  int i;
  unsigned char mask;
  point dp;
  int paf = 1;

  set_huge( &dp.x, 0 );
  set_huge( &dp.y, 0 );
  copy_huge( &dp.x, &p1->x );
  copy_huge( &dp.y, &p1->y );
  for ( i = k->size; i; i-- )
  {
    for ( mask = 0x01; mask; mask <<= 1 )
    {
      if ( k->rep[ i - 1 ] & mask )
      {
        if ( paf )
        {
```

```
        paf = 0;
        copy_huge( &p1->x, &dp.x );
        copy_huge( &p1->y, &dp.y );
      }
      else
      {
        add_points( p1, &dp, p );
      }
    }
    // double dp
    double_point( &dp, a, p );
    }
  }

  free_huge( &dp.x );
  free_huge( &dp.y );
}
```

You might want to compare this implementation to the multiply function presented in Listing 3-41. There is, of course, no divide equivalent. If there were, ECC wouldn't be cryptographically secure.

## Implementing ECDSA

Now you have enough ammunition to put together an implementation of ECDSA. Recall that DSA signature generation involved the computation of two numbers $r$ and $s$ from the parameters $g$, $p$, and $q$. ECDSA signatures are similar. In essence, the modular multiplications are replaced by point multiplications. The *generator* is a point on an elliptic curve; $r$ is that point multiplied by a random integer $k$; and $s$ is computed exactly the same way as in DSA. The only elliptic-curve function involved is in the computation of $r$. In code, this is shown in Listing 4-39.

**Listing 4-39:** "ecdsa.c" elliptic-curve DSA signature generation

```
void ecdsa_sign( elliptic_curve *params,
                 huge *private_key,
                 unsigned int *hash,
                 int hash_len,
                 dsa_signature *signature )
{
  unsigned char K[] = {
    0x9E, 0x56, 0xF5, 0x09, 0x19, 0x67, 0x84, 0xD9, 0x63, 0xD1, 0xC0,
    0xA4, 0x01, 0x51, 0x0E, 0xE7, 0xAD, 0xA3, 0xDC, 0xC5, 0xDE, 0xE0,
    0x4B, 0x15, 0x4B, 0xF6, 0x1A, 0xF1, 0xD5, 0xA6, 0xDE, 0xCE
  };
  huge k;
  point X;
  huge z;
```

*(Continued)*

```
    // This should be a random number between 0 and n-1
    load_huge( &k, ( unsigned char * ) K, sizeof( K ) );

    set_huge( &X.x, 0 );
    set_huge( &X.y, 0 );
    copy_huge( &X.x, &params->G.x );
    copy_huge( &X.y, &params->G.y );

    multiply_point( &X, &k, &params->a, &params->p );

    set_huge( &signature->r, 0 );
    copy_huge( &signature->r, &X.x );
    divide( &signature->r, &params->n, NULL ); // r = x1 % n

    // z is the L_n leftmost bits of hash - cannot be longer than n
    load_huge( &z, ( unsigned char * ) hash,
        ( ( hash_len * 4 ) < params->n.size ) ? ( hash_len * 4 ) : params->n.size );

    // s = k^-1 ( z + r d_a ) % n
    inv( &k, &params->n );
    set_huge( &signature->s, 0 );
    copy_huge( &signature->s, private_key );
    multiply( &signature->s, &signature->r );
    add( &signature->s, &z );
    multiply( &signature->s, &k );
    divide( &signature->s, &params->n, NULL );

    free_huge( &k );
    free_huge( &z );
    free_huge( &X.x );
    free_huge( &X.y );
}
```

You can see a lot of parallels between the DSA signature verification routine and the ECDSA signature verification routine in Listing 4-40.

**Listing 4-40:** "ecdsa.c" elliptic-curve DSA signature verification

```
int ecdsa_verify( elliptic_curve *params,
        point *public_key,
        unsigned int *hash,
        int hash_len,
        dsa_signature *signature )
{
    huge z;
    huge w;
    point G;
    point Q;
    int match;

    // w = s^-1 % n
```

```
set_huge( &w, 0 );
copy_huge( &w, &signature->s );
inv( &w, &params->n );

// z is the L_n leftmost bits of hash - cannot be longer than n
load_huge( &z, ( unsigned char * ) hash,
  ( ( hash_len * 4 ) < params->n.size ) ? ( hash_len * 4 ) : params->n.size );

// u1 = zw % n
multiply( &z, &w );
divide( &z, &params->n, NULL );  // u1 = z

// u2 = (rw) % q
multiply( &w, &signature->r );
divide( &w, &params->n, NULL ); // u2 = w

// (x1,y1) = u1 * G + u2 * Q
set_huge( &G.x, 0 );
set_huge( &G.y, 0 );
set_huge( &Q.x, 0 );
set_huge( &Q.y, 0 );
copy_huge( &G.x, &params->G.x );
copy_huge( &G.y, &params->G.y );
copy_huge( &Q.x, &public_key->x );
copy_huge( &Q.y, &public_key->y );

multiply_point( &G, &z, &params->a, &params->p );
multiply_point( &Q, &w, &params->a, &params->p );
add_points( &G, &Q, &params->p );

// r = x1 % n
divide( &G.x, &params->n, NULL );

match = !compare( &G.x, &signature->r );

free_huge( &z );
free_huge( &w );
free_huge( &G.x );
free_huge( &G.y );
free_huge( &Q.x );
free_huge( &Q.y );

return match;
}
```

Here, as in signature generation, modular exponentiation has been replaced with elliptic-curve addition and multiplication operations.

## Generating ECC Keypairs

One point glossed over thus far is that of the elliptic-curve parameters themselves. In fact, generating elliptic-curve parameters is so complex, so time consuming, and so hard to get right that the NIST publishes a list of approved *named curves* for use in elliptic curve operations. Of course, the actual keypairs — the secret integer and the public point — are generated per-user from the parameters. Generating a keypair is actually pretty simple: Pick a random large integer $d$ and multiply it by the point $G$. The result of the multiplication is the public key, and $d$ is the private key.

To illustrate how to use this, you can borrow an elliptic curve from RFC 4754 that includes some ECDSA examples. The test routine is shown in Listing 4-41.

**Listing 4-41:** "ecdsa.c" test routine

```
#ifdef TEST_ECDSA
int main( int argc, char *argv[ ] )
{
  // ECC parameters
  unsigned char P[] = {
0xFF, 0xFF, 0xFF, 0xFF, 0x00, 0x00, 0x00, 0x01, 0x00, 0x00, 0x00, 0x00, 0x00,
0x00, 0x00, 0x00, 0x00, 0x00, 0x00, 0x00, 0xFF, 0xFF, 0xFF, 0xFF, 0xFF, 0xFF,
0xFF, 0xFF, 0xFF, 0xFF, 0xFF, 0xFF
  };
  unsigned char b[] = {
0x5A, 0xC6, 0x35, 0xD8, 0xAA, 0x3A, 0x93, 0xE7, 0xB3, 0xEB, 0xBD, 0x55, 0x76,
0x98, 0x86,  0xBC, 0x65, 0x1D, 0x06, 0xB0, 0xCC, 0x53, 0xB0, 0xF6, 0x3B, 0xCE,
0x3C, 0x3E, 0x27, 0xD2, 0x60, 0x4B
  };
  unsigned char q[] = {
0xFF, 0xFF, 0xFF, 0xFF, 0x00, 0x00, 0x00, 0x00, 0xFF, 0xFF, 0xFF, 0xFF, 0xFF,
0xFF, 0xFF, 0xFF, 0xBC, 0xE6, 0xFA, 0xAD, 0xA7, 0x17, 0x9E, 0x84, 0xF3, 0xB9,
0xCA, 0xC2, 0xFC, 0x63, 0x25, 0x51
  };
  unsigned char gx[] = {
    0x6B, 0x17, 0xD1, 0xF2, 0xE1, 0x2C, 0x42, 0x47, 0xF8, 0xBC, 0xE6, 0xE5,
0x63,
    0xA4, 0x40, 0xF2, 0x77, 0x03, 0x7D, 0x81, 0x2D, 0xEB, 0x33, 0xA0, 0xF4,
0xA1,
    0x39, 0x45, 0xD8, 0x98, 0xC2, 0x96
  };
  unsigned char gy[] = {
0x4F, 0xE3, 0x42, 0xE2, 0xFE, 0x1A, 0x7F, 0x9B, 0x8E, 0xE7, 0xEB, 0x4A, 0x7C,
0x0F, 0x9E, 0x16, 0x2B, 0xCE, 0x33, 0x57, 0x6B, 0x31, 0x5E, 0xCE, 0xCB, 0xB6,
0x40, 0x68, 0x37, 0xBF, 0x51, 0xF5
  };

  // key
  unsigned char w[] = { 0xDC, 0x51, 0xD3, 0x86, 0x6A, 0x15, 0xBA, 0xCD, 0xE3,
    0x3D, 0x96, 0xF9, 0x92, 0xFC, 0xA9, 0x9D, 0xA7, 0xE6, 0xEF, 0x09, 0x34, 0xE7,
```

```
    0x09, 0x75, 0x59, 0xC2, 0x7F, 0x16, 0x14, 0xC8, 0x8A, 0x7F };

    elliptic_curve curve;
    ecc_key A;
    dsa_signature signature;

    digest_ctx ctx;

    load_huge( &curve.p, ( unsigned char * ) P, sizeof( P ) );
    set_huge( &curve.a, 3 );
    curve.a.sign = 1;
    load_huge( &curve.b, b, sizeof( b ) );
    load_huge( &curve.G.x, gx, sizeof( gx ) );
    load_huge( &curve.G.y, gy, sizeof( gy ) );
    load_huge( &curve.n, q, sizeof( q ) );

    // Generate new public key from private key "w" and point "G"
    load_huge( &A.d, w, sizeof( w ) );
    set_huge( &A.Q.x, 0 );
    set_huge( &A.Q.y, 0 );
    copy_huge( &A.Q.x, &curve.G.x );
    copy_huge( &A.Q.y, &curve.G.y );
    multiply_point( &A.Q, &A.d, &curve.a, &curve.p );

    new_sha256_digest( &ctx );
    update_digest( &ctx, "abc", 3 );
    finalize_digest( &ctx );

    ecdsa_sign( &curve, &A.d, ctx.hash, ctx.hash_len, &signature );

    printf( "R:" );
    show_hex( signature.r.rep, signature.r.size );
    printf( "S:" );
    show_hex( signature.s.rep, signature.r.size );

    if ( !ecdsa_verify( &curve, &A.Q, ctx.hash, ctx.hash_len, &signature ) )
    {
      printf( "Signatures don't match.\n" );
    }
    else
    {
      printf( "Signature verified.\n" );
    }

    return 0;
}
#endif
```

Like the DSA test routine output, this one isn't particularly interesting, but it demonstrates the concept:

```
jdavies@localhost$ ./ecdsa
```

```
R:
cb28e0999b9c7715fd0a80d8e47a77079716cbbf917dd72e97566ea1c066957c
S:
86fa3bb4e26cad5bf90b7f81899256ce7594bb1ea0c89212748bff3b3d5b0315
Verifying
Signature verified.
```

If you ran this on your own computer, you may have noticed that it was slow. Murderously slow, in fact. Each point-multiplication operation requires between $log_2k$ and $2 * log_2k$ modular inversions, each of which involves many operations in its own right. Nor can you speed the thing up by precomputing some inversions and reusing them because $\lambda$ is going to be different for each call. The whole process, including the generation of the public key, took me three minutes on a relatively modern computer running Windows Vista, and this was a 256-bit key — although, for ECC, that's actually pretty long whereas for RSA or DSA it would be unusably short.

**NOTE** Incidentally, on the same computer, the same code, compiled with GCC even with optimizations off, ran in less than one minute when I booted over to Linux, so ECC isn't entirely to blame here.

So, what's the point of ECC, then? The idea was that it was supposed to be faster. Actually, there's been quite a bit of research in speeding up the somewhat naïve implementation presented here. These techniques generally involve translating the point to be multiplied from the two-dimensional coordinate system presented here into a three-dimensional coordinate system, performing equivalent operations, and then transforming them back to the two-dimensional coordinate system, all the while taking into account the prime-field you're working in.

The implementation is even more complex than the *simple* multiplication routine presented above, and involves orders of magnitude more operations (but you can trade lots of operations to get rid of just one modular inversion and still be ahead). The Jacobian projection is one such popular transformation; I don't cover it here, but it can speed up elliptic-curve operations by an order of magnitude to bring it to parity with modular exponentiation operations. Because ECC offers equivalent security with far fewer public-key bits, this makes ECC an attractive choice for public-key cryptography operations, which will probably become more and more important in the future.

# CHAPTER 5

# Creating a Network of Trust Using X.509 Certificates

Chapters 3 and 4 discussed public and private keypairs and reviewed their importance to secure communications over insecure channels. Until now, where these keys come from and how they're exchanged has been mostly glossed over. Where the keys come from is the topic of this chapter. This chapter also includes some further discussion on authentication.

You're probably familiar with the term *certificate*, even if you're fuzzy on the details. You've undoubtedly visited web sites that have reported errors such as "this website's certificate is no longer valid" or "this website's host name does not match its certificate's host name" or "this certificate was not signed by a trusted CA." If you're like most Internet users, you generally ignore these warnings, although in some cases they can indicate something important.

Fundamentally, the certificate is a holder for a public key. Although it contains a lot more information about the subject of the public key — in the case of web sites, that would be the DNS name of the site which has the corresponding private key — the primary purpose of the certificate is to present the user agent with a public key that should then be used to encrypt a symmetric key that is subsequently used to protect the remainder of the connection's traffic.

At this point, you may have at least a hazy idea of how most of the concepts of the past three chapters can be put together to establish a secure communications link: First, a symmetric algorithm and key is chosen, and then the key is exchanged using public-key techniques. Finally, everything is encrypted using the secret symmetric key and authenticated using an HMAC with another secret key. However, the digital signatures examined in Chapter 4 haven't come into play yet. How are these used and why are they important? Digital signatures are how certificates are authenticated and how you can determine whether or not to trust a certificate. This is examined in much greater detail later in this chapter.

## Putting It Together: The Secure Channel Protocol

Armed with symmetric encryption and some method of secure key exchange, such as public key encryption of the symmetric encryption key, you have enough to implement a secure channel against passive eavesdroppers. Assuming that an attacker can see, but not modify, your data, you could adopt the simple secure channel protocol shown in Figure 5-1.

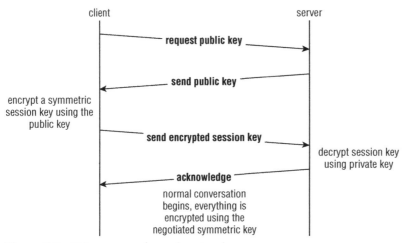

**Figure 5.1:** Naïve secure channel protocol

Even if an attacker can view all packets exchanged, all he sees is that the public key was requested and what the public key was — which, by definition, is not a secret. From that point forward, everything is encrypted and, assuming the encryption method is unbreakable, the remainder of the session is secure.

However, a more dangerous form of attack is called a *man-in-the middle* attack and is carried out by an adversary who can not only view traffic, but also can intercept and modify it. Consider the scenario shown in Figure 5-2.

The problem here is that the client implicitly trusts that the public key belongs to the server. Solving this trust issue surrounds most of the complexity associated with SSL/TLS. The remainder of this book is spent looking at how to get around this problem.

The solution adopted by SSL requires the use of a trusted intermediary. This trusted intermediary digitally signs the public key of the server — using the algorithms discussed in Chapter 4 — and the client must verify this signature. Such a signed public key is called a *certificate*, and a trusted intermediary responsible for signing certificates is called a *certificate authority (CA)*. The client must have access to the public key of the CA so that it can authenticate the signature before accepting the key as genuine. Web browsers have a list of trusted CAs with their public keys built in for just this purpose.

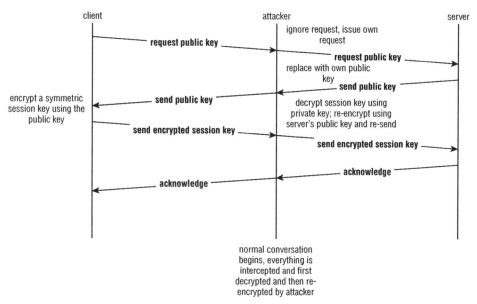

**Figure 5.2:** Man-in-the-middle attack

This buys a bit of security against a man-in-the-middle attack, but not much. After all, if the server can get a certificate signed by the trusted CA, you must assume that the attacker, if sufficiently motivated, could do so too. He could present himself to the CA as a legitimate business, for example. This makes his job a bit more difficult, but hardly insurmountable.

What you really need is some way to associate the public key with the server you're connecting to. Thus, a properly formatted certificate needs to have not only the public key of the server included, but also the domain name of the server that the public key belongs to, all signed by the trusted intermediary.

This foils the man-in-the-middle attack. The client requests a certificate from the server, and the man in the middle replaces it with his own. The client then validates the attacker's certificate as legitimate — it's signed by a trusted CA — but observes that the domain doesn't match that of www.server.com, as expected. Nor can the attacker forge a certificate with the domain name www .server.com — this is protected by the digital signature. If he obtains a digitally signed certificate from the CA, with the domain name www.attacker.com, and then changes his own domain in the certificate to www.server.com, the hash code in the signature won't match the hash code of the contents of the certificate, and the client rejects it on this basis.

So, at a bare minimum, in order to protect yourself against man-in-the-middle attacks, you need a trusted CA and a certificate format that includes the domain name, the public key and a digital signature issued by the CA. Now, imagine that a few years go by, and the administrator of the server figures that it's time to reissue the certificate. After all, technology changes, and certificate security holes are found from time to time. And who knows? Some hacker could have broken into the system and stolen the private key without the administrator's knowledge.

Unfortunately, the administrator can't reissue the certificate. Assuming that there's a problem with the certificate — the private key has been compromised or the certificate technology is outdated and includes a security flaw — and the server installs a new certificate, the man in the middle strikes again. When the client tries to connect, the attacker substitutes the old, and presumably weaker, certificate for the new one. The client has no way to authenticate this certificate; the domain is correct, and so is the issuer's digital signature.

To partially guard against this, certificates also include a *validity period*: a *not before* date and a *not after* date. It's the responsibility of the client to check that the certificate's not after date does not fall in the past. If the date is in the past, the client should not connect to the server.

As you can imagine, this is really only half a solution. Imagine that the private key has been compromised and the server administrator knows that the private key been compromised. He should immediately stop allowing use of the compromised certificate. The validity period guarantees that clients stop using the certificate at some point in the future, but you really want a way to accelerate that date. Again, that can't be forced, because a man in the middle can just replace any new certificate with an old one, right up until the end of the validity period.

To fight against this, CAs are responsible for keeping a list of *revoked* certificates that is called a *certificate revocation list* (CRL). The client periodically checks this list. But wait — checks it for what? How can you uniquely identify a certificate? As they've been specified so far, you can't; you need one more field in the certificate format, the *serial ID*. This is a number, unique within a CA, assigned to each certificate. When a certificate is known or believed to be compromised, its serial number is added to the CRL. If the man in the middle tries to replace a new certificate with an old one, the client recognizes that the serial number has been revoked and rejects the connection.

Finally, it's unlikely that everybody on the Internet will use a single CA. That means that the client, when presented with a certificate, needs some way to know whose public key to use to verify the signature. As such, each certificate also includes an *issuer* that uniquely identifies the CA. The client decides whether or not to trust the issuer dynamically.

# Encoding with ASN.1

Certificates need to be precisely defined. Although this sort of structured data is now usually represented and defined in XML, certificates have been around for quite a while, longer than XML. They're specified instead using a syntax referred to as *Abstract Syntax Notation* (ASN), or ASN.1 (the .1 being the version of Abstract Syntax Notation). ASN serves the same purpose as a DTD or an XSD might serve in an XML context; it describes how elements are nested within one another, what order they must occur in, and what type each is. Official ASN.1 looks quite a bit like a C `struct` definition, although the differences are significant enough that you can't map directly from one to another.

The certificate format that SSL/TLS uses is defined and maintained by the *International Telecommunication Union* (ITU) in a series of documents they just refer to as the *X series*. The documents themselves can be found at `http://www.itu.int/rec/T-REC-X/en`. Each one has a number, and the corresponding document/standard is referred to as X.*nnn* where *nnn* is a number. So, for instance, if you want to see the official standard for X.509, you look under `http://www.itu.int/rec/T-REC-X.509/en`. I'll refer to several of these specifications by number throughout this chapter.

You may notice that the specifications presented here aren't always specific to SSL/TLS. They were developed independently and adopted later by the Internet consortium. As such, the specifications contain quite a few elements that aren't necessarily relevant to the subject matter of this book itself; I'll mention some of these elements here but refer the interested reader to other sources for details.

## Understanding Signed Certificate Structure

ASN.1 is used to describe the structure of an X.509 certificate, which is the official standard for public-key certificates and the format on which TLS 1.0 relies. X.509 has been through three revisions; the current, at the time of this writing, revision of X.509 is 3. The top-level structure of an X.509v3 certificate is shown in Listing 5-1.

**Listing 5-1:** X.509 Certificate structure declaration

```
SEQUENCE {
    version      [0] EXPLICIT Version DEFAULT v1,
    serialNumber     CertificateSerialNumber,
    signature        AlgorithmIdentifier,
    issuer       Name,
    validity         Validity,
    subject      Name,
    subjectPublicKeyInfo SubjectPublicKeyInfo,
    issuerUniqueID [1] IMPLICIT UniqueIdentifier OPTIONAL,
            -- If present, version shall be v2 or v3
```

*(Continued)*

```
subjectUniqueID [2] IMPLICIT UniqueIdentifier OPTIONAL,
            -- If present, version shall be v2 or v3
extensions   [3] EXPLICIT Extensions OPTIONAL
            -- If present, version shall be v3

}
```

*Excerpted from* http://www.ietf.org/rfc/rfc2459.txt

The syntax is given in ASN.1. ASN.1 syntax isn't covered completely here; however, you have to understand a fair bit of it to analyze X.509 because X.509 makes use of most of ASN.1. See http://luca.ntop.org/Teaching/Appunti/asn1.html for a complete overview of ASN.1 syntax.

The first line here in the top-level structure of the X.509v3 certificate is SEQUENCE. An ASN.1 SEQUENCE is analogous to a C struct, which may be confusing to a C programmer because *sequence* sounds more like an array. An ASN.1 sequence groups other elements. As you can see, this sequence contains 10 subelements. The most important of these, of course, is the seventh, subjectPublicKeyInfo, because the primary purpose of a certificate is to transmit a public key.

Each subelement is presented with a name followed by a type — just like a C struct, but inverted. Each of these is examined in detail in the following sections. I'll go over the meaning of each at a high-level, and then come back and show you how to parse a real certificate; if some of this seems a bit abstract, the code samples at the end of this chapter should clear up the intent behind all of these elements.

### Version

```
version     [0] EXPLICIT Version DEFAULT v1
```

The version is an integer between 0 and 2, with 0 representing version 1, 1 representing version 2, 2 representing version 3, and so on. The version number indicates how to parse the remaining structures. For example, the comments at the bottom that indicate issuerUniqueId, subjectUniqueId, and extensions cannot be present if the version is less than 2. However, the original X.509 specification didn't include a version number, so it's necessary for the parser to first check to see if a version number is present. If no version number is present, the parser should assume that the version number is 0 (that is, v1). That's the meaning of the EXPLICIT DEFAULT v1 in the declaration.

The type Version itself is defined in the specification as

```
Version ::= INTEGER { v1(0), v2(1), v3(2) }
```

This tells you that the version field is an integer and that it can take on three discrete values.

### serialNumber

```
serialNumber      CertificateSerialNumber
```

As discussed in the section "Putting It Together: The Secure Channel Protocol" earlier in this chapter, certificates are signed by CAs. The process of signing a certificate is often referred to as *issuing* a certificate, and the signer is referred to as the *issuer*, although this terminology is a bit misleading. Each signer is required to assign a unique serial number to each certificate issued. The serial number is not necessarily globally unique, but it can safely be assumed that VeriSign (a popular CA), for example, never reuses a serial number. Two different CAs may issue two certificates with identical serial numbers, but the same CA never will. The `CertificateSerialNumber` is defined as an `INTEGER`.

### signature

```
signature      AlgorithmIdentifier,
```

An X.509 certificate must have been signed by a CA. Whether that CA is trusted or not is a matter for the client to decide. In fact, for testing purposes, it's often useful to create *self-signed* certificates, in which case the certificate is digitally signed by the private key corresponding to the public key that it contains.

Whoever signed the certificate, the signature algorithm used must be identified by this field. The declaration for an algorithm identifier is

```
AlgorithmIdentifier ::= SEQUENCE {
    algorithm         OBJECT IDENTIFIER,
    parameters        ANY DEFINED BY algorithm OPTIONAL }
```

Here you see a new type you haven't come across before: the *object identifier* (OID). OIDs are used quite a bit in the X.509 standard and anything else that's based on ASN.1. OIDs are actually murderously complex and describe a hierarchy of just about anything you can think of. Fortunately, you don't really need to fully understand OIDs. You can treat them simply as byte arrays and keep track of the mappings of these byte arrays and their meanings.

Recall from the Chapter 4 that digitally signing a sequence of bytes involves first securely hashing those bytes using a secure hash algorithm such as MD5 or SHA and then encrypting the bytes using a private key. Thus, a digital signature algorithm identifier must identify both the secure hashing algorithm applied as well as the encrypting algorithm. Given MD5 and SHA for secure hashing algorithms and RSA and DSS for private-key encryption algorithms, you end up with four separate algorithm identifiers. However, because MD5 is not specified for use with DSS, there are only three algorithm identifiers, which are shown in Table 5-1.

**Table 5-1:** Signing Algorithm OIDs

| HASH ALGORITHM IDENTIFIER | ENCRYPTION ALGORITHM | OBJECT IDENTIFIER |
|---|---|---|
| MD5 | RSA | 2A 86 48 86 F7 0D 01 01 04 |
| SHA-1 | RSA | 2A 86 48 86 F7 0D 01 01 05 |
| SHA-1 | DSS | 2A 86 52 CE 38 04 03 |

See X.690 and RFC 2313 for more details on how these values are determined. All you particularly care about is that the third field of the certificate (or the second, if the version number was not supplied) is equal to one of these three-byte sequences. You use this value as a switch to validate the signature of the certificate.

> **NOTE**   You may be wondering: "What about ECDSA?" Well, that's sort of complicated. The topic of elliptic-curve cryptography (ECC) in X.509 is revisited in Chapter 9. In general, ECC is not explicitly supported by any version of TLS < 1.2, and supporting it in any version can get a bit hairy.

---

**OIDs**

If you read any of the ITU X series specification documents, you'll notice that the OIDs are not given in hexadecimal form as they are in Table 5-1. Instead, they're given in a *dotted-decimal* form such as 1.2.840.113549.1.1.4. However, in order to be used, they must be converted to the hexadecimal forms shown in this book. The X.690 specification details this conversion authoritatively. You don't actually need to know how to convert from these dotted-decimal numbers to the normalized hexadecimal forms in order to use them. I've converted all of the ones you need to know but if you're curious, read on.

An OID in X.509 is a leaf in a very, very large tree structure. For example, the OID for the MD5withRSA signature algorithm is 1.2.840.113549.1.1.4. Each number in this very long digit string identifies an element in a large hierarchy. 1 represents iso; 1.2 represents iso/memberBody; 1.2.840 represents iso/member-body/usa and so on. All in all, the OID in this example represents iso/memberBody/usa/rsadsi/pkcs/pkcs1/MD5. Each number only has meaning relative to what came before it. The RSA corporation controls the 1.2.840.113549 *namespace* and they use 1.1.4 to identify rsa with pkcs #1 padding md5.

So how do you get from 1.2.840.113549.1.1.4 to 2A 86 48 86 F7 0D 01 01 04? Well, the 01 01 04 part is pretty obvious: This is the byte representation of the digits 1.1.4. But as you can see, even the third numeral, 840, is too large to fit into a single byte. Rather than include separators, they adopted a variable-length encoding scheme (The X.500 family of specifications, which includes X.509, is big on variable-length encoding schemes). The 86 48 represents 840, and the 86 F7 0D represents 113549. The encoding scheme used here is this: If the high-order bit is 1 then the other seven bits in this byte should be concatenated with the *next* byte. If the high-order bit is 0 then this is the last byte in the identifier. So 840, in binary, is 1101001000. This is longer than seven bits, so break it up into chunks of seven or less:

```
110   1001000
```

Now, add the high-order bits (and pad the first one):

```
10000110   01001000
```

Or hexadecimal 86 48.

The decoder then sees the first byte, recognizes that the high-order bit is 1, continues on to the next byte, sees that the high-order bit is zero, and concatenates the seven lower-order bits of the two constituent bytes back into the value 1101001000, or decimal 840. Likewise, 113549 encodes to 11011101110001101 in binary. This requires 20 bits to encode, so you use three bytes ($\left\lceil\frac{20}{7}\right\rceil = 3$), with the high-order bits of the first two being set to 1, which tells the decoder that this should be concatenated with the next byte:

```
10000110 11110111 00001101
```

Or 86 F7 0D in hexadecimal.

Is your head spinning yet? Actually, it gets worse. Notice that the hex encoding of the "1.2" on the very beginning of the OID is a single byte: 2A. To save space, X.690 dictates that the first byte encodes two numeric elements according to the algebraic equation $Z = 40X + Y$. So, 1.2 is 40 * 1 + 2 = 42 (0x2A). On the unpacking side, it's safe to assume that if the byte is in the range 0–40, the decoded value should be 0.(byte); if it's in the range of 41–80, it should be 1.(byte − 40); if it is in the range of 81–120, it should be 2.(byte − 80); and so on. Obviously, this limits the range of values that can be encoded by the first byte.

Fortunately, I've done all of the conversion for you, so you don't have to understand any of this to code around it. All you need to know is that the unique byte sequence 2A 86 48 86 F7 0D 01 01 04 represents the MD5withRSA signature algorithm.

There is also an optional section for parameters. DSS includes a few parameters, so you re-examine this when DSA is covered. Notice that the `ANY DEFINED BY algorithm` indicates that if the object identifier is one of the two RSA algorithms, the `parameters` field is not present.

### issuer

```
issuer        Name
```

If you found the subject of OIDs slightly complicated, hold on to your hat as you examine X.509 *distinguished names*. You've likely seen a distinguished name written out at some point in long form, such as

```
CN=Joshua Davies,OU=Architecture,O=Travelocity,L=Southlake,ST=Texas,C=USA
```

You may even be familiar with the meanings of the terse one- and two-letter codes shown in the example, but in case you aren't, they expand to the long names shown in Table 5-2.

**Table 5-2:** An Expanded X.509 Distinguished Name

| TWO-LETTER CODE | LONG NAME | VALUE |
| --- | --- | --- |
| CN | Common Name | Joshua Davies |
| OU | Organizational Unit | Architecture |
| O | Organization | Travelocity |
| L | Locality, usually a city name | Southlake |
| ST | State | Texas |
| C | Country | USA |

As you can see, this identifies, fairly uniquely, an individual person. In the case of an X.509 certificate, a distinguished name is used to identify the issuer. Here's an example issuer name:

```
CN = VeriSign Class 3 Extended Validation SSL SGC CA,
OU = Terms of use at https://www.verisign.com/rpa (c)06,
OU = VeriSign Trust Network, O = VeriSign, Inc., C = US
```

This is the issuer string on the certificate that identifies the `Travelocity` `.com` web site at the time of this writing. As you can see, the `CN` (*common name*) doesn't actually identify a person; it identifies an entity. The `OU` field appears twice and is used to transmit data not actually related to the organizational unit. However, it identifies an issuer well enough for the receiver to decide if it wants to trust it or not. However, see the discussion later in this chapter about the `issuerUniqueId` field for more on this topic.

You can see this yourself. As way of example, follow these steps:

In FireFox:

1. Navigate to a secure page.

2. Double-click the lock icon, and click the View button. The Issued By section details the contents of the "issuer" field in the X.509 certificate that the server presented to negotiate the secure connection in the first place.

Using Microsoft's Internet Explorer 8:

1. Navigate to a secure page.

2. Click the lock icon on the URL bar, select View Certificates. The Certificate dialog appears as shown in Figure 5-3.

3. Click the Details tab, and click Issuer.

One thing you may notice about the two distinguished name examples I've given is that not every field appears in each distinguished name because at least some of them are optional. In fact, technically speaking, all of them are optional. If you look at the declaration of the `Name` type, which `issuer` is, you see that it's defined generically:

```
Name ::= CHOICE {
  RDNSequence }
  RDNSequence ::= SEQUENCE OF RelativeDistinguishedName
  RelativeDistinguishedName ::=
   SET OF AttributeTypeAndValue
  AttributeTypeAndValue ::= SEQUENCE {
   type   AttributeType,
   value  AttributeValue }
  AttributeType ::= OBJECT IDENTIFIER
  AttributeValue ::= ANY DEFINED BY AttributeType
```

**Figure 5.3:** Example of an Issuer field

A name is an RDNSequence, which is a SEQUENCE OF another type, the RelativeDistinguishedName. Remember earlier when SEQUENCE was compared to a C struct, which may be confusing because SEQUENCE sounds like a repeating field? Well, SET OF, which RelativeDistinguishedName is defined as, is a repeating field.

What this all means is that a name is a variable-length array of AttributeTypeAndValue structures. The attribute type is an OID, and the attribute value can be any type, depending on its OID. Again, you don't need to care much about the encoding structure of OIDs; you just need to care about their values and what they map to. As you can probably guess, CN, O, OU, L, ST, and C each have their own OID values. They're not represented as string values anywhere in the certificate. These OIDs are shown in Table 5-3.

**Table 5-3:** DistinguishedName OIDs

| LONG NAME | OID |
|---|---|
| CommonName | 0x55, 0x04, 0x03 |
| CountryName | 0x55, 0x04, 0x06 |
| LocalityName | 0x55, 0x04, 0x07 |
| StateOrProvinceName | 0x55, 0x04, 0x08 |
| OrganizationName | 0x55, 0x04, 0x0A |
| OrganizationalUnitName | 0x55, 0x04, 0x0B |

Although the actual type of the attribute value of each depends on the OID, all of the OIDs you typically see (within the distinguished name, at least) have attribute values whose types are strings. Notice also that these OIDs are only three bytes long, whereas the OIDs of the algorithm identifiers shown earlier are each nine bytes long. See X.520 for more detail on the attribute type OIDs (as well as many, many more attribute types — distinguished names are permitted to be very detailed, although they're usually relatively simple).

For now, you just have to identify an issuer well enough to make a trust decision, or provide this same information to the user and let the user make this decision. If you've ever come across the error message "The certificate is signed by an unrecognized CA or one you have chosen not to trust" while browsing the web, your browser is telling you that you should take a look at the "issued by" field.

### validity

```
validity        Validity
```

Recall the purpose and concept of *validity period* — the validity period represents a time window outside of which the certificate should be considered suspect. You've likely come across the error message "The web site's certificate has expired" while browsing. This is actually a much less serious condition than an untrusted issuer. You know that the certificate was valid at some point in the past; it's just due to be resissued. If it's not terribly old, you can probably trust it.

**TRACKING CERTIFICATE VALIDITY PERIODS**

Keeping track of validity periods and expiration dates, and ensuring that certificates get reissued before their expiration date, can be an onerous responsibility for a website administrator. Expired certificates are a user annoyance when a web server presents one — the user is presented with an ominous error message and given the option to continue or abort. However, in automated communications, such as secured web services, where a program is making a secure connection to another program, certificate expiration can be fatal.

One day your web services are connecting to one another as they should be; the next day they're failing for no apparent reason with a "certificate expired" error message buried in a log file somewhere. No certificate-based library I'm aware of gives you any warning that a certificate is about to expire (as nice as that would be).

One way to get around this is to have all certificates that protect program-to-program services expire on the same day — for instance, you can have all the test environment certificates expire on Feb. 1, and all the production environment certificates expire on Mar. 1. This way, you'll get some warning and when your test environment certificates start expiring and you'll know it's time to start reissuing your production environment certificates.

How is validity represented in X.509, then?

```
Validity ::= SEQUENCE {
    notBefore    Time,
    notAfter     Time }
Time ::= CHOICE {
    utcTime      UTCTime,
    generalTime  GeneralizedTime }
```

There are two `Time` values, each of which can either be a `UTCTime` or a `GeneralizedTime`. Each is a year, followed by a month, a day, an hour, a minute, a second, and the letter Z. The only difference between the two is that generalized time uses a four-digit year and `UTCTime` a two-digit year. A `UTCTime` is 13 bytes long; a `GeneralizedTime` is 15. Lengths are discussed later in the chapter, when representations are covered.

So, with a two-digit year, the client has to do a bit of detective work to figure out if 35 expired a very, very long time ago, or if it will expire in 25 years. Because no X.509 certificates were issued in 1935, it's safe to assume that a year of 35 means 2035. In fact, the specification mandates that all certificates issued before 2050 must use `UTCTime`, so if the year is less than 50, it's in the 21st century. After the year 2050, CA's are supposed to begin using `GeneralizedTime`, with a four-digit year. However, having lived through the Y2K "crisis," I have faith that computer programmers will not actually fix this two-digit year problem until a few years before it actually does become a problem — sometime around the year 2080.

## subject

```
    subject      Name
```

The subject, like the issuer, is a relative distinguished name. It includes an optional number of identifying fields, hopefully enough to identify the subject of the certificate. But, now that you mention it, who is the subject? If I have a certificate that identifies me, personally, the subject name (the CN field) should be my name, but if I'm connecting to a web site named www.whizbang.com, the subject field should identify that web site somehow.

As it turns out, this is actually poorly specified. The compromise here has been to insert the domain name into the CN field of the subject name and allow the client to compare the domain name it thinks it's connecting to against the domain name listed in the CN field of the certificate's subject. However, this is imperfect. Consider an e-commerce site that controls three different domains: shop.whizbang.com, purchase.whizbang.com and orders.whizbang.com. SSL certificates are expensive to obtain — at least, those issued by reputable CAs — and something of a hassle to maintain. The site administrator has to keep track of expiration dates and ensure that the certificates get reissued within a reasonable timeframe. As the administrator of whizbang.com, you'd really want one certificate that authenticates all of the site's servers. After all, www.whizbang.com almost certainly identifies multiple physical IP addresses.

As a result, it's acceptable for the certificate's subject's CN field to include a wildcard, such as *.whizbang.com. This actually creates other problems. If you can convince a CA to register you a certificate with a subject name including CN=*.com, you can masquerade as any site on the Internet, and the browser has no way of differentiating your certificate from the legitimate owner of the site. Although authorities are smart enough to check for this, security researcher Moxie Marlinspike, in his paper "Null Prefix Attacks Against SSL Certificates," detailed an interesting vulnerability not in the protocol itself but in most implementations of it. An attacker requests a certificate whose common name was *\0.badguy.com. Note the insertion of the null-terminator \0 in the domain name. Because he owns the top-level domain name badguy.com, the CA issues the certificate. However, a C-based client implementation almost certainly loads the common name into a string field and does a strcmp to determine equality — reading the common name as * or "any website". This is something that implementers of the TLS protocol need to be aware of; the length of the string needs to be checked, and null terminators before the actual end of the string should be removed. If you're lucky, the CA checks for this as well. You shouldn't rely on luck, though; as the implementer, make sure you protect your users against lazy CA's.

RFC 2247 extends the X.509 subject name to explicitly include domain-name components, split out according to the DNS hierarchy, so that www.whizbang.com becomes DC=www,DC=whizbang,DC=com. This new DC (domain-name component) attribute has OID 0.9.2342.19200300.100.1.25 and is not particularly common; most sites still instead use the CN field to identify their domain names. This is part of a chicken-and-egg problem; some older clients don't recognize the DC component, so to interoperate with them, sites identify themselves using the CN field. Because so few sites advertise DC components, there's little incentive for clients to recognize it. At the time of this writing, neither Firefox 3.6.3 nor Internet Explorer 8 properly recognize the DC field in the subject name, although RFC 3280 states that recognizing it is mandatory. If the DC field correctly identifies the domain name, but the CN does not (or is missing), a security exception is still reported. The DC field is more common in LDAP-based certificates; perhaps someday in the future, web browsers will make use of it.

A recent Internet-wide security analysis by Qualys Research found "22 million SSL servers with certificates that are completely invalid because they do not match the domain name on which they reside" (see `http://www .esecurityplanet.com/features/article.php/3890171/SSL-Certificates-In-Use-Today-Arent-All-Valid.htm`), although some of this is likely caused by virtual hosting rather than truly invalid SSL certificates.

### subjectPublicKeyInfo

```
subjectPublicKeyInfo SubjectPublicKeyInfo
```

Here is the heart of the certificate — the public key that it presents. On the client side, when the certificate is received, you use the issuer, validity period, and the subject field to decide whether you trust the public key well enough to use it to perform a key exchange. If the subject matches the host you think you're connecting to, the certificate hasn't expired, and the issuer is one you trust, you have reasonable assurance that there's no man in the middle and you can go forward with the key exchange and, presumably, trade sensitive information over the now-secured channel.

The definition for `SubjectPublicKeyInfo` is

```
SubjectPublicKeyInfo ::= SEQUENCE {
    algorithm       AlgorithmIdentifier,
    subjectPublicKey   BIT STRING }
```

The `AlgorithmIdentifier`, it should come as no surprise, includes an OID. Two possible values of interest are shown in Table 5-4.

**Table 5-4:** Public-Key Algorithm OIDs

| ALGORITHM IDENTIFIER | OID |
| --- | --- |
| RSA | 2A 86 48 86 F7 0D 01 01 01 |
| Diffie-Hellman | 2A 86 48 CE 3E 02 01 |

**NOTE** Elliptic-curve Diffie-Hellman support in X.509 certificates is examined in Chapter 9.

The public key itself is defined here as a simple bit string. Recall from Chapter 4, though, that you need some pretty specific information in a pretty specific format to do key exchanges, For RSA, for example, you need the modulus $n$ and the public exponent $e$. So, as it turns out, the BIT STRING here actually encodes another ASN.1 formatted value, whose contents vary depending on the value of the algorithm identifier. For RSA, this is

```
RSAPublicKey ::= SEQUENCE {
    modulus       INTEGER, -- n
    publicExponent    INTEGER -- e -- }
```

So, after decoding the OID, you then need to ASN.1 decode the bit string as yet another ASN.1 value to extract the actual public key.

If you recall, regular (e.g. non-elliptic-curve) Diffie-Hellman key exchange doesn't involve a public key the way RSA does. There were two parameters needed, though: the generator $g$ and the field parameter $p$. The contents of the public key field, in this case, is simply:

```
DHPublicKey ::= INTEGER -- public key, y = g^x mod p
```

Of course, the public $y$ value is useless to the client without $g$ and $p$. You might expect to see them in the public key structure, as you see with $n$ in the `RSAPublicKey`, but instead the Diffie-Hellman generator and group are passed as algorithm parameters. Notice in the declaration of algorithm in `SubjectPublicKeyInfo` that the type is actually `AlgorithmIdentifier`. This includes an OID identifying the algorithm, but allows optional parameters to be included:

```
AlgorithmIdentifier ::= SEQUENCE {
    algorithm       OBJECT IDENTIFIER,
    parameters      ANY DEFINED BY algorithm OPTIONAL }
```

The parameters field is empty for RSA, but for DH, it's defined as

```
DomainParameters ::= SEQUENCE {
     p     INTEGER, -- odd prime, p=jq +1
     g     INTEGER, -- generator, g
     q     INTEGER, -- factor of p-1
     j     INTEGER OPTIONAL, -- subgroup factor
     validationParms ValidationParms OPTIONAL }

     ValidationParms ::= SEQUENCE {
       seed        BIT STRING,
       pgenCounter   INTEGER }
```

## HOW TO AVOID A SMALL SUBGROUP ATTACK USING THE DIFFIE-HELLMAN KEY

If you recall the discussion of Diffie-Hellman key exchange in Chapter 3, you may remember that $p$ and $g$ are the only two parameters that you need in order to perform a key exchange. Each side chooses a random secret number $a$ or $b$, sends the other side $y = g^a \% p$, and the receiving side computes $y^b \% p$ to complete the key agreement (refer back to Chapter 3 if this is still a bit fuzzy). So — you may wonder — what are those extra parameters, $q$, $j$, and *validationParms* for? Well, when $p$ and $g$ are fixed parameters — used over and over for multiple key exchanges — a poorly chosen $p$ value can open the user to an attack called the *small subgroup attack*, described by Chae Hoon Lim and Pil Joon Lee in their paper, "A Key Recovery Attack on Discrete Log-based Schemes Using a Prime Order Subgroup." The attack itself is mathematically complex, and I won't go into the details here. As it turns out, SSL/TLS ordinarily uses

> Diffie-Hellman key exchange in such a way that guarding against the small sub-group attack is unnecessary; this will be examined in more detail in Chapter 8. If you're curious, and would like to see more detail on how these parameters may be used to guard against small subgroup attacks, you may refer to RFC 2631.

### extensions

```
extensions   [3] EXPLICIT Extensions OPTIONAL
            -- If present, version shall be v3
```

Finally, there is the generic `extensions` field introduced in X.509v3 — in fact, this was the only addition to X.509v3. Certificate extensions, if present — which they almost always are these days — are appended here. `extensions` is a nested `SEQUENCE` of object identifiers, optionally followed by data (depending on the object identifier).

This book doesn't go through all the available certificate extensions. RFC 5280, section 4.2 lists all of the standard ones, but be aware that two entities can agree on non-standard extensions as well. There are, however, a handful of particularly important ones.

The `extensions` type is defined as

```
Extensions ::= SEQUENCE SIZE (1..MAX) OF Extension
```

and the extension type itself is defined as

```
Extension ::= SEQUENCE {
    extnID    OBJECT IDENTIFIER,
    critical  BOOLEAN DEFAULT FALSE,
    extnValue OCTET STRING }
```

Each extension has a unique object identifier; this object identifier determines how the `extnValue` is parsed, or if it's even present. Additionally, there's a `critical` field. If an extension is marked critical, and the reader doesn't recognize it, it must reject the entire certificate; otherwise, unrecognized extensions can be ignored. Most extensions are not marked critical.

The Subject Alternative Name extension (OID 55 1D 11) is a useful, but not widely used, extension. This extension offers a place to specifically identify a server's domain name; it also supports e-mail addresses, IP addresses, other directory names, and so on. Because the domain name is explicit, the common-name field no longer needs to be assumed to be the domain name. Unfortunately, this extension has failed to catch on, chiefly for the same reason the DC component in the subject name failed to catch on; to support older clients, servers must continue to set the common name to be the same as domain name. (In fact, it's unclear what, if anything, ought to be in the CN component of a certificate's subject when the certificate identifies a web site, if not the domain name.)

There are additional certificate extensions throughout the remainder of this chapter. Each one is encoded according to the `Extension` structure defined above, and is identified uniquely by an OID. Incidentally, all of the extension OIDs start with 55 1D.

## Signed Certificates

Now, as you browse over the list of fields described in the certificate structure from Listing 5-1, you may have noticed that although a signing algorithm is included, a signature isn't. As you recall from Chapter 4, a signature is generated when a byte sequence is hashed and the hash is encrypted using a private key. So, one thing that must be agreed upon before a signature can be generated is exactly which bytes are hashed. In this case, it's the bytes of the certificate structure — technically, the certificate's DER encoding (described later). So, there's another outer structure defined, which includes the certificate, the signature algorithm (again), and the signature value itself, as shown in Listing 5-2.

**Listing 5-2:** X.509 signed certificate declaration

```
Certificate ::= SEQUENCE {
    tbsCertificate      TBSCertificate,
    signatureAlgorithm  AlgorithmIdentifier,
    signatureValue      BIT STRING }
```

The certificate structure defined here is properly referred to as the TBSCertificate. TBS stands for *To Be Signed*, although the ones examined here have already been signed. If you think about the overall lifecycle of a certificate, this nomenclature makes sense. First, the certificate requester (e.g. the website owner) generates a public/private keypair and wraps up that information in a To-be-signed certificate structure. This is sent off to the CA, which signs it (after verifying it) and returns the whole certificate back, complete with its digital signature.

The signature algorithm is — in fact, must be — the exact same as the OID given in the TBSCertificate itself. The signature, of course, is a bit string. The use of a bit string — the ASN.1 equivalent of a void pointer — runs into the same definitional problem with subjectPublicKeyInfo; the precise contents vary depending on the signature algorithm itself. Therefore, again, the BIT STRING itself is another ASN.1-defined structure, depending on the algorithm identifier.

> **NOTE** A certificate can legally be signed by the private key corresponding to the public key contained within it. This sort of certificate is called a *self-signed* certificate. After all, my certificate is signed by a CA, but who signs their certificates? As a result, all *top-level* certificates are self-signed this way. How the client decides which self-signed top-level certificates to trust is not defined by the SSL specification. In the context of a web browser, for example, there's always a list of trusted CAs that can be updated by the user.

You can see which CAs your browser trusts. If you're using Internet Explorer 8, for instance, go to Tools ➢ Internet Options ➢ Publishers, and click the Trusted Root Certification Authorities tab, as shown in Figure 5-4:

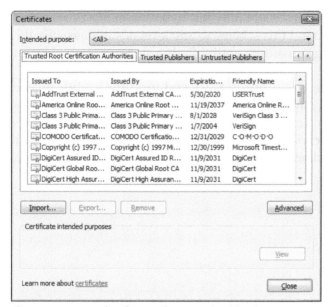

**Figure 5.4:** Sample of trusted root authorities in IE 8

X.509 is designed to allow delegation of signing authority. A top-level CA can issue and sign a certificate to, for instance, a "west coast" authority and an "east coast" authority. These authorities can sign certificates on behalf of the top-level CA. The receiver first verifies that the lowest-level certificate is valid according to the delegated authority's certificate. Then it checks the signature of the delegated authority against that of the root-level authority as illustrated in Figure 5-5.

**Figure 5.5:** Certificate authority delegation

This way, the verifier — for example, the web client — only needs to keep track of a small number of root CAs. A handful of trusted root authorities can certify other authorities, and the client only has to be aware of a dozen or so root authorities. You can extend this scheme to any level of sub-delegates; the client just goes on checking signatures until it finds a signature issued by an authority it already trusts.

Unfortunately, this system was put in place and used for a while before somebody identified a fatal flaw. The problem is that every certificate includes a public key, and any public key can sign another certificate. Therefore, there's nothing stopping an unscrupulous site administrator from using a regular server certificate to sign another certificate, as shown in Figure 5-6, for example.

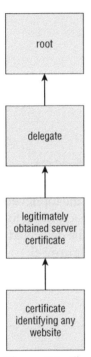

**Figure 5.6:** Illegitimate delegation

As a result, almost all clients are designed to require that each certificate be signed by a trusted authority and to reject delegated signatures.

The Key Usage certificate extension — OID 55 1D 0F — was introduced to allow this sort of delegated signature scheme in a safe way; this (critical) extension encodes a bit string, each of whose eight bits is either set or unset to identify that the public-key contained in this certificate may or may not be used for a particular purpose. Of course, there's nothing stopping an unscrupulous user from using the key for a nonspecified purpose anyway, but the receiver can check the key usage bit and determine whether to allow the sender to do so. The most important bit is bit 5, which, if set, identifies this certificate as a legitimate signing authority. Presumably, the issuing CA only allows this bit to be set if it trusts the requester to be responsible and sign other certificates on behalf of the CA itself.

### Summary of X.509 Certificates

I've covered a lot of ground in this section, and it's easy to get lost in all of the details. To summarize: when your browser warns you about certificate errors, it's referring to an X.509 certificate that was presented by the target web site to identify itself. Such a certificate must be presented in order to guard against man-in-the-middle attacks. An X.509 certificate itself is a mapping of an entity name (e.g. a person or a website) to a public key. This mapping has a validity period and is vouched for by a trusted entity called a certificate authority. As long as all of these elements are present, you have a legitimate certificate. The X.509 specification takes it a step further and tells you what order they should be stored in and what form they should take.

## Transmitting Certificates with ASN.1 Distinguished Encoding Rules (DER)

Quite a bit has been said so far about the abstract structure of a certificate without discussing how one is actually represented in byte form. The translation of primitive (ASN.1) types to byte representation is described according to a set of rules. Technically, these rules are independent of ASN.1 itself. I mentioned earlier that a certificate is the sort of thing that would probably be represented in XML these days — there is, in fact, a set of rules to encode ASN.1 in XML format! However, by far the most common encoding, and the one that SSL relies on, is called the *Distinguished Encoding Rules* (DER). The *distinguished* differentiates the rules from another set called the *basic* encoding rules. Fundamentally, the distinguished rules are more restrictive than the basic rules. For example, the basic rules allow the encoder to use more bytes than necessary to specify lengths (if the encoder wants all lengths to be encoded in a fixed set of bytes, for example). For the most part, the differences are superficial, and the *basic encoding rules* (BER) won't be specifically covered here.

The DER describes how to format integers, strings, dates, object identifiers, bit strings, sequences and sets — as well as several others, but these are the ones that are pertinent to the present discussion about X.509 certificates. See X.690 for a complete listing of DER encoding rules.

### Encoded Values

Every encoded value is represented as a type, followed by the value's length, followed by the actual contents of the value itself; the representation of the value depends on the type. So, for example, the type `integer` is byte 02. DER allows for multi-byte types as well — and has complex rules on how to encode and recognize them — but X.509 doesn't need to make use of them and sticks with single-byte types. Therefore, the integer value 5 is encoded, according to DER, as

```
02 01 05
```

That's type 2 (integer), one byte in length, value 5. The integer value 65535 is encoded as

```
02 02 FF FF
```

That's type 2, two bytes, value 0xFFFF equals 65535. The length byte tells you when to stop reading the value and start looking for another tag.

So far, so good. It's pretty simple. OID's are just as simple to encode. They're stored just like integers, but they have a type of 6 instead of 2. Otherwise, they're encoded the same way: type, length, value. The OID common name (in the subject and issuer distinguished name fields) of 55 04 03 is represented as

```
06 03 55 04 03
```

The length byte tells you that there are three bytes of OID.

### Strings and Dates

Strings and dates are both encoded similarly. The type code for a date is either 23 or 24; 23 is a generalized — four-digit year — time. 24 is a UTC — two-digit year — time. Although the type actually includes enough information to infer the length — you know that generalized times are 15 digits, and UTC times are 13 — for consistency's sake the lengths are included as well. After that, the year, month, day, hour, minute, second and Z are included in ASCII format. So the date Feb. 23, 2010, 6:50:13 is encoded in UTC time as

| 17 | 0d | 31 | 30 | 30 | 32 | 32 | 33 | 30 | 36 | 35 | 30 | 31 | 33 | 5A |
|-----|--------|---|---|---|---|---|---|---|---|---|---|---|---|---|
| tag | length | 1 | 0 | 0 | 2 | 2 | 3 | 0 | 6 | 5 | 0 | 1 | 3 | Z |

and is encoded in generalized time as

| 16 | 0f | 32 | 30 | 31 | 30 | 30 | 32 | 32 | 33 | 30 | 36 | 35 | 30 | 31 | 33 | 5A |
|-----|--------|---|---|---|---|---|---|---|---|---|---|---|---|---|---|---|
| tag | length | 2 | 0 | 1 | 0 | 0 | 2 | 2 | 3 | 0 | 6 | 5 | 0 | 1 | 3 | Z |

Strings are also coded this way. However, there are quite a few different string types to account for different byte encodings (among other things). The official specification is actually not proscriptive about which type of string should be used, and you actually see different kinds. However, the most common are IA5Strings (type 22) and printable strings (type 19), which you can treat interchangeably. Given, for example, the country code "US" in a name field, the encoding would be

```
13 02 55 53
```

which is the ASCII representation of the string "US."

## Bit Strings

So far, DER is pretty straightforward, and everything except bit strings, sequences and sets has been covered. Bit strings are just like strings, with one minor difference. Their type is 3 to distinguish them from printable strings, but the encoding is exactly the same: tag, length, contents. The only difference between bit strings and character strings is that bit strings don't necessarily have to end on an eight-bit boundary, so they have an extra byte to indicate how much padding was included. In practice, this is always 0 because all useful bit patterns are eight-bit aligned anyway.

However, as you recall from the discussion of public key algorithms and signature values, bit strings contain nested ASN.1 structures. All the examples of DER-encoded values examined so far have been able to get away with representing their length with a single byte, but a nested ASN.1 structure is bound to be larger than this. So how are lengths greater than 255 represented?

Actually, a single-length byte can only represent 127 byte values. The high-order bit is reserved. If it's 1, then the low order seven bits represent not the length of the value, but the length of the length — that is, how many of the bytes following encode the length of the subsequently following value. So, if a bit string is 512 bytes long, the DER-encoded representation looks like Table 5-5:

**Table 5-5:** ASN.1 Encoding of Long Values

| TAG NUMBER | NUMBER OF LENGTH BYTES | ACTUAL LENGTH VALUE | BITS OF PADDING | VALUE |
| --- | --- | --- | --- | --- |
| 03 | 83 | 02 00 00 | 00 | (512 bytes of value) |

Technically, a value doesn't have to be a bit string to have a length greater than 127; integers, strings, and OIDs could, at least in theory. In practice, though, this never happens.

## Sequences and Sets: Grouping and Nesting ASN.1 Values

So, you're almost ready to start encoding an entire X.509 certificate. There are two missing pieces, though. Notice that there are several sequences nested inside other sequences, and sets nested inside sequences (and sequences nested inside sets...). Sets and sequences are what ASN.1 calls a *constructed type* — that is, a type containing other types. Technically, they're encoded the same way other values are. They start with a tag, are followed by a variable number of length bytes, and are then followed by their contents. However, for constructed types, the contents themselves are further ASN.1-encoded tags. Sequences are identified by tag 0x30, and sets are identified by tag 0x31. Any tag value whose sixth bit is 1 is a constructed tag and the parser must recognize that it contains additional ASN.1-encoded data.

### ASN.1 Explicit Tags

Finally, turn back and look at the definition of the tbsCertificate. Notice that the first field is an optional version number, and the second field is a required `serialNumber`, and they're both numeric. When parsing a certificate, then, you know for certain that the first value you come across is a number, but you have to check the value of the first value to determine how to interpret the first value! Clearly this is not an optimal way to go about parsing certificates.

To get around this, ASN.1 also allows for explicit tags. Notice in the definition of the `tbsCertificate` that `Version` is listed as [0] EXPLICIT.

```
SEQUENCE {
    version       [0] EXPLICIT Version DEFAULT v1,
    serialNumber    CertificateSerialNumber,
```

So far, tags have been presented as randomly distributed identifiers. Actually, the first two bits of a tag identify its *tag class*. In X.509 you come across two types of tag classes: *universal* (00) and *context-specific* (10). (The other two are *application* and *private* and are not used in X.509 certificates.) Context-specific tags are *explicit* tags. So, to create an explicit tag 0, OR 0 with 1000 0000 (0x80). This is also a constructed tag — its contents are the actual version number — so the sixth bit is set to 1 (OR 0x20).

### A Real-World Certificate Example

An example might help clear up any remaining confusion here. To see an actual certificate, you can download one from any SSL-enabled site, or create a new one. The latest version of IE makes it a bit difficult to directly download a certificate, but it's still fairly straightforward with Firefox:

1. Navigate to a secure site.
2. Click the lock icon.
3. Select Security ➤ View Certificate.
4. Click the Details tab, shown in figure 5-7, and then click the Export button.

### Using OpenSSL to Generate an RSA KeyPair and Certificate

To keep the first example simple, go ahead and just create a new certificate. OpenSSL has a `req` option that enables you to generate a self-signed certificate. Do so and then examine its contents.

```
jdavies@home:ssl$ openssl req -x509 -newkey rsa:512 -keyout key.der -keyform der \
  -out cert.der -outform der
Generating a 512 bit RSA private key
.....++++++++++++
........++++++++++++
```

```
writing new private key to 'key.der'
Enter PEM pass phrase:
Verifying - Enter PEM pass phrase:
-----
You are about to be asked to enter information that will be incorporated
into your certificate request.
What you are about to enter is what is called a Distinguished Name or a DN.
There are quite a few fields but you can leave some blank
For some fields there will be a default value,
If you enter '.', the field will be left blank.
-----
Country Name (2 letter code) [AU]:US
State or Province Name (full name) [Some-State]:TX
Locality Name (eg, city) []:Southlake
Organization Name (eg, company) [Internet Widgits Pty Ltd]:Travelocity
Organizational Unit Name (eg, section) []:Architecture
Common Name (eg, YOUR name) []:Joshua Davies
Email Address []:joshua.davies@travelocity.com
```

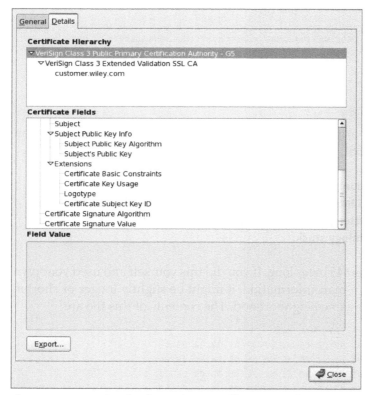

**Figure 5.7:** Downloading/exporting a certificate in Firefox

Notice that it created two output files: a key file, containing the encrypted private key, and a cert file, containing the certificate. It doesn't make much sense to generate a new public key without a private key to go with it. The structure of this key file is revisited later.

Also, notice the parameters: `-keyform` and `-outform`. There are two options here, `der` and `pem`. `der` is, unsurprisingly, the ASN.1 DER-encoded representation of the certificate or key file. `pem`, which stands for *Privacy Enhanced Mail,* is a Base-64 encoded representation of the DER-encoded certificate with a header and a footer. A `pem`-encoded certificate file looks like this:

```
-----BEGIN CERTIFICATE-----
MIIDUjCCAvygAwIBAgIJAMdcnerewaJQMA0GCSqGSIb3DQEBBQUAMIGkMQswCQYD
VQQGEwJVUzEOMAwGA1UECBMFVGV4YXMxEjAQBgNVBAcTCVNvdXRobGFrZTEUMBIG
...
AwEB/zANBgkqhkiG9w0BAQUFAANBAKf3QiQgbre9DSq4aeED9v0nonEHXPRsU79j
13q/IUMlhmtuZ4SIlNAPvRdZ6DUIvWqVVJbt15Bm7MKo7KCMarc=
-----END CERTIFICATE-----
```

And a `pem`-encoded key file looks like this:

```
-----BEGIN RSA PRIVATE KEY-----
Proc-Type: 4,ENCRYPTED
DEK-Info: DES-EDE3-CBC,DF6F51939AF51B22

+cvob7sZl6Ew8/iBqNUF1Q40B14mYzw43cS08/xpzbqtkczYfiQeYN8N4dl8h3tp
VzoeCoRKsBKtl89NtpzTJocv33vgcaTFHt1BXBnOPxrQALhyV1x4ADIoW5e7rvsW
...
RmyqjA8BH9JeCPzvJlmir55OYB9aCQBTR3+mAlvVrnx5eng1f0YCw/tneXJor3jT
IgYBcTpEvug5qeGVl27UA2cI/lcCuNQ0Cjdfztlhhmo=
-----END RSA PRIVATE KEY-----
```

These structures are more amenable to being transmitted in e-mail than DER-encoded files. SSL always deals in DER-encoded files, though.

> **NOTE**  You'll encounter the term PEM every once in a while as you read through the official Internet documentation on certificates. Privacy-Enhanced Mail was the first attempt to apply X.509 certificates in an Internet context, so some of the terminology stuck.

The `cert.der` file is 845 bytes long. If you did this yourself and used your own name, location, and e-mail information, it might be slightly longer or shorter, but should be in this same neighborhood. The contents of this file are

```
jdavies@home:ssl$ od -t x1 cert.der
0000000 30 82 03 49 30 82 02 f3 a0 03 02 01 02 02 09 00
0000020 ca 30 e1 8f 77 8d a2 81 30 0d 06 09 2a 86 48 86
0000040 f7 0d 01 01 05 05 00 30 81 a1 31 0b 30 09 06 03
0000060 55 04 06 13 02 55 53 31 0b 30 09 06 03 55 04 08
0000100 13 02 54 58 31 12 30 10 06 03 55 04 07 13 09 53
0000120 6f 75 74 68 6c 61 6b 65 31 14 30 12 06 03 55 04
0000140 0a 13 0b 54 72 61 76 65 6c 6f 63 69 74 79 31 15
0000160 30 13 06 03 55 04 0b 13 0c 41 72 63 68 69 74 65
0000200 63 74 75 72 65 31 16 30 14 06 03 55 04 03 13 0d
```

```
0000220 4a 6f 73 68 75 61 20 44 61 76 69 65 73 31 2c 30
0000240 2a 06 09 2a 86 48 86 f7 0d 01 09 01 16 1d 6a 6f
0000260 73 68 75 61 2e 64 61 76 69 65 73 40 74 72 61 76
0000300 65 6c 6f 63 69 74 79 2e 63 6f 6d 30 1e 17 0d 31
0000320 30 30 33 30 32 32 32 34 36 32 33 5a 17 0d 31 30
0000340 30 34 30 31 32 32 34 36 32 33 5a 30 81 a1 31 0b
0000360 30 09 06 03 55 04 06 13 02 55 53 31 0b 30 09 06
0000400 03 55 04 08 13 02 54 58 31 12 30 10 06 03 55 04
0000420 07 13 09 53 6f 75 74 68 6c 61 6b 65 31 14 30 12
0000440 06 03 55 04 0a 13 0b 54 72 61 76 65 6c 6f 63 69
0000460 74 79 31 15 30 13 06 03 55 04 0b 13 0c 41 72 63
0000500 68 69 74 65 63 74 75 72 65 31 16 30 14 06 03 55
0000520 04 03 13 0d 4a 6f 73 68 75 61 20 44 61 76 69 65
0000540 73 31 2c 30 2a 06 09 2a 86 48 86 f7 0d 01 09 01
0000560 16 1d 6a 6f 73 68 75 61 2e 64 61 76 69 65 73 40
0000600 74 72 61 76 65 6c 6f 63 69 74 79 2e 63 6f 6d 30
0000620 5c 30 0d 06 09 2a 86 48 86 f7 0d 01 01 01 05 00
0000640 03 4b 00 30 48 02 41 00 e0 13 38 0f 83 b6 ef 06
0000660 70 f5 5b aa 3a 2b cf 8e 95 ff 91 b1 90 03 52 51
0000700 69 73 de a7 fa 97 fb 56 0d b9 e9 0f e8 30 22 8c
0000720 5e f0 1f 07 f0 dc cc 61 b8 01 0e b1 b0 58 ef b5
0000740 b4 54 16 70 eb 59 b4 bf 02 03 01 00 01 a3 82 01
0000760 0a 30 82 01 06 30 1d 06 03 55 1d 0e 04 16 04 14
0001000 2d f1 04 e4 46 1d 72 ef bb a7 ce 05 58 4c 31 f1
0001020 ff 8e 4e 2e 30 81 d6 06 03 55 1d 23 04 81 ce 30
0001040 81 cb 80 14 2d f1 04 e4 46 1d 72 ef bb a7 ce 05
0001060 58 4c 31 f1 ff 8e 4e 2e a1 81 a7 a4 81 a4 30 81
0001100 a1 31 0b 30 09 06 03 55 04 06 13 02 55 53 31 0b
0001120 30 09 06 03 55 04 08 13 02 54 58 31 12 30 10 06
0001140 03 55 04 07 13 09 53 6f 75 74 68 6c 61 6b 65 31
0001160 14 30 12 06 03 55 04 0a 13 0b 54 72 61 76 65 6c
0001200 6f 63 69 74 79 31 15 30 13 06 03 55 04 0b 13 0c
0001220 41 72 63 68 69 74 65 63 74 75 72 65 31 16 30 14
0001240 06 03 55 04 03 13 0d 4a 6f 73 68 75 61 20 44 61
0001260 76 69 65 73 31 2c 30 2a 06 09 2a 86 48 86 f7 0d
0001300 01 09 01 16 1d 6a 6f 73 68 75 61 2e 64 61 76 69
0001320 65 73 40 74 72 61 76 65 6c 6f 63 69 74 79 2e 63
0001340 6f 6d 82 09 00 ca 30 e1 8f 77 8d a2 81 30 0c 06
0001360 03 55 1d 13 04 05 30 03 01 01 ff 30 0d 06 09 2a
0001400 86 48 86 f7 0d 01 01 05 05 00 03 41 00 1b 63 7b
0001420 f5 13 ef 2e 3d 56 22 3d a2 4c d5 0e 31 8d 0c 25
0001440 bb 24 30 fd a3 20 f5 a3 b5 7d 1b cb 1e a8 bd b0
0001460 ce 78 8b e7 5e 7a ac 66 2c 6d 06 06 e8 e3 06 24
0001500 ca d5 ce 0d 99 1a 7c 37 53 4d d3 be 83
```

It's worth taking the time to break this file down into its constituent parts. As discussed above, the first byte is a tag. 0x30 is a sequence, as you would expect — this should be a signed certificate sequence. This tag is followed by its length. Because the high-order bit of the length byte (0x82) is 1, this indicates that the next two bytes are the length of the sequence. These bytes are 0x0349, or decimal 841. This looks right — four bytes of the 845-byte file are the sequence and length tag, the remaining 841 are its content. The next byte is another sequence (0x30). Remember that the first element of a signed certificate is a `tbsCertificate`, which is itself a sequence. Again, the length takes up two bytes of the input stream, and is 0x02F3, or decimal 755. That leaves 86 bytes, toward the end, to contain the signature. Recall from Chapter 4 that this is about the right length for a 512-bit RSA signature value.

Table 5-6 presents an annotated breakdown of this certificate.

**Table 5-6:** Disassembled Certificate

| BYTE CONTENTS | ASN.1 MEANING | X.509 CERTIFICATE MEANING |
|---|---|---|
| 30 82 03 49 | 841 byte sequence | Certificate |
| 30 82 02 f3 | 755 byte sequence | TBSCertificate |
| a0 03 | 3 byte explicit tag | 0 |
| 02 01 02 | 1 byte integer | version number 3 |
| 02 09 00 ca 30 e1 8f 77 8d a2 81 | 9 byte integer | Serial Number |
| 30 0d | 13 byte sequence | Algorithm Identifier |
| 06 09 2a 86 48 f7 0d 01 01 01 05 | 9 byte OID | SHA-1 with RSA Encryption |
| 05 00 | Empty space filler | |
| 30 81 a1 | 161 byte sequence | Issuer Name |
| 31 0b | 11 byte set | AttributeTypeAndValue |
| 30 09 | 9 byte sequence | AttributeTypeAndValue |
| 06 03 55 04 06 | 3 byte OID | id-at-countryName |
| 13 02 55 53 | 2 byte string | US |
| 31 0b | 11 byte set | AttributeTypeAndValue |
| 30 09 | 9 byte sequence | AttributeTypeAndValue |
| 06 03 44 04 08 | 3 byte OID | id-at-stateOrProvinceName |
| 13 02 54 58 | 2 byte string | TX |
| 31 12 | 18 byte set | AttributeTypeAndValue |
| 30 10 | 16 byte sequence | AttributeTypeAndValue |
| 06 03 55 04 07 | 3 byte OID | id-at-localityName |
| 13 09 53 6f 75 74 68 6c 61 6b 65 | 9 byte string | Southlake |
| 31 14 | 20 byte set | AttributeTypeAndValue |

| 30 12 | 18 byte sequence | AttributeTypeAndValue |
|---|---|---|
| 06 03 55 04 0a | 3 byte OID | id-at-organizationName |
| 13 0b 54 72 61 76 65 6c 6f 63 69 74 79 | 11 byte string | Travelocity |
| 31 15 | 21 byte set | AttributeTypeAndValue |
| 30 13 | 19 byte sequence | AttributeTypeAndValue |
| 06 03 55 04 0b | 3 byte OID | id-at-organizationalUnit-Name |
| 13 0c 41 72 63 68 69 74 65 63 74 75 72 65 | 12 byte string | Architecture |
| 31 16 | 22 byte set | AttributeTypeAndValue |
| 30 14 | 20 byte sequence | AttributeTypeAndValue |
| 06 03 55 04 03 | 3 byte OID | id-at-commonName |
| 13 0d 4a 6f 73 68 75 61 20 44 61 76 69 65 73 | 13 byte string | Joshua Davies |
| 30 1e | 31 byte sequence | Validity |
| 17 0d 31 30 30 33 30 32 32 32 34 36 32 33 5a | 13 byte UTC time | notBefore=100302224623Z |
| 17 0d 31 30 30 34 30 31 32 32 34 36 32 33 5a | 13 byte UTC time | notAfter =100401224623Z |
| 30 81 a1 | 161 byte sequence | subject name |
| 31 0b | 11 byte set | AttributeTypeAndValue |
| 30 09 | 9 byte sequence | AttributeTypeAndValue |
| 06 03 55 04 06 | 3 byte OID | id-at-countryName |
| 13 02 55 53 | 2 byte string | US |
| 31 0b | 11 byte set | AttributeTypeAndValue |
| 30 09 | 9 byte sequence | AttributeTypeAndValue |
| 06 03 44 04 08 | 3 byte OID | id-at-stateOrProvinceName |
| 13 02 54 58 | 2 byte string | TX |
| 31 12 | 18 byte set | AttributeTypeAndValue |
| 30 10 | 16 byte sequence | AttributeTypeAndValue |
| 06 03 55 04 07 | 3 byte OID | id-at-localityName |
| 13 09 53 6f 75 74 68 6c 61 6b 65 | 9 byte string | Southlake |
| 31 14 | 20 byte set | AttributeTypeAndValue |

*Continued*

**Table 5-6** *(continued)*

| BYTE CONTENTS | ASN.1 MEANING | X.509 CERTIFICATE MEANING |
|---|---|---|
| 30 12 | 18 byte sequence | AttributeTypeAndValue |
| 06 03 55 04 0a | 3 byte OID | id-at-organizationName |
| 13 0b 54 72 61 76 65 6c 6f 63 69 74 79 | 11 byte string | Travelocity |
| 31 15 | 21 byte set | AttributeTypeAndValue |
| 30 13 | 19 byte sequence | AttributeTypeAndValue |
| 06 03 55 04 0b | 3 byte OID | id-at-organizationalUnit-Name |
| 13 0c 41 72 63 68 69 74 65 63 74 75 72 65 | 12 byte string | Architecture |
| 31 16 | 22 byte set | AttributeTypeAndValue |
| 30 14 | 20 byte sequence | AttributeTypeAndValue |
| 06 03 55 04 03 | 3 byte OID | id-at-commonName |
| 13 0d 4a 6f 73 68 75 61 20 44 61 76 69 65 73 | 13 byte string | Joshua Davies |
| 30 5c | 92 byte sequence | SubjectPublicKeyInfo |
| 30 0d | 13 byte sequence | AlgorithmIdentifier |
| 06 09 2a 86 48 f7 0d 01 01 01 | 9 byte OID | RSA |
| 05 00 | 0 byte filler | |
| 03 4b | 75 byte bit string | subjectPublicKey |
| 00 30 48 02 41 00 … | | ASN.1 encoded public key bit string |
| a3 82 01 0a | 266 byte explicit tag 3 | extensions |
| 30 82 01 06 | 262 byte sequence | Extension |
| 30 1d | 29 byte sequence | Extension |
| 06 03 55 1d 0e | 3 byte OID | Subject Key Identifier |
| 04 16 04 14 2d f1 04 e4 46 1d 72 ef bb a7 ce 05 58 4c 31 f1 ff 8e 4e 2e | 22 byte octet string | |
| 30 81 d6 | 214 byte sequence | Extension |
| 06 03 55 1d 23 | 3 byte OID | Authority key identifier |

| 04 81 ce | 206 byte octet string | |
| --- | --- | --- |
| 30 81 cb 80 14 2d … | | |
| 30 0d | 13 byte sequence | Signature Algorithm |
| 06 09 2a 86 48 86 f7 0d 01 01 05 | 9 byte OID | RSA with SHA-1 |
| 05 00 | 0 byte filler | |
| 03 41 00 1b 63 7b … | 65 byte string | signatureValue |

Note that the interpretation of the second column is automatic and requires no context. However, the interpretation of the third column — the actual certificate contents — requires that you keep close track of the sequences, sets, and so on and match them against the definition. One frustrating thing about ASN.1 DER-encoded strings is that they don't carry any identifying information with them. You can often recognize a DER-encoded file by the 30 byte that (usually) starts it, but if you don't have some external information indicating what type of file it is, you'll never be able to figure out what sort of file you're looking at.

### Using OpenSSL to Generate a DSA KeyPair and Certificate

The example certificate in the previous section included an RSA public key. Although this is by far the most common certificate form, OpenSSL allows you to generate certificates that include DSA keys as well. (It does not, at the time of this writing, allow the creation of a certificate with Diffie-Hellman parameters as discussed earlier). The process is slightly more involved, though. First, you must create a set of DSA parameters ($p$, $q$, and $g$):

```
[jdavies@localhost ssl]$ openssl dsaparam 512
-out dsaparam.cer
Generating DSA parameters, 512 bit long prime

This could take some time

..+................+.....+++++++++++++++++++++++++++++++++++++++++++++++++*

.......+..+...........+......................................+.....+..+.......
...
.......+..+.....+.......................+.............+....+.+.....+...........
...
.+.+.......+...........................................+....+..+.+......+..+..+..
...
.+............+...+..........+.............................+.............+..........
...
+.......+...+.............+.....+.....+++++++++++++++++++++++++++++++++++++++++
+++
++++*
```

You pass this in to your certificate request:

```
[jdavies@localhost ssl]$ openssl req -x509 -newkey dsa:dsaparam.cer -keyout \
  dsakey.der -keyform der -out dsacert.der -outform der
Generating a 512 bit DSA private key
writing new private key to 'dsakey.der'
Enter PEM pass phrase:
Verifying - Enter PEM pass phrase:
-----
You are about to be asked to enter information that will be incorporated
into your certificate request.
What you are about to enter is what is called a Distinguished Name or a DN.
There are quite a few fields but you can leave some blank
For some fields there will be a default value,
If you enter '.', the field will be left blank.
-----
Country Name (2 letter code) [GB]:US
State or Province Name (full name) [Berkshire]:Texas
Locality Name (eg, city) [Newbury]:Southlake
Organization Name (eg, company) [My Company Ltd]:Travelocity
Organizational Unit Name (eg, section) []:Architecture
Common Name (eg, your name or your server's hostname) []:Joshua Davies
Email Address []:joshua.davies@travelocity.com
```

# Developing an ASN.1 Parser

By now, you're probably itching to see some code. You develop code to parse an X.509 certificate in two parts; first, deconstruct the DER-encoded ASN.1 structure into its constituent parts and then interpret these parts as an X.509 certificate. ASN.1-encoded values can be represented naturally as nodes of the form shown in Listing 5-3.

**Listing 5-3:** "asn1.h" asn1struct definition

```
struct asn1struct
{
  int constructed;  // bit 6 of the identifier byte
  int tag_class;    // bits 7-8 of the identifier byte
  int tag;          // bits 1-5 of the identifier byte
  int length;
  const unsigned char *data;
  struct asn1struct *children;
  struct asn1struct *next;
};
```

## Converting a Byte Stream into an ASN.1 Structure

The first five elements ought to be relatively straightforward if you understood the description of ASN.1 DER in the previous section. The last two are used to navigate the hierarchy. Each `asn1struct` is part of a linked list of other `asn-1struct` structures, and each one optionally points to the head of another linked list that is its child. So, after parsing, the first part of the certificate is represented in memory as shown in Figure 5-8.

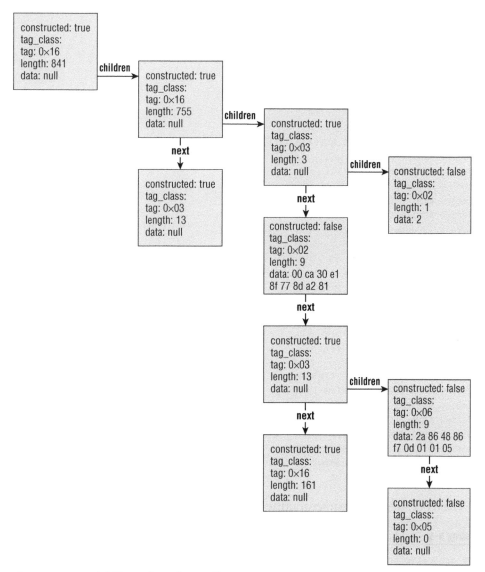

**Figure 5.8:** Partial illustration of a certificate structure

As you can see, locating a node is a matter of starting at the root, and traversing any number of `children` or `nexts` until you reach the one you're looking for. The tree structure is preserved by the use of the `children` pointers. Define a handful of constants to clarify the code as shown in Listing 5-4.

**Listing 5-4:** "asn1.h" constants

```
#define ASN1_CLASS_UNIVERSAL 0
#define ASN1_CLASS_APPLICATION 1
#define ASN1_CONTEXT_SPECIFIC 2
#define ASN1_PRIVATE 3

#define ASN1_BER 0
#define ASN1_BOOLEAN 1
#define ASN1_INTEGER 2
#define ASN1_BIT_STRING 3
#define ASN1_OCTET_STRING 4
#define ASN1_NULL 5
#define ASN1_OBJECT_IDENTIFIER 6
#define ASN1_OBJECT_DESCRIPTOR 7
#define ASN1_INSTANCE_OF_EXTERNAL 8
#define ASN1_REAL 9
#define ASN1_ENUMERATED 10
#define ASN1_EMBEDDED_PPV 11
#define ASN1_UTF8_STRING 12
#define ASN1_RELATIVE_OID 13
// 14 & 15 undefined
#define ASN1_SEQUENCE 16
#define ASN1_SET 17
#define ASN1_NUMERIC_STRING 18
#define ASN1_PRINTABLE_STRING 19
#define ASN1_TELETEX_STRING 20
#define ASN1_T61_STRING 20
#define ASN1_VIDEOTEX_STRING 21
#define ASN1_IA5_STRING 22
#define ASN1_UTC_TIME 23
#define ASN1_GENERALIZED_TIME 24
#define ASN1_GRAPHIC_STRING 25
#define ASN1_VISIBLE_STRING 26
#define ASN1_ISO64_STRING 26
#define ASN1_GENERAL_STRING 27
#define ASN1_UNIVERSAL_STRING 28
#define ASN1_CHARACTER_STRING 29
#define ASN1_BMP_STRING 30
```

The recursive ASN.1 parser routine itself is surprisingly simple (see Listing 5-5).

**Listing 5-5:** "asn1.c" asn1parse

```
int asn1parse( const unsigned char *buffer,
               int length,
               struct asn1struct *top_level_token )
{
  unsigned int tag;
  unsigned char tag_length_byte;
  unsigned long tag_length;
  const unsigned char *ptr;
```

```
const unsigned char *ptr_begin;
struct asn1struct *token;

ptr = buffer;
token = top_level_token;

while ( length )
{
 ptr_begin = ptr;
 tag = *ptr;
 ptr++;
 length--;

 // High tag # form (bits 5-1 all == "1"), to encode tags > 31. Not used
 // in X.509
 if ( ( tag & 0x1F ) == 0x1F )
 {
   tag = 0;
   while ( *ptr & 0x80 )
   {
     tag <<= 8;
     tag |= *ptr & 0x7F;
   }
 }

 tag_length_byte = *ptr;
 ptr++;
 length--;

 // TODO this doesn't handle indefinite-length encodings (according to
 // ITU-T X.690, this never occurs in DER, only in BER, which X.509 doesn't
 // use)
 if ( tag_length_byte & 0x80 )
 {
   const unsigned char *len_ptr = ptr;
   tag_length = 0;
   while ( ( len_ptr - ptr ) < ( tag_length_byte & 0x7F ) )
   {
     tag_length <<= 8;
     tag_length |= *(len_ptr++);
     length--;
   }
   ptr = len_ptr;
 }
 else
 {
   tag_length = tag_length_byte;
 }

 // TODO deal with "high tag numbers"
 token->constructed = tag & 0x20;
```

*(Continued)*

```
      token->tag_class = ( tag & 0xC0 ) >> 6;
      token->tag = tag & 0x1F;
      token->length = tag_length;
      token->data = ptr;
      token->children = NULL;
      token->next = NULL;

      if ( tag & 0x20 )
      {
        token->length = tag_length + ( ptr - ptr_begin );

        token->data = ptr_begin;

        // Append a child to this tag and recurse into it
        token->children = ( struct asn1struct * )
          malloc( sizeof( struct asn1struct ) );
        asn1parse( ptr, tag_length, token->children );
      }

      ptr += tag_length;
      length -= tag_length;

      // At this point, we're pointed at the tag for the next token in the buffer.
      if ( length )
      {
        token->next = ( struct asn1struct * ) malloc( sizeof( struct asn1struct ) );
        token = token->next;
      }
    }

  return 0;
}
```

This routine is passed a complete certificate structure, so the whole thing must be resident in memory before this routine is called; this approach might need to be revisited in, say, a handheld device where memory is constrained. It reads through the whole buffer, recognizing ASN.1 structures, and allocating `asn1struct` instances to represent them.

1. Check to see if this is a multi-byte tag:

```
        if ( ( tag & 0x1F ) == 0x1F )
        {
          tag = 0;
          while ( *ptr & 0x80 )
          {
            tag <<= 8;
```

```
        tag |= *ptr & 0x7F;
    }
}
```

X.509 doesn't define any of these, but you ought to recognize them for completeness — if for no other reason than to be able to safely ignore them if you happen to come across one.

2. Parse out the length of the structure itself; this is always present. If the first byte is a multi-length byte, the processing is a bit complex in part because of the endian-ness issue.

```
if ( tag_length_byte & 0x80 )
{
  const unsigned char *len_ptr = ptr;
  tag_length = 0;
  while ( ( len_ptr - ptr ) < ( tag_length_byte & 0x7F ) )
  {
    tag_length <<= 8;
    tag_length |= *(len_ptr++);
    length--;
  }
  ptr = len_ptr;
}
else
{
  tag_length = tag_length_byte;
}
```

3. Now that you know the type of tag and the length of its contents — whether they are data or other ASN.1 structures — you can start filling out the asn1struct instance:

```
token->constructed = tag & 0x20;
token->tag_class = ( tag & 0xC0 ) >> 6;
token->tag = tag & 0x1F;
token->length = tag_length;
token->data = ptr;
token->children = NULL;
token->next = NULL;
```

4. Now the tricky part — if this is a constructed tag, its contents are more ASN.1 structures, which must be appended to the children list. If it is then allocate a new structure to store the children and recursively call this routine:

```
if ( tag & 0x20 )
{
  token->length = tag_length + ( ptr - ptr_begin );
```

```
              token->data = ptr_begin;

              token->children = ( struct asn1struct * )
                malloc( sizeof( struct asn1struct ) );
              asn1parse( ptr, tag_length, token->children );
            }
```

5. When it returns, or if it wasn't called because the tag was a non-constructed tag, you're either at the end of the data or you're pointing at the next element relative to the one that was just parsed.

```
        if ( length )
        {
          token->next = ( struct asn1struct * )
            malloc( sizeof( struct asn1struct ) );
          token = token->next;
        }
```

6. If there is another element to parse, allocate space for it, update the target `token` pointer, and loop back around to process this element. When you're finished the supplied `top_level_token` structure points to the root of a fully parsed ASN.1 tree.

7. Finally, because a lot of memory is allocated by the ASN.1 parsing process, define a function to recursively go through and clean it all up as shown in Listing 5-6.

**Listing 5-6:** "asn1.c" asn1free

```
/**
 * Recurse through the given node and free all of the memory that was allocated
 * by asn1parse. Don't free the "data" pointers, since that points to memory
 * that was not allocated by asn1parse.
 */
void asn1free( struct asn1struct *node )
{
  if ( !node )
  {
    return;
  }

  asn1free( node->children );
  free( node->children );
  asn1free( node->next );
  free( node->next );
}
```

As you can see, the recursive definition of the `asn1struct` structure makes cleanup and traversal very straightforward.

## The asn1parse Code in Action

To see this code in action, put together a sample `main` routine as in Listing 5-7 that takes as input a certificate file (or any other ASN.1 DER-encoded file) and output the ASN.1 structure elements.

**Listing 5-7:** "asn1.c" test routine

```
#ifdef TEST_ASN1
int main( int argc, char *argv[ ] )
{
  int certificate_file;
  struct stat certificate_file_stat;
  unsigned char *buffer, *bufptr;
  int buffer_size;
  int bytes_read;

  struct asn1struct certificate;

  if ( argc < 2 )
  {
    fprintf( stderr, "Usage: %s <certificate file>\n", argv[ 0 ] );
    exit( 0 );
  }

  if ( ( certificate_file = open( argv[ 1 ], O_RDONLY ) ) == -1 )
  {
    perror( "Unable to open certificate file" );
    return 1;
  }

  // Slurp the whole thing into memory
  if ( fstat( certificate_file, &certificate_file_stat ) )
  {
    perror( "Unable to stat certificate file" );
    return 2;
  }

  buffer_size = certificate_file_stat.st_size;
  buffer = ( char * ) malloc( buffer_size );
```

*(Continued)*

```
  if ( !buffer )
  {
    perror( "Not enough memory" );
    return 3;
  }

  bufptr = buffer;

  while ( bytes_read = read( certificate_file, ( void * ) buffer,
                certificate_file_stat.st_size ) )
  {
    bufptr += bytes_read;
  }
  asn1parse( buffer, buffer_size, &certificate );

  asn1show( 0, &certificate );

  asn1free( &certificate );

  return 0;
}
#endif
```

This invokes the asn1show routine in Listing 5-8.

**Listing 5-8:** "asn1.c" asn1show

```
static char *tag_names[] = {
  "BER",                      // 0
  "BOOLEAN",                  // 1
  "INTEGER",                  // 2
  "BIT STRING",               // 3
  "OCTET STRING",             // 4
  "NULL",                     // 5
  "OBJECT IDENTIFIER",        // 6
  "ObjectDescriptor",         // 7
  "INSTANCE OF, EXTERNAL",    // 8
  "REAL",                     // 9
  "ENUMERATED",               // 10
  "EMBEDDED PPV",             // 11
  "UTF8String",               // 12
  "RELATIVE-OID",             // 13
  "undefined(14)",            // 14
  "undefined(15)",            // 15
  "SEQUENCE, SEQUENCE OF",    // 16
  "SET, SET OF",              // 17
  "NumericString",            // 18
  "PrintableString",          // 19
  "TeletexString, T61String", // 20
```

```
"VideotexString",           // 21
"IA5String",                // 22
"UTCTime",                  // 23
"GeneralizedTime",          // 24
"GraphicString",            // 25
"VisibleString, ISO64String", // 26
"GeneralString",            // 27
"UniversalString",          // 28
"CHARACTER STRING",         // 29
"BMPString"                 // 30
};

void asn1show( int depth, struct asn1struct *certificate )
{
  struct asn1struct *token;
  int i;

  token = certificate;

  while ( token )
  {
    for ( i = 0; i < depth; i++ )
    {
      printf( " " );
    }
    switch ( token->tag_class )
    {
      case ASN1_CLASS_UNIVERSAL:
        printf( "%s", tag_names[ token->tag ] );
        break;
      case ASN1_CLASS_APPLICATION:
        printf( "application" );
        break;
      case ASN1_CONTEXT_SPECIFIC:
        printf( "context" );
        break;
      case ASN1_PRIVATE:
        printf( "private" );
        break;
    }
    printf( " (%d:%d) ", token->tag, token->length );

    if ( token->tag_class == ASN1_CLASS_UNIVERSAL )
    {
      switch ( token->tag )
      {
        case ASN1_INTEGER:
          break;
```

*(Continued)*

```
      case ASN1_BIT_STRING:
      case ASN1_OCTET_STRING:
      case ASN1_OBJECT_IDENTIFIER:
        {
          int i;

          for ( i = 0; i < token->length; i++ )
          {
            printf( "%.02x ", token->data[ i ] );
          }
        }
        break;
    case ASN1_NUMERIC_STRING:
    case ASN1_PRINTABLE_STRING:
    case ASN1_TELETEX_STRING:
    case ASN1_VIDEOTEX_STRING:
    case ASN1_IA5_STRING:
    case ASN1_UTC_TIME:
    case ASN1_GENERALIZED_TIME:
    case ASN1_GRAPHIC_STRING:
    case ASN1_VISIBLE_STRING:
    case ASN1_GENERAL_STRING:
    case ASN1_UNIVERSAL_STRING:
    case ASN1_CHARACTER_STRING:
    case ASN1_BMP_STRING:
    case ASN1_UTF8_STRING:
    {
      char *str_val = ( char * ) malloc( token->length + 1 );
      strncpy( str_val, ( char * ) token->data, token->length );
       str_val[ token->length ] = 0;
      printf( " %s", str_val );
      free( str_val );
    }
      break;
    default:
      break;
  }
}

printf( "\n" );
if ( token->children )
{
  asn1show( depth + 1, token->children );
}
token = token->next;
}
}
```

If you run this on a DER-encoded certificate file, you get an output similar to Table 5-6 (this was, in fact, how that table was generated). However, when most software saves certificate files, it doesn't do it in DER form; it uses PEM form instead. To use this parsing routine to see the contents of a PEM-encoded file, you can call the `base64decode` routine from Chapter 1 to convert PEM to DER as in Listing 5-9.

**Listing 5-9:** "asn1.c" pem_decode

```c
int pem_decode( unsigned char *pem_buffer, unsigned char *der_buffer )
{
  unsigned char *pem_buffer_end, *pem_buffer_begin;
  unsigned char *bufptr = der_buffer;
  int buffer_size;
  // Skip first line, which is always "-----BEGIN CERTIFICATE-----".

  if ( strncmp( pem_buffer, "-----BEGIN", 10 ) )
  {
    fprintf( stderr,
       "This does not appear to be a PEM-encoded certificate file\n" );
    exit( 0 );
  }

  pem_buffer_begin = pem_buffer;
  pem_buffer= pem_buffer_end = strchr( pem_buffer, '\n' ) + 1;

  while ( strncmp( pem_buffer, "-----END", 8 ) )
  {
    // Find end of line
    pem_buffer_end = strchr( pem_buffer, '\n' );
    // Decode one line out of pem_buffer into buffer
    bufptr += base64_decode( pem_buffer,
      ( pem_buffer_end - pem_buffer ) -
      ( ( *( pem_buffer_end - 1 ) == '\r' ) ? 1 : 0 ),
      bufptr );
    pem_buffer = pem_buffer_end + 1;
  }

  buffer_size = bufptr - der_buffer;

  return buffer_size;
}
```

Change the test `main` routine to accept either PEM or DER form:

```c
if ( argc < 3 )
{
  fprintf( stderr, "Usage: %s [-der|-pem] <certificate file>\n", argv[ 0 ] );
  exit( 0 );
}
if ( ( certificate_file = open( argv[ 2 ], O_RDONLY ) ) == -1 )
{
...
}
```

*(Continued)*

```
if ( !( strcmp( argv[ 1 ], "-pem" ) ) )
{
  // XXX this overallocates a bit, since it sets aside space for markers, etc.
  unsigned char *pem_buffer = buffer;
  buffer = (unsigned char * ) malloc( buffer_size );
  buffer_size = pem_decode( pem_buffer, buffer );
  free( pem_buffer );
}

asn1parse( buffer, buffer_size, &certificate );
```

You now have a working ASN.1 parser that can be used to read and interpret X.509 certificates. You could stop here, and write code like this:

```
root->next->next->children->next->children->next->data
```

to look up the values of specific elements in the tree, but to make your code have any semblance of readability, you should really continue to parse this ASN.1 tree into a proper X.509 structure.

## Turning a Parsed ASN.1 Structure into X.509 Certificate Components

The X.509 structure is decidedly more complex than the ASN.1 structure; define it to mirror the ASN.1 definition. To keep the implementation easy to digest, the code is presented for RSA certificates — by far the most common case — and then extended to support DSA and Diffie-Hellman. The structure definitions are shown in Listing 5-10.

**Listing 5-10:** "x509.h" structure definitions

```
typedef enum
{
  rsa,
  dh
}
algorithmIdentifier;

typedef enum
{
  md5WithRSAEncryption,
  shaWithRSAEncryption
}
signatureAlgorithmIdentifier;

/**
 * A name (or "distinguishedName") is a list of attribute-value pairs.
 * Instead of keeping track of all of them, just keep track of
 * the most interesting ones.
 */
typedef struct
```

```
{
  char *idAtCountryName;
  char *idAtStateOrProvinceName;
  char *idAtLocalityName;
  char *idAtOrganizationName;
  char *idAtOrganizationalUnitName;
  char *idAtCommonName;
}
name;

typedef struct
{
  // TODO deal with the "utcTime" or "GeneralizedTime" choice.
  time_t notBefore;
  time_t notAfter;
}
validity_period;

typedef huge uniqueIdentifier;

typedef struct
{
  algorithmIdentifier algorithm;
  rsa_key rsa_public_key;
}
public_key_info;

typedef huge objectIdentifier;

typedef struct
{
  int version;
  huge serialNumber; // This can be much longer than a 4-byte long allows
  signatureAlgorithmIdentifier signature;
  name issuer;
  validity_period validity;
  name subject;
  public_key_info subjectPublicKeyInfo;
  uniqueIdentifier issuerUniqueId;
  uniqueIdentifier subjectUniqueId;
  int certificate_authority; // 1 if this is a CA, 0 if not
}
x509_certificate;

typedef struct
{
  x509_certificate tbsCertificate;
  signatureAlgorithmIdentifier algorithm;
  huge signature_value;
}
signed_x509_certificate;
```

Compare the x509_certificate structure in Listing 5-10 with the official ITU definition shown in Listing 5-1 and signed_x509_certificate with Listing 5-2. The goal of the certificate parsing process is to take a "blob" of unstructured bytes and turn it into a signed_x509_certificate instance. As you can see above, there's quite a bit of unallocated memory in this structure definition, so the first thing you need is an initializer function, as shown in Listing 5-11.

**Listing 5-11:** "x509.c" init_x509_certificate

```
void init_x509_certificate( signed_x509_certificate *certificate )
{
  set_huge( &certificate->tbsCertificate.serialNumber, 1 );
  memset( &certificate->tbsCertificate.issuer, 0, sizeof( name ) );
  memset( &certificate->tbsCertificate.subject, 0, sizeof( name ) );
  certificate->tbsCertificate.subjectPublicKeyInfo.rsa_public_key.modulus =
    malloc( sizeof( huge ) );
  certificate->tbsCertificate.subjectPublicKeyInfo.rsa_public_key.exponent =
    malloc( sizeof( huge ) );
  set_huge(
    certificate->tbsCertificate.subjectPublicKeyInfo.rsa_public_key.modulus,
    0 );
  set_huge(
    certificate->tbsCertificate.subjectPublicKeyInfo.rsa_public_key.exponent,
    0 );
  set_huge( &certificate->signature_value, 0 );
  certificate->tbsCertificate.certificate_authority = 0;
}
```

You also need, of course, a companion "free" function as shown in Listing 5-12.

**Listing 5-12:** "x509.c" free_x509_certificate

```
static void free_x500_name( name *x500_name )
{
  if ( x500_name->idAtCountryName ) { free( x500_name->idAtCountryName ); }
  if ( x500_name->idAtStateOrProvinceName ) { free( x500_name-
>idAtStateOrProvinceName ); }
  if ( x500_name->idAtLocalityName ) { free( x500_name->idAtLocalityName ); }
  if ( x500_name->idAtOrganizationName ) { free( x500_name->idAtOrganizationName
); }
  if ( x500_name->idAtOrganizationalUnitName ) { free( x500_name-
>idAtOrganizationalUnitName ); }
  if ( x500_name->idAtCommonName ) { free( x500_name->idAtCommonName ); }
}

void free_x509_certificate( signed_x509_certificate *certificate )

{
  free_huge( &certificate->tbsCertificate.serialNumber );
  free_x500_name( &certificate->tbsCertificate.issuer );
```

```
  free_x500_name( &certificate->tbsCertificate.subject );
  free_huge(
   certificate->tbsCertificate.subjectPublicKeyInfo.rsa_public_key.modulus );
  free_huge(
   certificate->tbsCertificate.subjectPublicKeyInfo.rsa_public_key.exponent );
  free(
   certificate->tbsCertificate.subjectPublicKeyInfo.rsa_public_key.modulus );
  free(
   certificate->tbsCertificate.subjectPublicKeyInfo.rsa_public_key.exponent );
  free_huge( &certificate->signature_value );
}
```

After the `signed_x509_certificate` structure has been properly initialized, parsing it involves invoking the `parse_asn1_certificate` function shown previously and then selectively copying `data` values from the `asn1struct` nodes into the appropriate locations in the `signed_x509_certificate` target. The top-level function that controls this whole process is in Listing 5-13.

**Listing 5-13:** "x509.c" parse_x509_certificate

```
int parse_x509_certificate( const unsigned char *buffer,
             const unsigned int certificate_length,
             signed_x509_certificate *parsed_certificate )
{
  struct asn1struct certificate;
  struct asn1struct *tbsCertificate;
  struct asn1struct *algorithmIdentifier;
  struct asn1struct *signatureValue;

  // First, read the whole thing into a traversable ASN.1 structure
  asn1parse( buffer, certificate_length, &certificate );

  tbsCertificate = ( struct asn1struct * ) certificate.children;

  algorithmIdentifier = ( struct asn1struct * ) tbsCertificate->next;
  signatureValue = ( struct asn1struct * ) algorithmIdentifier->next;
  if ( parse_tbs_certificate( &parsed_certificate->tbsCertificate,
     tbsCertificate ) )
  {
    fprintf( stderr, "Error trying to parse TBS certificate\n" );
    return 42;
  }
  if ( parse_algorithm_identifier( &parsed_certificate->algorithm,
                  algorithmIdentifier ) )
  {
    return 42;
  }

  if ( parse_signature_value( parsed_certificate, signatureValue ) )
  {
    return 42;
```

```
  }

  asn1free( &certificate );

  return 0;
}
```

## Joining the X.509 Components into a Completed X.509 Certificate Structure

According to the ITU specification, the top level node should be a structure containing three child nodes — the TBS certificate, the signature algorithm identifier, and the signature value itself. First, parse the tbsCertificate in Listing 5-14, which is where the most interesting information is anyway. Afterward, the algorithm identifier and signature values are parsed, as was shown in Listing 5-13.

**Listing 5-14:** "x509.c" parse_tbs_certificate

```
static int parse_tbs_certificate( x509_certificate *target,
               struct asn1struct *source )
{
  struct asn1struct *version;
  struct asn1struct *serialNumber;
  struct asn1struct *signatureAlgorithmIdentifier;
  struct asn1struct *issuer;
  struct asn1struct *validity;
  struct asn1struct *subject;
  struct asn1struct *publicKeyInfo;
  struct asn1struct *extensions;

  // Figure out if there's an explicit version or not; if there is, then
  // everything else "shifts down" one spot.
  version = ( struct asn1struct * ) source->children;

  if ( version->tag == 0 && version->tag_class == ASN1_CONTEXT_SPECIFIC )
  {
    struct asn1struct *versionNumber =
     ( struct asn1struct * ) version->children;

    // This will only ever be one byte; safe
    target->version = ( *versionNumber->data ) + 1;
    serialNumber = ( struct asn1struct * ) version->next;
  }
  else
  {
    target->version = 1; // default if not provided
    serialNumber = ( struct asn1struct * ) version;
  }

  signatureAlgorithmIdentifier = ( struct asn1struct * ) serialNumber->next;
```

```
issuer = ( struct asn1struct * ) signatureAlgorithmIdentifier->next;
validity = ( struct asn1struct * ) issuer->next;
subject = ( struct asn1struct * ) validity->next;
publicKeyInfo = ( struct asn1struct * ) subject->next;
extensions = ( struct asn1struct * ) publicKeyInfo->next;

if ( parse_huge( &target->serialNumber, serialNumber ) ) { return 2; }
if ( parse_algorithm_identifier( &target->signature,
                  signatureAlgorithmIdentifier ) )
  { return 3; }
if ( parse_name( &target->issuer, issuer ) ) { return 4; }
if ( parse_validity( &target->validity, validity ) ) { return 5; }
if ( parse_name( &target->subject, subject ) ) { return 6; }
if ( parse_public_key_info( &target->subjectPublicKeyInfo, publicKeyInfo ) )
  { return 7; }
if ( extensions )
{
  if ( parse_extensions( target, extensions ) ) { return 8; }
}

return 0;
}
```

The only thing that makes the tbsCertificate structure tricky to parse is the version number. The original designers of the X.509 structure didn't see fit to include a version number in it, so the version was added later on, necessitating an explicit tag as discussed previously. So, if the tag class of the first node is context-specific and the tag is explicit tag 0, it must be the version number and the serial number follows as the next element. Otherwise, the version of the certificate is 1 and the serial number is the first element. To mix things up just a bit more, the version number, if present, is contained within the explicit tag, so you need to look for the first child of the explicit tag. Almost all certificates you find on the public Internet these days include a version tag, but you must be prepared to deal with a very, very old one.

Also, version 1 is identified by the number 0, version 2 by the number 1, and version 3 by the number 2. I think they're just messing with your head.

Whether a version number was supplied or not, the next element is the serial number. Go ahead and parse this into a huge structure as shown in Listing 5-15, although it is just treated as a byte array; you won't be performing any huge math on it.

**Listing 5-15:** "x509.c" parse_huge

```
static int parse_huge( huge *target, struct asn1struct *source )
{
  target->sign = 0;
  target->size = source->length;
  target->rep = ( char * ) malloc( target->size );
```

*(Continued)*

```
  memcpy( target->rep, source->data, target->size );

  return 0;
}
```

## Parsing Object Identifiers (OIDs)

Following the serial number is the algorithm identifier of the signature. This is an OID and can take on several possible values; each value is unique and identifies a digest algorithm/digital signature algorithm pair. For now, only support two: MD5 with RSA and SHA-1 with RSA, as shown in Listing 5-16.

**Listing 5-16:** "x509.c" parse_algorithm_identifier

```
static const unsigned char OID_md5WithRSA[] =
  { 0x2A, 0x86, 0x48, 0x86, 0xF7, 0x0D, 0x01, 0x01, 0x04 };
static const unsigned char OID_sha1WithRSA[] =
  { 0x2A, 0x86, 0x48, 0x86, 0xF7, 0x0D, 0x01, 0x01, 0x05 };

static int parse_algorithm_identifier( signatureAlgorithmIdentifier *target,
                  struct asn1struct *source )
{
  struct asn1struct *oid = ( struct asn1struct * ) source->children;

  if ( !memcmp( oid->data, OID_md5WithRSA, oid->length ) )
  {
    *target = md5WithRSAEncryption;
  }
  else if ( !memcmp( oid->data, OID_sha1WithRSA, oid->length ) )
  {
    *target = shaWithRSAEncryption;
  }
  else
  {
    int i;
    fprintf( stderr, "Unsupported or unrecognized algorithm identifier OID " );
    for ( i = 0; i < oid->length; i++ )
    {
      fprintf( stderr, "%.02x ", oid->data[ i ] );
    }
    fprintf( stderr, "\n" );
    return 2;
  }

  return 0;
}
```

Remember that OIDs are being hardcoded in expanded form so that you can just do a memcmp to identify them.

## Parsing Distinguished Names

Following the signature algorithm identifier is the issuer name. Name parsing is by far the most involved part of X.509 certificate management. Recall that an X.509 distinguished name is a list of components such as CN, O, OU, each of which is identified by its own OID and may or may not be present. None of them is required, and any of them can appear more than once. However, for all practical purposes, the names you'll be looking at have exactly one each of a country name, a state/province name, a city/locality name, an organization name, an organizational unit name and, most importantly, a common name. As such the structure for the name only contains pointers for this data and throws away any additional information; a more robust implementation than the one shown in Listing 5-17 would be much more complex.

**Listing 5-17:** "x509.c" parse_name

```
static unsigned char OID_idAtCommonName[] = { 0x55, 0x04, 0x03 };
static unsigned char OID_idAtCountryName[] = { 0x55, 0x04, 0x06 };
static unsigned char OID_idAtLocalityName[] = { 0x55, 0x04, 0x07 };
static unsigned char OID_idAtStateOrProvinceName[] = { 0x55, 0x04, 0x08 };
static unsigned char OID_idAtOrganizationName[] = { 0x55, 0x04, 0x0A };
static unsigned char OID_idAtOrganizationalUnitName[] = { 0x55, 0x04, 0x0B };

/**
 * Name parsing is a bit different. Loop through all of the
 * children of the source, each of which is going to be a struct containing
 * an OID and a value. If the OID is recognized, copy its contents
 * to the correct spot in "target". Otherwise, ignore it.
 */
static int parse_name( name *target, struct asn1struct *source )
{
  struct asn1struct *typeValuePair;
  struct asn1struct *typeValuePairSequence;
  struct asn1struct *type;
  struct asn1struct *value;

  target->idAtCountryName = NULL;
  target->idAtStateOrProvinceName = NULL;
  target->idAtLocalityName = NULL;
  target->idAtOrganizationName = NULL;
  target->idAtOrganizationalUnitName = NULL;
  target->idAtCommonName = NULL;

  typeValuePair = source->children;
  while ( typeValuePair )
  {
    typeValuePairSequence = ( struct asn1struct * ) typeValuePair->children;
    type = ( struct asn1struct * ) typeValuePairSequence->children;
```

*(Continued)*

```
      value = ( struct asn1struct * ) type->next;

      if ( !memcmp( type->data, OID_idAtCountryName, type->length ) )
      {
        target->idAtCountryName = ( char * ) malloc( value->length + 1 );
        memcpy( target->idAtCountryName, value->data, value->length );
        target->idAtCountryName[ value->length ] = 0;
      }
      else if ( !memcmp( type->data, OID_idAtStateOrProvinceName, type->length ) )
      {
        target->idAtStateOrProvinceName = ( char * ) malloc( value->length + 1 );
        memcpy( target->idAtStateOrProvinceName, value->data, value->length );
        target->idAtStateOrProvinceName[ value->length ] = 0;
      }
      else if ( !memcmp( type->data, OID_idAtLocalityName, type->length ) )
      {
        target->idAtLocalityName = ( char * ) malloc( value->length + 1 );
        memcpy( target->idAtLocalityName, value->data, value->length );
        target->idAtLocalityName[ value->length ] = 0;
      }
      else if ( !memcmp( type->data, OID_idAtOrganizationName, type->length ) )
      {
        target->idAtOrganizationName = ( char * ) malloc( value->length + 1 );
        memcpy( target->idAtOrganizationName, value->data, value->length );
        target->idAtOrganizationName[ value->length ] = 0;
      }
      else if ( !memcmp( type->data, OID_idAtOrganizationalUnitName,
               type->length ) )
      {
        target->idAtOrganizationalUnitName = ( char * )
          malloc( value->length + 1 );
        memcpy( target->idAtOrganizationalUnitName, value->data, value->length );
        target->idAtOrganizationalUnitName[ value->length ] = 0;
      }
      else if ( !memcmp( type->data, OID_idAtCommonName, type->length ) )
      {
        target->idAtCommonName = ( char * ) malloc( value->length + 1 );
        memcpy( target->idAtCommonName, value->data, value->length );
        target->idAtCommonName[ value->length ] = 0;
      }
      else
      {
       int i;

       // This is just advisory - NOT a problem
       printf( "Skipping unrecognized or unsupported name token OID of " );
       for ( i = 0; i < type->length; i++ )
       {
         printf( "%.02x ", type->data[ i ] );
       }
       printf( "\n" );
      }
```

```
    typeValuePair = typeValuePair->next;
  }

  return 0;
}
```

As you can see, after you've decided how to represent a distinguished name, parsing it isn't complex, although it is a bit tedious.

Following the issuer name is the validity structure that tells the user between which dates the certificate is valid. It is parsed in Listing 5-18.

**Listing 5-18:** "parse_validity"

```
static int parse_validity( validity_period *target, struct asn1struct *source )
{
  struct asn1struct *not_before;
  struct asn1struct *not_after;
  struct tm not_before_tm;
  struct tm not_after_tm;

  not_before = source->children;

  not_after = not_before->next;
  // Convert time instances into time_t
  if ( sscanf( ( char * ) not_before->data, "%2d%2d%2d%2d%2d%2d",
      &not_before_tm.tm_year, &not_before_tm.tm_mon, &not_before_tm.tm_mday,
      &not_before_tm.tm_hour, &not_before_tm.tm_min, &not_before_tm.tm_sec ) < 6 )
  {
    fprintf( stderr, "Error parsing not before; malformed date." );
    return 6;
  }
  if ( sscanf( ( char * ) not_after->data, "%2d%2d%2d%2d%2d%2d",
      &not_after_tm.tm_year, &not_after_tm.tm_mon, &not_after_tm.tm_mday,
      &not_after_tm.tm_hour, &not_after_tm.tm_min, &not_after_tm.tm_sec ) < 6 )
  {
    fprintf( stderr, "Error parsing not after; malformed date." );
    return 7;
  }

  not_before_tm.tm_year += 100;
  not_after_tm.tm_year += 100;
  not_before_tm.tm_mon -= 1;
  not_after_tm.tm_mon -= 1;

  // TODO account for TZ information on end
  target->notBefore = mktime( &not_before_tm );
  target->notAfter = mktime( &not_after_tm );

  return 0;
}
```

Following the validity period is the subject name; this is parsed using the same routine as the issuer name.

Finally, it's time to parse the element you've been waiting this whole time to see — the public key itself, which is the one piece of information that you can't complete a secure key exchange without. Because the designers of the X.509 structure wanted to leave room for arbitrary public encryption algorithms, the structure is a bit more complex than you might expect; the public key node starts with an OID that indicates what to do with the rest. For now, to keep things relatively simple, just look at the RSA specification.

The element following the algorithm identifier OID is a bit string. This bit string is itself an ASN.1 DER-encoded value and must be parsed. Its contents vary depending on the algorithm. For RSA, the contents are a single sequence containing two integers — the first is the public exponent and the second is the modulus (of course, the private exponent is not included).

RSA public key info parsing is shown in Listing 5-19.

**Listing 5-19:** "x509.c" parse_public_key_info

```c
static const unsigned char OID_RSA[] =
  { 0x2A, 0x86, 0x48, 0x86, 0xF7, 0x0D, 0x01, 0x01, 0x01 };

static int parse_public_key_info( public_key_info *target,
                  struct asn1struct *source )
{
  struct asn1struct *oid;
  struct asn1struct *public_key;
  struct asn1struct public_key_value;

  oid = source->children->children;
  public_key = source->children->next;

  // The public key is a bit string encoding yet another ASN.1 DER-encoded
  // value - need to parse *that* here
  // Skip over the "0" byte in the public key.
  if ( asn1parse( public_key->data + 1,
         public_key->length - 1,
         &public_key_value ) )
  {
    fprintf( stderr,
      "Error; public key node is malformed (not ASN.1 DER-encoded)\n" );
    return 5;
  }

  if ( !memcmp( oid->data, &OID_RSA, sizeof( OID_RSA ) ) )
  {
    target->algorithm = rsa;

    parse_huge( target->rsa_public_key.modulus, public_key_value.children );
```

```
    parse_huge( target->rsa_public_key.exponent, public_key_value.children->next );
    // This is important. Most times, the response includes a trailing 0 byte
    // to stop implementations from interpreting it as a twos-complement
    // negative number. However, in this implementation, this causes the
    // results to be the wrong size, so they need to be contracted.
    contract( target->rsa_public_key.modulus );
    contract( target->rsa_public_key.exponent );
  }
  else
  {
    fprintf( stderr, "Error; unsupported OID in public key info.\n" );
    return 7;
  }

  asn1free( &public_key_value );

  return 0;
}
```

The only potential surprise in this routine is the "skip over the 0 byte" part. What's the 0 byte? Well, the subject public key is declared as an ASN.1 bit string. The DER encoding of a bit string starts with a length — just like any other ASN.1 value — but a bit string can be any length; it doesn't necessarily need to be a multiple of eight bits. Because DER encoding requires that the result be normalized to eight-bit octets, the first byte of any bit string following the length is the amount of padding bits that were added to the bit string to pad it up to a multiple of eight. In the case of an RSA public key, the result is always a multiple of eight, so this byte is always 0.

**NOTE** Technically, you really ought to verify that this is the case, but, practically speaking, you never see a public key value that's not a multiple of eight bits. If you actually find an example "in the wild" that contradicts this code, I'd like to know about it.

## Parsing Certificate Extensions

Optionally, and only if the version of the certificate is greater than or equal to three, the public key information can be followed by a sequence of extensions. Practically speaking, all certificates that you come across on today's Internet include extensions; RFC 2459 dedicates 19 pages to describing a subset of the available X.509 certificate extensions. Although many of them are important, I'm just showing you how to deal with extensions in general and focus on one — perhaps the most important one: the *key usage* extension that enables the receiver to determine if the certificate is allowed to sign other certificates or not.

First, if extensions are present, loop through them as in Listing 5-20.

**Listing 5-20:** "x509.c" parse_extensions

```
static int parse_extensions( x509_certificate *certificate,
             struct asn1struct *source )
{
  // Parse each extension; if one is recognized, update the certificate
  // in some way
  source = source->children->children;
  while ( source )
  {
    if ( parse_extension( certificate, source ) )
    {
      return 1;
    }
    source = source->next;
  }

  return 0;
}
```

An extension consists of an OID, an optional `critical` marker, and another optional `data` section whose interpretation varies depending on the OID. Parsing of the actual extension is shown in Listing 5-21.

**Listing 5-21:** "x509.c" parse_extension

```
static int parse_extension( x509_certificate *certificate,
             struct asn1struct *source )
{
  struct asn1struct *oid;
  struct asn1struct *critical;
  struct asn1struct *data;

  oid = ( struct asn1struct * ) source->children;
  critical = ( struct asn1struct * ) oid->next;
  if ( critical->tag == ASN1_BOOLEAN )
  {
    data = ( struct asn1struct * ) critical->next;
  }
  else
  {
    // critical defaults to false
    data = critical;
    critical = NULL;
  }
  // TODO recognize and parse extensions - there are several

  return 0;
}
```

The first tag is always an OID; the second can be a boolean value, in which case it indicates whether the extension should be considered critical or not.

Because the default of this optional value is false, for all intents and purposes if it's present then the extension is critical.

What differentiates a critical from a non-critical extension? According to the specification, if an implementation does not recognize an extension that is marked critical, it should reject the whole certificate. Otherwise, the extension can be safely ignored. Note that the implementation presented here is not compliant, for this reason.

How the data field is interpreted depends on the OID. It's always declared as an OCTET STRING; for all defined extensions, this is an string of bytes whose contents must in turn be parsed as an ASN.1 DER-encoded structure (the X.509 people clearly weren't really aiming for optimal efficiency).

This book doesn't have enough space to cover all, or even most, X.509 extensions. One worth examining is the key usage extension, though. If the OID is 2.5.29.15 then the extension describes key usage, and the final field is a bit field. The bits are interpreted in big-endian order, and the most important is bit 5. If bit 5 is set then the certificate is a CA and can legitimately sign other certificates. Presumably, the signing CA checked that this was truly the case before signing the certificate. Processing the key usage bit is shown in Listing 5-22.

**Listing 5-22:** "x509.c" parse_extension with key usage recognition

```
static const unsigned char OID_keyUsage[] = { 0x55, 0x1D, 0x0F };
#define BIT_CERT_SIGNER 5
...
  }
  if ( !memcmp( oid->data, OID_keyUsage, oid->length ) )
  {
    struct asn1struct key_usage_bit_string;
    asn1parse( data->data, data->length, &key_usage_bit_string );
    if ( asn1_get_bit( key_usage_bit_string.length,
             key_usage_bit_string.data,
             BIT_CERT_SIGNER ) )
    {
      certificate->certificate_authority = 1;
    }
    asn1free( &key_usage_bit_string );
  }
  // TODO recognize and parse other extensions - there are several
```

As you can see, the data node is itself another ASN.1-encoded structure, which must be parsed when the key usage OID is encountered. In the case of key usage, the contents of this ASN.1 structure are a single-bit string. Bit strings can be a tad complex because they're permitted by ASN.1 to be of arbitrary length. The first byte of the data field is the number of padding bits that were added to pad up to an eight-bit boundary. Implement a handling function as shown in Listing 5-23 to retrieve the value of a single bit from an ASN.1 bit string.

**Listing 5-23:** "asn1.c" asn1_get_bit

```c
int asn1_get_bit( const int length,
          const unsigned char *bit_string,
          const int bit )
{
  if ( bit > ( ( length - 1 ) * 8 ) )
  {
    return 0;
  }
  else
  {
    return bit_string[ 1 + ( bit / 8 ) ] & ( 0x80 >> ( bit % 8 ) );
  }
}
```

Another potentially useful extension is the `subjectAltName` extension 2.5.29.17. Look over the definition of the `subjectName`. It specifies a country, a state, a city, an organizational unit. This is a pretty good qualifier for a person, but fairly irrelevant for a web site. Or an e-mail address. Or an IP address. Or any of a dozen other entities that you might want to identify with a certificate. Therefore, the `subjectAltName` extension allows the certificate to simply identify, for instance, a domain name. If the `subjectAltName` extension is present, the `subjectName` can actually be empty. However, the `subjectAltName` extension is pretty rare, so in general the `subjectName`'s CN field identifies the domain name of the bearer site. Of course, there's also an `IssuerAltName` (OID 2.5.29.18), which serves the same purpose and is equally rare.

The last extension examined here has to do with certificate validation. The entire trust model outlined in this chapter hinges on how accurately CAs vet certificate requests. The `CertificatePolicies` extension 2.5.29.32 provides a way for the CA to indicate how it goes about verifying that the requester of a certificate is, in fact, the entity it purports to be. Recently, the CA/Browser forum began compiling a list of CAs that perform what is called *extended validation.* Extended validation just indicates that a CA has made extraordinary efforts to ensure that it is signing a certificate on behalf of the true owner of the identity in question. Recent browsers have begun displaying a green bar in addition to the traditional padlock icon to tell the user that the certificate is not only valid, but that it has been signed by an extended validation CA.

A complete X.509 implementation should recognize all of the extensions listed in RFC 5280.

The extensions mark the end of the `TBSCertificate`. There are two fields left in the signed certificate structure: the signature algorithm and the signature itself. The signature algorithm is an OID, and must match the signature algorithm listed in the `tbsCertificate`. The signature, of course, is a bit string whose interpretation varies depending on the signature algorithm. For RSA, it's simply a large integer, parsed in Listing 5-24.

**Listing 5-24:** "x509.c" parse_signature_value

```
static int parse_signature_value( signed_x509_certificate *target,
               struct asn1struct *source )
{
  parse_huge( &target->signature_value, source );
  contract( &target->signature_value );

  return 0;
}
```

## Signature Verification

You're not *quite* done yet. Remember that you also have to be able to verify this signature; just ensuring that it's there isn't enough. You must also check that it is a proper digital signature of the hash of the tbsCertificate bytes. So, after parsing the entire certificate, you must hash it and store the hash for later inspection. Extend parse_x509_certificate to do so as shown in Listing 5-25.

**Listing 5-25:** "x509.c" parse_x509_certificate with stored hash

```
typedef struct
{
  x509_certificate tbsCertificate;
  unsigned int *hash; // hash code of tbsCertificate
  int hash_len;
  signatureAlgorithmIdentifier algorithm;
  huge signature_value;
}
signed_x509_certificate;

int parse_x509_certificate( const unsigned char *buffer,
             const unsigned int certificate_length,
             signed_x509_certificate *parsed_certificate )
{
  struct asn1struct certificate;
  struct asn1struct *tbsCertificate;
  struct asn1struct *algorithmIdentifier;
  struct asn1struct *signatureValue;
  digest_ctx digest;
...
  switch ( parsed_certificate->algorithm )
  {
    case md5WithRSAEncryption:
      new_md5_digest( &digest );
      break;
    case shaWithRSAEncryption:
      new_sha1_digest( &digest );
      break;
    default:
```

*(Continued)*

```
            break;
    }

    update_digest( &digest, tbsCertificate->data, tbsCertificate->length );
    finalize_digest( &digest );

    parsed_certificate->hash = digest.hash;
    parsed_certificate->hash_len = digest.hash_len;

    asn1free( &certificate );
...
```

Notice that, although `tbsCertificate` is a structure type, the data itself is still made available by the ASN.1 parsing routine (Listing 5-5), which means that you can easily write code to securely hash the DER-encoded representation of the `tbsCertificate`.

## Validating PKCS #7-Formatted RSA Signatures

Validating a certificate involves finding the public key of the issuer, using it to run the digital signature algorithm on the computed hash, and then verifying that it matches the signature included in the certificate itself. When the RSA algorithm is used for signing a certificate, the hash value itself is concatenated onto the OID representing the signing algorithm and stored in an ASN.1 sequence. This is then DER encoded, and the whole thing is encrypted with the private key. This is called PKCS #7, which is officially documented by RSA labs at `http://www.rsa.com/rsalabs/node.asp?id=2129`. The code to unwrap the signed hash code and compare it to the previously computed one is shown in Listing 5-26.

**Listing 5-26:** "x509.c" validate_certificate_rsa

```
/**
 * An RSA signature is an ASN.1 DER-encoded PKCS-7 structure including
 * the OID of the signature algorithm (again), and the signature value.
 */
static int validate_certificate_rsa( signed_x509_certificate *certificate,
                    rsa_key *public_key )
{
  unsigned char *pkcs7_signature_decrypted;
  int pkcs7_signature_len;
  struct asn1struct pkcs7_signature;
  struct asn1struct *hash_value;
  int valid = 0;

  pkcs7_signature_len = rsa_decrypt( certificate->signature_value.rep,
    certificate->signature_value.size, &pkcs7_signature_decrypted,
    public_key );

  if ( pkcs7_signature_len == -1 )
```

```
  {
    fprintf( stderr, "Unable to decode signature value.\n" );
    return valid;
  }
  if ( asn1parse( pkcs7_signature_decrypted, pkcs7_signature_len,
      &pkcs7_signature ) )
  {
    fprintf( stderr, "Unable to parse signature\n" );
    return valid;
  }

  hash_value = pkcs7_signature.children->next;

  if ( memcmp( hash_value->data, certificate->hash, certificate->hash_len ) )
  {
    valid = 0;
  }
  else
  {
    valid = 1;
  }

  asn1free( &pkcs7_signature );

  return valid;
}
```

## Verifying a Self-Signed Certificate

How to map issuers to public keys is outside the scope of the implementation; browsers ship with a (long) list of trusted root CAs and their known public keys, which are compared to the issuer each time a certificate is received. To illustrate the concept, though, you can go ahead and write code to verify a self-signed certificate in Listing 5-27, such as those that are distributed by the CAs to the browsers to begin with. Like the ASN.1 test routine, this routine expects a DER- or PEM-encoded certificate file and outputs the contents of the file. This time, though, it does a lot more interpretation and actually produces useful, meaningful content.

**Listing 5-27:** "x509.c" main routine

```
#ifdef TEST_X509
int main( int argc, char *argv[ ] )
{
  int certificate_file;
  struct stat certificate_file_stat;
  char *buffer, *bufptr;
  int buffer_size;
  int bytes_read;
```

*(Continued)*

```
int error_code;

signed_x509_certificate certificate;

if ( argc < 3 )
{
  fprintf( stderr, "Usage: x509 [-pem|-der] [certificate file]\n" );
  exit( 0 );
}

if ( ( certificate_file = open( argv[ 2 ], O_RDONLY ) ) == -1 )
{
  perror( "Unable to open certificate file" );
  return 1;
}

// Slurp the whole thing into memory
if ( fstat( certificate_file, &certificate_file_stat ) )
{
  perror( "Unable to stat certificate file" );
  return 2;
}

buffer_size = certificate_file_stat.st_size;
buffer = ( char * ) malloc( buffer_size );
if ( !buffer )
{
  perror( "Not enough memory" );
  return 3;
}

bufptr = buffer;

while ( ( bytes_read = read( certificate_file, ( void * ) buffer,
              buffer_size ) ) )
{
  bufptr += bytes_read;
}

if ( !strcmp( argv[ 1 ], "-pem" ) )
{
  // XXX this overallocates a bit, since it sets aside space for markers, etc.
  unsigned char *pem_buffer = buffer;
  buffer = (unsigned char * ) malloc( buffer_size );
  buffer_size = pem_decode( pem_buffer, buffer );
  free( pem_buffer );
}

// now parse it
init_x509_certificate( &certificate );
if ( !( error_code = parse_x509_certificate( buffer, buffer_size,
                        &certificate ) ) )
```

```
  {
    printf( "X509 Certificate:\n" );
    display_x509_certificate( &certificate );

    // Assume it's a self-signed certificate and try to validate it that
    switch ( certificate.algorithm )
    {
     case md5WithRSAEncryption:
     case shaWithRSAEncryption:
       if ( validate_certificate_rsa( &certificate,
        &certificate.tbsCertificate.subjectPublicKeyInfo.rsa_public_key ) )
       {
         printf( "Certificate is a valid self-signed certificate.\n" );
       }
       else
       {
         printf( "Certificate is corrupt or not self-signed.\n" );
       }
       break;
    }
  }
  else
  {
    printf( "error parsing certificate: %d\n", error_code );
  }

  free_x509_certificate( &certificate );
  free( buffer );
  return 0;
}
#endif
```

This invokes the companion `display_x509_certificate` function in Listing 5-28.

**Listing 5-28:** "x509.c" display_x509_certificate

```
static void output_x500_name( name *x500_name )
{
  printf( "C=%s/ST=%s/L=%s/O=%s/OU=%s/CN=%s\n",
    ( x500_name->idAtCountryName ? x500_name->idAtCountryName : "?" ),
    ( x500_name->idAtStateOrProvinceName ? x500_name->idAtStateOrProvinceName :
"?" ),
    ( x500_name->idAtLocalityName ? x500_name->idAtLocalityName : "?" ),
    ( x500_name->idAtOrganizationName ? x500_name->idAtOrganizationName : "?" ),
    ( x500_name->idAtOrganizationalUnitName ? x500_name-
>idAtOrganizationalUnitName : "?" ),
    ( x500_name->idAtCommonName ? x500_name->idAtCommonName : "?" ) );
}

static void print_huge( huge *h )
{
```

```
    show_hex( h->rep, h->size );
}

static void display_x509_certificate( signed_x509_certificate *certificate )
{
  printf( "Certificate details:\n" );
  printf( "Version: %d\n", certificate->tbsCertificate.version );
  printf( "Serial number: " );
  print_huge( &certificate->tbsCertificate.serialNumber );
  printf( "issuer: " );
  output_x500_name( &certificate->tbsCertificate.issuer );
  printf( "subject: " );
  output_x500_name( &certificate->tbsCertificate.subject );
  printf( "not before: %s", asctime( gmtime(
   &certificate->tbsCertificate.validity.notBefore ) ) );
  printf( "not after: %s", asctime( gmtime(
   &certificate->tbsCertificate.validity.notAfter ) ) );
  printf( "Public key algorithm: " );
  switch ( certificate->tbsCertificate.subjectPublicKeyInfo.algorithm )
  {
    case rsa:
      printf( "RSA\n" );
      printf( "modulus: " );
      print_huge(
        certificate->tbsCertificate.subjectPublicKeyInfo.rsa_public_key.modulus );
      printf( "exponent: " );
      print_huge(
        certificate->tbsCertificate.subjectPublicKeyInfo.rsa_public_key.exponent );
      break;
    case dh:
      printf( "DH\n" );
      break;
    default:
      printf( "?\n" );
      break;
  }

  printf( "Signature algorithm: " );

  switch ( certificate->algorithm )
  {
    case md5WithRSAEncryption:
      printf( "MD5 with RSA Encryption\n" );
      break;
    case shaWithRSAEncryption:
      printf( "SHA-1 with RSA Encryption\n" );
      break;
  }
```

```
  printf( "Signature value: " );

  switch ( certificate->algorithm )
  {
    case md5WithRSAEncryption:
    case shaWithRSAEncryption:
      print_huge( &certificate->signature_value );
      break;
  }
  printf( "\n" );

  if ( certificate->tbsCertificate.certificate_authority )
  {
    printf( "is a CA\n" );
  }
  else
  {
    printf( "is not a CA\n" );
  }
}
```

Now, you can parse the test certificate you generated.

```
[jdavies@localhost ssl]$ ./x509 -der cert.der
Skipping unrecognized or unsupported name token OID of 2a 86 48 86 f7 0d 01 09 01
Skipping unrecognized or unsupported name token OID of 2a 86 48 86 f7 0d 01 09 01
X509 Certificate:
Certificate details:
Version: 3
Serial number: 0ca30e18f778da281
issuer: C=US/ST=TX/L=Southlake/O=Travelocity/OU=Architecture/CN=Joshua Davies
subject: C=US/ST=TX/L=Southlake/O=Travelocity/OU=Architecture/CN=Joshua Davies
not before: Wed Mar 3 04:46:23 2010
not after: Fri Apr 2 03:46:23 2010
Public key algorithm: RSA
modulus: e013380f83b6ef0670f55baa3a2bcf8e95ff91b1900352516973dea7fa97fb560db9e90f
e830228c5ef01f07f0dccc61b8010eb1b058efb5b4541670eb59b4bf
exponent: 10001
Signature algorithm: SHA-1 with RSA Encryption
Signature value: 1b637bf513ef2e3d56223da24cd50e318d0c25bb2430fda320f5a3b57d1bcb1e
a8bdb0ce788be75e7aac662c6d0606e8e30624cad5ce0d991a7c37534dd3be83
Certificate hash (fingerprint): ac7d5752 30586fb4 3c106b90 60af5eb5 939147f1
certificate is not a CA.
01 ff ff ff ff ff ff ff ff ff ff ff ff ff ff ff ff ff ff ff ff ff ff ff ff ff ff
00 30 21 30 09 06 05 2b 0e 03 02 1a 05 00 04 14 52 57 7d ac b4 6f 58 30 90 6b 10
3c b5 5e af 60 f1 47 91 93 00
Certificate is a valid self-signed certificate.
```

### Adding DSA Support to the Certificate Parser

Go ahead and add support for DSA as well. This is mostly academic because DSA-signed certificates are extremely rare "in the wild," at least for SSL. Because servers present certificates primarily to prepare for key exchange, and DSA can't be used for this purpose, there's not much point in presenting a certificate with a DSA public key to an SSL client. A CA, on the other hand, could use DSA; the purpose of a root certificate is to sign other certificates, and this is the one thing DSA can do. However, at the time of this writing no CA does — at least none of those implicitly trusted by major browser vendors.

However, it's worthwhile to see how it's done so that you can see how different signature algorithms change the parsing semantics. In addition, common or not, support for DSA certificates is required by TLS. First of all, the structure definitions change slightly as shown in Listing 5-29.

**Listing 5-29:** "x509.h" with DSA support

```
typedef enum
{
  rsa,
  dsa,
  dh
}
algorithmIdentifier;

typedef enum
{
  md5WithRSAEncryption,
  shaWithRSAEncryption,
  shaWithDSA
}
signatureAlgorithmIdentifier;
...
typedef struct
{
  algorithmIdentifier algorithm;
  // RSA parameters, only if algorithm == rsa
  rsa_key rsa_public_key;

  // DSA or DH parameters, only if algorithm == dsa
  dsa_params dsa_parameters;

  // DSA parameters, only if algorithm == dsa
  huge dsa_public_key;
}
public_key_info;
...
typedef struct
{
  x509_certificate tbsCertificate;
```

```
    unsigned int *hash; // hash code of tbsCertificate
    int hash_len;
    signatureAlgorithmIdentifier algorithm;
    huge rsa_signature_value;
    dsa_signature dsa_signature_value;
}
signed_x509_certificate;
```

Notice that no attempt was made to have the DSA and RSA public keys or signatures share the same memory space. An RSA public key is two distinct numbers *e* and *n*, whereas a DSA public key is a single number *y*. DSA also defines parameters whereas RSA does not. Conversely, a DSA signature is two distinct numbers *r* and *s*, whereas an RSA signature is a single number. There's just no commonality there. If you want to be a stickler for space optimization, you could force the declarations of these structures to include a single `signature` and `public key` element, but the code that interpreted them would be such a mess it would hardly be worth it. Here, one or the other is left empty, and it is up to the invoker to check the `algorithm` value to determine which to ignore.

Of course, you need to modify the `parse_algorithm_identifier` routine to recognize DSA; there's no MD5 with DSA, so there's only one new algorithm to identify in Listing 5-30.

**Listing 5-30:** "x509.c" parse_algorithm_identifier with DSA support

```
static const unsigned char OID_sha1WithRSA[] =
  { 0x2A, 0x86, 0x48, 0x86, 0xF7, 0x0D, 0x01, 0x01, 0x05 };
static const unsigned char OID_sha1WithDSA[] =
  { 0x2A, 0x86, 0x48, 0xCE, 0x38, 0x04, 0x03 };

static int parse_algorithm_identifier( signatureAlgorithmIdentifier *target,
                                        struct asn1struct *source )
{
…
}
else if ( !memcmp( oid->data, OID_sha1WithDSA, oid->length ) )
{
  *target = shaWithDSA;
}
else
{
```

The top-level `parse_x509_certificate` function must likewise invoke a different routine to parse the signature value depending on the signature algorithm as shown in Listing 5-31.

**Listing 5-31:** "x509.c" parse_x509_certificate with DSA support

```
int parse_x509_certificate( const unsigned char *buffer,
             const unsigned int certificate_length,
```

*(Continued)*

```
                 signed_x509_certificate *parsed_certificate )
{
...
  switch ( parsed_certificate->algorithm )
  {
   case md5WithRSAEncryption:
   case shaWithRSAEncryption:
     if ( parse_rsa_signature_value( parsed_certificate, signatureValue ) )
     {
       return 42;
     }
    break;
   case shaWithDSA:
     if ( parse_dsa_signature_value( parsed_certificate, signatureValue ) )
     {
       return 42;
     }
...
  switch ( parsed_certificate->algorithm )
  {
    case md5WithRSAEncryption:
      new_md5_digest( &digest );
      break;
    case shaWithRSAEncryption:
    case shaWithDSA:
      new_sha1_digest( &digest );
      break;
    default:
      break;
  }
...
```

Note that the parse_signature_value routine is now named parse_rsa_sig-
nature_value. The new parse_dsa_signature_value shown in Listing 5-32 is
pretty much like the parse_rsa_signature_value routine except that it expects
two values.

**Listing 5-32:** "x509.c" parse_dsa_signature_value

```
static int parse_dsa_signature_value( signed_x509_certificate *target,
                  struct asn1struct *source )
{
 struct asn1struct dsa_signature;

 if ( asn1parse( source->data + 1, source->length - 1, &dsa_signature ) )
 {
  fprintf( stderr, "Unable to parse ASN.1 DER-encoded signature.\n" );
  return 1;
 }

 parse_huge( &target->dsa_signature_value.r, dsa_signature.children );
```

```
parse_huge( &target->dsa_signature_value.s, dsa_signature.children->next );

asn1free( &dsa_signature );

return 0;
}
```

Most of the complexity in dealing with DSA certificates is in parsing the public key information. An RSA public key is simply two numbers. A DSA public key is a single number, but the algorithm also requires parameters. For no clear reason, the X.509 designers split the parameters and the public key into two separate ASN.1 sequences, with different parent elements, so the parsing code gets a bit involved in Listing 5-33.

**Listing 5-33:** "x509.c" public key info parsing with DSA support

```
static const unsigned char OID_RSA[] =
  { 0x2A, 0x86, 0x48, 0x86, 0xF7, 0x0D, 0x01, 0x01, 0x01 };
static const unsigned char OID_DSA[] =
  { 0x2A, 0x86, 0x48, 0xCE, 0x38, 0x04, 0x01 };
...
static int parse_public_key_info( public_key_info *target,
                struct asn1struct *source )
{
...
 if ( !memcmp( oid->data, &OID_RSA, sizeof( OID_RSA ) ) )
 {
...
 }
 else if ( !memcmp( oid->data, &OID_DSA, sizeof( OID_DSA ) ) )
 {
  struct asn1struct *params;
  target->algorithm = dsa;

  parse_huge( &target->dsa_public_key, &public_key_value );

  params = oid->next;
  parse_dsa_params( target, params );
 }
```

Finally, parsing the DSA params themselves in Listing 5-34 is simple after you've identified the node.

**Listing 5-34:** "tls.c" parse_dsa_params

```
static int parse_dsa_params( public_key_info *target, struct asn1struct *source )
{
 struct asn1struct *p;
 struct asn1struct *q;
 struct asn1struct *g;
```

*(Continued)*

```
p = source->children;
q = p->next;
g = q->next;

parse_huge( &target->dsa_parameters.p, p );
parse_huge( &target->dsa_parameters.q, q );
parse_huge( &target->dsa_parameters.g, g );

return 0;
}
```

To test this, you have to generate your own DSA certificate; this was shown in the section "Using OpenSSL to Generate a DSA KeyPair and Certificate" earlier. Extend the certificate display routine just a bit as shown in Listing 5-35, and you can output the details of this certificate:

**Listing 5-35:** "x509.c" display_x509_certificate

```
static void display_x509_certificate( signed_x509_certificate *certificate )
{
...
printf( "Public key algorithm: " );
switch ( certificate->tbsCertificate.subjectPublicKeyInfo.algorithm )
{
...
  case dsa:
   printf( "DSA\n" );
   printf( "y: " );
   print_huge(
    &certificate->tbsCertificate.subjectPublicKeyInfo.dsa_public_key );
   printf( "p: " );
   print_huge(
    &certificate->tbsCertificate.subjectPublicKeyInfo.dsa_parameters.p );
   printf( "q: " );
   print_huge(
    &certificate->tbsCertificate.subjectPublicKeyInfo.dsa_parameters.q );
   printf( "g: " );
   print_huge(
    &certificate->tbsCertificate.subjectPublicKeyInfo.dsa_parameters.g );
   break;
...
switch ( certificate->algorithm )
{
...
  case shaWithDSA:
   printf( "SHA-1 with DSA\n" );
   break;
}
...
printf( "Signature value: " );
```

```
switch ( certificate->algorithm )
{
...
  case shaWithDSA:
   printf( "\n\tr:" );
   print_huge( &certificate->dsa_signature_value.r );
   printf( "\ts:" );
   print_huge( &certificate->dsa_signature_value.s );
   break;
}
```

Finally, extend the test main routine in Listing 5-36 to attempt a self-signature validation if the signature algorithm is DSA.

**Listing 5-36:** "x509.c" main routine

```
int main( int argc, char *argv[ ] )
{
...
  switch ( certificate.algorithm )
  {
...
    case shaWithDSA:
     if ( validate_certificate_dsa( &certificate ) )
     {
      printf( "Certificate is a valid self-signed certificate.\n" );
     }
     else
     {
      printf( "Certificate is corrupt or not self-signed.\n" );
     }
```

DSA certificate validation is actually simpler than RSA certificate validation because the signature value is not an encrypted ASN.1 DER-encoded structure like RSA's; the DSA signature algorithm doesn't allow this. It also doesn't allow the algorithm OID to be embedded in the signature value the way RSA does, though. The validation is shown in Listing 5-37.

**Listing 5-37:** "x509.c" validate_certificate_dsa

```
static int validate_certificate_dsa( signed_x509_certificate *certificate )
{
 return dsa_verify(
  &certificate->tbsCertificate.subjectPublicKeyInfo.dsa_parameters,
  &certificate->tbsCertificate.subjectPublicKeyInfo.dsa_public_key,
  certificate->hash,
  certificate->hash_len * 4,
  &certificate->dsa_signature_value );
}
```

This covers RSA and DSA signature validation and RSA key exchange. What about Diffie-Hellman? X.509 does define a certificate structure that includes the Diffie-Hellman parameters; however, this is even rarer in practice than the nonexistent DSA certificate. You can't even use OpenSSL to generate such a certificate. I won't cover it here; if you're so inclined, though, it wouldn't be hard to add support for it.

There's one big, big problem with all of the X.509 parsing code presented in this chapter. You probably noticed it while you were reading it: There's no error checking. At each step, the code assumes that there is, for instance, a `children` `.next.next.children.next` structure as required by the X.509 definition. The code should include a lot more error checking to validate that the parsed ASN.1 structure correctly conforms to the expected X.509 structure. As is the technical book author's prerogative, though, I'll leave that as an exercise for the reader (or you could just download the code from the companion website at `www.wiley.com/go/ImplementingSSL`, which does include the aforementioned error checking).

# Managing Certificates

The primary purpose of a certificate is to communicate a public key. The additional data — the subject name, the issuer name, the signature, the extensions, and so on — are present to allow the receiver of the certificate to verify that the bearer is legitimately in possession of the private key that corresponds with the included public key. Overall, this is referred to as a *public key infrastructure* (PKI). Public-key cryptography itself was originally developed to permit a secure key exchange to occur over an insecure medium with no prior off-line communication; however, PKI requires that the identities — that is, the public keys — of the trusted CAs be set up before secure communications can be established. How this is done is outside the scope of SSL/TLS. Browsers come preconfigured with a list of trusted CAs, for instance, with an option to allow the user to import new ones. It's up to the user to verify that new public keys are correct and trustworthy, and to keep track of the trustworthiness of the top-level CAs. Although this is not part of the SSL/TLS flow, there is a set of best practices that has grown around PKI and certificate management.

## How Authorities Handle Certificate Signing Requests (CSRs)

The CA is vouching for the legitimacy of a certificate. In the context of the world-wide web, CAs are typically for-profit businesses; their reputation, and business viability, depends on how accurately they vet certificates prior to signing them and thus providing their seal of approval. However, it's perfectly acceptable, in a corporate intranet environment, to establish a local CA and let it sign certificates that are only trusted within the local network. An entity wishing to act as a CA must simply create a new key pair, generate a certificate that contains the public key, sign the certificate with the private key, and publish the self-signed certificate.

How the receivers decide which authorities to trust is not part of the PKI specification, but how a would-be certificate holder gets a signature is. First, of course, the hopeful certificate holder must generate his own keypair. The public key and the subject's name are wrapped up into a PKCS #10 *certificate signing request* (*CSR*). The whole certificate signing request itself is signed with the private key, but the private key isn't shared with the CA. Signing the request with the private key prevents a malicious man in the middle from intercepting the CSR, substituting his own public key in the request itself, and obtaining a signed certificate in somebody else's name. In essence, the signature proves that whoever generated the request has access to the private key that corresponds with the public key, without ever revealing the actual private key.

The CA should, of course, verify the signature with the public key, but should also verify, in some unspecified offline manner, that the requester is actually the correct holder of the name in the CN field of the subject name. If the certificate identifies an individual, perhaps the CA would request that the individual appear in person and present a driver's license with a name that matches the CN field and a state that matches the ST field. If the certificate identifies a web site, the CA might perform a WHOIS query against the ARIN database for the domain in question to determine who the registered owner is and demand a driver's license in that name.

After the identity of the requester has been verified, the CA creates an X.509 certificate that includes the public key and subject name, as well as the serial number, validity period, issuer's name as well as any extra attributes that may be appropriate, such as key usage, and, of course, the signature using the CA's private key. The final certificate can safely be returned over a cleartext channel with no further authentication. This certificate is now public data and by design contains no sensitive information.

The PKCS #10 format won't be examined in detail here. The official specification can be downloaded from `http://www.rsa.com/rsalabs/node.asp?id=2132`, and the OpenSSL `req` command can be used to generate a new CSR.

## Correlating Public and Private Keys Using PKCS #12 Formatting

Notice that the private key itself doesn't appear anywhere in the certificate format, nor the CSR format. (This a good thing!) As you can imagine, when dealing with several certificates, it can become difficult to keep track of which private keys correspond to which public keys; some certificates expire, some need to be revoked due to a key compromise, some domains have their own certificates for security purposes, and so on. If you lose track of which private key goes with which certificate, you're pretty much out of luck; it would be nice to store them together so you can always go back to the source.

Storing the keys, of course, must be done in a secure way. The private key may be the most sensitive bit of information in the entire system. The PKCS #12 format was designed as a standardized way to transmit any arbitrary bit of data securely — by encrypting it in a standardized way — but in practice it is generally used to store certificates and their corresponding private keys. The PKCS #12 format was standardized from an older, de facto standard named PFX. As such, many applications that generate PKCS #12 files give them the extension .pfx. If you export a certificate and private key from Internet Explorer, for instance, you get a .pfx file.

The PKCS #12 format is actually extremely general — a bit too general, in fact. The top-level structure consists of a version number, a sequence of bit strings, and a MAC over the whole thing. It's up to the reader of the file to interpret the bit strings to figure out if they're encrypted and what they contain.

## Blacklisting Compromised Certificates Using Certificate Revocation Lists (CRLs)

After a CA has applied its signature to a certificate, that signature can never be revoked, ever. The signature is a mathematical operation performed over the certificate data; if it's valid today, it will be valid a million years from now. So what can the holder of a certificate do if, for whatever reason, its private key is compromised?

Depending on the usage pattern of the certificate, this could be very bad news for the rightful owner of the certificate. Of course, if the certificate holder knows about the compromise, the certificate can be taken out of use and a new one generated. However, the key thief can use the old certificate and private key to sign any document he likes, masquerading as the rightful certificate holder.

Every certificate has an expiration date to guard against this. Even if the rightful holder is unaware of the breach, the certificate eventually expires and a new certificate, with a new public key (one would hope) is generated. However, if the certificate holder is aware of a breach, it is irresponsible not to notify the users of the certificate that it should be revoked prior to its expiration date.

CAs came up with half a solution with *certificate revocation lists (CRLs)*. The CA maintains a list of the serial numbers of certificates that have been identified by their owners as no longer applicable. The users of the certificates are responsible for checking this list on a periodic basis and comparing the serial number of each received certificate against the list of revoked serial numbers. The format for a CRL is, of course, an ASN.1 syntax; it starts with a header identifying the CA, the date it was published, and a list of serial numbers and revocation dates.

VeriSign's current CRL, as an example, is 125K and includes more than 3600 certificates, some of which were revoked more than two years ago. The idea behind CRLs is that a user downloads each trusted CA's CRL on a periodic basis. However, there's no real upper bound on how large a CRL may grow. It might be reasonable to try to keep a handle on the size of the file by removing a certificate from the CRL after its validity period had passed, but an actual compromised certificate is a far greater security risk than one that is simply expired. A compromised certificate should never be used, under any circumstances; an expired certificate may be used, if the receiver trusts the certificate holder. As a result, it's necessary for the CA to keep a certificate on its CRL list for a fairly long period of time. To keep the size of the download somewhat manageable, the specification allows the CA to distribute "delta" CRL's that only include newly revoked certificates. This is still problematic, as the user of the CRL has no way of knowing when it's safe to stop keeping track of an expired certificate, whereas the CA knows, for instance, that a certificate expired six years ago and can probably be safely removed from the list. The downloader only knows the serial number of the certificate; he has no way of knowing whether it was revoked 10 years ago or last Tuesday.

You may be wondering where to go to find the CRL associated with a CA. It would seem reasonable that the location of the CRL would be set up when the CA itself was listed as trusted, but this doesn't allow a CA to move its CRL location, ever. The X.509 certificate form has an extension that allows the CA to indicate where the CRL ought to be downloaded from. This does introduce one potential confusion, though: The extension doesn't permit the CA to indicate the date that the CRL distribution point changed. Remember that the CRL is associated with the CA that signed the certificate. If the client downloads two certificates signed by the same CA, but with two different CRL URLs, which one should be used? There are no clear guidelines in the specifications. This isn't a problem if you don't mind downloading the entire CRL each time you want to validate a certificate, but it can be a problem if you're trying to use deltas or if the CRL distribution point is temporarily unreachable.

How does the legitimate holder of a certificate inform a CA that a certificate is compromised and should be revoked? The CSR format described earlier includes an optional attributes section in which the requester can provide a *challenge password* that must be supplied at any later time in order to perform subsequent certificate management, including revocation.

## Keeping Certificate Blacklists Up-to-Date with the Online Certificate Status Protocol (OCSP)

As detailed in the previous section, there are quite a few problems with using CRLs as a means of notifying consumers of the revocation of certificates. In addition to some of the management/ambiguity problems, there's also the problem of freshness. If a private key has been compromised, the potential users of that certificate probably want to know about it right away. To accomplish this, the client has to download the entire CRL, or at least a delta (if the CA supports them) every time a new certificate is encountered. The *Online Certificate Status Protocol* (OCSP) was developed to enable the client to look up the status of a certificate by serial ID.

The details can be found in RFC 2560 and aren't covered in depth here. The user supplies the serial number of the certificate along with a hash of the issuer's distinguished name as well as its public key. The issuer name and public key are included so that a single OCSP can report on multiple CAs. The OCSP server returns, at a minimum, a status of "good" or "revoked."

Of course, this all works only if the OCSP server itself is online. If the server is not available, the user has a decision to make: abandon the connection attempt, or go ahead with a potentially revoked certificate? Ideally, the client should have a CRL handy to verify in case the OCSP server is unavailable.

## Other Problems with Certificates

Whenever a flaw is found in SSL, it's almost always related to certificates.

Even when certificates are implemented "perfectly" human behavior often renders them moot. All browsers, at the time of this writing, allow a user to ignore a mismatched domain name or a certificate past its validity period. Users are presented with cryptic warning messages and allowed to continue, which most of them do — even the ones who ought to know better. Still, PKI is what we have to guard against man-in-the-middle attacks. At a bare minimum, an implementation of TLS must be prepared to parse certificates to extract the server's public key.

# A Usable, Secure Communications Protocol: Client-Side TLS

Armed with symmetric encryption to protect sensitive data from eavesdroppers, public-key encryption to exchange keys securely over an insecure medium, message authentication to ensure message integrity, and certificates and their digital signatures to establish trust, it's possible to create a secure protocol that operates over an insecure line without any prior interaction between parties. This is actually pretty amazing when you think about it. You can assume that anybody who's interested in snooping on your traffic has full and complete access to it. Nevertheless, it's possible to securely send data such that only the intended recipient can read it, and be assured, within reason, that you're communicating with the intended recipient and not an impostor.

Even with all the pieces in place, though, it's possible to get this subtly wrong. This is why the TLS protocol was developed — even if you use the strongest cryptography, key exchange, MAC and signature algorithms available, you can still leave yourself vulnerable by improper use of random numbers, improper seeding of random number generation, improper verification of parameters, and a lot of other, subtle, easy-to-overlook flaws. TLS was designed as a standard for secure communications. You must, of course, use strong, secure cryptographic algorithms; the best way to ensure this is to use standard algorithms that were designed and have been thoroughly reviewed by security professionals for years. To ensure that you're using them correctly, your best bet is to also follow a standard protocol that was also designed and has been thoroughly reviewed by security professionals for years.

## FROM SSLV2 TO TLS 1.2: THE HISTORY OF THE SSL PROTOCOL

SSL is currently on its fifth revision over its fifteen-year history, and has undergone one name change and one ownership change in that time period. This book focuses mainly on TLS 1.0, which is the version in most widespread use. This section looks over the history of the protocol at a high level. This overview is a helpful segue into the details of TLS 1.0 — some elements of TLS 1.0 make the most sense if you understand the problems with its predecessors that it means to solve.

### SSLv2: The First Widespread Attempt at a Secure Browser Protocol

In 1995, most people had never heard of a "web browser." The Internet itself had been a reality for quite a while, but it was clear to a handful of visionaries that the World Wide Web is what would bring networked computing to the masses. Marc Andreessen had written Mosaic, the first graphical web browser, while at the University of Illinois. At the time, Mosaic was incredibly popular, so Andreessen started a company named Netscape which was going to create the computing platform of the future — the Netscape browser (and its companion server).

The World Wide Web was to become the central platform for the fledgling "e-commerce" industry. There was one problem, though — its users didn't trust it with their sensitive data. In 1995, Kipp Hickman, then an employee of Netscape Communications, drafted the first public revision of SSLv2, which was at the time viewed as an extension to HTTP that would allow the user to establish a secure link on a nonsecure channel using the concepts and techniques examined in previous chapters.

Although SSLv2 mostly got it right, it overlooked a couple of important details that rendered it, while not useless, not as secure as it ought to have been. The details of SSLv2 aren't examined in detail here, but if you're curious, Appendix C includes a complete examination of the SSLv2 protocol.

The cracks in SSLv2 were identified after it was submitted for peer review, and Netscape withdrew it, following up with SSLv3 in 1996. However, by this time, in spite of the fact that it was never standardized or ratified by the IETF, SSLv2 had found its way into several commercial browser and server implementations. Although its use has been deprecated for a decade, you may still run across it from time to time. However, it's considered to be too unsafe to the extent that the Payment Card Industry, which regulates the use of credit cards on the Internet, no longer permits websites that support SSLv2 to even accept credit cards.

### SSL 3.0, TLS 1.0, and TLS 1.1: Successors to SSLv2

The IETF was much happier with the SSLv3 proposal; however, it made a few superficial changes before formally accepting it. The most significant superficial change was that, for whatever reason, they decided to change the name from the widespread, recognizable household name "SSL" to the somewhat awkward "TLS." SSLv3.1 became TLS v1.0. To this day, the version numbers transmitted and published in a TLS connection are actually SSL versions, not TLS versions. TLS 1.0 was formally specified by RFC 2246 in 1999.

Although SSLv3 was also never officially ratified by the IETF, SSLv3 and TLS 1.0 are both widespread. Most current commercial implementations of SSL/TLS support both SSLv3 and TLS 1.0; TLS also includes a mechanism to negotiate the highest version supported. SSLv3 and TLS 1.0, although similar except for some cosmetic differences, are not interoperable — a client that only supports SSLv3 cannot establish a secure connection with a server that only supports TLS 1.0. However, a client that supports both can ask for TLS 1.0 and be gracefully downgraded to SSLv3.

At the time of this writing, SSLv3 and TLS 1.0 are by far the most widespread implementations of the protocol. In 2006, a new version, 1.1, was released in RFC 4346; it's not radically different than TLS 1.0, and the few differences are examined at the end of this chapter. Two years later, TLS 1.2 was released, and it was a major revision; TLS 1.2 is covered in depth in Chapter 9.

This chapter focuses on TLS 1.0. A complete implementation of the client-side of TLS 1.0 is presented here in some detail.

## Implementing the TLS 1.0 Handshake (Client Perspective)

As much as possible, TLS aims to be completely transparent to the upper-layer protocol. Effectively, this means that it tries to be completely transparent to the application programmer; the application programmer implements the protocol in question as if TLS was not being used. As long as nothing goes wrong, TLS succeeds admirably in this goal; although, as you'll see, if something does go wrong, everything fails miserably and the developer is left scratching his head, trying to figure out what he missed.

Of course, TLS can't be completely transparent. The application must indicate in some way that it wants to negotiate a secure channel. Perhaps surprisingly, TLS doesn't specify how the application should do this nor does it even provide any guidance. Remembering that SSL was initially developed as an add-on to HTTP, this makes some sense. The protocol designers weren't thinking about applicability to other protocols at the time. In fact, they didn't even specify how to use HTTP with SSL, assuming that there was only way to do so. It actually wasn't until 2000 that Eric Rescorla finally drafted RFC 2818 that describes how it should be done.

TLS requires that the handshake — a secure key exchange — takes place before it can protect anything. Effectively the question is when the handshake should take place; anything that's transmitted before the handshake is complete is transmitted in plaintext and is theoretically interceptable. HTTPS takes an extreme position on this. The very first thing that must take place on the channel is

the TLS handshake; no HTTP data can be transmitted until the handshake
is complete.

You can probably spot a problem with this approach. HTTP expects the very
first byte(s) on the connection to be an HTTP command such as GET, PUT, POST,
and so on. The client has to have some way of warning the server that it's going
to start with a TLS negotiation rather than a plaintext HTTP command. The
solution adopted by HTTPS is to require secure connections to be established
on a separate port. If the client connects on port 80, the next expected communication is a valid HTTP command. If the client connects on port 443, the next
expected communication is a TLS handshake after which, if the handshake
is successful, an encrypted, authenticated valid HTTP command is expected.

## Adding TLS Support to the HTTP Client

To add TLS support to the HTTP client developed in Chapter 1, you define four
new top-level functions as shown in Listing 6-1.

**Listing 6-1:** "tls.h" top-level function prototypes

```
/**
 * Negotiate an TLS channel on an already-established connection
 * (or die trying).
 * @return 1 if successful, 0 if not.
 */
int tls_connect( int connection,
                 TLSParameters *parameters );


/**
 * Send data over an established TLS channel.  tls_connect must already
 * have been called with this socket as a parameter.
 */
int tls_send( int connection,
              const char *application_data,
              int length,
              int options,
              TLSParameters *parameters );
/**
 * Received data from an established TLS channel.
 */
int tls_recv( int connection,
              char *target_buffer,
              int buffer_size,
              int options,
              TLSParameters *parameters );

/**
 * Orderly shutdown of the TLS channel (note that the socket itself will
```

```
 * still be open after this is called).
 */
int tls_shutdown( int connection, TLSParameters *parameters );
```

The primary "goal" of tls_connect is to fill in the TLSParameters structure that is passed in. It contains, among other things, the negotiated encryption and authentication algorithms, along with the negotiated keys. Because this structure is large and complex, it is built up incrementally throughout the course of this chapter; the bulk of this chapter is dedicated to filling out the tls_connect function and the TLSParamaters structure.

To apply these to an HTTP connection, open it as usual but immediately call tls_connect, which performs a TLS handshake. Afterward, assuming it succeeds, replace all calls to send and recv with tls_send and tls_recv. Finally, just before closing the socket, call tls_shutdown. Note that SSLv2 didn't have a dedicated shutdown function — this opened the connection to subtle attacks.

In order to support HTTPS, the first thing you'll need to do is to modify the main routine in http.c to start with a TLS handshake as shown in Listing 6-2.

**Listing 6-2:** "https.c" main routine

```
#define HTTPS_PORT      443
...
int main( int argc, char *argv[ ] )
{
  int client_connection;
  char *host, *path;
  struct hostent *host_name;
  struct sockaddr_in host_address;
  int port = HTTPS_PORT;

  TLSParameters tls_context;
...
  printf( "Connection complete; negotiating TLS parameters\n" );

  if ( tls_connect( client_connection, &tls_context ) )
  {
    fprintf( stderr, "Error: unable to negotiate TLS connection.\n" );
    return 3;
  }

  printf( "Retrieving document: '%s'\n", path );

  http_get( client_connection, path, host, &tls_context );
  display_result( client_connection, &tls_context );

  tls_shutdown( client_connection, &tls_context );
...
```

Here, `http_get` and `display_result` change only slightly, as shown in Listing 6-3; they take an extra parameter indicating the new `tls_context`, and they call `tls_send` and `tls_recv` to send and receive data; otherwise, they're identical to the functions presented in Chapter 1:

**Listing 6-3:** "https.c" http_get and display_result

```
int http_get( int connection, const char *path, const char *host,
              TLSParameters *tls_context )
{
  static char get_command[ MAX_GET_COMMAND ];

  sprintf( get_command, "GET /%s HTTP/1.1\r\n", path );
  if ( tls_send( connection, get_command,
       strlen( get_command ), 0, tls_context ) == -1 )
  {
    return -1;
  }

  sprintf( get_command, "Host: %s\r\n", host );
  if ( tls_send( connection, get_command,
       strlen( get_command ), 0, tls_context ) == -1 )
  {
    return -1;
  }

  strcpy( get_command, "Connection: Close\r\n\r\n" );
  if ( tls_send( connection, get_command,
       strlen( get_command ), 0, tls_context ) == -1 )
  {
    return -1;
  }

  return 0;
}
void display_result( int connection, TLSParameters *tls_context )
{
...
  while ( ( received = tls_recv( connection, recv_buf,
            BUFFER_SIZE, 0, tls_context ) ) >= 0 )
  {
    recv_buf[ received ] = '\0';
    printf( "data: %s", recv_buf );
  }
...
```

Notice that the proxy negotiation part of `http_get` is missing from Listing 6-3. Negotiating proxies is a major complication for SSL; by now you can probably see why. The proxy performs the HTTP connection on behalf of the client and then returns the results back to it. Unfortunately this is by definition a man-in-the-middle attack. HTTPS can, of course, be extended to work correctly behind a proxy. This topic is revisited in Chapter 10.

Otherwise, this is it. After the `tls_connect`, `tls_send`, `tls_recv`, and `tls_shutdown` routines are complete, this client is HTTPS-compliant. If you are inclined to extend `display_result` to parse the HTML response and build a renderable web page, you can do so without giving a single thought to whether or not the connection is secure. If you add support for POST, HEAD, PUT, DELETE, and so on into the client-side implementation, you do so just as if the connection was plaintext; just be sure to call `tls_send` instead of `send`. Of course, you should probably extend this to actually pay attention to the protocol and perform a TLS connection only if the user requested "https" instead of "http." I'll leave that as an exercise for you if you're interested.

## Understanding the TLS Handshake Procedure

Most of the complexity is in the handshake; after the handshake has been completed, sending and receiving is just a matter of encrypting/decrypting, MAC'ing/verifying data before/after it's received. At a high-level, the handshake procedure is as shown in Figure 6-1.

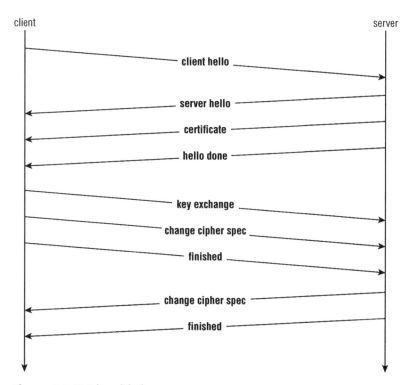

**Figure 6-1:** TLS handshake

The client is responsible for sending the *client hello* that gets the ball rolling and informs the server, at a minimum, what version of the protocol it understands and what *cipher suites* (cryptography, key exchange, and authentication triples) it is capable of working with. It also transmits a unique random number, which is important to guard against replay attacks and is examined in depth later.

The server selects a cipher suite, generates its own random number, and assigns a session ID to the TLS connection; each connection gets a unique session ID. The server also sends enough information to complete a key exchange. Most often, this means sending a certificate including an RSA public key.

The client is then responsible for completing the key exchange using the information the server provided. At this point, the connection is secured, both sides have agreed on an encryption algorithm, a MAC algorithm, and respective keys. Of course, the whole process is quite a bit more complex than this, but you may want to keep this high-level overview in mind as you read the remainder of this chapter.

## TLS Client Hello

Every step in the TLS handshake is responsible for updating some aspect of the TLSParameters structure. As you can probably guess, the most important values are the MAC secret, the symmetric encryption key, and, if applicable, the initialization vector. These are defined in the ProtectionParameters structure shown in Listing 6-4.

**Listing 6-4:** "tls.h" ProtectionParameters

```
typedef struct
{
  unsigned char *MAC_secret;
  unsigned char *key;
  unsigned char *IV;
  ...
}
ProtectionParameters;
```

### *Tracking the Handshake State in the TLSParameters Structure*

TLS actually allows a different MAC secret, key, and IV to be established for the sender and the receiver. Therefore, the TLSParameters structure keeps track of two sets of ProtectionParameters as shown in Listing 6-5.

**Listing 6-5:** "tls.h" TLSParameters

```
#define TLS_VERSION_MAJOR 3
#define TLS_VERSION_MINOR 1
```

```
#define MASTER_SECRET_LENGTH  48
typedef unsigned char master_secret_type[ MASTER_SECRET_LENGTH ];

#define RANDOM_LENGTH 32
typedef unsigned char random_type[ RANDOM_LENGTH ];

typedef struct
{
  master_secret_type    master_secret;
  random_type           client_random;
  random_type           server_random;

  ProtectionParameters  pending_send_parameters;
  ProtectionParameters  pending_recv_parameters;
  ProtectionParameters  active_send_parameters;
  ProtectionParameters  active_recv_parameters;

  // RSA public key, if supplied
  public_key_info       server_public_key;

  // DH public key, if supplied (either in a certificate or ephemerally)
  // Note that a server can legitimately have an RSA key for signing and
  // a DH key for key exchange (e.g. DHE_RSA)
  dh_key                server_dh_key;
...
}
TLSParameters;
```

TLS 1.0 is SSL version 3.1, as described previously. The `pending_send_parameter` and `pending_recv_parameters` are the keys currently being exchanged; the TLS handshake fills these out along the way, based on the computed master secret. The master secret, server random, and client random values are likewise provided by various hello and key exchange messages; the public keys' purpose ought to be clear to you by now.

What about this `active_send_parameters` and `active_recv_parameters`? After the TLS handshake is complete, the pending parameters become the active parameters, and when the active parameters are non-null, the parameters are used to protect the channel. Separating them this way simplifies the code; you could get away with a single set of `send` and `recv` parameters in the `TLSParameters` structure, but you'd have to keep track of a lot more state in the handshake code.

Both the `TLSParameters` and `ProtectionParameters` structures are shown partially filled out in Listings 6-4 and 6-5; you add to them along the way as you develop the client-side handshake routine.

As always, you need a couple of initialization routines, shown in Listing 6-6.

**Listing 6-6:** "tls.c" init_parameters

```
static void init_protection_parameters( ProtectionParameters *parameters )
{
  parameters->MAC_secret = NULL;
  parameters->key = NULL;
  parameters->IV = NULL;
…
}
static void init_parameters( TLSParameters *parameters )
{
  init_protection_parameters( &parameters->pending_send_parameters );
  init_protection_parameters( &parameters->pending_recv_parameters );
  init_protection_parameters( &parameters->active_send_parameters );
  init_protection_parameters( &parameters->active_recv_parameters );

  memset( parameters->master_secret, '\0', MASTER_SECRET_LENGTH );
  memset( parameters->client_random, '\0', RANDOM_LENGTH );
  memset( parameters->server_random, '\0', RANDOM_LENGTH );
…
}
```

So, `tls_connect`, shown partially in Listing 6-7, starts off by calling `init_parameters`.

**Listing 6-7:** "tls.c" tls_connect

```
/**
 * Negotiate TLS parameters on an already-established socket.
 */
int tls_connect( int connection,
                 TLSParameters *parameters )
{
  init_parameters( parameters );
  // Step 1. Send the TLS handshake "client hello" message
  if ( send_client_hello( connection, parameters ) < 0 )
  {
    perror( "Unable to send client hello" );
    return 1;
  }
…
```

Recall from the overview that the first thing the client should do is send a client hello message. The structure of this message is defined in Listing 6-8.

**Listing 6-8:** "tls.h" client hello structure

```
typedef struct
{
  unsigned char major, minor;
}
ProtocolVersion;
```

```
typedef struct
{
  unsigned int   gmt_unix_time;
  unsigned char  random_bytes[ 28 ];
}
Random;

/**
 * Section 7.4.1.2
 */
typedef struct
{
  ProtocolVersion client_version;
  Random random;
  unsigned char session_id_length;
  unsigned char *session_id;
  unsigned short cipher_suites_length;
  unsigned short *cipher_suites;
  unsigned char compression_methods_length;
  unsigned char *compression_methods;
}
ClientHello;
```

Listing 6-9 shows the first part of the send_client_hello function, which is responsible for filling out a ClientHello structure and sending it on to the server.

**Listing 6-9:** "tls.c" send_client_hello

```
/**
 * Build and submit a TLS client hello handshake on the active
 * connection.  It is up to the caller of this function to wait
 * for the server reply.
 */
static int send_client_hello( int connection, TLSParameters *parameters )
{
  ClientHello       package;
  unsigned short    supported_suites[ 1 ];
  unsigned char     supported_compression_methods[ 1 ];
  int               send_buffer_size;
  char              *send_buffer;
  void              *write_buffer;
  time_t            local_time;
  int               status = 1;

  package.client_version.major = TLS_VERSION_MAJOR;
  package.client_version.minor = TLS_VERSION_MINOR;
  time( &local_time );
  package.random.gmt_unix_time = htonl( local_time );
  // TODO - actually make this random.
  // This is 28 bytes, but client random is 32 - the first four bytes of
```

*(Continued)*

```
// "client random" are the GMT unix time computed above.
memcpy( parameters->client_random, &package.random.gmt_unix_time, 4 );
memcpy( package.random.random_bytes, parameters->client_random + 4, 28 );
package.session_id_length = 0;
package.session_id = NULL;
// note that this is bytes, not count.
package.cipher_suites_length = htons( 2 );
supported_suites[ 0 ] = htons( TLS_RSA_WITH_3DES_EDE_CBC_SHA );
package.cipher_suites = supported_suites;
package.compression_methods_length = 1;
supported_compression_methods[ 0 ] = 0;
package.compression_methods = supported_compression_methods;
```

**NOTE** Notice that the client `random` isn't entirely random — the specification actually mandates that the first four bytes be the number of seconds since January 1, 1970. Fortunately, C has a built-in time function to compute this. The remaining 28 bytes are supposed to be random. The most important thing here is that they be different for each connection.

The session ID is left empty, indicating that a new session is being requested (session reuse is examined in Chapter 8). To complete the `ClientHello` structure, the supported cipher suites and compression methods are indicated. Only one of each is given here: For the cipher suite, it's RSA key exchange; 3DES (EDE) with CBC for encryption; and SHA-1 for MAC. The compression method selected is "no compression." TLS allows the client and sender to agree to compress the stream before encrypting.

You may be wondering, legitimately, what compression has to do with security. Nothing, actually — however, it was added to TLS and, at the very least, both sides have to agree not to compress. If the stream is going to be compressed, however, it is important that compression be applied before encryption. One property of secure ciphers is that they specifically not be compressible, so if you try to compress after encrypting, it will be too late.

### Describing Cipher Suites

So, what about this `TLS_RSA_WITH_3DES_EDE_CBC_SHA` value? Strictly speaking, it's not always safe to "mix and match" encryption functions with key exchange and MAC functions, so TLS defines them in triples rather than allowing the two sides to select them à la carte. As a result, each allowed triple has a unique identifier: `TLS_RSA_WITH_3DES_EDE_CBC_SHA` is 10 or 0x0A hex. Go ahead and define a `CipherSuiteIdentifier` enumeration as shown in Listing 6-10.

**Listing 6-10:** "tls.h" CipherSuiteIdentifier list

```
typedef enum
{
  TLS_NULL_WITH_NULL_NULL             = 0x0000,
```

```
    TLS_RSA_WITH_NULL_MD5                     = 0x0001,
    TLS_RSA_WITH_NULL_SHA                     = 0x0002,
    TLS_RSA_EXPORT_WITH_RC4_40_MD5            = 0x0003,
    TLS_RSA_WITH_RC4_128_MD5                  = 0x0004,
    TLS_RSA_WITH_RC4_128_SHA                  = 0x0005,
    TLS_RSA_EXPORT_WITH_RC2_CBC_40_MD5        = 0x0006,
    TLS_RSA_WITH_IDEA_CBC_SHA                 = 0x0007,
    TLS_RSA_EXPORT_WITH_DES40_CBC_SHA         = 0x0008,
    TLS_RSA_WITH_DES_CBC_SHA                  = 0x0009,
    TLS_RSA_WITH_3DES_EDE_CBC_SHA             = 0x000A,

    ...
} CipherSuiteIdentifier;
```

Notice the NULL cipher suites 0, 1 and 2. TLS_NULL_WITH_NULL_NULL indicates that there's no encryption, no MAC and no key exchange. This is the default state for a TLS handshake — the state it starts out in. Cipher suites 1 and 2 allow a non-encrypted, but MAC'ed, cipher suite to be negotiated. This can actually be pretty handy when you're trying to debug something and you don't want to have to decrypt what you're trying to debug. Unfortunately for the would-be debugger, for obvious security reasons, most servers won't allow you to negotiate this cipher suite by default.

There's no particular rhyme or reason to the identifiers assigned to the various cipher suites. They're just a sequential list of every combination that the writers of the specification could think of. They're not even grouped together meaningfully; the RSA key exchange cipher suites aren't all in the same place because after the specification was drafted, new cipher suites that used the RSA key exchange method were identified. It would certainly have been nicer, from an implementer's perspective, if they had allocated, say, three bits to identify the key exchange, five bits to identify the symmetric cipher, two for the MAC, and so on.

Additional cipher suites are examined later on. For now, you're just writing a client that understands only 3DES, RSA, and SHA-1.

### Flattening and Sending the Client Hello Structure

Now that the ClientHello message has been built, it needs to be sent on. If you look at RFC 2246, which describes TLS, you see that the formal description of the client hello message looks an awful lot like the C structure defined here. You may be tempted to try to just do something like this:

```
send( connection, ( void * ) &package, sizeof( package ), 0 );
```

This is tempting, but your compiler thwarts you at every turn, expanding some elements, memory-aligning others, and generally performing unexpected optimizations that cause your code to run faster and work better (the nerve!). Although it is possible to include enough compiler directives to force this structure to appear in memory just as it needs to appear on the wire, you'd be, at the very least, locking yourself into a specific platform. As a result, you're better off manually flattening the structure to match the expected wire-level interface as shown in Listing 6-11:

**Listing 6-11:** "tls.c" send_client_hello (continued in Listing 6-13)

```
// Compute the size of the ClientHello message after flattening.
send_buffer_size = sizeof( ProtocolVersion ) +
   sizeof( Random ) +
   sizeof( unsigned char ) +
   ( sizeof( unsigned char ) * package.session_id_length ) +
   sizeof( unsigned short ) +
   ( sizeof( unsigned short ) * 1 ) +
   sizeof( unsigned char ) +
   sizeof( unsigned char );

write_buffer = send_buffer = ( char * ) malloc( send_buffer_size );

write_buffer = append_buffer( write_buffer, ( void * )
   &package.client_version.major, 1 );
write_buffer = append_buffer( write_buffer, ( void * )
   &package.client_version.minor, 1 );
write_buffer = append_buffer( write_buffer, ( void * )
   &package.random.gmt_unix_time, 4 );
write_buffer = append_buffer( write_buffer, ( void * )
   &package.random.random_bytes, 28 );
write_buffer = append_buffer( write_buffer, ( void * )
   &package.session_id_length, 1 );
if ( package.session_id_length > 0 )
{
  write_buffer = append_buffer( write_buffer,
     ( void * )package.session_id,
     package.session_id_length );
}
write_buffer = append_buffer( write_buffer,
   ( void * ) &package.cipher_suites_length, 2 );
write_buffer = append_buffer( write_buffer,
   ( void * ) package.cipher_suites, 2 );
write_buffer = append_buffer( write_butter,
   ( void * ) &package.compression_methods_length, 1 );
if ( package.compression_methods_length > 0 )
{
  write_buffer = append_buffer( write_buffer,
      ( void * ) package.compression_methods, 1 );
}
```

The append_buffer function, in Listing 6-12, is a convenience routine designed to be called incrementally as in Listing 6-11.

**Listing 6-12:** "tls.c" append buffer

```
/**
 * This is just like memcpy, except it returns a pointer to dest + n instead
 * of dest, to simplify the process of repeated appends to a buffer.
 */
static char *append_buffer( char *dest, char *src, size_t n )
{
  memcpy( dest, src, n );
  return dest + n;
}
```

This flattened structure is illustrated in Figure 6-2.

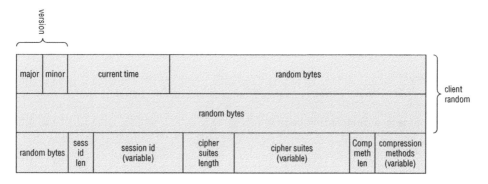

**Figure 6-2:** Client hello structure

Finally, the client hello is sent off in Listing 6-13:

**Listing 6-13:** "tls.c" send_client_hello (continued from Listing 6-11)

```
  assert( ( ( char * ) write_buffer - send_buffer ) == send_buffer_size );

  status = send_handshake_message( connection, client_hello, send_buffer,
     send_buffer_size );

  free( send_buffer );

  return status;
}
```

Notice that `send` still isn't called. Instead, you invoke `send_handshake_message`. Like TCP and IP, and network programming in general, TLS is an onion-like nesting of headers. Each handshake message must be prepended with a header indicating its type and length. The definition of the handshake header is shown in Listing 6-14.

**Listing 6-14:** "tls.h" handshake structure

```
/**
 * Handshake message types (section 7.4)
 */
typedef enum
{
  hello_request = 0,
  client_hello = 1,
  server_hello = 2,
  certificate = 11,
  server_key_exchange = 12,
  certificate_request = 13,
  server_hello_done = 14,
  certificate_verify = 15,
  client_key_exchange = 16,
  finished = 20
}
HandshakeType;

/**
 * Handshake record definition (section 7.4)
 */
typedef struct
{
  unsigned char      msg_type;
  unsigned int       length;       // 24 bits(!)
}
Handshake;
```

This structure is illustrated in Figure 6-3.

**Figure 6-3:** TLS handshake header

The send_handshake_message function that prepends this header to a hand-shake message is shown in Listing 6-15.

**Listing 6-15:** "tls.c" send_handshake_message

```
static int send_handshake_message( int connection,
                                   int msg_type,
                                   const unsigned char *message,
                                   int message_len )
{
  Handshake      record;
  short          send_buffer_size;
  unsigned char *send_buffer;
```

```
   int            response;

   record.msg_type = msg_type;
   record.length = htons( message_len ) << 8; // To deal with 24-bits...
   send_buffer_size = message_len + 4; // space for the handshake header

   send_buffer = ( unsigned char * ) malloc( send_buffer_size );
   send_buffer[ 0 ] = record.msg_type;
   memcpy( send_buffer + 1, &record.length, 3 );
   memcpy( send_buffer + 4, message, message_len );

   response = send_message( connection, content_handshake,
                    send_buffer, send_buffer_size );

   free( send_buffer );

   return response;
}
```

This would be a bit simpler except that, for some strange reason, the TLS designers mandated that the length of the handshake message must be given in a 24-bit field, which no compiler that I'm aware of can generate. Of course, on a big-endian machine, this wouldn't be a problem; just truncate the high-order byte of a 32-bit integer and you'd have a 24-bit integer. Unfortunately, most general purpose computers these days are little-endian, so it's necessary to convert it and then truncate it.

But send_handshake_message *still* doesn't call send! TLS mandates not only that every handshake message be prepended with a header indicating its type and length, but that every message, including the already-prepended handshake messages, be prepended with yet *another* header indicating *its* type and length!

So, finally, define yet another header structure and some supporting enumerations in Listing 6-16.

**Listing 6-16:** "tls.h" TLSPlaintext header

```
/** This lists the type of higher-level TLS protocols that are defined */
typedef enum {
  content_change_cipher_spec = 20,
  content_alert = 21,
  content_handshake = 22,
  content_application_data = 23
}
ContentType;

typedef enum { warning = 1, fatal = 2 } AlertLevel;

/**
 * Enumerate all of the error conditions specified by TLS.
```

*(Continued)*

```
*/
typedef enum
{
  close_notify = 0,
  unexpected_message = 10,
  bad_record_mac = 20,
  decryption_failed = 21,
  record_overflow = 22,
  decompression_failure = 30,
  handshake_failure = 40,
  bad_certificate = 42,
  unsupported_certificate = 43,
  certificate_revoked = 44,
  certificate_expired = 45,
  certificate_unknown = 46,
  illegal_parameter = 47,
  unknown_ca = 48,
  access_denied = 49,
  decode_error = 50,
  decrypt_error = 51,
  export_restriction = 60,
  protocol_version = 70,
  insufficient_security = 71,
  internal_error = 80,
  user_canceled = 90,
  no_renegotiation = 100
}
AlertDescription;

typedef struct
{
  unsigned char level;
  unsigned char description;
}
Alert;

/**
 * Each packet to be encrypted is first inserted into one of these structures.
 */
typedef struct
{
  unsigned char   type;
  ProtocolVersion version;
  unsigned short  length;
}
TLSPlaintext;
```

There are four types of TLS messages defined: handshake messages, alerts, data, and "change cipher spec," which is technically a handshake message, but is broken out for specific implementation types that are examined later. Also, the protocol version is included on every packet.

The TLS Message header is illustrated in Figure 6-4.

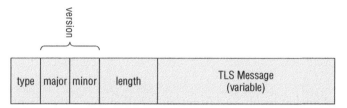

**Figure 6-4:** TLS Message header

Notice that this header is added to *every* packet that is sent over a TLS connection, not just the handshake messages. If, after handshake negotiation, either side receives a packet whose first byte is not greater than or equal to 20 and less than or equal to 23 then something has gone wrong, and the whole connection should be terminated.

Finally, you need one last send function that prepends *this* header on top of the handshake message as shown in Listing 6-17.

**Listing 6-17:** "tls.c" send_message

```
static int send_message( int connection,
                         int content_type,
                         const unsigned char *content,
                         short content_len )
{
  TLSPlaintext header;
  unsigned char *send_buffer;
  int send_buffer_size;

  send_buffer_size = content_len;
  send_buffer_size +=5;

  send_buffer = ( unsigned char * ) malloc( send_buffer_size );

  header.type = content_type;
  header.version.major = TLS_VERSION_MAJOR;
  header.version.minor = TLS_VERSION_MINOR;
  header.length = htons( content_len );
  send_buffer[ 0 ] = header.type;
  send_buffer[ 1 ] = header.version.major;
  send_buffer[ 2 ] = header.version.minor;
  memcpy( send_buffer + 3, &header.length, sizeof( short ) );
  memcpy( send_buffer + 5, content, content_len );
```

*(Continued)*

```
if ( send( connection, ( void * ) send_buffer,
     send_buffer_size, 0 ) < send_buffer_size )
{
  return -1;
}

free( send_buffer );

return 0;
}
```

At this point, the actual socket-level `send` function is called. Now the client hello message, with its handshake message header, with *its* TLS header, are sent to the server for processing. After all of this prepending, the final wire-level structure is as shown in Figure 6-5.

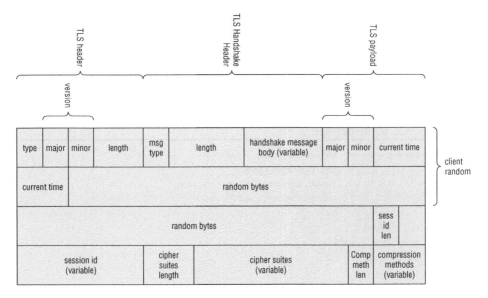

**Figure 6-5:** TLS Client Hello with all headers

## TLS Server Hello

The server should now select one of the supported cipher suites and respond with a server hello response. The client is required to block, waiting for an answer; nothing else can happen on this socket until the server responds. Expand `tls_connect`:

```
// Step 2. Receive the server hello response
if ( receive_tls_msg( connection, parameters ) < 0 )
{
  perror( "Unable to receive server hello" );
  return 2;
}
```

The function `receive_tls_msg`, as you can probably imagine, is responsible for reading a packet off the socket, stripping off the TLS header, stripping off the handshake header if the message is a handshake message, and processing the message itself. This is shown in Listing 6-18.

**Listing 6-18:** "tls.c" receive_tls_msg

```
/**
 * Read a TLS packet off of the connection (assuming there's one waiting)
 * and try to update the security parameters based on the type of message
 * received.  If the read times out, or if an alert is received, return an error
 * code; return 0 on success.
 * TODO - assert that the message received is of the type expected (for example,
 * if a server hello is expected but not received, this is a fatal error per
 * section 7.3).
 * returns -1 if an error occurred (this routine will have sent an
 * appropriate alert). Otherwise, return the number of bytes read if the packet
 * includes application data; 0 if the packet was a handshake.  -1 also
 * indicates that an alert was received.
 */
static int receive_tls_msg( int connection,
                            TLSParameters *parameters )
{
  TLSPlaintext  message;
  unsigned char *read_pos, *msg_buf;
  unsigned char header[ 5 ];  // size of TLSPlaintext
  int bytes_read, accum_bytes;

  // STEP 1 - read off the TLS Record layer
  if ( recv( connection, header, 5, 0 ) <= 0 )
  {
    // No data available; it's up to the caller whether this is an error or not.
    return -1;
  }

  message.type = header[ 0 ];
  message.version.major = header[ 1 ];
  message.version.minor = header[ 2 ];
  memcpy( &message.length, header + 3, 2 );
  message.length = htons( message.length );
```

## *Adding a Receive Loop*

First, the TLSPlaintext header is read from the connection and validated. The error handling here leaves a bit to be desired, but ignore that for the time being. If everything goes correctly, `message.length` holds the number of bytes remaining in the current message. Because TCP doesn't guarantee that all bytes are available right away, it's necessary to enter a receive loop in Listing 6-19:

**Listing 6-19:** "tls.c" receive_tls_msg (continued in Listing 6-21)

```
msg_buf = ( char * ) malloc( message.length );

// keep looping & appending until all bytes are accounted for
accum_bytes = 0;
while ( accum_bytes < message.length )
{
  if ( ( bytes_read = recv( connection, ( void * ) msg_buf,
        message.length - accum_bytes, 0 ) ) <= 0 )
  {
    int status;
    perror( "While reading a TLS packet" );

    if ( ( status = send_alert_message( connection,
          illegal_parameter ) ) )
    {
      free( msg_buf );
      return status;
    }
    return -1;
  }
  accum_bytes += bytes_read;
  msg_buf += bytes_read;
}
```

This loop, as presented here, is vulnerable to a denial of service attack. If the server announces that 100 bytes are available but never sends them, the client hangs forever waiting for these bytes. There's not much you can do about this, though. You can (and should) set a socket-level timeout, but if it expires, there's not much point in continuing the connection.

### Sending Alerts

Notice that if `recv` returns an error, a function `send_alert_message` is invoked. Remember the four types of TLS messages? *Alert* was one of them. This is how clients and servers notify each other of unexpected conditions. In theory, an alert can be recoverable — *expired certificate* is defined as an alert, for example — but this poses a problem for the writer of a general-purpose TLS implementation. If the client tells the server that its certificate has expired then in theory the server could present a new certificate that hadn't expired. But why did it send an expired certificate in the first place, if it had one that was current? In general, all alerts are treated as fatal errors.

Alerts are also frustratingly terse. As you can see, if the client wasn't able to receive the entire message, it just returns an *illegal parameter* with no further context. Although it logs a more detailed reason, the server developer probably doesn't have access to those logs and has no clue what he did wrong. It would certainly be nice if the TLS alert protocol allowed space for a descriptive error message.

`send_alert_message` is shown in Listing 6-20.

**Listing 6-20:** "tls.c" send_alert_message

```
static int send_alert_message( int connection,
                               int alert_code )
{
  char buffer[ 2 ];

  // TODO support warnings
  buffer[ 0 ] = fatal;
  buffer[ 1 ] = alert_code;

  return send_message( connection, content_alert, buffer, 2 );
}
```

By reusing the `send_message` routine from above, sending an alert message is extremely simple.

## Parsing the Server Hello Structure

Assuming nothing went wrong, the message has now been completely read from the connection and is contained in `msg_buf`. For the moment, the only type of message you're interested in is `content_handshake`, whose parsing is shown in Listing 6-21:

**Listing 6-21:** "tls.c" receive_tls_msg (continued from Listing 6-19)

```
  read_pos = msg_buf;

  if ( message.type == content_handshake )
  {
    Handshake handshake;

    // Now, read the handshake type and length of the next packet
    // TODO - this fails if the read, above, only got part of the message
    read_pos = read_buffer( ( void * ) &handshake.msg_type,
             ( void * ) read_pos, 1 );
    handshake.length = read_pos[ 0 ] << 16 | read_pos[ 1 ] << 8 | read_pos[ 2 ];

    read_pos += 3;

    // TODO check for negative or unreasonably long length
    // Now, depending on the type, read in and process the packet itself.
    switch ( handshake.msg_type )
    {
      // Client-side messages
      case server_hello:
```

*(Continued)*

```
      read_pos = parse_server_hello( read_pos, handshake.length,
          parameters );
      if ( read_pos == NULL )  /* error occurred */
      {
        free( msg_buf );
        send_alert_message( connection, illegal_parameter );
        return -1;
      }
      break;
    default:
      printf( "Ignoring unrecognized handshake message %d\n",
        handshake.msg_type );
      // Silently ignore any unrecognized types per section 6
      // TODO However, out-of-order messages should result in a fatal alert
      // per section 7.4
      read_pos += handshake.length;
      break;
    }
  }
  else
  {
    // Ignore content types not understood, per section 6 of the RFC.
    printf( "Ignoring non-recognized content type %d\n", message.type );
  }

  free( msg_buf );

  return message.length;
}
```

As I'm sure you can imagine, you fill this out quite a bit more throughout this chapter. For now, though, just focus on the `parse_server_hello` function. The *Server Hello* message is illustrated in Figure 6-6.

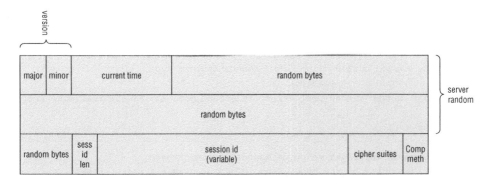

**Figure 6-6:** Server Hello structure

As with the client hello, go ahead and define a structure to hold its value in Listing 6-22.

**Listing 6-22:** "tls.h" ServerHello structure

```
typedef struct
{
  ProtocolVersion    server_version;
  Random             random;
  unsigned char      session_id_length;
  unsigned char      session_id[ 32 ]; // technically, this len should be dynamic.
  unsigned short     cipher_suite;
  unsigned char      compression_method;
}
ServerHello;
```

Because the TLSParameters were passed into the receive_tls_message function, the parse_server_hello can go ahead and update the ongoing state as it's parsed, as in Listing 6-23.

**Listing 6-23:** "tls.c" parse_server_hello

```
static char *parse_server_hello( char *read_pos,
                                 int pdu_length,
                                 TLSParameters *parameters )
{
  ServerHello hello;

  read_pos = read_buffer( ( void * ) &hello.server_version.major,
    ( void * ) read_pos, 1 );
  read_pos = read_buffer( ( void * ) &hello.server_version.minor,
    ( void * ) read_pos, 1 );
  read_pos = read_buffer( ( void * ) &hello.random.gmt_unix_time,
    ( void * ) read_pos, 4 );
  // *DON'T* put this in host order, since it's not used as a time!  Just
  // accept it as is
  read_pos = read_buffer( ( void * ) hello.random.random_bytes,
    ( void * ) read_pos, 28 );
  read_pos = read_buffer( ( void * ) &hello.session_id_length,
    ( void * ) read_pos, 1 );
  read_pos = read_buffer( ( void * ) hello.session_id,
    ( void * ) read_pos, hello.session_id_length );
  read_pos = read_buffer( ( void * ) &hello.cipher_suite,
    ( void * ) read_pos, 2 );
  hello.cipher_suite = ntohs( hello.cipher_suite );

  // TODO check that these values were actually in the client hello
  // list.
  parameters->pending_recv_parameters.suite = hello.cipher_suite;
  parameters->pending_send_parameters.suite = hello.cipher_suite;

  read_pos = read_buffer( ( void * ) &hello.compression_method,
    ( void * ) read_pos, 1 );
  if ( hello.compression_method != 0 )
```

*(Continued)*

```
  {
    fprintf( stderr, "Error, server wants compression.\n" );
    return NULL;
  }

  // TODO - abort if there's more data here than in the spec (per section
  // 7.4.1.2, forward compatibility note)
  // TODO - abort if version < 3.1 with "protocol_version" alert error

  // 28 random bytes, but the preceding four bytes are the reported GMT unix
  // time
  memcpy( ( void * ) parameters->server_random, &hello.random.gmt_unix_time, 4
);
  memcpy( ( void * ) ( parameters->server_random + 4 ),
    ( void * ) hello.random.random_bytes, 28 );
  return read_pos;
}
```

Note that if the server asked for compression, this function returns null because this implementation doesn't support compression. This is recognized by the calling routine and is used to generate an alert. Here the terseness of the TLS alert protocol shows. If the server asked for compression, it just gets back a nondescript *illegal parameter* but receives no indication of which parameter was illegal. It certainly would be more robust if you were allowed to tell it which parameter you were complaining about. This is generally not a problem for *users* of TLS software — if you get an illegal parameter while using, say, a browser, that means that the programmer of the browser did something wrong — but is a hassle when developing/testing TLS software like the library developed in this book. When developing, therefore, it's best to test against a client or server with its debug levels set to maximum so that if you do get back an illegal parameter (or any other nondescript alert message), you can go look at the server logs to see what you actually did wrong.

This routine stores the server random, of course, because it is needed later on in the master secret computation. Primarily, though, it sets the values `pending_send_parameters` and `pending_recv_parameters` with the selected suite. Expand the definition of `ProtectionParameters` to keep track of this in Listing 6-24.

**Listing 6-24:** "tls.h" ProtectionParameters with cipher suite

```
typedef struct
{
  unsigned char *MAC_secret;
  unsigned char *key;
  unsigned char *IV;
  CipherSuiteIdentifier suite;
}
ProtectionParameters;
```

Recall that `CipherSuiteIdentifier` was defined as part of the client hello.

`parse_server_hello` is something of the opposite of `send_client_hello` and it even makes use of a function complementary to `append_buffer`, shown in Listing 6-25.

**Listing 6-25:** "tls.c" read_buffer

```
static char *read_buffer( char *dest, char *src, size_t n )
{
  memcpy( dest, src, n );
  return src + n;
}
```

## Reporting Server Alerts

What if the server doesn't happen to support `TLS_RSA_WITH_3DES_EDE_CBC_SHA` (or any of the cipher suites on the list the client sends)? It doesn't return a `server_hello` at all; instead it responds with an alert message. You need to be prepared to deal with alerts at any time, so extend `receive_tls_message` to handle alerts as shown in Listing 6-26.

**Listing 6-26:** "receive_tls_message" with alert support

```
static int receive_tls_msg( int connection,
                            TLSParameters *parameters )
{
...
  if ( message.type == content_handshake )
  {
    ...
  }
  else if ( message.type == content_alert )
  {
    while ( ( read_pos - decrypted_message ) < decrypted_length )
    {
      Alert alert;

      read_pos = read_buffer( ( void * ) &alert.level,
        ( void * ) read_pos, 1 );
      read_pos = read_buffer( ( void * ) &alert.description,
        ( void * ) read_pos, 1 );

      report_alert( &alert );

      if ( alert.level == fatal )
      {
        return -1;
      }
    }
  }
}
```

Notice that alert level is checked. If the server specifically marks an alert as a fatal, the handshake is aborted; otherwise, the handshake process continues. Effectively this means that this implementation is ignoring warnings, which is technically a Bad Thing. However, as noted previously, there's really not much that can be done about the few alerts defined as warnings anyway. In any case, the alert itself is written to `stdout` via the helper function `report_alert` in Listing 6-27.

**Listing 6-27:** "tls.c" report_alert

```
static void report_alert( Alert *alert )
{
  printf( "Alert - " );

  switch ( alert->level )
  {
    case warning:
      printf( "Warning: " );
      break;
    case fatal:
      printf( "Fatal: " );
      break;
    default:
      printf( "UNKNOWN ALERT TYPE %d (!!!): ", alert->level );
      break;
  }

  switch ( alert->description )
  {
    case close_notify:
      printf( "Close notify\n" );
      break;
    case unexpected_message:
      printf( "Unexpected message\n" );
      break;
    case bad_record_mac:
      printf( "Bad Record Mac\n" );
      break;
    ...
    default:
      printf( "UNKNOWN ALERT DESCRIPTION %d (!!!)\n", alert->description );
      break;
  }
```

## TLS Certificate

According to the handshake protocol, the next message after the server hello ought to be the certificate that both identifies the server and provides a public key for key exchange. The client, then, should accept the server hello and immediately start waiting for the certificate message that follows.

The designers of TLS recognized that it is somewhat wasteful to rigidly separate messages this way, so the TLS format actually allows either side to concatenate multiple handshake messages within a single TLS message. This capability was one of the big benefits of TLS over SSLv2. Remember the TLS header that included a message length which was then followed by the seemingly superfluous handshake header that included essentially the same length? This is why it was done this way; a single TLS header can identify multiple handshake messages, each with its own independent length. Most TLS implementations do take advantage of this optimization, so you must be prepared to handle it.

This slightly complicates the design of `receive_tls_msg`, though. The client must now be prepared to process multiple handshake messages within a single TLS message. Modify the `content_handshake` handler to keep processing the TLS message until there are no more handshake messages remaining as in Listing 6-28.

**Listing 6-28:** "tls.c" receive_tls_msg with multiple handshake support

```
if ( message.type == content_handshake )
{
  while ( ( read_pos - decrypted_message ) < decrypted_length )
  {
    Handshake handshake;
    read_pos = read_buffer( ( void * ) &handshake.msg_type,
      ( void * ) read_pos, 1 );
...

    switch ( handshake.msg_type )
    {
...

      case certificate:
        read_pos = parse_x509_chain( read_pos, handshake.length,
          &parameters->server_public_key );
        if ( read_pos == NULL )
        {
          printf( "Rejected, bad certificate\n" );
          send_alert_message( connection, bad_certificate );
          return -1;
        }
        break;
```

Notice that the call is made, not directly to the `parse_x509_certificate` function developed in Chapter 5, but to a new function `parse_x509_chain`. TLS actually allows the server to pass in not just its own certificate, but the signing certificate of its certificate, and the signing certificate of *that* certificate, and so on, until a top-level, self-signed certificate is reached. It's up to the client to determine whether or not it trusts the top-level certificate. Of course, each certificate after the first should be checked to ensure that it includes the "is a certificate authority" extension described in Chapter 5 as well.

Therefore, the TLS *certificate* handshake message starts off with the length of the certificate chain so that the receiver knows how many bytes of certificate follow. If you are so inclined, you can infer this from the length of the handshake message and the ASN.1 structure declaration that begins each certificate, but explicitness can never hurt.

Certificate chain parsing, then, consists of reading the length of the certificate chain from the message, and then reading each certificate in turn, using each to verify the last. Of course, the first must also be verified for freshness and domain name validity. At a bare minimum, though, in order to complete a TLS handshake, you need to read and store the public key contained within the certificate because it's required to perform the key exchange. Listing 6-29 shows a bare-bones certificate chain parsing routine that doesn't actually verify the certificate signatures or check validity parameters.

**Listing 6-29:** "x509.c" parse_x509_chain

```
/**
 * This is called by "receive_server_hello" when the "certificate" PDU
 * is encountered.  The input to this function should be a certificate chain.
 * The most important certificate is the first one, since this contains the
 * public key of the subject as well as the DNS name information (which
 * has to be verified against).
 * Each subsequent certificate acts as a signer for the previous certificate.
 * Each signature is verified by this function.
 * The public key of the first certificate in the chain will be returned in
 * "server_public_key" (subsequent certificates are just needed for signature
 * verification).
 * TODO verify signatures.
 */
char *parse_x509_chain( unsigned char *buffer,
                        int pdu_length,
                        public_key_info *server_public_key )
{
  int pos;
  signed_x509_certificate certificate;
  unsigned int chain_length, certificate_length;
  unsigned char *ptr;
  ptr = buffer;

  pos = 0;

  // TODO this won't work on a big-endian machine
  chain_length = ( *ptr << 16 ) | ( *( ptr + 1 ) << 8 ) | ( *( ptr + 2 ) );
  ptr += 3;

  // The chain length is actually redundant since the length of the PDU has
  // already been input.
  assert ( chain_length == ( pdu_length - 3 ) );
```

```
while ( ( ptr - buffer ) < pdu_length )
{
  // TODO this won't work on a big-endian machine
  certificate_length = ( *ptr << 16 ) | ( *( ptr + 1 ) << 8 ) |
    ( *( ptr + 2 ) );
  ptr += 3;

  init_x509_certificate( &certificate );

  parse_x509_certificate( ( void * ) ptr, certificate_length, &certificate );
  if ( !pos++ )
  {
    server_public_key->algorithm =
      certificate.tbsCertificate.subjectPublicKeyInfo.algorithm;
    switch ( server_public_key->algorithm )
    {
      case rsa:
        server_public_key->rsa_public_key.modulus = ( huge * ) malloc( sizeof(
          huge ) );
        server_public_key->rsa_public_key.exponent = ( huge * ) malloc(
          sizeof( huge ) );
        set_huge( server_public_key->rsa_public_key.modulus, 0 );
        set_huge( server_public_key->rsa_public_key.exponent, 0 );
        copy_huge( server_public_key-> rsa_public_key.modulus,
          certificate.tbsCertificate.subjectPublicKeyInfo.
          rsa_public_key.modulus );
        copy_huge( server_public_key-> rsa_public_key.exponent,
          certificate.tbsCertificate.subjectPublicKeyInfo.
          rsa_public_key.exponent );
        break;
      default:
        break;
    }
  }

  ptr += certificate_length;

  // TODO compute the hash of the certificate so that it can be validated by
  // the next one

  free_x509_certificate( &certificate );
}

return ptr;
}
```

This blindly accepts whatever certificate is presented by the server. It doesn't check the domain name parameter of the subject name, doesn't check to see that it's signed by a trusted certificate authority, and doesn't even verify that the validity period of the certificate contains the current date. Clearly, an industrial-strength TLS implementation needs to do at least all of these things.

## TLS Server Hello Done

After the certificate the server should send a *hello done* message — at least that's what happens in the most common type of TLS handshake being examined here. This indicates that the server will not send any more unencrypted handshake messages on this connection.

This may seem surprising, but if you think about it, there's nothing more for the server to do. It has chosen a cipher suite acceptable to the client and provided enough information — the public key — to complete a key exchange in that cipher suite. It's incumbent on the client to now come up with a key and exchange it. Parsing the server hello done message is trivial, as in Listing 6-30.

**Listing 6-30:** "tls.c" receive_tls_message with server hello done support

```
switch ( handshake.msg_type )
{
...
   case server_hello_done:
     parameters->server_hello_done = 1;
     break;
```

As you can see, there's really nothing there; the server hello done message is just a marker and contains no data. Note that this will almost definitely be piggy-backed onto a longer message that contains the server hello and the server certificate.

This routine just sets a flag indicating that the server hello done message has been received. Add this flag to TLSParameters as shown in Listing 6-31; it's used internally to track the state of the handshake.

**Listing 6-31:** "tls.h" TLSParameters with state tracking included

```
typedef struct
{
...
  int                   server_hello_done;
}
TLSParameters;
```

Finally, recall that this whole process was being controlled by tls_connect. It sent a client hello message and then received the server hello. Due to piggy-backing of handshake messages, though, that call to receive probably picked up all three expected messages and processed them, culminating in the setting of server_hello_done. This isn't guaranteed, though; the server could legitimately split these up into three separate messages (the server you develop in the next chapter does this, in fact). To handle either case, modify `tls_connect` to keep receiving TLS messages until `server_hello_done` is set, as in Listing 6-32.

**Listing 6-32:** "tls.c" tls_connect multiple handshake messages

```
// Step 2. Receive the server hello response (will also have gotten
// the server certificate along the way)
parameters->server_hello_done = 0;
while ( !parameters->server_hello_done )
{
  if ( receive_tls_msg( connection, parameters ) < 0 )
  {
    perror( "Unable to receive server hello" );
    return 2;
  }
}
```

## TLS Client Key Exchange

Now it's time for the client to do a key exchange, which is the most critical part of the whole TLS handshake. You might reasonably expect that if RSA is used as a key exchange method then the client selects a set of keys, encrypts them, and sends them on. If DH was used as a key exchange method, both sides would agree on $Z$ and that would be used as the key. As it turns out, however, TLS mandates a bit more complexity here; the key exchange is used to exchange a *premaster secret*, which is expanded using a pseudo-random function into a *master secret* which is used for keying material. This procedure guards against weaknesses in the client's key generation routines.

### Sharing Secrets Using TLS PRF (Pseudo-Random Function)

In several places during the TLS negotiation, the algorithm calls for a lot of data to be generated deterministically so that both sides agree on the same result, based on a seed. This process is referred to as *pseudo-random*, just like the software pseudo-random generator that's built into every C implementation. TLS has a fairly complex pseudo-random function called the PRF that generates data from a seed in such a way that two compliant implementations, given the same seed data, generate the same data, but that the output is randomly distributed and follows no observable pattern.

It should come as no surprise at this point that this pseudo-random function is based on secure hash algorithms, which deterministically generate output from input in a non-predictable way. TLS's PRF is actually based on the HMAC algorithm. It takes as input three values: the *seed*, a *label*, and a *secret*. The seed and the label are both used as input to the HMAC algorithm.

The PRF for TLS v1.0 involves both MD5 and SHA-1 (and the use of these specific hash algorithms is hard-coded into the specification). MD5 and SHA-1 are each used, along with the HMAC algorithm specified in Chapter 4, to generate an arbitrary quantity of output independently. Then the results of both the MD5 HMAC and the SHA HMAC are XORed together to produce the final result. The secret is split up so that the MD5 routine gets the first half and the SHA routine gets the second half:

Consider using the triple ("abcd", "efgh", "ijkl" ) to generate 40 bytes of output through the PRF as shown in Figure 6-7.

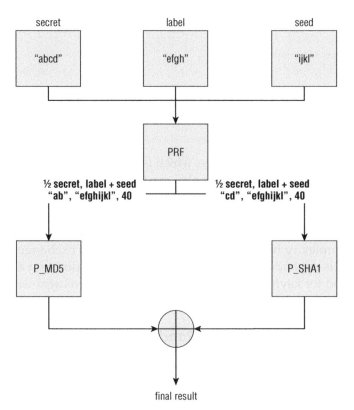

**Figure 6-7:** TLS's pseudo-random function

So what are these P_MD5 and P_SHA1 blocks that are XORed together to produce the final result? Well, if you recall from Chapter 4, MD5 produces 16 bytes of output, regardless of input length, and SHA-1 produces 20. If you want to produce an arbitrary amount of data based on the secret, the label, and the seed using these hashing algorithms, you have to call them more than once. Of course, you have to call them with different data each time, otherwise you get the same 16 bytes back each time. P_[MD5|SHA1] actually use the HMAC algorithm, again, to produce the input to the final HMAC algorithm. So what goes into the HMAC algorithms that go into the HMAC algorithms? More HMAC output, of course! The seed is HMAC'ed once to produce the HMAC input for the first $n$ bytes (where $n$ is 16 or 20 depending on the algorithm), and then that is HMAC'ed again to produce the input for the next $n$ bytes.

All of this sounds almost self-referential, but it actually does work. Figure 6-8 shows the P_MD5 algorithm, illustrated out to three iterations (to produce 48 = 16 * 3 bytes of output).

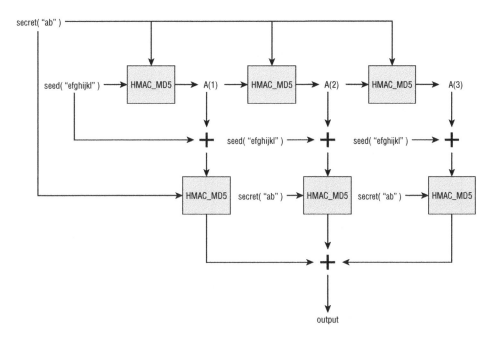

**Figure 6-8:** P_MD5

So, given a secret of "ab" and a seed of "efghijkl", A(1) is HMAC_MD5("ab", "efghijkl"), or 0xefe3a7027ddbdb424cabd0935bfb3898. A(2), then, is HMAC_MD5( "ab", 0xefe3a7027ddbdb424cabd0935bfb3898), or 0xda55f448c81b 93ce1231cb7668bee2a2. Because you need 40 bytes of output, and MD5 only produces 16 per iteration, you need to iterate three times to produce 48 bytes and throw away the last 8. This means that you need A(3) as well, which is HMAC_MD5( "ab", A(2) = 0xda55f448c81b93ce1231cb7668bee2a2), or 0xbfa8ec7eda156ec26478851358c7a1fa.

With all the As computed, you now have enough information to feed into the "real" HMAC operations that generate the requisite 48 bytes of output. The final 48 bytes of output (remembering that you discard the last 8) are

```
HMAC( "ab", A(1) . "efghijkl" ) .
HMAC( "ab", A(2) . "efghijkl" ) .
HMAC( "ab", A(3), "efghijkl" )
```

Notice that the secret and the seed are constant throughout each HMAC operation; the only difference in each are the A values. These operations produce the 48 output bytes:

```
0x1b6ca10d18faddfbeb92b2d95f55ce2607d6c81ebe4b96d
1bec81813b9a0275725564781eda73ac521548d7d1f982c17
```

P_SHA1 is identical. It just replaces the SHA-1 hash algorithm with the MD5 hash algorithm. Because SHA-1 produces 20 bytes of output per iteration, though, it's only necessary to iterate twice and none of the output is discarded. P_SHA is fed the exact same seed, but only the last half of the secret, as diagrammed in Figure 6-9.

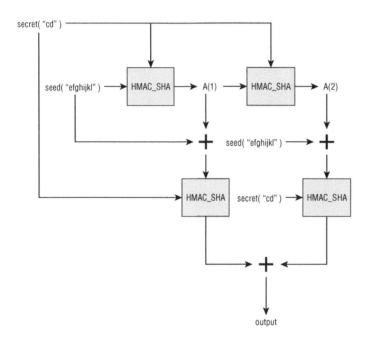

**Figure 6-9:** P_SHA1

This produces the 40 bytes:

```
0xcbb3de5db9295cdb68eb1ab18f88939cb3146849fe167cf8f9ec5f131790005d7f27b
2515db6c590
```

Finally, these two results are XORed together to produce the 40-byte pseudo-random combination:

```
0xd0df7f50a1d381208379a868d0dd5dbab4c2a057405dea2947244700ae30270
a5a71f5d0b011ff55
```

Notice that there's no predictable repetition here, and no obvious correlation with the input data. This procedure can be performed to produce any arbitrarily large amount of random data that two compliant implementations, both of which share the secret, can reproduce consistently.

In code, this is shown in Listing 6-33.

**Listing 6-33:** "prf.c" PRF function

```
/**
 * P_MD5 or P_SHA, depending on the value of the "new_digest" function
 * pointer.
 * HMAC_hash( secret, A(1) + seed ) + HMAC_hash( secret, A(2) + seed ) + ...
 * where + indicates concatenation and A(0) = seed, A(i) =
 * HMAC_hash( secret, A(i - 1) )
 */
static void P_hash( const unsigned char *secret,
                    int secret_len,
                    const unsigned char *seed,
                    int seed_len,
                    unsigned char *output,
                    int out_len,
                    void (*new_digest)( digest_ctx *context ) )
{
  unsigned char *A;
  int hash_len; // length of the hash code in bytes
  digest_ctx A_ctx, h;
  int adv;
  int i;
  new_digest( &A_ctx );
  hmac( secret, secret_len, seed, seed_len, &A_ctx );

  hash_len = A_ctx.hash_len * sizeof( int );
  A = malloc( hash_len + seed_len );
  memcpy( A, A_ctx.hash, hash_len );
  memcpy( A + hash_len, seed, seed_len );

  i = 2;

  while ( out_len > 0 )
  {
    new_digest( &h );
    // HMAC_Hash( secret, A(i) + seed )
    hmac( secret, secret_len, A, hash_len + seed_len, &h );
    adv = ( h.hash_len * sizeof( int ) ) < out_len ?
      h.hash_len * sizeof( int ) : out_len;
    memcpy( output, h.hash, adv );
    out_len -= adv;
    output += adv;
    // Set A for next iteration
    // A(i) = HMAC_hash( secret, A(i-1) )
    new_digest( &A_ctx );
    hmac( secret, secret_len, A, hash_len, &A_ctx );
    memcpy( A, A_ctx.hash, hash_len );
```

*(Continued)*

```
    }

    free( A );
}

/**
 * P_MD5( S1, label + seed ) XOR P_SHA1(S2, label + seed );
 * where S1 & S2 are the first & last half of secret
 * and label is an ASCII string.  Ignore the null terminator.
 *
 * output must already be allocated.
 */
void PRF( const unsigned char *secret,
          int secret_len,
          const unsigned char *label,
          int label_len,
          const unsigned char *seed,
          int seed_len,
          unsigned char *output,
          int out_len )
{
  int i;
  int half_secret_len;
  unsigned char *sha1_out = ( unsigned char * ) malloc( out_len );
  unsigned char *concat = ( unsigned char * ) malloc( label_len + seed_len );
  memcpy( concat, label, label_len );
  memcpy( concat + label_len, seed, seed_len );

  half_secret_len = ( secret_len / 2 ) + ( secret_len % 2 );
  P_hash( secret, half_secret_len, concat, ( label_len + seed_len ),
    output, out_len, new_md5_digest );
  P_hash( secret + ( secret_len / 2 ), half_secret_len, concat,
    ( label_len + seed_len ), sha1_out, out_len, new_sha1_digest );

  for ( i = 0; i < out_len; i++ )
  {
    output[ i ] ^= sha1_out[ i ];
  }

  free( sha1_out );
  free( concat );
}
```

To see the PRF in action, put together a short test `main` routine in Listing 6-34.

**Listing 6-34:** "prf.c" main routine

```
#ifdef TEST_PRF
int main( int argc, char *argv[ ] )
```

```
{
  unsigned char *output;
  int out_len, i;
  int secret_len;
  int label_len;
  int seed_len;
  unsigned char *secret;
  unsigned char *label;
  unsigned char *seed;

  if ( argc < 5 )
  {
    fprintf( stderr,
      "usage: %s [0x]<secret> [0x]<label> [0x]<seed> <output len>\n",
      argv[ 0 ] );
    exit( 0 );
  }

  secret_len = hex_decode( argv[ 1 ], &secret );
  label_len = hex_decode( argv[ 2 ], &label );
  seed_len = hex_decode( argv[ 3 ], &seed );
  out_len = atoi( argv[ 4 ] );
  output = ( unsigned char * ) malloc( out_len );

  PRF( secret, secret_len,
       label, label_len,
       seed, seed_len,
       output, out_len );

  for ( i = 0; i < out_len; i++ )
  {
    printf( "%.02x", output[ i ] );
  }
  printf( "\n" );

  free( secret );
  free( label );
  free( seed );
  free( output );

  return 0;
}
#endif
```

You can try out the PRF, although it's not earth-shatteringly interesting:

```
[jdavies@localhost ssl]$ ./prf secret label seed 20
b5baf4722b91851a8816d22ebd8c1d8cc2e94d55
```

### Creating Reproducible, Unpredictable Symmetric Keys with Master Secret Computation

The client selects the premaster secret and sends it to the server (or agrees on it, in the case of DH key exchange). The premaster secret is, as the name implies, secret — in fact, it's really the only important bit of handshake material that's hidden from eavesdroppers. However, the premaster secret itself isn't used as a session key; this would open the door to replay attacks. The premaster secret is combined with the *server random* and *client random* values exchanged earlier in the handshake and then run through the PRF to generate the *master secret*, which is used, indirectly, as the keying material for the symmetric encryption algorithms and MACs that actually protect the data in transit.

Given, for example, a premaster secret

```
030102030405060708090a0b0c0d0e0f101112131415161718191a1b1c1d1e
1f202122232425262728292a2b2c2d2e2f
```

a client random

```
4af0a381000000000000000000000000000000000000000000000000000000000000
```

and a server random

```
4af0a3818ff72033b852b9b9c09e7d8045ab270eabc74e11d565ece018c9a5ec
```

you would compute the final master secret from which the actual keys are derived using — you guessed it — the PRF.

Remember that the PRF takes three parameters: a secret, a label, and a seed. The premaster secret is the secret, the label is just the unimaginative text string `"master secret"`, and the seed is the client random and the server random concatenated one after the other, client random first.

The PRF is the XOR of the SHA-1 and the MD5 HMACs of the secret and the label concatenated with the seed, expanded out iteratively. With the PRF function defined above, master secret expansion is actually simple to code, as in Listing 6-35.

**Listing 6-35:** "tls.c" master secret computation

```
/**
 * Turn the premaster secret into an actual master secret (the
 * server side will do this concurrently) as specified in section 8.1:
 * master_secret = PRF( pre_master_secret, "master secret",
 * ClientHello.random + ServerHello.random );
 * ( premaster_secret, parameters );
 * Note that, with DH, the master secret len is determined by the generator (p)
 * value.
 */
static void compute_master_secret( const unsigned char *premaster_secret,
                                    int premaster_secret_len,
                                    TLSParameters *parameters )
```

```
{
  const char *label = "master secret";
  PRF( premaster_secret, premaster_secret_len,
       label, strlen( label ),
       // Note - cheating, since client_random & server_random are defined
       // sequentially in the structure
       parameters->client_random, RANDOM_LENGTH * 2,
       parameters->master_secret, MASTER_SECRET_LENGTH );
}
```

## RSA Key Exchange

After the server hello done has been received, the server believes that the client has enough information to complete the key exchange specified in the selected cipher suite. If the key exchange is RSA, this means that the client now has the server's public key. It's the client's problem whether to trust that key or not, based on the certificate chain.

The client should thus send a key exchange as shown in Listing 6-36, in `tls_connect`.

**Listing 6-36:** "tls.c" tls_connect with key exchange

```
// Step 3. Send client key exchange, change cipher spec (7.1) and encrypted
// handshake message
if ( !( send_client_key_exchange( connection, parameters ) ) )
{
  perror( "Unable to send client key exchange" );
  return 3;
}
```

`send_client_key_exchange` is slightly complex because RSA and DH key exchanges are so different. For now, just focus on RSA in Listing 6-37.

**Listing 6-37:** "tls.c" send_client_key_exchange

```
/**
 * Send the client key exchange message, as detailed in section 7.4.7
 * Use the server's public key (if it has one) to encrypt a key. (or DH?)
 * Return true if this succeeded, false otherwise.
 */
static int send_client_key_exchange( int connection, TLSParameters *parameters )
{
  unsigned char *key_exchange_message;
  int key_exchange_message_len;
  unsigned char *premaster_secret;
  int premaster_secret_len;

  switch ( parameters->pending_send_parameters.suite ) {
    case TLS_NULL_WITH_NULL_NULL:
      // XXX this is an error, exit here
      break;
```

*(Continued)*

```
    case TLS_RSA_WITH_NULL_MD5:
    case TLS_RSA_WITH_NULL_SHA:
...
    case TLS_RSA_WITH_DES_CBC_SHA:
    case TLS_RSA_WITH_3DES_EDE_CBC_SHA:
    case TLS_RSA_WITH_AES_128_CBC_SHA:
    case TLS_RSA_WITH_AES_256_CBC_SHA:
      premaster_secret_len = MASTER_SECRET_LENGTH;
      premaster_secret = malloc( premaster_secret_len );
      key_exchange_message_len = rsa_key_exchange(
        &parameters->server_public_key.rsa_public_key,
        premaster_secret, &key_exchange_message );
      break;
    default:
      return 0;
  }

  if ( send_handshake_message( connection, client_key_exchange,
       key_exchange_message, key_exchange_message_len ) )
  {
    free( key_exchange_message );
    return 0;
  }

  free( key_exchange_message );

  // Now, turn the premaster secret into an actual master secret (the
  // server side will do this concurrently).
  compute_master_secret( premaster_secret, premaster_secret_len, parameters );

  // XXX - for security, should also "purge" the premaster secret from
  // memory.
  calculate_keys( parameters );

  free( premaster_secret );

  return 1;
}
```

The goal of the key exchange is to exchange a premaster secret, turn it into a master secret, and use that to calculate the keys that are used for the remainder of the connection. As you can see, `send_client_key_exchange` starts by checking if the key exchange method is RSA. If the key exchange method is RSA, `send_client_key_exchange` calls `rsa_key_exchange` to build the appropriate handshake message. `compute_master_secret` has already been examined in Listing 6-35, and `calculate_keys` is examined later in Listing 6-41.

This routine goes ahead and lets the `rsa_key_exchange` function select the premaster secret. There's no reason why `send_client_key_exchange` couldn't do this, and pass the premaster secret into `rsa_key_exchange`. However, this configuration makes DH key exchange easier to support because the upcoming `dh_key_exchange` necessarily has to select the premaster secret, due to the nature of the Diffie-Hellman algorithm.

The `rsa_key_exchange` message is built in Listing 6-38.

**Listing 6-38:** "tls.c" rsa_key_exchange

```
int rsa_key_exchange( rsa_key *public_key,
                      unsigned char *premaster_secret,
                      unsigned char **key_exchange_message )
{
  int i;
  unsigned char *encrypted_premaster_secret = NULL;
  int encrypted_length;

  // first two bytes are protocol version
  premaster_secret[ 0 ] = TLS_VERSION_MAJOR;
  premaster_secret[ 1 ] = TLS_VERSION_MINOR;
  for ( i = 2; i < MASTER_SECRET_LENGTH; i++ )
  {
    // XXX SHOULD BE RANDOM!
    premaster_secret[ i ] = i;
  }

  encrypted_length = rsa_encrypt( premaster_secret, MASTER_SECRET_LENGTH,
    &encrypted_premaster_secret, public_key );

  *key_exchange_message = ( unsigned char * ) malloc( encrypted_length + 2 );
  (*key_exchange_message)[ 0 ] = 0;
  (*key_exchange_message)[ 1 ] = encrypted_length;
  memcpy( (*key_exchange_message) + 2, encrypted_premaster_secret,
    encrypted_length );

  free( encrypted_premaster_secret );

  return encrypted_length + 2;
}
```

This function takes as input the RSA public key, generates a "random" premaster secret, encrypts it, and returns both the premaster secret and the key exchange message. The format of the key exchange message is straightforward; it's just a two-byte length followed by the PKCS #1 padded, RSA encrypted premaster secret. Notice that the specification mandates that the first two bytes of the premaster secret must be the TLS version — in this case, 3.1. In theory, the server is supposed to verify this. In practice, few servers do the verification because there are a few buggy TLS implementations floating around that they want to remain compatible with.

Now the only thing left to do is to turn the master secret into a set of keys. The amount, and even the type, of keying material needed depends on the cipher suite. If the cipher suite uses SHA-1 HMAC, the MAC requires a 20-byte key; if MD5, it requires a 16-byte key. If the cipher suite uses DES, it requires an 8-byte key; if AES-256, it requires a 32-byte key. If the encryption algorithm uses CBC, initialization vectors are needed; if the algorithm is a stream algorithm, no initialization vector is involved.

Rather than build an enormous switch/case statement for each possibility, define a `CipherSuite` structure as in Listing 6-39.

**Listing 6-39:** "tls.h" CipherSuite structure

```
typedef struct
{
  CipherSuiteIdentifier id;

  int                   block_size;
  int                   IV_size;
  int                   key_size;
  int                   hash_size;

  void (*bulk_encrypt)( const unsigned char *plaintext,
                        const int plaintext_len,
                        unsigned char ciphertext[],
                        void *iv,
                        const unsigned char *key );
  void (*bulk_decrypt)( const unsigned char *ciphertext,
                        const int ciphertext_len,
                        unsigned char plaintext[],
                        void *iv,
                        const unsigned char *key );
  void (*new_digest)( digest_ctx *context );
}
CipherSuite;
```

This includes everything you need to know about a cipher suite; by now, the utility of declaring the encrypt, decrypt, and hash functions with identical signatures in the previous chapters should be clear. Now, for each supported cipher suite, you need to generate a `CipherSuite` instance and index it as shown in Listing 6-40.

**Listing 6-40:** "tls.c" cipher suites list

```
static CipherSuite suites[] =
{
  { TLS_NULL_WITH_NULL_NULL, 0, 0, 0, 0, NULL, NULL, NULL },
  { TLS_RSA_WITH_NULL_MD5, 0, 0, 0, MD5_BYTE_SIZE, NULL, NULL, new_md5_digest },
  { TLS_RSA_WITH_NULL_SHA, 0, 0, 0, SHA1_BYTE_SIZE, NULL, NULL, new_sha1_digest },
  { TLS_RSA_EXPORT_WITH_RC4_40_MD5, 0, 0, 5, MD5_BYTE_SIZE, rc4_40_encrypt,
```

```
    rc4_40_decrypt, new_md5_digest },
  { TLS_RSA_WITH_RC4_128_MD5, 0, 0, 16, MD5_BYTE_SIZE, rc4_128_encrypt,
    rc4_128_decrypt, new_md5_digest },
  { TLS_RSA_WITH_RC4_128_SHA, 0, 0, 16, SHA1_BYTE_SIZE, rc4_128_encrypt,
    rc4_128_decrypt, new_sha1_digest },
  { TLS_RSA_EXPORT_WITH_RC2_CBC_40_MD5, 0, 0, 0, MD5_BYTE_SIZE, NULL, NULL,
    new_md5_digest },
  { TLS_RSA_WITH_IDEA_CBC_SHA, 0, 0, 0, SHA1_BYTE_SIZE, NULL, NULL,
    new_sha1_digest },
  { TLS_RSA_EXPORT_WITH_DES40_CBC_SHA, 0, 0, 0, SHA1_BYTE_SIZE, NULL, NULL,
    new_sha1_digest },
  { TLS_RSA_WITH_DES_CBC_SHA, 8, 8, 8, SHA1_BYTE_SIZE, des_encrypt, des_decrypt,
    new_sha1_digest },
  { TLS_RSA_WITH_3DES_EDE_CBC_SHA, 8, 8, 24, SHA1_BYTE_SIZE, des3_encrypt,
    des3_decrypt, new_sha1_digest },
...
```

Because these instances are referred to by position, you have to list each one, even if it's not supported. Notice, for example, that `TLS_RSA_WITH_IDEA_CBC_SHA` is declared, but left empty. It is never used by this implementation, but by allocating space for it, the rest of the code is allowed to refer to elements in the `CipherSuite` structure by just referencing the `suites` array.

If you wanted to create a key for a 3DES cipher suite, for example, you could invoke

```
suites[ TLS_RSA_WITH_3DES_EDE_CBC_SHA ].key_size
```

In fact, because the `CipherSuiteIdentifier` was added to `ProtectionParameters`, the key computation code can just invoke

```
suites[ parameters->suite ].key_size
```

when it needs to know how much keying material to retrieve from the master secret.

Now, recall that `MASTER_SECRET_LENGTH` is 48 bytes, regardless of cipher suite. If the selected cipher suite is AES 256, CBC, with SHA-1, you need 136 bytes of keying material — 32 bytes each for the client and server keys, 16 bytes each for the initialization vectors, and 20 bytes each for the MAC secrets. Therefore, the master secret itself must be expanded. As you can probably guess, this is done via the PRF; the only difference between the use of the PRF in key calculation and the use of the PRF in master secret expansion is that the label passed in is `"key expansion"` rather than `"master secret"`.

The key calculation routine is shown in Listing 6-41.

**Listing 6-41:** "tls.c" calculate_keys

```
/**
  6.3: Compute a key block, including MAC secrets, keys, and IVs for client & server.
Notice that the seed is server random followed by client random (whereas for master
secret computation, it's client random followed by server random).  Sheesh!
```

*(Continued)*

```
*/
static void calculate_keys( TLSParameters *parameters )
{
  // XXX assuming send suite & recv suite will always be the same
  CipherSuite *suite = &( suites[ parameters->pending_send_parameters.suite ] );
  const char *label = "key expansion";
  int key_block_length =
    suite->hash_size * 2 +
    suite->key_size * 2 +
    suite->IV_size * 2;
  char seed[ RANDOM_LENGTH * 2 ];
  unsigned char *key_block = ( unsigned char * ) malloc( key_block_length );
  unsigned char *key_block_ptr;
  ProtectionParameters *send_parameters = &parameters->pending_send_parameters;
  ProtectionParameters *recv_parameters = &parameters->pending_recv_parameters;

  memcpy( seed, parameters->server_random, RANDOM_LENGTH );
  memcpy( seed + RANDOM_LENGTH, parameters->client_random, RANDOM_LENGTH );

  PRF( parameters->master_secret, MASTER_SECRET_LENGTH,
    label, strlen( label ),
    seed, RANDOM_LENGTH * 2,
    key_block, key_block_length );

  send_parameters->MAC_secret = ( unsigned char * ) malloc( suite->hash_size );
  recv_parameters->MAC_secret = ( unsigned char * ) malloc( suite->hash_size );
  send_parameters->key = ( unsigned char * ) malloc( suite->key_size );
  recv_parameters->key = ( unsigned char * ) malloc( suite->key_size );
  send_parameters->IV = ( unsigned char * ) malloc( suite->IV_size );
  recv_parameters->IV = ( unsigned char * ) malloc( suite->IV_size );

  key_block_ptr = read_buffer( send_parameters->MAC_secret, key_block,
    suite->hash_size );
  key_block_ptr = read_buffer( recv_parameters->MAC_secret, key_block_ptr,
    suite->hash_size );
  key_block_ptr = read_buffer( send_parameters->key, key_block_ptr,
    suite->key_size );
  key_block_ptr = read_buffer( recv_parameters->key, key_block_ptr,
    suite->key_size );
  key_block_ptr = read_buffer( send_parameters->IV, key_block_ptr,
    suite->IV_size );
  key_block_ptr = read_buffer( recv_parameters->IV, key_block_ptr,
    suite->IV_size );

  free( key_block );
}
```

**NOTE** One interesting point to note about this key generation routine: It assumes that all keys are equally valid. If you recall from Chapter 2, strictly speaking, DES requires that each byte of its keys be parity adjusted. If you

**were implementing TLS with a strictly correct DES implementation, you'd need to recognize this fact and parity adjust the generated key (e.g. ensure an even number of 1 bits), or you'd get an inexplicable error when you tried to use it.**

### *Diffie-Hellman Key Exchange*

TLS 1.0 supports Diffie-Hellman key exchange in addition to RSA key exchange. Remember that, in Diffie-Hellman key exchange, neither side gets to pick the negotiated secret, but both sides end up computing the same value. This works out in the context of TLS key exchange; both sides can agree on the premaster secret, which is expanded to the master secret, which is expanded to the keying material.

Add support for DH key exchange in `send_client_key_exchange` as shown in Listing 6-42.

**Listing 6-42:** "tls.c" send_client_key_exchange with Diffie-Hellman key exchange

```
switch ( parameters->pending_send_parameters.suite ) {
  case TLS_NULL_WITH_NULL_NULL:
    // XXX this is an error, exit here
    break;
...
  case TLS_DH_DSS_EXPORT_WITH_DES40_CBC_SHA:
  case TLS_DH_DSS_WITH_DES_CBC_SHA:
  case TLS_DH_DSS_WITH_3DES_EDE_CBC_SHA:
...
    premaster_secret_len = parameters->server_dh_key.p.size;
    premaster_secret = malloc( premaster_secret_len );
    key_exchange_message_len = dh_key_exchange( &parameters->server_dh_key,
      premaster_secret, &key_exchange_message );
    break;
```

The Diffie-Hellman key exchange procedure continues as described in Chapter 3. Recall that you didn't code a specific Diffie-Hellman routine because it was essentially just a couple of calls to `mod_pow`. These calls can be integrated into a premaster secret exchange as shown in Listing 6-43.

**Listing 6-43:** "tls.c" dh_key_exchange

```
/**
 * Just compute Yc = g^a % p and return it in "key_exchange_message".  The
 * premaster secret is Ys ^ a % p.
 */
int dh_key_exchange( dh_key *server_dh_key,
                     unsigned char *premaster_secret,
                     unsigned char **key_exchange_message )
{
  huge Yc;
  huge Z;
```

*(Continued)*

```
    huge a;
    int message_size;
    short transmit_len;

    // TODO obviously, make this random, and much longer
    set_huge( &a, 6 );
    mod_pow( &server_dh_key->g, &a, &server_dh_key->p, &Yc );
    mod_pow( &server_dh_key->Y, &a, &server_dh_key->p, &Z );

    // Now copy Z into premaster secret and Yc into key_exchange_message
    memcpy( premaster_secret, Z.rep, Z.size );
    message_size = Yc.size + 2;
    transmit_len = htons( Yc.size );
    *key_exchange_message = malloc( message_size );
    memcpy( *key_exchange_message, &transmit_len, 2 );
    memcpy( *key_exchange_message + 2, Yc.rep, Yc.size );

    free_huge( &Yc );
    free_huge( &Z );
    free_huge( &a );

    return message_size;
}
```

If you've been following closely, you may be wondering where the server's dh_key value — the $p$, $g$ and $Y$ values that this key exchange relies on — come from? Although it's possible to get one from a certificate (it's officially defined, anyway), practically speaking this never happens. Instead, there's a specific *server key exchange* handshake type where the server can provide these values as well as authenticate them. This is examined in Chapter 8.

## TLS Change Cipher Spec

After the key exchange has been successfully completed, the client should send a *change cipher spec* message. Although change cipher spec can never be legally sent outside of the context of a handshake, it's not declared as a handshake message. Why? According to the specification,

> *"To help avoid pipeline stalls, ChangeCipherSpec is an independent TLS Protocol content type, and is not actually a TLS handshake message."*

This isn't made particularly clear, but it appears that they're concerned with the possibility of an implementation that automatically piggy-backs handshake messages into one large TLS message doing so with change cipher spec messages and having the other side lose this.

The change cipher spec message is a marker message, just like *server hello done* was, that doesn't include any data. It is a major milestone in the handshake process, though, because the reception of a change cipher spec message tells the other side that the key exchange has completed, and every subsequent message sent by this peer is encrypted and authenticated using it. Note that neither side should assume that the negotiated parameters are in place before receiving a change cipher spec message — it's entirely possible that, although a change cipher spec message is expected, an alert could appear in plaintext instead.

So, at this point in the key exchange, the client should send a change cipher spec and make its pending *send* parameters active, but not touch the pending *receive* parameters. This is shown in Listing 6-44.

**Listing 6-44:** "tls.c" send_change_cipher_spec

```
static int send_change_cipher_spec( int connection, TLSParameters *parameters )
{
  char          send_buffer[ 1 ];
  send_buffer[ 0 ] = 1;
  send_message( connection, content_change_cipher_spec, send_buffer, 1 );

  memcpy( &parameters->active_send_parameters,
          &parameters->pending_send_parameters,
          sizeof( ProtectionParameters ) );

  init_protection_parameters( &parameters->pending_send_parameters );

  return 1;
}
```

As promised, this is pretty simple. The server then sends a change cipher spec of its own, and this should be accounted for as in Listing 6-45.

**Listing 6-45:** "tls.c" receive_tls_msg with support for change cipher spec

```
...
  if ( message.type == content_handshake )
  {
...
  }
  else if ( message.type == content_change_cipher_spec )
  {
    while ( ( read_pos - decrypted_message ) < decrypted_length )
    {
      unsigned char change_cipher_spec_type;

      read_pos = read_buffer( ( void * ) &change_cipher_spec_type,
        ( void * ) read_pos, 1 );

      if ( change_cipher_spec_type != 1 )
      {
        printf( "Error - received message ChangeCipherSpec, but type != 1\n" );
        exit( 0 );
      }
```

```
      else
      {
        memcpy( &parameters->active_recv_parameters,
                &parameters->pending_recv_parameters,
                sizeof( ProtectionParameters ) );
        init_protection_parameters( &parameters->pending_recv_parameters );
      }
    }
  }
```

Now, when the server sends its `change_cipher_spec` message, the pending receive parameters are updated and made the active receive parameters. Technically, the change cipher spec messages can "cross" on the wire. The server may legally send its change cipher spec message as soon as it receives a proper key exchange from the client; it doesn't strictly have to wait until the client sends a change cipher spec.

## TLS Finished

So, the key exchange has been completed, both sides have agreed that the pending parameters are now the active parameters. It's time to start using the connection, right?

Well, that's what the designers of SSLv2 thought, too. As it turns out, this was the fatal flaw in SSLv2. After the key exchange had completed, the connection was used immediately to transfer data. The problem with this is that it doesn't take into account man-in-the-middle attacks that occur before the key exchange. Although the key exchange protocol designed around X.509 certificates does an admirable job of protecting against man-in-the-middle attacks against the public key, the malicious man in the middle can intercept and modify all the exchanges prior to this.

How can an attacker use this to his advantage? Well, he could, for instance, change the client hello message to list only one possibility for a cipher suite — DES with MD5 MAC. If he has a DES-cracking machine, the key exchange can proceed, and he can decode the communications at his leisure.

In general, both sides need a way to strongly authenticate that what they sent was what was received. The way TLS accomplishes this is to require both sides to send a *finished* message before the handshake can be considered complete. Both of these finished messages must be sent before the negotiated parameters can be used for application data, and the finished messages themselves are sent using the negotiated encryption and authentication parameters. The contents of this finished message are a 12-byte *verify* array whose contents are based on the hash of the contents of all of the handshake messages to this point.

### Computing the Verify Message

To compute this verify message, then, it's necessary to keep a running hash of every byte that's sent or received with a message type of *handshake*. This is, incidentally, why I spent so much time in Chapter 4 on creating an "updateable" HMAC function; without the updateable HMAC function, it would have been necessary here to buffer all this data and pass it as a gigantic memory array into the HMAC function.

Instead, following these steps:

1. Add a pair of `digest_ctx` objects to the `TLSParameters` as shown in Listing 6-46; the verify data is actually based on a combination of both MD5 and SHA (similar to the PRF).

**Listing 6-46:** "tls.h" TLSParameters with digest contexts

```
typedef struct
{
...
  int                  server_hello_done;
  digest_ctx           md5_handshake_digest;
  digest_ctx           sha1_handshake_digest;
}
TLSParameters;
```

2. At the top of `tls_connect`, initialize them both, in Listing 6-47.

**Listing 6-47:** "tls.c" tls_connect with handshake digests

```
int tls_connect( int connection,
                 TLSParameters *parameters )
{
  init_parameters( parameters );

  new_md5_digest( &parameters->md5_handshake_digest );
  new_sha1_digest( &parameters->sha1_handshake_digest );
```

3. Modify `send_handshake_message`, as shown in Listing 6-48, to update the running digest every time a handshake message is sent.

**Listing 6-48:** "tls.c" send_handshake_message with handshake digest update

```
static int send_handshake_message( int connection,
                                    int msg_type,
                                    const unsigned char *message,
                                    int message_len,
                                    TLSParameters *parameters )
{
...
  update_digest( &parameters->md5_handshake_digest, send_buffer,
    send_buffer_size );
```

*(Continued)*

```
update_digest( &parameters->sha1_handshake_digest, send_buffer,
  send_buffer_size );

response = send_message( connection, content_handshake, send_buffer,
  send_buffer_size );
```

4. Because `send_handshake_message` now takes a new parameter — the `TLSParameters` — update the invocations to it to include this, as shown in Listing 6-49.

**Listing 6-49:** "tls.c" send_handshake_message updates

```
static int send_client_hello( int connection, TLSParameters *parameters )

{

...

  status = send_handshake_message( connection, client_hello, send_buffer,
    send_buffer_size, parameters );

...

static int send_client_key_exchange( int connection, TLSParameters *parameters )

{
...

  if ( send_handshake_message( connection, client_key_exchange,

      key_exchange_message, key_exchange_message_len, parameters ) )

  {
```

5. Update the running digest within `receive_tls_message`, if the type of the message is `content_handshake`, as in Listing 6-50.

**Listing 6-50:** "tls.c" receive_tls_message with handshake digest update

```
static int receive_tls_msg( int connection,
                            TLSParameters *parameters )
{
...
  if ( message.type == content_handshake )
  {
    while ( ( read_pos - decrypted_message ) < decrypted_length )
    {
      Handshake handshake;
      // Keep track of beginning of message for handshake digest update below
      const unsigned char *handshake_msg_start = read_pos;

...

      update_digest( &parameters->md5_handshake_digest, handshake_msg_start,
        handshake.length + 4 );
      update_digest( &parameters->sha1_handshake_digest, handshake_msg_start,
        handshake.length + 4 );
    }
```

6. With the handshake digest defined and updated, the client can send its `finished` message, in Listing 6-51.

**Listing 6-51:** "tls.c" tls_connect with client finished message

```
if ( !( send_change_cipher_spec( connection, parameters ) ) )
{
  perror( "Unable to send client change cipher spec" );
  return 4;
}

// This message will be encrypted using the newly negotiated keys
if ( !( send_finished( connection, parameters ) ) )
{
  perror( "Unable to send client finished" );
  return 5;
}
```

7. `send_finished` itself is straightforward, as shown in Listing 6-52.

**Listing 6-52:** "tls.c" send_finished

```
static int send_finished( int connection,
                          TLSParameters *parameters )
{
  unsigned char verify_data[ VERIFY_DATA_LEN ];

  compute_verify_data( "client finished", parameters, verify_data );
  send_handshake_message( connection, finished, verify_data, VERIFY_DATA_LEN,
    parameters );

  return 1;
}
```

8. Of course, as you can likely guess, the challenge is in the computation of `verify data`. This is shown in Listing 6-53.

**Listing 6-53:** "tls.c" compute_verify_data

```
/**
 * 7.4.9:
 * verify_data = PRF( master_secret, "client finished", MD5(handshake_messages)
 * + SHA-1(handshake_messages)) [0..11]
 *
 * master_secret = PRF( pre_master_secret, "master secret", ClientHello.random +
 *   ServerHello.random );
 * always 48 bytes in length.
 */
#define VERIFY_DATA_LEN 12

static void compute_verify_data( const char *finished_label,
                                 TLSParameters *parameters,
```

*(Continued)*

```
                                char *verify_data )
{
  unsigned char handshake_hash[ ( MD5_RESULT_SIZE * sizeof( int ) ) +
                                ( SHA1_RESULT_SIZE * sizeof( int ) ) ];

  finalize_digest( &parameters->md5_handshake_digest );
  finalize_digest( &parameters->sha1_handshake_digest );

  memcpy( handshake_hash, parameters->md5_handshake_digest.hash, MD5_BYTE_SIZE
);
  memcpy( handshake_hash + MD5_BYTE_SIZE, parameters->sha1_handshake_digest.hash,
    SHA1_BYTE_SIZE );

  PRF( parameters->master_secret, MASTER_SECRET_LENGTH,
       finished_label, strlen( finished_label ),
       handshake_hash,
       MD5_RESULT_SIZE * sizeof( int ) + SHA1_RESULT_SIZE * sizeof( int ),
       verify_data, VERIFY_DATA_LEN );
}
```

The verify data is a PRF expansion of "client finished" with both hashes concatenated next to one another. The result is 12 bytes, and both sides end up computing the same value.

9. Of course, the client must wait for the server to send its `finished` message as well. Update `tls_connect` to wait for the `server_finished` as shown in Listing 6-54.

**Listing 6-54:** "tls.c" tls_connect with server finished support

```
parameters->server_finished = 0;
while ( !parameters->server_finished )
{
  if ( receive_tls_msg( connection, parameters ) < 0 )
  {
    perror( "Unable to receive server finished" );
    return 6;
  }
}
```

**NOTE**  This call will also be the first time the client receives the change cipher spec message.

10. This requires that you also add a `server_finished` flag, similar to the `server_hello_done` flag, in `TLSParameters`, in Listing 6-55:

**Listing 6-55:** "tls.c" TLSParameters

```
typedef struct
{
```

```
...
  int                   server_hello_done;
  int                   server_finished;
...
}
TLSParameters;
```

11. Update `tls_receive_message` to process the `server_finished` message in Listing 6-56.

**Listing 6-56:** "tls.c" tls_receive_message with server finished support

```
        switch ( handshake.msg_type )
        {
...
          case finished:
            {
              read_pos = parse_finished( read_pos, handshake.length, parameters );
              if ( read_pos == NULL )
              {
                send_alert_message( connection, illegal_parameter );
                return -1;
              }
            }
            break;
```

12. Now you can parse the finished message, in Listing 6-57.

**Listing 6-57:** "tls.c" parse_finished

```
static unsigned char *parse_finished( unsigned char *read_pos,
                                      int pdu_length,
                                      TLSParameters *parameters )
{
  unsigned char verify_data[ VERIFY_DATA_LEN ];

  parameters->server_finished = 1;

  compute_verify_data( "server finished", parameters, verify_data );

  if ( memcmp( read_pos, verify_data, VERIFY_DATA_LEN ) )
  {
    return NULL;
  }

  return read_pos + pdu_length;
}
```

Here, `compute_verify_data` is called again to recompute the verification data, and the received data is compared with the computed data.

### Correctly Receiving the Finished Message

Unfortunately, `parse_finished`, in Listing 6-57, doesn't work. The handshake digests were finalized when `verify_data` was called the first time around, but they need to be finalized again when the server sends its finished message. And because the server's finished message is based on a hash including the *client's* finished message you can't just reuse the original hashes; the server sends verification of a different hash code.

Therefore, it's necessary to modify `compute_verify_data` so that it doesn't operate on the running hash. The easiest way to do this is to make a temporary copy and operate on that temporary copy, as in Listing 6-58.

**Listing 6-58:** "tls.c" compute_verify_data with temporary copy

```
void compute_handshake_hash( TLSParameters *parameters, unsigned char
*handshake_hash )
{
  digest_ctx tmp_md5_handshake_digest;
  digest_ctx tmp_sha1_handshake_digest;

  // "cheating".  Copy the handshake digests into local memory (and change
  // the hash pointer) so that we can finalize twice (again in "recv")
  memcpy( &tmp_md5_handshake_digest, &parameters->md5_handshake_digest,
    sizeof( digest_ctx ) );
  memcpy( &tmp_sha1_handshake_digest, &parameters->sha1_handshake_digest,
    sizeof( digest_ctx ) );

  tmp_md5_handshake_digest.hash = ( unsigned int * ) malloc( MD5_BYTE_SIZE );
  tmp_sha1_handshake_digest.hash = ( unsigned int * ) malloc( SHA1_BYTE_SIZE );
  memcpy( tmp_md5_handshake_digest.hash, parameters->md5_handshake_digest.hash,
    MD5_BYTE_SIZE );
  memcpy( tmp_sha1_handshake_digest.hash, parameters->sha1_handshake_digest.hash,
    SHA1_BYTE_SIZE );

  finalize_digest( &tmp_md5_handshake_digest );
  finalize_digest( &tmp_sha1_handshake_digest );

  memcpy( handshake_hash, tmp_md5_handshake_digest.hash, MD5_BYTE_SIZE );
  memcpy( handshake_hash + MD5_BYTE_SIZE, tmp_sha1_handshake_digest.hash,
    SHA1_BYTE_SIZE );

  free( tmp_md5_handshake_digest.hash );
  free( tmp_sha1_handshake_digest.hash );
}

static void compute_verify_data( const char *finished_label,
                                 TLSParameters *parameters,
                                 char *verify_data )
{
  // Per 6.2.3.1 - encrypted data should always be followed by a MAC
```

```
unsigned char handshake_hash[ ( MD5_RESULT_SIZE * sizeof( int ) ) +
                             ( SHA1_RESULT_SIZE * sizeof( int ) ) ];

compute_handshake_hash( parameters, handshake_hash );

// First, compute the verify data
PRF( parameters->master_secret, MASTER_SECRET_LENGTH,
    finished_label, strlen( finished_label ),
    handshake_hash,
    MD5_RESULT_SIZE * sizeof( int ) + SHA1_RESULT_SIZE * sizeof( int ),
    verify_data, VERIFY_DATA_LEN );
}
```

Now, the same `compute_verify_data` function can be used both when sending and receiving finished messages.

That's it, right? The key exchange is complete, and the finished messages have been exchanged and verified. Everything is in place except for the small matter of actually encrypting and MAC'ing the data.

## Secure Data Transfer with TLS

Conceptually, applying TLS is simple after the keys have been agreed upon. First, the whole block of data to be sent, including the TLS message header, is run through the MAC algorithm and the result is appended to the message. There's a chicken-and-the-egg problem here, though. The MAC includes the TLS header, which includes the length of the following buffer, which includes the MAC in its length. So when MAC'ing, what length is used? The transmitted length is the length of the content, plus the MAC; what's MAC'ed is just the length of the content.

If the bulk encryption algorithm requires padding, the length also indicates padding. Again, the MAC buffer does not reflect the padding length. And, of course, the whole thing — header, padding, MAC and all — are encrypted using the bulk encryption algorithm in force before being sent.

### Assigning Sequence Numbers

As a protection against replay attacks, each packet is also assigned a sequence number. The sequence numbers start at 0 whenever a `change_cipher_spec` is received and is incremented each time a new `TLSMessage` is sent or received. Each side maintains a separate counter, and this counter is prepended to each message before MAC'ing it.

Declare the sequence number as shown in Listing 6-59 and initialize it as shown in Listing 6-60.

**Listing 6-59:** "tls.h" ProtectionParameters with seq_num

```
typedef struct
{
…

  unsigned long          seq_num;
}
ProtectionParameters;
```

**Listing 6-60:** "tls.c" init_protection_parameters with seq_num

```
void init_protection_parameters( ProtectionParameters *parameters )
{
  parameters->MAC_secret = NULL;
  parameters->key = NULL;
  parameters->IV = NULL;

  parameters->seq_num = 0;
  parameters->suite = TLS_NULL_WITH_NULL_NULL;
}

static int send_change_cipher_spec( int connection, TLSParameters *parameters )
{
  send_message( connection, content_change_cipher_spec, send_buffer, 1,
              &parameters->active_send_parameters );
…
  // Per 6.1: The sequence number must be set to zero whenever a connection
  // state is made the active state... the first record which is transmitted
  // under a particular connection state should use sequence number 0.
  parameters->pending_send_parameters.seq_num = 0;

  memcpy( &parameters->active_send_parameters,
          &parameters->pending_send_parameters,
          sizeof( ProtectionParameters ) );
…
static int receive_tls_msg( int connection,
                            TLSParameters *parameters )
{
…
  else if ( message.type == content_change_cipher_spec )
  {
…
      if ( change_cipher_spec_type != 1 )
      {
        printf( "Error - received message of type ChangeCipherSpec, but type !=
1\n" );
        exit( 0 );
      }
      else
      {
        parameters->pending_recv_parameters.seq_num = 0;
```

```
memcpy( &parameters->active_recv_parameters,
        &parameters->pending_recv_parameters,
        sizeof( ProtectionParameters ) );
```
...

Note that the sequence number is never transmitted, encrypted or otherwise; it's just prepended to the MAC buffer before the packet is MAC'ed. Therefore, given a content buffer of "content", the buffer that is MAC'ed looks like this:

| SEQUENCE NUM | MESSAGE TYPE | VERSION | CONTENT LENGTH | CONTENT |
|---|---|---|---|---|
| 4 bytes | 1 byte | 2 bytes | 2 bytes | variable |

A digest is produced over this data.
What's actually transmitted, on the other hand, is

| MESSAGE TYPE | VERSION | CONTENT LEN + MAC LEN + PADDING LEN | CONTENT | MAC |
|---|---|---|---|---|
| 1 byte | 2 bytes | 2 bytes | variable | variable |

But this is, of course, encrypted before sending. Notice that the buffer is MAC'ed first and then encrypted. The order is clearly important so that the other side can correctly receive it.

## Supporting Outgoing Encryption

To support encryption — outgoing — the only function that needs to be updated is the `send_message` function. In order to apply the active cipher suite, it needs to be sent the active `ProtectionParameters` so that it can check to see what cipher suite is active, and apply that cipher suite. Remember that `TLS_NULL_WITH_NULL_NULL` is a valid cipher suite, and it's the one that's active when the handshake first starts. It just tells `send_message` to do no MAC nor encrypt. In this way, there's always a cipher suite active, even if it's a "do nothing" cipher suite.

The first thing `send_message` must do is to create the MAC buffer and compute the MAC. To do this, follow these steps:

1. Check for an active digest and apply it to the contents as shown in Listing 6-61.

**Listing 6-61:** "tls.c" send_message with MAC support

```
static int send_message( int connection,
                         int content_type,
                         const unsigned char *content,
                         short content_len,
```

(Continued)

```
                          ProtectionParameters *parameters )
{
  TLSPlaintext header;
  unsigned char *send_buffer;
  int send_buffer_size;
  unsigned char *mac = NULL;
  digest_ctx digest;
  CipherSuite *active_suite;

  active_suite = &suites[ parameters->suite ];

  if ( active_suite->new_digest )
  {
    // Allocate enough space for the 8-byte sequence number, the 5-byte pseudo
    // header, and the content.
    unsigned char *mac_buffer = malloc( 13 + content_len );
    int sequence_num;

    mac = ( unsigned char * ) malloc( active_suite->hash_size );
    active_suite->new_digest( &digest );

    memset( mac_buffer, 0x0, 8 );
    sequence_num = htonl( parameters->seq_num );
    memcpy( mac_buffer + 4, &sequence_num, sizeof( int ) );

    // These will be overwritten below
    header.type = content_type;
    header.version.major = 3;
    header.version.minor = 1;
    header.length = htons( content_len );
    mac_buffer[ 8 ] = header.type;
    mac_buffer[ 9 ] = header.version.major;
    mac_buffer[ 10 ] = header.version.minor;
    memcpy( mac_buffer + 11, &header.length, sizeof( short ) );

    memcpy( mac_buffer + 13, content, content_len );
    hmac( parameters->MAC_secret,
          active_suite->hash_size,
          mac_buffer, 13 + content_len,
          &digest );

    memcpy( mac, digest.hash, active_suite->hash_size );

    free( mac_buffer );
  }

  send_buffer_size = content_len + active_suite->hash_size;
...

  parameters->seq_num++;
```

```
free( send_buffer );

return 0;
}
```

If the current active protection parameters include a digest, a MAC buffer is built as described above, MAC'ed, and thrown away; after the MAC itself has been computed, the MAC buffer is immaterial to the remainder of the function.

2. Check to see if the active cipher suite has a block size (that is, is not a stream cipher). If so, add any required padding, as shown in Listing 6-62.

**Listing 6-62:** "tls.c" send_message with padding support

```
unsigned char padding_length = 0;
...
send_buffer_size = content_len + active_suite->hash_size;

if ( active_suite->block_size )
{
  padding_length = active_suite->block_size -
    ( send_buffer_size % active_suite->block_size );
  send_buffer_size += padding_length;
}

// Add space for the header, but only after computing padding
send_buffer_size +=5;
```

3. Build the actual send buffer. Recall Listing 6-15 where send_message was initially defined; the send buffer was simply the TLS header followed by the contents, verbatim. Now, it's the TLS header, followed by the contents, followed by any required padding, followed by the MAC. The updated send buffer is shown in Listing 6-63.

**Listing 6-63:** "tls.c" send buffer

```
send_buffer = ( unsigned char * ) malloc( send_buffer_size );
if ( mac )
{
  memcpy( send_buffer + content_len + 5, mac, active_suite->hash_size );
  free( mac );
}

if ( padding_length > 0 )
{
  unsigned char *padding;
  for ( padding = send_buffer + send_buffer_size - 1;
        padding > ( send_buffer + ( send_buffer_size - padding_length - 1 ) );
        padding-- )
```

*(Continued)*

```
  {
    *padding = ( padding_length - 1 );
  }
}

header.type = content_type;
header.version.major = 3;
header.version.minor = 1;
header.length = htons( content_len + active_suite->hash_size + padding_length );
```

4. The send buffer itself needs to be encrypted if the cipher suite calls for it (remember that TLS_NULL_WITH_MD5 is a legitimate cipher suite that calls for authentication but no encryption). The encryption is shown in Listing 6-64.

**Listing 6-64:** "tls.c" send_message with encryption

```
memcpy( send_buffer + 5, content, content_len );

if ( active_suite->bulk_encrypt )
{
  unsigned char *encrypted_buffer = malloc( send_buffer_size );
  // The first 5 bytes (the header) aren't encrypted
  memcpy( encrypted_buffer, send_buffer, 5 );
  active_suite->bulk_encrypt( send_buffer + 5, send_buffer_size - 5,
    encrypted_buffer + 5, parameters->IV, parameters->key );
  free( send_buffer );
  send_buffer = encrypted_buffer;
}

if ( send( connection, ( void * ) send_buffer, send_buffer_size, 0 ) <
    send_buffer_size )
```

The original send buffer is encrypted and then thrown away; the encrypted buffer is the send buffer, which is what's transmitted over the wire. Notice that the header itself is not encrypted; this is necessary so that the receiver knows how many bytes to process in the current packet. Everything following the header is encrypted, though.

## Adding Support for Stream Ciphers

The encryption routine in Listing 6-64 almost works, but not quite. Recall from the calculate_keys routine in Listing 6-41 that if the cipher suite called for an initialization vector, one was computed, but otherwise, parameters->IV was left as a null pointer. This is fine for block ciphers, but causes a failure if you try to use this routine for the RC4 routine, which expects a state vector in this position.

**NOTE** The state vector was developed in Chapter 2, in Listing 2-47.

You might try to get around this by changing the IV size in the cipher suite declaration to 256 so that you'd get a state vector here. Unfortunately, this won't work: You'd get 256 pseudo-random bytes rather than an array of 0's as `rc4_encrypt` expects on its first call. The ideal way to handle this would be to define a `cipher_init` routine that should be called on first invocation. However, the simple hack in Listing 6-65 works well enough:

**Listing 6-65:** "tls.c" calculate_keys with a special RC4 exception

```
static void calculate_keys( TLSParameters *parameters )

{
...
  switch ( suite->id )
  {
    case TLS_RSA_EXPORT_WITH_RC4_40_MD5:
    case TLS_RSA_WITH_RC4_128_MD5:
    case TLS_RSA_WITH_RC4_128_SHA:
    case TLS_DH_anon_EXPORT_WITH_RC4_40_MD5:
    case TLS_DH_anon_WITH_RC4_128_MD5:
      {
      rc4_state *read_state = malloc( sizeof( rc4_state ) );
      rc4_state *write_state = malloc( sizeof( rc4_state ) );
      read_state->i = read_state->j = write_state->i = write_state->j = 0;
      send_parameters->IV = ( unsigned char * ) read_state;
      recv_parameters->IV = ( unsigned char * ) write_state;
      memset( read_state->S, '\0', RC4_STATE_ARRAY_LEN );
      memset( write_state->S, '\0', RC4_STATE_ARRAY_LEN );
      }
      break;
    default:
      break;
  }

  free( key_block );
```

At this point, `send_parameters->IV` is no longer necessarily an IV, but a void pointer to the state of the cipher suite. Although the code would be clearer if it were renamed, the specification refers specifically to IV in several places, so leave it this way.

## Updating Each Invocation of send_message

Of course, because you're now applying the active encryption function to every sent message, you must also go through and update each invocation of `send_message` to include the active `ProtectionParameters`, as in Listing 6-66.

**Listing 6-66:** "tls.c" with protection parameters sent to send_message

```
static int send_handshake_message( int connection,
                                    int msg_type,
                                    const unsigned char *message,
                                    int message_len,
                                    TLSParameters *parameters )
{
...

  return send_message( connection, content_handshake, send_buffer,
    send_buffer_size, &parameters->active_send_parameters );
...
static int send_alert_message( int connection,
                               int alert_code,
                               ProtectionParameters *parameters )
{
...

  return send_message( connection, content_alert, buffer, 2, parameters );
...
static int send_change_cipher_spec( int connection, TLSParameters *parameters )
{
...

  send_message( connection, content_change_cipher_spec, send_buffer, 1,
            &parameters->active_send_parameters );
...
static int receive_tls_msg( int connection,
                            TLSParameters *parameters )
{
...

      if ( ( status = send_alert_message( connection, illegal_parameter,
            &parameters->active_send_parameters ) ) )
...
        read_pos = parse_server_hello( read_pos, handshake.length, parameters
);
        if ( read_pos == NULL )  /* error occurred */
        {
          send_alert_message( connection, illegal_parameter,
            &parameters->active_send_parameters );
...
        read_pos = parse_finished( read_pos, handshake.length, parameters );
        if ( read_pos == NULL )
        {
          send_alert_message( connection, illegal_parameter,
            &parameters->active_send_parameters );
```

Notice that the alert messages need to be updated, too. If an alert is sent after a handshake has completed, the alert itself must be encrypted. Although this won't come up during an initial handshake, send_alert_message must include a ProtectionParameters value because send_message does.

## Decrypting and Authenticating

Just as encryption was handled entirely within `send_message`, decrypting can be handled entirely within `receive_tls_msg`. This time, you don't even need to update the parameter list because it already accepts a `TLSParameters`; it just needs to look at the active receive parameters and apply them as necessary. Decryption and authentication is shown in Listing 6-67.

**Listing 6-67:** "tls.c" receive_tls_msg with decrypt support

```
static int receive_tls_msg( int connection,
                            TLSParameters *parameters )
{
  TLSPlaintext  message;
  unsigned char *read_pos, *msg_buf, *decrypted_message, *encrypted_message;
  unsigned char header[ 5 ];  // size of TLSPlaintext
  int bytes_read, accum_bytes;
  int decrypted_length;
// Read header as usual - header is not encrypted
...
    encrypted_message = ( char * ) malloc( message.length );

    // keep looping & appending until all bytes are accounted for
    accum_bytes = 0;

    msg_buf = encrypted_message;
    while ( accum_bytes < message.length )
    {
// Read the buffer as before, but update encrypted_message now
...
    }
    // If a cipherspec is active, all of "encrypted_message" will be encrypted.
    // Must decrypt it before continuing.  This will change the message length
    // in all cases, since decrypting also involves verifying a MAC (unless the
    // active cipher spec is NULL_WITH_NULL_NULL).
    decrypted_message = NULL;
    decrypted_length = tls_decrypt( header, encrypted_message, message.length,
      &decrypted_message, &parameters->active_recv_parameters );

    free( encrypted_message );

    if ( decrypted_length < 0 )
    {
      send_alert_message( connection, bad_record_mac,
        &parameters->active_send_parameters );
      return -1;
    }
    parameters->active_recv_parameters.seq_num++;
  }
```

*(Continued)*

```
    read_pos = decrypted_message;
    if ( message.type == content_handshake )
    {
...
    }
    free( decrypted_message );

    return decrypted_length;
}
```

And everything else stays the same; at this point, the message has been decrypted and can be processed just as if it had been received in plaintext. In fact, this code is necessary to process a server finished handshake message because, per the specification, server finished is *always* sent using the active cipher spec.

The heavy lifting of decryption is handled by tls_decrypt, which is responsible for not only decrypting the buffer, but verifying its MAC as well. If the MAC doesn't verify, tls_decrypt returns –1; otherwise it returns the length of the decrypted buffer. As mentioned earlier, this is always different than the original buffer length, even for stream ciphers, as the tls_decrypt function strips off the MAC after decrypting the block.

Without further ado, tls_decrypt itself is presented in Listing 6-68.

**Listing 6-68:** "tls.c" tls_decrypt

```
/**
 * Decrypt a message and verify its MAC according to the active cipher spec
 * (as given by "parameters").  Free the space allocated by encrypted message
 * and allocate new space for the decrypted message (if decrypting is "identity",
 * then decrypted will point to encrypted).  The caller must always issue a
 * "free decrypted_message".
 * Return the length of the message, or -1 if the MAC doesn't verify.  The return
 * value will almost always be different than "encrypted_length", since it strips
 * off the MAC if present as well as bulk cipher padding (if a block cipher
 * algorithm is being used).
 */
static int tls_decrypt( const unsigned char *header, // needed for MAC verification
                        unsigned char *encrypted_message,
                        short encrypted_length,
                        unsigned char **decrypted_message,
                        ProtectionParameters *parameters )
{
    short decrypted_length;
    digest_ctx digest;
    unsigned char *mac_buffer;
    int sequence_number;
    short length;
    CipherSuite *active_suite = &( suites[ parameters->suite ] );
```

```
*decrypted_message = ( unsigned char * ) malloc( encrypted_length );

if ( active_suite->bulk_decrypt )
{
  active_suite->bulk_decrypt( encrypted_message, encrypted_length,
    *decrypted_message, parameters->IV, parameters->key );
  decrypted_length = encrypted_length;
  // Strip off padding
  if ( active_suite->block_size )
  {
    decrypted_length -= ( (*decrypted_message)[ encrypted_length - 1 ] + 1 );
  }
}
else
{
  // Do nothing, no bulk cipher algorithm chosen.
  // Still have to memcpy so that "free" in caller is consistent
  decrypted_length = encrypted_length;
  memcpy( *decrypted_message, encrypted_message, encrypted_length );
}

// Now, verify the MAC (if the active cipher suite includes one)
if ( active_suite->new_digest )
{
  active_suite->new_digest( &digest );

  decrypted_length -= ( digest.hash_len * sizeof( int ) );

  // Allocate enough space for the 8-byte sequence number, the TLSPlainText
  // header, and the fragment (e.g. the decrypted message).
  mac_buffer = malloc( 13 + decrypted_length );
  memset( mac_buffer, 0x0, 13 + decrypted_length );
  sequence_number = htonl( parameters->seq_num );
  memcpy( mac_buffer + 4, &sequence_number, sizeof( int ) );

  // Copy first three bytes of header; last two bytes reflected the
  // message length, with MAC attached.  Since the MAC was computed
  // by the other side before it was attached (obviously), that MAC
  // was computed using the original length.
  memcpy( mac_buffer + 8, header, 3 );
  length = htons( decrypted_length );
  memcpy( mac_buffer + 11, &length, 2 );
  memcpy( mac_buffer + 13, *decrypted_message, decrypted_length );

  hmac( parameters->MAC_secret, digest.hash_len * sizeof( int ),
    mac_buffer, decrypted_length + 13, &digest );

  if ( memcmp( digest.hash,
               (*decrypted_message) + decrypted_length,
               digest.hash_len * sizeof( int ) ) )
```

*(Continued)*

```
  {
    return -1;
  }

  free( mac_buffer );
}

  return decrypted_length;
}
```

This is essentially the inverse of the encryption performed in `send_message`. There aren't any real surprises here; the buffer is decrypted and a MAC buffer is built and verified. The MAC buffer is built the same as it is in `send_message`; if you're so inclined, you could probably refactor this into a common routine and share it between the two. After the local MAC has been computed, verifying it is just a matter of comparing it, byte-for-byte, with the MAC that the server sent.

> **NOTE** Technically, there's a security flaw in this implementation. According to the specification, if the padding byte is *x* then it must be preceded by *x* bytes of the byte *x*. This implementation doesn't explicitly verify this so a determined attacker can attempt to take advantage of this and determine the length of the original plaintext.
>
> This vulnerability is highly theoretical and discussed in more detail at `http://www.openssl.org/~bodo/tls-cbc.txt`; on the other hand, it's trivial to defend against as long as you're aware of it — just verify that the padding bytes equal the padding length.

## TLS Send

That's it. The TLS handshake is complete, and `tls_connect` returns control back up to the calling function, which, in this case, is the main routine of the HTTPS utility. From this point on, nothing can be sent on this connection unless it's encrypted, authenticated, and prepended with a correct TLS header. So, as you recall from Listing 6-3, each call to the socket-level `send` function is replaced with a call to `tls_send`. With the infrastructure developed in the previous sections, this is simple to implement, in Listing 6-69.

**Listing 6-69:** "tls.c" tls_send

```
int tls_send( int connection,
              const char *application_data,
              int length,
              int options,
              TLSParameters *parameters )
{
  send_message( connection, content_application_data, application_data, length,
    &parameters->active_send_parameters );
```

```
    return length;
}
```

This is nothing but a wrapper around `send_message`, which examines the active protection parameters and applies them to the data buffer before sending it on.

## TLS Receive

`tls_recv`, shown in Listing 6-70, can take advantage of the decrypt support added to `receive_tls_message`. However, `receive_tls_message` expected to handle the received packet after decrypting it. `tls_recv` wants the data itself, so `receive_tls_message` also needs to be updated as shown in Listing 6-71 to optionally pass back a chunk of decrypted data.

**Listing 6-70:** "tls_recv"

```
int tls_recv( int connection, char *target_buffer, int buffer_size, int options,
            TLSParameters *parameters )
{
  int bytes_decrypted = 0;

  bytes_decrypted = receive_tls_msg( connection, target_buffer, buffer_size,
    parameters );

  return bytes_decrypted;
}
```

**Listing 6-71:** "receive_tls_msg" with optional response buffer

```
static int receive_tls_msg( int connection,
                            char *buffer,
                            int bufsz,
                            TLSParameters *parameters )
{
  if ( message.type == content_handshake )
  {
...
  else if ( message.type == content_application_data )
  {
    memcpy( buffer, decrypted_message, decrypted_length );
  }
...
```

This means that the invocations of `receive_tls_msg` in `tls_connect` must also be updated to pass a null pointer, shown in Listing 6-72.

**Listing 6-72:** "tls.c" tls_connect with receive_tls_msg calls updated

```
int tls_connect( int connection,
                 TLSParameters *parameters )
{
```

```
...
  while ( !parameters->server_hello_done )
  {
    if ( receive_tls_msg( connection, NULL, 0, parameters ) < 0 )
...
  while ( !parameters->server_finished )
  {
    if ( receive_tls_msg( connection, NULL, 0, parameters ) < 0 )
...
```

This change is just necessary to satisfy the compiler; at no point does `receive_tls_msg` actually check this pointer for NULL. If a handshake message is expected and application data arrives, you get an unhelpful segmentation violation.

There's still a problem here. If you glance back at the implementation of `display_result` in Listing 6-3, you notice that it calls for a buffer of data at a time — in this case, 255 bytes. However, there's no guarantee that this much data is available in the next TLS packet, nor is there a guarantee that there isn't more. Therefore, whenever the application calls `tls_recv` with a buffer set to receive a chunk of application data, the routine must check to see if there's any left over from a previous call, as well as store any that was decrypted but that the user didn't ask for.

To accommodate variable-length input, follow these steps:

1. Add a buffer to the end of the `TLSParameters` structure as shown in Listing 6-73.

**Listing 6-73:** "tls.h" TLSParameters with buffering support

```
typedef struct
{
...
  char                *unread_buffer;
  int                 unread_length;
}
TLSParameters;
```

2. `receive_tls_msg` must also be updated to check this buffer for any unread bytes whenever the application asks for more data, as well as to buffer any data that was decrypted but that the user didn't ask for. This is shown in Listing 6-74.

**Listing 6-74:** "tls.c" receive_tls_msg with buffering support

```
void init_parameters( TLSParameters *parameters,
                      int renegotiate )
{
...
  parameters->server_hello_done = 0;
  parameters->server_finished = 0;
```

```
  parameters->unread_buffer = NULL;
  parameters->unread_length = 0;
}

static int receive_tls_msg( int connection,
                            char *buffer,
                            int bufsz,
                            TLSParameters *parameters )
{
...
  int bytes_read, accum_bytes;
  int decrypted_length;

  // First, check to see if there's any data left over from a previous read.
  // If there is, pass that back up.
  // This means that if the caller isn't quick about reading available data,
  // TLS alerts can be missed.
  if ( parameters->unread_buffer != NULL )
  {
    decrypted_message = parameters->unread_buffer;
    decrypted_length = parameters->unread_length;
    parameters->unread_buffer = NULL;
    parameters->unread_length = 0;

    message.type = content_application_data;
  }
  else
  {
    if ( recv( connection, header, 5, 0 ) <= 0 )
...
  }

  read_pos = decrypted_message;
...
  else if ( message.type == content_application_data )
  {
    if ( decrypted_length <= bufsz )
    {
      memcpy( buffer, decrypted_message, decrypted_length );
    }
    else
    {
      // Need to hang on to a buffer of data here and pass it back for the
      // next call
      memcpy( buffer, decrypted_message, bufsz );
      parameters->unread_length = decrypted_length - bufsz;
      parameters->unread_buffer = malloc( parameters->unread_length );
      memcpy( parameters->unread_buffer, decrypted_message + bufsz,
        parameters->unread_length );
```

*(Continued)*

```
        decrypted_length = bufsz;
    }
  }
}
```

Now, if there's any data left over from a previous call, as much as the caller asked for is returned. If there's less than the caller asked for, only what's available is returned; the caller must invoke another call if it wants the next chunk of data. This could be made more robust — and more complicated — if it went ahead and read the next available `TLSMessage`, concatenated *that* on top of whatever it had buffered, and tried to fill up the buffer the client requested. Of course, in any case, if the caller requested less data than is available in the buffer, the remaining data must be held on to. `receive_tls_message` accomplishes this by masquerading any buffered data as `decrypted_message`; whether the client consumes all of it or not, it ends up in the `decrypted_length <= bufsz` else-case and is rebuffered.

If you closely compared the `display_result` listing of 6-3 to the `display_result` Listing 1-7 in Chapter 1, you may have noticed one seemingly trivial difference: The plaintext HTTP routine reads until `recv` returns 0 bytes, indicating EOF. The secured implementation reads until `tls_recv` returns less than 0. Why?

To frustrate attackers, it's acceptable for compliant TLS implementations to return empty packets consisting of nothing but padding. When this function receives such a packet, it removes the padding and the MAC and reports the returned data length as 0.

"So," you must certainly be wondering, "if `tls_recv` can't return 0 to indicate an EOF condition, how does TLS handle an end-of-stream?" Read on.

## Implementing TLS Shutdown

SSLv2 didn't have a specific shutdown mechanism; when either side was done using the connection, it just issued a regular TCP FIN packet. The problem with this was that it's easy for a man in the middle to generate a FIN packet; it's not encrypted or authenticated in any way. This can be used to perform truncation attacks as detailed in Chapter 4.

As a result, TLS has a special way to indicate shutdown. The side wishing to shut the connection down sends an alert with the `close_notify` code of 0. Because this is a TLS message, it's subject to the standard encryption and authentication values currently in force and is protected. `tls_shutdown` is shown in Listing 6-75.

**Listing 6-75:** "tls.c" tls_shutdown

```
int tls_shutdown( int connection, TLSParameters *parameters )
{
  send_alert_message( connection, close_notify,
```

```
    &parameters->active_send_parameters );
  if ( parameters->unread_buffer )
  {
    free( parameters->unread_buffer );
  }
  free_protection_parameters( &parameters->pending_send_parameters );
  free_protection_parameters( &parameters->pending_recv_parameters );
  free_protection_parameters( &parameters->active_send_parameters );
  free_protection_parameters( &parameters->active_recv_parameters );

  return 1;
}
```

This routine goes ahead and frees any memory that was allocated by the connection; it mostly relies on `free_protection_parameters` to free the MAC secrets, keys, and IVs. This is shown in Listing 6-76.

**Listing 6-76:** "tls.c" free_protection_parameters

```
static void free_protection_parameters( ProtectionParameters *parameters )
{
  if ( parameters->MAC_secret )
  {
    free( parameters->MAC_secret );
  }
  if ( parameters->key )
  {
    free( parameters->key );
  }
  if ( parameters->IV )
  {
    free( parameters->IV );
  }
}
```

Another benefit of the dedicated TLS shutdown protocol is that either side can switch back to plaintext if desired without severing the connection. This could potentially be useful if for regulatory reasons some data had to be sent in the clear. I'm not aware of any applications that take advantage of this, but it's nice to know that the flexibility is there if you need it.

## Examining HTTPS End-to-End Examples (TLS 1.0)

You can, and should, compile the code presented in this chapter and try to connect to a few different public secure websites. You may have to scrounge around to find one that doesn't require a context to be previously established; your bank's login landing page might be a good choice (if it's not SSL enabled, consider a different bank).

For illustration purposes, though, you can also run an instance of the Apache web server locally, configure it to accept HTTPS connections, and connect to it. The *tcpdump* utility can be used to monitor exactly what's passed back and forth over a socket connection.

**NOTE** See Appendix B for a brief overview on installing and configuring tcpdump.

## Dissecting the Client Hello Request

Now you can run your `https` command-line client to connect to an SSL-enabled website and monitor the packets exchanged. After invoking tcpdump to run in the background, start up an instance of `https`:

```
[jdavies@localhost ssl]$ ./https https://localhost/index.html
```

The tcpdump output starts with the standard expected TCP 3-way handshake:

```
[root@localhost ssl]# /usr/sbin/tcpdump -i lo -s 0 -X tcp port 443
tcpdump: verbose output suppressed, use -v or -vv for full protocol decode
listening on lo, link-type EN10MB (Ethernet), capture size 65535 bytes
12:37:03.937423 IP localhost.localdomain.56047 > localhost.localdomain.https: S
506618802:506618802(0) win 32792
<mss 16396,sackOK,timestamp 12673266 0,nop,wscale 7>
        0x0000:  4500 003c 0340 4000 4006 397a 7f00 0001   E..<.@@.@.9z....
        0x0010:  7f00 0001 daef 01bb 1e32 63b2 0000 0000   .........2c.....
        0x0020:  a002 8018 cf4a 0000 0204 400c 0402 080a   .....J....@.....
        0x0030:  00c1 60f2 0000 0000 0103 0307             ..`.........
12:37:03.937430 IP localhost.localdomain.https > localhost.localdomain.56047: S
505995792:505995792(0) ack 506618803 win 32768
<mss 16396,sackOK,timestamp 12673267 12673266,nop,wscale 7>
        0x0000:  4500 003c 0000 4000 4006 3cba 7f00 0001   E..<..@.@.<.....
        0x0010:  7f00 0001 01bb daef 1e28 e210 1e32 63b3   .........(...2c.
        0x0020:  a012 8000 6d64 0000 0204 400c 0402 080a   ....md....@.....
        0x0030:  00c1 60f3 00c1 60f2 0103 0307             ..`...`.....
12:37:03.937459 IP localhost.localdomain.56047 > localhost.localdomain.https: .
        ack 1 win 257 <nop,nop,timestamp 12673267 12673267>
        0x0000:  4500 0034 0341 4000 4006 3981 7f00 0001   E..4.A@.@.9.....
        0x0010:  7f00 0001 daef 01bb 1e32 63b3 1e28 e211   .........2c..(..
        0x0020:  8010 0101 5587 0000 0101 080a 00c1 60f3   ....U........`.
        0x0030:  00c1 60f3                                 ..`.
```

After the three-way handshake is complete, the TLS protocol takes over:

- The first actual packet exchanged is the client hello. The client hello starts at byte 0x0035. The first five bytes of the data packet is the TLS header 160301002d. 0x16 is the type of the message (content_handshake); 0x0301 is the version of SSL (3.1); and 0x002d is the length of the contained packet — 45 bytes. *Every* packet sent over this connection must now start with a TLS header.

- Next is the handshake header 0x01000029. 0x01 is the handshake message type (client hello), and 0x000029 is the strange three-byte length that indicates that the actual payload is 41 bytes.

- Following this, finally, is the client hello message itself. The first two bytes are the protocol version 0x0301 again, followed by 32 bytes of random data (although as you can see the data isn't particularly random in this case). Remember that the random structure is required to begin with a four-byte "seconds since January 1, 1970" time, followed by 28 actually random bytes. As you can see, this is passed in the clear. Anything you can see with tcpdump, a malicious intruder can see with a packet sniffer as well.

After the random bytes, a 0 byte is supplied indicating that no session ID follows. The session ID structure is followed by the cipher suites list, which must be supplied. First the two-byte length of the cipher suites indicates that there are two bytes of cipher suite (that is, one cipher suite). This length declaration is followed by the cipher suite list itself — here 0x002F, which is the single cipher suite TLS_RSA_WITH_AES_128_CBC_SHA. Notice that the length of 2 indicates that there follows two *bytes* of cipher suites, which is one cipher suite because each suite is two bytes long. The client hello message ends with the list of supported compression methods, which is simply "no compression."

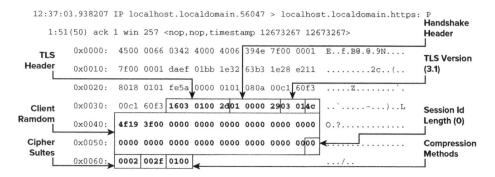

```
12:37:03.938207 IP localhost.localdomain.56047 > localhost.localdomain.https: P
    1:51(50) ack 1 win 257 <nop,nop,timestamp 12673267 12673267>
0x0000:  4500 0066 0342 4000 4006 394e 7f00 0001   E..f.B@.@.9N....
0x0010:  7f00 0001 daef 01bb 1e32 63b3 1e28 e211   .........2c..(..
0x0020:  8018 0101 fe5a 0000 0101 080a 00c1 60f3   .....Z........`.
0x0030:  00c1 60f3 1603 0100 2d01 0000 2903 014c   ..`.......-...)..L
0x0040:  4f19 3f00 0000 0000 0000 0000 0000 0000   O.?.............
0x0050:  0000 0000 0000 0000 0000 0000 0000 0000   ................
0x0060:  0002 002f 0100                            .../..
```

After the client hello, the server acknowledges the packet according to the standard rules of TCP.

```
12:37:03.938244 IP localhost.localdomain.https > localhost.localdomain.56047: .
    ack 51 win 256 <nop,nop,timestamp 12673267 12673267>
0x0000:  4500 0034 82e2 4000 4006 b9df 7f00 0001   E..4..@.@.......
0x0010:  7f00 0001 01bb daef 1e28 e211 1e32 63e5   .........(...2c.
0x0020:  8010 0100 5556 0000 0101 080a 00c1 60f3   ....UV........`.
0x0030:  00c1 60f3                                  ..`.
```

Because this is a book about SSL/TLS and not about TCP, packet acknowledgments are omitted from the remainder of this section.

## Dissecting the Server Response Messages

The server then sends back the server hello, certificate and server hello done messages. Notice that in this case, they're not included in a single TLS packet, although the specification allows for this. This single TCP packet includes three individual top-level TLS messages.

The first is of length 75 bytes (0x004a) and contains a handshake message of type 2 (server hello). The server hello packet, of course, starts with the version number 0x0301, followed by the 32-byte server random structure. Servers normally assign a session ID to every connection, so the session ID in this case is non-empty; it is 32 bytes long and is equal to 07e76fed29bfc73b710b0c2757fcd 1a7b325561b232906ceb3d8a0347f3bd2f5. The server hello finishes out by selecting a cipher suite and a compression method. Obviously it chose 0x002F and 0x00, respectively, because those were the only two choices it was given. If it didn't recognize, or didn't support, any of these choices then this server hello message would have instead been an alert.

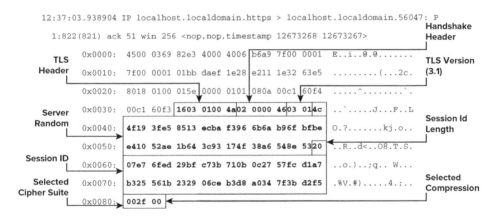

```
12:37:03.938904 IP localhost.localdomain.https > localhost.localdomain.56047: P
     1:822(821) ack 51 win 256 <nop,nop,timestamp 12673268 12673267>
```

A server hello is generally followed by a server certificate message. This is not necessarily always the case, as you see in Chapter 8, but generally it is. Here the TLS header indicates that the following message is 344 (0x02d8) bytes long and is a server handshake certificate message (handshake message 0x0b). This message in turns starts out with a three-byte length declaration — 0x0002d1 indicating that the following certificate *chain* is 337 bytes long. After this is yet another length declaration 0x0002ce, indicating that the first certificate in this certificate chain — in this case, the only certificate in this chain — is 334 bytes long. Finally, the ASN.1 DER representation of the server's certificate follows.

```
          16 0301 02d8 0b00 02d4 0002 d100    ./.............
0x0090:  02ce 3082 02ca 3082 0274 a003 0201 0202    ..0...0..t......
0x00a0:  0900 a72f c757 5f51 e56f 300d 0609 2a86    .../.W_Q.oO...*.
0x00b0:  4886 f70d 0101 0505 0030 7931 0b30 0906    H........0y1.0..
....
```

The server's side of the exchange is rounded out by the server hello done message. As shown in the next line of code, this contains no actual data; it's just a TLS header indicating that the packet is four bytes whose contents are an empty handshake message of type `0x0e`.

```
0x0360:   1603 0100 040e 0000 00                     . . . . . . . . .
```

## Dissecting the Key Exchange Message

If the client was able to parse the certificate and has decided to trust it, and the certificate contains enough information to satisfy the key exchange method in the selected cipher suite, it must now send a key exchange message. Because the key exchange method in this case is RSA, this involves making up a random premaster secret, encrypting it using the public key that the server sent in the certificate message, and sending that on.

After the standard TLS header and handshake message header, an RSA key exchange message starts with a two-byte length, followed by the data. Because the key used here is 512 bits, the RSA-encrypted data is also 512 bits, 64 bytes.

```
12:37:04.007143 IP localhost.localdomain.56047 > localhost.localdomain.https: P
   51:126(75) ack 822 win 270 <nop,nop,timestamp 12673336 12673268>
        0x0000:   4500 007f 0344 4000 4006 3933 7f00 0001   E....D@.@.93....
        0x0010:   7f00 0001 daef 01bb 1e32 63e5 1e28 e546   .........2c..(.F
        0x0020:   8018 010e fe73 0000 0101 080a 00c1 6138   .....s........a8
        0x0030:   00c1 60f4 1603 0100 4610 0000 4200 407a   ..`.....F...B.@z
        0x0040:   8d74 369f 97e3 86e4 494f 5e71 1e0f 2059   .t6.....IO^q...Y
        0x0050:   6583 04d2 d432 ce33 1067 251c 5a4b edef   e....2.3.g%.ZK..
        0x0060:   d149 935b 9256 1a20 959a b9e4 0427 175e   .I.[.V.......'.^
        0x0070:   6d70 cd0d af00 e3c2 c977 ab11 5af5 f7      mp.......w..Z..
```

Because I have access to the private key that corresponds with the public key used in this exchange, I can decrypt this message using the `rsa` code developed in Chapter 3. If I didn't have this private key then I'd be out of luck trying to interpret this or any subsequent message in this connection. Of course, the private key appears nowhere in this exchange; the security of TLS hinges around this fact. The private key exponent is

```
EAFF403432CBD12A7F7174C209F5364398E62F4A1B8F9B7C32B6CE190E716696D3E866E09
AF5367743EA5CC7903515D05D667E5480C562BCC0821F4A670B27F9
```

and the modulus is

```
EEB4761CAAE2E34F56CBC3AFE479E88589A9AB398250687ADE502D53EEFAD78C6E3CF8946
301095BD0BD7A60089737E2F1BB40A152E12DDCDBC95BD86661DA4F
```

so the RSA-encrypted message can be decoded as

```
[jdavies@localhost ssl]$ ./rsa -d \
0xEEB4761CAAE2E34F56CBC3AFE479E88589A9AB398250687ADE502D53EEFAD78\
C6E3CF8946301095BD0BD7A60089737E2F1BB40A152E12DDCDBC95BD86661DA4F \
```

```
0xEAFF403432CBD12A7F7174C209F5364398E62F4A1B8F9B7C32B6CE190E71669\
6D3E866E09AF5367743EA5CC7903515D05D667E5480C562BCC0821F4A670B27F9 \
0x7a8d74369f97e386e4494f5e711e0f2059658304d2d432ce331067251c5a4be\
defd149935b92561a20959ab9e40427175e6d70cd0daf00e3c2c977ab115af5f7
02 02 03 04 05 06 07 08 09 0a 0b 0c 0d 0e 00 03 01 02 03 04 05 06 07 08 09 0a 0b
0c 0d 0e 0f 10 11 12 13 14 15 16 17 18 19 1a 1b 1c 1d 1e 1f 20 21 22 23 24 25 26
27 28 29 2a 2b 2c 2d 2e 2f 00
03010203040506070809a0b0c0d0e0f10111213141516171819191a1b1c1d1e1f2021222324252627
28292a2b2c2d2e2f
```

After stripping off the padding, you're left with a premaster secret whose first two bytes are the SSL version 0301 and then the premaster secret which, in this case, isn't particularly secure.

According to the protocol, the client must now send a change cipher spec message. This is a pretty boring message, consisting of a single byte:

```
12:37:04.046440 IP localhost.localdomain.56047 > localhost.localdomain.https: P
   126:185(59) ack 822 win 270 <nop,nop,timestamp 12673376 12673376>
        0x0000:  4500 006f 0345 4000 4006 3942 7f00 0001   E..o.E@.@.9B....
        0x0010:  7f00 0001 daef 01bb 1e32 6430 1e28 e546   .........2d0.(.F
        0x0020:  8018 010e fe63 0000 0101 080a 00c1 6160   .....c........a`
        0x0030:  00c1 6160 1403 0100 0101
```

Notice that the message type is 14, not 16; change cipher spec is a separate top-level type. Other than this, it's just the single, plain byte 0x01.

## Decrypting the Encrypted Exchange

Change cipher spec is followed by a finished message. This message is encrypted using the newly negotiated parameters, so must be decrypted. My network stack decided to aggregate these two messages into a single TCP push, but there's no particular reason why it would have to be this way.

The finished message starts with the standard, expected (unencrypted) TLS message header, and tells the recipient that the message that follows is 48 bytes long. Everything following the header is encrypted using the negotiated session keys.

```
                                   1603 0100 301c   ..a`..........0.
        0x0040:  e1a2 aaf3 1267 749d b1e7 701d 8f95 98d8   .....gt...p.....
        0x0050:  cd65 526b 90a4 d8d0 7536 1dd4 6a26 4787   .eRk....u6..j&G.
        0x0060:  4f49 5ac7 8c89 7dcc 1ee3 ad37 b25e 8d     OIZ...}....7.^.
```

Because you know the private key that was used for the key exchange, you know the premaster secret. Therefore, you can work forward and discover the master secret and the key material. Recall that the master secret was generated by applying the PRF to the premaster secret. Specifically, the PRF takes three input parameters: the secret, the label, and the seed. Recall that, for master secret computation, the label is the fixed string `"master secret"`, and the seed is the client random followed by the server random. The secret is, of course, the premaster secret.

You can reproduce the master secret with this information:

```
[jdavies@localhost ssl]$ ./prf \
0x030102030405060708090a0b0c0d0e0f101112131415161718\
191a1b1c1d1e1f202122232425262728292a2b2c2d2e2f "master secret" \
0x4c4f193f0000000000000000000000000000000000000000000000000000000\
4c4f193fe58513ecbaf3966b6ab96fbfbee41052ae1b643c93174f38a6548e53 48
2dee06e1ba5e41722dd1c24286ae5a0cfbd89b38bd4688fa
fb97c3dc05a2647be55490ba733406807df8023ae75d0a0a
```

The master secret is always exactly 48 bytes long.

The master secret itself isn't used for key material; instead, it's used as a seed into the PRF again. The PRF also needs to know how many bytes to generate in order to determine how many times to iterate. How many bytes are needed for the selected cipher suite? AES-128 uses 16-byte keys, and a 16-byte block size, so you need 32 bytes of keying material and 32 bytes of IV — one of each for each side of the conversation. SHA-1 uses a 20-byte MAC key, so you need 40 bytes of MAC secret; this works out to 104 bytes of keying material.

You can reproduce the keys by running the PRF algorithm with this input:

```
[jdavies@localhost ssl]$ ./prf \
0x2dee06e1ba5e41722dd1c24286ae5a0cfbd89b38bd4688\
fafb97c3dc05a2647be55490ba733406807df8023ae75d0a0a "key expansion" \
0x4c4f193fe58513ecbaf3966b6ab96fbfbee41052ae1b643c93174f38a6548e\
534c4f193f0000000000000000000000000000000000000000000000000000000 104
3a1ee25b3fa7efb9a2c8f112de47c3276917a2bbb0f81a9a389dbc82c3fc2a073e97aa31087f312
96dbb1276d318c6551ef8245888420cf4c2a545f7a8515c42c367599cdd52cf6ef6bb0cc22615db
9c0d93ad3c21d2f58ed18324dbfb7645103f191455421cceca
```

Notice that the seed in this case is the server random, followed by the client random, whereas for the master secret expansion, it was the other way around. If you overlook this fact, you will end up tearing your hair out for days trying to figure out why your code isn't working. (Don't ask me how I know).

The key material block starts with the MAC secrets, then the keys, then the initialization vectors, so this works out to what is shown in Table 6-1.

**Table 6-1:** The Key Material Block

| PURPOSE | CLIENT/WRITE | SERVER/READ |
|---|---|---|
| MAC secret | 3a1ee25b3fa7efb9a2c8f112de 47c3276917a2bb | b0f81a9a389dbc82c3f c2a073e97aa31087f3129 |
| Encryption Key | 6dbb1276d318c6551e f8245888420cf4 | c2a545f7a8515c42c367599cd d52cf6e |
| Initialization Vector | f6bb0cc22615db9c 0d93ad3c21d2f58e | d18324dbfb7645103f 191455421cceca |

Armed with the keys and initialization vectors, you can go ahead and decrypt the 48-byte finished message:

```
[jdavies@localhost ssl]$ ./aes -d 0x6dbb1276d318c6551ef8245888420cf4 \
0xf6bb0cc22615db9c0d93ad3c21d2f58e \
0x1ce1a2aaf31267749db1e7701d8f9598d8cd65526b90a4d8\
d075361dd46a2647874f495ac78c897dcc1ee3ad37b25e8d
1400000ce3945aa7b226794d96cfcaf7b79febcb41c2bd7b48a77d7b26f
958296dc1467c0b0b0b0b0b0b0b0b0b0b0b0b0b
```

This is, as expected, a handshake message of type 0x14 (finished), followed by a three-byte length indicating that the message is 12 bytes long. If you recall, this is correct; the finished message is 12 bytes, generated by the PRF, seeded with the hash values of all of the handshake messages up to this point.

However, the message body is significantly longer. It includes 20 bytes of MAC and an extra 12 bytes of padding, because 4+12+20 (header + contents + MAC) is equal to 36, which is not an even multiple of the 16-byte block size. Notice that there are 12 bytes of padding, but the value of the padding byte is 0x0b (11); there's always one byte on the end that indicates how much padding there is, which isn't actually considered padding.

You can verify the MAC as well. Remember that the MAC is the HMAC function of the sequence number, the TLS header, and the contents. Because this is the first securely exchanged packet, the sequence number is 0. However, be careful. If you try to do this

```
[jdavies@localhost ssl]$ ./hmac -sha1 \
0x3a1ee25b3fa7efb9a2c8f112de47c3276917a2bb \
0x00000000000000001601010030140000ce3945aa7b226794d96cfcaf7
dfc0e0ef8c50a3bc3f9db3d87168a99ce3c4f99d
```

you'll get the wrong answer. The MAC is actually b79febcb41c2bd7b48a77d 7b26f958296dc1467c; what went wrong?

Remember that the MAC was generated from the sequence number and what the TLS header *would have* looked like, had there been no encryption or MAC — that is, the length before padding and MAC. So, to get the correct answer, you have to subtract the 32 bytes of MAC and padding from the length in the TLS header and compute:

```
[jdavies@localhost ssl]$ ./hmac -sha1 \
0x3a1ee25b3fa7efb9a2c8f112de47c3276917a2bb \
0x00000000000000001603010001014000000ce3945aa7b226794d96cfcaf7
b79febcb41c2bd7b48a77d7b26f958296dc1467c
```

The server receives the finished message, decrypts it, verifies the MAC, and compares the verify data of e3945aa7b226794d96cfcaf7 to what it has computed so far. It then responds with its own change cipher spec and finished message:

```
12:37:04.047107 IP localhost.localdomain.https > localhost.localdomain.56047: P
    822:881(59) ack 185 win 256 <nop,nop,timestamp 12673376 12673376>
        0x0000:  4500 006f 82e6 4000 4006 b9a0 7f00 0001  E..o..@.@.......
```

```
0x0010:   7f00 0001 01bb daef 1e28 e546 1e32 646b   .........(.F.2dk
0x0020:   8018 0100 fe63 0000 0101 080a 00c1 6160   .....c........a`
0x0030:   00c1 6160 1403 0100 0101 1603 0100 30c8   ..a`..........0.
0x0040:   5afc e4c0 1560 ec3b 4db9 6185 f4f4 f1b1   Z....`.;M.a.....
0x0050:   bcb1 3528 c8a6 5862 f512 30e6 02d5 62a8   ..5(..Xb..0...b.
0x0060:   6e4d f925 8048 d19b 0a2d 6296 4b6c e9      nM.%.H...-b.Kl.
```

The finished message is encrypted just as the client's was, but because you know the keys you can decrypt it:

```
[jdavies@localhost ssl]$ ./aes -d 0xc2a545f7a8515c42c367599cdd52cf6e \
0xd18324dbfb7645103f191455421cceca \
0xc85afce4c01560ec3b4db96185f4f4f1b1bcb13528c8a65\
862f51230e602d562a86e4df9258048d19b0a2d62964b6ce9
1400000c45c4904ac71a5948a7198e18b8618774e12b8f58f49216bcf
59a914f236b6fef0b0b0b0b0b0b0b0b0b0b0b0b0b0b0
```

Of course, you must use the second set of keys to decrypt this properly. You can verify the MAC as well.

Also, notice that, in this case, the verify data is 45c4904ac71a5948a7198e18 — it does *not* match the verify data that the client sent. Why not? Because the client's finished message is included in the computation of the verify data that the server sends.

## Exchanging Application Data

The TLS handshake is complete; it's time for the top-level protocol, in this case HTTP, to take over. The TLS header is present, but this time, it identifies application data:

```
12:37:04.049299 IP localhost.localdomain.56047 > localhost.localdomain.https: P
185:238(53) ack 881 win 270 <nop,nop,timestamp 12673378 12673376>
        0x0000:   4500 0069 0347 4000 4006 3946 7f00 0001   E..i.G@.@.9F....
        0x0010:   7f00 0001 daef 01bb 1e32 646b 1e28 e581   .........2dk.(..
        0x0020:   8018 010e fe5d 0000 0101 080a 00c1 6162   .....]........ab
        0x0030:   00c1 6160 1703 0100 301d 6070 ca35 be42   ..a`....0.`p.5.B
        0x0040:   29da cf8a 9654 391c 08a5 981a 8d15 e87a   )....T9........z
        0x0050:   c058 437c 834d 957a d446 b9eb dd78 f392   .XC|.M.z.F...x..
        0x0060:   0375 de85 e852 b6e6 c0                     .u...R...
```

This is decrypted just like the finished message was. However, remember that the initialization vector used to decrypt this packet is the last 16 bytes of the previously sent packet:

```
[jdavies@localhost ssl]$ ./aes -d 0x6dbb1276d318c6551ef8245888420cf4 \
0x874f495ac78c897dcc1ee3ad37b25e8d \
0x1d6070ca35be4229dacf8a9654391c08a5981a8d15e87ac\
058437c834d957ad446b9ebdd78f3920375de85e852b6e6c0
474554202f696e6465782e68746d6c20485454502f312e310d0a200e496b9e2dadcf20bb5c9
2c4047baf348b1f7b0101
```

After the MAC is verified and removed and the padding is stripped off, the payload of 474554202f696e6465782e68746d6c20485454502f312e310d0a is handed off to the HTTP protocol. This is just the ASCII encoding of "GET /index.html HTTP/1.0" and the CRLF delimiter. HTTP doesn't indicate its length; the TLS header gave the TLS layer enough information to decrypt and strip off the MAC, but it's up to HTTP to figure out what to do with this message.

The server's response is omitted here. After the server has responded, though, it sends

```
12:37:04.089204 IP localhost.localdomain.https > localhost.localdomain.56047: P
   1291:1328(37) ack 344 win 256 <nop,nop,timestamp 12673418 12673418>
        0x0000:  4500 0059 82ea 4000 4006 b9b2 7f00 0001   E..Y..@.@.......
        0x0010:  7f00 0001 01bb daef 1e28 e71b 1e32 650a   .........(...2e.
        0x0020:  8018 0100 fe4d 0000 0101 080a 00c1 618a   .....M........a.
        0x0030:  00c1 618a 1503 0100 20ae dd34 8655 8551   ..a........4.U.Q
        0x0040:  3836 6592 0d73 dcda 4770 9798 dc2a c22c   86e..s..Gp...*.,
        0x0050:  79da e8c2 0945 6c4f 61                    y....ElOa
```

As you can see from the header, this is an alert. Of course, it's encrypted, but you know by now that this is a close_notify alert. This is followed by the normal TCP shutdown.

# Differences Between SSL 3.0 and TLS 1.0

As mentioned previously, TLS is a minor revision to SSL 3.0, which was a major overhaul of SSLv2. There are few differences between SSL 3.0 and TLS 1.0; TLS defined a handful of new alert types and removed support for the Fortezza key exchange algorithm.

**WHAT IS FORTEZZA?**

Fortezza was the U.S. government's aborted attempt at a *key escrow* system. The idea was that you could use as strong cryptography as you liked, but you had to share a copy of the private key with the U.S. government in case it ever needed to decrypt something that you had exchanged. This didn't go over well with the U.S. public and went over even less well with users in foreign countries.

The U.S. government has not resurrected a key escrow system since the failure of Fortezza. Whether this means that they've decided that it's not nice to snoop on people or whether they've found but kept secret a fundamental flaw in the cryptographic protocols that TLS relies on that allows them to decrypt your data at will is for you to decide.

The most significant difference, and what necessitated a new version, was the introduction of the PRF. SSL 3.0 had a premaster secret, just like TLS 1.0, but it became the master secret by taking the MD5 hash of the premaster secret plus the SHA hash of the letter A plus the premaster secret, the client random, and the server random, followed by the same MD5 hash with A replaced by BB, and the same MD5 hash again with CCC instead of BB. The finished messages, the other place where the PRF shows up in TLS, were based directly on MD5 and SHA-1 hashes as well.

There's not much reason to go into any more detail on SSLv3 here. Because SSLv3 and TLS 1.0 are almost identical, it's a good bet that any server that supports one supports the other.

## Differences Between TLS 1.0 and TLS 1.1

The TLS 1.0 protocol stood untouched for seven years after it was standardized in 1999. In 2006, Tim Dierks and Eric Rescorla drafted RFC 4346, specifying TLS 1.1 and making TLS 1.0 obsolete.

By and large, TLS 1.1 is not a significant change from TLS 1.0. It added some new cipher suites and some clarifications and implementation notes, but the most important change is that initialization vectors are no longer computed from the master secret; instead, they're prepended to each packet.

Why, you ask? Well, each record's IV is the most recently transmitted block. Although an attacker can't decrypt the packet, even a passive eavesdropper can see what the next IV is going to be. The attack is complex, but a dedicated attacker who can inject known plaintext into the stream can guess what the last plaintext block is and verify his guess by injecting a specially crafted plaintext block into the stream. It's not clear under what circumstances an attacker might be able to inject known plaintext, but not have access to the keys; perhaps he's sniffing traffic coming out of a call center, calls that call center, makes up an account ID, and hopes that that account ID is the next packet on a live session.

Theoretical or not, this is an easy enough attack to defend against, so TLS 1.1 does so. TLS 1.1 is not particularly common on the public Internet, even today, four years after it was drafted.

Two years after TLS 1.1 was drafted, it was made obsolete by RFC 5246, which specifies TLS 1.2. TLS 1.2 was a major modification of the TLS protocol and Chapter 9 is devoted to detailing the changes it introduced.

# Adding Server-Side TLS 1.0 Support

The previous chapter examined the TLS protocol in detail from the perspective of the client. This chapter examines the server's role in the TLS exchange. Although you should have a pretty good handle by now on what's expected of the server, the implementation includes a few gotchas that you should be aware of.

The good news is that you can reuse most of the code from the previous chapter; the supporting infrastructure behind encrypting and authenticating is exactly the same for the server as for the client. For the most part, implementing the server's view of the handshake involves sending what the client received and receiving what the client sent. After the handshake is complete, `tls_send`, `tls_recv`, and `tls_shutdown` work exactly as they do on the client side.

## Implementing the TLS 1.0 Handshake from the Server's Perspective

You need to have a way to verify the server-side code, so add HTTPS support to the simple web server developed in Chapter 1. The startup and listen routine doesn't change at all. Of course, it's listening on port 443 instead of port 80, but otherwise, the main routine in Listing 7-1 is identical to the one in Listing 1-18.

**Listing 7-1:** "ssl_webserver.c" main routine

```
#define HTTPS_PORT 443
...
  local_addr.sin_port = htons( HTTPS_PORT );
...
  while ( ( connect_sock = accept( listen_sock,
                                ( struct sockaddr * ) &client_addr,
                                &client_addr_len ) ) != -1 )
  {
    process_https_request( connect_sock );
  }
```

As you can see, there's nothing TLS-specific here; you're just accepting connections on a different port.

`process_https_request` is just like `process_http_request`, except that it starts with a call to `tls_accept` in Listing 7-2.

**Listing 7-2:** "ssl_webserver.c" process_https_request

```
static void process_https_request( int connection )

{
  char *request_line;
  TLSParameters tls_context;

  if ( tls_accept( connection, &tls_context ) )
  {
    perror( "Unable to establish SSL connection" );
  }
  else
  {
    request_line = read_line( connection, &tls_context );

    if ( strncmp( request_line, "GET", 3 ) )
    {
      // Only supports "GET" requests
      build_error_response( connection, 400, &tls_context );
    }
    else
    {
      // Skip over all header lines, don't care
      while ( strcmp( read_line( connection, &tls_context ), "" ) )
      {
        printf( "skipped a header line\n" );
      }

      build_success_response( connection, &tls_context );
    }

    tls_shutdown( connection, &tls_context );
```

```
  }

#ifdef WIN32
  if ( closesocket( connection ) == -1 )
#else
  if ( close( connection ) == -1 )
#endif
  {
    perror( "Unable to close connection" );
  }
}
```

And, of course, `read_line`, `build_error_response`, and `build_success_response` must be updated to invoke `tls_send` and `tls_recv` instead of `send` and `recv` as in Listing 7-3.

**Listing 7-3:** "ssl_webserver.c" send and read modifications

```
char *read_line( int connection, TLSParameters *tls_context )
{
…
  while ( ( size = tls_recv( connection, &c, 1, 0, tls_context ) ) >= 0 )
  {
…
static void build_success_response( int connection, TLSParameters *tls_context )
{
…
  if ( tls_send( connection, buf, strlen( buf ), 0, tls_context ) < strlen( buf ) )
…
static void build_error_response( int connection,
                                  int error_code,
                                  TLSParameters *tls_context )
{
  if ( tls_send( connection, buf, strlen( buf ), 0, tls_context ) < strlen( buf ) )
  {
```

Other than `tls_accept`, all of the support functions referenced here were implemented in Chapter 6 and can be used exactly as is.

Notice the HTTPS protocol at work. The server accepts a connection and then immediately waits for a client hello message; if any attempt is made to send any other data, an error occurs. Although this is not strictly required by the TLS protocol itself, it is common when integrating TLS into an existing protocol.

`tls_accept` is a mirror image of `tls_connect`; it must wait for a client hello. (Remember that the client must always initiate the TLS handshake.) After the hello is received, the server responds with hello, certificate, and hello done messages back-to-back, waits for the client's change cipher-spec and finished message, sends its own, and returns. This is shown in Listing 7-4.

**Listing 7-4:** "tls.c" tls_accept

```c
int tls_accept( int connection,
                TLSParameters *parameters )
{
  init_parameters( parameters );
  parameters->connection_end = connection_end_server;

  new_md5_digest( &parameters->md5_handshake_digest );
  new_sha1_digest( &parameters->sha1_handshake_digest );

  // The client sends the first message
  parameters->got_client_hello = 0;
  while ( !parameters->got_client_hello )
  {
    if ( receive_tls_msg( connection, NULL, 0, parameters ) < 0 )
    {
      perror( "Unable to receive client hello" );
      send_alert_message( connection, handshake_failure,
        &parameters->active_send_parameters );
      return 1;
    }
  }
  if ( send_server_hello( connection, parameters ) )
  {
    send_alert_message( connection, handshake_failure,
      &parameters->active_send_parameters );
    return 2;
  }

  if ( send_certificate( connection, parameters ) )
  {
    send_alert_message( connection, handshake_failure,
      &parameters->active_send_parameters );
    return 3;
  }

  if ( send_server_hello_done( connection, parameters ) )
  {
    send_alert_message( connection, handshake_failure,
      &parameters->active_send_parameters );
    return 4;
  }

  // Now the client should send a client key exchange, change cipher spec, and
  // an encrypted "finalize" message
  parameters->peer_finished = 0;
  while ( !parameters->peer_finished )
  {
    if ( receive_tls_msg( connection, NULL, 0, parameters ) < 0 )
```

```
  {
    perror( "Unable to receive client finished" );
    send_alert_message( connection, handshake_failure,
      &parameters->active_send_parameters );
    return 5;
  }
}

// Finally, send server change cipher spec/finished message
if ( !( send_change_cipher_spec( connection, parameters ) ) )
{
  perror( "Unable to send client change cipher spec" );
  send_alert_message( connection, handshake_failure,
    &parameters->active_send_parameters );
  return 6;
}

// This message will be encrypted using the newly negotiated keys
if ( !( send_finished( connection, parameters ) ) )
{
  perror( "Unable to send client finished" );
  send_alert_message( connection, handshake_failure,
    &parameters->active_send_parameters );
  return 7;
}

// Handshake is complete; now ready to start sending encrypted data
return 0;
}
```

This listing should be easy to follow if you understood `tls_connect` (Listing 6-7). It starts by initializing its own handshake digest pair so that it can validate the final *finished* message as described in Chapter 6. It also references three new `TLSParameter` members that you haven't seen yet:

- `connection_end`: This requires a bit of explanation. Recall from Listing 6-37 that, when calculating keys, the first *mac-length* bytes were the client's MAC secret, and the next *mac-length* bytes were the server's. If you want to reuse the same code to compute keys, you must keep track of whether you are the client or the server, to know which keys to put into the `active_send_parameters` and which to put into the `active_recv_parameters`. Because `tls_accept` is only invoked by a TLS server, and `tls_connect` is only invoked by a TLS client, it's safe to set this flag here to control common functions.

- `got_client_hello`: Serves the same purpose in `tls_accept` as `got_server_hello` did in `tls_connect`. Each call to `receive_tls_message` processes the next available TLS message, regardless of what type it is — alert, data, handshake — so you must keep processing messages until you get the one you were expecting.

■ `peer_finished`. The same as `server_finished`. In fact, you should delete `server_finished` from the `TLSParameters` structures and rename it `peer_finished`; the finished messages are identical whether they came from the client or from the server, so handling them is exactly the same either way.

Define these new members in Listing 7-5.

**Listing 7-5:** "tls.h" TLSParameters with server-side support

```
typedef enum { connection_end_client, connection_end_server } ConnectionEnd;

typedef struct
{
    ConnectionEnd           connection_end;
    master_secret_type      master_secret;
    random_type             client_random;
    random_type             server_random;

    ProtectionParameters    pending_send_parameters;
    ProtectionParameters    active_send_parameters;
    ProtectionParameters    pending_recv_parameters;
    ProtectionParameters    active_recv_parameters;

    public_key_info         server_public_key;

    dh_key                  server_dh_key;

    // Internal state
    int                     got_client_hello;
    int                     server_hello_done;
    int                     peer_finished;
    digest_ctx              md5_handshake_digest;
    digest_ctx              sha1_handshake_digest;

    char                    *unread_buffer;
    int                     unread_length;
}
TLSParameters;
```

Change references from `server_finished` to `peer_finished` and change the verify data label depending on the connection end in Listing 7-6.

**Listing 7-6:** "tls.c" peer_finished

```
static unsigned char *parse_finished( unsigned char *read_pos,
                                       int pdu_length,
                                       TLSParameters *parameters )
{
```

```
    unsigned char verify_data[ VERIFY_DATA_LEN ];

    parameters->peer_finished = 1;
    compute_verify_data(
      parameters->connection_end == connection_end_client ?
      "server finished" : "client finished",
      parameters, verify_data );
…
int tls_connect( int connection,
                 TLSParameters *parameters )
{
…
    parameters->peer_finished = 0;
    while ( !parameters->peer_finished )
    {
      if ( receive_tls_msg( connection, NULL, 0, parameters ) < 0 )
```

And finally update the initialization routine in Listing 7-7.

**Listing 7-7:** "tls.c" init_parameters

```
static void init_parameters( TLSParameters *parameters )
{
…
  // Internal state
  parameters->got_client_hello = 0;
  parameters->server_hello_done = 0;
  parameters->peer_finished = 0;
...
int tls_connect( int connection,
                 TLSParameters *parameters )
{
  init_parameters( parameters );
  parameters->connection_end = connection_end_client;
```

## TLS Client Hello

Of course, a client hello can be received by receive_tls_message now, so it must be added in Listing 7-8.

**Listing 7-8:** "tls.c" receive_tls_message with client_hello

```
static int receive_tls_msg( int connection,
                            char *buffer,
                            int bufsz,
                            TLSParameters *parameters )
{
…
    switch ( handshake.msg_type )
    {
```

*(Continued)*

```
...
          // Server-side messages
          case client_hello:
            if ( parse_client_hello( read_pos, handshake.length,
                                     parameters ) == NULL )

            {

              send_alert_message( connection, illegal_parameter,
                &parameters->active_send_parameters );

              return -1;

            }

            read_pos += handshake.length;

            break;
...
```

Parsing and processing the client hello message involves, at a bare minimum, selecting one of the offered cipher suites. The easiest way to do this is to cycle through the list of cipher suites that the client offers and select the first one that the server understands. Note that this is not necessarily the best strategy; ideally the server would select the strongest suite that both sides understand. On the other hand, client designers can meet server designers halfway and sort the cipher suite list by cipher strength so that the server's cipher selection code can be simpler. The specification states that the client hello should include its "favorite cipher first." However, there are no suggestions on what criteria it ought to use in selecting a favorite. This does imply that the server probably ought to select the first one it recognizes, but does not actually mandate this.

Parsing the client hello message is shown in Listing 7-9.

**Listing 7-9:** "tls.c" parse_client_hello

```
static char *parse_client_hello( char *read_pos,
                                 int pdu_length,
                                 TLSParameters *parameters )
{
  int i;
  ClientHello hello;

  read_pos = read_buffer( ( void * ) &hello.client_version.major,
    ( void * ) read_pos, 1 );
  read_pos = read_buffer( ( void * ) &hello.client_version.minor,
    ( void * ) read_pos, 1 );
  read_pos = read_buffer( ( void * ) &hello.random.gmt_unix_time,
    ( void * ) read_pos, 4 );
  // *DON'T* put this in host order, since it's not used as a time!  Just
  // accept it as is
```

```
read_pos = read_buffer( ( void * ) hello.random.random_bytes,
  ( void * ) read_pos, 28 );
read_pos = read_buffer( ( void * ) &hello.session_id_length,
  ( void * ) read_pos, 1 );
hello.session_id = NULL;
if ( hello.session_id_length > 0 )
{
  hello.session_id = ( unsigned char * ) malloc( hello.session_id_length );
  read_pos = read_buffer( ( void * ) hello.session_id, ( void * ) read_pos,
    hello.session_id_length );
  // TODO if this is non-empty, the client is trying to trigger a restart
}
read_pos = read_buffer( ( void * ) &hello.cipher_suites_length,
  ( void * ) read_pos, 2 );
hello.cipher_suites_length = ntohs( hello.cipher_suites_length );
hello.cipher_suites = ( unsigned short * ) malloc( hello.cipher_suites_length
);
read_pos = read_buffer( ( void * ) hello.cipher_suites,
                        ( void * ) read_pos,
                        hello.cipher_suites_length );
read_pos = read_buffer( ( void * ) &hello.compression_methods_length,
  ( void * ) read_pos, 1 );
hello.compression_methods = ( unsigned char * ) malloc(
  hello.compression_methods_length );
read_pos = read_buffer( ( void * ) hello.compression_methods,
                        ( void * ) read_pos,
                        hello.compression_methods_length );
```

This reuses the read_buffer function from Listing 6-21 to fill in the ClientHello structure.

After this structure is filled in, the server must select a cipher suite.

```
for ( i = 0; i < hello.cipher_suites_length; i++ )
{
  hello.cipher_suites[ i ] = ntohs( hello.cipher_suites[ i ] );
  if ( hello.cipher_suites[ i ] < MAX_SUPPORTED_CIPHER_SUITE &&

      suites[ hello.cipher_suites[ i ] ].bulk_encrypt != NULL )
  {
    parameters->pending_recv_parameters.suite = hello.cipher_suites[ i ];
    parameters->pending_send_parameters.suite = hello.cipher_suites[ i ];
    break;
  }
}

if ( i == MAX_SUPPORTED_CIPHER_SUITE )
{
  return NULL;
}

parameters->got_client_hello = 1;
```

The specification isn't clear on exactly what the server should do if the client doesn't offer any supported cipher suites; OpenSSL just closes the connection without sending an alert. This implementation returns NULL here, which ultimately triggers a `handshake failed` alert back in the `tls_accept` code.

Finally, record the client random for the key exchange step and clean up.

```
memcpy( ( void * ) parameters->client_random, &hello.random.gmt_unix_time, 4 );
memcpy( ( void * ) ( parameters->client_random + 4 ),
  ( void * ) hello.random.random_bytes, 28 );

free( hello.cipher_suites );
free( hello.compression_methods );

if ( hello.session_id )
{
  free( hello.session_id );
}

return read_pos;
}
```

## TLS Server Hello

Sending a server hello is pretty much the same as sending a client hello; the only difference between the two structures is that the server hello only has space for one cipher suite and one compression method. This is shown in Listing 7-10.

**Listing 7-10:** "tls.c" send_server_hello

```
static int send_server_hello( int connection, TLSParameters *parameters )

{
  ServerHello      package;
  int              send_buffer_size;
  char             *send_buffer;
  void             *write_buffer;
  time_t           local_time;

  package.server_version.major = 3;
  package.server_version.minor = 1;
  time( &local_time );
  package.random.gmt_unix_time = htonl( local_time );
  // TODO - actually make this random.
  // This is 28 bytes, but server random is 32 - the first four bytes of
  // "server random" are the GMT unix time computed above.
  memcpy( parameters->server_random, &package.random.gmt_unix_time, 4 );
  memcpy( package.random.random_bytes, parameters->server_random + 4, 28 );
  package.session_id_length = 0;
  package.cipher_suite = htons( parameters->pending_send_parameters.suite );
  package.compression_method = 0;

  send_buffer_size = sizeof( ProtocolVersion ) +
```

```
          sizeof( Random ) +
          sizeof( unsigned char ) +
          ( sizeof( unsigned char ) * package.session_id_length ) +
          sizeof( unsigned short ) +
          sizeof( unsigned char );

  write_buffer = send_buffer = ( char * ) malloc( send_buffer_size );

  write_buffer = append_buffer( write_buffer,
                          ( void * ) &package.server_version.major, 1 );
  write_buffer = append_buffer( write_buffer,
                          ( void * ) &package.server_version.minor, 1 );
  write_buffer = append_buffer( write_buffer,
                          ( void * ) &package.random.gmt_unix_time, 4 );
  write_buffer = append_buffer( write_buffer,
                          ( void * ) &package.random.random_bytes, 28 );
  write_buffer = append_buffer( write_buffer,
                          ( void * ) &package.session_id_length, 1 );
  if ( package.session_id_length > 0 )
  {
    write_buffer = append_buffer( write_buffer, ( void * )package.session_id,
      package.session_id_length );
  }
  write_buffer = append_buffer( write_buffer,
                          ( void * ) &package.cipher_suite, 2 );
  write_buffer = append_buffer( write_buffer,
                          ( void * ) &package.compression_method, 1 );

  assert( ( ( char * ) write_buffer - send_buffer ) == send_buffer_size );

  send_handshake_message( connection, server_hello, send_buffer,
                          send_buffer_size, parameters );

  free( send_buffer );

  return 0;
}
```

The selected cipher suite is copied from `pending_send_parameters` and bundled off to the client. Notice that the session ID sent by this implementation is empty; this is permissible per the specification and indicates to the client that this server either does not support session resumption or does not intend to resume this session.

## TLS Certificate

After the server hello is sent, the server should send a certificate, if the cipher spec calls for one (which is the case in the most common cipher specs). Because the certificate normally must be signed by a certificate authority in order to be accepted, it's usually pre-generated and signed, and it must be loaded from disk to be presented to the user. There's no realistic way to generate a new certificate with a new public key "on the fly."

Recall that the certificate handshake message was the length of the chain, followed by the length of the certificate, followed by the certificate, followed by (optionally) another length of a certificate/certificate, and so on. The simplest case is a certificate chain consisting of one certificate, so the certificate must be loaded from disk, the length must be checked, prepended twice, and the whole array serialized as a TLS handshake message. This is shown in Listing 7-11.

**Listing 7-11:** "tls.c" send_certificate

```c
static int send_certificate( int connection, TLSParameters *parameters )
{
  short send_buffer_size;
  unsigned char *send_buffer, *read_buffer;
  int certificate_file;
  struct stat certificate_stat;
  short cert_len;
  if ( ( certificate_file = open( "cert.der", O_RDONLY ) ) == -1 )
  {
    perror( "unable to load certificate file" );
    return 1;
  }

  if ( fstat( certificate_file, &certificate_stat ) == -1 )
  {
    perror( "unable to stat certificate file" );
    return 1;
  }

  // Allocate enough space for the certificate file, plus 2 3-byte length
  // entries.
  send_buffer_size = certificate_stat.st_size + 6;
  send_buffer = ( unsigned char * ) malloc( send_buffer_size );
  memset( send_buffer, '\0', send_buffer_size );
  cert_len = certificate_stat.st_size + 3;
  cert_len = htons( cert_len );
  memcpy( ( void * ) ( send_buffer + 1 ), &cert_len, 2 );

  cert_len = certificate_stat.st_size;
  cert_len = htons( cert_len );
  memcpy( ( void * ) ( send_buffer + 4 ), &cert_len, 2 );

  read_buffer = send_buffer + 6;
  cert_len = certificate_stat.st_size;

  while ( ( read_buffer - send_buffer ) < send_buffer_size )
  {
    int read_size;
    read_size = read( certificate_file, read_buffer, cert_len );
```

```
    read_buffer += read_size;
    cert_len -= read_size;
  }

  if ( close( certificate_file ) == -1 )
  {
    perror( "unable to close certificate file" );
    return 1;
  }

  send_handshake_message( connection, certificate, send_buffer,
                          send_buffer_size, parameters );

  free( send_buffer );

  return 0;
}
```

This loads the file cert.der from the current directory into memory, builds a certificate handshake message, and sends it on. Notice the use of `fstat` to allocate a buffer of exactly the right size for the certificate file, along with two three-byte length fields. The first length field is three more than the second because it includes the second length in its count. Of course, all of the lengths need to be given in network, not host, order. Although there's no three-byte integral type, it's doubtful that a certificate is going to be greater than 65,536 bytes in length, so this code just assumes two byte lengths and pads with an extra 0 to satisfy the formatting requirements.

You can almost certainly see an obvious performance improvement here; nothing in this packet changes from one handshake to the next. Although the code as presented here permits the server administrator to update the certificate without a server restart, the performance hit of loading the entire thing from file to satisfy every single HTTP connection is probably not worth this flexibility. This message ought to be cached in memory and sent from cache after it's generated the first time.

## TLS Server Hello Done

As you can see from Listing 7-12, there's not much to the server hello done message:

**Listing 7-12:** "tls.c" send_server_hello_done

```
static int send_server_hello_done( int connection, TLSParameters *parameters )
{
  send_handshake_message( connection, server_hello_done, NULL, 0, parameters );

  return 0;
}
```

## TLS Client Key Exchange

If you look back at Listing 7-4, you see that after the server sends the hello done message, it waits for the client to respond with a key exchange message. This should contain either an RSA-encrypted premaster secret or the last half of a Diffie-Hellman handshake, depending on the key exchange method chosen. In general, the server certificate is expected to have contained enough information for the client to do so. (You see in the next chapter what happens if this is not the case.)

So add the `client_key_exchange` message to `receive_tls_message` in Listing 7-13.

**Listing 7-13:** "tls.c" receive_tls_msg with client_key_exchange

```
static int receive_tls_msg( int connection,
                            char *buffer,
                            int bufsz,
                            TLSParameters *parameters )
{
…

    switch ( handshake.msg_type )
    {
…

      case client_key_exchange:
        read_pos = parse_client_key_exchange( read_pos, handshake.length,
          parameters );
        if ( read_pos == NULL )
        {
          send_alert_message( connection, illegal_parameter,
            &parameters->active_send_parameters );
          return -1;
        }
        break;
```

`parse_client_key_exchange` reads the premaster secret, expands it into a master secret and then into key material, and updates the pending cipher spec. Remember that the pending cipher spec cannot be made active until a change cipher spec message is received.

TLS 1.0 supports two different key exchange methods: RSA and Diffie-Hellman. To process an RSA client key exchange, the server must use the private key to decrypt the premaster secret that the client encrypts and sends. To process a DH client key exchange, the server must compute $z = Y_c^a \% p$; $Y_c$ will have been sent in the client key exchange message. However, the server must have sent $g$, $p$, and $Y_s = g^a \% p$ in the first place. Although there's a provision in the X.509 specification to allow the server to send this information in the certificate itself, I'm not aware of any software that generates a Diffie-Hellman certificate. In fact, the specification for Diffie-Hellman certificates puts $p$ and $g$ in the certificate, which makes perfect sense, but it also puts $Y_s$ in the certificate.

Because the whole certificate must be signed by a certificate authority, this means that the corresponding secret value *a* must be used over and over for multiple handshakes; ideally, you'd want to select a new one for each connection.

Does this mean that Diffie-Hellman key exchange is never used in TLS? It doesn't, but it does mean that it's usually used in a slightly more complex way, which is examined in the next chapter. This section instead simply focuses on the conceptually simpler RSA key exchange.

### RSA Key Exchange and Private Key Location

RSA key exchange, then, consists of loading the private key corresponding to the public key previously transmitted in the certificate message, decrypting the client key exchange message, and extracting the premaster key. After this has been done, the `compute_master_secret` and `calculate_keys` functions from the previous chapter can be used to complete the key exchange (with one minor difference, detailed later, to account for the fact that this is now the server and the read and write keys must be swapped). You know how RSA decryption works; the `rsa_decrypt` function was developed in Listing 3-20; the padding used by TLS is the same PKCS #1.5 padding implemented there.

However, where does the private key come from in the first place? It's obviously not in the certificate. Recall from Chapter 5 that when you generated your own test self-signed certificate, you actually output two files: cert.der and key.der. key.der contained the private key. A DER-encoded file is a binary file that you can't read without special software, but a PEM (Base64-encoded) key file — which is actually the default in OpenSSL if you don't specifically ask for DER — can be loaded in a standard text editor.

```
-----BEGIN RSA PRIVATE KEY-----
Proc-Type: 4,ENCRYPTED
DEK-Info: DES-EDE3-CBC,BD1FF235EA6104E1

rURbzE1gnHP0Pcq6SeXvMeP6b5pNmJSpJxCZtuBkC0iTNwRRwICcv0pVNTgkut1U
sCnstPyVh/JRU94KQKS0e471Jsq8FKFYqhpDuu1gq7eUGnajFnIh2UvNASVSit6i
6VpJAAs8y1wrt93FfiCMyKiYYGYAOEaE2paDJ4E8zjyVB253BoXDY4PUHpuZDQpL
Oxd2mplnTI+5wLomXwW4hjRpX61xfg7ed2RKw00jSx89dkqTgI3jv2VoYqzO88Rb
EnQp+2+iSEo+CYvhO26c7c12hGzW0P0fE5o1OYnUv5WFPnjBmheWRkAj+K2eeS6w
qMTsv1OzKR02gxMWt1JQc2JmnUCfypjTcf9FSGHQKaPSDqbs/1/m+U9DzuzD6NUH
/EUWR6m1WxQiORzDUtHrTZ3tJmuGGUEhpqIjpFsL//0=
-----END RSA PRIVATE KEY-----
```

As the headers indicate, this file is encrypted by default; if you recall, you were prompted for a password before this was generated.

OpenSSL does have an option to write an encrypted RSA private key file in plaintext.

```
[jdavies@localhost ssl]$ openssl rsa -in key.pem -out key_decoded.pem
writing RSA key
```

Now the contents of the same key are output in a nice, neat, PEM-encoded ASN.1 structure like the ones you're used to.

```
-----BEGIN RSA PRIVATE KEY-----
MIIBOwIBAAJBALGybTND0yjFYJBkXg3cFpYy/C76CFtoqOAyLEjH8RRcPCt6CsTo
bxaDC1Lmdaxddti4fbpRG+RPS8gVeCrzvwECAwEAAQJBAJrPX+Oxy11R1/bz+h0J
CYSBlsM2geFhJP9ttrcRui6JWQlbEHHQiF1OI9sedv6hDbgynUKdh+Lgo4KHzCTD
OYECIQDZ/iNMPqXJDNBd8JBHNsJIqU+tNWPS7wjvp/ivcCcVDQIhANCtu6MGz9tQ
S7DkyIYQxuvtxFQsIzir62b6yx2KV7zFAiBatPrvEOpfHCvfyufeGhUBsyHqStr8
vGYVgulh5uL8SQIgVCdLvQHZPutRquoITjBj1+8JtpwaFBeYle3bjW0l1rUCIQDV
dUNImB3h18TEB3RwSFoTufh+UlaqBHnXLR8HiTPs6g==
-----END RSA PRIVATE KEY-----
```

To read and use this, it's just a matter of writing code to parse it and extract the private key exponent. This is shown in Listing 7-14.

**Listing 7-14:** "privkey.c" parse_private_key

```
/**
 * Parse the modulus and private exponent from the buffer, which
 * should contain a DER-encoded RSA private key file.  There's a
 * lot more information in the private key file format, but this
 * app isn't set up to use any of it.
 * This, according to PKCS #1 (note that this is not in pkcs #8 format), is:
 * Version
 * modulus (n)
 * public exponent (e)
 * private exponent (d)
 * prime1 (p)
 * prime2 (q)
 * exponent1 (d mod p-1)
 * exponent2 (d mod q-1)
 * coefficient (inverse of q % p)
 * Here, all we care about is n & d.
 */
int parse_private_key( rsa_key *privkey,
                       const unsigned char *buffer,
                       int buffer_length )
{
  struct asn1struct private_key;
  struct asn1struct *version;
  struct asn1struct *modulus;
  struct asn1struct *public_exponent;
  struct asn1struct *private_exponent;

  asn1parse( buffer, buffer_length, &private_key );

  version = ( struct asn1struct * ) private_key.children;
  modulus = ( struct asn1struct * ) version->next;
  // Just read this to skip over it
  public_exponent = ( struct asn1struct * ) modulus->next;
  private_exponent = ( struct asn1struct * ) public_exponent->next;
```

```
  privkey->modulus = malloc( sizeof( huge ) );
  privkey->exponent = malloc( sizeof( huge ) );
  load_huge( privkey->modulus, modulus->data, modulus->length );
  load_huge( privkey->exponent, private_exponent->data, private_exponent->length );

  asn1free( &private_key );

  return 0;
}
```

This is a regular ASN.1 parsing routine of the kind examined in Chapter 5. It takes as input a DER-encoded buffer that it parses and uses to fill out the `privkey` argument, a pointer to an `rsa_key` structure. Remember that an RSA private key is structurally no different than an RSA public key, so the same structure is used to represent both here. Notice that the input is DER-encoded; the caller must ensure either that the file is loaded from the disk that way or that it's passed through the `pem_decode` routine from Listing 5-7 before being passed to `parse_private_key`.

The private key structure, as indicated by the comments to this function, contains quite a bit more information than just the modulus and the private exponent; these numbers in theory could be used to support a more optimized `rsa_decrypt` routine than the one presented in Chapter 3.

If you want to see this in action, you can put together a test `main` routine as shown in Listing 7-15.

**Listing 7-15:** "privkey.c" test main routine

```
#ifdef TEST_PRIVKEY
int main( int argc, char *argv[ ] )
{
  rsa_key privkey;
  unsigned char *buffer;
  int buffer_length;

  if ( argc < 3 )
  {
    fprintf( stderr, "Usage: %s [-pem|-der] <rsa private key file>\n", argv[ 0 ] );
    exit( 0 );
  }

  if ( !( buffer = load_file_into_memory( argv[ 2 ], &buffer_length ) ) )
  {
    perror( "Unable to load file" );
    exit( 1 );
  }

  if ( !strcmp( argv[ 1 ], "-pem" ) )
  {
    // XXX this overallocates a bit, since it sets aside space for markers, etc.
```

*(Continued)*

```
    unsigned char *pem_buffer = buffer;
    buffer = (unsigned char * ) malloc( buffer_length );
    buffer_length = pem_decode( pem_buffer, buffer );
    free( pem_buffer );
  }

  parse_private_key( &privkey, buffer, buffer_length );

  printf( "Modulus:" );
  show_hex( privkey.modulus->rep, privkey.modulus->size );
  printf( "Private Exponent:" );
  show_hex( privkey.exponent->rep, privkey.exponent->size );

  free( buffer );

  return 0;
}
#endif
```

This relies on the simple utility function `load_file_into_memory` shown in Listing 7-16.

**Listing 7-16:** "file.c" load_file_into_memory

```
/**
 * Read a whole file into memory and return a pointer to that memory chunk,
 * or NULL if something went wrong.  Caller must free the allocated memory.
 */
char *load_file_into_memory( char *filename, int *buffer_length )
{
  int file;
  struct stat file_stat;
  char *buffer, *bufptr;
  int buffer_size;
  int bytes_read;

  if ( ( file = open( filename, O_RDONLY ) ) == -1 )
  {
    perror( "Unable to open file" );
    return NULL;
  }

  // Slurp the whole thing into memory
  if ( fstat( file, &file_stat ) )
  {
    perror( "Unable to stat certificate file" );
    return NULL;
  }

  buffer_size = file_stat.st_size;

  buffer = ( char * ) malloc( buffer_size );
```

```
if ( !buffer )
{
  perror( "Not enough memory" );
  return NULL;
}

bufptr = buffer;

while ( ( bytes_read = read( file, ( void * ) buffer, buffer_size ) ) )
{
  bufptr += bytes_read;
}

close( file );

if ( buffer_length != NULL )
{
  *buffer_length = buffer_size;
}

return buffer;
}
```

### Supporting Encrypted Private Key Files

If you run `privkey` on the previously generated private key file, you see the modulus and private exponent of your RSA key:

```
[jdavies@localhost ssl]$ ./privkey -pem key_decoded.pem
Modulus:b1b26d3343d328c56090645e0ddc169632fc2efa085b68a8e0322c48c7f1145c3c2
b7a0ac4e86f16830b52e675ac5d76d8b87dba511be44f4bc815782af3bf01
Private Exponent:9acf5fe3b1cb5d51d7f6f3fa1d0909848196c33681e16124ff6db6b711ba2e8959
095b1071d0885d4e23db1e76fea10db8329d429d87e2e0a38287cc24c33981
```

Still, it seems a shame to require that the server user keep the private key stored in plaintext on a disk somewhere. As you can see from the header on the original, encrypted key file, this is encrypted using DES, which you have code to decrypt. Why not go ahead and implement the code to decrypt the encrypted file?

The file, by default, starts with two bits of information:

```
Proc-Type: 4,ENCRYPTED
DEK-Info: DES-EDE3-CBC,BD1FF235EA6104E1
```

First, the Proc-Type tells you that the file is encrypted. The DEK-Info gives you the encryption algorithm, followed by an initialization vector.

Note that the key contents themselves are PKCS #1 formatted, but the extra header information is OpenSSL/PEM-specific. In fact, if you use OpenSSL to save the key file itself in DER format, you lose the encryption. Because there's no way to communicate the required initialization vector and encryption algorithm, OpenSSL saves you from shooting yourself in the foot and always stores a DER-encoded key file unencrypted, even if you ask for encryption.

A more standardized format, *PKCS #8*, describes essentially the same information. Although OpenSSL supports the format, there's no way to generate a key file in PKCS #8 format on an initial certificate request. You can convert an OpenSSL to a PKCS #8 private key via:

```
[jdavies@localhost ssl]$ openssl pkcs8 -topk8 -in key.der -out key.pkcs8 \
  -outform der
Enter pass phrase for key.der:
Enter Encryption Password:
Verifying - Enter Encryption Password:
```

This, by default, encrypts the file using DES; other encryption options are possible, of course. The output is a triply nested ASN.1 DER encoded structure. At the bottom layer of nesting is, of course, the PKCS #1-formatted private key, which the `parse_private_key` routine of Listing 7-14 can parse correctly. That structure is bit-string encoded and wrapped up as shown in Figure 7-1 in another structure that includes an OID identifying the type of private key — for example, to allow a non-RSA private key, such as DSA, to be included instead.

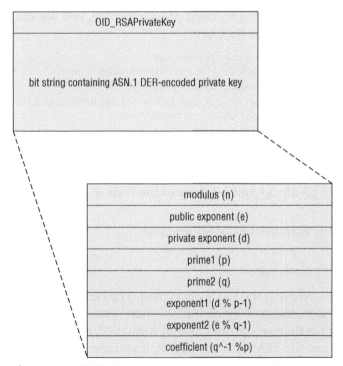

**Figure 7-1:** PKCS #8 contents

This whole structure is bit-string encoded, encrypted, and wrapped up in the final, third, ASN.1 structure shown in Figure 7-2 that indicates the encryption method used and enough information to decrypt it before processing. This section bears a bit more explanation.

Recall from Chapter 2 that you examined examples of symmetric encryption where a passphrase such as `"password"` or `"encrypt_thisdata"` was used as a key input to the encryption algorithms. However, using human-readable text such as this is actually a bad idea when you want to protect data. An attacker knows that the keyspace is limited to the printable-ASCII character set that the user can type on the keyboard. However, you can't exactly require your users to type characters not available on their keyboards either. *PKCS #5* describes a solution to this conundrum called *password-based encryption* (PBE). The idea here is to take the user's input and feed it into a one-way hash function to securely generate a key whose bits are far better distributed than the limited range of the available printable-ASCII character set.

By itself, this doesn't accomplish anything, though. An attacker can still easily mount a dictionary attack on the one-way hash function; the rainbow tables examined in Chapter 4 are perfect for this. Not only is the user's typed input fed into the hash function to generate the keying material, a *salt* is added to this to thwart dictionary attacks.

However, as you recall, salts/initialization vectors must be distributed non-securely so that both sides know what they are, and PKCS #5 is no exception. Therefore, a determined attacker (and remember we're talking about protecting the keys to the kingdom — the server's private key — here) could still mount a dictionary attack using the unencrypted salt value. He couldn't take advantage of a pre-computed rainbow table, but still, the input space of printable-ASCII characters is far smaller than the entire space of potential hash inputs. Especially considering that users generally pick bad passwords that follow the typing and spelling conventions of their native spoken languages, the attacker can probably mount an offline attack in a few weeks to a month. To slow the attacker down a bit, PKCS #5 finally mandates that the output from the first hash be rehashed and the output of *that* hash be rehashed, over and over again, up to a specified iteration count. Typically this is a large number, in the thousands – it's not a big deal for somebody with access to the correct passphrase to do a few thousand hashes, but it is a big deal for an attacker who has a large key space to search through. Finally, after all that hashing, the key material is taken from the final resultant hash value.

The top-level PKCS #8 structure indicates what encryption algorithm was used to encrypt the actual private key data — for instance "password-based encryption using the MD5 hash function and the DES encryption function." In the case of DES with MD5, because MD5 produces 16 bytes of output, the DES key is the first eight bytes of this output, and the initialization vector is the last eight bytes.

Thus, the final PKCS #8 structure looks like this:

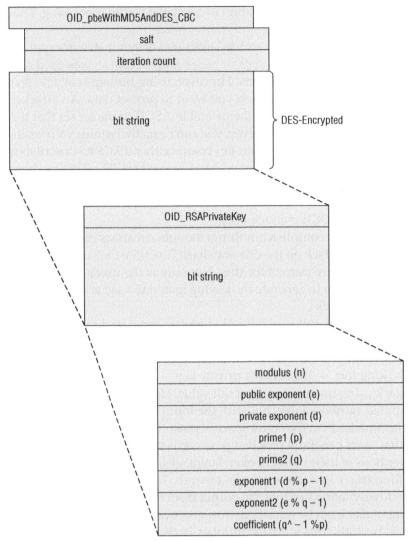

**Figure 7-2:** PKCS #8-encoded private key file

To decode this, then, you must first unwrap the top level structure and then decrypt it to reveal the second level structure, and finally unwrap that to reveal the key. Listing 7-17 illustrates this process for the case of an RSA private key encrypted using PBE with DES/MD5.

**Listing 7-17:** "privkey.c" parse_pkcs8_private_key

```
static unsigned char OID_pbeWithMD5andDES_CBC[] =
   { 0x2a, 0x86, 0x48, 0x86, 0xf7, 0x0d, 0x01, 0x05, 0x03 };
```

```c
static unsigned char OID_RSAPrivateKey [] =
  { 0x2a, 0x86, 0x48, 0x86, 0xf7, 0x0d, 0x01, 0x01, 0x01 };

int parse_pkcs8_private_key( rsa_key *privkey,
                             const unsigned char *buffer,
                             const int buffer_length,
                             const unsigned char *passphrase )
{
  struct asn1struct pkcs8_key;
  struct asn1struct private_key;
  struct asn1struct *encryptionId;
  struct asn1struct *salt;
  struct asn1struct *iteration_count;
  struct asn1struct *encrypted_key;
  struct asn1struct *key_type_oid;
  struct asn1struct *priv_key_data;
  digest_ctx initial_hash;
  int counter;
  unsigned char passphrase_hash_in[ MD5_RESULT_SIZE * sizeof( int ) ];
  unsigned char passphrase_hash_out[ MD5_RESULT_SIZE * sizeof( int ) ];
  unsigned char *decrypted_key;

  asn1parse( buffer, buffer_length, &pkcs8_key );

  encryptionId = pkcs8_key.children->children;
  if ( memcmp( OID_pbeWithMD5andDES_CBC, encryptionId->data,
               encryptionId->length ) )
  {
    fprintf( stderr, "Unsupported key encryption algorithm\n" );
    asn1free( &pkcs8_key );
    return 1;
  }
  // TODO support more algorithms
  salt = encryptionId->next->children;
  iteration_count = salt->next;
  encrypted_key = pkcs8_key.children->next;

  // ugly typecasting
  counter = ntohs( *iteration_count->data );

  new_md5_digest( &initial_hash );
  update_digest( &initial_hash, passphrase, strlen( passphrase ) );
  update_digest( &initial_hash, salt->data, salt->length );
  finalize_digest( &initial_hash );
  memcpy( passphrase_hash_out, initial_hash.hash,
    initial_hash.hash_len * sizeof( int ) );
  while ( --counter )
  {
    memcpy( passphrase_hash_in, passphrase_hash_out,
      sizeof( int ) * MD5_RESULT_SIZE );
```

*(Continued)*

```
    md5_hash( passphrase_hash_in,
      sizeof( int ) * MD5_RESULT_SIZE,
      ( unsigned int * ) passphrase_hash_out );
  }
  decrypted_key = ( unsigned char * ) malloc( encrypted_key->length );
  des_decrypt( encrypted_key->data, encrypted_key->length, decrypted_key,
    ( unsigned char * ) passphrase_hash_out + DES_KEY_SIZE,
    ( unsigned char * ) passphrase_hash_out );

  // sanity check
  if ( decrypted_key[ encrypted_key->length - 1 ] > 8 )
  {
    fprintf( stderr, "Decryption error, bad padding\n");
    asn1free( &pkcs8_key );
    free( decrypted_key );
    return 1;
  }
  asn1parse( decrypted_key,
    encrypted_key->length - decrypted_key[ encrypted_key->length - 1 ],
    &private_key );
  free( decrypted_key );
  key_type_oid = private_key.children->next->children;
  if ( memcmp( OID_RSAPrivateKey, key_type_oid->data, key_type_oid->length ) )
  {
    fprintf( stderr, "Unsupported private key type" );
    asn1free( &pkcs8_key );
    asn1free( &private_key );
  }

  priv_key_data = private_key.children->next->next;

  parse_private_key( privkey, priv_key_data->data, priv_key_data->length );

  asn1free( &pkcs8_key );
  asn1free( &private_key );

  return 0;
}
```

The first part is pretty straightforward; at this point, you're dealing with an ASN.1 DER-encoded structure just like the ones you examined in Chapter 5. Parse it with `asn1parse` and extract the information, after making sure that the encryption algorithm is actually the one supported by this routine.

```
asn1parse( buffer, buffer_length, &pkcs8_key );

encryptionId = pkcs8_key.children->children;
if ( memcmp( OID_pbeWithMD5andDES_CBC, encryptionId->data,
             encryptionId->length ) )
{
```

```
      fprintf( stderr, "Unsupported key encryption algorithm\n" );
      asn1free( &pkcs8_key );
      return 1;
  }
  // TODO support more algorithms
  salt = encryptionId->next->children;
  iteration_count = salt->next;
  encrypted_key = pkcs8_key.children->next;
```

The same caveat about error checking from Chapter 5 applies here, although
at the very least, you're not dealing with data transmitted by some random
stranger over the Internet. A mistake here is likely to be user or programmer
error rather than a malicious attack.

Next, decrypt the encrypted private key structure following the PKCS #5
structure.

```
  // ugly typecasting
  counter = ntohs( *iteration_count->data );

  // Since the passphrase can be any length, not necessarily 8 bytes,
  // must use a digest here.
  new_md5_digest( &initial_hash );
  update_digest( &initial_hash, passphrase, strlen( passphrase ) );
  update_digest( &initial_hash, salt->data, salt->length );
  finalize_digest( &initial_hash );
  memcpy( passphrase_hash_out, initial_hash.hash,
    initial_hash.hash_len * sizeof( int ) );
  while ( --counter )
  {
    memcpy( passphrase_hash_in, passphrase_hash_out,
      sizeof( int ) * MD5_RESULT_SIZE );
    // Since MD5 always outputs 8 bytes, input size is known; can
    // use md5_hash directly in this case; no need for a digest.
    md5_hash( passphrase_hash_in,
      sizeof( int ) * MD5_RESULT_SIZE,
      ( unsigned int * ) passphrase_hash_out );
  }
  decrypted_key = ( unsigned char * ) malloc( encrypted_key->length );
  des_decrypt( encrypted_key->data, encrypted_key->length, decrypted_key,
    ( unsigned char * ) passphrase_hash_out + DES_KEY_SIZE,
    ( unsigned char * ) passphrase_hash_out );
```

If PBE was used elsewhere in this program, this section might be useful to
extract as a separate function call; it's instead included inline here:

1. The initial hash is built as the concatenation of the passphrase, which was
   passed as an argument to the function, and the salt, which was part of the
   key file itself.

2. This hash is hashed over and over, `counter` times, to generate the keying
   material.

3. This keying material, along with the encrypted structure, is passed into `des_decrypt`. This process is illustrated in Figure 7-3.

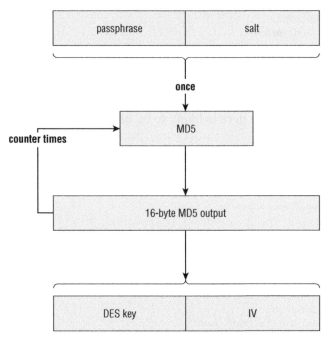

**Figure 7-3:** PKCS #5 password-based encryption

### Checking That Decryption was Successful

If the passphrase was wrong, you still get back a data block here; it's probably a bad idea to blindly continue with the data without first checking that it decrypted correctly. Fortunately, there's a simple way to check for success with a reasonable degree of accuracy. Remember that DES data is always block-aligned. If the input is already eight-byte aligned, an extra eight bytes of padding is always added to the end. Therefore, if the last byte of the decrypted data is not between 1 and 8, then the decryption process failed. Of course, it could fail and still have a final byte in the range between 1 and 8. Technically speaking, you ought to go ahead and check the padding bytes themselves as well to minimize the chance of a false positive.

```
// sanity check
if ( decrypted_key[ encrypted_key->length - 1 ] > 8 )
{
  fprintf( stderr, "Decryption error, bad padding\n");
  asn1free( &pkcs8_key );
  free( decrypted_key );
  return 1;
}
```

Finally, the decrypted data must be ASN.1 parsed. After parsing, double-check that OID really declares it as an RSA private key before passing it on to the previously examined `parse_private_key` routine to extract the actual key value.

```
asn1parse( decrypted_key,
  encrypted_key->length - decrypted_key[ encrypted_key->length - 1 ],
  &private_key );
free( decrypted_key );
key_type_oid = private_key.children->next->children;
if ( memcmp( OID_RSAPrivateKey, key_type_oid->data, key_type_oid->length ) )
{
  fprintf( stderr, "Unsupported private key type" );
  asn1free( &pkcs8_key );
  asn1free( &private_key );
}

priv_key_data = private_key.children->next->next;

parse_private_key( privkey, priv_key_data->data, priv_key_data->length );
```

## Completing the Key Exchange

Now that you can read a stored private key from disk, whether it's stored unencrypted or in the standardized PKCS #8 format (they're also sometimes stored in PKCS #12 format, which isn't examined here), you can complete the key exchange, as shown in Listing 7-18.

**Listing 7-18:** "tls.c" parse_client_key_exchange

```
/**
 * By the time this is called, "read_pos" points at an RSA encrypted (unless
 * RSA isn't used for key exchange) premaster secret.  All this routine has to
 * do is decrypt it.  See "privkey.c" for details.
 * TODO expand this to support Diffie-Hellman key exchange
 */
static unsigned char *parse_client_key_exchange( unsigned char *read_pos,
                                                 int pdu_length,
                                                 TLSParameters *parameters )
{
  int premaster_secret_length;
  unsigned char *buffer;
  int buffer_length;
  unsigned char *premaster_secret;
  rsa_key private_key;

  // TODO make this configurable
  // XXX this really really should be buffered
  if ( !( buffer = load_file_into_memory( "key.pkcs8", &buffer_length ) ) )
  {
    perror( "Unable to load file" );
```

*(Continued)*

```
    return 0;
  }

  parse_pkcs8_private_key( &private_key, buffer, buffer_length, "password" );

  free( buffer );

  // Skip over the two length bytes, since length is already known anyway
  premaster_secret_length = rsa_decrypt( read_pos + 2, pdu_length - 2,
    &premaster_secret, &private_key );

  if ( premaster_secret_length <= 0 )
  {
    fprintf( stderr, "Unable to decrypt premaster secret.\n" );
    return NULL;
  }

  free_huge( private_key.modulus );
  free_huge( private_key.exponent );
  free( private_key.modulus );
  free( private_key.exponent );

  // Now use the premaster secret to compute the master secret.  Don't forget
  // that the first two bytes of the premaster secret are the version 0x03 0x01
  // These are part of the premaster secret (8.1.1 states that the premaster
  // secret for RSA is exactly 48 bytes long).
  compute_master_secret( premaster_secret, MASTER_SECRET_LENGTH, parameters );

  calculate_keys( parameters );

  return read_pos + pdu_length;
}
```

This should be easy to follow. The private key is loaded into memory and parsed; the private key is then used to decrypt the premaster secret. Of course, the same points about storing and buffering the private key apply here as they did to the certificate in the previous section.

The master secret computation and key calculation are almost identical on the server side as on the client side. The only difference is that, now, as the server, the read and write keys are reversed. Because you want to go ahead and use the exact same `tls_send` and `tls_recv` functions as before, remember that `tls_send` is looking for the write key, and `tls_recv` is looking for the read key. This means that you have to add a check in `calculate_keys` to determine if the current process is the client or the server and adjust accordingly in Listing 7-19.

**Listing 7-19:** "tls.c" calculate_keys with server support

```
static void calculate_keys( TLSParameters *parameters )
{
…
  if ( parameters->connection_end == connection_end_client )
```

```
{
  key_block_ptr = read_buffer( send_parameters->MAC_secret, key_block,
    suite->hash_size );
  key_block_ptr = read_buffer( recv_parameters->MAC_secret, key_block_ptr,
    suite->hash_size );
  key_block_ptr = read_buffer( send_parameters->key, key_block_ptr,
    suite->key_size );
  key_block_ptr = read_buffer( recv_parameters->key, key_block_ptr,
    suite->key_size );
  key_block_ptr = read_buffer( send_parameters->IV, key_block_ptr,
    suite->IV_size );
  key_block_ptr = read_buffer( recv_parameters->IV, key_block_ptr,
    suite->IV_size );
}
else  // I'm the server
{
  key_block_ptr = read_buffer( recv_parameters->MAC_secret, key_block,
    suite->hash_size );
  key_block_ptr = read_buffer( send_parameters->MAC_secret, key_block_ptr,
    suite->hash_size );
  key_block_ptr = read_buffer( recv_parameters->key, key_block_ptr,
    suite->key_size );
  key_block_ptr = read_buffer( send_parameters->key, key_block_ptr,
    suite->key_size );
  key_block_ptr = read_buffer( recv_parameters->IV, key_block_ptr,
    suite->IV_size );
  key_block_ptr = read_buffer( send_parameters->IV, key_block_ptr,
    suite->IV_size );
}
```

The benefit of this approach is that `tls_recv` and `tls_send` work exactly as before. They don't care whether they're operating in the context of a client or a server.

## TLS Change Cipher Spec

After receiving the key exchange and parsing it correctly, the server must send a *change cipher spec* message. It can't send one until the key exchange is complete because it doesn't know the keys. This message informs the client that it is starting to encrypt every following packet, and it expects the client to do the same.

The `send_change_cipher_spec` function is the same one shown in Listing 6-40; it looks exactly the same when the server sends it as it does when the client sends it.

## TLS Finished

Finally, the server sends its *finished* message. Recall from Listing 7-4 that the client sends its finished message before the server does. Making sure to keep this ordering straight is important because one of the finished messages includes the other one in the handshake digest. The protocol would have worked just as well if the client waited for the server to send its finished message first, but it's critical that they both agree on the order for interoperability.

The `send_finished` code from Listing 6-48 can be used almost as is; the only difference between a client finished and a server finished is that the label input to the PRF by the server is the string `"server finished"`, rather than the string `"client finished"`. This necessitates one small change to the `send_finished` function shown in Listing 7-20.

**Listing 7-20:** "tls.c" send_finished with server support

```
static int send_finished( int connection,
                          TLSParameters *parameters )
{
  unsigned char verify_data[ VERIFY_DATA_LEN ];

  compute_verify_data(
    parameters->connection_end == connection_end_client ?
      "client finished" : "server finished",
    parameters, verify_data );
```

And that's it. Everything else continues on just as it would have if this were a client connection; TLS doesn't care which endpoint you are after the handshake is complete.

You can run this `ssl_webserver` and connect to it from a standard browser; the response is the simple "Nothing here" message that was hardcoded into it. You'll have problems with Firefox and IE, unfortunately, because they (still!) try to negotiate an SSLv2 connection before "falling back" to TLS 1.0. Most TLS implementations are set up to recognize and reject SSLv2 connections; this one simply hangs if an SSLv2 connection request is submitted. Of course, the HTTPS client from Chapter 6 should connect with no problems.

You can (and should!) disable SSLv2 support within IE8:

1. Go to Tools ➢ Internet Options ➢ Advanced, and scroll down to the Security section.

2. Uncheck the boxes Use SSL 2.0 and Use SSL 3.0

3. Check the Use TLS 1.0 box, which is unchecked by default. Your Internet Options should look like Figure 7-4.

You should now be able to run the `ssl_webserver` example and connect to it from your browser. The page just states "Nothing here," but if you're feeling adventurous, you can easily change this to display anything you can think of.

If you run into otherwise inexplicable problems, ensure that the certificate file and the key file match. It's very easy to accidentally change a certificate file and forget to change the key file. One way to ensure that you've got the right key file for your certificate file is to compare the RSA moduli of each. If they're the same, the files are matches.

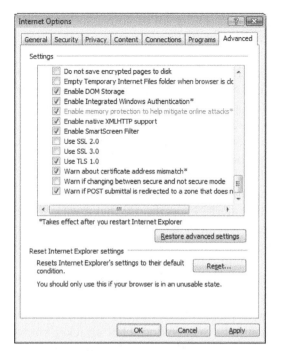

**Figure 7-4:** IE8 Internet Options

Also ensure that your client doesn't request one of the Diffie-Hellman key exchange protocols; this server doesn't support those yet. This is addressed in Chapter 8.

## Avoiding Common Pitfalls When Adding HTTPS Support to a Server

The server must pay closer attention to security than the client. If the client is compromised, one user's data is exposed; if the server is compromised, many users' data is at risk. The developer of the server code must be more careful to guard against security hazards such as data left over in shared cache lines. The topic of secure programming can, and does, span entire books. If you're developing code that will be deployed and used in a multi-user environment, you must be aware of these dangers.

When RSA is used for key exchange, the private key is especially vulnerable to attack. Ensuring that it's stored encrypted on disk using a solid, secure encryption method such as PKCS #5 is a good start. However, the private key itself must also necessarily be stored in memory, and you must take care to ensure that other users of the shared system that the server runs on can't, for example, force a core dump and then read the decrypted key at their leisure.

Although a lazy system administrator can render all of your cautious coding moot, you must still ensure that a diligent system administrator's efforts don't go to waste.

Daniel Bleichenbacher discovered an interesting attack on the RSA private key. This attack wasn't on the server, but on most common implementations of TLS. His idea was to ignore the supplied public key and instead pass a specifically chosen bit string in the client key exchange message. At this point, the server has no choice but to attempt to decrypt it using its private key; it almost certainly retrieves gibberish. Because the server expects a PKCS 1.5-padded premaster secret, it first checks that the first byte is the expected padding byte 0x02; if it isn't, it issues an alert immediately.

Bleichenbacher took advantage of this alert — specifically that it was, at the time, always implemented as a different alert message than the alert that would occur later if a bad record MAC occurred. What would happen is that, most of the time, the server would immediately send an alert indicating that the RSA decryption failed. However, occasionally, the decrypted message would accidentally appear as a valid, padded message. The rest would decrypt in a garbled, unpredictable way, and the subsequent *finished* message would result in a bad record MAC, but the damage would have been done. The attacker knew that the chosen ciphertext did decrypt to a correctly padded message, even if he didn't know what that message was. In this way, TLS was leaking bits of information about the private key, which an attacker could exploit with about a million carefully chosen key exchanges.

The solution to this attack is simple: ignore padding errors and continue on with the key exchange, letting the final finished message failure abort the handshake. This way, the attacker doesn't know if the key exchange decrypted to a properly padded message or not. The implementation presented here doesn't address this, and is susceptible to the Bleichenbacher attack. If you want to tighten up the code to defend against the attack, you can either modify `rsa_decrypt` itself to go ahead and perform a decryption even if the padding type is unrecognized, but still return an error code, or modify `parse_client_key_exchange` to fill the premaster secret buffer with random values on a decryption failure and just continue on with the handshake, allowing the finished verification to cause the handshake to fail.

## When a Browser Displays Errors: Browser Trust Issues

Of course, if you tried to connect to the SSL-secured web server described in this chapter, you almost definitely received some variant of the error message shown in Figure 7-5.

**Figure 7-5:** Certificate Error Message

The error messages make sense. The server is using the self-signed certificate that you generated in Chapter 5, which is certainly not trusted. If you're so inclined, you can add it as a trusted certificate; go to Tools ➢ Internet Options ➢ Content ➢ Certificate ➢ Trusted Root Certification Authorities. (See Figure 7-6.)

**Figure 7-6:** Trusted root certification authorities

Click the Import button and follow the instructions in Figure 7-7 to import cert.der into your trusted certificates list.

**Figure 7-7:** New trusted certification authority

This clears up the first error that the certificate was issued by an untrusted certificate authority (it was issued by itself, actually). The browser still complains that the certificate was issued for a different website's address. You should understand by now that this means that the browser is connecting to localhost, but the certificate's subject has a CN of Joshua Davies. There's nothing stopping you, of course, from issuing a new certificate whose CN field is localhost, which makes this error disappear as well. As long as the certificate is signed by a trusted authority, the browser accepts anything that matches. If you click Continue to This Website, however, your browser remembers that you trust this certificate and automatically connects to it the next time you request it. IE 8 at least has the sense to display a red URL bar and provide a Certificate Error popup.

Watch the server and keep track of how an untrusted certificate error is handled. The client goes ahead and completes the handshake, but then immediately shuts down the connection. It then displays an error message to the user. If the user clicks through, it begins an entirely new SSL session, but this time with a security exception indicating that this site is to be trusted even if something looks wrong.

The only other common error message you might come across is "This site's certificate has expired." Of the error messages you might see, this one is probably the most benign, although it's certainly a headache for a server administrator because most TLS implementations give you no warning when a certificate is close to expiration. One day your site is working just fine; the next day the traffic has dropped to practically zero because your customers are being presented with a scary error message and bailing out. If you don't keep close track of logged error messages, you might have to spend some time investigating before you realize you've had yet another certificate expire.

# CHAPTER 8

# Advanced SSL Topics

The prior two chapters examined the TLS handshake process in detail, walking through each message that each side must send and receive. So far, you've looked at the most common use of SSL/TLS — a server-authenticated RSA key exchange. However, there are actually quite a few more options available to the user when performing a TLS handshake. Some potential scenarios are simpler, and some are more complex than those presented so far — it's possible to connect without authenticating the server, or to force the client to authenticate itself, or to employ different key exchange mechanisms. It's even possible to bypass the handshake completely, if secure parameters have already been negotiated. This chapter looks at the less common — or not strictly required — but still important aspects of the TLS handshake.

## Passing Additional Information with Client Hello Extensions

Peek back to the definition of the handshake messages defined in Chapter 6. Although each one is prepended with a length, most of them — with the exception of the certificate message — have lengths that are fixed or that can easily be inferred from their structure. The client hello message, for instance, is a fixed two bytes of version information, 32 bytes of random data, and three variable-length structures each of which includes their length. The receiver can easily figure out where the record ends without being given an explicit length.

So, why restate the length? Well, the designers of the protocol anticipated, correctly, that they might not have covered all the bases when they described the handshake, so they allowed extra data to be appended to the client hello handshake message. This is the reason why the code in the last chapter handles the parsing of client hello messages differently than all the other messages. In fact, if you tried using TCPdump to sniff your own browser's traffic, you probably noticed some of these extensions in its client hello messages. The TLS protocol designers didn't, however, specify what form these extensions should take. This wasn't actually standardized until years later, when RFC 3546 was drafted.

One of the most important of these standardized extensions is the *server name identification* (SNI) extension. It's common in today's Internet for low-traffic websites to share a hosting provider. There's no particular reason why a blog that gets a few hundred hits a day needs a dedicated server; it can share bandwidth (and costs) with several other sites on a single host. However, this can pose problems for TLS. Each physical server on the Internet has its own IP address, even if that physical host maps to multiple domains. So, for instance, if a shared hosting provider had three hosts named `www.hardware.com`, `www.books.com`, and `www.computers.com`, all hosted from a single physical server, each one would resolve to the same IP address.

This doesn't seem like a problem for TLS until you consider that TLS must send a certificate whose domain name matches the requested domain name to avoid the man-in-the-middle attack described in Chapter 5. However, TLS doesn't know what domain was requested. Domain names are for people; computers deal in IP addresses. Therefore, the client has to have some way to notify the server that it should present the certificate for `www.books.com` rather than the certificate for `www.computers.com`; wildcard certificates don't help here, because it's specifically prohibited to generate a wildcard of the form `*.com` — for obvious reasons.

Therefore, the client is optionally permitted to indicate with a client hello extension the name of the host it's trying to connect to, and all modern browsers do this. It's easy to add client hello extension parsing to the `parse_client_hello` routine from Listing 7-9 as shown in Listing 8-1.

**Listing 8-1:** "tls.c" parse_client_hello with client hello extension support

```
static char *parse_client_hello( char *read_pos,
                                  int pdu_length,
                                  TLSParameters *parameters )
{
  char *init_pos;

  init_pos = read_pos; // keep track of start to check for extensions
```

...

```
    free( hello.session_id );
  }

  // Parse client hello extensions
  if ( ( read_pos - init_pos ) < pdu_length )
  {
    read_pos = parse_client_hello_extensions( read_pos, parameters );
  }

  return read_pos;
}
```

Client hello extensions are, of course, a list of extensions; like every other variable-length list in TLS, the extensions list is preceded by the byte count (not the item count!) of the list that follows. The extensions themselves are as open-ended as possible; each starts with a two-byte extension identifier and another variable-length *blob* of data whose contents depend on the extension identifier. The interpretation of this blob varies greatly from one extension to the next. In many cases, it's yet another variable-length list of data, but in other cases it's a simple numeric type, and sometimes it's empty if the extension is just a marker that indicates that a certain feature is supported.

This book won't exhaustively cover all the available client hello extensions. Of those that are covered, most are discussed as they come up rather than in this section. They'll make more sense that way. However, Listings 8-2 and 8-3 illustrate the parsing of the server name extension:

**Listing 8-2:**  "tls.c" parse_client_hello_extensions

```
typedef enum
{
  server_name = 0
}
ExtensionType;

static char *parse_client_hello_extensions( char *read_pos,
                                            TLSParameters *parameters )
{
  unsigned short extensions_size, extension_data_size;
  char *init_pos;
  ExtensionType type;

  read_pos = read_buffer( ( void * ) &extensions_size, ( void * ) read_pos, 2 );
  extensions_size = ntohs( extensions_size );
  init_pos = read_pos;

  while ( ( read_pos - init_pos ) < extensions_size )
```

*(Continued)*

```
  {
    read_pos = read_buffer( ( void * ) &type, ( void * ) read_pos, 2 );
    read_pos = read_buffer( ( void * ) &extension_data_size,
      ( void * ) read_pos, 2 );
    type = ntohs( type );
    extension_data_size = ntohs( extension_data_size );

    switch ( type )
    {
      case server_name:
        parse_server_name_extension( read_pos, extension_data_size,
          parameters );
        printf( "Got server name extension\n" );
        break;
      default:
        printf( "warning, skipping unsupported client hello extension %d\n",
          type );
        break;
    }

    read_pos += extension_data_size;
  }

  return read_pos;
}
```

**Listing 8-3:** "tls.c" parse_server_name_extension

```
typedef enum
{
  host_name = 0
}
NameType;

static void parse_server_name_extension( unsigned char *data,
                                         unsigned short data_len,
                                         TLSParameters *parameters )
{
  unsigned short server_name_list_len;
  unsigned char name_type;
  unsigned char *data_start;

  data = read_buffer( ( void * ) &server_name_list_len, ( void * ) data, 2 );
  server_name_list_len = ntohs( server_name_list_len );

  data_start = data;

  data = read_buffer( ( void * ) &name_type, ( void * ) data, 1 );

  switch ( name_type )
  {
    case host_name:
```

```
        {
          unsigned short host_name_len;
          unsigned char *host_name;
          data = read_buffer( ( void * ) &host_name_len,
            ( void * ) data, 2 );
          host_name_len = ntohs( host_name_len );
          host_name = malloc( host_name_len + 1 );
          data = read_buffer( ( void * ) host_name,
            ( void * ) data, host_name_len );
          host_name[ host_name_len ] = '\0';
          printf( "got host name '%s'\n", host_name );
          // TODO store this and use it to select a certificate
          // TODO return an "unrecognized_name" alert if the host name
          // is unknown
          free( host_name );
        }
        break;
      default:
        // nothing else defined by the spec
        break;
  }
}
```

As you can see from these listings, there's nothing particularly different about
the server name extension — it's a triply-nested list. Each list is prepended with
a two-byte length that needs to be converted from network order to host order
before the list can be processed, as usual. A client hello with a server name
extension is illustrated in Figure 8-1. Compare this to the plain client hello in
Figure 6-2.

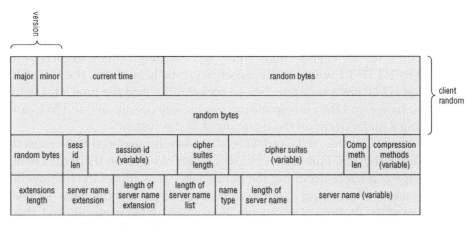

**Figure 8-1:** Client Hello with SNI

Strangely, the server name extension itself allows for a list of host names. It's
not clear how the server ought to behave if one of the names was recognized,
but another wasn't, or if both were recognized and correspond, for example,

to available certificates. Prefer the first? Prefer the last? I know of no TLS client that supports SNI but also sends more than one host name. OpenSSL, reasonably enough, regards it as an error if you pass more than one (prior to version 1.0, though, OpenSSL just ignores this).

The implementation presented in this book is only capable of sending one certificate, so all this code does is print out the host name it receives from the client and throws away the negotiated server name. A more robust implementation would, of course, keep track of this. If the server recognized, accepted, and understood the server name extension, it should include an empty server-name extension in its own hello message, to let the client know that the extension was recognized. This might prompt the client, for instance, to tighten its security requirements if the received certificate was invalid. Of course, this wouldn't be useful against a malicious server, but might expose an innocently misconfigured one.

There are quite a few other extensions defined; RFC 3546 defines six, and there are several others that are fairly common and are examined later.

## Safely Reusing Key Material with Session Resumption

Recall in Chapter 6 that the server was responsible for assigning a unique session ID to each TLS connection. However, if you browse through the remainder of the handshake, that session ID is never used again. Why does the server generate it, then?

SSL, since v2, has always supported session resumption. Remember that SSL was originally conceived as an HTTP add-on; it was only later retrofitted to other protocols. It was also designed back when HTTP 1.0 was state-of-the-art, and HTTP 1.0 required the web client — the browser — to close the socket connection to indicate the end of request. This meant that a lot of HTTP requests needed to be made for even a single web page. Although this was corrected somewhat in HTTP 1.1 with pipelining of requests/keepalives, the fact still remains that HTTP has a very low data-to-socket ratio. Add the time it takes to do a key exchange and the corresponding private key operations, and SSL can end up being a major drain on the throughput of the system.

To get a handle on this, SSL, and TLS, allow keying material to be reused across multiple sockets. This works by passing an old session ID in the client hello message and short-circuiting the handshake. This allows the lifetime of the SSL session — the keying material that's used to protect the data — to be independent of the lifetime of the socket. Regardless of the protocol used, this is a good thing. After a 128-bit key has been successfully negotiated, depending on the cipher spec, it can be used to protect potentially hundreds of thousands of bytes of content. There's no reason to throw away these carefully negotiated keys just because the top-level protocol itself has ended.

Figure 8-2 shows that the certificate, hello done, and key exchange messages have all been elided. Because the client and the server have already negotiated a master secret, there's no reason to resend these parameters.

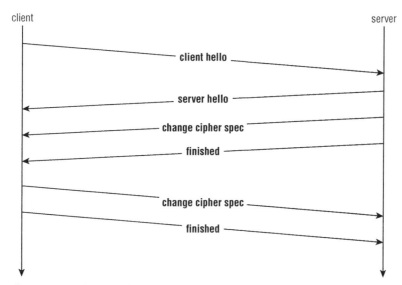

**Figure 8-2:** Shortened session resumption handshake sequence

Interestingly, when the handshake is shortened for session resumption, the server sends the finished message first, whereas for a normal handshake as shown back in Figure 6-1, it's the client. This is a nod to efficiency: The server needn't wait for the client to send a key exchange before it computes its finished message, so it can go ahead and pipeline all three of its messages in a single burst if the server is willing to renegotiate.

## Adding Session Resumption on the Client Side

What if the server isn't willing to renegotiate? According to the specification, the server should go ahead and silently begin a new handshake, and send its certificate and hello done message. It's technically up to the client if it wants to abort at this point, or go ahead and just negotiate a new session. In most cases, the client wants to continue anyway. It's hard to imagine a scenario where a client wouldn't want to negotiate a new session in this case. All TLS-based software that I'm familiar with automatically does so, without prompting or notifying the user. It's possible, though, that some particularly security-conscious (say, military) software somewhere may say, "Hey, you gave me this session ID two minutes ago, and now you're not willing to resume it? Something's wrong here, I'm bailing," and notify the user to investigate what could possibly be a security breach.

### *Requesting Session Resumption*

To add session resumption to the TLS client from Chapter 6, modify the TLSParameters structure from Listing 6-5 to include an optional session ID as shown in Listing 8-4:

**Listing 8-4:** "tls.h" TLSParameters with session ID

```
#define MAX_SESSION_ID_LENGTH 32

typedef struct
{
...

  int                  session_id_length;
  unsigned char        session_id[ MAX_SESSION_ID_LENGTH ];
}
TLSParameters;
```

## *Adding Session Resumption Logic to the Client*

Now, go ahead and define a new top-level function called tls_resume that renegotiates a previously negotiated session. If you were so inclined, you could probably work this into the logic of tls_connect from Listing 6-7, but it's clearer to just define a new function. tls_resume is shown in Listing 8-5.

**Listing 8-5:** "tls.c" tls_resume

```
int tls_resume( int connection,
                int session_id_length,
                const unsigned char *session_id,
                const unsigned char *master_secret,
                TLSParameters *parameters )
{
  init_parameters( parameters );
  parameters->connection_end = connection_end_client;
  parameters->session_id_length = session_id_length;
  memcpy( &parameters->session_id, session_id, session_id_length );

  new_md5_digest( &parameters->md5_handshake_digest );
  new_sha1_digest( &parameters->sha1_handshake_digest );

  // Send the TLS handshake "client hello" message
  if ( send_client_hello( connection, parameters ) < 0 )
  {
    perror( "Unable to send client hello" );
    return 1;
  }

  // Receive server hello, change cipher spec & finished.
  parameters->server_hello_done = 0;
```

```
  parameters->peer_finished = 0;
  while ( !parameters->peer_finished )
  {
    if ( receive_tls_msg( connection, NULL, 0, parameters ) < 0 )
    {
      perror( "Unable to receive server finished" );
      return 6;
    }

    if ( server_hello_done )
    {
      // Check to see if the server agreed to resume; if not,
      // abort, even though the server is probably willing to continue
      // with a new session.
      if ( memcmp( session_id, &parameters->session_id, session_id_length ) )
      {
        printf( "Server refused to renegotiate, exiting.\n" );
        return 7;
      }
      else
      {
        memcpy( parameters->master_secret, master_secret,
          MASTER_SECRET_LENGTH );
        calculate_keys( parameters );
      }
    }
  }

  if ( !( send_change_cipher_spec( connection, parameters ) ) )
  {
    perror( "Unable to send client change cipher spec" );
    return 4;
  }

  if ( !( send_finished( connection, parameters ) ) )
  {
    perror( "Unable to send client finished" );
    return 5;
  }

  return 0;
}
```

This is pretty close to `tls_connect` from Chapter 6; the differences are, of course, that it doesn't send a `client_key_exchange` message, and it has some special processing when the `server_hello_done` message is received:

```
  if ( server_hello_done )
  {
    if ( memcmp( session_id, &parameters->session_id, session_id_length ) )
    {
```

*(Continued)*

```
      printf( "Server refused to renegotiate, exiting.\n" );
      return 7;
    }
    else
    {
      memcpy( parameters->master_secret, master_secret,
        MASTER_SECRET_LENGTH );
      calculate_keys( parameters );
    }
  }
```

First, it checks to see if the session ID returned by the server matches the one offered by the client. If not, the server is unable to or is unwilling to renegotiate this session. This code aborts if this is the case; normally you'd want to just continue on with the handshake and negotiate new keys. However, for experimental purposes, you should be more interested in ensuring that a resumption succeeded. This way, if you mistype the session ID, for instance, you get an immediate error.

### Restoring the Previous Session's Master Secret

If the server is willing to resume, the client has to reproduce the master secret, so it had better have it handy. If it does, it can just perform the calculate keys routine. You could do this with the premaster secret, the master secret, or the keying material itself, but it's easiest to work with the master secret. Notice that the finished messages start over "from scratch" when a session resumes; neither side needs to keep track of the digest from the original handshake.

None of the subordinate functions except `send_client_hello` and `parse_server_hello` are aware that they are participating in a resumption instead of an initial handshake. `send_client_hello`, of course, needs to send the ID of the session it's trying to resume as shown in Listing 8-6.

**Listing 8-6:** "tls.c" send_client_hello with session resumption

```
static int send_client_hello( int connection, TLSParameters *parameters )

{
...
  memcpy( package.random.random_bytes, parameters->client_random + 4, 28 );
  if ( parameters->session_id_length > 0 )
  {
    package.session_id_length = parameters->session_id_length;
    package.session_id = parameters->session_id;
  }
  else
  {
    package.session_id_length = 0;
    package.session_id = NULL;
```

```
    }
    package.cipher_suites_length = htons( 2 );
```

If the client supports any extensions, it re-sends them here. This is important if the session ID is not recognized and the server starts a new handshake. It needs to be able to see all of the original extensions. Of course, if the client negotiates an extension the first time around, you should assume it's still in effect if the session is resumed.

## Testing Session Resumption

You must update `parse_server_hello`, of course, to store the session ID assigned by the server as shown in Listing 8-7.

**Listing 8-7:** "tls.c" parse_server_hello with session ID support

```
memcpy( ( void * ) ( parameters->server_random + 4 ), ( void * )
  hello.random.random_bytes, 28 );

parameters->session_id_length = hello.session_id_length;
memcpy( parameters->session_id, hello.session_id, hello.session_id_length );
```

Go ahead and expand the https example from Listing 6-2 to allow the user to pass in a session ID/master secret combination from a prior session for resumption. The session ID is unique to the target server. If you try to pass a session ID to a different server, the session ID will almost certainly not be recognized, and if it is, you don't know what the master secret was, so the session resumption fails when the server tries to verify your finished message. The modified https example is shown in Listing 8-8.

**Listing 8-8:** "https.c" main routine with session resumption

```
int main( int argc, char *argv[ ] )
{
...
  int master_secret_length;
  unsigned char *master_secret;
  int session_id_length;
  unsigned char *session_id;
...
  proxy_host = proxy_user = proxy_password = host = path =
    session_id = master_secret = NULL;
  session_id_length = master_secret_length = 0;

  for ( ind = 1; ind < ( argc - 1 ); ind++ )
  {
    if ( !strcmp( "-p", argv[ ind ] ) )
    {
      if ( !parse_proxy_param( argv[ ++ind ], &proxy_host, &proxy_port,
```

*(Continued)*

```
              &proxy_user, &proxy_password ) )
      {
        fprintf( stderr, "Error - malformed proxy parameter '%s'.\n", argv[ 2 ] );
        return 2;
      }
    }
    else if ( !strcmp( "-s", argv[ ind ] ) )
    {
      session_id_length = hex_decode( argv[ ++ind ], &session_id );
    }
    else if ( !strcmp( "-m", argv[ ind ] ) )
    {
      master_secret_length = hex_decode( argv[ ++ind ], &master_secret );
    }
  }

  if ( ( ( master_secret_length > 0 ) && ( session_id_length == 0 ) ) ||
       ( ( master_secret_length == 0 ) && ( session_id_length > 0 ) ) )
  {
    fprintf( stderr, "session id and master secret must both be provided.\n" );
    return 3;
  }
...
  if ( session_id != NULL )
  {
    if ( tls_resume( client_connection, session_id_length,
         session_id, master_secret, &tls_context ) )
    {
      fprintf( stderr, "Error: unable to negotiate SSL connection.\n" );
      if ( close( client_connection ) == -1 )
      {
        perror( "Error closing client connection" );
        return 2;
      }
      return 3;
    }
  }
  else
  {
    if ( tls_connect( client_connection, &tls_context ) )
    {
...
  if ( session_id != NULL )
  {
    free( session_id );
  }
```

```
if ( master_secret != NULL )
{
  free( master_secret );
}
```

Other than calling `tls_resume` instead of `tls_connect`, nothing else changes. As far as the rest of the library is concerned, it's as if the socket was never closed. Of course, if you actually want to try this out, you need to know what the session ID and master secret are; you can go ahead and print them out just after performing the TLS shutdown:

```
tls_shutdown( client_connection, &tls_context );

printf( "Session ID was: " );
show_hex( tls_context.session_id, tls_context.session_id_length );
printf( "Master secret was: " );
show_hex( tls_context.master_secret, MASTER_SECRET_LENGTH );

if ( close( client_connection ) == -1 )
```

### Viewing a Resumed Session

The following code illustrates a network trace of a resumed session:

```
debian:/home/jdavies/devl/test/c/ssl# tcpdump -s 0 -X -i lo tcp port 8443
tcpdump: verbose output suppressed, use -v or -vv for full protocol decode
listening on lo, link-type EN10MB (Ethernet), capture size 65535 bytes
… (omitted initial handshake)
21:54:05.568241 IP localhost.37289 > localhost.8443: Flags [P.], ack 1, win 257,
options [nop,nop,TS val 274087 ecr 274087], length 82
```

Here, the client hello message looks like the client hello message in Chapter 6, except that, this time, the session ID is non-empty.

```
21:54:05.568432 IP localhost.8443 > localhost.37289: Flags [P.], ack 83, win
256, options [nop,nop,TS val 274087 ecr 274087], length 130
        0x0000:  4500 00b6 f2e1 4000 4006 495e 7f00 0001   E.....@.@.I^....
        0x0010:  7f00 0001 20fb 91a9 d260 dc47 d246 a65c   .........`.G.F.\
        0x0020:  8018 0100 feaa 0000 0101 080a 0004 2ea7   ...............
        0x0030:  0004 2ea7 1603 0100 4a02 0000 4603 014c   ........J...F..L
        0x0040:  743f 7dc9 fc4e af63 d94b e2e0 672e 5a0d   t?}..N.c.K..g.Z.
        0x0050:  ea6b 91da 9e2f 2f48 f733 23d5 4b0d 8720   .k.../\/H.3#.K...
        0x0060:  be2e b988 f5bc 6412 5981 35f7 7e3b 2128   ......d.Y.5.~;!(
        0x0070:  f8cc 4e6f fc52 77fd a687 2ac5 0f1e cbbb   ..No.Rw...*.....
        0x0080:  000a 0014 0301 0001 0116 0301 0028 1d95   .............(..
        0x0090:  a8c8 56f3 841b 0046 4e40 29d9 6b83 036b   ..V....FN@).k..k
        0x00a0:  c30f 624e c3b9 fc32 d8f2 9d1e 8ae5 6b18   ..bN...2......k.
        0x00b0:  cb75 d7a7 d311                            .u....
```

The server responds with a server hello message containing the identical session ID. If the session ID is different here, the client should begin negotiating a new connection. If the session ID is the same, however, the client should expect the server hello to be followed immediately by a change cipher spec message, followed by a server finished.

The client follows up with its own change cipher spec and server finished message; this is followed immediately by encrypted application data, as shown here:

```
21:54:05.572924 IP localhost.37289 > localhost.8443: Flags [P.], ack 131, win
265, options [nop,nop,TS val 274088 ecr 274087], length 6
        0x0000:  4500 003a 88b2 4000 4006 b409 7f00 0001   E..:..@.@.......
        0x0010:  7f00 0001 91a9 20fb d246 a65c d260 dcc9   .........F.\.`..
        0x0020:  8018 0109 fe2e 0000 0101 080a 0004 2ea8   ...............
        0x0030:  0004 2ea7 1403 0100 0101                  .........
21:54:05.613696 IP localhost.37289 > localhost.8443: Flags [P.], ack 131, win
265, options [nop,nop,TS val 274098 ecr 274098], length 196
        0x0000:  4500 00f8 88b3 4000 4006 b34a 7f00 0001   E.....@.@..J...
        0x0010:  7f00 0001 91a9 20fb d246 a662 d260 dcc9   .........F.b.`..
        0x0020:  8018 0109 feec 0000 0101 080a 0004 2eb2   ...............
        0x0030:  0004 2eb2 1603 0100 2892 32f1 da76 4138   ........(.2..vA8
        0x0040:  cb21 3a05 15f0 803b 34d3 e308 f12c 7aee   .!:....;4....,z.
        0x0050:  634f 9246 924d f6bd d646 9c92 3879 a882   cO.F.M...F..8y..
        0x0060:  2e17 0301 0030 0127 7be8 e387 2b97 5f9c   .....0.'{...+._.
        0x0070:  8d2b 02fe 8587 a91a ef3a fa53 fb54 d577   .+.......:.S.T.w
        0x0080:  e62a 44fd 5e0d eaf1 769f c2a2 619c 27aa   .*D.^...v...a.'.
        0x0090:  d619 fc02 3d81
...
```

# Adding Session Resumption on the Server Side

How about supporting session resumption on the server side? The server has to do quite a bit more work than the client. It must remember each session ID it assigns and the master key associated with each.

### Assigning a Unique Session ID to Each Session

The first change you must make to support server-side session resumption
is to assign a unique session ID to each session. Recall that in Chapter 7, each
server hello message is sent with an empty session ID, which the client should
interpret as "server unable to resume session." The changes to assign unique
session IDs to each session are shown in Listing 8-9.

**Listing 8-9:** "tls.c" server-side session resumption support

```
static int next_session_id = 1;

static int send_server_hello( int connection, TLSParameters *parameters )
{
  ServerHello      package;
...
  memcpy( package.random.random_bytes, parameters->server_random + 4, 28 );

  if ( parameters->session_id_length == 0 )
  {
    // Assign a new session ID
    memcpy( parameters->session_id, &next_session_id, sizeof( int ) );
    parameters->session_id_length = sizeof( int );
    next_session_id++;
  }

  package.session_id_length = parameters->session_id_length;
```

Here, I've gone ahead and made `next_session_id` a static variable. This could
potentially create some threading problems if I was using this in a multithreaded
application. The session ID in this case is a monotonically increasing 4-byte
identifier. I also didn't bother correcting for host ordering, so if this is run on a
little-endian machine, the first session ID shows up as 0x01000000, the second
as 0x02000000, and so on. This increase doesn't really matter in this case, as long
as each is unique. Finally, notice that the code checks whether a session ID has
already been assigned before assigning one. This will be the case, when session
resumption is added in Listing 8-15, if a session is being resumed.

### Adding Session ID Storage

To actually store these, you need some internal data structure that can easily
map session IDs to master secret values. As a nod to efficiency, go ahead and
make this a hash table. First, declare a storage structure and a static instance to
contain it as shown in Listing 8-10.

**Listing 8-10:** "tls.c" session storage hash table

```
#define HASH_TABLE_SIZE 100

typedef struct StoredSessionsList_t
```

*(Continued)*

```
{
  int session_id_length;
  unsigned char session_id[ MAX_SESSION_ID_LENGTH ];
  unsigned char master_secret[ MASTER_SECRET_LENGTH ];
  struct StoredSessions_list_t *next;
}
StoredSessionsList;

static StoredSessionsList *stored_sessions[ HASH_TABLE_SIZE ];
```

This structure simply contains the session ID and the master secret, which is the bare minimum amount of information you need to resume a prior session.

Because this is a static variable (again, not thread safe), it must be initialized on startup by the `init_tls` function shown in Listing 8-11.

**Listing 8-11:** "tls.c" init_tls

```
void init_tls()
{
  int i = 0;

  for ( i = 0; i < HASH_TABLE_SIZE; i++ )
  {
    stored_sessions[ i ] = NULL;
  }
}
```

First of all, you need to store each successfully negotiated session in this structure. Listing 8-12 illustrates how to find the correct placement in the hash map for the master secret. By forcing the session IDs themselves to be numeric values, the hash function is simply the session ID modulo the size of the hash table.

**Listing 8-12:** "tls.c" remember_session

```
/**
 * Store the session in the stored sessions cache
 */
static void remember_session( TLSParameters *parameters )
{
  if ( parameters->session_id_length > 0 )
  {
    int session_id;
    StoredSessionsList *head;
    memcpy( &session_id, parameters->session_id, sizeof( int ) );
    head = stored_sessions[ session_id % HASH_TABLE_SIZE ];
    if ( head == NULL )
    {
      head = stored_sessions[ session_id % HASH_TABLE_SIZE ] =
        malloc( sizeof( StoredSessionsList ) );
    }
    else
```

```
  {
    while ( head->next != NULL )
    {
      head = ( StoredSessionsList * ) head->next;
    }
    head->next = malloc( sizeof( StoredSessionsList ) );
    head = ( StoredSessionsList * ) head->next;
  }

  head->session_id_length = parameters->session_id_length;
  memcpy( head->session_id, &session_id, head->session_id_length );
  memcpy( head->master_secret, parameters->master_secret,
    MASTER_SECRET_LENGTH );
  head->next = NULL;
  }
}
```

Figure 8-3 illustrates how this would be laid out in memory if you stored, for example, six sessions with IDs 100, 106, 199, 200, 299, and 599. Each entry in the `stored_sessions` array is a pointer to a linked list of every session whose ID is equal to its index, mod 100.

If you've ever studied data structures, this common technique for balancing storage space with lookup speed ought to look familiar. Listing 8-13 is the corresponding retrieval function.

**Listing 8-13:** "tls.c" find_stored_session

```
/**
 * Check to see if the requested session ID is stored in the local cache.
 * If the session ID is recognized, parameters will be updated to include
 * it, and the master secret will be stored in the parameters.
 * If it is not recognized, the session
 * ID in the parameters will be left empty, indicating that a new handshake
 * should commence.
 */
static void find_stored_session( int session_id_length,
                                 const unsigned char *session_id,
                                 TLSParameters *parameters )
{
  int session_id_num;
  StoredSessionsList *head;

  if ( session_id_length > sizeof( int ) )
  {
    // Definitely didn't come from this server.
    return;
  }

  memcpy( &session_id_num, session_id, session_id_length );
  for ( head = stored_sessions[ session_id_num % HASH_TABLE_SIZE ];
```

*(Continued)*

```
      head != NULL;
      head = ( StoredSessionsList * ) head->next )
{
  if ( !memcmp( session_id, head->session_id, session_id_length ) )
  {
    parameters->session_id_length = session_id_length;
    memcpy( parameters->session_id, head->session_id, session_id_length );
    memcpy( parameters->master_secret, head->master_secret,
      MASTER_SECRET_LENGTH );
    break;
  }
 }
}
```

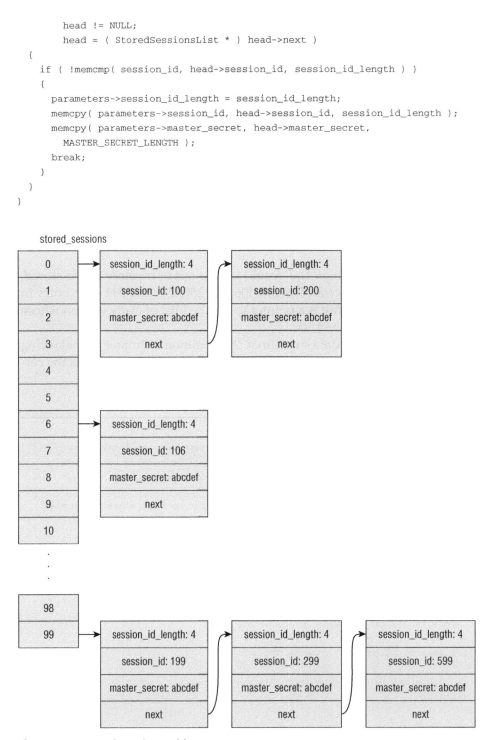

**Figure 8-3:** stored_sessions table

Notice that `find_stored_session` doesn't actually return anything. If it finds an entry corresponding to the request session, it updates the `TLSParameters` structure with the corresponding master secret and continues on. It's up to the caller to check to see if the `TLSParameters` structure was updated or not.

### Modifying parse_client_hello to Recognize Session Resumption Requests

To make use of these new functions, `parse_client_hello` must first be modified to check to see if the client is attempting a renegotiation as shown in Listing 8-14.

**Listing 8-14:** "tls.c" parse_client_hello with session resumption support

```
static char *parse_client_hello( char *read_pos,
                                 int pdu_length,
                                 TLSParameters *parameters )
{
…
  free( hello.compression_methods );

  if ( hello.session_id_length > 0 )
  {
    find_stored_session( hello.session_id_length, hello.session_id,
      parameters );
  }

  if ( hello.session_id )
```

This just invokes `find_stored_session_id` if the client passes one in. If the requested session ID is found, the `parameters` structure now contains the master secret and the session ID that has been found. If not, nothing is done and the handshake should continue as if no session ID had been suggested. An unrecognized session ID is not necessarily an error — the client could just be trying to resume an old session.

Correspondingly, `tls_accept` must be updated to check this condition and perform the shortened handshake if the client is resuming as in Listing 8-15.

**Listing 8-15:** "tls.c" tls_accept with session resumption support

```
int tls_accept( int connection,
                TLSParameters *parameters )
{
…
  parameters->got_client_hello = 0;
  while ( !parameters->got_client_hello )
  {
    if ( receive_tls_msg( connection, NULL, 0, parameters ) < 0 )
    {
```

*(Continued)*

```
    perror( "Unable to receive client hello" );
    send_alert_message( connection, handshake_failure,
      &parameters->active_send_parameters );
    return 1;
  }
}
if ( parameters->session_id_length > 0 )
{
  // Client asked for a resumption, and this server recognized the
  // session id.  Shortened handshake here.  "parse_client_hello"
  // will have already initiated calculate keys.
  if ( send_server_hello( connection, parameters ) )
  {
    send_alert_message( connection, handshake_failure,
      &parameters->active_send_parameters );
    return 3;
  }

  // Can't calculate keys until this point because server random
  // is needed.
  calculate_keys( parameters );

  // send server change cipher spec/finished message
  // Order is reversed when resuming
  if ( !( send_change_cipher_spec( connection, parameters ) ) )
  {
    perror( "Unable to send client change cipher spec" );
    send_alert_message( connection, handshake_failure,
      &parameters->active_send_parameters );
    return 7;
  }

  // This message will be encrypted using the newly negotiated keys
  if ( !( send_finished( connection, parameters ) ) )
  {
    perror( "Unable to send client finished" );
    send_alert_message( connection, handshake_failure,
      &parameters->active_send_parameters );
    return 8;
  }

  parameters->peer_finished = 0;
  while ( !parameters->peer_finished )
  {
    if ( receive_tls_msg( connection, NULL, 0, parameters ) < 0 )
    {
      perror( "Unable to receive client finished" );
      send_alert_message( connection, handshake_failure,
        &parameters->active_send_parameters );
      return 6;
    }
```

```
    }
  }
  else
  {
    if ( send_server_hello( connection, parameters ) )
```

If the session isn't being resumed — that is, it's new — the `tls_accept` must also remember it for future resumptions as shown in Listing 8-16.

**Listing 8-16:** "tls.c" tls_accept with session storage

```
    if ( !( send_finished( connection, parameters ) ) )
    {
      perror( "Unable to send client finished" );
      send_alert_message( connection, handshake_failure,
        &parameters->active_send_parameters );
      return 7;
    }

    // Handshake is complete; now ready to start sending encrypted data

    // IFF the handshake was successful, put it into the sesion ID cache
    // list for reuse.
    remember_session( parameters );
  }
```

The only other change that needs to made here is that `init_parameters` must initialize the session ID to be empty, as in Listing 8-17.

**Listing 8-17:** "tls.c" init_parameters with session resumption support

```
static void init_parameters( TLSParameters *parameters )
{
...
  parameters->session_id_length = 0;
}
```

## Drawbacks of This Implementation

This implementation is by no means perfect, or complete. After a session is added to the hash table, it's never removed until the server shuts down. Not only is this an operational problem — its memory consumption grows without bounds until it crashes — it's also a security problem because a session can be resumed days or even weeks afterward. This won't be a significant problem for the use you put this server to, but it would be for a highly available server.

The TLS specification, RFC 2246, mandates that if a session was not shut down correctly — if the client didn't send a *close notify* alert before shutting down the socket — then the session should be marked non-resumable and attempts to resume it should fail. From section 7.2.1 of the RFC, which discusses the `close_notify` alert:

*close_notify*

*This message notifies the recipient that the sender will not send any more messages on this connection. The session becomes unresumable if any connection is terminated without proper close_notify messages with level equal to warning.*

This was not widely implemented, and later versions of the specification rescinded this requirement. However, to be technically compliant with RFC 2246, this implementation ought to include this requirement when the negotiated protocol version is 3.1.

There's also a theoretical problem with this implementation. The server remembers the session ID and the master secret, and nothing else. What happens if the client sends a hello request with the same session ID, but a different set of cipher suites? What if, for example, the original session used RC4/MD5, but the new client hello only includes AES/SHA-1? In this case, it actually does work correctly because the master secret is just expanded as many times as it needs to be to generate the appropriate keying material. If the client is requesting the wrong cipher suite, though, you should just abandon the connection because it's most likely that somebody is trying to do something nasty.

A more robust server implementation should also keep track of which client hello extensions are successfully negotiated and ensure that the second hello request includes those same extensions. Depending on the negotiated extension, omitting it on a resumption request might be a fatal error.

## Avoiding Fixed Parameters with Ephemeral Key Exchange

Chapter 6 states that after the server hello, the server should follow up with a certificate for key exchange. Technically, this isn't always true. Recall from Chapter 5 that although X.509 defines and allows the server to provide Diffie-Hellman parameters — $Ys$, $p$ and $g$ — in a certificate, the reality of Diffie-Hellman is that it works best when $Ys$ is computed from a different secret value $a$ for each instance. If the key exchange parameters aren't in the certificate, is the certificate strictly necessary?

As it turns out, no. There is a class of cipher suites referred to as *ephemeral* cipher suites that don't expect a key to be supplied in a certificate at all. Instead, the server sends a *server key exchange* message that contains the key exchange parameters — normally a set of Diffie-Hellman parameters. This way, each connection gets its own, unique, key exchange parameters which are never stored anywhere after the connection ends.

## Supporting the TLS Server Key Exchange Message

To support ephemeral key exchange on the client side, the client must be prepared to accept either a certificate or a server key exchange message. As you can probably guess, implementing this first involves adding a new case arm to receive_tls_msg, shown in Listing 8-18.

**Listing 8-18:** "tls.c" receive_tls_msg with server key exchange

```
static int receive_tls_msg( int connection,
                            char *buffer,
                            int bufsz,
                            TLSParameters *parameters )
{
...
      switch ( handshake.msg_type )
      {
...
        case server_key_exchange:
          read_pos = parse_server_key_exchange( read_pos, parameters );
          if ( read_pos == NULL )
          {
            send_alert_message( connection, handshake_failure,
              &parameters->active_send_parameters );
            return -1;
          }
          break;
```

The optional server key exchange message is sent after the server hello. Both the certificate and the server key exchange handshake messages are optional, as indicated by the dashed lines in Figure 8-4.

Recall from Listing 6-37 that the send_client_key_exchange was coded to perform Diffie-Hellman key exchange if the cipher suite called for it, so the only thing left to do in parse_server_key_exchange is to store the Diffie-Hellman parameters for the subsequent key exchange as shown in Listing 8-19.

**Listing 8-19:** "tls.c" parse_server_key_exchange

```
static char *parse_server_key_exchange( unsigned char *read_pos,
                                        TLSParameters *parameters )
{
  short length;
  int i;
  unsigned char *dh_params = read_pos;

  for ( i = 0; i < 3; i++ )
  {
    memcpy( &length, read_pos, 2 );
    length = ntohs( length );
```

*(Continued)*

```
   read_pos += 2;
   switch ( i )
   {
   case 0:
     load_huge( &parameters->server_dh_key.p, read_pos, length );
     break;
   case 1:
     load_huge( &parameters->server_dh_key.g, read_pos, length );
     break;
   case 2:
     load_huge( &parameters->server_dh_key.Y, read_pos, length );
     break;
   }
   read_pos += length;
 }

 return read_pos;
}
```

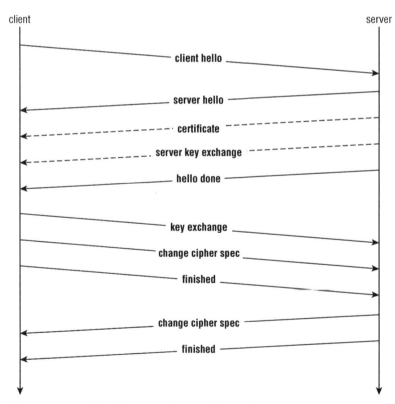

**Figure 8-4:** TLS handshake with server key exchange

   The server key exchange message is just a list of parameters; the receiver must know how to interpret them. Each element $p$, $g$, and $Ys$ are given as variable-length structures so, in TLS style, are prepended by their lengths. Here you can see, they're each loaded into `huge` structures.

That's it; you already added support for the rest of the Diffie-Hellman key exchange in Listing 6-42. It was just a matter of getting the parameters to complete the exchange.

You can use this on a live server. The cipher suites that are named `DH_anon_xxx` work correctly with this code, as is, if the server supports the cipher suite. Wait — "if the server supports them"? Why wouldn't the server support them? Well, the name of the cipher suite offers a clue: `DH_anon`. This means that the handshake is anonymous and no protection against man-in-the-middle attacks is offered. How could you even check? There's no certificate, so there's no common name to compare to the domain name. Even if there were, there'd be no signature to verify with a trusted public key.

### Authenticating the Server Key Exchange Message

Strictly speaking, it's not necessarily the case that certificate messages and server key exchange messages are mutually exclusive. Remember DSA certificates, which didn't seem terribly useful because you couldn't use the DSA public key for a key exchange? This is what they're useful for. A DSA certificate can provide a public key that can be used to verify a signature over a set of ephemeral Diffie-Hellman parameters. This same certificate can include a verifiable common name and a trusted signature. The signature itself can even be an RSA signature (which is fortunate, because I have yet to find a certificate authority that uses DSA to sign certificates).

In fact, the server can even send an RSA certificate before sending the server key exchange message in support of a Diffie-Hellman key exchange. You may wonder why anybody would want to go to all this trouble if they've already gotten an RSA certificate that can be used directly to do a key exchange, but remember that Diffie-Hellman achieves perfect forward secrecy. If RSA is used for key exchange, and the server's private key is ever compromised, every communication that is protected by that key is at risk.

Therefore, TLS defines another set of cipher suites called `DHE_DSS_xxx` for Diffie-Hellman with a DSA signature and `DHE_RSA_xxx` for Diffie-Hellman with an RSA signature. In both cases, the server key exchange is preceded by a certificate bearing either a DSA public key or an RSA public key. (There are also `DH_xxx` cipher suites that skip the server key exchange and expect the Diffie-Hellman parameters to appear in the certificate itself. As has been noted, this is rare).

As presented so far, though, this is still vulnerable to a man-in-the-middle attack. You can verify that the certificate belongs to the site you believe you're connecting to, but you can't verify that the key exchange parameters are the ones that were sent by the server itself. The man in the middle can replace the server's DH parameters with his own and you have no way of detecting this.

After you verify the certificate and decide to trust this connection, the man in the middle takes over, drops the connection to the server, and you complete the handshake with the falsified server, none the wiser.

Therefore, the specification enables the server key exchange to be signed by the public key in the certificate. This optional signature immediately follows the key exchange parameters if present; it is present for any key exchange except for the anonymous types.

Extend the `parse_server_key_exchange` function from Listing 8-19 as shown in Listing 8-20 to recognize this signature if it is present and verify it. If it is present but doesn't verify according to the previously received certificate, return NULL, which causes the calling `tls_receive_message` to fail with the *illegal parameter* handshake alert.

**Listing 8-20:**  "tls.c" parse_server_key_exchange with signature verification

```
static char *parse_server_key_exchange( unsigned char *read_pos,
                                         TLSParameters *parameters )
{
...
  for ( i = 0; i < 4; i++ )
...
    case 3:
      // The third element is the signature over the first three, including their
      // length bytes
      if ( !verify_signature( dh_params,
             ( read_pos - 2 - dh_params ),
             read_pos, length, parameters ) )
      {
        return NULL;
      }
      break;
  }
}
```

The signature type depends on the type of public key in the certificate. TLS defines two: RSA and DSA. Recall from Chapter 3 that an RSA signature is a secure hash of the data to be signed, encrypted with the private key. TLS actually takes a slightly more paranoid approach to RSA signatures, and encrypts both the MD5 and the SHA-1 hash, presumably to guard against a compromise of either hash function. Unfortunately, both are fairly weak today, and TLS 1.0 doesn't provide a way to negotiate a stronger hash function. Recall from Chapter 5 that the X.509 certificate signature included the OID of the corresponding hash function in its signature; TLS 1.0, unfortunately, didn't follow suit.

To verify an RSA signature over the server key exchange parameters, implement the `verify_signature` function in Listing 8-21.

**Listing 8-21:** "tls.c" verify_signature

```
static int verify_signature( unsigned char *message,
                             int message_len,
                             unsigned char *signature,
                             int signature_len,
                             TLSParameters *parameters )
{
  unsigned char *decrypted_signature;
  int decrypted_signature_length;
  digest_ctx md5_digest;
  digest_ctx sha1_digest;

  new_sha1_digest( &sha1_digest );
  update_digest( &sha1_digest, parameters->client_random, RANDOM_LENGTH );
  update_digest( &sha1_digest, parameters->server_random, RANDOM_LENGTH );
  update_digest( &sha1_digest, message, message_len );
  finalize_digest( &sha1_digest );

  new_md5_digest( &md5_digest );
  update_digest( &md5_digest, parameters->client_random, RANDOM_LENGTH );
  update_digest( &md5_digest, parameters->server_random, RANDOM_LENGTH );
  update_digest( &md5_digest, message, message_len );
  finalize_digest( &md5_digest );

  decrypted_signature_length = rsa_decrypt( signature, signature_len,
    &decrypted_signature,
    &parameters->server_public_key.rsa_public_key );

  if ( memcmp( md5_digest.hash, decrypted_signature, MD5_BYTE_SIZE ) ||
       memcmp( sha1_digest.hash, decrypted_signature + MD5_BYTE_SIZE,
               SHA1_BYTE_SIZE ) )
  {
    return 0;
  }

  free( decrypted_signature );

  return 1;
}
```

Each digest is over the two random values and then the parameters; incorporating the random values this way prevents replay attacks. The whole signature process is illustrated in Figure 8-5.

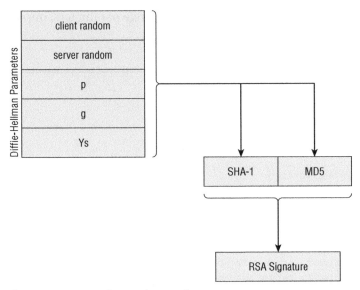

**Figure 8-5:** Server key exchange signature

## *Examining an Ephemeral Key Exchange Handshake*

Here is an illustration of an abbreviated DHE/RSA/DES/SHA-1 handshake.

```
debian:/home/jdavies/devl/test/c/ssl# tcpdump -s 0 -X -i lo tcp port 8443
tcpdump: verbose output suppressed, use -v or -vv for full protocol decode
listening on lo, link-type EN10MB (Ethernet), capture size 65535 bytes
… (omitted TCP handshake) …
21:35:48.344479 IP localhost.59349 > localhost.8443: Flags [P.], ack 1, win 257,
options [nop,nop,TS val 4294952080 ecr 4294952080], length 50
        0x0000:  4500 0066 6dde 4000 4006 ceb1 7f00 0001   E..fm.@.@.......
        0x0010:  7f00 0001 e7d5 20fb aa9d a94d ab00 752a   ...........M..u*
        0x0020:  8018 0101 fe5a 0000 0101 080a ffff c490   .....Z..........
        0x0030:  ffff c490 1603 0100 2d01 0000 2903 014c   ........-...)..L
        0x0040:  758c b400 0000 0000 0000 0000 0000 0000   u...............    TLS_DHE_RSA_
        0x0050:  0000 0000 0000 0000 0000 0000 0000 0000   ................    WITH_DES_CBC_
        0x0060:  0002 0015 0100                             ......              SHA
```

This is an ordinary client hello message, just like the one in Chapter 6. The only noteworthy point here is that the only offered cipher suite is an ephemeral Diffie-Hellman cipher.

```
21:35:48.345236 IP localhost.8443 > localhost.59349: Flags [P.], ack 51, win
256, options [nop,nop,TS val 4294952080 ecr 4294952080], length 1158
        0x0000:  4500 04ba b1bb 4000 4006 8680 7f00 0001   E.....@.@.......
        0x0010:  7f00 0001 20fb e7d5 ab00 752a aa9d a97f   ..........u*....
```

```
0x0020:  8018 0100 02af 0000 0101 080a ffff c490    ...............
0x0030:  ffff c490 1603 0100 4a02 0000 4603 014c    ........J...F..L
0x0040:  758c b47e 27e1 3d63 09fa 4c62 83c8 a510    u..~'.=c..Lb....
0x0050:  72a1 9a98 4c4e 186d 000b c059 31c1 4220    r...LN.m...Y1.B.
0x0060:  1823 08ca b7af a651 a39a f8e4 56c2 5934    .#.....Q....V.Y4
0x0070:  2ffd c57b aafe 12f9 bff3 9b0f 85ef 08a9    /..{............
0x0080:  0015 0016 0301 0357 0b00 0353 0003 5000    .......W...S..P.
… (omitted certificate) …
```

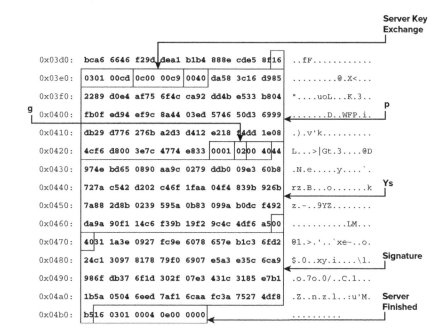

```
0x03d0:  bca6 6646 f29d dea1 b1b4 888e cde5 8f16    ..fF............
0x03e0:  0301 00cd 0c00 00c9 0040 da58 3c16 d985    .........@.X<...
0x03f0:  2289 d0e4 af75 6f4c ca92 dd4b e533 b804    "....uoL...K.3..
0x0400:  fb0f ed94 ef9c 8a44 03ed 5746 50d3 6999    .......D..WFP.i.
0x0410:  db29 d776 276b a2d3 d412 e218 f4dd 1e08    .).v'k..........
0x0420:  4cf6 d800 3e7c 4774 e833 0001 0200 4044    L...>|Gt.3....@D
0x0430:  974e bd65 0890 aa9c 0279 ddb0 09e3 60b8    .N.e...y.....`.
0x0440:  727a c542 d202 c46f 1faa 04f4 839b 926b    rz.B...o.......k
0x0450:  7a88 2d8b 0239 595a 0b83 099a b0dc f492    z.-..9YZ........
0x0460:  da9a 90f1 14c6 f39b 19f2 9c4c 4df6 a500    ...........LM...
0x0470:  4031 1a3e 0927 fc9e 6078 657e b1c3 6fd2    @1.>.'..`xe~..o.
0x0480:  24c1 3097 8178 79f0 6907 e5a3 e35c 6ca9    $.0..xy.i....\l.
0x0490:  986f db37 6f1d 302f 07e3 431c 3185 e7b1    .o.7o.0/..C.1...
0x04a0:  1b5a 0504 6eed 7af1 6caa fc3a 7527 4df8    .Z..n.z.l..:u'M.
0x04b0:  b516 0301 0004 0e00 0000                    ..........
```

The server hello and certificate messages occur as before; however, instead of being followed immediately by server done, they're followed by a server key exchange message that identifies the Diffie-Hellman values *p*, *g*, and *Ys*. The length declarations of each are highlighted in the preceding code. This is followed by the RSA signature of the MD5 hash of client random, server random, and the remainder of the server key exchange, followed by the SHA-1 hash of the client random, the server random, and the remainder of the message. The client should use the public key of the certificate — which should have been verified using the public key of a trusted certificate — to verify these key exchange parameters.

```
21:35:48.449922 IP localhost.59349 > localhost.8443: Flags [P.], ack 1159, win
275, options [nop,nop,TS val 4294952106 ecr 4294952080], length 12
0x0000:  4500 0040 6de0 4000 4006 ced5 7f00 0001    E..@m.@.@.......
0x0010:  7f00 0001 e7d5 20fb aa9d a97f ab00 79b0    ..............y.
0x0020:  8018 0113 fe34 0000 0101 080a ffff c4a0    .....4..........
0x0030:  ffff c490 1603 0100 0710 0000 0300 0140    ...............@
```

The server hello done is always followed by a client key exchange, whether the key exchange was an ephemeral one or not. In this case, the client key exchange is significantly shorter than in the case of an RSA key exchange, especially because the "secret" value $A$ was hardcoded to be 6 by this implementation. Because $g$ is 2 (see the preceding code), $Yc = 2^6 \%p = 64$. To complete the key exchange, the server must compute $64^B \%p$. I can't show you this computation because I don't know what $B$ was. No matter how hard I try, I shouldn't be able to figure it out. The client must compute $Ys^6 \%p$ to settle on the premaster secret.

The remainder of the handshake continues as in the RSA key exchange case; now that the premaster secret has been successfully exchanged, the client sends a change cipher spec, followed by a finished message, which the server reciprocates as shown below.

```
21:35:48.488513 IP localhost.59349 > localhost.8443: Flags [P.], ack 1159, win
275, options [nop,nop,TS val 4294952116 ecr 4294952116], length 51
        0x0000:  4500 0067 6de1 4000 4006 cead 7f00 0001  E..gm.@.@.......
        0x0010:  7f00 0001 e7d5 20fb aa9d a98b ab00 79b0  ..............y.
        0x0020:  8018 0113 fe5b 0000 0101 080a ffff c4b4  .....[..........
        0x0030:  ffff c4b4 1403 0100 0101 1603 0100 28ac  ..............(.
        0x0040:  cc09 37ea 64f2 4677 68e8 0025 bf96 f1df  ..7.d.Fwh..%....
        0x0050:  92f3 f83a b5a9 cb9e 6672 e245 4687 2259  ...:...fr.EF."Y
        0x0060:  9135 c6f2 707a b6                        .5..pz.
21:35:48.488901 IP localhost.8443 > localhost.59349: Flags [P.], ack 114, win
256, options [nop,nop,TS val 4294952116 ecr 4294952116], length 51
        0x0000:  4500 0067 b1be 4000 4006 8ad0 7f00 0001  E..g..@.@.......
        0x0010:  7f00 0001 20fb e7d5 ab00 79b0 aa9d a9be  ..........y.....
        0x0020:  8018 0100 fe5b 0000 0101 080a ffff c4b4  .....[..........
        0x0030:  ffff c4b4 1403 0100 0101 1603 0100 2827  ..............('
        0x0040:  a9bf 753d f061 2e90 62b3 5cfa 19f8 52f4  ..u=.a..b.\...R.
        0x0050:  4ad5 6a59 5d4e 5bba 7f89 3ce3 9e25 c15f  J.jY]N[...<..%._
        0x0060:  5e1d 0ef8 a8ce 22                        ^....."
```

This works for all of the DHE_RSA_xxx cipher suites — that is, those whose certificate includes an RSA public key. What about the DHE_DSS_xxx cipher suites?

If you recall from Listing 6-5, the TLSParameters structure is declared to have space only for an RSA public key. If the server returns a DSA public key, it is ignored. Back then, that was a sensible decision because you were just focusing on RSA-based key exchanges, but now you can actually do something with a DSA certificate.

To support DSA verification, change the TLSParameters server_public_key type from an rsa_key to the public_key_info structure that is defined in Listing 5-26. This has a section for either an rsa_key or a dsa key, plus the required dsa params. This is shown in Listing 8-22.

**Listing 8-22:** "tls.h" TLSParameters with dsa key support

```
typedef struct
{
```

```
...
  ProtectionParameters   active_recv_parameters;

  public_key_info        server_public_key;
  dh_key                 server_dh_key;
...
}
TLSParameters;
```

Pass this into `parse_x509_chain` when parsing the certificate message as shown in Listing 8-23.

**Listing 8-23:** "tls.c" receive_tls_message with DSA key support

```
static int receive_tls_msg( int connection,
                            char *buffer,
                            int bufsz,
                            TLSParameters *parameters )
{
...
      case certificate:
        read_pos = parse_x509_chain( read_pos, handshake.length,
          &parameters->server_public_key );
```

Modify `send_client_key_exchange` to recognize this new level of indirection as in Listing 8-24.

**Listing 8-24:** "tls.c" send_client_key_exchange

```
static int send_client_key_exchange( int connection, TLSParameters *parameters )
{
...
    key_exchange_message_len = rsa_key_exchange(
      &parameters->server_public_key.rsa_public_key,
      premaster_secret, &key_exchange_message );
```

Because `parse_x509_chain` has to update the `server_public_key` structure rather than just an RSA key structure, make the appropriate modifications as shown in Listing 8-25.

**Listing 8-25:** "x509.c" parse_x509_chain with DSA support

```
char *parse_x509_chain( unsigned char *buffer,
                        int pdu_length,
                        public_key_info *server_public_key )
{
...
  if ( !pos++ )
  {
    // Copy public key information into target on first cert only
    server_public_key->algorithm =
      certificate.tbsCertificate.subjectPublicKeyInfo.algorithm;
```

*(Continued)*

```
switch ( server_public_key->algorithm )
{
  case rsa:
    server_public_key->rsa_public_key.modulus =
      ( huge * ) malloc( sizeof( huge ) );
    server_public_key->rsa_public_key.exponent =
      ( huge * ) malloc( sizeof( huge ) );
    set_huge( server_public_key->rsa_public_key.modulus, 0 );
    set_huge( server_public_key->rsa_public_key.exponent, 0 );
    copy_huge( server_public_key->rsa_public_key.modulus,
      certificate.tbsCertificate.subjectPublicKeyInfo.rsa_public_key.modulus
    );
    copy_huge( server_public_key->rsa_public_key.exponent,
      certificate.tbsCertificate.subjectPublicKeyInfo.rsa_public_key.exponent
    );
    break;
  case dsa:
    set_huge( &server_public_key->dsa_parameters.g, 0 );
    set_huge( &server_public_key->dsa_parameters.p, 0 );
    set_huge( &server_public_key->dsa_parameters.q, 0 );
    set_huge( &server_public_key->dsa_public_key, 0 );
    copy_huge( &server_public_key->dsa_parameters.g,
      &certificate.tbsCertificate.subjectPublicKeyInfo.dsa_parameters.g );
    copy_huge( &server_public_key->dsa_parameters.p,
      &certificate.tbsCertificate.subjectPublicKeyInfo.dsa_parameters.p );
    copy_huge( &server_public_key->dsa_parameters.q,
      &certificate.tbsCertificate.subjectPublicKeyInfo.dsa_parameters.q );
    copy_huge( &server_public_key->dsa_public_key,
      &certificate.tbsCertificate.subjectPublicKeyInfo.dsa_public_key );
    break;
  default:
    // Diffie-Hellman certificates not supported in this implementation
    break;
}
```

This just copies the relevant parts of the certificate's `subjectPublicKeyInfo` values into the one in `TLSParameters`.

Modify `verify_signature` itself to verify a DSA signature when appropriate. Recall from Chapter 4 that a DSA signature by its nature is computed over a single hash value; you can't safely play games with concatenated hash values using DSA like TLS does with RSA. The `dsa_verify` function of Listing 4-33 just returns a true or false; you don't "decrypt" anything. Also, a DSA signature is not just a single number; it is two numbers, *r* and *s*. To keep them straight, TLS mandates that they be provided in ASN.1 DER-encoded form.

Modify `verify_signature` as shown in Listing 8-26 to verify DSA signatures if the certificate contains a DSA public key.

**Listing 8-26:** "tls.c" verify_signature

```
static int verify_signature( unsigned char *message,
                             int message_len,
```

```
                              unsigned char *signature,
                              int signature_len,
                              TLSParameters *parameters )
{
  // This is needed for RSA or DSA
  digest_ctx sha1_digest;

  new_sha1_digest( &sha1_digest );
  update_digest( &sha1_digest, parameters->client_random, RANDOM_LENGTH );
  update_digest( &sha1_digest, parameters->server_random, RANDOM_LENGTH );
  update_digest( &sha1_digest, message, message_len );
  finalize_digest( &sha1_digest );

  if ( parameters->server_public_key.algorithm == rsa )
  {
    unsigned char *decrypted_signature;
    int decrypted_signature_length;
    digest_ctx md5_digest;

    decrypted_signature_length = rsa_decrypt( signature, signature_len,
      &decrypted_signature,
      &parameters->server_public_key.rsa_public_key );

    // If the signature algorithm is RSA, this will be the md5 hash, followed by
    // the sha-1 hash of: client random, server random, params).
    // If DSA, this will just be the sha-1 hash
    new_md5_digest( &md5_digest );

    update_digest( &md5_digest, parameters->client_random, RANDOM_LENGTH );
    update_digest( &md5_digest, parameters->server_random, RANDOM_LENGTH );
    update_digest( &md5_digest, message, message_len );
    finalize_digest( &md5_digest );

    if ( memcmp( md5_digest.hash, decrypted_signature, MD5_BYTE_SIZE ) ||
         memcmp( sha1_digest.hash, decrypted_signature + MD5_BYTE_SIZE,
                 SHA1_BYTE_SIZE ) )
    {
      return 0;
    }

    free( decrypted_signature );
  }
  else if ( parameters->server_public_key.algorithm == dsa )
  {
    struct asn1struct decoded_signature;
    dsa_signature received_signature;

    asn1parse( signature, signature_len, &decoded_signature );
    set_huge( &received_signature.r, 0 );
    set_huge( &received_signature.s, 0 );
    load_huge( &received_signature.r, decoded_signature.children->data,
      decoded_signature.children->length );
```

*(Continued)*

```
    load_huge( &received_signature.s,
      decoded_signature.children->next->data,
      decoded_signature.children->next->length );
    asn1free( &decoded_signature );

    if ( !dsa_verify( &parameters->server_public_key.dsa_parameters,
                      &parameters->server_public_key.dsa_public_key,
                      sha1_digest.hash,
                      SHA1_BYTE_SIZE,
                      &received_signature ) )
    {
      free_huge( &received_signature.r );
      free_huge( &received_signature.s );
      return 0;
    }

    free_huge( &received_signature.r );
    free_huge( &received_signature.s );
  }

  return 1;
}
```

Notice that the SHA-1 digest is computed regardless of the signature type; it is needed whether the signature is an RSA or DSA signature.

DHE is not very common; most servers still prefer RSA for key exchange, and those that do support DHE still present an RSA, rather than a DSA, certificate. This doesn't mean that RSA has an advantage over Diffie-Hellman for key exchange; RSA also uses the same private key over and over, for potentially millions and millions of handshakes. There's no particular reason why certificate-based Diffie-Hellman can't be used, or why the server key exchange can't include an RSA key which was different for each connection instead of DH parameters. However, the fact that RSA can be used for both signature generation and encryption meant that it was more common in certificates, so this has ended up being the way it was most often used.

## Verifying Identity with Client Authentication

In almost all cases — unless the cipher suite is one of the DH_anon_XXX cipher suites — the server is required to present a certificate, signed by a certificate authority, whose subject name's CN field matches the DNS name to which the client is trying to connect. This is always useful to guard against man-in-the-middle attacks; without this certificate, there's no way, at all, to be sure that a malicious attacker didn't hijack your connection during the handshake.

But what about the reverse situation? The server has no way of verifying that the client is really who it says it is. This may or may not be important, but most applications that use TLS to protect the privacy and authenticity of communications also require that the client authenticate itself through some means such as a shared password.

If you think about it, this is sort of archaic. All of the problems of synchronizing shared keys apply to shared passwords. Because you have public-key cryptography and PKI, why not use it?

Imagine, for instance, an online bank that creates its own internal CA and then uses that CA to sign customer's certificate requests at a physical branch location (after authenticating them physically by verifying a driver's license, fingerprints, and so on). The customer can then install that CA's root certificate and his own signed certificate on his computer and use that to prove his identity in addition to the primitive username/password authentication method currently used. (You need both methods to guard against the damage of a private key compromise.)

TLS allows for this. The server can demand a certificate and refuse to complete the handshake unless the client provides one, signed by a suitable certificate authority. RSA Data Security's *RSA Key Manager* (RKM) product uses this technique to authenticate requests from applications, but it's not as widespread as it could be. This is a shame, because it's a very good, secure way to authenticate users. If a bank started requiring this sort of "mutual authentication," I would definitely put all of *my* money in it.

TLS describes two additional handshake messages to support client authentication.

■ The *CertificateRequest* handshake message is sent by the server to the client, notifying the client that it expects the client to authenticate itself with a certificate. The Certificate message sent by the client is exactly the same format as the certificate message sent by the server.

■ the *CertificateVerify* message, the second new handshake message, is sent by the client to prove that it is, in fact, in possession of the private key corresponding to the public key in the certificate itself.

## Supporting the CertificateRequest Message

The *CertificateRequest* handshake message is sent by the server after sending its own certificate and, if applicable, server key exchange.

**NOTE** If the server did not send a certificate — for example, if it is performing an anonymous key exchange — it may not request a certificate from the client.

The designers of TLS could have designed the certificate request to have been defined as a simple *marker request* like the hello done and ChangeCipherSpec messages were. However, to streamline things a bit, the TLS designers allowed the server to indicate what sorts of certificates it would accept, and by which CAs. This makes some sense. The most likely use case for a client-side authentication is a private CA, not one of the public, shared, pre-trusted (and expensive!) ones. As long as the CA's private key is kept private, it's no less secure than a public CA. In fact, it might be more secure.

The format of the `CertificateRequest` message is first a list of the types of certificates it accepts; TLS 1.0 defines four: `rsa_sign`, `dss_sign`, `rsa_fixed_dh`, and `dss_fixed_dh`. Following this is a list of the ASN.1 DER-encoded distinguished names of the certificate authorities that the server trusts. The specification is silent on whether this list must contain any entries or is allowed to be empty, and what to do if the list of trusted CAs is empty. Some implementations respond with an empty list to indicate that any CA is trusted. Although this sort of defeats the purpose, you should be aware that it is a possible condition.

### Adding Certificate Request Parsing Capability for the Client

The client has no way of knowing when a server might demand a client certificate, so it has to be ready to handle the request, whether by supplying a certificate or by aborting the connection. Add a new flag to `TLSParameters` as shown in Listing 8-27.

**Listing 8-27:** "tls.h" TLSParameters with certificate request flag

```
typedef struct
{
...
  int                    peer_finished;
  int                    got_certificate_request;
  digest_ctx             md5_handshake_digest;
...
}

TLSParameters;
```

Of course, as with all potential handshake messages, you need to add a new conditional in `receive_tls_msg` as shown in Listing 8-28.

**Listing 8-28:** "tls.c" receive_tls_msg with certificate request support

```
static int receive_tls_msg( int connection,
                            char *buffer,
                            int bufsz,
                            TLSParameters *parameters )
{
...
        case certificate_request: // Abort if server requests a certificate?
          read_pos = parse_certificate_request( read_pos, parameters );
          break;
...
```

The certificate request message indicates what sort of certificates the server is capable of receiving and what CAs it trusts to sign one. This implementation isn't robust enough to associate potential certificates with their signers; it just hardcodes a single certificate and always returns that, if asked for any certificate. This has to be good enough for the server. However, to illustrate the layout of the certificate request message, go ahead and add code to parse it as shown in Listing 8-29.

**Listing 8-29:** "tls.c" parse_certificate_request

```c
#define MAX_CERTIFICATE_TYPES 4

typedef enum
{
  rsa_signed = 1,
  dss_signed = 2,
  rsa_fixed_dh = 3,
  dss_fixed_dh = 4
}
certificate_type;

typedef struct
{
  unsigned char certificate_types_count;
  certificate_type supported_certificate_types[ MAX_CERTIFICATE_TYPES ];
}
CertificateRequest;

static unsigned char *parse_certificate_request( unsigned char *read_pos,
                                                 TLSParameters *parameters )
{
  int i;
  int trusted_roots_length;
  unsigned char *init_pos;
  CertificateRequest request;

  read_pos = read_buffer( &request.certificate_types_count, read_pos, 1 );
  for ( i = 0; i < request.certificate_types_count; i++ )
  {
    read_pos = read_buffer(
      ( void * ) &request.supported_certificate_types[ i ], read_pos, 1 );
  }

  read_pos = read_buffer( ( void * ) &trusted_roots_length, read_pos, 2 );
  trusted_roots_length = htons( trusted_roots_length );
  init_pos = read_pos;
  while ( ( ( read_pos - init_pos ) < trusted_roots_length )
  {
    int dn_length;
    struct asn1struct dn_data;
```

*(Continued)*

```
    name dn;
    read_pos = read_buffer( ( void * ) &dn_length, read_pos, 2 );
    dn_length = htons( dn_length );
    asn1parse( read_pos, dn_length, &dn_data );
    parse_name( &dn, &dn_data );

    printf( "Server trusts issuer: C=%s/ST=%s/L=%s/O=%s/OU=%s/CN=%s\n",
      dn.idAtCountryName, dn.idAtStateOrProvinceName,
      dn.idAtLocalityName, dn.idAtOrganizationName,
      dn.idAtOrganizationalUnitName, dn.idAtCommonName );

    asn1free( &dn_data );
    read_pos += dn_length;
  }

  parameters->got_certificate_request = 1;

  return read_pos;
}
```

## Handling the Certificate Request

The certificate request is split into two parts. The first is a variable-length list of recognized certificate types; the values defined by TLS 1.0 are described by the enumeration `certificate_types`. The second part is a variable-length list of ASN.1 DER-encoded X.509 distinguished names (whew!) of trusted CAs. Notice in Listing 8-29 that the `CertificateRequest` structure defined in this book's implementation has a section to store the received certificate types but not the CA names. You can — and a robust implementation certainly should — store them for downstream processing, but the memory management gets fairly complex and adds little to the discussion here because this code ignores the information. Still, for your edification, the list of trusted CAs is parsed and printed out. In most common use cases, there is only a single trusted CA here.

The only really important bit of this routine is the setting of the `got_certifi-cate_request` flag. This indicates to the `tls_connect` routine that it must send a certificate. If, and only if, the server sends a certificate request, the client should send a certificate. The client certificate message is in exactly the same format as the server certificate; the code can be reused as is, as shown in Listing 8-30.

**Listing 8-30:** "tls.c" tls_connect with support for certificate requests

```
  // Step 2. Receive the server hello response (will also have gotten
  // the server certificate along the way)
  parameters->server_hello_done = 0;
  parameters->got_certificate_request = 0;
  while ( !parameters->server_hello_done )
  {
    if ( receive_tls_msg( connection, NULL, 0, parameters ) < 0 )
```

```
  {
    perror( "Unable to receive server hello" );
    return 2;
  }
}


// Certificate precedes key exchange
if ( parameters->got_certificate_request )
{
  send_certificate( connection, parameters );
}
```

The `send_certificate` routine is exactly the same as the one from Listing 7-11; there's no difference between the two at all.

> **NOTE** Because the certificate name is hardcoded into this routine, if you run the server from Chapter 7 from the same directory as you run the client, you actually return the same certificate that the server uses for key exchange! Obviously, this isn't the way things normally work, but it's good enough for illustration purposes.

## Supporting the Certificate Verify Message

The code presented in Listing 8-30 won't quite work, though. Consider; the client has presented a certificate whose common name is, for example, "Joshua Davies." The certificate is signed by a trusted CA. It's also passed in the clear, so any eavesdropper who's listening in can capture it and reuse it, masquerading as this "Joshua Davies" fellow. Recall that the server's certificate was tied to a domain name; the client could verify that the CN component of the certificate's subject name matches the domain name to which it is connecting. The server can't do that with the client's certificate; the client is likely to be mobile and probably won't *have* a domain name.

Therefore, there's one last thing the client needs to do in order to satisfy a certificate request. It must use the private key that corresponds to the server's public key to sign a secure hash of the handshake messages that have been exchanged so far.

This should sound familiar; it's the same thing that was done for the `finished` message in Listing 6-53. In fact, the code to build the `CertificateVerify` handshake message is pretty similar to the code to compute the verify data in the finished message. The only real difference is that instead of iterating the secure hash through the PRF, the secure hash is signed using the private key.

### Refactoring rsa_encrypt to Support Signing

Recall from Chapter 4 that RSA signatures are data encrypted using an RSA private key. This is almost exactly the same as RSA encryption, except that the block type is slightly different; rather than padding with random bytes, the padding section contains all 1's.

Why is this? Well, imagine that the same RSA key was used to decrypt private data as well as to sign messages. To keep the example small and simple, use small values — the mini-key pair e = 79, d = 1019, and n = 3337 from Chapter 3 works nicely. Now, let's say you encrypted your secret number, 42, using the public key *e* and *n*, which works out to 2,973. So far, so good; an eavesdropper without access to *d* can't recover your secret number 42. All he saw was 2,973, which is useless to him.

However, he can trick the private key holder into revealing it. He can ask the private key holder to please sign his credit card number, which happens to be 2,973. Now, the private key holder computes $2973^d$ % n, which is your secret number 42. Oops.

To guard against this, PKCS #1 mandates that signatures and encryptions be padded differently. It's the responsibility of the signer to add this padding before signing anything.

It's easy to refactor the `rsa_encrypt` routing from Listing 3-17 to support signing and encrypting correctly. Extract everything except the padding into a separate routing called `rsa_process` that takes a `block_type` as an argument, and call it from `rsa_encrypt` and `rsa_sign` as shown in Listing 8-31.

**Listing 8-31:** "rsa.c" rsa_encrypt and rsa_sign

```
int rsa_process( unsigned char *input,
                 unsigned int len,
                 unsigned char **output,
                 rsa_key *public_key,
                 unsigned char block_type )
{
...

    memcpy( padded_block + ( modulus_length - block_size ), input, block_size );
    // set block type
    padded_block[ 1 ] = block_type;

    for ( i = 2; i < ( modulus_length - block_size - 1 ); i++ )
    {
      if ( block_type == 0x02 )
      {
        // TODO make these random
        padded_block[ i ] = i;
      }
      else
      {
        padded_block[ i ] = 0xFF;
      }
    }
```

```
      load_huge( &m, padded_block, modulus_length );
…
}


int rsa_encrypt( unsigned char *input,
                 unsigned int len,
                 unsigned char **output,
                 rsa_key *public_key )
{
  return rsa_process( input, len, output, public_key, 0x02 );
}


int rsa_sign( unsigned char *input,
              unsigned int len,
              unsigned char **output,
              rsa_key *private_key )
{
  return rsa_process( input, len, output, private_key, 0x01 );
}
```

Now you can use this signature routine to generate the certificate verify message as shown in Listing 8-32.

**Listing 8-32:** "tls.c" send_certificate_verify

```
static int send_certificate_verify( int connection,
                                    TLSParameters *parameters )
{
  unsigned char *buffer;
  int buffer_length;
  rsa_key private_key;
  digest_ctx tmp_md5_handshake_digest;
  digest_ctx tmp_sha1_handshake_digest;
  unsigned short handshake_signature_len;
  unsigned char *handshake_signature;
  unsigned short certificate_verify_message_len;
  unsigned char *certificate_verify_message;

  unsigned char handshake_hash[ ( MD5_RESULT_SIZE * sizeof( int ) ) +
                                ( SHA1_RESULT_SIZE * sizeof( int ) ) ];

  compute_handshake_hash( parameters, handshake_hash );

  memcpy( handshake_hash, tmp_md5_handshake_digest.hash, MD5_BYTE_SIZE );
  memcpy( handshake_hash + MD5_BYTE_SIZE, tmp_sha1_handshake_digest.hash,
    SHA1_BYTE_SIZE );

  if ( !( buffer = load_file_into_memory( "key.der", &buffer_length ) ) )
  {
    perror( "Unable to load file" );
    return 0;
```

*(Continued)*

```
  }

  parse_private_key( &private_key, buffer, buffer_length );
  free( buffer );

  handshake_signature_len = ( unsigned short ) rsa_sign( handshake_hash,
    MD5_BYTE_SIZE + SHA1_BYTE_SIZE, &handshake_signature,
    &private_key );

  certificate_verify_message_len = handshake_signature_len +
    sizeof( unsigned short );
  certificate_verify_message = ( unsigned char * )
    malloc( certificate_verify_message_len );
  // copying this "backwards" so that I can use the signature len
  // as a numeric input but then htons it to send on.
  memcpy( ( void * ) ( certificate_verify_message + 2 ),
    ( void * ) handshake_signature, handshake_signature_len );
  handshake_signature_len = htons( handshake_signature_len );
  memcpy( ( void * ) certificate_verify_message,
    ( void * ) &handshake_signature_len, sizeof( unsigned short ) );

  send_handshake_message( connection, certificate_verify,
    certificate_verify_message, certificate_verify_message_len, parameters );

  free( certificate_verify_message );
  free( handshake_signature );

  return 1;
}
…
int tls_connect( int connection,
                 TLSParameters *parameters )
{
…
  if ( !( send_client_key_exchange( connection, parameters ) ) )
  {
    perror( "Unable to send client key exchange" );
    return 3;
  }

  // Certificate verify comes after key exchange
  if ( parameters->got_certificate_request )
  {
    if ( !send_certificate_verify( connection, parameters ) )
    {
      perror( "Unable to send certificate verify message" );
      return 3;
    }
  }
```

```
if ( !( send_change_cipher_spec( connection, parameters ) ) )
```

Almost all of this logic was discussed in the `compute_verify_data` routine in Listing 6-53 and the `parse_client_key_exchange` in Listing 7-18. The only thing new here is the formatting of the certificate verify message; this is just the length of the signature, followed by the signature bytes. Network byte ordering makes this a bit more complex than you might expect it to be, but otherwise there's not much to it. The full handshake, with optional client authentication, is shown in Figure 8-6.

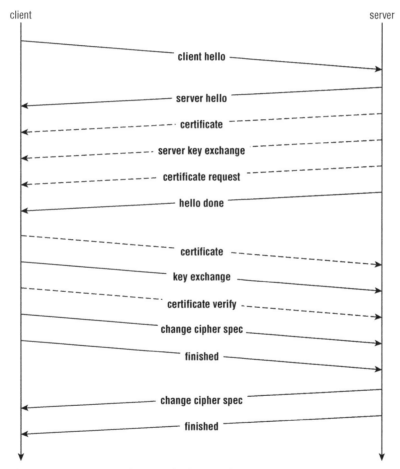

**Figure 8-6:** TLS handshake with client authentication

As you can see, a full TLS handshake can take as many as 13 independent messages. However, by taking advantage of message concatenation, this can be reduced to four network round trips. This is still quite a few, considering that the TCP handshake itself already used up three. You can see why session resumption is important.

### Testing Client Authentication

You can use OpenSSL to test client authentication because you'll probably find it very difficult to locate a server on the public Internet that requests and accepts client certificates. The process for even getting OpenSSL's test server `s_server` to accept client certificates is a complicated one:

1. Create a root cert; you did this in Chapter 5 via

   ```
   openssl req -x509 -newkey rsa:512 -out root_cert.pem -keyout root_key.pem
   ```

2. Copy this into a special directory; call it "trusted_certs" (for example).

3. OpenSSL requires that all root certificates be named according to a special convention — the name should be a hash of the subject name followed by a number. You can see the hash of the subject name by running the command

   ```
   openssl x509 -hash -in root_cert.pem -noout
   6018de75
   ```

   `6018de75` is the hash in this case. Rename (or symbolically link, if your system supports it) the root certificate to `6018de75.0`.

4. Create a certificate that the client passes back in.

   1. First, create a CSR:

      ```
      openssl req -newkey rsa:512 -out client_csr.pem -keyout client_key.pem
      ```

      Notice that the same command, `req`, is used to create a CSR as was used to create the self-signed root certificate above. The difference between the creation of the CSR and of the root CA is that the CSR-creation command omits the `-x509` parameter.

   2. Sign the CSR using the root certificate you generated in step 1. This is an involved process; OpenSSL supports it as a demonstration of how it can be done. OpenSSL recommends that you not actually use the software for this purpose except for testing, although apparently some entities do use this as a full-blown CA.

   3. To configure your own mini-CA, you need to first create a file called `ca.cnf` as shown in Listing 8-33.

**Listing 8-33:** "ca.cnf"

```
[ ca ]
default_ca = CA_default

[ CA_default ]
```

```
database=index.txt
serial=serial
policy=policy_any

[ policy_any ]
commonName=supplied
```

**NOTE** These files are required to complete a CSR signature; if you want to know more about what they're for and what other options are available, consult the OpenSSL documentation.

4. You also need an empty `index.txt` file

```
touch index.txt
```

or, on a windows system

```
fsutil file createnew index.txt 0
```

and a file name `serial` with the next serial number in it. Because this is a new "certificate authority," the first serial number it issues is serial number 1:

```
echo 01 > serial
```

5. With this very minimal infrastructure, you can now sign your CSR using the root CA file:

```
[jdavies@localhost trusted_certs]$ openssl ca -config ca.cnf -cert root_
cert.pem \
 -keyfile root_key.pem -in client_csr.pem -out client_cert.pem -outdir .
-md sha1 \
 -days 365
Using configuration from ca.cnf
Enter pass phrase for root_key.pem:
Check that the request matches the signature
Signature ok
The Subject's Distinguished Name is as follows
countryName           :PRINTABLE:'US'
stateOrProvinceName   :PRINTABLE:'TX'
localityName          :PRINTABLE:'Southlake'
organizationName      :PRINTABLE:'Architecture'
organizationalUnitName:PRINTABLE:'Travelocity'
commonName            :PRINTABLE:'Joshua Davies Client'
emailAddress          :IA5STRING:'joshua.davies@travelocity.com'
Certificate is to be certified until Aug 11 22:31:21 2011 GMT (365 days)
Sign the certificate? [y/n]:y
```

*(Continued)*

```
1 out of 1 certificate requests certified, commit? [y/n]y

Write out database with 1 new entries

Data Base Updated
```

This produces the `client_cert.pem` file that you pass back to the server from the client. You may also have noticed that it modifies the index.txt and serial files that you created earlier.

6. Start up the `openssl s_server` with client certificate support active:

```
openssl s_server -tls1 -accept 8443 -cert cert.pem -key key.pem -Verify 1 \
   -CApath trusted_certs/ -CAfile trusted_certs/root_cert.pem -www
```

This tells the server to demand a certificate that has been signed by `root_cert.pem`. Notice that the server does not need access to the root certificate's private key to do this; the public key is sufficient to verify a signature, just not to generate one. Also notice that the certificate presented by the server for its own authentication need not be — shouldn't be, in fact — the same as the root certificate that signs client certificates.

### *Viewing a Mutually-Authenticated TLS Handshake*

The following is an examination of a network capture of a mutually authenticated handshake.

```
debian:/home/jdavies/devl/test/c/ssl# tcpdump -s 0 -X -i lo tcp port 8443
tcpdump: verbose output suppressed, use -v or -vv for full protocol decode
listening on lo, link-type EN10MB (Ethernet), capture size 65535 bytes
… (omitted TCP handshake) …
21:43:42.754999 IP localhost.40795 > localhost.8443: Flags [P.], ack 1, win 257,
options [nop,nop,TS val 103385 ecr 103385], length 50
        0x0000:  4500 0066 5ad5 4000 4006 e1ba 7f00 0001   E..fZ.@.@.......
        0x0010:  7f00 0001 9f5b 20fb c914 c90b c8dd 0009   .....[..........
        0x0020:  8018 0101 fe5a 0000 0101 080a 0001 93d9   .....Z..........
        0x0030:  0001 93d9 1603 0100 2d01 0000 2903 014c   ........-...)..L
        0x0040:  758e 8e00 0000 0000 0000 0000 0000 0000   u...............
        0x0050:  0000 0000 0000 0000 0000 0000 0000 0000   ................
        0x0060:  0002 002f 0100                            .../..
21:43:42.755151 IP localhost.8443 > localhost.40795: Flags [P.], ack 51, win
256, options [nop,nop,TS val 103385 ecr 103385], length 1124
        0x0000:  4500 0498 93d1 4000 4006 a48c 7f00 0001   E.....@.@.......
        0x0010:  7f00 0001 20fb 9f5b c8dd 0009 c914 c93d   .......[.......=
        0x0020:  8018 0100 028d 0000 0101 080a 0001 93d9   ................
        0x0030:  0001 93d9 1603 0100 4a02 0000 4603 014c   ........J...F..L
        0x0040:  758e 8eae 5199 0c93 dbff 9c76 d32f 9066   u...Q......v./.f
        0x0050:  f168 1527 02ba 4f7e f5d0 fd0f d343 5f20   .h.'..O~.....C_.
        0x0060:  7ed6 9019 4e6a 3807 55b2 7e5b 4f72 c0b1   ~...Nj8.U.~[Or..
        0x0070:  d6bc df1d e49b c57b 9ea1 fd0f 1cb5 85e1   .......{........
        0x0080:  002f 0016 0301 0357 0b00 0353 0003 5000   ./.....W...S..P.
        0x0090:  034d 3082 0349 3082 02f3 a003 0201 0202   .M0..I0.........
        0x00a0:  0900 b5b5 d921 2707 fe0e 300d 0609 2a86   .....!'...0...*.
```

```
         0x00b0:  4886 f70d 0101 0505 0030 81a1 310b 3009   H........0..1.0.
         0x00c0:  0603 5504 0613 0255 5331 0b30 0906 0355   ..U....US1.0...U
… (omitted server certificate) …
```

**Certificate Request**

```
         0x03b0:  92bd fd6e dc5a 552f ecd3 90c5 6580 2796   ...n.ZU/....e.'.    Certificate
         0x03c0:  b99c f8ba 0958 972b 9360 6001 3abe 3ee4   .....X.+.``.:.>.
         0x03d0:  bca6 6646 f29d dea1 b1b4 888e cde5 8f16   ..fF............    List of Certificate
         0x03e0:  0301 00b4 0d00 00ac 0301 0240 00a6 00a4   ...........@....    Authorities
         0x03f0:  3081 a131 0b30 0906 0355 0406 1302 5553   0..1.0...U....US
         0x0400:  310b 3009 0603 5504 0813 0254 5831 1230   1.0...U....TX1.0
         0x0410:  1006 0355 0407 1309 536f 7574 686c 616b   ...U....Southlak
         0x0420:  6531 1430 1206 0355 040a 130b 5472 6176   e1.0...U....Trav
         0x0430:  656c 6f63 6974 7931 1530 1306 0355 040b   elocity1.0...U..
         0x0440:  130c 4172 6368 6974 6563 7475 7265 3116   ..Architecture1.
         0x0450:  3014 0603 5504 0313 0d4a 6f73 6875 6120   0...U....Joshua.
… (omitted certificate authorities) …
```

Here, the client hello, server hello, and server certificate are exchanged as always. However, the server certificate is followed by a certificate request, which lists the acceptable certificate types and the certificate authorities, by DER-encoded subject name, that the server recognizes.

```
21:43:42.756657 IP localhost.40795 > localhost.8443: Flags [P.], ack 1125, win
274, options [nop,nop,TS val 103386 ecr 103385], length 860
         0x0000:  4500 0390 5ad7 4000 4006 de8e 7f00 0001   E...Z.@.@.......
         0x0010:  7f00 0001 9f5b 20fb c914 c93d c8dd 046d   .....[.....=...m    Certificate
         0x0020:  8018 0112 0185 0000 0101 080a 0001 93da   ................
         0x0030:  0001 93d9 1603 0103 570b 0003 5300 0350   ........W...S..P
         0x0040:  0003 4d30 8203 4930 8202 f3a0 0302 0102   ..M0..I0........
         0x0050:  0209 00b5 b5d9 2127 07fe 0e30 0d06 092a   ......!'...0...*
         0x0060:  8648 86f7 0d01 0105 0500 3081 a131 0b30   .H........0..1.0
         0x0070:  0906 0355 0406 1302 5553 310b 3009 0603   ...U....US1.0...
         0x0080:  5504 0813 0254 5831 1230 1006 0355 0407   U....TX1.0...U..
… (omitted client certificate) …
         0x0350:  4b20 8c96 7f7a d456 d9e0 5176 54e6 b850   K....z.V..QvT..P
         0x0360:  1692 bdfd 6edc 5a55 2fec d390 c565 8027   ....n.ZU/....e.'
         0x0370:  96b9 9cf8 ba09 5897 2b93 6060 013a be3e   ......X.+.``.:.>
         0x0380:  e4bc a666 46f2 9dde a1b1 b488 8ecd e58f   ...fF...........
```

The client responds, of course, with a certificate. Notice that the message is the exact same format — down to the same handshake message type — that the server sent.

```
21:43:42.826911 IP localhost.40795 > localhost.8443: Flags [P.], ack 1125, win
274, options [nop,nop,TS val 103403 ecr 103396], length 75
        0x0000:  4500 007f 5ad8 4000 4006 e19e 7f00 0001   E...Z.@.@.......
        0x0010:  7f00 0001 9f5b 20fb c914 cc99 c8dd 046d   .....[.........m
        0x0020:  8018 0112 fe73 0000 0101 080a 0001 93eb   .....s..........
        0x0030:  0001 93e4 1603 0100 4610 0000 4200 4092   ........F...B.@.
        0x0040:  7029 733b 045d dc11 0944 9189 588d a503   p)s;.]...D..X...
        0x0050:  62ae 134b 81cc 5d85 aab1 bc7b 7855 b291   b..K..]....{xU..
        0x0060:  8ca2 b919 7d3e ad58 9ba3 781b c6ee 564f   ....}>.X..x...VO
        0x0070:  ac15 1de4 a83a 8a77 c7bb d112 f964 6f     .....:.w.....do
21:43:44.786284 IP localhost.40795 > localhost.8443: Flags [P.], ack 1125, win
274, options [nop,nop,TS val 103893 ecr 103403], length 75
        0x0000:  4500 007f 5ad9 4000 4006 e19d 7f00 0001   E...Z.@.@.......
        0x0010:  7f00 0001 9f5b 20fb c914 cce4 c8dd 046d   .....[.........m
        0x0020:  8018 0112 fe73 0000 0101 080a 0001 95d5   .....s..........
        0x0030:  0001 93eb 1603 0100 460f 0000 4200 4016   ........F...B.@.
        0x0040:  7c3c 9b7a a26d 300d b155 b494 ef9e f96c   |<.z.m0..U.....l
        0x0050:  a09b 262a bab7 409f dc93 79e1 cc4d 3565   ..&*..@...y..M5e
        0x0060:  2f55 c50a ed35 8c8c 1d49 ab5e 4678 cd58   /U...5...I.^Fx.X
        0x0070:  4d01 aca8 d312 7b74 21ff b2eb 5595 bd     M.....{t!...U..
```

**Certificate Verify**

The client certificate is followed first by a key exchange — in this case, an ordinary RSA key exchange of the sort in Chapter 6 — and then a certificate verify message. This is an RSA signature of the MD5, followed by the SHA-1, hash of all of the handshake messages that preceded this message. The remainder of the handshake proceeds as normal, assuming the server accepts the certificate and its verification.

You may have been struck by the utility of the server indicating a list of certificate authorities it trusts. Why can't the client do the same thing? Although TLS 1.0 itself doesn't allow for this, RFC 3546 defines client hello extension 3, *trusted CA keys,* to pass a list of CA identities that it trusts; if the server doesn't have any certificates signed by any of the trusted CAs it can just abort the connection and not waste time completing the handshake.

It's also permissible, if the client and server are both able to negotiate it via client hello extension 4, *client certificate URL,* for the client to pass, rather than an entire certificate in its certificate message, a URL from which the server should download its certificate. This isn't a security risk, because the client follows up with the *certificate verification* message after the key exchange; this proves that the client is in possession of the certificate's private key and that the client is not replaying an older verification message.

# Dealing with Legacy Implementations: Exportable Ciphers

Export-grade ciphers don't necessarily belong in a chapter called "advanced" TLS; they're actually regressed. In 1999, when the TLS 1.0 specification was drafted, the U.S. government classified cryptography as munitions, right along with machine guns, hand grenades, rocket launchers, and thermonuclear warheads. Exporting software capable of strong cryptography was subject to the same regulations as weapons capable of killing millions of people. From the perspective of the U.S. Department of Defense, this made a certain amount of sense — if enemy combatants could communicate securely during wartime, it was entirely possible that millions of American soldiers could be killed. Or at least I assume that's what they must have been thinking.

Finally recognizing that foreign software developers could just as easily develop and distribute secure software and that U.S. software developers were actually being put at a global disadvantage, the U.S. government has since relaxed its stance on export of strong cryptography. However, *export-grade cryptography* — that is, weak cryptography — was a fixed feature of SSL and TLS. TLS 1.0 declares certain ciphers as *exportable*, and any software that met U.S. export requirements at that time had to be certified as only supporting exportable cipher suites.

There's no reason to expend any significant effort to support export-grade ciphers, but you should be aware that they exist. The next two sections examine briefly, at a very high level, how export-grade SSL differs from domestic. If you do happen to connect to an extremely old implementation that only supports exportable ciphers, you may receive alert 60: export restriction. I recommend simply refusing to connect to such a server.

## Export-Grade Key Calculation

The main difference between exportable cipher suites and non-exportable — U.S. customers only — cipher suites is in the key calculation. Remember that, in the ordinary case, the key calculation routine first figures out how much keying material is needed and then runs the PRF to generate that much keying material from the exchanged 48-byte master secret. In the case of export-grade cryptography, the PRF was only allowed to generate five bytes (!) for the read and write keys.

The initialization vectors don't come from the PRF expansion of the keying material at all, but instead come from a PRF expansion of the text string "IV block" and the two random values — the master secret isn't used in IV calculation at all. In code, this looks like Listing 8-34.

**Listing 8-34:** Example export-grade initialization vector calculation

```
unsigned char *iv_block = ( unsigned char * )
  malloc( suites[ parameters->pending_send_parameters.suite ].IV_size * 2
);
PRF( "", 0,    // empty secret, anybody can compute
     "IV block", strlen( "IV block" ),
     parameters->client_random, RANDOM_LENGTH * 2,
     iv_block,
     suites[ parameters->pending_send_parameters.suite ].IV_size * 2 );
memcpy( parameters->pending_send_parameters.IV, iv_block, 8 );
memcpy( parameters->pending_recv_parameters.IV, iv_block + 8, 8 );
```

This means that any eavesdropper can compute the initialization vectors from the client and server random values. Why the U.S. government insisted on this concession is a bit of a mystery; recall from Chapter 6 that TLS 1.1 actually puts the initialization vector for each individual TLS packet in plaintext with no appreciable loss of security. Perhaps the NSA is aware of an attack on block ciphers in CBC mode that requires nothing other than knowledge of the IV to mount — if so, TLS 1.1 and TLS 1.2 are completely vulnerable to this attack. If such an attack exists, it hasn't been made public. Of course, if there were such an attack, stream ciphers such as RC4 would have an edge because they don't make use of initialization vectors or CBC.

Now, there's not much you can do with a five-byte key. This is actually enough for RC4, but it's not sufficient for any of the other ciphers that have been examined in this book. Remember that DES, for example, needs exactly eight bytes. Therefore, there's a second key expansion step to turn the temporary five-byte keys that came from the master secret into the final actual keys. The key block material is computed just as in a non-export cipher, but the final keys are run through the PRF a second time as shown in Listing 8-35:

**Listing 8-35:** Example of export-grade key generation

```
PRF( write_key, 5,
     "client write key", strlen( "client write key" ),
     parameters->client_random, RANDOM_LENGTH * 2,
     parameters->pending_send_parameters.key,
     suites[ parameters->pending_send_parameters.suite ].key_size );
PRF( read_key, 5,
     "server write key", strlen( "server write key" ),
     parameters->client_random, RANDOM_LENGTH * 2,
     parameters->pending_recv_parameters.key,
     suites[ parameters->pending_recv_parameters.suite ].key_size );
```

Notice that the secret here is the weak five-byte key that was computed by the master secret expansion. An attacker would only need to run the PRF on all $2^{40}$ possible input values to brute-force the key. In 1999, this would have taken a few days. On modern hardware, it can be done in minutes.

## Step-up Cryptography

There are yet more restrictions on export-grade ciphers. If RSA is used for key exchange, the modulus can be no larger than 512 bits. Of course, the same restrictions were put on DH key agreement; the exchanged parameters — $Yc$ and $Ys$ — could not be longer than 512 bits.

However, implementations were actually allowed to present certificates with public keys whose moduli were longer than 512 bits; they just couldn't use those for key exchange. So, you may ask, how was key exchange performed in this case? Actually, if the selected cipher was an exportable one, the certificate could contain an arbitrarily sized public key, but the server was required to turn around and send an ephemeral *RSA* key in a server key exchange message! Recall that the server key exchange message permitted the ephemeral key to be signed by the public key in the certificate. So, in this case, the long key signed the short key. In fact, it is entirely permissible for the certificate to contain a DSS key that signs a shorter ephemeral RSA key. This scenario was referred to as *server gated* or *step up* cryptography. You might still come across the term from time to time in older documentation, but be aware that the U.S. government has relaxed its export restrictions and no commercial CA sells server gated certificates anymore.

In theory, this approach could also be used in modern TLS to permit RSA key exchange to achieve perfect forward secrecy as does Diffie-Hellman. A certificate with a fixed RSA key could be presented, followed by a server key exchange message with a (strong) ephemeral RSA key. However, the TLS 1.0 specification states that the server key exchange message "is sent by the server only when the server certificate message (if sent) does not contain enough data to allow the client to exchange a premaster secret." In other words, sending a server key exchange message when the selected cipher suite is neither an ephemeral Diffie-Hellman key exchange method nor an exportable RSA key exchange is an error. Internet Explorer actually accepts such an out-of-place server key exchange message, although Firefox and Chrome (correctly, per the spec) reject it as invalid.

# Discarding Key Material Through Session Renegotiation

In some ways, session renegotiation is the opposite of session resumption. Session resumption exists to allow a client to reuse previously negotiated keying material so that the negotiated keys don't "go to waste." Session renegotiation, on the other hand, is a way for either side to indicate that it believes that the keying material has been used plenty, thanks, so it's time to establish some new ones.

Whereas only the client can initiate a session resumption — by including a previously agreed-upon session identifier in its client hello — either side can initiate session renegotiation. After a TLS session has been established, the client can issue a new client hello at any time. This new client hello should be encrypted using the currently active cipher suite. The server recognizes an out-of-place client hello message as an indication that it should perform a renegotiation; the remainder of the handshake proceeds as normal, except that all messages are encrypted. Of course, when the change cipher spec message is received, the keying material — and potentially the cipher suite itself — changes.

## Supporting the Hello Request

What about the server? How does it initiate a session renegotiation? Does it just send a server hello message unprompted? TLS could have been designed this way, but remember that the client and server random values are part of the handshake process. If you're going to go to all the trouble to renegotiate new keying material, you might as well go ahead and change the random values as well. Therefore, TLS defines one last handshake message type: the *Hello Request*. This is a simple marker message that tells the client that it should send a new client hello and begin a new handshake. The client should be prepared to receive this message at any time.

The handshake hash should be reset when a hello request is received; the finished message is the digest of all handshake messages that constituted the current handshake, not all handshake messages that have occurred on the current connection.

Adding support for session renegotiation is actually pretty simple. As always, add a new case to handle it in `receive_tls_message` in Listing 8-36.

**Listing 8-36:** "tls.c" receive_tls_message with session renegotiation support

```
static int receive_tls_msg( int connection,
                            char *buffer,
                            int bufsz,
                            TLSParameters *parameters )
{
...
        case hello_request: // Tell the client to start again from the beginning
          // No data in the hello request, nothing to parse
          if ( parameters->connection_end != connection_end_client )
          {
            // This shouldn't be sent to a server, and it shouldn't
            // be sent until the first negotiation is complete.
            send_alert_message( connection, unexpected_message,
              &parameters->active_send_parameters );
            return -1;
          }
```

```
                      // Per the spec, this isn't an error, just ignore if
                      // currently negotiating
                      if ( parameters->peer_finished )
                      {
                        // recursive, but the check for peer_finished above
                        // prevents infinite recursion.
                        tls_connect( connection, parameters );
                      }
                      else
                      {
                        read_pos += handshake.length;
                      }
                      break;
```

The hello request is just a marker; there's no data contained within it, so there's nothing to parse. After it's received, first make sure that it was sent by the server; a client cannot legally send this message. Next, check to see if the current handshake has completed — if peer_finished hasn't been received, ignore the hello request and continue on. Otherwise, invoke tls_connect. The check for peer_finished prevents infinite recursion.

This almost works. The only problem with this routine is that tls_connect resets the active cipher suite. Remember that the renegotiation should happen using the currently active cipher suite. So, you have to have a way to indicate to the tls_connect routine to initialize most, but not all, of the parameters.

The easiest way to support this is to simply pass a renegotiate flag into tls_connect as in Listing 8-37.

**Listing 8-37:** "tls.c" tls_connect with renegotiate flag

```
void init_parameters( TLSParameters *parameters,
                      int renegotiate )
{
  init_protection_parameters( &parameters->pending_send_parameters );
  init_protection_parameters( &parameters->pending_recv_parameters );
  if ( !renegotiate )
  {
    init_protection_parameters( &parameters->active_send_parameters );
    init_protection_parameters( &parameters->active_recv_parameters );
  }
…

int tls_connect( int connection,
                 TLSParameters *parameters,
                 int renegotiate )
  init_parameters( parameters, renegotiate );
```

This just warns the init_parameters routine not to reset the currently active parameters; they stay in place until the renegotiation has completed successfully.

## Renegotiation Pitfalls and the Client Hello Extension 0xFF01

Believe it or not, session renegotiation was found to be problematic. After all, if negotiating a handshake in the clear is secure, then negotiating a handshake using a previously negotiated cipher suite must be that much more secure, right? In 2009, Marsh Ray and Steve Dispensa detailed a series of attacks that could be used against session renegotiation (`http://extendedsubset.com/ Renegotiating_TLS.pdf`). The essential problem had nothing to do with session renegotiation per se, but instead with the way that it was commonly deployed across secure websites.

This is not a theoretical, academic attack — this attack breaks most protocols that use TLS. It works like this: Imagine that the attacker has compromised a router somewhere, or has falsely advertised himself as a wireless hotspot, and the victim is routing all traffic through the attacker. The attacker can change, add, or delete packets at will. This is the essence of the man-in-the-middle attack that TLS strives so hard to guard against. Now the victim, being security conscious, connects to his banking site securely — the attacker cannot modify the TLS handshake in any way without being detected. Let's say the victim just wants to check his bank balance, so he logs in:

```
POST /bank/login.cgi HTTP/1.1
Host: www.bank.com
Connection: Close

user=josh&password=secret

HTTP/1.1 200 OK
Set-Cookie: session=12345

<html>
<head><title>Welcome</title></head>
<body>
<a href="checkbalance.cgi">check bank balance</a>
<a href="transferfunds.cgi">transfer money</a>
</body>
</html>
```

So far, so good. The attacker can't eavesdrop on any of this because it's protected by the negotiated TLS parameters. The attacker does know, however, that the victim is connected to IP address 192.168.0.1, which he can determine is the IP address of bank.com through a DNS lookup. Now, the victim clicks on "check bank balance." In the absence of an active attack, this should result in a TLS negotiation, followed by the HTTP query:

```
GET /bank/login.cgi HTTP/1.1
Host: www.bank.com
Connection: Close
Cookie: session=12345
```

Notice that the session cookie, set by the server in the login response, is used to correlate this request with the previous login and authenticate that whatever action is taken next is done on behalf of a user whose ID is "josh." Because the connection is secure, the browser first sends a TLS Client Hello message. The attacker sees this and intercepts it. He then begins his own TLS connection with www.bank.com, which accepts his connection. Once the connection is established, he submits the following HTTP request

```
GET /bank/transferfunds.cgi?amount=1000000&destinationAccount=98765
x-ignore-header:
```

with no trailing CRLF. The attacker then allows the victim's original Client Hello request to pass through. He intercepts each message and encrypts it using his own active cipher state. The victim negotiates what appears to him as a brand-new TLS connection. Meanwhile, to the bank this looks like a legitimate renegotiation — remember that TLS renegotiation can be initiated at any time by the client, whenever it sends a new Client Hello.

Once this negotiation is complete, the attacker cannot eavesdrop on the victim's traffic, but it doesn't matter — the damage has been done. The victim sends his original request, but to the server it looks like this:

```
GET /bank/transferfunds.cgi?amount=1000000&destinationAccount=98765
x-ignore-header: (slight pause for renegotiation) GET /bank/login.cgi HTTP/1.1
Host: www.bank.com
Connection: Close
Cookie: session=12345
```

The x-ignore-header is included to trick the server into ignoring the client's actual GET command. The cookie is correct, so the bank goes ahead and transfers the money. This technique only allows the man-in-the-middle to prepend data — but as you can see, that's enough to mount a devastating attack.

### Defending Against the Renegotiation Attack

The problem here is that the server has no way of verifying that the request that preceded the renegotiation came from the same source that actually performed the renegotiation. A malicious attacker can intercept a client request, block it, submit his own request — for something that only an authenticated client can do — and then allow the client to complete the authenticated renegotiation.

The server automatically resubmits the last request, without first checking to be sure that it came from the same entity that performed the renegotiation. In general, an attacker can splice any arbitrary data onto the beginning of a secure connection and neither side has a way to detect it.

When this flaw was identified, the quick fix solution was to disable session renegotiation completely. However, renegotiation in general is a useful feature, so work began on patching the security hole. In February, 2010, RFC 5746 was released and it introduced a new client hello extension, extension 0xFF01, which permitted secure renegotiation. The solution is simple; if renegotiating, include the secure renegotiation *Client Hello* extension with the verify data of the connection that is in effect. An attacker can't fake this; if either side does not believe that it should be renegotiating, it detects the non-empty verify data and aborts the connection. Likewise, if the verify data is wrong, this is detected by the side that accepted the renegotiation request. If a client is capable of secure renegotiation, it must always include an empty 0xFF01 extension in its initial client hello.

During an initial negotiation, the client will send a secure renegotiation extension with one byte of *renegotiation info*; the single byte 0. The server must indicate that it understands secure renegotiation by responding with its own renegotiation extension. It's permissible for the *Server Hello* response to send its own extensions — as long as the client has indicated that it will understand them.

When the client is ready to perform a renegotiation, it must send a *Client Hello* with the 12 bytes of verify data that it sent with its most recent *finished* message. The server must respond with not only the client's verify data, but also its own verify data as well — the server will respond back with 24 bytes of verify data.

For example, consider the handshake that was examined at the end of Chapter 6. The last two TLS handshake messages were the *client finished* and the *server finished* message, which included the encrypted verify data on the client side of `e3945aa7b226794d96cfcaf7` and of `45c4904ac71a5948a7198e18` on the server side. Remember from Listing 6-53 that the verify data is computed using the PRF and the master secret — an attacker without access to the master secret cannot reproduce the verify data, nor can he eavesdrop on it, because it was transmitted encrypted. However, both the legitimate client and server have access to the master secret, as well as the verify data values themselves. An example of a secure renegotiation is illustrated in Figure 8-7.

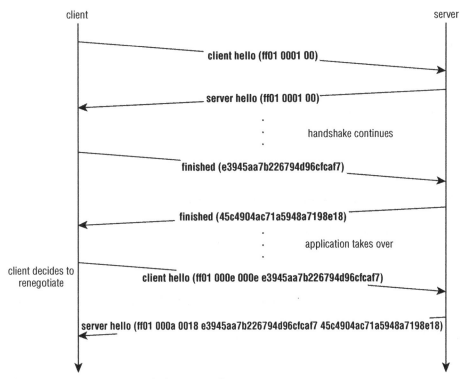

**Figure 8-7:** Secure renegotiation example

## *Implementing Secure Renegotiation*

To add secure renegotiation to the TLS client:

1. Add parameters to keep track of the client and server verify data, as well as a flag to indicate whether both sides support secure renegotiation, as shown in Listing 8-38.

**Listing 8-38:** "tls.h" TLSParameters with saved verify data

```
typedef struct
{
…
  int                 support_secure_renegotiation;
  unsigned char       client_verify_data[ VERIFY_DATA_LEN ];
  unsigned char       server_verify_data[ VERIFY_DATA_LEN ];
}
TLSParameters;
```

2. Expand `init_parameters` as shown in Listing 8-39.

**Listing 8-39:** "tls.c" init_parameters with saved verify data

```
void init_parameters( TLSParameters *parameters,
                      int renegotiate )
{
  init_protection_parameters( &parameters->pending_send_parameters );
  init_protection_parameters( &parameters->pending_recv_parameters );
  if ( !renegotiate )
  {
    init_protection_parameters( &parameters->active_send_parameters );
    init_protection_parameters( &parameters->active_recv_parameters );
    // Always assume secure renegotiation to begin
    parameters->support_secure_renegotiation = 1;
    memset( parameters->client_verify_data, '\0', VERIFY_DATA_LEN );
    memset( parameters->server_verify_data, '\0', VERIFY_DATA_LEN );
  }
  ...
```

3. Record the verify data when it is sent or received as shown in Listing 8-40.

**Listing 8-40:** "tls.c" Saving verify data

```
static int send_finished( int connection,
                          TLSParameters *parameters )
{
  unsigned char verify_data[ VERIFY_DATA_LEN ];

  compute_verify_data(
    parameters->connection_end == connection_end_client ? "client finished" :
"server finished",
    parameters, verify_data );

  // Record the verify data for later secure renegotiation
  memcpy( parameters->connection_end == connection_end_client ?
    parameters->client_verify_data : parameters->server_verify_data,
    verify_data, VERIFY_DATA_LEN );
...
static unsigned char *parse_finished( unsigned char *read_pos,
                                      int pdu_length,
                                      TLSParameters *parameters )
{
  unsigned char verify_data[ VERIFY_DATA_LEN ];

  parameters->peer_finished = 1;

  compute_verify_data(
    parameters->connection_end == connection_end_client ? "server finished" :
"client finished",
    parameters, verify_data );
```

```
// Record the verify data for later secure renegotiation
memcpy( parameters->connection_end == connection_end_client ?
  parameters->server_verify_data : parameters->client_verify_data,
  verify_data, VERIFY_DATA_LEN );
```

4. Add client hello extension capabilities to `send_client_hello` as shown in Listing 8-41.

**Listing 8-41:** "tls.c" client hello extension capability

```
typedef enum
{
  server_name = 0,
  secure_renegotiation = 0xFF01
}
ExtensionType;

static unsigned short add_client_hello_extensions( unsigned char **extensions,
                                                   TLSParameters *parameters,
                                                   int renegotiating )
{
  unsigned char *write_ptr;
  unsigned short extensions_length;
  unsigned short extension_type;

  unsigned char *renegotiation_extension;
  unsigned short renegotiation_extension_length;

  extensions_length = 0;

  if ( parameters->support_secure_renegotiation )
  {
    renegotiation_extension_length =
      add_renegotiation_extension( &renegotiation_extension,
      renegotiating, parameters );
    extensions_length += renegotiation_extension_length +
      sizeof( unsigned short ) + 2;
  }

  if ( extensions_length )
  {
    write_ptr = *extensions = ( unsigned char * ) malloc(
      extensions_length );
    memset( *extensions, '\0', extensions_length );

    // Insert the renegotiation extension
    extension_type = htons( secure_renegotiation );
    write_ptr = append_buffer( write_ptr, ( void * ) &extension_type,
      sizeof( unsigned short ) );
```

*(Continued)*

```
          renegotiation_extension_length = htons( renegotiation_extension_length );
          write_ptr = append_buffer( write_ptr,
            ( void *) &renegotiation_extension_length,
            sizeof( unsigned short ) );
          write_ptr = append_buffer( write_ptr, renegotiation_extension,
            ntohs( renegotiation_extension_length ) );

          free( renegotiation_extension );
      }

    return extensions_length;
}

static int send_client_hello( int connection,
                              TLSParameters *parameters,
                              int renegotiating )
{
...

    unsigned char *extensions;
    unsigned short extensions_length;
...

    extensions_length = add_client_hello_extensions( &extensions,
      parameters, renegotiating );

    send_buffer_size = sizeof( ProtocolVersion ) +
        sizeof( Random ) +
        sizeof( unsigned char ) +
        ( sizeof( unsigned char ) * package.session_id_length ) +
        sizeof( unsigned short ) +
        ( sizeof( unsigned short ) * 1 ) +
        sizeof( unsigned char ) +
        sizeof( unsigned char ) +
        extensions_length + sizeof( unsigned short );   // extensions support
...

    extensions_length = htons( extensions_length );
    write_buffer = append_buffer( write_buffer, ( void * ) &extensions_length,
      2 );
    write_buffer = append_buffer( write_buffer, ( void * ) extensions,
      ntohs( extensions_length ) );
    free( extensions );

    assert( ( ( char * ) write_buffer - send_buffer ) == send_buffer_size );

    status = send_handshake_message( connection, client_hello, send_buffer,
      send_buffer_size, parameters );
```

This logic is the inverse of the logic that was discussed in Listing 8-2.

5. Add the secure renegotiation extension to every client hello request as shown in Listing 8-42.

**Listing 8-42:** "tls.c" secure renegotiation extension

```
static unsigned short add_renegotiation_extension(
                          unsigned char **renegotiation_extension,
                          int renegotiating,
                          TLSParameters *parameters )
{
  unsigned char *write_ptr;
  unsigned char data_length;
  unsigned short renegotiation_length;

  if ( renegotiating )
  {
    renegotiation_length =
      ( parameters->connection_end == connection_end_client ?
        VERIFY_DATA_LEN : ( VERIFY_DATA_LEN * 2 ) );

    write_ptr = *renegotiation_extension = ( unsigned char * ) malloc(
      renegotiation_length + 1 );

    data_length = renegotiation_length;
    write_ptr = append_buffer( write_ptr, ( void * ) &data_length,
      sizeof( unsigned char ) );
    write_ptr = append_buffer( write_ptr,
      parameters->client_verify_data, renegotiation_length );

    return renegotiation_length + 1;
  }
  else
  {
    renegotiation_length = 1;

    write_ptr = *renegotiation_extension = ( unsigned char * ) malloc(
      renegotiation_length );

    write_ptr = append_buffer( write_ptr,
      parameters->client_verify_data, renegotiation_length );

    return 1;
  }
}
```

At this point, the client will send an empty renegotiation extension of 0xFF01 0001 00 on every initial handshake — this tells the server both that the client is capable and interested in performing secure renegotiation. As coded in Listing 8-42, this extension would allow for the server to support secure renegotiation as well, because it checks the connection end. The code in this book won't illustrate implementing secure renegotiation on the server, but it should be fairly clear at this point how you would go about doing so.

6. If the server is also capable and willing, it must respond with the exact same extension. So far, you haven't added support to parse server hello extensions, so you must do so now as in Listing 8-43.

**Listing 8-43:** "tls.c" parse_server_hello with extensions recognition

```
static char *parse_server_hello( char *read_pos, int pdu_length, TLSParameters
*parameters )
{
  int extensions_length;
  char *server_hello_begin = read_pos;
...
  extensions_length = pdu_length - ( read_pos - server_hello_begin );

  if ( extensions_length )
  {
    read_pos = parse_server_hello_extensions( read_pos, extensions_length,
      parameters );

    // Abort the handshake if the extensions didn't parse.
    if ( read_pos == NULL )
    {
      return NULL;
    }
  }

memcpy( ( void * ) parameters->server_random,
  &hello.random.gmt_unix_time, 4 );
memcpy( ( void * ) ( parameters->server_random + 4 ),
  ( void * ) hello.random.random_bytes, 28 );
```

7. When parsing server hello extensions, just skip over the ones that aren't recognized as shown in Listing 8-44. Technically, this violates the RFC 5246, which states:

*An extension type MUST NOT appear in the ServerHello unless the same extension type appeared in the corresponding ClientHello. If a client receives an extension type in ServerHello that it did not request in the associated ClientHello, it MUST abort the handshake with an unsupported_extension fatal alert.*

In reality, you won't see server extensions other than the secure renegotiation extension anyway.

**Listing 8-44:** "tls.c" parse_server_hello_extensions

```
static char *parse_server_hello_extensions( char *read_pos,
                                            int extensions_length,
                                            TLSParameters *parameters )
{
  unsigned short advertised_extensions_length;
```

```
    unsigned short extension_type;
    unsigned short extension_length;

    parameters->support_secure_renegotiation = 0;

    read_pos = read_buffer( ( void * ) &advertised_extensions_length,
      read_pos, sizeof( unsigned short ) );
    advertised_extensions_length = ntohs( advertised_extensions_length );
    extensions_length -= 2;

    assert( advertised_extensions_length == extensions_length );
    while ( extensions_length )
    {
      read_pos = read_buffer( ( void * ) &extension_type, read_pos,
        sizeof( unsigned short ) );
      read_pos = read_buffer( ( void * ) &extension_length, read_pos,
        sizeof( unsigned short ) );

      extensions_length -= 4;

      extension_type = ntohs( extension_type );
      extension_length = ntohs( extension_length );

      if ( extension_type == secure_renegotiation )
      {
        parameters->support_secure_renegotiation = 1;
        if ( !parse_renegotiation_info( read_pos, extension_length, parameters ) )
        {
          return NULL;
        }
      }

      read_pos += extension_length;
      extensions_length -= extension_length;
    }

    return read_pos;
}
```

8. The only extension you're interested in for now is the secure renegotiation
   extension 0xFF01. Parse it as shown in Listing 8-45.

**Listing 8-45:** "tls.c" parse_renegotiation_info

```
/**
 * Compare the server renegotiation data with the stored
 * verify data.  If this is the first negotiation attempt,
 * this data should be set to 0.
 */
static int parse_renegotiation_info( const char *read_pos,
                                     const int extension_length,
```

*(Continued)*

```
                                    TLSParameters *parameters )
{
  return !( memcmp( parameters->client_verify_data, read_pos + 1,
     extension_length - 1 ) );
}
```

If the server did not respond with the correct client verify data *and* server verify data, reject the renegotiation and abort the connection.

This implementation will allow renegotiation even if the server didn't respond with an 0xFF01 extension indicating that it understood secure renegotiation. This is probably a bad idea; if the server doesn't understand secure renegotiation, the client should not try to renegotiate at all. What if the server tries? What should a security-conscious TLS client do if the server sends a HelloRequest, but is not capable of secure renegotiation? The client is strictly allowed, by the rules of the specification, to ignore a HelloRequest — but most likely, a server that sends one is going to expect a ClientHello in response. The best option in this case would be to abort with a `no_renegotiation` alert, close the socket entirely, and start a new handshake.

# CHAPTER 9

# Adding TLS 1.2 Support to Your TLS Library

TLS 1.2 was formally specified in 2008 after several years of debate. It represents a significant change to its predecessor TLS 1.1 — mostly in terms of increased security options and additional cipher suite choices. This chapter details the changes that you need to make to the TLS 1.0 implementation of the previous three chapters to make it compliant with TLS 1.2.

The next two sections detail the message-format level changes that TLS 1.2 introduced. I move quickly here, assuming a good familiarity with the material in the previous three chapters — if you don't remember what the PRF is or what messages are involved in the TLS handshake, you may want to jump back and briefly review at least Chapter 6. Alternatively, if you're more interested in what TLS 1.2 does, rather than how it does it, you can skip ahead to the section in the chapter on AEAD encryption.

## Supporting TLS 1.2 When You Use RSA for the Key Exchange

This section covers changes sufficient enough to support TLS 1.2 in the most straightforward case: when RSA is used directly for key exchange. To do so, you would follow these basic steps.

1. Obviously, you should change the version number declared in the header file from 3.1 to 3.3 as shown in Listing 9-1.

**Listing 9-1:** "tls.h" TLS 1.2 version declaration

```
#define TLS_VERSION_MAJOR 3
#define TLS_VERSION_MINOR 3
```

2. After this, you need to make the code TLS 1.1 compliant. If you recall from Chapter 6, the most significant difference between TLS 1.0 and TLS 1.1 is that, for CBC-based block ciphers, TLS 1.1 prepends the IV to each block rather than computing it from the master secret. TLS 1.2 does this as well.

3. You can go ahead and remove the IV calculation from the `calculate_keys` routine if you're so inclined. However, it's not really important that you do; for TLS 1.1+, computing an unused set of IVs just becomes a few wasted clock cycles.

4. You do, however, have to modify `send_message` and `tls_decrypt` to prepend the IVs and recognize them, respectively.

The necessary changes to `send_message` are shown in Listing 9-2.

**Listing 9-2:** "tls.c" send_message with explicit IVs

```
// Finally, write the whole thing out as a single packet.
if ( active_suite->bulk_encrypt )
{
  unsigned char *encrypted_buffer = malloc( send_buffer_size +
    active_suite->IV_size );
  int plaintext_len;
  // TODO make this random
  memset( parameters->IV, '\0', active_suite->IV_size );
  // The first 5 bytes (the header) and the IV aren't encrypted
  memcpy( encrypted_buffer, send_buffer, 5 );
  memcpy( encrypted_buffer + 5, parameters->IV, active_suite->IV_size );

  plaintext_len = 5 + active_suite->IV_size;

  active_suite->bulk_encrypt( send_buffer + 5,
    send_buffer_size - 5, encrypted_buffer + plaintext_len,
    parameters->IV, parameters->key );
  free( send_buffer );
  send_buffer = encrypted_buffer;
  send_buffer_size += active_suite->IV_size;
```

As you can see, there's not much to change, here; just make sure to overwrite the IV with random bytes before encrypting, and put the IV in between the send buffer header and the encrypted data. You may wonder why you should keep the IV pointer in `parameters` at all given that the IV is being generated randomly each time a message is sent. Well, don't forget that the IV parameter was used as a generic state area for stream ciphers such as RC4 and needs to be kept intact, because RC4 looks just the same in TLS 1.1+ as it does in TLS 1.0.

5. Listing 9-3 details the converse changes that you must make to `tls_decrypt` to properly decode buffers that are written this way.

**Listing 9-3:** "tls.c" tls_decrypt with explicit IVs

```
CipherSuite *active_suite = &( suites[ parameters->suite ] );

encrypted_length -= active_suite->IV_size;
*decrypted_message = ( unsigned char * ) malloc( encrypted_length );
if ( active_suite->bulk_decrypt )
{
  if ( active_suite->IV_size )
  {
    memcpy( parameters->IV, encrypted_message, active_suite->IV_size );
  }

  active_suite->bulk_decrypt( encrypted_message + active_suite->IV_size,
    encrypted_length, *decrypted_message,
    parameters->IV, parameters->key );
```

To decrypt, it's even easier; just check to see if the cipher suite calls for an IV, and, if so, copy the first `IV_size` bytes of the message into the `parameters->IV`.

If you change the `TLS_MINOR_VERSION` to 2, you actually now have a TLS 1.1-compliant implementation. You can probably easily see how this code could have been structured to allow the same function to service TLS 1.1 and TLS 1.0 with a handful of `if` statements. You might even want to try to do this as an exercise.

**NOTE** Note that this code makes no attempt at checking versions. If a client asks for version 3.1, it gets version 3.3, which is actually an error. To be properly compliant, the server should either negotiate the version requested by the client, or the highest version it supports. It can never negotiate a version higher than was requested.

## TLS 1.2 Modifications to the PRF

The code in the previous section is still not TLS 1.2 compliant. TLS 1.2 made two significant structural changes to the message formats. The first was a change in the PRF.

Remember from Listing 6-33 that the TLS PRF defined a P_hash function that took as input a label and a seed, and securely generated an arbitrary number of bytes based on a hash function. In TLS 1.1 and earlier, this P_hash function was called twice; once with the hash function MD5, and once with the hash function SHA-1. The two calls each got half of the secret, and the outputs were XORed together to create the final output. Getting the PRF right is by far the most difficult part of implementing TLS.

If you're cringing in terror at what new horrors might await you with the complexity of TLS 1.2's modifications to the PRF, you'll be pleasantly surprised that TLS 1.2 actually simplifies the PRF. The P_hash function stays the same, but it's no longer a combination of two separate hash functions. You just call P_hash one time, give it the whole secret, and return the results directly as the output.

You may be wondering, of course, which hash function you should use if you're calling P_hash just one time. MD5 or SHA-1? Actually, TLS 1.2 makes this configurable; there's a new client hello extension that enables the client to suggest a hash function that should be used. If the client doesn't suggest one, though, both sides should default to SHA-256. Modify the PRF function from Listing 6-29 as shown in Listing 9-4.

**Listing 9-4:** "prf.c" PRF2

```
void PRF( const unsigned char *secret,
          int secret_len,
          const unsigned char *label,
          int label_len,
          const unsigned char *seed,
          int seed_len,
          unsigned char *output,
          int out_len )
{
  unsigned char *concat = ( unsigned char * ) malloc( label_len + seed_len );
  memcpy( concat, label, label_len );
  memcpy( concat + label_len, seed, seed_len );
  P_hash( secret, secret_len, concat, label_len + seed_len, output,
    out_len, new_sha256_digest );

  free( concat );
}
```

As you can see, you almost don't need a PRF function anymore; you could just as easily change the callers to directly invoke P_hash because PRF isn't really adding any value anymore. Leaving it in place minimizes the changes to other code, though; everything else can stay just as it is.

## TLS 1.2 Modifications to the Finished Messages Verify Data

You may recall from Listing 6-53 that there was one other data value that depended on the combination of an MD5 and an SHA-1 hash: the verify data in the finished message. And yes, sure enough, this changes in TLS 1.2 as well. Rather than tracking the MD5 and SHA-1 hashes of the handshake messages and then running those hashes through the PRF to generate the finished message, TLS 1.2 instead tracks a single hash; the same one that the PRF uses (the one negotiated in the client hello or the default SHA-256). It still hashes all handshake messages, and does so in the same way as TLS 1.1.

To support the TLS 1.2 finished message, follow these steps:

1. Modify TLSParameters as shown in Listing 9-5 to keep track of an SHA-256 digest.

**Listing 9-5:** "tls.h" TLSParameters

```
int                 got_certificate_request;
digest_ctx          sha256_handshake_digest;

char                *unread_buffer;
```

2. Of course, the two digest updates in send_handshake_message and receive_tls_msg must be changed to update this digest as shown in Listing 9-6.

**Listing 9-6:** "tls.c" SHA-256 digest update

```
int send_handshake_message( int connection,
                            int msg_type,
                            const unsigned char *message,
                            int message_len,
                            TLSParameters *parameters )
{
…
  memcpy( send_buffer + 1, &record.length, 3 );
  memcpy( send_buffer + 4, message, message_len );

  update_digest( &parameters->sha256_handshake_digest,
    send_buffer, send_buffer_size );
  response = send_message( connection, content_handshake, send_buffer,
    send_buffer_size, &parameters->active_send_parameters );
…
static int receive_tls_msg( int connection,
                            char *buffer,
```

*(Continued)*

```
                             int bufsz,
                             TLSParameters *parameters )
{
...

     update_digest( &parameters->sha256_handshake_digest,
       handshake_msg_start, handshake.length + 4 );
   }
 }
 else if ( message.type == content_alert )
```

3. Finally, tls_resume and tls_connect must both be changed to initialize this digest rather than the two parallel digests that they initialized in Chapters 6 and 8. Listing 9-7 demonstrates.

**Listing 9-7:** "tls.c" TLS 1.2 handshake digest initialization

```
int tls_resume( int connection,
                int session_id_length,
                const unsigned char *session_id,
                const unsigned char *master_secret,
                TLSParameters *parameters )
{
  init_parameters( parameters, 0 );
  parameters->connection_end = connection_end_client;
  parameters->session_id_length = session_id_length;
  memcpy( &parameters->session_id, session_id, session_id_length );

  new_sha256_digest( &parameters->sha256_handshake_digest );
...
int tls_connect( int connection,
                 TLSParameters *parameters,
                 int renegotiate )
{
  init_parameters( parameters, renegotiate );
  parameters->connection_end = connection_end_client;

  new_sha256_digest( &parameters->sha256_handshake_digest );
...
int tls_accept( int connection,
                TLSParameters *parameters )
{
  init_parameters( parameters, 0 );
  parameters->connection_end = connection_end_server;

  new_sha256_digest( &parameters->sha256_handshake_digest );
...
```

Of course, if you want to implement this code to support TLS 1.0 through TLS 1.2 concurrently, you'd have some conditional logic to initialize the handshake digests depending on the version of TLS.

# Impact to Diffie-Hellman Key Exchange

As mentioned previously, the changes in the previous section are sufficient to support TLS 1.2 in the most straightforward case: when RSA is used directly for key exchange. However, there's one other significant structural change that was introduced by TLS 1.2 that impacts ephemeral Diffie-Hellman (DHE) key exchange suites. Recall that when DHE is used for key exchange the server must sign the DH parameters $g$, $p$, and $Ys$ with the private key corresponding to the public key in the server's certificate. Prior to TLS 1.2, the type of signature was implied. If the server certificate included an RSA key, the client knew that the signature was an RSA signature. If the certificate was a DSA key, the client knew to perform a DSA signature check.

This works, but in the long-term is a bit of a burden on the implementer. It would be nice if each signature included an indicator of what type it is; this is exactly what TLS 1.2 added to the inline signatures. Additionally, recall from Listing 8-21 that RSA signatures were RSA-encrypted concatenations of the MD5 hash followed by the SHA-1 hash. TLS 1.2 changes this here, just as it does in the PRF; an RSA signature is an encrypted representation of a single hash — SHA-256 unless a client hello extension has negotiated a different hash. The hash algorithm is also identified in the encrypted data, just like an X.509 signature is. This is redundant; the signature first declares the hash algorithm, and then the signature itself redeclares it. Why was it done this way? DSA has no provision for including a declaration of a hash algorithm, so TLS 1.2 adds it before the signature as well.

## Parsing Signature Types

To parse these new signature types, modify the `verify_signature` code from Listing 8-21 as shown in Listing 9-8 to first read off the hash and signature algorithm and then to ASN.1-decode the decrypted RSA signature value to locate the actual signed hash code. (DSS validation stays the same, as it must.)

**Listing 9-8:** "tls.c" TLS 1.2 signature verification

```
int verify_signature( unsigned char *message,
                       int message_len,
                       unsigned char *signature,
                       int signature_len,
                       TLSParameters *parameters )
{
...
  digest_ctx sha_digest;

  new_sha256_digest( &sha_digest );
```

*(Continued)*

```
...
if ( parameters->server_public_key.algorithm == rsa )
{
  unsigned char *decrypted_signature;
  int decrypted_signature_length;
  struct asn1struct rsa_signature;
  decrypted_signature_length = rsa_decrypt( signature, signature_len,
    &decrypted_signature,
    &parameters->server_public_key.rsa_public_key );

  // TLS 1.2; no longer includes MD-5, just SHA-256,
  // but the RSA signature also includes the signature scheme,
  // so must be DER-decoded
  asn1parse( decrypted_signature, decrypted_signature_length,
    &rsa_signature );
  if ( memcmp( sha_digest.hash, rsa_signature.children->next->data,
              SHA256_BYTE_SIZE ) )
  {
    asn1free( &rsa_signature );
    free( decrypted_signature );
    return 0;
  }

  asn1free( &rsa_signature );
  free( decrypted_signature );
}
```

Notice that the MD5 computation has been removed here; it's no longer needed. The implementation in Listing 9-8 also completely ignores the declared hash algorithm; it's included as an OID as the first child of the top-level structure. The implementation ought to verify that the declared hash algorithm is SHA-256 and, in theory, compute a separate hash if it isn't. Because no other hash algorithms are supported here, this check is omitted. If the server gives back, say, SHA-384, the hashes don't match and an alert is thrown.

The signature structures also prepend the signature and hash algorithms, but they don't do so as full-blown X.509 OIDs (fortunately). Instead, an enumeration of supported algorithms is declared as shown in Listing 9-9.

**Listing 9-9:** "tls.h" signature and hash algorithms

```
typedef enum
{
  none = 0,
  md5 = 1,
  sha1 = 2,
  sha224 = 3,
  sha256 = 4,
  sha384 = 5,
  sha512 = 6
```

```
}
HashAlgorithm;

typedef enum
{
  anonymous = 0,
  sig_rsa = 1,
  sig_dsa = 2,
  sig_ecdsa = 3
}
SignatureAlgorithm;
```

This is less extensible, but significantly easier to code, than the X.509 OID structure.

Modify `parse_server_key_exchange` from Listing 8-19 as shown in Listing 9-10 to read the hash and signature algorithm from the beginning of the packet. Note that this implementation reads, but completely ignores, the declared signature and hash algorithms; a proper, robust implementation verifies that the algorithm is one that has a public key to verify with and, if the hash algorithm is not SHA-256, the implementation computes that hash or throws an alert indicating that it can't.

**Listing 9-10:** "tls.c" parse_server_key_exchange with signature and hash algorithm declaration

```
static char *parse_server_key_exchange( unsigned char *read_pos,
                                        TLSParameters *parameters )
{
  short length;
  int i;
  unsigned char *dh_params = read_pos;
  HashAlgorithm hash_alg;
  SignatureAlgorithm sig_alg;

  // TLS 1.2 read off the signature and hash algorithm
  hash_alg = read_pos[ 0 ];
  sig_alg = read_pos[ 1 ];
  read_pos += 2;

  for ( i = 0; i < 4; i++ )
```

These changes are necessary to support ephemeral key exchange algorithms. Because the structure of the message itself changes, you must be ready to at least look in a different place for the key exchange parameters.

Finally, remember that if the server wants a client certificate, the client must also send back a *certificate verify* message with its own signature. To save the client the trouble of sending a certificate whose public key the server cannot use to verify a signature, the certificate request message was changed in TLS

1.2 to include a list of supported signature and hash algorithms. The enumerations from Listing 9-9 are reused here. To properly parse the certificate request, modify the `parse_certificate_request` routine from Listing 8-29 as shown in Listing 9-11:

**Listing 9-11:** "tls.c" parse_certificate_request with TLS 1.2 support

```
#define MAX_CERTIFICATE_TYPES 4

typedef enum
{
  rsa_signed = 1,
  dss_signed = 2,
  rsa_fixed_dh = 3,
  dss_fixed_dh = 4
}
certificate_type;

#define MAX_SIGNATURE_ALGORITHMS  28

typedef struct
{
  HashAlgorithm hash;
  SignatureAlgorithm signature;
}
SignatureAndHashAlgorithm;

typedef struct
{
  unsigned char certificate_types_count;
  certificate_type supported_certificate_types[ MAX_CERTIFICATE_TYPES ];
  unsigned char signature_algorithms_length;
  SignatureAndHashAlgorithm
  supported_signature_algorithms[ MAX_SIGNATURE_ALGORITHMS ];
}
CertificateRequest;

static unsigned char *parse_certificate_request( unsigned char *read_pos,
                                                 TLSParameters *parameters )
{
…
    read_pos = read_buffer(
      ( void * ) &request.supported_certificate_types[ i ], read_pos, 1 );
  }

  read_pos = read_buffer( &request.signature_algorithms_length, read_pos, 2 );
  for ( i = 0; i < request.signature_algorithms_length; i++ )
  {
    read_pos = read_buffer( ( void * )
      &request.supported_signature_algorithms[ i ].hash, read_pos, 1 );
```

```
    read_pos = read_buffer( ( void * )
      &request.supported_signature_algorithms[ i ].signature, read_pos, 1 );
}

  read_pos = read_buffer( ( void * ) &trusted_roots_length, read_pos, 2 );
```

The supported signature/hash algorithms list occurs between the list of supported certificate types and the list of trusted root authorities. The length of the list is declared as being two bytes, even though there are only $7 \times 4 = 28$ possible combinations of signature and hash algorithms; the length is declared to be this long for future extensibility. In a full-featured implementation, the signature and hash algorithms are used to select an appropriate certificate, end the handshake prematurely, or just decline to supply a certificate and see what happens.

Now, it may occur to you that it's not very fair for the server to list its supported signature and hash algorithms while the client is left at the mercy of whatever the server supports, and you'd be right. RFC 5246 also standardizes a new client hello extension that enables the client to list its supported signature and hash algorithms; this extension takes the same form as the list of signature and hash algorithms in the certificate request (see Listing 8-29). This new extension is extension number 13 and is documented in section 7.4.1.4.1 of the TLS 1.2 specification.

To summarize, TLS 1.2 differs from TLS 1.0, at the message-format level, in the following ways:

- Initialization vectors are explicitly declared at the start of each message for block ciphers.

- The client can negotiate, by way of a new hello extension, a stronger hash algorithm to be used whenever the algorithm itself calls for one.

- The PRF is based on a single hash, rather than a combination of MD-5 and SHA-1. If no stronger hash algorithm is negotiated, the default is SHA-256.

- The *finished* message's *verify data* is also based on SHA-256 instead of MD-5 and SHA-1.

- Signatures computed over handshake messages such as the *server key exchange* and *certificate verify* declare their hash and signature algorithms explicitly.

The changes described in this section are, at a minimum, what you need to change in order to support TLS 1.2. Of course, there's no significant benefit to making these changes just to upgrade to TLS 1.2 if you don't take advantage of the cool new features that it includes. The following two sections examine the most significant cryptographic advances introduced by TLS 1.2: Authenticated Encryption with Associated Data (AEAD) ciphers and Elliptic-Curve Cryptography (ECC) support.

# Adding Support for AEAD Mode Ciphers

TLS 1.0 defined two cipher modes: block and stream. The primary reason for the distinction is that block ciphers need an IV and padding whereas block ciphers don't. TLS 1.2 describes a third cipher mode — *Authenticated Encryption with Associated Data* (AEAD) — that is often described as combining the authentication with the encryption in one fell swoop. I find this description somewhat misleading; AEAD ciphers encrypt the data and then MAC it, just like block and stream ciphers do. However, the main difference is that an AEAD cipher describes both a protection and an authentication method that must be used as an inseparable unit.

## Maximizing Throughput with Counter Mode

Recall from Chapter 2 that the simplest way to apply a block cipher is the *electronic code book* (ECB) mode: chop the input into blocks and process each one according to the block cipher itself. This mode has some problems, though, because identical input blocks become identical output blocks. Because most block ciphers operate on relatively short block sizes, an attacker can spot a lot of similarities in a large block of plaintext encrypted with a single key. *Cipher block chaining* (CBC), the preferred mode of SSL and TLS, combats this by XORing each block, before encryption, with the encrypted prior block. Yet another mode, *output feedback* (OFB), inverts CBC and, rather than encrypting the plaintext and then XORing it with the initialization vector, encrypts the initialization vector over and over again, XORing it with the plaintext and turning a block cipher into a stream cipher.

> **STREAM CIPHERS VERSUS BLOCK CIPHERS**
>
> Stream ciphers have some advantages in some contexts. With stream ciphers, there's no padding, so the ciphertext length is the same as the plaintext length. On the other hand, this can be a vulnerability as well. If the ciphertext is as long as the plaintext, a passive eavesdropper can determine the length of the plaintext, which is a problem in many contexts. In HTTPS, for instance, the browser usually sends a fixed-length block of header and preamble, with the only variable-length part of the request being the page being requested. If an eavesdropper knows the length of the plaintext, he can likely narrow down the actual requested page to a short list. Block ciphers have an advantage because the padding doesn't necessarily have to be the minimum amount that makes a full block; if you need three bytes of padding to satisfy an eight-byte block, you can choose to provide 3, 11, 19, 27, and so on up to 251 blocks of padding to frustrate such an attack.

> You could, of course, define a stream cipher that allows optional padding, but that sort of defeats the purpose. The principal benefit of a stream cipher is that you can transmit data as soon as it becomes available and not wait for an entire block.

*Counter (CTR) mode* , illustrated in Figure 9-1, is similar to OFB, but instead of encrypting an initialization vector over and over again, it encrypts a monotonically increasing sequence called a *nonce* and XOR's that with the plaintext to produce the ciphertext. This approach has an advantage over CBC and OFB because it's infinitely parallelizable. If you have 10 dedicated AES chips that can encrypt a block in a single clock cycle, you can encrypt 10 blocks in a single clock cycle with CTR mode; this is not the case with CBC and OFB because the final output of each block depends on all of the blocks that preceded it. Additionally, if you lose one block somewhere in the middle, you can't recover the following block if you're using CBC and OFB, but you can recover it with CTR mode.

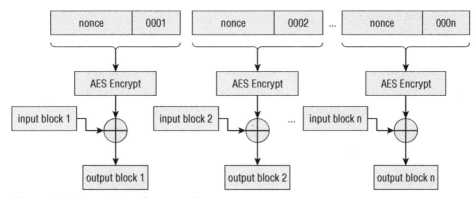

**Figure 9-1:** Counter mode encryption

Listing 9-12 illustrates how to modify the AES-CBC sample from Listing 2-42 to work in CTR mode.

**Listing 9-12:** AES-CTR mode

```
void aes_ctr_encrypt( const unsigned char *input,
                      int input_len,
                      unsigned char *output,
                      void *iv,
                      const unsigned char *key )
{
  unsigned char *nonce = ( unsigned char * ) iv;
```

*(Continued)*

```
unsigned char input_block[ AES_BLOCK_SIZE ];
unsigned int next_nonce;
int block_size;

while ( input_len )
{
  block_size = ( input_len < AES_BLOCK_SIZE ) ? input_len : AES_BLOCK_SIZE;
  aes_block_encrypt( nonce, input_block, key, 16 );
  xor( input_block, input, block_size );  // implement CTR
  memcpy( ( void * ) output, ( void * ) input_block, block_size );

  memcpy( ( void * ) &next_nonce, ( void * ) ( nonce + 12 ),
    sizeof( unsigned int ) );
  // Have to preserve byte ordering to be NIST compliant
  next_nonce = ntohl( next_nonce );
  next_nonce++;
  next_nonce = htonl( next_nonce );
  memcpy( ( void * ) ( nonce + 12 ), ( void * ) &next_nonce,
    sizeof( unsigned int ) );
  input += block_size;
  output += block_size;
  input_len -= block_size;
}
}
```

If you compare Listing 9-12 with Listing 2-42, you notice a few key differences:

- Of course, the IV is referred to as a *nonce* to fit the terminology used in the CTR-mode specification.

- The input itself is never encrypted; only the nonce is. The input is XORed with the encrypted nonce output.

This function expects to be passed in a 16-byte value, the first 12 bytes of which should be randomly chosen, but not necessarily kept secret, and the last 4 bytes of which should be all zeros. Each block computation is followed by an increment of the nonce; the last 4 bytes are treated as a four-byte integer, incremented, and updated in-place.

Also notice that the input does *not* need to be block-aligned. CTR mode turns a block cipher into a stream cipher. Because the nonce is the only thing that's encrypted, it's the only thing that has to be an even multiple of the block size. This implementation is hard-coded to use the 128-bit AES encryption algorithm; of course, you can modify this or make it configurable if you are so inclined.

One particularly interesting point about the CTR mode is that the *exact* same routine is used to decrypt. Recall from Chapter 2 that AES isn't a reversible cipher like DES is, but when you use AES in CTR mode, AES doesn't need to be reversible. Because the counter is what's encrypted at each step, re-creating it and encrypting it again, XORing each such encrypted block with the ciphertext recovers the plaintext. In fact, if you try to use `aes_decrypt` here, you end up getting the wrong answer.

Nonce selection is crucial with CTR mode, though. You can never, ever reuse a nonce with the same key. In CBC mode, reusing an initialization vector was sort of bad. With CTR mode, it's catastrophic. Consider the CTR-mode encryption of the ASCII string "Hello, World!!" (`0x68656c6c6f20776f726c642121`) with the key `0x404142434445464748494a4b4c4d4e4f` and a nonce of `0x10111213141516`. This encrypts, in CTR mode, to `0xfb35f1556ac63f6f226935cd57`. So far, so good; an attacker can't determine anything about the plaintext from the ciphertext.

Later, though, you encrypt the plaintext "Known Plaintxt" (`0x4b6e6f776e20506c616e747874`), which the attacker knows. Using the same key and the same nonce (starting from counter 0), this encrypts to `0xd83ef24e6bc6186c316b259402`. Unfortunately, if the attacker now XOR's the first cipher text block with the second, and then XOR's this with the known input, he recovers p1. This attack is illustrated in Table 9-1. This vulnerability has nothing to do with the strength of the cipher or the choice of the key; it's a fixed property of CTR mode itself. As long as you keep incrementing the counter, you're safe. As soon as the counter is reset (or wraps) back to 0, you *must* change the nonce.

**Table 9-1:** Recovering unknown plaintext from known plaintext when a nonce is reused

| PURPOSE | VALUE |
|---|---|
| cipher text block 2 (c1) | 0xfb35f1556ac63f6f226935cd57 |
| cipher text block 1 (c2) | 0xd83ef24e6bc6186c316b259402 |
| c1⊕c2 | 0x230b031b010027031302105955 |
| plain text 2 (p2) | 0x4b6e6f776e20506c616e747874 |
| p2⊕c1⊕c2 | 0x68656c6c6f20776f726c642121 |

As usual, the implementation presented by this book completely disregards this critical security advice and reuses the same hardcoded nonce over and over again for the sake of illustration. However, at least you can get around this security hole by making sure never to reuse a nonce. There's another problem with CTR mode that you can't solve, at least not within CTR mode.

Consider the plaintext `0xAB` and the CTR-mode key stream byte `0x34`. XORed together, they become the cipher text `0xB2`. So far, so good; the attacker can't recover the plaintext `0xAB` without the keystream byte `0x34` and can't learn anything about the plaintext from the ciphertext. But say that the attacker does know that the first nibble is "A", and he wants to change it to a "C" (pretend this is a really simple protocol where C is an identifier representing the attacker and B is a value indicating that A or C should get a million dollars). Because "A" XOR "C" is "2", he can XOR the first nibble of the cipher text with 2 to produce 0x82. When the recipient decrypts it, he applies the keystream byte 0x34 and reveals 0xCB.

This is called a *bit-flipping* attack, and CTR mode is particularly vulnerable to it. If the attacker knows part of the plaintext, he can change it to anything he wants by XORing the known plaintext with the desired plaintext and then XORing that with the ciphertext. Of course, you can probably guess the solution: a MAC. This is why AEAD ciphers are so named; they use a cipher mode that must be combined with a MAC function.

## Reusing Existing Functionality for Secure Hashes with CBC-MAC

Chapter 4 focuses on HMAC to provide Message Authentication Codes; HMAC is a widely used, intensively scrutinized MAC algorithm. It isn't, however, the only way to generate a secure MAC. Recall from Chapter 4 what sort of qualities you should look for in a good MAC algorithm. It should be impossible:

- To reverse-engineer. Knowing the input and the MAC should not make it any easier to discover the shared MAC key.
- For somebody without the shared key to generate a valid MAC.
- To deliberately construct a message such that it shares a MAC with another message.
- To engineer two separate messages that share a MAC.

Of course, to be cryptographically correct, you must replace the word "impossible" with "computationally infeasible" in the requirements, but this is the essence of a keyed-MAC construction. The second two requirements are met by the use of secure hash algorithms; the first two come from the HMAC construct itself.

Similar to the concept of using OFB or CTR mode to convert a block cipher into a stream cipher, CBC-MAC converts a block cipher into a secure keyed-MAC construction. The construct itself is simple; you can probably guess how it works. Encrypt the input using the block cipher in CBC mode — start with an IV of all zeros. Throw away all output blocks except the last; this is your MAC. Notice that a secure hash of the input is not computed or required with CBC-MAC. You can actually implement this using the aes_encrypt function from Listing 2-42 directly, but to be a bit more memory efficient, you should write a separate function that only uses a single block of output, as shown in Listing 9-13.

**Listing 9-13:** aes_cbc_mac

```
#define MAC_LENGTH      8

void aes_cbc_mac( const unsigned char *key,
                  int key_length,
                  const unsigned char *text,
                  int text_length,
                  unsigned char *mac )
{
  unsigned char input_block[ AES_BLOCK_SIZE ];
  unsigned char mac_block[ AES_BLOCK_SIZE ];

  memset( mac_block, '\0', AES_BLOCK_SIZE );

  while ( text_length >= AES_BLOCK_SIZE )
  {
    memcpy( input_block, text, AES_BLOCK_SIZE );
    xor( input_block, mac_block, AES_BLOCK_SIZE );
    aes_block_encrypt( input_block, mac_block, key, key_length );
    text += AES_BLOCK_SIZE;
    text_length -= AES_BLOCK_SIZE;
  }

  memcpy( mac, mac_block, MAC_LENGTH );
}
```

If you compare Listing 9-13 to Listing 2-42, you see that the only difference here — besides different variable names — is that the output is copied to the same mac_block over and over again. The mac output pointer can't be used for this purpose because it's not guaranteed to be the same length as an AES block; if you need fewer bytes of MAC, you discard the least-significant bytes of the final AES block. Of course, if you need a longer MAC, you must use a different MAC function; the output of the CBC-MAC is bounded by the block size of the underlying block cipher. The process is illustrated in Figure 9-2.

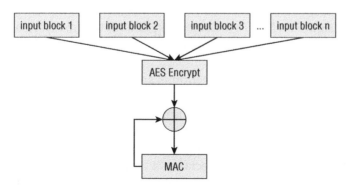

**Figure 9-2:** CBC-MAC

However, CBC-MAC fails to provide all of the requirements for a secure MAC.

- It satisfies the first and second requirements. You cannot discover the key from the output, and somebody without the key cannot generate a valid MAC.

- It fails to satisfy the last two requirements; it is possible to deliberately engineer collisions this way.

Therefore, CBC-MAC must be used with an encryption algorithm; the MAC itself must be protected by a cipher.

## Combining CTR and CBC-MAC into AES-CCM

AES-CCM uses AES in CTR mode to achieve encryption and the same algorithm in CBC-MAC mode to achieve authentication (CCM just stands for Counter with CBC-MAC). AES-CCM is specified by the U.S. government's NIST at `http://csrc .nist.gov/publications/nistpubs/800-38C/SP800-38C.pdf`. Both encryption and MAC are used with the same key to provide a simultaneously encrypted and authenticated block. The length of the output is the same as that of the input, plus the chosen length of the MAC.

The length of the MAC is variable; as noted previously, you can make it any length you want, up to the length of an AES block. However, both sides must agree, before exchanging any data, what this length is; although the MAC length affects the output, it's not recoverable from the ciphertext. Therefore, the length must generally be fixed at implementation time, or exchanged out of band. To keep things relatively simple, you fix it at eight bytes.

Conceptually, AES-CCM is simple — CTR mode and CBC-MAC are both fairly easy to understand. However, as they say, "the devil is in the details." Actually implementing AES-CCM according to the standard is fairly complex, because everything has to be just-so to achieve proper interoperability. Most of the complexity in CCM surrounds the MAC. Remember from Chapter 4 that a good MAC function must include the length of the input somehow; MD5 and SHA both append a padding block terminated with the length of the input, in bits. This ensures that a single 0 bit MAC's to something different than, say, two 0 bits. CCM uses CBC-MAC with such a length, but the length is prepended rather than appended.

In fact, the first input block to the MAC function is an entire 16-byte block of header information. This header information is never encrypted, but is just used to initialize the MAC. The first byte of this header information declares both the length of the MAC and the number of bytes that encode the length of the input. In other words, if the length of the input is encoded in a four-byte integer, then the first byte of the header block declares "4". (This also means that the length of the input must be known before encryption begins. AES-CCM does not lend itself to "running" computations.)

The remaining 15 bytes of the header block are split between the nonce and the actual length of the input. Therefore, if the number of bytes that encode the length of the input is 4, then the nonce is 11 bytes. The encoding of the first byte is particularly complex, to keep things packed tightly; to simplify, just hardcode the value `0x1F`, which declares — in a very roundabout way — that the MAC is 8 bytes long, and the length of the length is also 8 bytes long. This implies that the nonce is 7 bytes long.

Therefore, if the nonce is `0x01020304050607` and the input length is 500 bytes, the header block looks like this:

```
0x1F 0x01020304050607 0x000000000000001F4
```

This should be fed into the CBC-MAC function to initialize it. After this initialization is complete, the CBC-MAC function operates on the input exactly as shown in Listing 9-13.

The first "input-length" bytes of output are the CTR-mode encryption of the input itself. The only stipulation that CCM places on the CTR mode is that the first byte of each nonce must be a declaration of the number of bytes that encode the length that was described in the header, followed by the nonce as was declared in the header, followed by an incrementing sequence that starts at 1 (not 0!).

Finally, the last "mac-length" bytes of output are, of course, the MAC, but before the MAC is output, it's counter-mode encrypted itself. It's encrypted with the counter at 0. The whole process is illustrated in Figure 9-3.

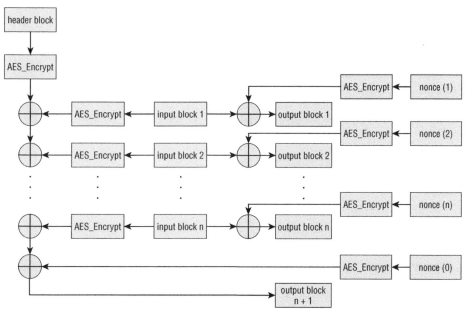

**Figure 9-3:** AES-CCM

If this is not quite clear, the code in Listing 9-14 should clarify.

**Listing 9-14:** "aes.c" aes_ccm_encrypt

```c
#define MAC_LENGTH 8
/**
 * This implements 128-bit AES-CCM.
 * The IV is the nonce; it should be seven bytes long.
 * output must be the input_len + MAC_LENGTH
 * bytes, since CCM adds a block-length header
 */
int aes_ccm_encrypt( const unsigned char *input,
                     int input_len,
                     unsigned char *output,
                     void *iv,
                     const unsigned char *key )
{
  unsigned char nonce[ AES_BLOCK_SIZE ];
  unsigned char input_block[ AES_BLOCK_SIZE ];
  unsigned char mac_block[ AES_BLOCK_SIZE ];
  unsigned int next_nonce;
  int block_size;
  unsigned int header_length_declaration;

  // The first input block is a (complicated) standardized header
  // This is just for the MAC; not output
  memset( input_block, '\0', AES_BLOCK_SIZE );
  input_block[ 0 ] = 0x1F;  // t = mac_length = 8 bytes, q = 8 bytes (so n = 7)
  header_length_declaration = htonl( input_len );
  memcpy( ( void * ) ( input_block + ( AES_BLOCK_SIZE - sizeof( int ) ) ),
    &header_length_declaration, sizeof( unsigned int ) );
  memcpy( ( void * ) ( input_block + 1 ), iv, 8 );

  // update the CBC-MAC
  memset( mac_block, '\0', AES_BLOCK_SIZE );
  xor( input_block, mac_block, AES_BLOCK_SIZE );
  aes_block_encrypt( input_block, mac_block, key, 16 );

  // Prepare the first nonce
  memset( nonce, '\0', AES_BLOCK_SIZE );
  nonce[ 0 ] = 0x07; // q hardcode to 8 bytes, so n = 7
  memcpy( ( nonce + 1 ), iv, 8 );

  while ( input_len )
  {
    // Increment counter
    memcpy( ( void * ) &next_nonce, ( void * ) ( nonce + 12 ),
      sizeof( unsigned int ) );
    // Preserve byte ordering, although not strictly necessary
    next_nonce = ntohl( next_nonce );
    next_nonce++;
```

```
next_nonce = htonl( next_nonce );
memcpy( ( void * ) ( nonce + 12 ), ( void * ) &next_nonce,
  sizeof( unsigned int ) );

// encrypt the nonce
block_size = ( input_len < AES_BLOCK_SIZE ) ? input_len : AES_BLOCK_SIZE;
aes_block_encrypt( nonce, input_block, key, 16 );
xor( input_block, input, block_size );  // implement CTR
memcpy( output, input_block, block_size );

// update the CBC-MAC
memset( input_block, '\0', AES_BLOCK_SIZE );
memcpy( input_block, input, block_size );
xor( input_block, mac_block, AES_BLOCK_SIZE );
aes_block_encrypt( input_block, mac_block, key, 16 );

// advance to next block
input += block_size;
output += block_size;
input_len -= block_size;
}

// Regenerate the first nonce
memset( nonce, '\0', AES_BLOCK_SIZE );
nonce[ 0 ] = 0x07; // q hardcode to 8 bytes
memcpy( ( nonce + 1 ), iv, 8 );

// encrypt the header and output it
aes_block_encrypt( nonce, input_block, key, AES_BLOCK_SIZE );

// MAC is the CBC-mac XOR'ed with S0
xor( mac_block, input_block, MAC_LENGTH );
memcpy( output, mac_block, MAC_LENGTH );

return 0;
}
```

The first section builds the CCM mode header in the `input_block`:

```
memset( input_block, '\0', AES_BLOCK_SIZE );
input_block[ 0 ] = 0x1F;  // t = mac_length = 8 bytes, q = 8 bytes (so n = 7)
header_length_declaration = htonl( input_len );
memcpy( ( void * ) ( input_block + ( AES_BLOCK_SIZE - sizeof( int ) ) ),
  &header_length_declaration, sizeof( unsigned int ) );
memcpy( ( void * ) ( input_block + 1 ), iv, 8 );
```

As always, the length of the length must be put in network byte order.
The next section updates the CBC-MAC with this header:

```
memset( mac_block, '\0', AES_BLOCK_SIZE );
xor( input_block, mac_block, AES_BLOCK_SIZE );
aes_block_encrypt( input_block, mac_block, key, 16 );
```

This is followed by a single loop through the input data that simultaneously performs the CTR-mode encryption and updates the CBC-MAC. This enables the encrypt-and-authenticate process to pass over the data only one time. Because CTR mode encryption encrypts the counter, and CBC-MAC encrypts the input itself, it's necessary to invoke `aes_block_encrypt` twice inside the loop. If you want to be hyper-efficient, you can modify `aes_block_encrypt` to accept two inputs and generate two outputs; you can then reuse the key schedule computation.

The order of things in the main loop of Listing 9-14 is only slightly different than those of Listings 9-12 and 9-13 (you may want to compare them before continuing). Because AES-CCM wants the first counter block to have the value of 1, the counter is initialized outside the loop and then incremented at the top instead of after encryption.

Finally, the MAC itself is encrypted in CTR mode with the 0 counter and output:

```
// Regenerate the first nonce
memset( nonce, '\0', AES_BLOCK_SIZE );
nonce[ 0 ] = 0x07; // q hardcode to 8 bytes
memcpy( ( nonce + 1 ), iv, 8 );

// encrypt the header and output it
aes_block_encrypt( nonce, input_block, key, AES_BLOCK_SIZE );

// MAC is the CBC-mac XOR'ed with S0
xor( mac_block, input_block, MAC_LENGTH );
memcpy( output, mac_block, MAC_LENGTH );
```

Although counter-mode makes a reversible cipher from any block cipher, you do still need a special decrypt routine for AES-CCM. The encryption routine generates the output and appends a MAC, so the decryption routine must be aware of the MAC and not output it. For robustness, the decryption routine should probably verify the MAC as well. However, the bulk of the routine is the same as the encryption routine, so it makes sense to combine them into one common routine and just pass in a flag indicating which operation is taking place: encrypt or decrypt.

Rename `aes_ccm_encrypt` to `aes_ccm_process` and add a `decrypt` flag to it as shown in Listing 9-15.

**Listing 9-15:** "aes.c" aes_ccm_process common routine for encrypt and decrypt

```
int aes_ccm_process( const unsigned char *input,
                     int input_len,
                     unsigned char *output,
                     void *iv,
                     const unsigned char *key,
                     int decrypt )
{
...
```

```
  unsigned int next_nonce;
  int process_len;
  int block_size;
…
  input_block[ 0 ] = 0x1F;   // t = mac_length = 8 bytes, q = 8 bytes (so n = 7)
  process_len = input_len - ( decrypt ? MAC_LENGTH : 0 );
  header_length_declaration = htonl( process_len );
…
  while ( process_len )
  {
    // Increment counter
    memcpy( ( void * ) &next_nonce, ( void * ) ( nonce + 12 ),
      sizeof( unsigned int ) );
…
    block_size = ( process_len < AES_BLOCK_SIZE ) ?
      process_len : AES_BLOCK_SIZE;
…
    // update the CBC-MAC
    memset( input_block, '\0', AES_BLOCK_SIZE );
    memcpy( input_block, decrypt ? output : input, block_size );
    xor( input_block, mac_block, AES_BLOCK_SIZE );
…
    output += block_size;
    process_len -= block_size;
  }
…
  if ( !decrypt )
  {
    xor( mac_block, input_block, MAC_LENGTH );
    memcpy( output, mac_block, MAC_LENGTH );
    return 1;
  }
  else
  {
    xor( input_block, input, MAC_LENGTH );
    if ( memcmp( mac_block, input_block, MAC_LENGTH ) )
    {
      return 0;
    }
    return 1;
  }

int aes_ccm_encrypt( const unsigned char *input,
                     int input_len,
                     unsigned char *output,
                     void *iv,
                     const unsigned char *key )
{
  return aes_ccm_process( input, input_len, output, iv, key, 0 );
}
```

*(Continued)*

```
int aes_ccm_decrypt( const unsigned char *input,
                     int input_len,
                     unsigned char *output,
                     void *iv,
                     const unsigned char *key )
{
  return aes_ccm_process( input, input_len, output, iv, key, 1 );
}
```

As you can see, most of the changes involve making sure to process only the ciphertext in decrypt mode. The big change is at the end; in decrypt mode, rather than outputting the MAC, you decrypt it and then compare the computed MAC with the one that was received. If they don't match, return false.

Note that there's nothing AES-specific about this routine; for optimum flexibility, you could pass a pointer to a block encrypt function and invoke that for each block. However, CCM with AES has been extensively studied and is believed to be secure; if you swap AES with some arbitrary block cipher function, you may not be so lucky. Your best bet for now is to only use CCM with AES.

## Maximizing MAC Throughput with Galois-Field Authentication

CBC-MAC has some theoretical problems, which are not serious enough to discount using it (AES-CCM is actually becoming pretty popular), but the problems are significant enough that professional cryptanalysts have spent effort trying to find improvements. Additionally, recall that one of the benefits of CTR mode is that it's infinitely parallelizable. Unfortunately, CBC-MAC has the same throughput problems that CBC encryption has, so CCM loses one of the main advantages of using CTR mode in the first place.

An alternative that avoids the problems with CBC-MAC is the GHASH authentication routine. GHASH is based on *Galois-Field* (GF) multiplication; i.e. multiplication in a finite field. The idea behind GHASH is to XOR each block with the previous block, but compute the GF($2^{128}$) multiplication in the fixed polynomial field $x^{128} + x^7 + x^2 + x + 1$. This may sound somewhat familiar — it's actually the same thing that you did to code the AES matrix multiplication, only it's relative to a different polynomial. The code to perform this multiplication is similar to the dot/xtime computation from Listing 2-36. The only real difference here, other than the new polynomial, is that GHASH computation is done over 128-bit fields rather than only 8.

If all of that doesn't mean much to you, don't worry; you can treat the GHASH function as a black box in the same way you treated the MD5 and SHA functions. It creates a probabilistically unique, impossible-to-reverse output from its input. How it does so is not as important as the fact that it does. Listing 9-16 shows the `gf_multiply` function.

**Listing 9-16:** "aes.c" gf_multiply

```
/**
 * "Multiply" X by Y (in a GF-128 field) and return the result in Z.
 * X, Y, and Z are all AES_BLOCK_SIZE in length.
 */
static void gf_multiply( const unsigned char *X,
                         const unsigned char *Y,
                         unsigned char *Z )
{
  unsigned char V[ AES_BLOCK_SIZE ];
  unsigned char R[ AES_BLOCK_SIZE ];
  unsigned char mask;
  int i, j;
  int lsb;

  memset( Z, '\0', AES_BLOCK_SIZE );
  memset( R, '\0', AES_BLOCK_SIZE );
  R[ 0 ] = 0xE1;
  memcpy( V, X, AES_BLOCK_SIZE );
  for ( i = 0; i < 16; i++ )
  {
    for ( mask = 0x80; mask; mask >>= 1 )
    {
      if ( Y[ i ] & mask )
      {
        xor( Z, V, AES_BLOCK_SIZE );
      }

      lsb = ( V[ AES_BLOCK_SIZE - 1 ] & 0x01 );
      for ( j = AES_BLOCK_SIZE - 1; j; j-- )
      {
        V[ j ] = ( V[ j ] >> 1 ) | ( ( V[ j - 1 ] & 0x01 ) << 7 );
      }
      V[ 0 ] >>= 1;

      if ( lsb )
      {
        xor( V, R, AES_BLOCK_SIZE );
      }
    }
  }
}
```

This is just another variant of the same double-and-add multiplication routine that has come up over and over again throughout this book — the counter variables i and mask iterate over the bits of the input Y and add x to the z computation whenever the input bit is 1 (you may want to refer to Listing 3-9 for a more detailed look at this format). The only big difference is that x — which is copied into the temporary variable v at the start of the routine — is right-shifted at each step and, if the least-significant bit of x is a 1, x is additionally XORed with the field polynomial $0xE1 \times 2^{120}$. The value of this polynomial is significant, in the number-theoretic sense, but you can just treat it as a *magic constant* that you must use to maintain compatibility with other implementations.

The GHASH routine, illustrated in Figure 9-4, takes as input a key that the specification calls H. It computes a variable-length MAC from its input by GF-multiplying each input block by H and XORing all of the resulting blocks to each other. If the last block is not block-length aligned, it's padded with 0's, and there's a single "pseudo-block" trailer that includes the 64-bit length of the input itself.

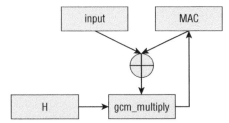

**Figure 9-4:** GHASH MAC algorithm

A standalone GHASH implementation is shown in Listing 9-17.

**Listing 9-17:** "aes.c" ghash

```
static void ghash( unsigned char *H,
                   unsigned char *X,
                   int X_len,
                   unsigned char *Y ) // Y is the output value
{
  unsigned char X_block[ AES_BLOCK_SIZE ];
  unsigned int input_len;
  int process_len;

  memset( Y, '\0', AES_BLOCK_SIZE );
  input_len = htonl( X_len << 3 ); // remember this for final block

  while ( X_len )
  {
    process_len = ( X_len < AES_BLOCK_SIZE ) ? X_len : AES_BLOCK_SIZE;
    memset( X_block, '\0', AES_BLOCK_SIZE );
    memcpy( X_block, X, process_len );
    xor( X_block, Y, AES_BLOCK_SIZE );
    gf_multiply( X_block, H, Y );

    X += process_len;
    X_len -= process_len;
  }
```

```
    // Hash the length of the ciphertext as well
    memset( X_block, '\0', AES_BLOCK_SIZE );
    memcpy( X_block + 12, ( void * ) &input_len, sizeof( unsigned int ) );
    xor( X_block, Y, AES_BLOCK_SIZE );
    gf_multiply( X_block, H, Y );
}
```

As you can see, it's not too complex after you've gotten `gf_multiply` working. The input is `gf_multiply`'ed, one block at a time, and each resulting block is XOR'ed with the last. Here, the block size is hardcoded as `AES_BLOCK_SIZE` because this is used in the context of AES. The terse variable names presented here match the specification so you can easily compare what this code is doing with what the specification declares.

## Combining CTR and Galois-Field Authentication with AES-GCM

AES-GCM is specified by `http://csrc.nist.gov/publications/nistpubs/800-38D/SP-800-38D.pdf` and in more detail in `http://www.csrc.nist.gov/groups/ST/toolkit/BCM/documents/proposedmodes/gcm/gcm-revised-spec.pdf`. It's a lot like AES-CCM, but it uses GHASH instead of CBC-MAC. It also MAC's the encrypted values rather than the plaintext, so although you can, in theory, try to write one über-routine that encapsulated both, you'd end up with such a mess of special cases it wouldn't really be worth it. AES-GCM also does away with AES-CCM's special *header block* and starts the encryption on counter block 2, rather than counter block 1; the MAC is encrypted with counter block 1 rather than counter block 0.

Listing 9-18 illustrates a combined CTR/GHASH implementation of AES-GCM. There are a lot of similarities between this and the AES-CCM implementation in Listing 9-14, but not *quite* enough to make it worth trying to combine them into a single common routine.

**Listing 9-18:** "aes.c" aes_gcm_encrypt

```
/**
 * This implements 128-bit AES-GCM.
 * IV must be exactly 12 bytes long and must consist of
 * 12 bytes of random, unique data.  The last four bytes will
 * be overwritten.
 * output must be exactly 16 bytes longer than input.
 */
int aes_gcm_encrypt( const unsigned char *input,
                     int input_len,
                     unsigned char *output,
                     void *iv,
```

*(Continued)*

```
                        const unsigned char *key )
{
  unsigned char nonce[ AES_BLOCK_SIZE ];
  unsigned char input_block[ AES_BLOCK_SIZE ];
  unsigned char zeros[ AES_BLOCK_SIZE ];
  unsigned char H[ AES_BLOCK_SIZE ];
  unsigned char mac_block[ AES_BLOCK_SIZE ];
  unsigned int next_nonce;
  int original_input_len;
  int block_size;

  memset( zeros, '\0', AES_BLOCK_SIZE );
  aes_block_encrypt( zeros, H, key, 16 );
  memcpy( nonce, iv, 12 );
  memset( nonce + 12, '\0', sizeof( unsigned int ) );

  // MAC initialization
  memset( mac_block, '\0', AES_BLOCK_SIZE );
  original_input_len = htonl( input_len << 3 ); // remember this for final block

  next_nonce = htonl( 1 );

  while ( input_len )
  {
    next_nonce = ntohl( next_nonce );
    next_nonce++;
    next_nonce = htonl( next_nonce );
    memcpy( ( void * ) ( nonce + 12 ), ( void * ) &next_nonce,
      sizeof( unsigned int ) );

    block_size = ( input_len < AES_BLOCK_SIZE ) ? input_len : AES_BLOCK_SIZE;
    aes_block_encrypt( nonce, input_block, key, 16 );
    xor( input_block, input, block_size );  // implement CTR
    memcpy( ( void * ) output, ( void * ) input_block, block_size );

    // Update the MAC; input_block contains encrypted value
    memset( ( input_block + AES_BLOCK_SIZE ) -
      ( AES_BLOCK_SIZE - block_size ), '\0',
      AES_BLOCK_SIZE - block_size );
    xor( input_block, mac_block, AES_BLOCK_SIZE );
    gf_multiply( input_block, H, mac_block );

    input += block_size;
    output += block_size;
    input_len -= block_size;
  }
  memset( input_block, '\0', AES_BLOCK_SIZE );
  memcpy( input_block + 12, ( void * ) &original_input_len,
    sizeof( unsigned int ) );
  xor( input_block, mac_block, AES_BLOCK_SIZE );
  gf_multiply( input_block, H, output );
```

```
// Now encrypt the MAC block and output it
memset( nonce + 12, '\0', sizeof( unsigned int ) );
nonce[ 15 ] = 0x01;
aes_block_encrypt( nonce, input_block, key, 16 );
xor( output, input_block, AES_BLOCK_SIZE );

return 0;
}
```

As you can see, the H parameter that GHASH requires is a block of all zeros, AES-encrypted with the shared key.

```
memset( zeros, '\0', AES_BLOCK_SIZE );
aes_block_encrypt( zeros, H, key, 16 );
memset( nonce + 12, '\0', sizeof( unsigned int ) );
```

The CTR-mode computation is identical to that of AES-CCM; the only difference is that the nonce counter starts at 2, rather than at 1. However, the MAC is different: AES-GCM MACs the encrypted output, instead of the plaintext as AES-CCM does. The only potentially confusing line of Listing 9-18, then, is this one:

```
memset( ( input_block + AES_BLOCK_SIZE ) -
    ( AES_BLOCK_SIZE - block_size ), '\0',
    AES_BLOCK_SIZE - block_size );
```

Because the MAC is computed over the encrypted output, and input_block currently contains the encrypted output (it was memcpy'd into output on the previous line), you can feed this block into the MAC computation. However, the GHASH MAC requires that a non-aligned block be zero-padded, whereas the CTR mode just drops any unused output. This complex line, then, zero pads the final block, if needed. Otherwise, this looks just like the GHASH computation in Listing 9-17, with somewhat more meaningful variable names.

Finally, the trailer is appended to the MAC:

```
memset( input_block, '\0', AES_BLOCK_SIZE );
memcpy( input_block + 12, ( void * ) &original_input_len,
    sizeof( unsigned int ) );
xor( input_block, mac_block, AES_BLOCK_SIZE );
gf_multiply( input_block, H, output );
```

Note that original_input_len is given in bits, not bytes — hence the << 3 at the start of the function.

Finally, the whole MAC is CTR-mode encrypted with nonce 1 (not nonce 0, as it was with AES-CCM), and output as the final block:

```
memset( nonce + 12, '\0', sizeof( unsigned int ) );
nonce[ 15 ] = 0x01;
aes_block_encrypt( nonce, input_block, key, 16 );
xor( output, input_block, AES_BLOCK_SIZE );
```

Of course, it's not particularly useful to write an encryption routine without a decryption routine. As with AES-CCM, decrypting is pretty much the same as encrypting, you just have to remember to authenticate the last block rather than decrypting and outputting it. In fact, the changes to support decryption in `aes_gcm_process` in Listing 9-19 are nearly identical to those to apply the same change to `aes_ccm_process` in Listing 9-15.

**Listing 9-19:** "aes.c" aes_gcm_process with encrypt and decrypt support

```
int aes_gcm_process( const unsigned char *input,
                     int input_len,
                     unsigned char *output,
                     void *iv,
                     const unsigned char *key,
                     int decrypt )
{
...
  int original_input_len;
  int process_len;
  int block_size;
...
  memset( nonce + 12, '\0', sizeof( unsigned int ) );

  process_len = input_len - ( decrypt ? AES_BLOCK_SIZE : 0 );

  // MAC initialization
  memset( mac_block, '\0', AES_BLOCK_SIZE );

  original_input_len = htonl( process_len << 3 );
...
  while ( process_len )
  {
...
    block_size = ( process_len < AES_BLOCK_SIZE ) ? process_len : AES_BLOCK_SIZE;
    aes_block_encrypt( nonce, input_block, key, 16 );

    xor( input_block, input, block_size );   // implement CTR
    memcpy( ( void * ) output, ( void * ) input_block, block_size );

    if ( decrypt )
    {
      // When decrypting, put the input - e.g. the ciphertext -
      // back into the input block for the MAC computation below
      memcpy( input_block, input, block_size );
    }

    // Update the MAC; input_block contains encrypted value
    memset( ( input_block + AES_BLOCK_SIZE ) -
...
    process_len -= block_size;
  }
```

```
...
  memset( nonce + 12, '\0', sizeof( unsigned int ) );
  nonce[ 15 ] = 0x01;

  if ( !decrypt )
  {
    gf_multiply( input_block, H, output );

    // Now encrypt the MAC block and output it
    aes_block_encrypt( nonce, input_block, key, 16 );
    xor( output, input_block, AES_BLOCK_SIZE );
  }
  else
  {
    gf_multiply( input_block, H, mac_block );

    // Now decrypt the final (MAC) block and compare it
    aes_block_encrypt( nonce, input_block, key, 16 );
    xor( input_block, input, AES_BLOCK_SIZE );

    if ( memcmp( mac_block, input_block, AES_BLOCK_SIZE ) )
    {
      return 1;
    }
  }

  return 0;
}

int aes_gcm_encrypt( const unsigned char *input,
                     int input_len,
                     unsigned char *output,
                     void *iv,
                     const unsigned char *key )
{
  return aes_gcm_process( input, input_len, output, iv, key, 0 );
}

int aes_gcm_decrypt( const unsigned char *input,
                     int input_len,
                     unsigned char *output,
                     void *iv,
                     const unsigned char *key )
{
  return aes_gcm_process( input, input_len, output, iv, key, 1 );
}
```

AES-CCM and AES-GCM are fairly simple to understand, but not necessarily simple to implement, due to the required precision surrounding their associated MACs. Fortunately, once you get the details all worked out, you can treat the functions as black boxes — plaintext goes in, ciphertext comes out. As long as you're careful to ensure that nonces are never reused with a single key, you can be confident that the encrypted data is safely protected.

## Authentication with Associated Data

By now you may be wondering, "If AEAD stands for Authenticated Encryption with Associated Data, what's the associated data part?" The *Associated Data* is data that should be authenticated along with the encrypted data, but not itself encrypted. If you remember the use of the MAC in TLS 1.0, it MAC'ed one additional piece of data that was not transmitted — the sequence number — and some that were transmitted but not encrypted. Because the main upside of AEAD is to incorporate the authentication into the encryption, you need to replicate the authentication of the original TLS 1.0 MAC.

The *associated data*, if present, is MAC'ed before the rest of the data stream, but in the case of CCM, after the header block. In order to process associated data during AES-CCM or AES-GCM, make the changes shown in Listing 9-20 to the encrypt and decrypt routines.

**Listing 9-20:** "aes.h" AES-CCM and AES-GCM with associated data support

```
int aes_ccm_encrypt( const unsigned char *input,
                     const int input_len,
                     const unsigned char *addldata,
                     const int addldata_len,
                     unsigned char output[],
                     void *iv,
                     const unsigned char *key )
{
  return aes_ccm_process( input, input_len, addldata, addldata_len,
    output, iv, key, 0 );
}

int aes_ccm_decrypt( const unsigned char *input,
                     const int input_len,
                     const unsigned char *addldata,
                     const int addldata_len,
                     unsigned char output[],
                     void *iv,
                     const unsigned char *key )
{
  return aes_ccm_process( input, input_len, addldata, addldata_len,
    output, iv, key, 1 );
}

int aes_gcm_encrypt( const unsigned char *plaintext,
                     const int input_len,
```

```
                    const unsigned char *addldata,
                    const int addldata_len,
                    unsigned char output[],
                    void *iv,
                    const unsigned char *key )
{
  return aes_gcm_process( input, input_len, addldata, addldata_len,
    output, iv, key, 0 );
}

int aes_gcm_decrypt( const unsigned char *input,
                    const int input_len,
                    const unsigned char *addldata,
                    const int addldata_len,
                    unsigned char output[],
                    void *iv,
                    const unsigned char *key )
{
  return aes_gcm_process( input, input_len, addldata, addldata_len,
    output, iv, key, 1 );
}
```

Now modify `aes_ccm_process` and `aes_gcm_process` to accept and authenticate the associated data. This is not too terribly complex; you just run the associated data through the MAC computation before beginning the encrypt/MAC process. The only complicating factor for CCM is that the first two bytes of the first block of associated data must include the length of the additional data. Remember that every time you MAC anything, you must include the length of what you're MAC'ing in the processing somehow to ensure that two inputs of differing lengths whose trailing bytes are all zeros MAC to different values (if the reason for this isn't clear, you might want to jump back and briefly review Chapter 4). AES-CCM with additional data support is shown in Listing 9-21.

**Listing 9-21:** "aes.c" aes_ccm_process with associated data

```
int aes_ccm_process( const unsigned char *input,
                    int input_len,
                    const unsigned char *addldata,
                    unsigned short addldata_len,
                    unsigned char *output,
                    void *iv,
                    const unsigned char *key,
                    int decrypt )
{
...
  memset( input_block, '\0', AES_BLOCK_SIZE );
  input_block[ 0 ] = 0x1F;  // t = mac_length = 8 bytes, q = 8 bytes (so n = 7)
```

*(Continued)*

```
    input_block[ 0 ] |= addldata_len ? 0x40 : 0x00;
...
  xor( input_block, mac_block, AES_BLOCK_SIZE );
  aes_block_encrypt( input_block, mac_block, key, 16 );

  if ( addldata_len )
  {
    int addldata_len_declare;
    int addldata_block_len;
    // First two bytes of addl data are the length in network order
    addldata_len_declare = ntohs( addldata_len );
    memset( input_block, '\0', AES_BLOCK_SIZE );
    memcpy( input_block, ( void * ) &addldata_len_declare,
      sizeof( unsigned short ) );
    addldata_block_len = AES_BLOCK_SIZE - sizeof( unsigned short );

    do
    {
      block_size = ( addldata_len < addldata_block_len ) ?
        addldata_len : addldata_block_len;

      memcpy( input_block + ( AES_BLOCK_SIZE - addldata_block_len ),
        addldata, block_size );

      xor( input_block, mac_block, AES_BLOCK_SIZE );
      aes_block_encrypt( input_block, mac_block, key, 16 );

      addldata_len -= block_size;
      addldata += block_size;
      addldata_block_len = AES_BLOCK_SIZE;
      memset( input_block, '\0', addldata_block_len );
    }
    while ( addldata_len );
  }

  // Prepare the first nonce
  memset( nonce, '\0', AES_BLOCK_SIZE );
```

Remember that, in CCM, there was a header that was MAC'ed before the data, and that the first byte of this header was a byte of flags. One of these flags indicates whether to expect associated data. The first change in Listing 9-21 sets the adata flag in the header that indicates that there is associated data in the first place; the remainder of the changes are contained in the if block. This if block just cycles through the additional data supplied (if any) and computes it into the MAC; the only thing that makes this a bit complex is that the first two bytes of the first block must be the length of the additional data, in network byte order.

To see this in action, go ahead and modify the AES test main routine to call aes_ccm_encrypt instead of aes_128_encrypt when the key size is 16 bytes,

and add a provision to optionally pass in some additional data as shown in
Listing 9-22.

**Listing 9-22:** "aes.c" main routine modified to accept associated data

```
#ifdef TEST_AES
int main( int argc, char *argv[ ] )
{
  unsigned char *key;
  unsigned char *input;
  unsigned char *iv;
  unsigned char *addl_data;
  int key_len;
  int input_len;
  int iv_len;
  int addldata_len;

  if ( argc < 5 )
  {
    fprintf( stderr, "Usage: %s [-e|-d] <key> <iv> <input> [<addl data>]\n",
      argv[ 0 ] );
    exit( 0 );
  }

  key_len = hex_decode( argv[ 2 ], &key );
  iv_len = hex_decode( argv[ 3 ], &iv );
  input_len = hex_decode( argv[ 4 ], &input );

  if ( argc > 5 )
  {
    addldata_len = hex_decode( argv[ 5 ], &addl_data );
  }
  else
  {
    addldata_len = 0;
    addl_data = NULL;
  }

  if ( !strcmp( argv[ 1 ], "-e" ) )
  {
    unsigned char *ciphertext = ( unsigned char * )
      malloc( input_len + MAC_LENGTH );

    if ( key_len == 16 )
    {
      aes_ccm_encrypt( input, input_len, addl_data, addldata_len, ciphertext,
        ( void * ) iv, key );
    }
...
  else if ( !strcmp( argv[ 1 ], "-d" ) )
```

*(Continued)*

```
  {
    unsigned char *plaintext = ( unsigned char * )
      malloc( input_len - MAC_LENGTH );

    if ( key_len == 16 )
    {
      if ( aes_ccm_decrypt( input, input_len, addl_data, addldata_len,
plaintext, ( void * ) iv, key ) )
      {
        fprintf( stderr, "Error, MAC mismatch.\n" );
      }
    }
...

    show_hex( plaintext, input_len - MAC_LENGTH );
    free( plaintext );
...
  free( iv );
  free( key );
  free( input );
  free( addl_data );

  return 0;
}
#endif
```

Now, you can see an AES-CCM encryption in action:

```
[jdavies@localhost ssl]$ ./aes -e "@ABCDEFGHIJKLMNO" "12345678" "tuvwxyz" "abc"
404855688058bb65f9c511
```

Here, `"@ABCDEFGHIJKLMNO"` is the key, `"12345678"` is the nonce, `"tuvwxyz"` is the associated data, and `"abc"` is the data to encrypt. The encrypted output — the CTR-mode part — is the three bytes `0x404855`. The remainder of the output is the eight-byte MAC `0x688058bb65f9c511`. This MAC is computed over first the header block `0x5f31323334353637380000000000003`. `0x5F` is the declaration that there is associated data, the MAC size is eight bytes, and that the declaration of the length of the input takes up seven bytes. This is followed by the nonce itself and the length of the input — in this case, three bytes. The associated data is then added to the MAC — this is `0x0007747576 7778797a00000000000000`. Notice that the first two bytes are the length of the associated data, followed by the zero-padded associated data itself. Finally, the plaintext input `"abc"` is added to the MAC (again, zero-padded). This final MAC block is AES-counter-mode encrypted with nonce 0: `0x3132333435363 7380000000000000000`.

This entire operation is illustrated in Figure 9-5.

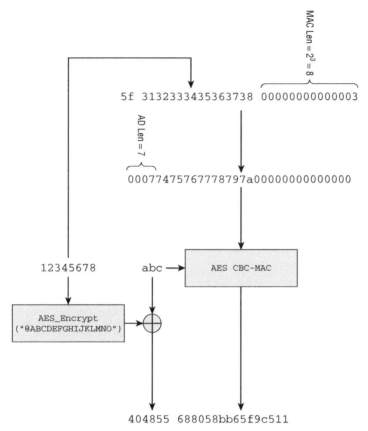

**Figure 9-5:** AES-CCM encryption example

Decrypting gives you back the original input:

```
[jdavies@localhost ssl]$ ./aes -d "@ABCDEFGHIJKLMNO" "123456789012" "tuvwxyz" \
0x404855688058bb65f9c511
616263
```

If the MAC is wrong, though, you just get back nothing:

```
[jdavies@localhost ssl]$ ./aes -d "@ABCDEFGHIJKLMNO" "123456789012" "tuvwxyz" \
0x404855688058bb65f9c5112
Error, MAC mismatch.
```

Technically, though, there's nothing stopping you, if you have the key, from writing a CTR-mode decryption routine and decrypting the first three bytes anyway. If you know the MAC is eight bytes, you know the input was three. You can decrypt, but not authenticate, the ciphertext even if you don't know what the additional data was; it's just used in the MAC computation.

AES-GCM with associated data is even easier; there's no length to prepend to the associated data, so you can just incorporate the associated data processing into the MAC just before encryption starts, as shown in Listing 9-23:

**Listing 9-23:** "aes.c" aes_gcm_process with associated data support

```
int aes_gcm_process( const unsigned char *input,
                     int input_len,
                     const unsigned char *addl_data,
                     unsigned short addldata_len,
                     unsigned char *output,
                     void *iv,
                     const unsigned char *key,
                     int decrypt )
{

...

  original_input_len = htonl( process_len << 3 ); // remember this for final
block

  while ( addldata_len )
  {
    block_size = ( addldata_len < AES_BLOCK_SIZE ) ?
      addldata_len : AES_BLOCK_SIZE;
    memset( input_block, '\0', AES_BLOCK_SIZE );
    memcpy( input_block, addl_data, block_size );
    xor( input_block, mac_block, AES_BLOCK_SIZE );
    gf_multiply( input_block, H, mac_block );

    addl_data += block_size;
    addldata_len -= block_size;
  }

  next_nonce = htonl( 1 );
...
```

However, remember from the previous section that the GCM MAC itself included a trailer block whose last eight bytes was the length, in bits, of the MAC'ed data. If you start including additional data in the MAC, you must declare that length as well. Because the trailer block is 16 bytes long, and the last 8 bytes are the length of the ciphertext, you can probably guess that the first 8 bytes are the length of the additional data. Modify aes_gcm_process as shown in Listing 9-24 to account for this.

**Listing 9-24:** "aes.c" aes_gcm_process with associated data length declaration

```
  int original_input_len, original_addl_len;
...
  original_input_len = htonl( process_len << 3 ); // remember this for final block
```

```
original_addl_len = htonl( addldata_len << 3 ); // remember this for final block
...
memset( input_block, '\0', AES_BLOCK_SIZE );
memcpy( input_block + 4, ( void * ) &original_addl_len,
  sizeof( unsigned int ) );
memcpy( input_block + 12, ( void * ) &original_input_len,
  sizeof( unsigned int ) );
```

You can see this in action, as well, if you modify the main routine to invoke aes_gcm_encrypt or aes_gcm_decrypt instead of aes_ccm:

```
[jdavies@localhost ssl]$ ./aes -e "@ABCDEFGHIJKLMNO" "12345678" "tuvwxyz" "abc"
87fd0515d242cf110c77b98055c3ad3196aec6
[jdavies@localhost ssl]$ ./aes -d "@ABCDEFGHIJKLMNO" "12345678" "tuvwxyz" \
0x87fd0515d242cf110c77b98055c3ad3196aec6
616263
```

Notice that the AES-GCM output for the same input is 8 bytes longer than the AES-CCM output because the AES-GCM routine included a 16-byte MAC, but AES-CCM's was just 8. There's no particular reason why it must be this way. This is the way they're shown in their relative specifications, so they were coded this way here. The MAC-length is variable, but remember that because the length itself is not included anywhere in the output, both sides must agree on what it must be before transmitting any data.

## Incorporating AEAD Ciphers into TLS 1.2

AEAD ciphers such as AES-CCM and AES-GCM are just different enough than block and stream ciphers, from the perspective of TLS 1.2, to warrant their own format. Both ciphers examined here are stream ciphers with a MAC, which is just like RC4 with SHA-1. However, AEAD ciphers must also transmit their nonce. Block ciphers do something similar with their IVs; they incorporate padding, but in theory you could implement an AEAD cipher by treating it as a block-ciphered structure with a 0-length input block.

In fact, you could get away with this for AES-CCM. If you declared the cipher as aes_ctr_(en/de)crypt, you could make the MAC function variable and replace the default HMAC operation with a CBC-MAC. This would actually work with the block ciphered encryption structure coded in Listing 6-64. However, this would fail for AES-GCM. AES-GCM computes a MAC over the ciphertext, rather than the plaintext. Although you could probably write code to maintain this as a special case, AEAD ciphers are designed to be treated as a black-box. You give it the plaintext and the key, and it gives you back an arbitrarily sized chunk of data that it promises to decrypt and authenticate, with the key, at a later date. To properly support AEAD, you must treat AEAD ciphers as yet another sort of cipher.

To this end, modify the `CipherSuite` structure declaration to include a section for AEAD ciphers as shown in Listing 9-25.

**Listing 9-25:** "tls.h" CipherSuite declaration with AEAD support

```
typedef struct
{
...
  void (*new_digest)( digest_ctx *context );
  int (*aead_encrypt)( const unsigned char *plaintext,
                       const int plaintext_len,
                       const unsigned char *addldata,
                       const int addldata_len,
                       unsigned char ciphertext[],
                       void *iv,
                       const unsigned char *key );
  int (*aead_decrypt)( const unsigned char *ciphertext,
                       const int ciphertext_len,
                       const unsigned char *addldata,
                       const int addldata_len,
                       unsigned char plaintext[],
                       void *iv,
                       const unsigned char *key );
}
CipherSuite;
```

Now, to add support for the standardized AES_GCM cipher mode, you must just add another element to the list of cipher `suites` declared in Listing 6-10. Unfortunately, RFC 5288 assigns the cipher suite ID `0x9C` to AES-GCM. Remember that the `suites` array is positional; if you skip an element, you have to insert a NULL placeholder. Cipher suite ID `0x9C` works out to element 156. Prior to this chapter, the last element in this array was 58. To keep up with this method of inserting new ciphers, you'd have to include 98 empty elements in this array. Instead, just expand the list as shown in Listing 9-26.

**Listing 9-26:** "tls.h" aes-gcm cipher suite

```
typedef enum
{
...
  TLS_DH_anon_WITH_AES_256_CBC_SHA  = 0x003A,

  TLS_RSA_WITH_AES_128_GCM_SHA256   = 0x009C,

  MAX_SUPPORTED_CIPHER_SUITE        = 0x009D
} CipherSuiteIdentifier
```

Now, rather than explicitly declaring this new cipher suite in the array initializer, add it to the `init_tls` call as shown in Listing 9-27.

**Listing 9-27:** "tls.c" init_tls with AES-GCM cipher suite

```
void init_tls()

{
…

  // Extra cipher suites not previously declared
  suites[ TLS_RSA_WITH_AES_128_GCM_SHA256 ].id = TLS_RSA_WITH_AES_128_GCM_
SHA256;
  suites[ TLS_RSA_WITH_AES_128_GCM_SHA256 ].block_size = 0;
  suites[ TLS_RSA_WITH_AES_128_GCM_SHA256 ].IV_size = 12;
  suites[ TLS_RSA_WITH_AES_128_GCM_SHA256 ].key_size = 16;
  suites[ TLS_RSA_WITH_AES_128_GCM_SHA256 ].hash_size = 16;
  suites[ TLS_RSA_WITH_AES_128_GCM_SHA256 ].bulk_encrypt = NULL;
  suites[ TLS_RSA_WITH_AES_128_GCM_SHA256 ].bulk_decrypt = NULL;
  suites[ TLS_RSA_WITH_AES_128_GCM_SHA256 ].new_digest = NULL;
  suites[ TLS_RSA_WITH_AES_128_GCM_SHA256 ].aead_encrypt = aes_gcm_encrypt;
  suites[ TLS_RSA_WITH_AES_128_GCM_SHA256 ].aead_decrypt = aes_gcm_decrypt;
}
```

This declares the new cipher suite TLS_RSA_WITH_AES_128_GCM_SHA256. "But wait," you may be saying, "what is this 'SHA256'? Doesn't AES-GCM declare its own MAC?" It does, in fact; RFC 5288 indicates that the SHA-256 should be used to control the PRF. This is in response to section 5 of RFC 5246, which states

> "New cipher suites MUST explicitly specify a PRF and, in general, SHOULD use the TLS PRF with SHA-256 or a stronger standard hash function."

At this point, all that's left to do is invoke the AEAD cipher when such a suite becomes active. This happens in the functions send_message, originally defined in Listing 6-64, and tls_decrypt, originally defined in Listing 6-68. You might want to peek back to their final definitions before continuing. After the digest routines, these are the two most complex functions in this book.

If you recall, send_message first computed a MAC over the data to be sent, prepended with a 64-bit sequence number. It then applies padding as necessary, prepends the IV in the case of a block cipher (TLS 1.1+), and encrypts the plaintext and the MAC before sending. AES-GCM is not much different, but a single call computes the ciphertext and the MAC, and the associated data is the sequence number and the header. The CipherSuite declaration from Listing 9-27 lists the new_digest as NULL, but the hash_size as 16. You can rewrite send_message to take advantage of this by calculating the associated data whenever the hash_size is non-zero as shown in Listing 9-28.

**Listing 9-28:** "tls.c" send_message with associated data support

```
int send_message( int connection,
                   int content_type,
                   const unsigned char *content,
```

*(Continued)*

```
                          short content_len,
                          ProtectionParameters *parameters )
{
...
  unsigned char *mac = NULL;
  unsigned char mac_header[ 13 ];
  digest_ctx digest;
...
  active_suite = &suites[ parameters->suite ];

  // Compute the MAC header always, since this will be used
  // for AEAD or other ciphers
  // Allocate enough space for the 8-byte sequence number, the 5-byte pseudo
  // header, and the content.

  // These will be overwritten below
  if ( active_suite->hash_size )
  {
    int sequence_num;
    memset( mac_header, '\0', 8 );
    sequence_num = htonl( parameters->seq_num );
    memcpy( mac_header + 4, &sequence_num, sizeof( int ) );

    header.type = content_type;
    header.version.major = TLS_VERSION_MAJOR;
    header.version.minor = TLS_VERSION_MINOR;
    header.length = htons( content_len );
    mac_header[ 8 ] = header.type;
    mac_header[ 9 ] = header.version.major;
    mac_header[ 10 ] = header.version.minor;
    memcpy( mac_header + 11, &header.length, sizeof( short ) );
  }

  if ( active_suite->new_digest )
  {
    unsigned char *mac_buffer = malloc( 13 + content_len );

    mac = ( unsigned char * ) malloc( active_suite->hash_size );
    active_suite->new_digest( &digest );
    memcpy( mac_buffer, mac_header, 13 );

    memcpy( mac_buffer + 13, content, content_len );
...
```

This change just creates a new mac_header buffer and pulls its computation out of the MAC computation so that it's accessible to the AEAD encryption function.

Of course, you must also do the encryption itself. This is a tad complex just because you're indexing into various places in various buffers but ultimately boils down to a call to AEAD encrypt with the plaintext, associated data, nonce, and key previously negotiated. This is shown in Listing 9-29.

**Listing 9-29:** "tls.c" send_message with AEAD encryption support

```
...
  if ( active_suite->bulk_encrypt || active_suite->aead_encrypt )
  {
    unsigned char *encrypted_buffer = malloc( send_buffer_size +
      active_suite->IV_size +
      ( active_suite->aead_encrypt ? active_suite->hash_size : 0 ) );
    int plaintext_len;
    // TODO make this random
    memset( parameters->IV, '\0', active_suite->IV_size );
    // The first 5 bytes (the header) and the IV aren't encrypted
    memcpy( encrypted_buffer, send_buffer, 5 );
    memcpy( encrypted_buffer + 5, parameters->IV, active_suite->IV_size );

    plaintext_len = 5 + active_suite->IV_size;
    if ( active_suite->bulk_encrypt )
    {
      active_suite->bulk_encrypt( send_buffer + 5,
        send_buffer_size - 5, encrypted_buffer + plaintext_len,
        parameters->IV, parameters->key );
    }
    else if ( active_suite->aead_encrypt )
    {
      active_suite->aead_encrypt( send_buffer + 5,
        send_buffer_size - 5 - active_suite->hash_size,
        mac_header, 13, ( encrypted_buffer + active_suite->IV_size + 5 ),
        parameters->IV, parameters->key );
    }

    free( send_buffer );
    send_buffer = encrypted_buffer;
    send_buffer_size += active_suite->IV_size;
  }
...
```

As you can see, other than allocating enough space in the target encryption buffer for the MAC, this isn't that much different than ordinary block cipher encryption.

Decrypting with AEAD cipher support is about the same. First, declare a mac_header independent of the MAC buffer and precompute it. However, remember that the length declared in the MAC header was the length of the data before padding or the MAC was added. For this reason, it's impossible, in the block cipher case, to precompute the MAC header before decrypting the data; you need to know how much padding was added, and you can't do that without decrypting. All this means is that a bit of code — the MAC header computation — must be duplicated in tls_decrypt as shown in Listing 9-30 whereas it was reused in send_message.

**Listing 9-30:** "tls.c" tls_decrypt with AEAD decryption

```
int tls_decrypt( const unsigned char *header, // need this for MAC verification
                 unsigned char *encrypted_message,
                 short encrypted_length,
                 unsigned char **decrypted_message,
                 ProtectionParameters *parameters )
{
...
  unsigned char *mac_buffer;
  unsigned char mac_header[ 13 ];
  int sequence_number;
...
  if ( active_suite->bulk_decrypt )
  {
...
  }
  else if ( active_suite->aead_decrypt )
  {
    if ( active_suite->IV_size )
    {
      memcpy( parameters->IV, encrypted_message, active_suite->IV_size );
    }

    decrypted_length = encrypted_length - active_suite->hash_size;

    // Compute the MAC header, which is the AD part.  This
    // has to be done separately here, since the length computation
    // is slightly different than in the block cipher case
    memset( mac_header, 0x0, 13 );
    sequence_number = htonl( parameters->seq_num );
    memcpy( mac_header + 4, &sequence_number, sizeof( int ) );

    memcpy( mac_header + 8, header, 3 );
    length = htons( decrypted_length );
    memcpy( mac_header + 11, &length, 2 );

    if ( active_suite->aead_decrypt( encrypted_message + active_suite->IV_size,
         encrypted_length, mac_header, 13, *decrypted_message,
         parameters->IV, parameters->key ) )
    {
      // MAC verification failed
      return -3;
    }
  }
}
```

Notice that if `aead_decrypt` returns a non-zero response, indicating a MAC failure, this routine returns −3, which triggers a "bad mac" error to be returned to the caller.

This implementation of AEAD is crucially flawed, though. It does exactly what I warned you earlier to never ever do, which is to reuse a nonce. There's no provision here to ever change the IV; because each call to `aead_encrypt` starts the nonce counter back over at 0, every record is encrypted with the same set of input. You can't let the counter run over from one record to the next, either. The other end fails to decrypt the message because the receiving code expects to start over from 2 (or 1, or whatever) at decryption time. However, the 12 bytes of nonce are controlled entirely by the sender. There's nothing stopping you from making the last four bytes of the nonce itself another counter, whose values do persist from one `aead_encrypt` to the next. In fact, you could go ahead and safely use the MAC `sequence_num` for exactly this purpose.

AES-CCM has not yet been assigned a cipher suite identifier in the TLS space; when and if such an identifier is assigned, its use would be exactly like the AES-GCM example shown here.

In actual practice, AEAD ciphers don't offer much benefit over block ciphers with strong MAC functions when implemented in software. Most of the interest in these ciphers surrounds dedicated hardware. AES-GCM can be parallelized to encrypt 10Gbps, which is more than enough to encrypt an HDMI video stream in real time. Intel's newest processors include a PCLMULQDQ instruction that is explicitly stated as being an optimization to support AES-GCM. Expect AEAD ciphers to be of great interest to embedded hardware implementers.

## Working ECC Extensions into the TLS Library

Strictly speaking, ECC is not unique to TLS 1.2; AEAD is, but ECC is not. Although TLS 1.2 is the first version of TLS to mention ECC specifically, RFC 4492, which defines the ECC extensions to TLS, was written with TLS 1.1 in mind. In fact, OpenSSL version 1.0, which was released in March of 2010, supports RFC 4492 ECC extensions but does not support TLS 1.1. Make sure that you have a good grasp of the ECC concepts presented in Chapters 3 and 4 before reading this section.

Recall that ECC is mostly of interest for public-key operations; ECC operations are used to exchange a symmetric key and validate signatures, but plain-old AES usually takes over from there. Key exchange is done via *elliptic-curve Diffie-Hellman* (ECDH), and signatures are verified using *elliptic-curve DSA* (ECDSA).

ECDH is analogous to integer Diffie-Hellman. Integer Diffie-Hellman has both sides agree on a starting point — an integer — and each side raises it to an arbitrary (secret) power, exchanging the results with one another. Each side then raises the result by the secret. The distributivity of exponentiation guarantees that each side arrives at the same answer; the difficulty of the discrete logarithm problem thwarts an attacker's attempt to look at the starting point and the result to try to work backward and discover one of the secret numbers.

ECDH works the same way; both sides agree to a starting point, in this case a point on an elliptic curve whose parameters are negotiated in the clear. Each side then multiplies that point by a secret number, shares the resulting point with the other, and completes the shared multiplication with its own secret number. Because ECC point multiplication is distributive, they both arrive at the same shared point, and because ECC division is a difficult problem to which no efficient solution is known, an attacker can't work backward to uncover the secret number.

As discussed in Chapter 8, this is actually good enough for a key exchange in plain view of a passive eavesdropper. However, in order to guard against man-in-the-middle attacks, at least one side must authenticate the other, and the key exchange parameters must be digitally signed. Digital signatures imply public keys, and public keys imply certificates. Therefore, a complete ECC key exchange solution additionally involves the exchange of a certificate bearing an ECDSA public key, which is then used to sign the ECDH parameters verifiably. As long as the client trusts the signer of the certificate (or the signer of the signer, and so on), the key exchange is authentic.

ECDSA is, of course, analogous to DSA. A DSA public/private keypair is just two numbers $x$ and $y$, along with a set of parameters $p$, $g$, and $q$. The signature is computed over a hash of the message and produces two numbers $r$ and $s$ — the verifier takes $p$, $g$, $q$, and $y$ and verifies that $r$ is correct for $s$ according to $y$.

An ECDSA public key is a point, and the private key is an integer. Of course, everything is relative to a curve that is defined in terms of two numbers $a$ and $b$, and a starting point $G$. The signer computes an $r$ and $s$ pair from the private key point; the verifier checks to see if $r$ and $s$ match according to the public key point. So, to support ECC, you must implement ECDH for key exchange and ECDSA for signature verification.

Note that there's no reason at all why you must use ECDH and ECDSA together. It's perfectly permissible — and even preferable, in some cases — for a server to present an RSA certificate and use the RSA key to sign a set of parameters for ECDH key exchange. Just like using an RSA key to sign a set of DH keys, this enables you to present an RSA certificate but still achieve perfect forward secrecy.

Most of the heavy lifting surrounding the ECC implementation is done in Chapter 4. However, to actually put it in practice, there are a couple of practical considerations. The first is the elliptic curve itself. Chapter 4 glossed over the selection of the $a$ and $b$ parameters that defined the curve, the generator point $G$, the prime field $p$, and the order $n$. As it turns out, it's not easy to create a correct set, and it's even harder to do so securely. Fortunately, you don't have to. The NIST has created a set of "named curves" that you can use. There's no particular danger in letting everybody share the same set of curves as long as everyone randomly chooses the secret parameters.

The Standards for Efficient Cryptography Group (SECG) lists the named curves and their values at `http://www.secg.org/download/aid-784/sec2-v2` `.pdf`. The names the groups gives to the curves are along the lines of `secp192r1`, which indicates that it's an SEC (Standards for Efficient Cryptography) prime-field curve, 192 bits long, and that it is randomly generated. You also might see `sectnnn` curves that identify characteristic 2 finite-field curves and `secpnnnk` curves that identify *Koblitz curves*. The distinction isn't particularly important here; this book focuses on the "secp" curves.

Some of the SECP curves come from an older NIST standard, which referred to the curves as simply `primennnvx` where *nnn* was the length of the parameters and *x* was just a version. `prime192v1` is identical to `secp192r1`, and `prime256v1` is identical to `secp256r1`.

Named curve support is straightforward, if slightly tedious. A 256-bit named curve such as secp256r1 is described by a list of six 256-bit (32-byte) numeric values. To support a little bit of diversity, go ahead and implement two named curves — prime192v1/secp192r1 and prime256v1/secp256r1 — as shown in Listing 9-31.

**Listing 9-31:** "ecc.c" get_named_curve

```
unsigned char prime192v1_P[] = {
  0xFF, 0xFF, 0xFF, 0xFF, 0xFF, 0xFF, 0xFF, 0xFF,
  0xFF, 0xFF, 0xFF, 0xFF, 0xFF, 0xFF, 0xFF, 0xFF,
  0xFF, 0xFF, 0xFF, 0xFF, 0xFF, 0xFF, 0xFF, 0xFF
};
unsigned char prime192v1_A[] = {
  0xFF, 0xFF, 0xFF, 0xFF, 0xFF, 0xFF, 0xFF, 0xFF,
  0xFF, 0xFF, 0xFF, 0xFF, 0xFF, 0xFF, 0xFF, 0xFF,
  0xFF, 0xFF, 0xFF, 0xFF, 0xFF, 0xFF, 0xFF, 0xFC
};
unsigned char prime192v1_B[] = {
  0x64, 0x21, 0x05, 0x19, 0xE5, 0x9C, 0x80, 0xE7,
  0x0F, 0xA7, 0xE9, 0xAB, 0x72, 0x24, 0x30, 0x49,
  0xFE, 0xB8, 0xDE, 0xEC, 0xC1, 0x46, 0xB9, 0xB1
};
unsigned char prime192v1_Gx[] = {
  0x18, 0x8D, 0xA8, 0x0E, 0xB0, 0x30, 0x90, 0xF6,
  0x7C, 0xBF, 0x20, 0xEB, 0x43, 0xA1, 0x88, 0x00,
  0xF4, 0xFF, 0x0A, 0xFD, 0x82, 0xFF, 0x10, 0x12
};
unsigned char prime192v1_Gy[] = {
  0x07, 0x19, 0x2B, 0x95, 0xFF, 0xC8, 0xDA, 0x78,
  0x63, 0x10, 0x11, 0xED, 0x6B, 0x24, 0xCD, 0xD5,
  0x73, 0xF9, 0x77, 0xA1, 0x1E, 0x79, 0x48, 0x11
};
unsigned char prime192v1_N[] = {
  0xFF, 0xFF, 0xFF, 0xFF, 0xFF, 0xFF, 0xFF, 0xFF,
```

*(Continued)*

```
    0xFF, 0xFF, 0xFF, 0xFF, 0x99, 0xDE, 0xF8, 0x36,
    0x14, 0x6B, 0xC9, 0xB1, 0xB4, 0xD2, 0x28, 0x31
};

unsigned char prime256v1_P[] = {
    0xFF, 0xFF, 0xFF, 0xFF, 0x00, 0x00, 0x00, 0x01,
    0x00, 0x00, 0x00, 0x00, 0x00, 0x00, 0x00, 0x00,
    0x00, 0x00, 0x00, 0x00, 0xFF, 0xFF, 0xFF, 0xFF,
    0xFF, 0xFF, 0xFF, 0xFF, 0xFF, 0xFF, 0xFF, 0xFF
};
unsigned char prime256v1_A[] = {
    0xFF, 0xFF, 0xFF, 0xFF, 0x00, 0x00, 0x00, 0x01,
    0x00, 0x00, 0x00, 0x00, 0x00, 0x00, 0x00, 0x00,
    0x00, 0x00, 0x00, 0x00, 0xFF, 0xFF, 0xFF, 0xFF,
    0xFF, 0xFF, 0xFF, 0xFF, 0xFF, 0xFF, 0xFF, 0xFC
};
unsigned char prime256v1_B[] = {
    0x5A, 0xC6, 0x35, 0xD8, 0xAA, 0x3A, 0x93, 0xE7,
    0xB3, 0xEB, 0xBD, 0x55, 0x76, 0x98, 0x86, 0xBC,
    0x65, 0x1D, 0x06, 0xB0, 0xCC, 0x53, 0xB0, 0xF6,
    0x3B, 0xCE, 0x3C, 0x3E, 0x27, 0xD2, 0x60, 0x4B
};
unsigned char prime256v1_Gx[] = {
    0x6B, 0x17, 0xD1, 0xF2, 0xE1, 0x2C, 0x42, 0x47,
    0xF8, 0xBC, 0xE6, 0xE5, 0x63, 0xA4, 0x40, 0xF2,
    0x77, 0x03, 0x7D, 0x81, 0x2D, 0xEB, 0x33, 0xA0,
    0xF4, 0xA1, 0x39, 0x45, 0xD8, 0x98, 0xC2, 0x96
};
unsigned char prime256v1_Gy[] = {
    0x4F, 0xE3, 0x42, 0xE2, 0xFE, 0x1A, 0x7F, 0x9B,
    0x8E, 0xE7, 0xEB, 0x4A, 0x7C, 0x0F, 0x9E, 0x16,
    0x2B, 0xCE, 0x33, 0x57, 0x6B, 0x31, 0x5E, 0xCE,
    0xCB, 0xB6, 0x40, 0x68, 0x37, 0xBF, 0x51, 0xF5
};
unsigned char prime256v1_N[] = {
    0xFF, 0xFF, 0xFF, 0xFF, 0x00, 0x00, 0x00, 0x00,
    0xFF, 0xFF, 0xFF, 0xFF, 0xFF, 0xFF, 0xFF, 0xFF,
    0xBC, 0xE6, 0xFA, 0xAD, 0xA7, 0x17, 0x9E, 0x84,
    0xF3, 0xB9, 0xCA, 0xC2, 0xFC, 0x63, 0x25, 0x51
};

int get_named_curve( const char *curve_name, elliptic_curve *target )
{
    if ( !strcmp( "prime192v1", curve_name ) ||
         !strcmp( "secp192r1", curve_name ) )
    {
        load_huge( &target->p, prime192v1_P, sizeof( prime192v1_P ) );
        load_huge( &target->a, prime192v1_A, sizeof( prime192v1_A ) );
        load_huge( &target->b, prime192v1_B, sizeof( prime192v1_B ) );
```

```
    load_huge( &target->G.x, prime192v1_Gx,
      sizeof( prime192v1_Gx ) );
    load_huge( &target->G.y, prime192v1_Gy,
      sizeof( prime192v1_Gy ) );
    load_huge( &target->n, prime192v1_N, sizeof( prime192v1_N ) );

    return 0;
  }
  else if ( !strcmp( "prime256v1", curve_name ) ||
            !strcmp( "secp256r1", curve_name ) )
  {
    load_huge( &target->p, prime256v1_P, sizeof( prime256v1_P ) );
    load_huge( &target->a, prime256v1_A, sizeof( prime256v1_A ) );
    load_huge( &target->b, prime256v1_B, sizeof( prime256v1_B ) );
    load_huge( &target->G.x, prime256v1_Gx,
      sizeof( prime256v1_Gx ) );
    load_huge( &target->G.y, prime256v1_Gy,
      sizeof( prime256v1_Gy ) );
    load_huge( &target->n, prime256v1_N, sizeof( prime256v1_N ) );

    return 0;
  }


  // Unsupported named curve

  return 1;
}
```

Of course, there's no rule that you must use a named curve. Everywhere that TLS calls for an elliptic curve, a provision is made to enable either side to declare a curve explicitly by providing the $p$, $a$, $b$, $G$, and $n$ values. However, named curves are far more common, so explicit curves aren't examined here.

## ECDSA Certificate Parsing

The first step in adding ECC support is parsing an ECDSA certificate — that is, an X.509 certificate whose public key info includes an ECDSA public key and a description of a curve to which the public key (a point on the curve) is relative. Recall from Chapter 5 that a certificate consists of eight elements: the version, the serial number, the signature algorithm, the issuer, the validity period, the subject, the subject's public key, and an optional set of extensions. Of these, only two are dependent on the public key algorithm: the signature algorithm and the public key itself.

First, add ECDSA as a valid algorithm identifier as shown in Listing 9-32 and then modify `parse_algorithm_identifier` from Listing 5-16 to accept SHA-256 with ECDSA as shown in Listing 9-33.

**Listing 9-32:** "x509.h" ecdsa algorithm identifier

```
typedef enum
{
  md5WithRSAEncryption,
  shaWithRSAEncryption,
  shaWithDSA,
  sha256WithECDSA
}
signatureAlgorithmIdentifier;
```

**Listing 9-33:** "x509.c" parse_algorithm_identifier with ECDSA support

```
static const unsigned char OID_md5WithRSA[] =
    { 0x2A, 0x86, 0x48, 0x86, 0xF7, 0x0D, 0x01, 0x01, 0x04 };
static const unsigned char OID_sha1WithRSA[] =
    { 0x2A, 0x86, 0x48, 0x86, 0xF7, 0x0D, 0x01, 0x01, 0x05 };
static const unsigned char OID_sha1WithDSA[] =
    { 0x2A, 0x86, 0x48, 0xCE, 0x38, 0x04, 0x03 };
static const unsigned char OID_sha256WithECDSA[] =
    { 0x2A, 0x86, 0x48, 0xCE, 0x3D, 0x04, 0x03, 0x02 };

static int parse_algorithm_identifier( signatureAlgorithmIdentifier *target,
                                       struct asn1struct *source )
{
  struct asn1struct *oid = ( struct asn1struct * ) source->children;
...
    else if ( !memcmp( oid->data, OID_sha256WithECDSA, oid->length ) )
    {
      *target = sha256WithECDSA;
    }
```

As you can see, there's nothing particularly complex or surprising here; you just recognize a new OID.

Although parsing the public key is not necessarily complex, it's odd in the context of ASN.1. An RSA public key is a bit-string representation of two numbers $n$ and $e$, both given in an ASN.1 structure, and both properly ASN.1 encoded with a tag and a length. A DSA public key is similarly encoded as a bit string representation of ASN.1 encoded data. An ECDSA key, however, is not. Although the public key is an ASN.1 bit string, it's not an ASN.1 encoded structure, but a different, incompatible ASNI X9.62 encoded structure. This was probably done for compatibility with existing software, or perhaps it was done in the IETF's ongoing quest to ensure that every specification ever written for any purpose is somehow relevant to TLS.

Fortunately, the X9.62 structure — at least in the context of an ECDSA public key — isn't too hard to parse. The first byte is an identifier whose value is either 3, meaning *compressed*, or 4, meaning *uncompressed*. An uncompressed ECC point lists the $x$ and $y$ values back-to-back with no delimiter or length declaration.

The parser must split the data in half and recognize that the first half is $x$ and the last half is $y$.

What about the compressed format? Well, if you think about it, it's somewhat redundant to provide the $y$ value. After all, an elliptic curve is defined by an algebraic formula that describes $y$ in terms of $x$. Technically speaking, all you really need to know is the $x$ value, along with the curve parameters themselves, and you can compute the $y$ value. The only wrinkle here is that there are two possible $y$ values for a given $x$ — one positive and one negative — because the formula is $y^2 = x^3 + ax + b$. A compressed point, then, is just the $x$ value with a single extra bit indicating whether the $y$ value is the positive or the negative one; the implementation must multiply out the elliptic curve to recover $y$. This book only deals with uncompressed points.

Modify the algorithm identifier as shown in Listing 9-34 to recognize the new public key algorithm type, and modify `parse_public_key_info` from Listing 5-19 as shown in Listing 9-35 to properly parse ECDSA public keys.

**Listing 9-34:** "x509.h" ECDSA algorithm identifier

```
typedef enum
{
  rsa,
  dsa,
  dh,
  ecdsa
}
algorithmIdentifier;

typedef struct
{
  algorithmIdentifier algorithm;
...

  elliptic_curve ecdsa_curve;
  point ecdsa_public_key;
}
public_key_info;
```

**Listing 9-35:** "x509.c" parse_public_key_info with ECDSA support

```
static const unsigned char OID_RSA[] =
  { 0x2A, 0x86, 0x48, 0x86, 0xF7, 0x0D, 0x01, 0x01, 0x01 };
static const unsigned char OID_DSA[] =
  { 0x2A, 0x86, 0x48, 0xCE, 0x38, 0x04, 0x01 };
static const unsigned char OID_DH[] =
  { 0x2A, 0x86, 0x48, 0xCE, 0x3E, 0x02, 0x01 };
static const unsigned char OID_ECDSA[] =
  { 0x2A, 0x86, 0x48, 0xCE, 0x3D, 0x02, 0x01 };
```

*(Continued)*

```
// A.K.A. secp192R1, AKA NIST P-192
static const unsigned char OID_PRIME192V1[] =
    { 0x2A, 0x86, 0x48, 0xCE, 0x3D, 0x03, 0x01, 0x01 };
static int parse_public_key_info( public_key_info *target,
                                    struct asn1struct *source )
{
...
  public_key = source->children->next;
  if ( !memcmp( oid->data, &OID_ECDSA, sizeof( OID_ECDSA ) ) )
  {
    // TODO this only supports named curves (actually, only one specific
    // curve).
    struct asn1struct *curve = oid->next;

    target->algorithm = ecdsa;

    if ( !memcmp( curve->data, &OID_PRIME192V1, sizeof( OID_PRIME192V1 ) ) )
    {
      // TODO generate a mapping of OIDs to curve names
      if ( get_named_curve( "prime192v1", &target->ecdsa_curve ) )
      {
        return 1;
      }
    }
    else
    {
      fprintf( stderr,
        "Error, unsupported named curve in ECDSA certificate\n" );
      return 1;
    }
    load_huge( &target->ecdsa_public_key.x, public_key->data + 2,
      ( public_key->length - 2 ) / 2 );
    load_huge( &target->ecdsa_public_key.y,
      ( public_key->data + 2 ) + ( ( public_key->length - 2 ) / 2 ),
      ( public_key->length - 2 ) / 2 );
    return 0;
  }
...
```

As you can see, the certificate doesn't refer to curve names by their actual names; it uses another alias in OID form. The named curve OID is inserted after the public key OID — if the OID is recognized, it's converted into a string curve name and the curve is populated into the `ecdsa_curve` parameter of the supplied `public_key_info` instance.

Now, if you go back and look at Listing 5-19 that parses the RSA public key info or Listing 5-32 that parses the DSA public key info, you see that the next step in both cases is to ASN.1 parse the bit string that contains the public key info. ECDSA keys are not ASN.1 encoded. They're instead encoded as shown in Figure 9-6.

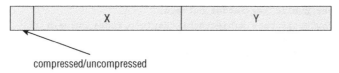

compressed/uncompressed

**Figure 9-6:** X9.62 ECC point encoding

The end of Listing 9-35 illustrates this parsing. Because every byte-aligned ASN.1 bit string must begin with a leading 0 byte as discussed in Chapter 5, the parsing must skip over this 0 byte and the "compressed/uncompressed" declaration. The remainder is split down the middle and the first half becomes the *x* point and the second half the *y* point.

Recall that the function `parse_x509_chain`, introduced in Listing 6-29, is responsible for parsing a certificate and copying its public key info into that of the `TLSParameters` structure. This must be modified as shown in Listing 9-36 to recognize the case of ECDSA.

**Listing 9-36:** "x509.c" parse_x509_chain with ECDSA support

```
char *parse_x509_chain( unsigned char *buffer,
                        int pdu_length,
                        public_key_info *server_public_key )
{
…
    switch ( server_public_key->algorithm )
    {
…
      case ecdsa:
        set_huge( &server_public_key->ecdsa_curve.a, 0 );
        set_huge( &server_public_key->ecdsa_curve.b, 0 );
        set_huge( &server_public_key->ecdsa_curve.G.x, 0 );
        set_huge( &server_public_key->ecdsa_curve.G.y, 0 );
        set_huge( &server_public_key->ecdsa_curve.p, 0 );
        set_huge( &server_public_key->ecdsa_curve.n, 0 );
        set_huge( &server_public_key->ecdsa_public_key.x, 0 );
        set_huge( &server_public_key->ecdsa_public_key.y, 0 );

        copy_huge( &server_public_key->ecdsa_curve.a,
          &certificate.tbsCertificate.subjectPublicKeyInfo.ecdsa_curve.a );
        copy_huge( &server_public_key->ecdsa_curve.b,
          &certificate.tbsCertificate.subjectPublicKeyInfo.ecdsa_curve.b );
        copy_huge( &server_public_key->ecdsa_curve.G.x,
          &certificate.tbsCertificate.subjectPublicKeyInfo.ecdsa_curve.G.x );
        copy_huge( &server_public_key->ecdsa_curve.G.y,
          &certificate.tbsCertificate.subjectPublicKeyInfo.ecdsa_curve.G.y );
        copy_huge( &server_public_key->ecdsa_curve.p,
          &certificate.tbsCertificate.subjectPublicKeyInfo.ecdsa_curve.p );
```

*(Continued)*

```
        copy_huge( &server_public_key->ecdsa_curve.n,
          &certificate.tbsCertificate.subjectPublicKeyInfo.ecdsa_curve.n );
        copy_huge( &server_public_key->ecdsa_public_key.x,
          &certificate.tbsCertificate.subjectPublicKeyInfo.ecdsa_public_key.x );
        copy_huge( &server_public_key->ecdsa_public_key.y,
          &certificate.tbsCertificate.subjectPublicKeyInfo.ecdsa_public_key.y );
        break;
...
```

What about the ECDSA signature itself? Actually, there's no special handling there; an ECDSA signature is two numbers, *r* and *s*, just like a DSA signature. There's no need for a special handler. Modify `parse_x509_certificate` to recognize this case as shown in Listing 9-37.

**Listing 9-37:** "x509.c" parse_x509_certificate with ECDSA signatures

```
int parse_x509_certificate( const unsigned char *buffer,
                            const unsigned int certificate_length,
                            signed_x509_certificate *parsed_certificate )
{
...
  switch ( parsed_certificate->algorithm )
  {
    case md5WithRSAEncryption:
    case shaWithRSAEncryption:
      if ( parse_rsa_signature_value( parsed_certificate, signatureValue ) )
      {
        return 42;
      }
      break;
    case shaWithDSA:
    case sha256WithECDSA:
      if ( parse_dsa_signature_value( parsed_certificate, signatureValue ) )
      {
        return 42;
      }
      break;
...
  switch ( parsed_certificate->algorithm )
  {
...
    case sha256WithECDSA:
      new_sha256_digest( &digest );
      break;
```

Remember that there's no particular reason that a certificate containing an ECDSA public key must be signed using ECDSA. In fact, it's likely that a commercially signed certificate is going to be signed using RSA because that's all that commercial CAs currently support.

You're unlikely to be able to find a server that presents an ECDSA certificate. However, as of version 1.0.0, OpenSSL enables you to create a self-signed ECDSA, certificate. First, generate a set of parameters; in other words, select a named curve:

```
[jdavies@localhost ssl]$ openssl ecparam -name prime192v1 -out ecprime192v1.pem
```

As you can see from the ASN.1 output, there's nothing in there except the OID of the named curve:

```
[jdavies@localhost ssl]$ ./asn1 -pem ecprime192v1.pem
0000: OBJECT IDENTIFIER (6:8) 2a 86 48 ce 3d 03 01 01
```

However, you can use this as input to the `req` command to generate a new ECDSA certificate:

```
[jdavies@localhost ssl]$ openssl req -x509 -newkey ec:ecprime192v1.pem \
  -keyout ecdsa_key.pem -out ecdsa_cert.pem -sha256
```

## ECDHE Support in TLS

To actually make use of this new certificate, you should extend the TLS implementation to support the ECDHE_ECDSA cipher suites. Not every cipher algorithm is supported with ECDHE_ECDSA key exchange (nor ECDH_RSA). In fact, the only algorithms standardized by RFC 4492 are RC4, 3DES, AES-128, and AES-256. These suites are given the identifiers `0xC007–0xC00A`. Because these are large numbers, you should instantiate them in the `init_tls` function just like the AEAD ciphers from Listing 9-27. The initialization of `TLS_ECDHE_ECDSA_WITH_AES_128_CBC_SHA` is shown in Listing 9-38.

**Listing 9-38:** "tls.c" init_tls with ECDHE_ECDSA support

```
void init_tls()
{
...
  suites[ TLS_ECDHE_ECDSA_WITH_AES_128_CBC_SHA ].id =
    TLS_ECDHE_ECDSA_WITH_AES_128_CBC_SHA;
  suites[ TLS_ECDHE_ECDSA_WITH_AES_128_CBC_SHA ].block_size = 16;
  suites[ TLS_ECDHE_ECDSA_WITH_AES_128_CBC_SHA ].IV_size = 16;
  suites[ TLS_ECDHE_ECDSA_WITH_AES_128_CBC_SHA ].key_size = 16;
  suites[ TLS_ECDHE_ECDSA_WITH_AES_128_CBC_SHA ].hash_size = SHA1_BYTE_SIZE;
  suites[ TLS_ECDHE_ECDSA_WITH_AES_128_CBC_SHA ].bulk_encrypt = aes_128_encrypt;
  suites[ TLS_ECDHE_ECDSA_WITH_AES_128_CBC_SHA ].bulk_decrypt = aes_128_decrypt;
  suites[ TLS_ECDHE_ECDSA_WITH_AES_128_CBC_SHA ].new_digest = new_sha1_digest;
  suites[ TLS_ECDHE_ECDSA_WITH_AES_128_CBC_SHA ].aead_encrypt = NULL;
  suites[ TLS_ECDHE_ECDSA_WITH_AES_128_CBC_SHA ].aead_decrypt = NULL;
}
```

You should have no problem filling in the remaining cipher suites; they all use SHA-1 MACs, so the only change is the `bulk_encrypt` and `bulk_decrypt` function pointers. There are no currently defined cipher suites that use both AEAD encryption and ECC key exchange.

If you look at the typical SSL handshake shown in Figure 6-1, you can see that the key exchange portion affects three messages: the certificate, which was addressed earlier, the client key exchange, and, optionally, the server key exchange. (It also affects the *client certificate* and *client certificate verify*, if client authentication is being used). Because the cipher suites being examined here are ECDHE cipher suites, the server is sending a key exchange message.

To complete its side of the ECDHE key exchange, the server must select a curve, choose a random number $b$, multiply the curve's generator point by $b$, and send the resulting point on to the client. It must also, of course, hang on to $b$ so that it can multiply the client's response point by this amount. Therefore, the server key exchange must consist of a curve — either explicitly or by name — and a point. Note that the selected curve does *not* have to be the same as the curve in the certificate. As always, the whole server key exchange is signed according to the previously exchanged certificate, unless an anonymous cipher suite is being used.

To support ECDH, you need a place to put the ephemeral key parameters:

1. Modify the TLSParameters, as shown in Listing 9-39.

**Listing 9-39:** "tls.h" TLSParameters with ECDH support

```
typedef struct
{
...
    dh_key                  server_dh_key;

    elliptic_curve          server_ecdh_params;
    point                   server_ecdh_key;

    int                     got_client_hello;
...
```

2. Modify the `parse_server_key_exchange` function from Listing 8-19 to read and populate these new parameters as shown in Listing 9-40.

**Listing 9-40:** "tls.c" parse_server_key_exchange with ECDH support

```
typedef enum
{
  secp192r1 = 19,
  secp256r1 = 23
}
named_curve;
typedef enum
{
```

```
  explicit_prime = 1,
  explicit_char2 = 2,
  named = 3
}
ec_curve_type;

typedef enum
{
  compressed = 3,
  uncompressed = 4
}
ec_point_type;

static char *parse_server_key_exchange( unsigned char *read_pos,
                                        TLSParameters *parameters )
{
  short length;
  int i;
  unsigned char *dh_params = read_pos;
  HashAlgorithm hash_alg;
  SignatureAlgorithm sig_alg;

  hash_alg = read_pos[ 0 ];
  sig_alg = read_pos[ 1 ];
  read_pos += 2;

  switch ( parameters->pending_send_parameters.suite )
  {
    case TLS_ECDHE_ECDSA_WITH_AES_128_CBC_SHA:
      {
        unsigned char curve_type;
        unsigned char curve;
        unsigned char public_key_length;
        unsigned char point_type;
        read_pos = read_buffer( ( void * ) &curve_type, read_pos, 1 );

        switch ( curve_type )
        {
          case named:
            // named curve takes up two bytes, but only one is populated
            read_pos += 1;
            read_pos = read_buffer( ( void * ) &curve, read_pos, 1 );
            switch ( curve )
            {
              case secp256r1:
                get_named_curve( "prime256v1",
                  &parameters->server_ecdh_params );
                break;
              default:
                fprintf( stderr, "error, unsupported named curve %d\n", curve );
```

*(Continued)*

```
                        return NULL;
            }
            break;
        default:
            fprintf( stderr, "Error, unsupported curve type %d.\n",
              curve_type );
            return NULL;
        }
        // Followed by a length-delimited (opaque) public key.
        read_pos = read_buffer( ( void * ) &public_key_length, read_pos, 1 );
        read_pos = read_buffer( ( void * ) &point_type, read_pos, 1 );
        if ( point_type == uncompressed )
        {
          load_huge( &parameters->server_ecdh_key.x, read_pos,
            ( public_key_length - 1 ) / 2 );
          load_huge( &parameters->server_ecdh_key.y,
            ( read_pos + ( ( public_key_length - 1 ) / 2 ) ),
            ( ( public_key_length - 1 ) / 2 ) );
          read_pos += ( public_key_length - 1 );

          // Read and verify the signature
          memcpy( &length, read_pos, 2 );
          length = ntohs( length );
          read_pos += 2;
          if ( !verify_signature( dh_params, ( read_pos - 2 - dh_params ),
                read_pos, length, parameters ) )
          {
            return NULL;
          }
          read_pos += length;
        }
        else
        {
          printf( "point type %d\n", point_type );
          fprintf( stderr, "Error, compressed ECDH public keys not supported.\n" );
          return NULL;
        }
      break;
    default:
      // XXX assume DHE if not ECDHE
      for ( i = 0; i < 4; i++ )
      {
```

Most of the logic here surrounds erroring out if any of the unsupported options are presented. This code handles the simplest case, when the server uses a named curve and presents the public key in uncompressed format. The first part of this is pretty similar to the public key parsing in Listing 9-35, which is unsurprising because both functions are parsing an ECC public key.

Although they are both for different algorithms — one for ECDSA, and the other for ECDH — the key itself is the same in both cases; a curve followed by a point on that curve. Both functions only accept named curves, although an option is defined in the specification to accept explicit curves. Of course, the public key parsing routine in the certificate code is looking for an OID. TLS has a simpler means of naming curves — each one is assigned a unique two-byte identifier. At present, only 25 are defined, but expect more to be defined over time.

The curve itself, whether presented by name or explicitly, is followed by the point that identifies the public key. This is encoded in the exact same ANSI X9.62 format that the certificate is coded in — one byte compressed/uncompressed marker, with the remaining bytes split in half between $x$ and $y$.

Finally, the whole parameter list — the curve specification and the public key point — are signed using the certificate's private key, and the signature follows the server key exchange parameters. This whole thing is passed into verify_signature. In the case of ECDSA, just like DSA, the signature is two values $r$ and $s$, encoded in ASN.1 DER format. Because an ECDSA signature looks just like a DSA signature, you can reuse a lot of the code from Listing 8-26 to verify an ECDSA signature, as shown in Listing 9-41.

**Listing 9-41:** "tls.c" verify_signature with ECDSA support

```
int verify_signature( unsigned char *message,
                      int message_len,
                      unsigned char *signature,
                      int signature_len,
                      TLSParameters *parameters )
{
…
  else if ( ( parameters->server_public_key.algorithm == dsa ) ||
            ( parameters->server_public_key.algorithm == ecdsa ) )
  {
    int verified;
…
    asn1free( &decoded_signature );

    if ( parameters->server_public_key.algorithm == dsa )
    {
      verified = dsa_verify( &parameters->server_public_key.dsa_parameters,
                      &parameters->server_public_key.dsa_public_key,
                      ( unsigned char * ) sha_digest.hash,
                      SHA1_BYTE_SIZE,
                      &received_signature );
    }
    else
    {
      digest_ctx sha256_digest;
```

*(Continued)*

```
        new_sha256_digest( &sha256_digest );
        update_digest( &sha256_digest, parameters->client_random, RANDOM_LENGTH );
        update_digest( &sha256_digest, parameters->server_random, RANDOM_LENGTH );
        update_digest( &sha256_digest, message, message_len );
        finalize_digest( &sha256_digest );

        verified = ecdsa_verify( &parameters->server_public_key.ecdsa_curve,
                        &parameters->server_public_key.ecdsa_public_key,
                        sha256_digest.hash,
                        SHA256_BYTE_SIZE,
                        &received_signature );
    }

    if ( !verified )
    {
      free_huge( &received_signature.r );
      free_huge( &received_signature.s );
      return 0;
    }
```

**NOTE**   The ECDSA verification routine itself was shown in Listing 4-40.

To support ECDHE on the client side, in the most common case of server-only authentication, the only thing left is to actually perform the key exchange. Modify send_client_key_exchange from Listing 6-33 to recognize ECDHE as an option, as shown in Listing 9-42.

**Listing 9-42:** "tls.c" send_client_key_exchange with ECDHE support

```
static int send_client_key_exchange( int connection, TLSParameters *parameters )
{
…
  switch ( parameters->pending_send_parameters.suite ) {
    case TLS_NULL_WITH_NULL_NULL:
…
    case TLS_ECDHE_ECDSA_WITH_AES_128_CBC_SHA:
      premaster_secret_len = parameters->server_ecdh_params.p.size;
      premaster_secret = malloc( premaster_secret_len );
      key_exchange_message_len = ecdh_key_exchange(
        &parameters->server_ecdh_key, &parameters->server_ecdh_params,
        premaster_secret, &key_exchange_message );
      break;
    default:
      break;
  }
```

The rest of send_client_key_exchange doesn't change in the case of ECDH; the key exchange function itself populates the handshake message and the premaster secret. All that's left is to implement the ECDH key exchange itself using the curve and the point specified by the server in the server key exchange, which is shown in Listing 9-43.

**Listing 9-43:** "tls.c" ecdh_key_exchange

```
int ecdh_key_exchange( point *server_ecdh_key,
                       elliptic_curve *curve,
                       unsigned char *premaster_secret,
                       unsigned char **key_exchange_message )
{
  ecc_key A;
  point K;

  set_huge( &A.d, 4 );  // TODO this should be random, and larger
  set_huge( &A.Q.x, 0 );
  set_huge( &A.Q.y, 0 );
  copy_huge( &A.Q.x, &curve->G.x );
  copy_huge( &A.Q.y, &curve->G.y );
  multiply_point( &A.Q, &A.d, &curve->a, &curve->p );

  // Response is now A.Q; put that into "key_exchange_message" as an
  // explicit point
  // XXX x & y must both be the same size for the encoding to work.
  *key_exchange_message = ( unsigned char * ) malloc( A.Q.x.size +
    A.Q.y.size + 2 );
  (*key_exchange_message)[ 0 ] = A.Q.x.size + A.Q.y.size + 1;
  (*key_exchange_message)[ 1 ] = 0x04;
  memcpy( (*key_exchange_message) + 2, A.Q.x.rep, A.Q.x.size );
  memcpy( (*key_exchange_message) + 2 + A.Q.x.size, A.Q.y.rep, A.Q.y.size );

  // Now compute the premaster secret from the server's point
  set_huge( &K.x, 0 );
  set_huge( &K.y, 0 );
  copy_huge( &K.x, &server_ecdh_key->x );
  copy_huge( &K.y, &server_ecdh_key->y );
  multiply_point( &K, &A.d, &curve->a, &curve->p );

  // The premaster secret is in K.x
  memcpy( premaster_secret, K.x.rep, curve->p.size );

  free_huge( &K.x );
  free_huge( &K.y );
  free_huge( &A.d );
  free_huge( &A.Q.x );
  free_huge( &A.Q.y );

  return A.Q.x.size + A.Q.y.size + 3;
}
```

The client responsibility in an ECDH key exchange — just as in an integer DH key exchange — is lighter than the server's; the client must just respond with a point. The implementation presented here is hardcoded to return the generator point * 4. A proper, secure implementation would naturally choose much larger numbers, and choose them randomly. The resulting point is encoded in ANSI X9.62 format; this is the handshake message itself. This same "secret" value 4 is then multiplied by the server's point; this is the shared, premaster secret. You may want to compare this to dh_key_exchange in Listing 6-43. In effect, the mod_pow calls are replaced by point multiplication calls, and the shared secret is retrieved from the x-coordinate of the shared point. Otherwise, these routines are very similar.

## ECC Client Hello Extensions

As you might imagine, it would be a shame if the client and the server went to all the trouble to try to perform an ECC key exchange only to find out that the server wanted to use a named curve that the client didn't support. It would be even worse to find out that the client and the server *do* share a named curve, but the server keeps picking the wrong one because it doesn't know which one the client supports.

To address this, RFC 4492 defines a new client hello extension, extension 10, which enables the client to list the named curves it supports. It uses the same two-byte characters for the curves that the server key exchange uses. The special values 0xFF01 and 0xFF02 denote explicit prime curves and explicit characteristic 2 curves, respectively. If either of these two values appears in the supported curves extension, this indicates that the client can accept explicit curves. The specification is silent on what the server should do if the client presents an elliptic-curve cipher suite, but does not indicate which named curves it supports. OpenSSL currently just defaults to secp256r1 in this case.

In addition, RFC 4492 defines a second client hello extension, extension 11, that enables the client to indicate what point formats it supports — compressed, uncompressed, or both. It would be strange for a client to support compressed but not uncompressed, and the specification states that all implementations must support uncompressed points, so it's somewhat redundant for the client to inform the server that it can support uncompressed points, but you can do so if you like.

## The Current State of TLS 1.2

One thing you may have noticed about this chapter was the conspicuous lack of examples. TLS 1.2 is still very new and hasn't found its way into very many TLS implementations yet. OpenSSL doesn't yet support it, although all the pieces are in place. GnuTLS does support TLS 1.2, but it's not enabled by default. To run a TLS 1.2-aware server:

```
[jdavies@localhost ssl]$ gnutls-serv -p 8443 --x509fmtder --x509certfile cert.der \
    --x509keyfile key.der --protocols TLS1.2
```

GnuTLS doesn't have an option to supply a password-protected key file, so you have to remove password protection from the key file if you've enabled it as is shown in Chapter 7. At the time of this writing, version 2.8.6 is also not quite RFC 5246 compliant, either; it's compliant to an earlier, draft specification. The most glaring difference is that it uses SHA-1 instead of SHA-256 to compute the PRF and the finalize data. This may be corrected by the time you read this, so you may want to double-check and see if this has been addressed yet. Even with TLS 1.2 support, it doesn't yet support any AEAD or ECC cipher suites.

OpenSSL 1.0.0 does support ECC, but only in the context of TLS 1.0. It doesn't yet even support TLS 1.1. To run an ECDHE-ECDSA-capable OpenSSL server, you must have an ECDSA certificate as discussed previously, and then run:

```
[jdavies@localhost openssl-1.0.0]$ apps/openssl s_server -tls1 -cipher \
    ECDHE-ECDSA-AES128-SHA -cert ecdsacert.pem -key ecdsakey.pem -accept 8443
```

If you want to test the code in the previous section against this server, though, you need to first ensure that everything else is TLS 1.0 compliant.

# CHAPTER 10

# Other Applications of SSL

So far, this book has been almost myopically focused on the application of TLS to HTTP. Although HTTP was the primary motivation for the development of SSL in the first place, and continues to be the principal driver behind its evolution, HTTP is not the only protocol that relies on SSL/TLS to provide privacy and authentication extensions. This chapter examines a few of these other applications, and looks at some of the ways that the HTTP-focused design decisions in TLS complicate its adaptation to other protocols.

## Adding the NTTPS Extension to the NTTP Algorithm

*Network News Transfer Protocol* (*NNTP*) is one of the oldest Internet protocols still in use. "In use" might be a charitable term — although the paramedics haven't pronounced NNTP dead, they've stopped resuscitating it and are just waiting for the heart monitor to stop beeping. I must admit I have a warm place in my heart for NNTP and the Usenet community that relied on it — before there was the National Center for Supercomputing Application's *Mosaic* or Mosaic's successor, *Netscape Communicator*, there was Usenet. I remember spending many hours in college, when I should have been working on programming assignments, in front of *tin*: the command-line, curses-based Unix Usenet reader. Although the newsgroups have since devolved into an unusable morass of spam, the early character-based Usenet is an example of what the Internet could be in its finest form. I blame high-speed connections and graphics-capable displays for the devolution of the once pure and beautiful Internet — now, you kids get off my lawn.

Although NNTP is an older protocol whose use is not nearly as widespread as it once was, it's useful as an example of an alternate means of initiating an SSL connection. HTTPS requires that you completely set up the SSL connection before a single byte of HTTP traffic can be sent. For this to be possible, the client must notify the server in some way of its intent to start with an SSL connection. HTTPS does this by assigning two separate ports to HTTP traffic. If the client wants a plaintext connection, it connects to port 80; if it wants SSL, it connects to port 443.

This is problematic in two ways:

▪ **The use of multiple ports:** If every protocol on the Internet needs two ports, the number of available ports is cut in half. TCP only allocates two bytes for the port number, which means that there are only 65,535 ports available to begin with.

▪ **Switching from plaintext to encrypted communication requires a connection change:** There's no provision in the TCP protocol for a connection to start using a new port. This isn't as bad with HTTP as with other protocols because HTTP is fundamentally stateless to begin with, but even HTTP has problems as a result. You've undoubtedly loaded a web page and have been presented with a security warning such as, "This page contains both secure and nonsecure items. Do you want to display the nonsecure items?" This happens when a web page is downloaded via HTTPS but some of the links within it are listed as using HTTP.

NNTP, defined in 1986 by RFC 977, was a stateful protocol. This was the only kind of protocol back in those days. The client software established a connection to the server on port 119 and sent text commands back and forth over this long-running socket connection. The socket itself would be held open until the session was complete. You could — and people did — interact with an NNTP server directly via telnet because the commands themselves were human-readable text.

At first, Usenet servers were provided by universities free of charge. Over time, though, Usenet traffic outgrew what could reasonably be provided for free, so commercial Usenet servers began to spring up, and they needed to support authentication to ensure that only paid-up users could send and receive. The original specification didn't provide for any means of client authentication, so RFC 2980 standardized an AUTHINFO extension to NNTP that allowed a user to provide a user name and password before issuing any commands.

Because you're reading a book about SSL/TLS, you can probably immediately spot the problem with this approach — NNTP is sent in the clear, with no provision for man-in-the-middle attacks or passive eavesdroppers. The simplest solution is to do what HTTP did and establish a new port for SSL-enabled connections. In fact, port 563 was assigned by the *Internet Assigned Numbers Authority* (IANA) for this purpose. A better approach, though, especially given that NNTP is a stateful protocol to begin with, is to establish a plaintext connection over port 119 and define a new command to switch to SSL. When the server receives this command, assuming the server recognizes, supports, and accepts it, the client should begin a TLS handshake as shown in Chapter 6.

NNTP uses the STARTTLS command for this purpose. When the client sends a STARTTLS command, the server must respond with response code 382 indicating that it supports TLS — if it doesn't, the client must either authenticate in the clear or terminate the connection. The server could even demand client-side authentication in this case, supplementing the password-based authentication described in RFC 2980. After the TLS handshake is complete, the NTTP session continues as it would have in the plaintext case, on the same socket that was originally established without TLS.

Although the same physical connection is used pre- and post-TLS negotiation, STARTTLS effectively resets all settings to what they were when the socket itself was first established. This is done because nothing that occurred prior to a successful TLS handshake can be trusted in a security-conscious setting; anything could have been modified by an active attacker, even if the client established the connection and immediately tried to submit a STARTTLS to secure it.

# Implementing "Multi-hop" SMTP over TLS and Protecting Email Content with S/MIME

After the World Wide Web itself, email is about as fundamental and ubiquitous as Internet usage gets. Email has been around even longer than NNTP, and much longer than SSL or TLS, so it suffers from the same eavesdropping and man-in-the-middle vulnerabilities as NNTP, but the vulnerabilities are compounded by the complexity of email itself.

## Understanding the Email Model

In the email model, individual users have mail boxes identified by email addresses such as `joshua.davies@ImplementingSSL.com`. These mail boxes are hosted by an email provider, typically at a different site than the actual user. A home email address, for example, is probably hosted by the user's Internet Service Provider. The email user connects periodically to check for new messages, but if a message is sent to a recognized email address, the hosting provider must store the message until the user connects to download it.

Additionally, the sender of the email doesn't generally establish a direct connection with the hosting provider of the recipient, but rather to his own hosting provider, who is responsible for correctly routing the email based on the email address domain. At a bare minimum, then, an email message probably passes through at least three distinct TCP connections, each unrelated to the other, and this can essentially occur at random times. The connection between the email's sender and his own hosting provider is governed by the SMTP protocol, and the connection between the receiver and his hosting provider is often governed by the POP protocol, although there are other protocols that can be used.

## The SSL/TLS Design and Email

The whole point of the SSL/TLS design is to protect against the dangers of message exposure when messages are subjected to multiple hops. However, SSL can't do that unless it has end-to-end control over a socket that starts and ends the logical transaction. The sender must authenticate that the receiver is the actual receiver and not an impostor before transmitting any sensitive information. This is impossible in the context of email because the receiver — the holder of the email address — is probably not online when the email is sent and cannot provide credentials in the form of a certificate. This means that the client must implicitly trust the SMTP server not to expose any sensitive details about the email message in question, as well as negotiate a secure connection with the receiver's hosting provider.

Does this mean that TLS is useless in the context of email? Not exactly, but it doesn't provide the sort of end-to-end confidentiality and integrity that you probably want from a secure email relay service. However, TLS is very useful for an SMTP server because it strongly authenticates the sender and ensures that the sender is who it says it is, and it authorizes sending email through the SMTP service itself. Of course, it's also useful for the client to establish that the SMTP server is not an impostor either, and to guard against eavesdroppers on the local network.

To this end, RFC 3207 describes the STARTTLS extension for SMTP for senders of email and RFC 2595 describes the same extension for POP for the receiver of the email. Still, it would be nice to protect the message itself. This is less of a concern in the context of NNTP, where messages are always public, than in email, where messages are almost always private.

There have been a number of attempts to design email security systems that address end-to-end privacy; PEM and PGP both enjoyed some measure of success at various times as de facto standards. S/MIME, described by RFC 5751, however, is the official IETF email security mechanism. S/MIME is not actually an application of TLS because TLS was designed under the assumption that both parties are online and capable of responding to each other's messages synchronously throughout the whole exchange (such as is the case with HTTP). However, S/MIME is closely related and has all the same pieces.

An email message, at the protocol level, looks quite a bit like an HTTP message. It starts with a set of name-value pair headers, delimited by a single CRLF pair, after which the message itself starts. In fact, email and HTTP share a lot of the same name-value pair headers — email messages can have `Content-Type`, `Content-Transfer-Encoding`, and so on. A simple email message may look like this:

```
Received:  from smtp.receiver.com ([192.168.1.1]) by smtp.sender.com
  with Microsoft SMTPSVC(6.0.3790.3959); Fri, 13 Aug 2010 04:58:25 -0500
Subject: I'm sending an email, do you like it?
Date: Fri, 13 Aug 2010 04:58:31 -0500
Message-ID: <12345@smtp.receiver.com>
From: "Davies, Joshua" <Joshua.Davies@ImplementingSSL.com>
To: "Reader, Avid" <reader@HopefullyABeachInMaui.com>

Hi there, I'm sending you an email.  What do you think of it?
```

This is a pretty simple (not to mention mundane) plaintext email. The `Received` header indicates the path that the email took from sender to receiver; you can have several such `Received` lines if the email was transferred over multiple relays, as most are. The `Subject` is what appears in the summary area, and the remaining headers ought to be fairly self-explanatory. The actual body of the email in this example is the single line of text after the blank line.

## Multipurpose Internet Mail Extensions (MIME)

All modern email readers, for better or for worse, support the *Multipurpose Internet Mail Extensions* (*MIME*) that allow the sender of the email to declare what are usually referred to by email reader software as *attachments* and which are offered as independent downloads to the message.

An email with attachments, at the wire-level, looks like this:

```
Received:  from smtp.receiver.com ([192.168.1.1]) by smtp.sender.com
  with Microsoft SMTPSVC(6.0.3790.3959); Fri, 2 Jul 2010 08:44:43 -0500
MIME-Version: 1.0
Content-Type: multipart/mixed;
       boundary="----_=_NextPart_001_01CB19EC.B9C71780"
Subject: This email contains an attachment
Date: Fri, 2 Jul 2010 08:44:23 -0500
Message-ID: <12345@smtp.receiver.com>
From: "Davies, Joshua" <joshua.davies@ImplementingSSL.com>
To: "Reader, Avid" <reader@HopefullyABeachInMaui.com>

This is a multi-part message in MIME format.
```

```
------_=_NextPart_001_01CB19EC.B9C71780
Content-Type: text/plain;
        charset="iso-8859-1"
Content-Transfer-Encoding: quoted-printable

Hi there, this email has an attachment.  I promise it's not a virus.

------_=_NextPart_001_01CB19EC.B9C71780
Content-Type: application/vnd.ms-excel;
        name="NotAVirus.xls"
Content-Transfer-Encoding: base64
Content-Description: NotAVirus.xls
Content-Disposition: attachment;
        filename="NotAVirus.xls"
```

```
0M8R4KGxGuEAAAAAAAAAAAAAAAAAAAAAPgADAP7/CQAGAAAAAAAAAAAAABAAAAKgAAAA
EAAA/v///wAAAD+////AAAAACkAAAD////////////////////////////////////////
/////////////////////////////////////////////////////////////////////
...
```

```
------_=_NextPart_001_01CB19EC.B9C71780--
```

This email contains a couple of new headers: MIME-Version and Content-Type. MIME-Version just indicates that the email reader must support MIME at a specific version; the second instructs the email reader how to parse the body of the email.

Content-Type should be followed by two strings that identify the type, separated by a forward-slash (/) delimiter, followed by a semicolon (;), followed by name-value parameters specific to the type itself. MIME content types are of the form text/html, text/xml, application/executable, image/jpeg. The first string identifies the broad classification of the type, and the second identifies a specialization of that class. In this case, the email's Content-Type is mulitpart/mixed, which indicates that the body itself consists of more than one mime type. The boundary="----_=_NextPart_001_01CB19EC.B9C71780" part indicates that the embedded MIME messages themselves are separated from each other by a long string that the email sender has verified doesn't occur within the message body itself.

There are two embedded MIME messages here:

- One of MIME type text/plain and a Content-Transfer-Encoding of quoted-printable
- Another of MIME type application/vnd.ms-excel and Content-Transfer-Encoding base64.

By convention, the email reader interprets the first message as text to display to the user in the body. The second, it makes available as a downloadable attachment. The attachment itself also declares a file name via the Content-Disposition header — this filename can be used, for example, to suggest a filename to save as if the user chooses to download the attachment.

## Protecting Email from Eavesdroppers with S/MIME

There's no reason an email with an attachment must be a `multi-part/mixed` type. If there's just one attachment and nothing else, the `Content-Type` of the email header can perfectly and legitimately be the type of the attachment; the email reader just shows nothing except an attachment with no accompanying text. S/MIME takes advantage of this by creating an `application/x-pkcs7-mime` MIME type. As you can likely guess, this is another ASN.1 encoded structure.

An S/MIME encoded email message looks like this:

```
Received:  from smtp.receiver.com ([192.168.1.1]) by smtp.sender.com
  with Microsoft SMTPSVC(6.0.3790.3959); Wed, 21 Apr 2010 12:42:48 -0500
MIME-Version: 1.0
Content-Transfer-Encoding: base64
Content-Disposition: attachment;
        filename="smime.p7m"
Content-class: urn:content-classes:message
Content-Type: application/x-pkcs7-mime;smime-type=enveloped-data;
        name=smime.p7m;
        smime-type=enveloped-data;
        name="smime.p7m"
Subject: This message will self-destruct in 15 seconds
Date: Wed, 21 Apr 2010 12:42:47 -0500
Message-ID: <12345@smtp.receiver.com>
From: "Davies, Joshua" <joshua.davies@ImplementingSSL.com>
To: "Reader, Avid" <reader@HopefullyABeachInMaui.com>
```

```
MIAGCSqGSIb3DQEHA6CAMIACAQAxggNGMIIBnwIBADCBhjB4MRMwEQYKCZImiZPyLGQBGRY
MRUwEwYKCZImiZPyLGQBGRYFc2FicmUxEjAQBgoJkiaJk/IsZAEZFgJhZDEWMBQGCgmSJom
ARkWBkdsb2JhbDEeMBwGA1UEAxMVU2FicmUgSW5jLiBJc3N1aW5nIENBQgo84HbtAAEABSy
CsqGSIb3DQEBAQUABIIBAKHiUib4D3g8bA1AyInu2CkcB75mgMI/Sb5mQjmMNPo7Q0ypV1n
```

Regarding this email:

- **Message body:** This is a base64 encoded PKCS #7 envelope for which the email reader software must have a legitimate certificate in order to display. The body is simply an attachment.

- **Headers:** These describe the attachment in enough detail for the receiving email reader to interpret and decode it.

- **Attachment:** This is named via the `Content-Disposition` header element in the email message itself — in the case of S/MIME, the filename is important. S/MIME dictates old DOS-style three-character file extensions that indicate the type of the file. `.p7m` stands for "PKCS #7 Message." (`.p7s`, in contrast, is a PKCS #7 signature file.) The filename itself is usually *smime*.

PKCS #7 is slightly more complicated to parse than the X.509 certificates examined in Chapter 5 because PKCS #7 allows indefinite-length encodings. In other words, it follows the *Canonical Encoding Rules* (CER) rather than the DER

(Distinguished Encoding Rules) that X.509 mandates. Indefinite-length encodings mean that the length is not explicitly output following that tag byte but instead, the application should read until it encounters two back-to-back 0 bytes. In other words, you process it just like a null-terminated C string, except that it has two null terminators instead of one. Parsing indefinitely encoded ASN.1 values can get somewhat complex because they can be nested inside one another.

The format of the message itself is currently described by RFC 5652, which refers to it as *Cryptographic Message Syntax* (CMS), a superset of PKCS #7.

---

**PARSING PKCS #7**

Parsing a PKCS #7-formatted S/MIME document is not for the faint of heart; I'll give an overview here, but if you're interested you should read the official specification document for complete details.

An S/MIME document body — such as the Base64-encoded .p7m part in the earlier example — is an ASN.1 sequence of what the specification refers to as *content types*. The most interesting case, and probably the most common, is when there is a single entry of content-type enveloped-data, which indicates that the content is encrypted. Of course, as you know, if anything is encrypted, a key is needed to decrypt it, so that key must be exchanged somehow. As you can probably guess, the key is exchanged using public-key techniques; if the sender has a certificate with the receiver's public RSA key, the content encryption key is encrypted using that key.

---

## Securing Email When There Are Multiple Recipients

What about emails with multiple recipients? If you've ever sent an email, you know that there are often many recipients, some on the To: line and some on the cc: line. If this is the case, only one key is used to encrypt the message content, but that same key is public-key encrypted multiple times in the recipientInfo section of the .p7m attachment.

An encrypted S/MIME attachment with two recipients and a DES-encrypted attachment, then, takes the general form shown in Figure 10-1.

So, if you have the private-key corresponding to one of the public keys, you decrypt the symmetric key and use it to decrypt the message body. Notice that the certificate is identified by serial number, which is unique to an issuer; therefore the issuer must also be specified.

**NOTE**   S/MIME also permits Key Agreement (for example, Diffie-Hellman) and pre-shared symmetric keys for encryption of the content encryption key.

Very often, when you finally decrypt the message body itself, you find that the contents are yet another S/MIME attachment! This is usually a plaintext email with a signature section, so that the recipient can authenticate the sender. S/MIME is a broad specification that permits messages to be signed but not encrypted and also covers certificate management.

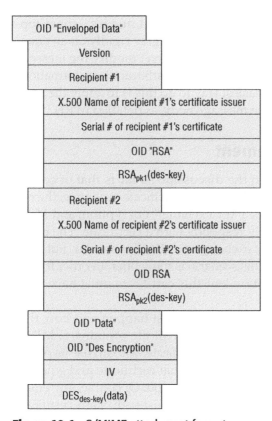

**Figure 10-1:** S/MIME attachment format

Signing email messages can be a bit complex, though. Recall from Chapter 4 that computing a digital signature consists of securely hashing a set of data and then encrypting it using a public-key encryption algorithm with the private key. Verifying that same signature involves computing that same hash over the same data, decrypting the encrypted hash using the public key, and verifying that they match. It's important to the process that both sides agree on exactly what the data being hashed is; if even one bit of data changes between the generation of the signature and the subsequent verification, the signature is rejected. In the context of TLS, this is not an issue, because the message format is rigidly defined. The data that is signed is the data that is received; it's streamed over an open, established socket immediately after it's signed

However, email is a different story. The signature is generated sometimes days before it's verified, and traditionally, email relay systems have assumed impunity to modify the email message itself however they see fit in order to route the message from one place to another. If an email gateway feels the need to Base64-encode an email message, or convert from EBCDIC to ASCII, or change the charset from ISO-8859-12 to UTF-8, it does so and lets the receiver sort it all out later. This is a problem for email readers in general, and it's a showstopper for email signatures. As a result, both sides must agree rigidly on an email format and ensure that intervening gateways either don't modify the message content, or that the receiver can reliably undo whatever arbitrary transformations may have been applied en route. The easiest way to do this is to apply the most restrictive set of transformations to the message body, as detailed in RFC 5751.

## S/MIME Certificate Management

One point that's been glossed over in the discussion so far is that of certificate management. TLS mandates a rigid means of certificate exchange; the client opens a connection and negotiates a key exchange, encryption, and MAC algorithm, and the server immediately responds with a certificate. The client uses that certificate to complete a key exchange. S/MIME is similar, but it's a delayed-reaction variant; the *client* in this scenario is the sender. In order for the sender to encrypt the content encryption key, this certificate must have been exchanged beforehand.

While TLS dictates specific rules on how this must happen and how this certificate must be validated and even what the certificate contains, S/MIME doesn't care at all; if you can uniquely identify a certificate, you can use its public key to encrypt. Whether you trust the validity of that certificate and whether you believe it belongs to the purported user is up to you. Of course, any email agent supporting S/MIME goes ahead and checks the trust-path of any certificate and warns you of any discrepancies in order to help you make a trust decision.

As you can see, neither TLS nor S/MIME is a complete solution to the email security problem — they're both required. TLS ensures that the SMTP server is really the SMTP server you think you're connecting to and that the SMTP headers themselves are private and not modified, and S/MIME (or some such equivalent) is required to ensure privacy of the email from the time it is written to the time it is received.

## Securing Datagram Traffic

It's somewhat ironic that SSL, originally designed as an add-on to the stateless HTTP protocol, is itself so stateful. Everything about SSL/TLS requires that a context be established and maintained from the start of the handshake to the end of the tear-down; the sequence numbers must be maintained from one record to the next, the initialization vectors for CBC ciphers (prior to TLS 1.0) must be carried forward, and so on.

This is perfectly acceptable in the context of TCP, which keeps track of its own sequence numbers and internally handles reordering of out-of-sequence packets and retransmission of lost packets. However, TCP provides these services at a cost in terms of per-packet overhead and per-socket handshake time. Although on modern networks this overhead is practically negligible, a lighter-weight alternative, called *User Datagram Protocol* (UDP), has been part of TCP/IP almost from the beginning. With UDP, a packet is built and sent across the network with almost no header or routing information — just enough to identify a source and a target machine and a port.

This section examines the application of TLS concepts to datagram traffic.

## Securing the Domain Name System

Chapter 1 presented, but didn't examine in-depth, the mapping between user-friendly hostnames and IP addresses. Ordinarily, a user doesn't connect to `http://64.170.98.32/index.html` but instead connects to `http://www.ietf.org/index.html`. This mapping of (arguably) human-readable domain names to machine-readable IP addresses is maintained by the *Domain Name System* (DNS). There's no automatic transformation that's applied here; the IP address isn't derived from the host name using some complex algorithm such as Base64; you can associate any host name with any IP address, as long as you can add an entry into the global DNS database.

This database is huge and must be widely distributed. DNS describes a hierarchical management system where the top-level keeps track of the registrars for the ending parts of a DNS name such as .org, .com, .gov, and so on. These registrars, in turn, keep track of the registrars for the next-level — the part that comes before the `.com`. You can nest these names as deeply as you can imagine until an *authoritative name server*, which maps a completed domain name back to an actual IP address, is found. This hierarchy is illustrated in Figure 10-2.

There are thirteen master copies of the important top-level database, named A-M, distributed throughout the world and continuously synchronized. The website `http://root-servers.org/` documents where these servers are physically located, what their IP addresses are, and who administers them. These copies are referred to as the *Root* DNS servers, and are considered authoritative. VeriSign, for example, operates the "J" root DNS servers, which have IP address 192.58.128.30. If VeriSign's root server states that `.org` is owned by a registrar at IP address XX.XX.XX.XX, then the Internet Corporation for Assigned Names and Numbers (ICANN)'s copy at 199.7.83.42 will say the same thing.

However, you probably don't (and probably shouldn't) request domain-name information from these root servers or the next-level registrars. Although each of these databases are replicated for load-balancing and redundancy purposes, there are many more *slave* copies of this same database distributed throughout the world. If you access the Internet through an ISP, for instance, your ISP almost certainly maintains a local cache of at least a subset of the master DNS data. You get the IP addresses of these local *name servers* when you get your own IP address at DHCP time. On a Linux system, you can see the IP addresses of the local copies under /etc/resolv.conf. On a Windows system, you can see them by going to Control Panel ➤ Connection Status ➤ Details and look under DNS Server. (Although I must warn you that this seems to change with every release of Windows, so you may have to hunt around a bit if you're on such a system.)

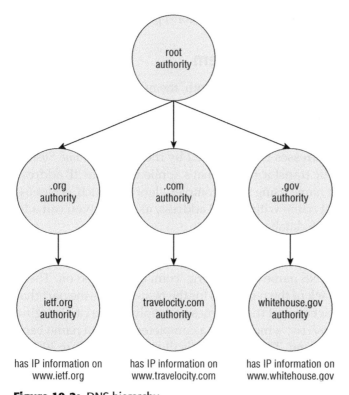

**Figure 10-2:** DNS hierarchy

So, when it comes time to resolve a human-readable, string host name to a machine-readable IP address, you typically call an operating system function, such as gethostbyname as illustrated in Listing 1-4. This function looks at /etc/resolv.conf (or wherever Windows hides it in its system registry), finds a name server, and asks it for the corresponding IP address. If the name server doesn't have the name/IP address pair cached already, it works backward through the domain name, first determining the authoritative name server for the top-level domain and then the authoritative name server for the next-level domain. When it finds an authoritative server for the actual requested host name, it issues a query to that server.

### Using the DNS Protocol to Query the Database

You may be curious, though, about how `gethostbyname` actually queries the database. These days, if I say *database*, you may start thinking about SQL and SELECT statements, but the DNS naming system, thankfully, predates the relational database craze and instead defines its own Internet protocol. This protocol is named, unsurprisingly, DNS, and is an interesting protocol in the way it structures requests and responses.

The DNS database is a collection of *resource records* (RR) as illustrated in Figure 10-3, each of which has a name, a type, a class, and a set of associated data that varies depending on the type. The most important type of resource record is type A, *Host Address*, which actually describes the mapping between a host name and an IP address. Type A, *Host Address*, RRs include an IP address in the associated data section. So, if a client has a host name for which it wants to query the corresponding IP address, it fills out as much information as it has on the RR, sends that to the server, and the server responds with as much information as *it* has — hopefully a completed record. The resource record itself is pretty open-ended — other available and common resource records include load-balancing information, redirect information, and mail server information.

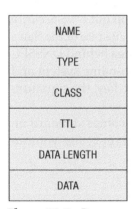

| NAME |
| TYPE |
| CLASS |
| TTL |
| DATA LENGTH |
| DATA |

**Figure 10-3:** Resource record format

### Disadvantages of the DNS Query

Normally, this query is submitted not with a TCP socket, but with a UDP (datagram) socket, on port 53. UDP Requests and responses aren't rigidly matched like they are in TCP. After you send a UDP request, you just wait for data — any data at all — to be returned with the ports reversed. If a client has multiple outstanding DNS queries, it is responsible for correlating the responses correctly. DNS mandates that every request has a unique transaction ID for this purpose.

Herein lies the problem. Any malicious user on the network can easily spoof a DNS reply; all he needs to know is the source port (the destination port is always 53) and the transaction ID, both of which can be obtained with a packet sniffer. TCP is harder to spoof this way (but not impossible); UDP's stateless nature makes it simple. All the attacker has to do is to respond faster than the name server. The name server's response is received and ignored at a later time.

This gets even worse when you consider that if a name server doesn't have an IP address for a given domain name, it queries the next-higher name server, up to the root servers. An attacker can respond to the name server with his own bogus record. If he does so, then the name server dutifully caches the wrong information and then hands it out to all of the clients that it services. This is called *DNS cache poisoning*. In 2008, security researcher Dan Kaminsky showed how to subvert this process completely and poison the authority record, thereby taking over not just individual hosts, but entire domains.

### Preventing DNS Cache Poisoning with DNSSEC

Although there are stopgaps to make DNS cache poisoning harder — better randomization of the transaction ID, wider variance of the request source port, and a check to see if multiple responses are received for the same query (a sure sign that something's amiss) — there have been efforts to roll out *DNS Security* (DNSSEC). This was specified back in 1999 by RFC 2535 and in spite of the flaws in the DNS system still has not been widely deployed. The idea behind DNSSEC is to deploy a public-key infrastructure around the domain-name system and sign each DNS record. If the receiver has a copy of a public key, the signature can be verified.

You can explore the DNS system using the `dig` tool that comes standard on all Unix systems. If you want to see the IP address for `www.ietf.org`, you can do this:

```
debian:ssl$ dig www.ietf.org

; <<>> DiG 9.3.4 <<>> www.ietf.org
;; global options:  printcmd
;; Got answer:
;; ->>HEADER<<- opcode: QUERY, status: NOERROR, id: 24804
;; flags: qr rd ra; QUERY: 1, ANSWER: 1, AUTHORITY: 0, ADDITIONAL: 0

;; QUESTION SECTION:
;www.ietf.org.                  IN      A
```

```
;; ANSWER SECTION:
www.ietf.org.          433      IN       A        64.170.98.32

;; Query time: 19 msec
;; SERVER: 209.18.47.61#53(209.18.47.61)
;; WHEN: Mon Sep 20 21:08:21 2010
;; MSG SIZE  rcvd: 46
```

This tells you that the IP address for `www.ietf.org` is `64.170.98.32`. You can also view signature information for this domain name:

```
debian:ssl$ dig @209.18.47.61 www.ietf.org +dnssec

; <<>> DiG 9.3.4 <<>> @209.18.47.61 www.ietf.org +dnssec
; (1 server found)
;; global options:  printcmd
;; Got answer:
;; ->>HEADER<<- opcode: QUERY, status: NOERROR, id: 63769
;; flags: qr rd ra; QUERY: 1, ANSWER: 2, AUTHORITY: 0, ADDITIONAL: 1

;; OPT PSEUDOSECTION:
; EDNS: version: 0, flags: do; udp: 4096
;; QUESTION SECTION:
;www.ietf.org.                  IN       A

;; ANSWER SECTION:
www.ietf.org.          1649     IN       A        64.170.98.32
www.ietf.org.          1649     IN       RRSIG    A 5 3 1800
   20110831142441 20100831132624 40452 ietf.org.
mukwwlQll9RPzlKkWKgI2TnOka17jFrkgtavMEITvU5r4xTAhbZxXA3K
mKAoK+d0OA0XiJC0u2GtsobAVtWVcrdqaeezllw/TppW+otIj43ZzJ6e
iKpytRJdFmJOS409mNLZaYjUgm6i154clMgmatOisLhX79snqQu18jG2
sRZE4faPmKw9kw9FNtOC8QuTCOGecTsmycuYpNbTxCSyD0Z4M1behKb9
rRzk1spXTBo6j2mn9vb8NYqY+Xa9JjLOe2Xw8bLGoQrdcB0+hBOBf4Od
+bdgMKMIE1scO9QFqQvTD345v1u2FygXFe0UgE1l6KDz+ZA4prkvzbfo yPy53w==

;; Query time: 15 msec
;; SERVER: 209.18.47.61#53(209.18.47.61)
;; WHEN: Mon Sep 20 21:05:31 2010
;; MSG SIZE  rcvd: 353
```

RFC 4034 details the format of this signature record, the `RRSIG` record type. Of course, a signature is useless without a corresponding public key with which to validate it. The public key is held by the next higher level's authoritative name server:

```
debian:ssl$ dig ietf.org dnskey
;; Truncated, retrying in TCP mode.
debian:ssl$ dig ietf.org dnskey +dnssec

; <<>> DiG 9.3.4 <<>> ietf.org dnskey +dnssec
```

```
;; global options:  printcmd
;; Got answer:
;; ->>HEADER<<- opcode: QUERY, status: NOERROR, id: 59127
;; flags: qr rd ra; QUERY: 1, ANSWER: 4, AUTHORITY: 0, ADDITIONAL: 1

;; OPT PSEUDOSECTION:
; EDNS: version: 0, flags: do; udp: 4096
;; QUESTION SECTION:
;ietf.org.                     IN      DNSKEY

;; ANSWER SECTION:
ietf.org.              1800    IN      DNSKEY  256 3 5
AwEAAdDECajHaTjfSoNTY58WcBah1BxPKVIHBz4IfLjfqMvium4lgKtK
ZLe97DgJ5/NQrNEGGQmr6fKvUj67cfrZUojZ2cGRizVhgkOqZ9scaTVX
NuXLM5Tw7VWOVIceeXAuuH2mPIiEV6MhJYUsW6dvmNsJ4XwCgNgroAmX
hoMEiWEjBB+wjYZQ5GtZHBFKVXACSWTiCtddHcueOeSVPi5WH94Vlubh
HfiytNPZLrObhUCHT6k0tNE6phLoHnXWU+6vpsYpz6GhMw/R9BFxW5Pd
PFIWBgoWk2/XFVRSKG9Lr61b2z1R126xeUwvw46RVy3hanV3vNO7LM5H niqaYclBbhk=
ietf.org.              1800    IN      DNSKEY  257 3 5
AwEAAavjQ1H6pE8FV8LGP0wQBFVL0EM9BRfqxz9p/sZ+8AByqyFHLdZc
HoOGF7CgB5OKYMvGOgysuYQloPlwbq7Ws5WywbutbXyG24lMWy4jijlJ
UsaFrS5EvUu4ydmuRc/TGnEXnN1XQkO+waIT4cLtrmcWjoY8Oqud6lDa
Jdj1cKr2nX1NrmMRowIu3DIVtGbQJmzpukpDVZaYMMAm8M5vz4U2vRCV
ETLgDoQ7rhsiD127J8gVExjO8B0113jCajbFRcMtUtFTjH4z7jXP2ZzD
cXsgpe4LYFuenFQAcRBR1E6oaykHR7rlPqqmw58nIELJUFoMcb/BdRLg byTeurFlnxs=
ietf.org.              1800    IN      RRSIG   DNSKEY 5 2 1800
   20110831142353 20100831132624 40452 ietf.org.
hbpdgpVd3DHrRcO7S5Y8YfLgw+dj8YSLPU43wRzt7TLx+hdLXC3H7BGk
5UZvjTIlYiIw5fokRzu1zNgKQX+89yRASf8oHX8EFW/GqIZ03Hduvorr
PbFyG3fw5Z5aMAeWTktwEQHc+OU0+m9srVT7fBndRXSWKNCg67NTbnKA
kNKUajSohpQu3I9HiiBaFIHPm7sZYlnurxnFOQHUJiA6WvU6B332oAto
AH9yBhV5ZK58GTg4t4KhAUD+w+oBdV4GXGVViGd0mCb2fN8OzJa9nb06
+A2DfAsW5zLBEBcP+yDO5ogKGN00atwI232Wfi5h7HDncHRri7Shg63C e6xiFA==
ietf.org.              1800    IN      RRSIG   DNSKEY 5 2 1800
   20110831142553 20100831132624 45586 ietf.org.
DhPTlnpVfvPUDUpz08zCXCDbNea8bu89Dok5mnyt1NXpP+OPZqZzXxDU
A/blHG6Z6ZYAqGUHbYhgPEz9XQBj/fZy0Jn2F8QVHgxkpL8+MEsDvGCd
t9o7kZoGd2eg3Hb0ImBMx59DLphHXwj3v0tOhEpZs25Pcul4QM5v7Pia
fXk+R5XQ4YtBQnI6FZYlUP2EthSWSasKmvzK4Dmky7m9sFsZrzRWNKsF
A+kvUPelbuz1m0WfsKBmh6klcok/BcVt4EluTeCoOloOra3t6JiPjrlv
MKtn2nUYmGFM6JJGN/K8CA7wtr93BwwpAjVkWftfmIOgPCi7X8uFosAq 3T0+JA==

;; Query time: 76 msec
;; SERVER: 209.18.47.61#53(209.18.47.61)
;; WHEN: Mon Sep 20 21:09:46 2010
;; MSG SIZE  rcvd: 1181
```

This provides authentication and integrity, but it doesn't provide confidentiality — although it's questionable what value confidentiality would provide a DNS lookup because all of the data is public.

Still, it seems a shame that every datagram-based protocol must invent its own means of securing its traffic, doesn't it?

## TLS Without TCP — Datagram TLS

In 2006, Nagendra Modadugu and Eric Rescorla drafted the *Datagram TLS* (*DTLS*) specification (`http://crypto.stanford.edu/~nagendra/papers/dtls.pdf`). Although you can't apply TLS directly to datagram traffic, the number of changes required to support it are surprisingly small. Whereas TLS's top-level encapsulating header includes just type, version and length, DTLS adds two fields:

- **Epoch:** This field increments whenever it receives a change cipher spec handshake message. This way, if the change cipher spec itself is lost, the server recognizes that the epoch has changed and knows something has gone wrong. Recognizing a dropped change cipher spec message is particularly important because that's the signal to start using encryption (or, in the case of a session renegotiation, to use new keying material).

- **Sequence number:** The purpose of this is obvious — to recognize dropped or out-of-order packets. TCP has one of these, too.

What about leftover cipher state? Prior to TLS 1.1, CBC-based ciphers used the last encrypted block as the IV for the next block — if one record is dropped, every subsequent record is undecryptable. TCP guards against this by providing automatic replay of dropped packets, but UDP has no such provision. Rather than require it, which would essentially force UDP to behave exactly like TCP in order to achieve any security, DTLS doesn't allow implicit IV's. They're a security hole anyway, so IV's are always output explicitly, TLS 1.1+ style. This also means that RC4, which carries state from one byte to the next, cannot be used with DTLS in any form; there's no safe way to explicitly output the current state of an RC4 cipher.

Interestingly, DTLS also requires that the client submit the ClientHello message twice. The first time, the server responds with a challenge "cookie" that the client must repeat in the second ClientHello. This proves that the client is actually receiving UDP packets at the given IP address and was designed to prevent *denial of service* (*DOS*) attacks.

From the implementer's perspective, the most difficult part of DTLS is the timeout and retransmit algorithm. Very similar to the one used by TCP, DTLS mandates a timeout and retransmit procedure with a sliding window. In fact, in a lot of ways, DTLS forces a UDP connection to behave like a TCP connection behaves. It hasn't yet been fully explored just how much overhead DTLS adds to a datagram connection and whether the extra overhead is worth DTLS or if the user might be better off just using TSL over TCP instead.

# Supporting SSL When Proxies Are Involved

If you tried to use the HTTPS example client from Chapter 6 from behind a web proxy, you were probably disappointed in the results. The TLS model doesn't work at all with the proxy model. When proxies are involved, the client connects to the proxy, tells the proxy which document it would like to view, and the proxy retrieves that document and returns it on behalf of the client. This works fine in the HTTP model; the client barely even needs to modify its behavior based on the proxy. Rather than establishing a socket connection to the target site, the client just establishes a socket connection to the proxy, submits essentially the same request it would normally submit, and the proxy forwards that request on to the target.

This breaks down completely when you want to use HTTPS. Remember that when using HTTPS, before you transmit a byte of HTTP data, the first thing you must do is complete a TLS handshake. This is important because the TLS handshake establishes that you're talking to the server you think you're talking to (or, more pedantically, an entity that has convinced a certificate authority that it legitimately owns a specific domain name). This is necessary to guard against man-in-the-middle attacks. Unfortunately, a proxy is, by definition, a man-in-the-middle. You may be inclined to trust it — most likely you don't have a choice in the matter — but TLS doesn't.

## Possible Solutions to the Proxy Problem

Other than just disallowing secure connections through proxies, the most obvious solution to this problem might be to establish an HTTPS connection to the proxy, forward the request, and allow it to establish an HTTPS connection to the target and continue as usual. This means that the proxy must be able to present a certificate signed by a certificate authority trusted by the browser, or the user needs to prepare to ignore untrusted certificate warnings. If the proxy presents a signed certificate, it needs to either purchase a top-level signed certificate, which is expensive, or it needs to distribute its own certificate authority to every browser that is configured to use it — which is administratively difficult.

Of course, you can always mandate that the browser never establish an HTTPS connection to the proxy; if it wants a secure document, it should establish a plain-old socket connection to the proxy and let the proxy deal with the secure negotiation. This presupposes, of course, that every node between the browser and the proxy is trusted because everything that passes to the proxy is passed in plaintext. This may or may not actually be the case.

A more serious problem with both of these approaches, however, is that the client itself can't see any certificate warnings. If the certificate is out of date, untrusted, or for a different domain than the one requested, only the proxy is aware of this. In addition, the proxy needs to know which CAs the client trusts, otherwise the client can't update its trust list. HTTP proxies are supposed to be pretty simple; — they have to handle huge volumes of requests, so you want to avoid adding any more complexity than necessary. Building the protocol extensions to enable the proxy to channel certificate warnings back to the client and respond to them is fairly complex.

Instead, the standard solution suggested by RFC 2817 is that HTTP proxies don't proxy secure documents at all — they proxy connections, instead. The proxy must accept the HTTP CONNECT command, which tells it not to establish an HTTP socket with a target host, but instead to establish an arbitrary socket connection. In effect, when the proxy receives a CONNECT command, rather than, for instance, a GET or a POST, it should complete the TCP three-way handshake with the target host on the target port, but from that point on it should *tunnel* all subsequent data unchanged.

This enables the client to complete the TLS handshake and respond appropriately to any certificate warnings, and so on, that may occur — the code itself doesn't change at all. The only trick is making sure to establish the tunneled connection before beginning the TLS handshake.

## Adding Proxy Support Using Tunneling

You can add proxy support to the HTTPS client from Chapter 6; After you understand how tunneling works, it's not terribly complicated. Instead of affixing a proxy authorization to each HTTP command, you instead issue a single HTTP CONNECT command before doing anything TLS-specific; the authorization string is attached to that command and forgotten afterward. If the CONNECT command succeeds, you just use the socket as if it was a direct connection to the target host, which, at this point, it is.

Recognizing the proxy parameters and parsing them doesn't change from HTTP to HTTPS. The only difference in the main routine is that you issue an HTTP CONNECT command after establishing the HTTP connection to the proxy and before sending a TLS handshake as shown in Listing 10-1.

**Listing 10-1:** "https.c" main routine with proxy support

```
if ( proxy_host )
{
  if ( !http_connect( client_connection, host, port, proxy_user,
                      proxy_password ) )
  {
    perror( "Unable to establish proxy tunnel" );
    if ( close( client_connection ) == -1 )
    {
      perror( "Error closing client connection" );
      return 2;
```

*(Continued)*

```
      }
      return 3;
    }
  }

  if ( tls_connect( client_connection, &tls_context ) )
  {
```

This makes use of the `http_connect` function shown in Listing 10-2.

**Listing 10-2:** "https.c" http_connect

```c
int http_connect( int connection,
                  const char *host,
                  int port,
                  const char *proxy_user,
                  const char *proxy_password )
{
  static char connect_command[ MAX_GET_COMMAND ];
  int received = 0;
  static char recv_buf[ BUFFER_SIZE + 1 ];
  int http_status = 0;

  sprintf( connect_command, "CONNECT %s:%d HTTP/1.1\r\n", host, port );
  if ( send( connection, connect_command,
             strlen( connect_command ), 0 ) == -1 )
  {
    return -1;
  }

  sprintf( connect_command, "Host: %s:%d\r\n", host, port );
  if ( send( connection, connect_command,
             strlen( connect_command ), 0 ) == -1 )
  {
    return -1;
  }

  if ( proxy_user )
  {
    int credentials_len = strlen( proxy_user ) +
                          strlen( proxy_password ) + 1;
    char *proxy_credentials = malloc( credentials_len );
    char *auth_string = malloc( ( ( credentials_len * 4 ) / 3 ) + 1 );
    sprintf( proxy_credentials, "%s:%s", proxy_user, proxy_password );
    base64_encode( proxy_credentials, credentials_len, auth_string );
    sprintf( connect_command, "Proxy-Authorization: BASIC %s\r\n",
             auth_string );
    if ( send( connection, connect_command,
               strlen( connect_command ), 0 ) == -1 )
    {
      free( proxy_credentials );
```

```
      free( auth_string );
      return -1;
    }
    free( proxy_credentials );
    free( auth_string );
  }

  sprintf( connect_command, "\r\n" );
  if ( send( connection, connect_command,
             strlen( connect_command ), 0 ) == -1 )
  {
    return -1;
  }

  // Have to read the response!
  while ( ( received = recv( connection, recv_buf,
                            BUFFER_SIZE, 0 ) ) > 0 )
  {
    if ( http_status == 0 )
    {
      if ( !strncmp( recv_buf, "HTTP", 4 ) )
      {
        http_status = atoi( recv_buf + 9 );
        printf( "interpreted http status code %d\n", http_status );
      }
    }

    if ( !strcmp( recv_buf + ( received - 4 ), "\r\n\r\n" ) )
    {
      break;
    }
  }

  return ( http_status == 200 );
}
```

This ought to look pretty familiar; the first half is the `http_get` function from Chapter 1 with a few details changed. If you're so inclined, you can probably see a way to consolidate these both into a single function. Notice that you still connect on port 80 to the proxy; the CONNECT command sent includes the desired port of 443.

Because CONNECT is an HTTP command, the proxy starts by returning an HTTP response. At the very least, you have to read it in its entirety so that the first `recv` command you invoke inside `tls_connect` doesn't start reading an HTTP response when it's expecting a ServerHello message. Of course, it's probably worthwhile to have a look at the response code as well, as in Listing 10-2. If you mistyped the password, or failed to provide a password to an authenticating proxy, you get a 407 error code. If this is the case, you should abort the connection attempt and report an error to the user.

One thing that's particularly interesting about this approach to supporting HTTPS through proxies is that it means that, in order to properly support HTTPS, the proxy must be capable of establishing arbitrary connections with arbitrary hosts as long as the authentication is completed properly. This capability can be used to tunnel any protocol through an HTTP proxy, although the client software has to be modified to support it.

# SSL with OpenSSL

It would be irresponsible of me to recommend using a tried-and-true SSL library, such as OpenSSL, but then not show you how to do so, especially if your desire is to do production-grade security work. Listing 10-3 reworks the HTTPS example from Chapter 6 using the OpenSSL library.

**Listing 10-3:** "https.c" with OpenSSL

```
#include <openssl/ssl.h>
...
int http_get( int connection,
              const char *path,
              const char *host,
              SSL *ssl )
{
  static char get_command[ MAX_GET_COMMAND ];

  sprintf( get_command, "GET /%s HTTP/1.1\r\n", path );
  if ( SSL_write( ssl, get_command, strlen( get_command ) ) == -1 )
  {
    return -1;
  }

  sprintf( get_command, "Host: %s\r\n", host );
  if ( SSL_write( ssl, get_command, strlen( get_command ) ) == -1 )
  {
    return -1;
  }

  strcpy( get_command, "Connection: Close\r\n\r\n" );
  if ( SSL_write( ssl, get_command, strlen( get_command ) ) == -1 )
  {
    return -1;
  }

  return 0;
}

void display_result( int connection, SSL *ssl )
```

```
{
  int received = 0;
  static char recv_buf[ BUFFER_SIZE + 1 ];
  while ( SSL_get_error( ssl,
          ( received = SSL_read( ssl, recv_buf, BUFFER_SIZE ) ) ) ==
          SSL_ERROR_NONE )
  {
    recv_buf[ received ] = '\0';
    printf( "data: %s", recv_buf );
  }
  printf( "\n" );
}

int main( int argc, char *argv[ ] )
{
...
  int ind;

  SSL_CTX *ctx;
  SSL *ssl;
  BIO *sbio;
  BIO *bio_err=0;
  SSL_METHOD *meth;

  if ( argc < 2 )
  {
    fprintf( stderr,
      "Usage: %s: [-p http://[username:password@]proxy-host:proxy-port]\
<URL>\n", argv[ 0 ] );
    return 1;
  }

  // OpenSSL-specific setup stuff
  SSL_library_init();
  SSL_load_error_strings();
  bio_err=BIO_new_fp(stderr,BIO_NOCLOSE);
  meth=SSLv23_method();
  ctx=SSL_CTX_new(meth);

  proxy_host = proxy_user = proxy_password = host = path = NULL;
... // set up the connection itself
  ssl=SSL_new(ctx);
  sbio=BIO_new_socket(client_connection,BIO_NOCLOSE);
  SSL_set_bio(ssl,sbio,sbio);

  if(SSL_connect(ssl)<=0)
  {
    fprintf( stderr, "Error: unable to negotiate SSL connection.\n" );
    if ( close( client_connection ) == -1 )
    {
```

*(Continued)*

```
      perror( "Error closing client connection" );
      return 2;
   }
   return 3;
}

http_get( client_connection, path, host, ssl );
display_result( client_connection, ssl );

SSL_CTX_free(ctx);

if ( close( client_connection ) == -1 )
```

You should have no trouble understanding the OpenSSL library after reading through the rest of this book; in fact, the source code itself should begin to make a lot of sense to you as well.

## Final Thoughts

Of course, the challenge is to ensure that TLS is implemented in a secure way — it's not enough to just use TLS. You must ensure that no sensitive information is leaked, that random numbers are properly seeded, and that private keys remain private, hidden behind secure passphrases. I can't count how many times I've seen a perfectly secure implementation rendered useless by a plaintext configuration file, containing the private key passphrase, checked into the source code control system.

The only advice I can offer here is to look at your application as an attacker might. An attacker always goes for the weakest part of your defense; so most likely the part that you've focused the most effort on securing is of the least interest to a smart attacker.

Finally, though, accept that security is ultimately a trade-off. They say that no home security system can keep out a determined intruder. The same is true of software security. You must balance security with usability. As long as that tradeoff is made deliberately, conscientiously, and collaboratively, with proper documentation, you've struck a decent balance; with any luck, malicious intruders will move past your system for lower-hanging fruit.

# Binary Representation of Integers: A Primer

If you know how to program in C, you must have spent some time looking at machine-level details, including binary number representations, as you learned it. This appendix covers some of these details that you were probably familiar with at one point, but have since (maybe willfully) forgotten.

## The Decimal and Binary Numbering Systems

Humans use a base-10 numbering system. Ten unique digits (including 0) represent the first nine ordinal numbers. After the ninth position, you use multiple digits to represent numerals. Anthropologists believe that the base-10 numbering system, which is ubiquitous in almost all human societies, came about because humans have 10 fingers. As it turns out, though, computers have just one such "finger" because they're electrical machines. I'll go out on a limb and assume you interact with electricity at least occasionally when you turn on a light switch — the switch is the counter which can be in two states: on and off. If it's on, electricity flows; if it's off, it doesn't.

To grossly oversimplify, a CPU is nothing but a series of interrelated electronic switches. Numbers are represented by unique combinations of multiple switches. One such switch can count two unique values. Two switches can count four: on-on, on-off, off-on and off-off. Three switches can count eight values, and $n$ switches can count $2^n$ values. Most modern computers are said to be *32-bit processors*, which means that the internal counters are composed of 32 switches each and are capable of counting up to $2^{32}$, or about 4.3 billion.

The binary numbering system works, at a logical level at least, just like the decimal system. With decimal numbers, the first nine digits are represented (for instance) by the Arabic numerals 1, 2, 3, 4, 5, 6, 7, 8, and 9. After 9, a *tens-place* is introduced, and 90 more unique numerals can be represented. After this, a *hundreds-place* is introduced, and 900 more unique numerals can be represented, and so on. Algebraically, the numeral 97,236 is $9 * 10^4 + 7 * 10^3 + 2 * 10^2 + 3 * 10^1 + 6 * 10^0$.

Binary numbers are usually represented with just two digits — 0 and 1 — corresponding to the off and on states of the internal hardware. It takes quite a few more digits to represent a number in binary than in decimal, but any number that can be expressed in one can be converted to the other. The binary number 11011010 is equal to $1 * 2^7 + 1 * 2^6 + 0 * 2^5 + 1 * 2^4 + 1 * 2^3 + 0 * 2^2 + 1 * 2^1 + 0 * 2^0 = 218$.

It's customary to delimit binary numbers at the byte level, where one byte consists of eight bits. There's no technical reason why this has to be eight bits (although hardware design is slightly easier when the number of bits is a power of 2). In the early days of computing, when communications providers charged by the bit (!), early airline reservation systems adopted a five-bit byte to save on communication costs.

## Understanding Binary Logical Operations

Binary numbers can be added, subtracted, multiplied and divided just like decimal numbers. Every computing device in existence has a dedicated circuit called an *Arithmetic Logical Unit (ALU)* whose purpose is to take as input two or more numbers in binary form and output the result of a mathematical operation on those numbers. This is done using more primitive operations on binary numbers — AND, OR, NOT, and XOR.

### The AND Operation

The AND operation operates at a bit-level. If both bits are 1, AND returns 1. If either bit is 0, AND returns 0. In other words, only if $x$ is on AND $y$ is on are $x$ AND $y$ on. C exposes the AND operation via the & operator, and it works on whole bytes. The result of C's & operator is the AND of each bit in the first operand with the corresponding bit in the second operand.

For example:

$$10101101 \ (173)$$
$$\&\ 01101011 \ (107)$$

$$\overline{\hspace{3cm}}$$

$$00101001 \ (41)$$

There's no mathematical relationship between the two operands and their output; the & operation just sets the bits that match in both operands. In C, this is useful to check the value of a single bit — if you compute $x$ & 00010000, you get 0 if the fifth bit (counting from the right) is unset, and you get 32 if it isn't. You can put this into a logical operation such as

```
if ( x & 00010000 ) { do_something(); }
```

because C considers non-zero to be "true."

## The OR Operation

The OR operation is sort of the opposite. If $x$ is on OR $y$ is on, then $x$ OR $y$ is on. If $x$ is off and $y$ is on, $x$ OR $y$ is on. If $x$ is on and $y$ is off, $x$ OR $y$ is on. The only way OR returns off is if $x$ and $y$ are both off. C exposes this via the | operator. This is useful to optionally set a bit without changing others. If you want to set the fifth bit of $x$, you can compute $x = x$ | 00010000. This won't change the values of the other bits but does force the fifth bit of $x$ to be 1 even if it was 0 before. For example,

$$10101101 \ (173)$$
$$|\ \ 01101011 \ (107)$$

$$\overline{\hspace{3cm}}$$

$$11101111 \ (239)$$

Compare this with the AND output in the previous section. Again, there's no mathematical relationship between the input and the output.

## The NOT Operation

The NOT operation, C's ~ operator, inverts a bit. 0 becomes 1 and 1 becomes 0.

## The XOR Operation

Finally, the *Exclusive OR* (*XOR*) operation is just like OR, except that if both bits are 1, the output is 0. For example,

$$10101101 \ (173)$$
$$\wedge \ \ 01101011 \ (107)$$
$$\overline{\phantom{xxxxxxxxxx}}$$
$$11000110 \ (198)$$

What makes XOR particularly interesting is that it's invertible; this important property is examined in depth in Chapter 2.

## Position Shifting of Binary Numbers

Binary numbers can also meaningfully be *shifted*. Shifting a binary number consists of moving all of the bits in one direction. Just as adding a zero to a decimal number multiplies it by 10, shifting the bits in a binary number to the left doubles its value. Similarly, shifting to the right halves it.

# Two's-Complement Representation of Negative Numbers

Because humans are so bad at performing mathematical computations, computers were invented to reliably add and subtract numbers. Although we've found a few additional purposes for which we can use computers, they're still fundamentally adding and subtracting machines. However, no computer can add or subtract infinitely. Every ALU has a register size that dictates how many bits represent a number; if an arithmetic operation needs more bits than the register size, the operation overflows, and wraps back around to a logically smaller number.

The idea behind two's-complement arithmetic is to split the available space in half, assigning one half positive numbers and the other negative numbers. Because, logically, negative numbers are smaller than positive numbers, you might guess that the first (*lowest*) half are the negative numbers and that the last half are the positive numbers. However, for compatibility with unsigned numbers, the first half are the positives, and the last half are the negatives.

Because the last (*greatest*) half of any binary number space is the half with the *most-significant-bit* (*MSB*) set, this provides an easy check for a negative number — if the MSB is set, the number is negative. This also simplifies the process of negating a number. If you just invert the bits — apply the NOT operation on all of them — you get the proper representation of the same number, with the sign reversed. This representation is called *one's complement* arithmetic. The only trick here is that if you invert 0 — binary 00000000 — you get 11111111. This is –0, which doesn't make any sense because 0 is neither negative nor positive. To get around this, *two's-complement* arithmetic inverts the number and adds one. This means that there is one more negative number than there are positive numbers.

Generally, you don't need to worry much about negative number representation or two's-complement arithmetic unless you're displaying a number; `printf`, for example, needs to know whether a number with its MSB set is a negative number or a very large positive number. The only other time this comes up is when you start shifting numbers. Remember that shifting to the right halves a binary number? Well, if that number is negative, you must preserve the sign bit to keep the number negative. Therefore, the shift operation behaves differently with a signed number than with an unsigned one; if an unsigned number is shifted right, the MSB becomes 0 in all cases. If a signed integer is shifted right, the MSB is preserved, and becomes the next-most-significant-bit.

Consider the binary number 10101101. Interpreted as an unsigned integer, this is decimal 173. Interpreted as a signed integer, this is –81; invert all of the bits except the sign bit and add one and you get 1010011. So, if the unsigned integer is divided in half, the answer should be 86, which 01010110 is if you right-shift each digit by 1 place and put a 0 in as the new MSB. However, the signed integer, shifted once to the right, should be –40, which is binary 11010110. And, if you shift 10101101 (–81) to the right, but keep the MSB as a 1, you'll get the correct answer.

For this reason, if you need to apply bit-shifting operations, which come up quite a bit in cryptographic programming, you need to pay careful attention to the *signed-ness* of your variables.

## Big-Endian versus Little-Endian Number Formats

*Bits* are usually segmented into bytes, which are eight bits. (Another term you'll come across eventually is the *nybble*, which is four bits. Get it? A small *byte* is a *nybble*). Bits within a byte are logically numbered right-to-left in increasing order, just like decimal numbers are; in the decimal number 97,236, the 6 is the *least-significant* digit, because changing it alters the numeric value the least. The 9 is the *most-significant* digit; if the fifth digit of your bank balance changes overnight, for example, you'll probably start investigating immediately.

Binary numbers have a most-significant and a least-significant digit; by convention, they're written ordered left-to-right in decreasing significance, but this convention has no bearing on how the computer hardware actually implements them. In fact, Intel hardware orders them the other way internally. This implementation detail isn't important except for the fact that when a number expands beyond the value 255 that a single eight-bit byte can represent, it expands not to the left, but to the right. What goes on inside a single byte is none of your concern. Unfortunately, it is your concern if you use multiple bytes to represent a number and you want to communicate with other software systems.

The reason you need to care about this is that the computer systems of the early Internet used what is called a *big-endian* numbering convention, where bytes are listed in decreasing order of significance, with the most significant byte occurring first. If you want to transmit a number to one of these systems, one byte at a time, you must transmit the most significant byte first. If your computer stores the least-significant byte first in memory, which is known as the *little-endian* convention, you must reverse these bytes before transmitting, or the other side will get the wrong answer.

Listing A-1 illustrates the problem with internal byte ordering.

**Listing A-1:** "endian.c"

```
#include <stdio.h>
#include <string.h>

int main( int argc, char *argv[ ] )
{
  int i;
  int x = 3494632738; // 32 bit integer
  unsigned char y[ 4 ];        // same integer in 8 bit chunks

  memcpy( y, &x, sizeof( int ) );

  printf( "%x\n", x );
  for ( i = 0; i < 4; i++ )
  {
    printf( "%.02x, ", y[ i ] );
  }
  printf( "\n" );
}
```

If you run this on a little-endian machine, you see this:

```
[jdavies@localhost c]$ ./endian
d04bdd22
22, dd, 4b, d0,
```

As you see, although the most-significant-byte-first representation is d04bdd22, its internal representation is backward, and starts with the least significant byte. Unfortunately, if you stream this or any other integer over a socket connection, you are streaming it one byte at a time, and therefore in the wrong order. You can find numerous references in this text to the functions htonl and htons which convert from host to network longs and shorts, respectively, and ntohl and ntohs which reverse this. Network order is always big-endian — the dominant computers of the early Internet (which almost nobody actually uses anymore) firmly established this. Host order is whatever the individual host wants it to be — and this is almost always little endian these days.

# Installing TCPDump
# and OpenSSL

The code developed in this book has been tested to work on both Windows and Linux systems. If you want to follow the examples, you also need both OpenSSL and TCPdump installed locally. If you're on a Linux system, OpenSSL may already be available. TCPDump you usually need to install yourself. This appendix goes through the installation process for both systems for both software packages.

## Installing TCPDump

*TCPDump* is a handy, versatile utility that can capture and display every byte that's exchanged on any given socket in a system. Obviously, if you're working with network protocols, this can be incredibly useful, although it's less useful when you're working with SSL/TLS-secured traffic. After all, the whole point of SSL/TLS is to protect users from these sorts of packet sniffers; TCPDump can come in handy, however, when debugging certificate verification problems or handshake problems.

TCPDump has its roots in Unix/Linux systems and as such is a command-line tool. You might find a more modern incarnation called *Ethereal* (also sometimes called *Wireshark*) preferable, especially if you're running a Windows system. However, the examples in this book use TCPDump strictly because its textual output lends itself much better to print.

## Installing TCPDump on a Windows System

WinDump — TCPDump for Windows — depends on a library named *pcap*, a packet capture library. You can download both WinDump and pcap at the same website: `http://www.winpcap.org/windump/install/default.htm`.

To install, follow these steps:

1. Download the WinPcap self-installer and run it. The first screen of the installer appears as shown in Figure B-1. Click Next.

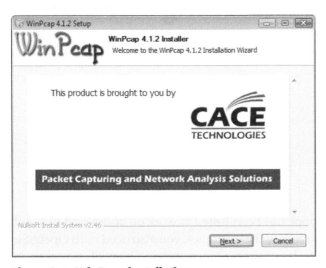

**Figure B-1 WinPcap installation**

2. Accept the defaults, including the Automatically Start Driver at Boot Time option.

3. After WinPcap has been successfully installed, download WinDump itself. This isn't distributed in an installable package, but is instead distributed simply as an executable. Download it and put it somewhere in your path; c:\windows\system32 will work.

Unfortunately, Windows doesn't provide an equivalent of Linux's loopback adapter. This means that if you want to sniff traffic, you have to sniff traffic remotely; either network two computers together and install the sample servers on a remote one, or connect to an external computer over the public Internet and sniff that traffic.

## Installing TCPDump on a Linux System

Your best bet on a Linux system is to just go ahead and install from source. The source distributions for libpcap and tcpdump are both available, at the time of this writing, from `http://www.tcpdump.org`. You need to install libpcap first, and tcpdump second; perform the standard

```
./config
make
sudo make install
```

on each.

The only potential challenge is that the kernel itself must have either the `CONFIG_PACKET` option built in, or the `af_packet` module available. Virtually all Linux distributions include a kernel with this option set. This is likely to only be a problem if you build your own custom kernel, in which case you may need to rebuild it.

Additionally, tcpdump must be run as root on a Linux system. An ordinary user can't communicate directly with the hardware in the way the tcpdump is required to in order to capture incoming packets.

# Installing OpenSSL

OpenSSL is a complete implementation of the client and server side of SSLv2, SSLv3, and TLS 1.0. It was developed from the SSLEay library originally written by Eric A. Young and Tim J. Hudson. At the time of this writing, the current version is 1.0.0. A complete OpenSSL installation also includes several useful utility programs that generate and display X.509 certificates, sign certificate requests, run test servers and clients, and so on. OpenSSL is the library that powers Apache's `mod_ssl`, which is still the most popular web server on the Internet. Many of this book's examples rely on OpenSSL utility programs, so you should have a version installed.

## Installing OpenSSL on a Windows System

OpenSSL is somewhat Unix/Linux-oriented, but you can install it on Windows. This just means that it runs on Windows; it's still entirely a command-line application, with no fancy graphical front-end. You need to roll up your sleeves and open a command prompt to do anything useful with OpenSSL.

As you probably know, Windows software is usually distributed in binary form, not in source code form as it traditionally is for Unix/Linux systems. Shining Light Productions maintains a binary distribution of OpenSSL that you can download from http://www.slproweb.com/products/Win32OpenSSL.html. This is a port of the main OpenSSL code to the Windows environment; every effort is made to ensure that both implementations are the same.

To install OpenSSL on a Windows system, use the following steps:

1. Download the Win32 OpenSSL vx.x.x installer; you should probably grab the latest one, but you need at least version 1.0.0 to follow all of the examples in this book.

2. Download the Visual C++ 2008 Redistributables package. There's a link to this on the Shining Light Productions site, but it takes you directly to the Microsoft download site; you must download this from Microsoft. Don't grab the latest version, either — grab the version that Win32 OpenSSL depends on.

3. Both the downloads are executable files; the Visual C++ 2008 redistributables download is called vcredist_x86.exe, and you should run it and follow the direction indicated by the graphical installer as shown in Figure B-2.

**Figure B-2  Visual C++ 2008 redistributables installation**

4. After this is complete, run the Win32OpenSSL-1_0_0a.exe installer. Accept the defaults and let it install into C:\OpenSSL-Win32.

## Installing OpenSSL on a Linux system

Your distribution may very well have OpenSSL installed already; check to see if you have it as well as what version you're running. However, you may want to download and build the latest copy from `http://www.openssl.org` anyway, just so that you have the most up-to-date code available. Just as with tcpdump, a source install is probably the easiest way to go; download the distributable and run

```
./config
make
sudo make install
```

You may want to skip the last step if you already have OpenSSL installed; you may have other products that rely on the version bundled with your distribution. If you don't install the custom binaries, you can find them under the `apps` directory of the distribution.

# Understanding the Pitfalls of SSLv2

With all the elements of a secure connection — cryptography, authentication, secure key exchange and message authentication — it should be a simple matter to put it all together securely, right? Well, as it turns out, even when all the pieces are in place, it's surprisingly easy to get subtly wrong. Just ask the original Netscape engineers who released SSLv2. On paper, they did everything right, but the protocol was found to have subtle, but fatal flaws after it had been widely released. To the credit of the Netscape protocol designers, everybody else thought that they had gotten everything right the first time around as well. It wasn't until the protocol had been intensively studied in action that the chinks in the armor began to show.

Because SSLv2 was widely disseminated before it was found to be flawed, it's interesting to start by examining exactly how it worked, and then move on to see what's wrong with the protocol. SSL was specified fairly rigorously and submitted as an IETF draft (`http://www.mozilla.org/projects/security/pki/nss/ssl/draft02.html`), but its flaws were discovered before it was accepted, so it's never been officially blessed by the IETF. Although SSLv2 has been deprecated, there are pockets of support for it, so you can easily find the protocol details.

This appendix details an SSLv2 implementation similar to the TLS implementation presented in Chapter 6. I've assumed you're familiar with Chapter 6; I discuss only the differences between the two implementations here. I do my best to avoid covering old ground, but since SSLv2 and TLS 1.0 have the same goals — to encrypt and authenticate a channel — it's unavoidable that some similar elements reappear here.

Listing C-1 details the SSL function prototypes. Notice that there's no `ssl_shutdown` routine; SSLv2 didn't explicitly mark the end of a secure session.

**Listing C-1:** "ssl.h" SSL function prototypes

```
int ssl_connect( int connection, SSLParameters *parameters );

int ssl_send( int connection, const char *application_data, int length,
              int options, SSLParameters *parameters );

int ssl_recv( int connection, char *target_buffer, int buffer_size,
              int options, SSLParameters *parameters );
```

You can modify the HTTP client implementation introduced in Chapter 1 as shown in Listing C-2 to be SSL-enabled by replacing socket-layer function calls with these new SSL library calls.

**Listing C-2:** "https.c" main routine with SSLv2 support

```
#define HTTPS_PORT        443
...
int main( int argc, char *argv[ ] )
{
...
  SSLParameters ssl_context;
...

  host_address.sin_family = AF_INET;
  host_address.sin_port = htons( HTTPS_PORT );
  memcpy( &host_address.sin_addr, host_name->h_addr_list[ 0 ],
    sizeof( struct in_addr ) );

  if ( connect( client_connection, ( struct sockaddr * ) &host_address,
                sizeof( host_address ) ) == -1 )
  {
    perror( "Unable to connect to host" );
    return 2;
  }

  if ( ssl_connect( client_connection, &ssl_context ) )
  {
    fprintf( stderr, "Error: unable to negotiate SSL connection.\n" );
    return 3;
  }

  http_get( client_connection, path, host, &ssl_context );

  display_result( client_connection, &ssl_context );
...
```

As you can see, the changes to the main routine, which establishes the HTTP connection, are fairly minimal. The changes to the `http_get` routine in Listing C-3 are similarly unobtrusive.

**Listing C-3:** "https.c" http_get with SSLv2 support

```
int http_get( int connection, const char *path, const char *host,
              SSLParameters *ssl_context )
{
  static char get_command[ MAX_GET_COMMAND ];

  sprintf( get_command, "GET /%s HTTP/1.1\r\n", path );

  if ( ssl_send( connection, get_command, strlen( get_command ),
                 0, ssl_context ) == -1 )
  {
    return -1;
  }

  sprintf( get_command, "Host: %s\r\n", host );
  if ( ssl_send( connection, get_command, strlen( get_command ),
                 0, ssl_context ) == -1 )
  {
    return -1;
  }

  strcpy( get_command, "Connection: Close\r\n\r\n" );
  if ( ssl_send( connection, get_command, strlen( get_command ),
                 0, ssl_context ) == -1 )
  {
    return -1;
  }

  return 0;
}
...
int display_result( int connection, SSLParameters *ssl_context )
{
  int received = 0;
  static char recv_buf[ BUFFER_SIZE + 1 ];

  // Can't exit when return value is 0 like in http.c, since empty SSL
  // messages can be sent (openssl does this)
  while ( ( received = ssl_recv( connection, recv_buf, BUFFER_SIZE,
                                 0, ssl_context ) ) >= 0 )
  {
    recv_buf[ received ] = '\0';
    printf( "data: %s", recv_buf );
  }
  printf( "\n" );
}
```

The application flow is exactly the same as before — in fact, other than the extra call to `ssl_connect` after the actual socket is connected, you could make this completely transparent by defining a few macros.

# Implementing the SSL Handshake

The bulk of the work in an SSL library is in the SSL handshake. When the `ssl_connect` function is called, the connection is unsecured. `ssl_connect` is primarily responsible for performing a secure key exchange and keeping track of the exchanged keys. Its job is to fill out the `SSLParameters` structure that's passed in as shown in Listing C-4.

**Listing C-4:** "ssl.h" SSLParameters declaration

```
// Technically, this is a variable-length parameter; the client can send
// between 16 and 32 bytes. Here, it's left as a fixed-length
// parameter.
#define CHALLENGE_LEN 16

typedef struct
{
  CipherSpec *active_cipher_spec;
  CipherSpec *proposed_cipher_spec;

  // Flow-control variables
  int got_server_hello;
  int got_server_verify;
  int got_server_finished;
  int handshake_finished;
  int connection_id_len;

  rsa_key server_public_key;

  unsigned char challenge[ CHALLENGE_LEN ];
  unsigned char *master_key;
  unsigned char *connection_id;

  void *read_state;
  void *write_state;
  unsigned char *read_key;
  unsigned char *write_key;
  unsigned char *read_iv;
  unsigned char *write_iv;
  int read_sequence_number;
  int write_sequence_number;

  unsigned char *unread_buffer;
  int           unread_length;
}
SSLParameters;
```

The `server_public_key` is the key with which RSA key exchange is performed as described in Chapter 3. (SSLv2 didn't support Diffie-Hellman key exchange.)

You should be familiar with the `read_key`, `write_key`, and `write_iv` from Chapter 2. There are a few internal variables to examine as you go through the implementation of `ssl_connect`.

The first two parameters are the `active_cipher_spec` and the `proposed_cipher_spec`. The `cipher_spec` describes exactly what encryption and MAC should be applied to each packet.

The format of a CipherSpec structure in Listing C-5 shouldn't be too surprising.

**Listing C-5:** "ssl.h" SSLv2 CipherSpec declaration

```
typedef struct
{
  int cipher_spec_code;

  int                    block_size;
  int                    IV_size;
  int                    key_size;
  int                    hash_size;
  void (*bulk_encrypt)( const unsigned char *plaintext,
                        const int plaintext_len,
                        unsigned char ciphertext[],
                        void *iv,
                        const unsigned char *key );
  void (*bulk_decrypt)( const unsigned char *ciphertext,
                        const int ciphertext_len,
                        unsigned char plaintext[],
                        void *iv,
                        const unsigned char *key );
  void (*new_digest)( digest_ctx *context );
}
CipherSpec;
```

Each cipher and MAC combination is identified by a unique, three-byte combination. SSLv2 defined 7 cipher/MAC combinations as shown in Listing C-6.

**Listing C-6:** "ssl.h" CipherSuite Declarations

```
#define SSL_CK_RC4_128_WITH_MD5                  0x800001
#define SSL_CK_DES_64_CBC_WITH_MD5               0x400006
#define SSL_CK_DES_192_EDE3_CBC_WITH_MD5         0xc00007
#define SSL_CK_RC4_128_EXPORT40_WITH_MD5         0x800002
#define SSL_CK_RC2_128_CBC_WITH_MD5              0x800003
#define SSL_CK_RC2_128_CBC_EXPORT40_WITH_MD5     0x800004
#define SSL_CK_IDEA_128_CBC_WITH_MD5             0x800005

#define SSL_PE_NO_CIPHER                     0x0100
#define SSL_PE_NO_CERTIFICATE                0x0200
#define SSL_PE_BAD_CERTIFICATE               0x0400
#define SSL_PE_UNSUPPORTED_CERTIFICATE_TYPE 0x0600
```

*(Continued)*

```
#define SSL_CT_X509_CERTIFICATE   1

#define SSL_MT_ERROR                  0
#define SSL_MT_CLIENT_HELLO           1
#define SSL_MT_CLIENT_MASTER_KEY      2
#define SSL_MT_CLIENT_FINISHED        3
#define SSL_MT_SERVER_HELLO           4
#define SSL_MT_SERVER_VERIFY          5
#define SSL_MT_SERVER_FINISHED        6
```

Because RC2 or IDEA weren't examined, they won't be supported here, although it should be fairly straightforward at this point how you might go about doing so. Notice that in all cases, the MAC algorithm is MD5; SHA is not supported in SSLv2. RC4 is supported, of course, and two other bulk cipher algorithms, DES and 3DES (identified here as DES_192_EDE3) are defined. In all cases, block ciphers use CBC chaining.

Also notice `SSL_CK_RC4_128_EXPORT40_WITH_MD5`. SSLv2 supports export-grade ciphers as discussed in Chapter 8, but it does so slightly differently than TLS does. The 128 in the cipher suite identifier, of course, identifies the key length in bits. However, `export40` mandates that only 40 bits of the key be protected by the key exchange algorithm; the remaining 88 bits are transmitted in the clear.

Add support for three of these ciphers in Listing C-7.

**Listing C-7:** "ssl.c" cipher spec declarations

```
#define NUM_CIPHER_SPECS  3
static CipherSpec specs[] =
{
  { SSL_CK_DES_64_CBC_WITH_MD5, 8, 8, 8, MD5_BYTE_SIZE, des_encrypt,
    des_decrypt, new_md5_digest },
  { SSL_CK_DES_192_EDE3_CBC_WITH_MD5, 8, 8, 24, MD5_BYTE_SIZE,
    des3_encrypt, des3_decrypt, new_md5_digest },
  { SSL_CK_RC4_128_WITH_MD5, 0, 0, 16, MD5_BYTE_SIZE, rc4_128_encrypt,
    rc4_128_decrypt, new_md5_digest }
};
```

So how does the SSL handshake work? First, the client advertises to the server which cipher specs it supports; it's not required to support all of them. The server responds by advising the client which specs *it* supports, as well as sending an X.509 certificate containing its public RSA key. Assuming there's at least one cipher spec that both sides understand, the client selects one, creates a key, encrypts it using the server's public key, and sends it on. This exchange is illustrated in Figure C-1.

As a double-check against man-in-the-middle attacks, the client also sends a *challenge* token, which the server must encrypt using the newly negotiated key before sending back the encrypted value, in its hello message. The client verifies that the decrypted token is the same as what was sent. If it's not, the handshake is rejected. Likewise, the server sends a *connection-id* that the client must send back, encrypted, after the key exchange succeeds.

The complete handshake is illustrated in Figure C-2.

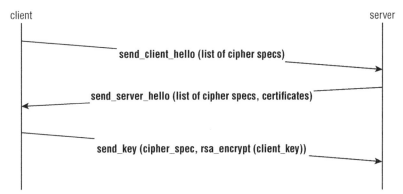

**Figure C-1:** SSLv2 opening handshake

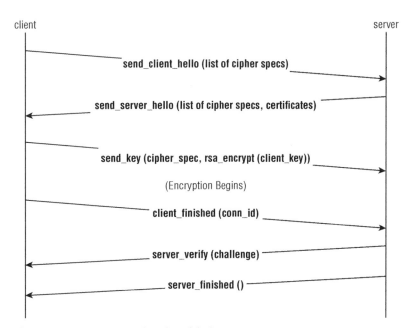

**Figure C-2:** SSLv2 complete handshake

The specification states that the client finished message should be sent before the server_verify is received. However, every working implementation sends the server_verify immediately after the key is received. This isn't a problem and doesn't affect the security of the implementation, but it is something that you need to be aware of when coding the SSLv2 handshake.

All six of these handshake messages are sent in the `ssl_connect` function. After the `server_finished` message has been received, the higher-level protocol begins.

The code for `ssl_connect` is shown in Listing C-8.

**Listing C-8:** "ssl.c" ssl_connect

```
int ssl_connect( int connection,
                 SSLParameters *parameters )
{
  init_parameters( parameters );

  if ( send_client_hello( connection, parameters ) == -1 )
  {
    return -1;
  }

  while ( !parameters->got_server_hello )
  {
    // set proposed_cipher_spec from server hello
    if ( receive_ssl_message( connection, NULL, 0, parameters ) == -1 )
    {
      return -1;
    }
  }

  // If proposed_cipher_spec is not set at this point, no cipher could
  // be negotiated
  if ( parameters->proposed_cipher_spec == NULL )
  {
    send_error( connection, SSL_PE_NO_CIPHER, parameters );
    return -1;
  }

  compute_keys( parameters );

  if ( send_client_master_key( connection, parameters ) == -1 )
  {
    return -1;
  }

  // From this point forward, everything is encrypted

  parameters->active_cipher_spec = parameters->proposed_cipher_spec;
  parameters->proposed_cipher_spec = NULL;

  if ( send_client_finished( connection, parameters ) == -1 )
  {
    return -1;
  }
```

```
  while ( !parameters->got_server_verify )
  {
    if ( receive_ssl_message( connection, NULL, 0, parameters ) == -1 )
    {
      return -1;
    }
  }

  while ( !parameters->got_server_finished )
  {
    if ( receive_ssl_message( connection, NULL, 0, parameters ) == -1 )
    {
      return -1;
    }
  }

  parameters->handshake_finished = 1;

  return 0;
}
```

The first call is to `init_parameters` in Listing C-9, which just resets all of the
`SSLParameters` values.

**Listing C-9:** "ssl.c" init_parameters

```
static void init_parameters( SSLParameters *parameters )
{
  int i;
  parameters->active_cipher_spec = NULL;
  parameters->proposed_cipher_spec = NULL;
  parameters->write_key = NULL;
  parameters->read_key = NULL;
  parameters->read_state = NULL;
  parameters->write_state = NULL;
  parameters->write_iv = NULL;
  parameters->read_iv = NULL;
  parameters->write_sequence_number = 0;
  parameters->read_sequence_number = 0;

  parameters->got_server_hello = 0;
  parameters->got_server_verify = 0;
  parameters->handshake_finished = 0;

  for ( i = 0; i < CHALLENGE_LEN; i++ )
  {
    // XXX this should be random
    parameters->challenge[ i ] = i;
  }

  parameters->master_key = NULL;
```

*(Continued)*

```
parameters->server_public_key.modulus = malloc( sizeof( huge ) );
parameters->server_public_key.exponent = malloc( sizeof( huge ) );
set_huge( parameters->server_public_key.modulus, 0 );
set_huge( parameters->server_public_key.exponent, 0 );

parameters->unread_buffer = NULL;
parameters->unread_length = 0;
}
```

You can easily match the remaining function calls with the sequence diagram in Figure C-2. If this function runs to completion, the caller can assume that a secure channel has been successfully negotiated and, for the most part, does not need to worry about it again. An implementation of each of the handshake functions is presented next.

## SSL Client Hello

The client is responsible for initiating an SSL handshake by sending the `ClientHello` message. If this isn't the first message that is sent, the server responds with an error and shuts down the socket. So what does this message look like? Listing C-10 defines in in C struct form.

**Listing C-10:** "ssl.h" ClientHello declaration

```
typedef struct
{
  unsigned char version_major;
  unsigned char version_minor;
  unsigned short cipher_specs_length;
  unsigned short session_id_length;
  unsigned short challenge_length;
  unsigned char *cipher_specs;
  unsigned char *session_id;
  unsigned char *challenge;
}
ClientHello;
```

I examine the specifics of the wire format in a minute, but first examine the contents of the client hello message. As you see, the client starts by announcing the version of SSL that it understands. You might expect this to be 2.0, but SSLv2 is actually version 0.2! Although SSLv2 was pretty widespread at one time, the designers considered it to be fairly experimental when it was proposed. It was never even actually officially "released."

Following the version number are the cipher specs that this client understands, a `sessionID`, and the `challenge` token. I have discussed the cipher specs and the challenge token, and session IDs are in place to support session resumption as detailed in Chapter 8.

Because each of the three parameters — cipher specs, session ID and challenge token — can be of variable length, length bytes are given for each before their values. You can build a client hello packet for a new, non-resumed, session as in Listing C-11.

**Listing C-11:** "ssl.c" send_client_hello

```
#define SSL_MT_CLIENT_HELLO                 1

static int send_client_hello( int connection,
                              SSLParameters *parameters )
{
  unsigned char *send_buffer, *write_buffer;
  int buf_len;
  int i;
  unsigned short network_number;
  int status = 0;
  ClientHello package;

  package.version_major = 0;
  package.version_minor = 2;
  package.cipher_specs_length = sizeof( specs ) / sizeof( CipherSpec );
  package.session_id_length = 0;
  package.challenge_length = CHALLENGE_LEN;

  // Each cipher spec takes up 3 bytes in SSLv2
  package.cipher_specs = malloc( sizeof( unsigned char ) * 3 *
    package.cipher_specs_length );
  package.session_id = malloc( sizeof( unsigned char ) *
    package.session_id_length );
  package.challenge = malloc( sizeof( unsigned char ) *
    package.challenge_length );

  buf_len = sizeof( unsigned char ) * 2 +
    sizeof( unsigned short ) * 3 +
    ( package.cipher_specs_length * 3 ) +
    package.session_id_length +
    package.challenge_length;

  for ( i = 0; i < package.cipher_specs_length; i++ )
  {
    memcpy( package.cipher_specs + ( i * 3 ),
      &specs[ i ].cipher_spec_code, 3 );
  }
  memcpy( package.challenge, parameters->challenge, CHALLENGE_LEN );

  write_buffer = send_buffer = malloc( buf_len );

  write_buffer = append_buffer( write_buffer,
    &package.version_major, 1 );
```

*(Continued)*

```
write_buffer = append_buffer( write_buffer,
  &package.version_minor, 1 );
network_number = htons( package.cipher_specs_length * 3 );
write_buffer = append_buffer( write_buffer,
  ( void * ) &network_number, 2 );
network_number = htons( package.session_id_length );
write_buffer = append_buffer( write_buffer,
  ( void * ) &network_number, 2 );
network_number = htons( package.challenge_length );
write_buffer = append_buffer( write_buffer,
  ( void * ) &network_number, 2 );
write_buffer = append_buffer( write_buffer, package.cipher_specs,
  package.cipher_specs_length * 3 );
write_buffer = append_buffer( write_buffer, package.session_id,
  package.session_id_length );
write_buffer = append_buffer( write_buffer, package.challenge,
  package.challenge_length );

status = send_handshake_message( connection, SSL_MT_CLIENT_HELLO,
  send_buffer, buf_len, parameters );

free( package.cipher_specs );
free( package.session_id );
free( package.challenge );
free( send_buffer );

return status;
}
```

This code should be straightforward to understand. First, fill out a `ClientHello` structure and then "flatten" it into a linear memory array with the byte ordering corrected. Then invoke `send_handshake_message` with a pointer to the flattened buffer.

Listing C-12 shows the `send_handshake_message` call. You pass in five parameters — the socket id (`connection`), the message type (client hello in this case), the buffer and its length, and finally the SSL parameters array you're building. This function is actually a small one.

**Listing C-12:** "ssl.c" send_handshake_message

```
static int send_handshake_message( int connection,
                                   unsigned char message_type,
                                   unsigned char *data,
                                   int data_len,
                                   SSLParameters *parameters )
{
  unsigned char *buffer;
  int buf_len;

  buf_len = data_len + 1;
```

```
  buffer = malloc( buf_len );
  buffer[ 0 ] = message_type;
  memcpy( buffer + 1, data, data_len );

  if ( send_message( connection, buffer, buf_len, parameters ) == -1 )
  {
    return -1;
  }

  free( buffer );

  return 0;
}
```

The `send_message` function in Listing C-13 actually writes something onto the socket itself.

**Listing C-13:** "ssl.c" send_message

```
static int send_message( int connection,
                         const unsigned char *data,
                         unsigned short data_len,
                         SSLParameters *parameters )
{
  unsigned char *buffer;
  int buf_len;
  unsigned short header_len;

  buf_len = data_len + 2;
  buffer = malloc( buf_len );
  header_len = htons( data_len );
  memcpy( buffer, &header_len, 2 );
  buffer[ 0 ] |= 0x80;  // indicate two-byte length
  memcpy( buffer + 2, data, data_len );

  if ( send( connection, ( void * ) buffer, buf_len, 0 ) < buf_len )
  {
    return -1;
  }

  free( buffer );

  return 0;
}
```

This function, like the last, just prepends yet another header in front of the data to be sent. This header consists of the two-byte length of the payload, followed by the payload. In the case of a handshake message, the first byte of the payload is a byte indicating which handshake message this is. Note that there's nothing to indicate that this is a handshake message to begin with. The receiver is supposed to keep track of where it is in the overall exchange. In other words, if the server hasn't gotten any data yet, it should assume that the next message it receives will be a `ClientHello` handshake message.

Every record transmitted over an SSL-secured channel must start with this header, including encrypted application data. When data is encrypted, the header is stripped off, the data is decrypted, and then it's passed up to the calling function.

The only potentially confusing part of the `send_message` function in Listing C-13 is this:

```
buffer[ 0 ] |= 0x80;   // indicate two-byte length
```

SSLv2 allows for two- or three-byte payload lengths. In a nod toward efficiency, the SSLv2 protocol designers borrowed a page from the ASN.1 protocol designers' playbook and used the first bit of the first byte to indicate the length of the length. If the most significant bit of the first byte is 1, this is a two-byte length. This function is extended for three-byte lengths later.

At this point, the server accepts the client hello, processes it or rejects it with an error, and sends back its own hello message.

## SSL Server Hello

The `ServerHello` message is structured as in Listing C-14.

**Listing C-14:** "ssl.h" ServerHello declaration

```
typedef struct
{
  unsigned char session_id_hit;
  unsigned char certificate_type;
  unsigned char server_version_major;
  unsigned char server_version_minor;
  unsigned short certificate_length;
  unsigned short cipher specs length;
  unsigned short connection_id_length;
  signed_x509_certificate certificate;
  unsigned char *cipher_specs;
  unsigned char *connection_id;
}
ServerHello;
```

The first byte, `session_id_hit`, is a true/false indicator of whether the session ID supplied was recognized by the server — 0 for false, 1 for true. Of course, if the client doesn't supply a session ID indicating a request for a brand-new session, `session_id_hit` is always 0.

The next byte is the `certificate_type`. This was added to support other certificates besides x.509, although no other certificate types were ever defined. This is followed by the version of SSL that the server understands. The specification isn't clear on what should be done if, in theory, the server understands a higher version of the protocol than the client, or if it doesn't understand the version that the client sent. However, this turned out to be a moot point. The next version of SSL was defined completely incompatibly with SSLv2, so version interoperability never came up. If the client sends an SSLv3+ handshake message to an SSLv2-only server, the server doesn't understand the message to begin with and immediately errors out. Likewise, if the client requests SSLv2, but the server would rather negotiate SSLv3 (which would be good advice), its only option is to reject the client hello with an error and hope the client retries with SSLv3 semantics. To complicate matters even further, there's no standard SSLv2 error message indicating that the protocol version requested isn't supported. As such, the only thing you ever see in these two bytes is 0, 2.

Finally, the server sends its variable length parameters — its certificate, its supported cipher specs, and its connection ID.

The certificate is in the format described in Chapter 5. Actually, the SSLv2 specification wasn't entirely clear on how the certificate should be encoded, but all implementations present the certificate in ANS.1 DER encoding. Notice that the definition only leaves room for one certificate — there's no concept of "certificate chaining" here. SSLv3/TLS 1.0 introduced certificate chaining, although without x.509v3 certificate extensions, this turned out to be a mistake.

The certificate is followed by a variable-length list of the cipher specs that the server supports. It's not clear whether this should be all of the ciphers that the server supports, or just the union of those that it supports with those that it knows the client supports. Remember, the client has already sent an exhaustive list of which ciphers it supports in its own hello message. However, it's unclear what use a client might make of the knowledge that the server supports a cipher that the client doesn't, so OpenSSL 0.9.8 returns the union of the two lists. Notice that SSLv2 lets the client finally select the cipher suite; SSLv3+ has the server do this — which actually makes more sense.

Finally, the server sends back a `connection_id` that serves the same purpose to the server that the `challenge` token served the client — to prevent replay attacks by forcing the client to encrypt a random value on each connection attempt. Note that the connection ID is *not* the session ID — that will be sent at the very end, in the server finished message.

After `ssl_connect` sends its `ClientHello` message, it waits until the server responds with a `ServerHello`:

```
while ( !parameters->got_server_hello )
{
  // set proposed_cipher_spec from server hello
```

```
        if ( receive_ssl_message( connection, NULL, 0, parameters ) == -1 )
        {
          return -1;
        }
      }
```

receive_ssl_message in Listing C-15 thus reads the data available from the socket, strips off the SSL header, and, if it's a handshake message, processes it.

**Listing C-15:** "ssl.c" receive_ssl_message

```c
static int receive_ssl_message( int connection,
                                char *target_buffer,
                                int target_bufsz,
                                SSLParameters *parameters )
{
  int status = 0;
  unsigned short message_len;
  unsigned short bytes_read;
  unsigned short remaining;
  unsigned char *buffer, *bufptr;

  // New message - read the length first
  if ( recv( connection, &message_len, 2, 0 ) <= 0 )
  {
    return -1;
  }

  message_len = ntohs( message_len );

  if ( message_len & 0x8000 )
  {
    // two-byte length
    message_len &= 0x7FFF;
  }
  // else TODO

  // Now read the rest of the message. This will fail if enough memory
  // isn't available, but this really should never be the case.
  bufptr = buffer = malloc( message_len );
  remaining = message_len;
  bytes_read = 0;
  while ( remaining )
  {
    if ( ( bytes_read = recv( connection, bufptr,
          remaining, 0 ) ) <= 0 )
    {
      return -1;
    }
    bufptr += bytes_read;
    remaining -= bytes_read;
```

```
  }

  if ( !parameters->handshake_finished )
  {
    switch ( buffer[ 0 ] )
    {
      case SSL_MT_ERROR:
        status = parse_server_error( parameters, buffer + 1 );
        return -1;
      case SSL_MT_SERVER_HELLO:
        status = parse_server_hello( parameters, buffer + 1 );
        if ( status == -1 )
        {
          send_error( connection,
                      SSL_PE_UNSUPPORTED_CERTIFICATE_TYPE,
                      parameters );
        }
        break;
      default:
        printf( "Skipping unrecognized handshake message %d\n",
          buffer[ 0 ] );
        break;
    }
  }

  free( buffer );

  return status;
}
```

First, read the length of the message. Remember that the first two or three bytes of every SSLv2 message must be the length of the following payload:

```
  if ( recv( connection, &message_len, 2, 0 ) <= 0 )
  {
    return -1;
  }

  message_len = ntohs( message_len );

  if ( message_len & 0x8000 )
  {
    // two-byte length
    message_len &= 0x7FFF;
  }
```

Because you know this is an SSLv2 connection, you know that at least two bytes should be available. Check the MSB of the first byte and, if it's 1, mask it out to get the actual length (you'll deal with the three-byte case below).

Next, read the whole payload into memory:

```
bufptr = buffer = malloc( message_len );
remaining = message_len;
bytes_read = 0;
while ( remaining )
{
  if ( ( bytes_read = recv( connection, bufptr,
         remaining, 0 ) ) <= 0 )
  {
    return -1;
  }
  bufptr += bytes_read;
  remaining -= bytes_read;
}
```

Finally, parse and handle the message. If the HandshakeFinished flag hasn't been set, then this message ought to be a handshake message, and the first byte should therefore be a handshake message type.

```
if ( !parameters->handshake_finished )
{
  switch ( buffer[ 0 ] )
  {
    case SSL_MT_ERROR:
      status = parse_server_error( parameters, buffer + 1 );
      return -1;
    case SSL_MT_SERVER_HELLO:
      status = parse_server_hello( parameters, buffer + 1 );
      if ( status == -1 )
      {
        send_error( connection,
                    SSL_PE_UNSUPPORTED_CERTIFICATE_TYPE,
                    parameters );
      }
      break;
    default:
      printf( "Skipping unrecognized handshake message %d\n",
        buffer[ 0 ] );
      break;
  }
}
```

The error message format is pretty simple as shown in Listing C-16: It's a two-byte error code. SSLv2 only defines four error codes, so one byte would have been more than enough, but the Netscape designers were being forward-thinking.

**Listing C-16:** "ssl.c" parse_server_error

```c
static int parse_server_error( SSLParameters *parameters,
                               unsigned char *buffer )
{
  unsigned short error_code;

  memcpy( &error_code, buffer, sizeof( unsigned short ) );
  error_code = ntohs( error_code );

  switch ( error_code )
  {
    case SSL_PE_NO_CIPHER:
      fprintf( stderr, "No common cipher.\n" );
      break;
    default:
      fprintf( stderr, "Unknown or unexpected error %d.\n",
        error_code );
      break;
  }

  return error_code;
}
```

Also notice that this routine only processes one type of error code, but there are three others spelled out in the specification: no certificate, bad certificate, and unsupported certificate. The server won't send any of these to the client — at least not in this implementation — so don't bother recognizing them.

The server hello message is accepted and parsed by the parse_server_hello function in Listing C-17.

**Listing C-17:** "ssl.c" parse_server_hello

```c
static int parse_server_hello( SSLParameters *parameters,
                               unsigned char *buffer )
{
  int i, j;
  int status = 0;
  ServerHello package;

  buffer = read_buffer( &package.session_id_hit, buffer, 1 );
  buffer = read_buffer( &package.certificate_type, buffer, 1 );
  buffer = read_buffer( &package.server_version_major, buffer, 1 );
  buffer = read_buffer( &package.server_version_minor, buffer, 1 );
  buffer = read_buffer( ( void * ) &package.certificate_length,
    buffer, 2 );
  package.certificate_length = ntohs( package.certificate_length );
  buffer = read_buffer( ( void * ) &package.cipher_specs_length,
    buffer, 2 );
```

*(Continued)*

```c
package.cipher_specs_length = ntohs( package.cipher_specs_length );
buffer = read_buffer( ( void * ) &package.connection_id_length,
  buffer, 2 );
package.connection_id_length = ntohs( package.connection_id_length );

// Only one of these was ever defined
if ( package.certificate_type == SSL_CT_X509_CERTIFICATE )
{
  init_x509_certificate( &package.certificate );
  if ( status = parse_x509_certificate( buffer,
      package.certificate_length, &package.certificate ) )
  {
    // Abort immediately if there's a problem reading the certificate
    return status;
  }
}
else
{
  printf( "Error - unrecognized certificate type %d\n",
          package.certificate_type );
  status = -1;
  return status;
}

buffer += package.certificate_length;
package.cipher_specs = malloc( package.cipher_specs_length );
buffer = read_buffer( package.cipher_specs, buffer,
  package.cipher_specs_length );
package.connection_id = malloc( package.connection_id_length );
buffer = read_buffer( package.connection_id, buffer,
  package.connection_id_length );

parameters->got_server_hello = 1;
// Copy connection ID into parameter state; this is needed for key
// computation, next
parameters->connection_id_len = package.connection_id_length;
parameters->connection_id = malloc( parameters->connection_id_len );
memcpy( parameters->connection_id, package.connection_id,
  parameters->connection_id_len );

// cycle through the list of cipher specs until one is found that
// matches
// XXX this will match the last one on the list
for ( i = 0; i < NUM_CIPHER_SPECS; i++ )
{
  for ( j = 0; j < package.cipher_specs_length; j++ )
  {
    if ( !memcmp( package.cipher_specs + ( j * 3 ),
                  &specs[ i ].cipher_spec_code, 3 ) )
    {
      parameters->proposed_cipher_spec = &specs[ i ];
```

```
      break;
    }
  }
}

// TODO validate the certificate/Check expiration date/Signer
copy_huge( parameters->server_public_key.modulus,
  package.certificate.tbsCertificate.subjectPublicKeyInfo.
  rsa_public_key.modulus );
copy_huge( parameters->server_public_key.exponent,
  package.certificate.tbsCertificate.subjectPublicKeyInfo.
  rsa_public_key.exponent );

free( package.cipher_specs );
free( package.connection_id );
free_x509_certificate( &package.certificate );

return status;
}
```

Part of the unflattening process involves a call to `parse_x509_certificate`, developed in Chapter 5. The process of parsing a certificate did not change between SSLv2 and TLS 1.2, although the certificate format itself grew a bit to include extensions and unique IDs.

Now, choose a cipher spec. Cycle through the list presented by the server and when you find one that's supported by this implementation, make that the `proposed_cipher_spec`. Also keep track of the connection ID, and the server's public RSA key.

Finally, if anything went wrong, `receive_ssl_message` will halt the process with an error message:

```
if ( status == -1 )
{
  send_error( connection,
              SSL_PE_UNSUPPORTED_CERTIFICATE_TYPE,
              parameters );
}
```

Sending an SSL error message in Listing C-18 is as simple as receiving one.

**Listing C-18:** "ssl.c" send_error

```
static int send_error( int connection,
                       unsigned short error_code,
                       SSLParameters *parameters )
{
  unsigned char buffer[ 3 ];
  unsigned short send_error;

  buffer[ 0 ] = SSL_MT_ERROR;
```

*(Continued)*

```
send_error = htons( error_code );
memcpy( buffer + 1, &send_error, sizeof( unsigned short ) );

if ( send_message( connection, buffer, 3, parameters ) == -1 )
{
  return -1;
}

return 0;
}
```

If a server hello response was received, and the certificate parsed OK, but the client and server had no common cipher specs, the `ssl_connect` responds with an error (note that the server could, and should, have done this instead of sending a server hello message):

```
if ( parameters->proposed_cipher_spec == NULL )
{
  send_error( connection, SSL_PE_NO_CIPHER, parameters );
  return -1;
}
```

If nothing has gone wrong, at this point you have a public key, a proposed cipher spec, and have exchanged both a challenge token and a connection ID. You now have enough information to compute keys.

## SSL Client Master Key

SSLv3+ generated keying material through a fairly complex pseudo-random function. SSLv2 didn't; instead, it just MD5-hashed a random master key along with the challenge token and the connection ID to produce as much keying material — read/write keys — as it needed. This master key is the same length as the cipher spec's symmetric key. Because you're only supporting three cipher specs here, this is easy to enumerate: 8 bytes for DES, 24 bytes for 3DES, and 16 bytes for 128-bit RC4.

Remember that the MD5 algorithm produces 16 bytes of output, regardless of the length of its input. For DES, that's as much key material as you need for both sides; each side needs 8 bytes. For RC4, you have to run the MD5 algorithm twice, and for 3DES, three times. So that you don't get the same key over and over again, you must also increment a counter on each run.

> **NOTE** The last published draft specification for SSLv2 (version 0.2, 1995) stated that the counter should not be used — that is, the byte itself should be omitted — for DES, which only requires 16 bytes of keying material. No implementation of SSLv2 ever followed this element of the specification; the code to omit this byte is shown in Listing C-19, but it's wrapped up in an `#if 0` to retain

compatibility with other SSLv2 implementations. Because the specification was never formally accepted by the IETF, the versions that don't follow it to the letter can't truly be said to be non-compliant; they had nothing to comply with.

Remember that the ssl_connect routine first invokes compute_keys and then send_client_master_key:

```
compute_keys( parameters );

if ( send_client_master_key( connection, parameters ) == -1 )
{
  return -1;
}
```

compute_keys in Listing C-19 creates a master secret and then runs the MD5 digest algorithm on it to generate the encryption keys.

**Listing C-19:** "ssl.c" compute_keys

```
static void compute_keys( SSLParameters *parameters )
{
  int i;
  digest_ctx md5_digest;
  int key_material_len;
  unsigned char *key_material, *key_material_ptr;
  char counter = '0';

  key_material_len = parameters->proposed_cipher_spec->key_size * 2;
  key_material_ptr = key_material = malloc( key_material_len );
  parameters->master_key = malloc(
    parameters->proposed_cipher_spec->key_size );

  for ( i = 0; i < parameters->proposed_cipher_spec->key_size; i++ )
  {
    // XXX should be random
    parameters->master_key[ i ] = i;
  }

// Technically wrong per the 1995 draft specification, but removed to
// maintain compatibility
#if 0
  if ( key_material_len <= 16 )
  {
    counter = '\0'; // don't use the counter here
  }
#endif

  while ( key_material_len )
  {
    new_md5_digest( &md5_digest );
```

*(Continued)*

```
    update_digest( &md5_digest, parameters->master_key,
      parameters->proposed_cipher_spec->key_size );
    if ( counter )
    {
      update_digest( &md5_digest, &counter, 1 );
      counter++;
    }
    update_digest( &md5_digest, parameters->challenge, CHALLENGE_LEN );
    update_digest( &md5_digest, parameters->connection_id,
      parameters->connection_id_len );

    finalize_digest( &md5_digest );

    memcpy( key_material_ptr, md5_digest.hash, MD5_BYTE_SIZE );
    key_material_ptr += MD5_BYTE_SIZE;
    key_material_len -= MD5_BYTE_SIZE;
  }

  parameters->read_key = malloc(
    parameters->proposed_cipher_spec->key_size );
  parameters->write_key = malloc(
    parameters->proposed_cipher_spec->key_size );
  memcpy( parameters->read_key, key_material,
    parameters->proposed_cipher_spec->key_size );
  memcpy( parameters->write_key, key_material +
    parameters->proposed_cipher_spec->key_size,
    parameters->proposed_cipher_spec->key_size );
  parameters->read_iv = malloc(
    parameters->proposed_cipher_spec->IV_size );
  parameters->write_iv = malloc(
    parameters->proposed_cipher_spec->IV_size );

  for ( i = 0; i < parameters->proposed_cipher_spec->IV_size; i++ )
  {
    // XXX these should be random
    parameters->read_iv[ i ] = i;
    parameters->write_iv[ i ] = i;
  }

  free( key_material );
}
```

First, figure out how much keying material you need: twice as much as the length of the key as specified in the cipher spec. Generate the master key, the same length as one key:

```
    key_material_len = parameters->proposed_cipher_spec->key_size * 2;
    key_material_ptr = key_material = malloc( key_material_len );
    parameters->master_key = malloc(
```

```
    parameters->proposed_cipher_spec->key_size );

  for ( i = 0; i < parameters->proposed_cipher_spec->key_size; i++ )
  {
    // XXX should be random
    parameters->master_key[ i ] = i;
  }
```

You need to store the master key because it is what is RSA encrypted and sent on to the server. Before you send it, though, go ahead and compute the keys themselves. The server needs to repeat the computation when it receives the RSA-encrypted master key:

```
  while ( key_material_len )
  {
    new_md5_digest( &md5_digest );

    update_digest( &md5_digest, parameters->master_key,
      parameters->proposed_cipher_spec->key_size );
    if ( counter )
    {
      update_digest( &md5_digest, &counter, 1 );
      counter++;
    }
    update_digest( &md5_digest, parameters->challenge, CHALLENGE_LEN );
    update_digest( &md5_digest, parameters->connection_id,
      parameters->connection_id_len );

    finalize_digest( &md5_digest );

    memcpy( key_material_ptr, md5_digest.hash, MD5_BYTE_SIZE );
    key_material_ptr += MD5_BYTE_SIZE;
    key_material_len -= MD5_BYTE_SIZE;
  }
```

Depending on how much keying material you need, cycle through the loop one to three times, creating a new digest, updating and finalizing it each time. The key material is stored in the temporary buffer `key_material`.

Next, copy the `key_material` buffer's contents into the read/write keys:

```
  parameters->read_key = malloc(
    parameters->proposed_cipher_spec->key_size );
  parameters->write_key = malloc(
    parameters->proposed_cipher_spec->key_size );
  memcpy( parameters->read_key, key_material,
    parameters->proposed_cipher_spec->key_size );
  memcpy( parameters->write_key, key_material +
    parameters->proposed_cipher_spec->key_size,
    parameters->proposed_cipher_spec->key_size );
```

```
Finally, generate the initialization vectors:
  parameters->read_iv = malloc(
    parameters->proposed_cipher_spec->IV_size );
  parameters->write_iv = malloc(
    parameters->proposed_cipher_spec->IV_size );

  for ( i = 0; i < parameters->proposed_cipher_spec->IV_size; i++ )
  {
    // XXX these should be random
    parameters->read_iv[ i ] = i;
    parameters->write_iv[ i ] = i;
  }
```

Notice that these values are not related to the master key — they're transmitted directly (in cleartext) to the server. This is generally not a problem because an attacker still needs to have access to the key in order to make use of the values. In fact, SSLv3 and TLS 1.0 computed the IVs from the master secret rather than transmitting them, which was later discovered to be a minor security flaw and TLS 1.1+ went back to transmitting them in cleartext just as SSLv2 did. (Although the flaw was related to carrying CBC state from one packet to the next, which SSLv2 also does.)

RC4 does not make use of an initialization vector, but it does need to keep track of its state from one call to the next. Insert a special RC4-only clause in here to support this case. If you have other stream ciphers, you should do something similar for them:

```
memcpy( parameters->write_key, key_material +
  parameters->proposed_cipher_spec->key_size,
  parameters->proposed_cipher_spec->key_size );


// Compute IV's (or, for stream cipher, initialize state vector)
if ( parameters->proposed_cipher_spec->cipher_spec_code ==
    SSL_CK_RC4_128_WITH_MD5 )
{
  rc4_state *read_state = malloc( sizeof( rc4_state ) );
  rc4_state *write_state = malloc( sizeof( rc4_state ) );
  read_state->i = read_state->j = write_state->i = write_state->j = 0;
  parameters->read_iv = NULL;
  parameters->write_iv = NULL;
  parameters->read_state = read_state;
  parameters->write_state = write_state;
  memset( read_state->S, '\0', RC4_STATE_ARRAY_LEN );
  memset( write_state->S, '\0', RC4_STATE_ARRAY_LEN );
}
else
{
  parameters->read_state = NULL;
```

```
        parameters->write_state = NULL;

    parameters->read_iv = malloc(
      parameters->proposed_cipher_spec->IV_size );
    parameters->write_iv = malloc(
      parameters->proposed_cipher_spec->IV_size );

    for ( i = 0; i < parameters->proposed_cipher_spec->IV_size; i++ )
    {
      // XXX these should be random
      parameters->read_iv[ i ] = i;
      parameters->write_iv[ i ] = i;
    }


}
```

Now that you have generated the master key and computed the session keys, the client must send the `client_master_key` message shown in Listing C-20.

**Listing C-20:** "ssl.h" ClientMasterKey declaration

```
typedef struct
{
  unsigned char cipher_kind[ 3 ];
  unsigned short clear_key_len;
  unsigned short encrypted_key_len;
  unsigned short key_arg_len;
  unsigned char *clear_key;
  unsigned char *encrypted_key;
  unsigned char *key_arg;
}
ClientMasterKey;
```

Note that the first element here is the cipher spec that has been chosen. In SSLv2, it's up to the client to select a cipher spec that both it and the server understand. It's important that this be transmitted at this point because the server needs to know how much key material to generate — that is, how many times to run the MD5 algorithm over the master key.

Three variable-length arguments follow the selected cipher spec. The clear_key, the encrypted_key, and the key_arg. Recall that SSLv2 specifically supports "export grade" ciphers such as RC4_128_EXPORT40. What this means is that 40 bits of the master key are encrypted and the other 88 bits are transmitted in cleartext. If the cipher spec calls for any unencrypted key material, the unencrypted bytes are transmitted in clear_key. This is the only difference between "export grade" and standard ciphers; the actual key is 128 bits (for example), but a potential attacker has 88 of them to start with.

The encrypted bytes are encrypted using the server's RSA key as described in Chapter 3. Finally, the key_arg is the optional area for the initialization vector.

The SSLv2 specification isn't clear on how many initialization vectors you should use. Should each side have its own initialization vector, or should the same one be used for both client and server? OpenSSL expects a single initialization vector that both sides start with (of course, they diverge immediately), so follow suit.

The `send_client_master_key` function is shown in Listing C-21.

**Listing C-21:** "ssl.c" send_client_master_key

```
static int send_client_master_key( int connection,
                                    SSLParameters *parameters )
{
  int status = 0;
  unsigned char *send_buffer, *write_buffer;
  int buf_len;
  unsigned short network_number;
  ClientMasterKey package;

  memcpy( package.cipher_kind,
    &parameters->proposed_cipher_spec->cipher_spec_code, 3 );
  package.clear_key_len = 0;  // not supporting export ciphers
  package.encrypted_key_len = rsa_encrypt( parameters->master_key,
    parameters->proposed_cipher_spec->key_size,
    &package.encrypted_key, &parameters->server_public_key );
  package.key_arg_len = parameters->proposed_cipher_spec->IV_size;

  package.clear_key = malloc( sizeof( unsigned char ) *
    package.clear_key_len );
  package.key_arg = malloc( sizeof( unsigned char ) *
    package.key_arg_len );

  memcpy( package.key_arg, parameters->read_iv,
    parameters->proposed_cipher_spec->IV_size );

  buf_len = sizeof( unsigned char ) * 3 +
    sizeof( unsigned short ) * 3 +
    package.clear_key_len +
    package.encrypted_key_len +
    package.key_arg_len;

  send_buffer = write_buffer = malloc( buf_len );

  write_buffer = append_buffer( write_buffer, package.cipher_kind, 3 );
  network_number = htons( package.clear_key_len );
  write_buffer = append_buffer( write_buffer,
    ( void * ) &network_number, 2 );
  network_number = htons( package.encrypted_key_len );
  write_buffer = append_buffer( write_buffer,
    ( void * ) &network_number, 2 );
```

```
network_number = htons( package.key_arg_len );
write_buffer = append_buffer( write_buffer,
  ( void * ) &network_number, 2 );
write_buffer = append_buffer( write_buffer, package.clear_key,
  package.clear_key_len );
write_buffer = append_buffer( write_buffer, package.encrypted_key,
  package.encrypted_key_len );
write_buffer = append_buffer( write_buffer, package.key_arg,
  package.key_arg_len );

status = send_handshake_message( connection,
  SSL_MT_CLIENT_MASTER_KEY, send_buffer, buf_len, parameters );

free( package.clear_key );
free( package.encrypted_key );
free( package.key_arg );
free( send_buffer );

return status;
}
```

First fill out a `ClientMasterKey` struct, flatten it, and then send it as an `SSL_MT_CLIENT_MASTER_KEY` handshake message. Notice that `clear_key` is always 0 (no support for export-grade ciphers), and that `rsa_encrypt`, from Chapter 3, is invoked to encrypt the master key. Otherwise, this works just like the previous two handshake messages.

## SSL Client Finished

As noted above, the specification makes it appear that the client should send `client_finished` before expecting the next message, a `server_verify`. Technically speaking, it doesn't really matter; neither of these two messages depends on the other. In general, the server sends the `server_verify` immediately without waiting for the `client_finished`, and the client sends `client_finished` without waiting for server verify, so these two messages can and do "pass" each other in transmit. Go ahead and follow the specification's advice and send the client finished before looking for the server verify.

`ClientFinished` is a pretty simple message, as shown in Listing C-22.

**Listing C-22:** "ssl.h" ClientFinished declaration

```
typedef struct
{
  unsigned char *connection_id;
}
ClientFinished;
```

As you can see, it just reflects the `connection_id` back to the server.

However, what makes this a bit more complicated, and useful, is that the whole `client_finished` message — and every subsequent packet transmitted over this connection — should be encrypted with the newly negotiated session keys. `ssl_connect` makes the "pending" cipher spec the active one:

```
parameters->active_cipher_spec = parameters->proposed_cipher_spec;
parameters->proposed_cipher_spec = NULL;
```

Sending the `client_finished` method in Listing C-23 is straightforward.

**Listing C-23:** "ssl.c" send_client_finished

```
static int send_client_finished( int connection,
                                 SSLParameters *parameters )
{
  int status = 0;
  unsigned char *send_buffer, *write_buffer;
  int buf_len;
  ClientFinished package;

  package.connection_id = malloc( parameters->connection_id_len );
  memcpy( package.connection_id, parameters->connection_id,
    parameters->connection_id_len );

  buf_len = parameters->connection_id_len;
  write_buffer = send_buffer = malloc( buf_len );

  write_buffer = append_buffer( write_buffer, package.connection_id,
    parameters->connection_id_len );

  status = send_handshake_message( connection, SSL_MT_CLIENT_FINISHED,
    send_buffer, buf_len, parameters );

  free( send_buffer );
  free( package.connection_id );

  return status;
}
```

There shouldn't be any surprises here. Fill in a structure, flatten it, and send it via `send_handshake_message`.

To actually support encryption, extend `send_message` in Listing C-24 to check to see if the `active_cipher_spec` parameter of the `SSLParameters` argument in non-null. If it is, it is used to encrypt and MAC the packet.

**Listing C-24:** "ssl.c" send_message with encryption support

```
if ( parameters->active_cipher_spec == NULL )
{
```

```
    // TODO support three-byte headers (when encrypting)
    buf_len = data_len + 2;
    buffer = malloc( buf_len );
    header_len = htons( data_len );
    memcpy( buffer, &header_len, 2 );
    buffer[ 0 ] |= 0x80;  // indicate two-byte length
    memcpy( buffer + 2, data, data_len );
}
else
{
  int padding = 0;
  unsigned char *encrypted, *encrypt_buf, *mac_buf;

  if ( parameters->active_cipher_spec->block_size )
  {
    padding = parameters->active_cipher_spec->block_size -
      ( data_len % parameters->active_cipher_spec->block_size );
  }

  buf_len = 3 + // sizeof header
            parameters->active_cipher_spec->hash_size + // sizeof mac
            data_len + // sizeof data
            padding; // sizeof padding
  buffer = malloc( buf_len );
  header_len = htons( buf_len - 3 );
  memcpy( buffer, &header_len, 2 );
  buffer[ 2 ] = padding;
  encrypt_buf = malloc( buf_len - 3 );
  encrypted = malloc( buf_len - 3 );
  memset( encrypt_buf, '\0', buf_len - 3 );

  // Insert a MAC at the start of "encrypt_buf"
  mac_buf = malloc( data_len + padding );
  memset( mac_buf, '\0', data_len + padding );
  memcpy( mac_buf, data, data_len );
  add_mac( encrypt_buf, mac_buf, data_len + padding, parameters );
  free( mac_buf );

  // Add the data (padding was already set to zeros)
  memcpy( encrypt_buf + parameters->active_cipher_spec->hash_size,
    data, data_len );

  // Finally encrypt the whole thing
  parameters->active_cipher_spec->bulk_encrypt( encrypt_buf,
    buf_len - 3, encrypted,
    parameters->write_state ? parameters->write_state :
                              parameters->write_iv,
    parameters->write_key );

  memcpy( buffer + 3, encrypted, buf_len - 3 );
```

*(Continued)*

```
    free( encrypt_buf );
    free( encrypted );
  }

  if ( send( connection, ( void * ) buffer, buf_len, 0 ) < buf_len )
  {
    return -1;
  }

  parameters->write_sequence_number++;

  free( buffer );
}
```

As you can see, the bulk of `send_message` is now handling encryption. Check to see if the active cipher spec requires that the message be padded to a certain multiple:

```
    if ( parameters->active_cipher_spec->block_size )
    {
      padding = parameters->active_cipher_spec->block_size -
        ( data_len % parameters->active_cipher_spec->block_size );
    }
```

In practice, `block_size` is always either 8 (for DES or 3DES) or 0 (for RC4).

Next, allocate enough space for the SSLv2 header, which now is three bytes instead of two, the MAC, the data itself, and the padding.

```
    buf_len = 3 + // sizeof header
              parameters->active_cipher_spec->hash_size + // sizeof mac
              data_len + // sizeof data
              padding; // sizeof padding
    buffer = malloc( buf_len );
    header_len = htons( buf_len - 3 );
    memcpy( buffer, &header_len, 2 );
    buffer[ 2 ] = padding;
    encrypt_buf = malloc( buf_len - 3 );
    encrypted = malloc( buf_len - 3 );
    memset( encrypt_buf, '\0', buf_len - 3 );
```

Notice the allocation of two buffers. `buffer` is the memory array that is actually sent over the connection. This is where the three-byte header is passed. Actually, the first two bytes are the length of the message, just as they were in the two-byte header. The third byte encodes the amount of padding on the end of the message, which is required to be present even if the cipher spec is a stream cipher.

**NOTE** Technically, this code is wrong. The next-to-most-significant bit in a three-byte header is reserved; if bit 6 is set to 1, then the message should be treated as a "security escape." What this might mean and what you might do when such a message is received has never been defined, so you don't have to worry about it. However, technically you ought to ensure that the size of the outgoing packet is never greater than 2^14 = 16,384 bytes.

The second buffer, `encrypted`, is the buffer that's passed into the bulk encryption routine. You may wonder why another buffer is needed for this purpose. After all, the input parameter `data` is the plaintext to be encrypted. Well, SSLv2 requires that you prepend this data with a MAC and then encrypt the whole thing.

So, the next thing to do is to generate the MAC in the first *mac-length* bytes of the `encrypt` buffer.

```
mac_buf = malloc( data_len + padding );
memset( mac_buf, '\0', data_len + padding );
memcpy( mac_buf, data, data_len );
add_mac( encrypt_buf, mac_buf, data_len + padding, parameters );
free( mac_buf );
```

As you can see, another buffer is used to MAC the data to be sent; this includes the plaintext data, plus the padding (the padding must be MAC'ed). Invoke `add_mac` in Listing C-25 to actually generate the MAC.

**Listing C-25:** "ssl.c" add_mac

```
static void add_mac( unsigned char *target,
                     const unsigned char *src,
                     int src_len,
                     SSLParameters *parameters )
{
  digest_ctx ctx;
  int sequence_number;

  parameters->active_cipher_spec->new_digest( &ctx );
  update_digest( &ctx, parameters->write_key,
    parameters->active_cipher_spec->key_size );
  update_digest( &ctx, src, src_len );
  sequence_number = htonl( parameters->write_sequence_number );
  update_digest( &ctx, ( unsigned char * ) &sequence_number,
    sizeof( int ) );
  finalize_digest( &ctx );

  memcpy( target, ctx.hash,
    parameters->active_cipher_spec->hash_size );
}
```

Notice that SSLv2 does *not* use the HMAC function. HMAC wasn't actually specified until 1997. Instead, SSLv2 uses a slightly weaker form that concatenates the write secret, the data, and a sequence number, and then securely hashes this combination of things.

Getting back to `send_message`, you have a data buffer with the MAC of the plaintext data. Now, from the `data` pointer that was passed into the function in the first place, copy the actual plaintext after it and encrypt the whole thing into the target buffer.

```
// Add the data (padding was already set to zeros)
memcpy( encrypt_buf + parameters->active_cipher_spec->hash_size,
  data, data_len );

// Finally encrypt the whole thing
parameters->active_cipher_spec->bulk_encrypt( encrypt_buf,
  buf_len - 3, encrypted,
  parameters->write_state ? parameters->write_state :
                          parameters->write_iv,
  parameters->write_key );
```

Now, the `encrypted` buffer contains the MAC, the plaintext, and the padding, all encrypted using the client write key. Finally, copy the encrypted data into the target `buffer`:

```
  memcpy( buffer + 3, encrypted, buf_len - 3 );

  free( encrypt_buf );
  free( encrypted );
}
```

The only other addition to `send_message` is the following, which updates the sequence number upon which the `add_mac` function relies:

```
parameters->write_sequence_number++;
```

The server receives this encrypted message, decrypts it using the negotiated keys, and verifies the MAC. If decryption and MAC verification succeed, the server finally verifies that the connection ID received matches the one that it sent.

What if any of these steps fail? The specification states that a MAC verify or decrypt error "is to be treated as if an 'I/O Error' had occurred (i.e. an unrecoverable error is asserted and the connection is closed)." However, it doesn't define any unrecoverable (or recoverable, for that matter) error codes describing this scenario. As a result, all existing implementations simply shut down the socket on error.

## SSL Server Verify

As discussed earlier, OpenSSL goes ahead and sends the `server_verify` as soon as the key exchange is complete, although the specification suggests that it should wait until the `client_finished` is received correctly. The `ServerVerify` message in Listing C-26 looks just like, and serves the same purpose as, the client finished message.

**Listing C-26:** "ssl.h" ServerVerify declaration

```
typedef struct
{
  unsigned char challenge[ CHALLENGE_LEN ];
}
ServerVerify;
```

**NOTE** There's also a server finished message that is *not* analogous to the client finished.

Here the server MACs, encrypts, and reflects back the client's challenge token. The client must verify that it can be decrypted, verified, and that it matches what the client sent initially. As discussed earlier, if anything goes wrong, no specific error code is sent. The connection is just closed.

After sending client_finished, ssl_connect starts looking for server_verify:

```
while ( !parameters->got_server_verify )
{
  if ( receive_ssl_message( connection, NULL, 0, parameters ) == -1 )
  {
    return -1;
  }
}
```

Of course, because the key exchange has been completed, this message is encrypted. You can still invoke receive_ssl_message here, but it has to be extended to handle encrypted incoming messages.

First of all, recognize and process the three-byte lengths described in the previous section as shown in Listing C-27.

**Listing C-27:** "ssl.c" receive_ssl_message with encryption support

```
  unsigned char padding_len = 0;
...
  if ( message_len & 0x8000 )
  {
    // two-byte length
    message_len &= 0x7FFF;
  }
  else
  {
    // three-byte length, include a padding value
    if ( recv( connection, &padding_len, 1, 0 ) <= 0 )
    {
      return -1;
    }
  }
```

As you may recall from the previous section, the first two bytes are the length of the payload, and the third byte is the length of the padding (if any).

Next, check to see if a cipher spec is active and if so, apply it:

```
    bufptr += bytes_read;
    remaining -= bytes_read;
  }


  // Decrypt if a cipher spec is active
  if ( parameters->active_cipher_spec != NULL )
  {
    unsigned char *decrypted = malloc( message_len );
    int mac_len = parameters->active_cipher_spec->hash_size;
    parameters->active_cipher_spec->bulk_decrypt( buffer, message_len,
      decrypted,
      parameters->read_state ? parameters->read_state :
                                parameters->read_iv,
      parameters->read_key );
    if ( !verify_mac( decrypted + mac_len, message_len - mac_len,
                      decrypted,  mac_len, parameters  ) )
    {
      return -1;
    }
    free( buffer );
    buffer = malloc( message_len - mac_len - padding_len );
    memcpy( buffer, decrypted + mac_len,
      message_len - mac_len - padding_len );
    message_len = message_len - mac_len, padding_len;

    free( decrypted );
  }


  parameters->read_sequence_number++;
```

This more or less parallels the changes made to `send_message`, in Listing C-24. First allocate a `decrypted` buffer and decrypt the whole packet into it. Next, the MAC is verified in Listing C-28.

**Listing C-28:** "ssl.c" verify_mac

```
static int verify_mac( const unsigned char *data,
                       int data_len,
                       const unsigned char *mac,
                       int mac_len,
                       SSLParameters *parameters )
{
  digest_ctx ctx;
  int sequence_number;
```

```
  parameters->active_cipher_spec->new_digest( &ctx );

  update_digest( &ctx, parameters->read_key,
    parameters->active_cipher_spec->key_size );
  update_digest( &ctx, data, data_len );
  sequence_number = htonl( parameters->read_sequence_number );
  update_digest( &ctx, ( unsigned char * ) &sequence_number,
    sizeof( int ) );
  finalize_digest( &ctx );

  return ( !memcmp( ctx.hash, mac, mac_len ) );
}
```

This works just like add_mac. In fact, the only differences here are that it uses the read_key as the first *n* bytes of the MAC buffer, and rather than memcpy-ing the resultant MAC to a target output buffer, it instead does a memcmp and returns a true or false.

If the MAC verifies properly, the decrypted data is copied into a target buffer and processed just as if it had been received as plaintext. Add a third "case arm" to the handshake processing switch:

```
  if ( !parameters->handshake_finished )
  {
    switch ( buffer[ 0 ] )
    {

...

      case SSL_MT_SERVER_VERIFY:
        status = parse_server_verify( parameters, buffer + 1 );
        break;
```

Parsing the ServerVerify, after it's been successfully decrypted, is straightforward, as shown in Listing C-29.

**Listing C-29:** "ssl.c" parse_server_verify

```
static int parse_server_verify( SSLParameters *parameters,
                                  const unsigned char *buf )
{
  ServerVerify package;

  memcpy( package.challenge, buf, CHALLENGE_LEN );

  parameters->got_server_verify = 1;

  return ( !memcmp( parameters->challenge, package.challenge,
    CHALLENGE_LEN ) );
}
```

Compare the challenge token sent back by the server with the challenge token sent in the "hello" message, and return an error code if they don't match. If the two tokens don't match, this error code is a signal to the outer function to close the socket.

## SSL Server Finished

At this point, the secure channel has been all but negotiated. The only thing remaining is the `server_finished` message. This also has only one field in Listing C-30.

**Listing C-30:** "ssl.h" ServerFinished declaration

```
typedef struct
{
  unsigned char *session_id;
}
ServerFinished;
```

This is the session ID, chosen by the server, that can be passed in a later `client_hello` message to resume this session.

The `ssl_connect` function waits until this is received and, after it has been, marks the handshake as complete:

```
    while ( !parameters->got_server_finished )
    {
      if ( receive_ssl_message( connection, NULL, 0, parameters ) == -1 )
      {
        return -1;
      }
    }

    parameters->handshake_finished = 1;
```

Server finished is the final case arm in `receive_ssl_message`'s handshake switch:

```
    if ( !parameters->handshake_finished )
    {
      switch ( buffer[ 0 ] )
      {
...
        case SSL_MT_SERVER_FINISHED:
          status = parse_server_finished( parameters, buffer + 1,
            message_len );
          break;
```

For this implementation, `parse_server_finished` in Listing C-31 is a formality because the session ID isn't stored anywhere.

**Listing C-31:** "ssl.c" parse_server_finished

```
static int parse_server_finished( SSLParameters *parameters,
                                  const unsigned char *buf,
                                  int buf_len )
{
  ServerFinished package;

  package.session_id = malloc( buf_len - 1 );
  memcpy( package.session_id, buf, buf_len - 1 );

  parameters->got_server_finished = 1;

  free( package.session_id );

  return 0;
}
```

At this point, `ssl_connect` returns with a successful status code, and the calling code continues processing as if no SSL handshake had been performed. The only difference, as shown earlier, is that instead of calling the socket-layer `send` and `recv` messages, it instead calls `ssl_send` and `ssl_recv`.

## SSL send

`ssl_send` in Listing C-32 is a pretty simple function.

**Listing C-32:** "ssl.c" ssl_send

```
int ssl_send( int connection, const char *application_data, int length,
              int options,  SSLParameters *parameters )
{
  return ( send_message( connection, application_data, length,
                         parameters ) );
}
```

All of the heavy lifting is done by the `send_message` function. If a key exchange has been successfully performed on the socket identified by `connection`, `send_message` pads, MAC's, and encrypts the `application_data`.

## SSL recv

`ssl_recv` in Listing C-33 is just as simple.

**Listing C-33:** "ssl.c" ssl_recv

```
int ssl_recv( int connection, char *target_buffer, int buffer_size,
              int options, SSLParameters *parameters )
{
  return receive_ssl_message( connection, target_buffer,
                              buffer_size, parameters );
}
```

However, because an SSL packet can be up to 16,384 bytes in length, either the caller should always supply a buffer of this length, or `ssl_recv` needs to deal with the case where the input buffer is smaller than the SSL packet. This means that it needs to remember what was left over but not read and passes that back to the caller on the next `ssl_recv`.

```
if ( !parameters->handshake_finished )
{

...

}
else
{
  // If the handshake is finished, the app should be expecting data;
  // return it
  if ( message_len > target_bufsz )
  {
    memcpy( target_buffer, buffer, target_bufsz );
    status = target_bufsz;

    // Store the remaining data so that the next "read" call just
    // picks it up
    parameters->unread_length = message_len - target_bufsz;
    parameters->unread_buffer = malloc( parameters->unread_length );
    memcpy( parameters->unread_buffer, buffer + target_bufsz,
            parameters->unread_length );
  }
  else
  {
    memcpy( target_buffer, buffer, message_len );
    status = message_len;
  }
}
```

Finally, near the top of `ssl_recv`, check to see if there was any unread data from the previous call:

```
if ( parameters->unread_length )
{
  buffer = parameters->unread_buffer;
  message_len = parameters->unread_length;
  parameters->unread_buffer = NULL;
  parameters->unread_length = 0;
}
else
{
  // New message - read the length first
  if ( read( connection, &message_len, 2, 0 ) <= 0 )
  {
    return -1;
```

SSLv2 didn't give any special treatment to connection closing as SSLv3 did, so closing the socket requires no special processing.

## Examining an HTTPS End-to-End Example

I'm sure you'd like to see this code in action. It's very unlikely that you can find a public website that accepts an SSLv2 connection, so if you want to see this code run you have to start a server locally. You can do this with OpenSSL; it has a built-in s_server command that is designed specifically to test implementations. You need to supply a path to a certificate and the corresponding private key; Chapter 5 discusses how to generate these.

On the command line, run

```
[jdavies@localhost ssl]$ openssl s_server -accept 8443 -cert cert.pem \
  -key key.pem
Enter pass phrase for key.pem:
Using default temp DH parameters
ACCEPT
```

Now, run the https application developed in this appendix:

```
[jdavies@localhost ssl]$ ./https https://localhost:8443/index.html
Connecting to host 'localhost' on port 8443
Connection complete; negotiating SSL parameters
Retrieving document: 'index.html'
sending: GET /index.html HTTP/1.1
Displaying Response...
data: HTTP/1.0 200 ok
Content-type: text/html

<HTML><BODY BGCOLOR="#ffffff">
<pre>

s_server -accept 8443 -cert cert.pem -key key.pem -www
Ciphers supported in s_server binary
...
```

## Viewing the TCPDump Output

To see what's going on beneath the hood, you can run the tcpdump application while you run the https application. You need to make sure to listen on the "loopback" interface because you're running both client and server on your localhost. If you listen on your actual Ethernet card, you won't see any traffic.

With tcpdump enabled, if you re-run the https command again, you see something like this:

```
[root@localhost ssl]# /usr/sbin/tcpdump -s 0 -x -i lo tcp port 8443
listening on lo, link-type EN10MB (Ethernet), capture size 65535 bytes
```

```
15:57:38.845640 IP localhost.localdomain.50704 >
localhost.localdomain.pcsync-https: S 2610069118:2610069118(0)
win 32792 <mss 16396,sackOK,timestamp 24215142 0,nop,wscale 7>
        0x0000:  4500 003c 0018 4000 4006 3ca2 7f00 0001
        0x0010:  7f00 0001 c610 20fb 9b92 7e7e 0000 0000
        0x0020:  a002 8018 0e99 0000 0204 400c 0402 080a
        0x0030:  0171 7e66 0000 0000 0103 0307
```

. . .

Recall however that the HTTPS protocol (but not necessarily SSL!) mandates that the very first packet sent after the connection is established must be an SSL ClientHello. The next packet, therefore, is

```
15:57:38.846983 IP localhost.localdomain.50704 >
localhost.localdomain.pcsync-https: P 1:37(36)
ack 1 win 257 <nop,nop,timestamp 24215144 24215142>
        0x0000:  4500 0058 001a 4000 4006 3c84 7f00 0001
        0x0010:  7f00 0001 c610 20fb 9b92 7e7f 9bb0 f1f9
        0x0020:  8018 0101 fe4c 0000 0101 080a 0171 7e68
        0x0030:  0171 7e66 8022 0100 0200 0900 0000 1006
        0x0040:  0040 0100 8007 00c0 0001 0203 0405 0607
        0x0050:  0809 0a0b 0c0d 0e0f
```

The TCP header ends at byte 0x0034, so the SSL data begins at 0x0035. If you refer to the specification for the ClientHello, you see that it starts with a version major and a version minor byte. However, this is preceded by a two-byte length field with the high-bit set to "1" to indicate that this is a two-, rather than three-, byte header. Removing the high-bit, you get a length of 34 bytes (0x22 = 34 base 10), which you can see matches the packet length. This is followed by the handshake type, a one-byte 0x01, which is the code for ClientHello. The receiver is responsible for keeping track of the fact that this is a new connection, and that a handshake message is expected.

The length header is followed by the ClientHello packet:

```
unsigned char version_major;       // 00
unsigned char version_minor;       // 02
unsigned short cipher_specs_length;  // 0009
unsigned short session_id_length;    // 0000
unsigned short challenge_length;   // 0010
unsigned char *cipher_specs;       // 0600400100800700c0
unsigned char *session_id;         // (empty)
unsigned char *challenge;          // 000102030405060708090a0b0c0d0e0f
```

You can compare this to the data that was loaded in the send_client_hello function; remember that the challenge, which actually ought to be a random number, is just an increasing sequence of bytes.

The server responds with its own hello, where it informs the client which ciphers it supports, and provides a public key, wrapped up in an X.509 certificate.

```
15:57:38.847302 IP localhost.localdomain.pcsync-https >
localhost.localdomain.50704: P 1:893(892) ack 37 win 256
<nop,nop,timestamp 24215144 24215144>
        0x0000:  4500 03b0 8fa0 4000 4006 a9a5 7f00 0001
        0x0010:  7f00 0001 20fb c610 9bb0 f1f9 9b92 7ea3
        0x0020:  8018 0100 01a5 0000 0101 080a 0171 7e68
        0x0030:  0171 7e68 837a 0400 0100 0203 5600 0900
        0x0040:  1030 8203 5230 8202 fca0 0302 0102 0209
        0x0050:  00c7 5c9d eade c1a2 5030 0d06 092a 8648
        0x0060:  86f7 0d01 0105 0500 3081 a431 0b30 0906
        0x0070:  0355 0406 1302 5553 310e 300c 0603 5504
        0x0080:  0813 0554 6578 6173 3112 3010 0603 5504
        0x0090:  0713 0953 6f75 7468 6c61 6b65 3114 3012
        0x00a0:  0603 5504 0a13 0b54 7261 7665 6c6f 6369
        0x00b0:  7479 3115 3013 0603 5504 0b13 0c41 7263
        ....
        0x0380:  bd17 59e8 3508 bd6a 9554 96ed 9790 66ec
        0x0390:  c2a8 eca0 8c6a b706 0040 0100 8007 00c0
        0x03a0:  b73b 8d2a 4c35 192b f6ff e87b 0137 8772
```

The length of this packet is 0x037A = 890 bytes; because the ServerHello packet includes the certificate, it's going to be fairly long. The type is 0x04, `ServerHello`. This is followed by the `ServerHello` packet:

```
    unsigned char session_id_hit;        // 00
    unsigned char certificate_type;      // 01 = SSL_CT_X509_CERTIFICATE
    unsigned char server_version_major;  // 00
    unsigned char server_version_minor;  // 02
    unsigned short certificate_length;   // 0356
    unsigned short cipher_specs_length;  // 0009
    unsigned short connection_id_length; // 0010
    signed_x509_certificate certificate; // (an entire DER-encoded X.509
                                         // certificate)
    unsigned char *cipher_specs;   // 0600400100800700c0
    unsigned char *connection_id;  // b73b8d2a4c35192bf6ffe87b01378772
```

The next packet is the client's master key message. The client selects a cipher spec from the ones presented by the server, generates a master key, encrypts it using the public key presented by the server, and sends it back:

```
15:57:38.915469 IP localhost.localdomain.50704 >
localhost.localdomain.pcsync-https: P 37:121(84) ack 893
win 271 <nop,nop,timestamp 24215212 24215144>
        0x0000:  4500 0088 001c 4000 4006 3c52 7f00 0001
        0x0010:  7f00 0001 c610 20fb 9b92 7ea3 9bb0 f575
        0x0020:  8018 010f fe7c 0000 0101 080a 0171 7eac
```

```
0x0030:    0171 7e68 8052 0206 0040 0000 0040 0008
0x0040:    8b78 24fb 8643 724b c052 5b9d 7460 ad16
0x0050:    ea68 5b82 70fe 138c 9701 8261 1ec7 055f
0x0060:    7a0b ecd9 8f25 008d 62c4 f8db 8bf5 6029
0x0070:    e797 1138 8b26 3c43 d889 164d 55fd cd22
0x0080:    0001 0203 0405 0607
```

Again, the length of the packet is 0x0052 = 82 bytes, and the message type is 0x02 = SSL_MT_CLIENT_MASTER_KEY.

```
unsigned char cipher_kind[ 3 ];      // 060040 =
                                     // SSL_CK_DES_64_CBC_WITH_MD5
unsigned short clear_key_len;        // 0000 (no cleartext key,
                                     // not an export cipher)
unsigned short encrypted_key_len;    // 0040
unsigned short key_arg_len;          // 0008 (8 bytes of IV)
unsigned char *clear_key;            // (empty)
unsigned char *encrypted_key;        // 8b7824fb8643724bc0525b9d7460ad16
                                     // ea685b8270fe138c970182611ec7055f
                                     // 7a0becd98f25008d62c4f8db8bf56029
                                     // e79711388b263c43d889164d55fdcd22

unsigned char *key_arg;              // 0001020304050607
```

To decrypt this, you need the private key, of course. Refer to Chapter 5 to see how to extract it from "key.pem" if you've forgotten. You can then use the rsa utility developed in Chapter 3 to decrypt this and verify that it is, indeed, the master key that was generated:

```
[jdavies@localhost ssl]$ ./rsa -d \
0xB8C4AB64DF20DCECB49C02ACECEA1B832742550267762E4CBE39EC3A0657E779A71\
2B9DE5048313CFDE01DFDACD12E999082E08FC3FFFFABA0816E3C54337AFF \
0x1DCD8343DB05C6FCDB490AD96FC1773C99798692C3B37956619CA030DFD30FFFF601\
CEE22444C1E32C9E89B37EB8C76AC9E49FA52C3AB463306A067C05B4B1B9 \
0x8b7824fb8643724bc0525b9d7460ad16ea685b8270fe138c970182611ec7055f7a0be\
cd98f25008d62c4f8db8bf56029e79711388b263c43d889164d55fdcd22
02 02 03 04 05 06 07 08 09 0a 0b 0c 0d 0e 0f 10 11 12 13 14 15 16 17 18
19 1a 1b 1c 1d 1e 1f 20 21 22 23 24 25 26 27 28 29 2a 2b 2c 2d 2e 2f 30
31 32 33 34 35 36 00 00 01 02 03 04 05 06 07 00
0001020304050607
```

Recall from Listing C-19 that 0001020304050607 is, in fact, the generated master key. At this point, the key exchange is complete, and every subsequent packet is encrypted using the chosen cipher.

Both sides now compute symmetric encryption keys. Remember that, in SSLv2, this is done by running the MD5 algorithm against the master key, the counter "0", the client's challenge, and the server's connection ID. You can see that this works out to

```
[jdavies@localhost ssl]$ ./digest -md5 \
0x0001020304050607300001020304050607080 90a0b0c0d0e0f\
b73b8d2a4c35192bf6ffe87b01378772
```

```
14f258c2fe6bf291b84ce9aeebc6d4d8
```

| | |
|---|---|
| **Master Key** | 0001020304050607 |
| **ASCII Zero** | 30 |
| **Challenge** | 000102030405060708090a0b0c0d0e0f |
| **Connection Id** | b73b8d2a4c35192bf6ffe87b01378772 |
| **Read Key** | 14f258c2fe6bf291 |
| **Write Key** | b84ce9aeebc6d4d8 |

According to the specification, the client should next respond with a client_finished message, but OpenSSL jumps the gun and sends its own server_verify. Because neither is dependent on the other, it doesn't matter what order they are received in:

```
15:57:38.916066 IP localhost.localdomain.pcsync-https >
localhost.localdomain.50704: P 893:936(43) ack 121
win 256 <nop,nop,timestamp 24215213 24215212>
        0x0000:  4500 005f 8fa1 4000 4006 acf5 7f00 0001
        0x0010:  7f00 0001 20fb c610 9bb0 f575 9b92 7ef7
        0x0020:  8018 0100 fe53 0000 0101 080a 0171 7ead
        0x0030:  0171 7eac 0028 0777 76d1 5c1e 94b1 d24d
        0x0040:  a349 b24c b342 af66 537b 0b19 154b 6daf
        0x0050:  2a36 064c a459 53b4 5c55 7c70 509a 14
```

However, the connection is now encrypted. A passive observer could follow along until this point, but without access to the keys — either the server's private key or the negotiated symmetric keys — he would be unable to figure out what the contents of this packet were, or even what type it is. You can decrypt it, though, because you know the keys. The first three bytes are sent in plain text; they are the length of the packet (0x0028), and the length of the padding (0x07). The rest is DES encrypted:

```
[jdavies@localhost ssl]$ ./des -d 0x14f258c2fe6bf291 \
0x0001020304050607 \
0x7776d15c1e94b1d24da349b24cb342af66537b0b19154b6daf\
2a36064ca45953b45c557c70509a14490d1f61abaf26ace8326d\
baa79b5f28050001020304050607080 90a0b0c0d0e0f00000000000000
```

You can see the seven bytes of padding, which should be removed:

```
490d1f61abaf26ace8326dbaa79b5f2805000102030405060708090a0b0c0d0e0f
```

Recall that every packet is prefixed with a 16-byte MD5 hash of the key, the data, the padding, and a sequence number (which starts at 1). You can verify the hash:

```
[jdavies@localhost ssl]$ ./digest -md5 \
0x14f258c2fe6bf291050001020304050607080809\
0a0b0c0d0e0f00000000000000000000000001
490d1f61abaf26ace8326dbaa79b5f28
```

| | |
|---|---|
| **Read Key** | 14f258c2fe6bf291 |
| **Payload** | 05000102030405060708090a0b0c0d0e0f |
| **Padding** | 00000000000000 |
| **Sequence Number** | 00000001 |

Because the MAC matches, the packet is accepted. The rest is a `server_verify` packet (type 0x05), which consists of the challenge echoed back to the client. The client sends its `ClientFinished` message, which consists of the `connection_ID`. The `connection_ID` can be decrypted similarly, using the write key instead of the read key:

```
15:57:38.916839 IP localhost.localdomain.50704 >
localhost.localdomain.pcsync-https: P 121:164(43)
ack 936 win 271 <nop,nop,timestamp 24215214 24215213>
        0x0000:  4500 005f 001e 4000 4006 3c79 7f00 0001
        0x0010:  7f00 0001 c610 20fb 9b92 7ef7 9bb0 f5a0
        0x0020:  8018 010f fe53 0000 0101 080a 0171 7eae
        0x0030:  0171 7ead 0028 0772 7318 5138 ed06 b8d1
        0x0040:  d324 e85d 9ac6 7342 41d0 d104 3f24 ac88
        0x0050:  6e3f e2d0 ae7f f45c b4cd f646 399c 5e
[jdavies@localhost ssl]$ ./des -d 0xb84ce9aeebc6d4d8 \
0x0001020304050607 \
0x7273185138ed06b8d1d324e85d9ac6734241d0d1043f24ac88\
6e3fe2d0ae7ff45cb4cdf646399c5e8b44c2a7fef149494ed138\
76c15ce73303b73b8d2a4c35192bf6ffe87b013787720000000000000000
[jdavies@localhost ssl]$ ./digest  md5 \
0xb84ce9aeebc6d4d803b73b8d2a4c35192bf6ffe87b01378772\
0000000000000000000002
8b44c2a7fef149494ed13876c15ce733
```

Notice that, when verifying the MAC, this is message #2 — the first (#0) was the client hello, and the second was the client master key message. You can verify that the payload consists of the `SSL_MT_CLIENT_FINISHED` byte (0x03) and the `connection_ID` received from the server, reflected back. If you send the wrong `connection_ID`, or if it fails to decrypt properly, the server will just close the connection.

To complete the handshake, the server sends an (encrypted) ServerFinished message. Notice that, to decrypt this packet, you need to keep track of the IV changes to do CBC correctly. The read IV is now b45c557c70509a14 — the last eight bytes that were sent by the server.

```
15:57:38.916884 IP localhost.localdomain.pcsync-https >
localhost.localdomain.50704: P 936:979(43) ack 164
win 256 <nop,nop,timestamp 24215214 24215214>
        0x0000:   4500 005f 8fa2 4000 4006 acf4 7f00 0001
        0x0010:   7f00 0001 20fb c610 9bb0 f5a0 9b92 7f22
        0x0020:   8018 0100 fe53 0000 0101 080a 0171 7eae
        0x0030:   0171 7eae 0028 07e1 227d cfc0 67d8 3e3b
        0x0040:   a0ec af96 31af 6ba9 089b 40b7 ad2b f6e9
        0x0050:   8272 2097 4a63 0981 1b60 7c28 512a cf
[jdavies@localhost ssl]$ ./des -d 0x14f258c2fe6bf291 \
0xb45c557c70509a14 \
0xe1227dcfc067d83e3ba0ecaf9631af6ba9089b40b7ad2bf6e9\
827220974a6309811b607c28512acf
852597cc4bd2463be5f8672e62b3a703060427efed281ba93999
9ff8a8f1f1ddd600000000000000
[jdavies@localhost ssl]$ ./digest -md5 \
0x14f258c2fe6bf291060427efed281ba939999ff8a8f1\
f1ddd6000000000000000000000002
852597cc4bd2463be5f8672e62b3a703
```

You can verify that the supplied session ID matches the one in the response page.

At this point, the handshake is complete, and the application takes over. The application acts as though nothing has changed; it submits an HTTP GET request just as if it had simply negotiated an unprotected connection. The SSL code takes care of encrypting and MAC'ing it.

```
15:57:38.917953 IP localhost.localdomain.50704 >
localhost.localdomain.pcsync-https: P 164:215(51)
ack 979 win 271 <nop,nop,timestamp 24215215 24215214>
        0x0000:   4500 0067 001f 4000 4006 3c70 7f00 0001
        0x0010:   7f00 0001 c610 20fb 9b92 7f22 9bb0 f5cb
        0x0020:   8018 010f fe5b 0000 0101 080a 0171 7eaf
        0x0030:   0171 7eae 0030 067b eb63 de21 6de7 ed5b
        0x0040:   45b7 969a 26a6 6d47 fbae 036d 4351 4def
        0x0050:   8e67 dcf3 c8e7 3ce4 52f7 9b26 f822 bad1
        0x0060:   942a 2ea0 6bb3 6e
[jdavies@localhost ssl]$ ./des -d 0x0xb84ce9aeebc6d4d8 \
0x5cb4cdf646399c5e \
0x7beb63de216de7ed5b45b7969a26a66d47fbae036d43514def8e6\
7dcf3c8e73ce452f79b26f822bad1942a2ea06bb36e
2d5720761aa3d1b19909972bd870e7c4474554202f696e6465782e68
746d6c20485454502f312e310d0a000000000000
```

The payload, after removing the MAC and the padding, is

| 47 | 45 | 54 | 20 | 2f | 69 | 6e | 64 | 65 | 78 | 2e | 68 | 74 | 6d | 6c |
|----|----|----|----|----|----|----|----|----|----|----|----|----|----|----|
| G | E | T |  | / | i | n | d | e | x | . | h | t | m | l |
| 20 | 48 | 54 | 54 | 50 | 2f | 31 | 2e | 31 | 0d | 0a |  |  |  |  |
|  | H | T | T | P | / | 1 | . | 1 | \r | \n |  |  |  |  |

which is exactly what would have been sent if there had been no SSL involved. The response from the server is similar. The remaining four packets are the standard TCP FIN/ACK FIN/ACK shutdown sequence. There is no SSL involved here.

## Problems with SSLv2

So, what's wrong with SSLv2? Everything is in place — encryption, MAC verification, certificate verification. Why was SSLv2 deprecated?

### Man-in-the-Middle Attacks

Man-in-the-middle attacks, which public-key cryptography and certificate authorizes are supposed to thwart, are discussed in Chapter 5. However, one significant weakness of SSLv2 is that the first few packets — the `ClientHello` and the `ServerHello` — aren't themselves protected against man-in-the-middle attacks. An attacker can insert himself in between the client and the server, and downgrade the connection by, for example, removing all encryption options except for DES, or even making it look as though the client can only support export-grade (that is, easily crackable) ciphers. The client never notices. Unless the client is specifically configured to never negotiate weak ciphers, the connection continues as requested.

### Truncation Attacks

SSLv2 uses the standard TCP shutdown mechanism (the FIN packet) to indicate that the connection is closed. An attacker can easily forge this packet, however, leading to the same sort of truncation problems that led to the use of MACs in the first place.

### Same Key Used for Encryption and Authentication

SSLv2 doesn't allow the peers to negotiate a separate encryption key versus a MAC key. This simplifies a brute-force attack because the attacker has additional data with which to attack the key.

## No Extensions

SSLv2 mandates, for example, RSA for key exchange and MD5 for MAC. There's no provision in the protocol itself for additional key exchange or MAC options (for instance, an actual HMAC).

# Index

Printed and bound by CPI Group (UK) Ltd, Croydon, CR0 4YY

27/10/2024

14580183-0003